LIGHT IN THE DALES

Volumes II and III

Light in the Dales comprises Volumes II and III of John Breay's original thesis entitled 'Northern Studies' in which he traces the agrarian background to the rise of political dissent in the northern dales in the sixteenth and seventeenth centuries and the change in political and religious ideals of the early Quakers in the dales from 1652.

VOL. I   The Quaker Registers of:

RAVENSTONEDALE:
  Births 1650-1836.
  Marriages 1656-1834.
  Burials 1659/60-1840.

GRISDALE & GARSDALE:
  Births 1651-1837.
  Births N.I.M. 1758-1837.
  Marriages 1666-1811.
  Burials 1662-1837.
  Burials N.I.M. 1752-1836.

(Volume I, published separately as a softback in 1994 and entitled *The Quaker Registers of Ravenstonedale, Grisedale and Garsdale 1650-1837* is available from R F G Hollett & Son, 6 Finkle Street, Sedbergh, Cumbria, LA10 5BZ (Tel: 015 396 10198), price £12.50 or £14.00 post paid).

Light in the Dales

Volumes II and III

The Agrarian Background to
the Rise of Political and Religious Dissent
in the Northern Dales
in the sixteenth and seventeenth centuries.

By the Revd J. Breay, M.A.

The Canterbury Press
Norwich

© Dr John and Mrs Wyn Hamilton, 1996

Volumes II & III first published 1996 by The Canterbury Press Norwich
(a publishing imprint of Hymns Ancient & Modern Limited,
a registered charity)
St Mary's Works, St Mary's Plain,
Norwich, Norfolk NR3 3BH

British Library Cataloguing in Publication Data

A catalogue record for this book is available
from the British Library

ISBN 1-85311-139-2

*Printed and bound in Great Britain by
The Lavenham Press Ltd, Lavenham, Suffolk*

To my sister
Mrs. Mary Bolton of Slaidburn,
whose encouragement, and the
support of many friends, have
been invaluable.

Volume II

Preface

It has long been debated, and rightly questioned by Quaker historians, as to how far the rise of political and religious dissent in the northern dales was conditioned by the agrarian troubles of the northern customary tenants from the Pilgrimage of Grace. Several writers have pointed to the Pilgrim grievances collated at York on 21st November 1536 and a number of tenant-right disputes in the following hundred years, notably the Kendal barony case of 1620, and the countess of Pembroke's Chancery case of 1650, as causing an increasing anger among the fellside farmers. On the other hand the Quaker historians have rightly demanded surer proof. The following work is an attempt to remedy the defect. In the realm of ideas St. John's College, Cambridge and archbishop Holgate of York were responsible for the early spread of Protestantism after the Dissolution of the religious houses.

These studies concentrate on a rough triangle of dales, and the Quaker community which grew out of them. The Gilbertine manor of Ravenstonedale looked toward Kirkby Stephen and the Eden Valley. So also did the Clifford manor of Mallerstang, the birthplace of John Knewstub. The monastic manors of upper Wensleydale became Crown manors, and with the Crown lordship of Middleham looked towards the great castle of Richmond. The monastic manors of Grisedale and Garsdale were let by the Crown to lord Scrope of Bolton, and looked towards Sedbergh and the Lune valley. The customary tenants of this rough triangle of dales held their lands by the ancient custom of tenant-right. Yet the story of the struggles between land lords and tenants in each dale was bitter though different. At the heart of the problem was the fall in the value of money. The tenants paid ancient rents fixed in the reign of Henry II; and periodically they paid

dropping fines on the change of tenants, and general fines on the death of the lord. As the value of money fell, lords demanded higher fines. In monastic days they were often no more than twice the annual ancient rent. By the end of the seventeenth century ten years ancient rent represented one year's improved rent; and many lords obtained two years' improved rent for a fine.

The second potent and disastrous factor creating a discontented tenantry was the division of farmholds in the second half of the sixteenth century. In the one dale of Mallerstang eleven primary farms or cowpastures were divided into 61 holdings. In the long run this created a distressed and discontented tenantry unable to resist years of bad harvest and disease. Though the majority of early Quakers came from these farms, a number of more substantial farmers embraced the cause. Church tithing was one more burden on poor people, and George Fox's attack on the whole system pointed to the hardship and bitterness of the old method of benefice endowment.

How far this old economy of maintaining land-lord and parson would have survived without the intervention of the Civil Wars is another matter. The inept rule of Charles I and his advisers, the imposition of Ship Money from 1635, the two short Scottish wars, and the two Civil Wars, and the compulsory provisioning on credit of the Scots armies from 1644-1646, created an atmosphere so disturbed in the dales, that many were ready for new ideas. When George Fox walked through Wensleydale, Grisedale, Garsdale and Dent in 1652 he was the catalyst who gave focus to the discontent of over an hundred years.

The last five chapters give the later history of customary tenant-right and its ultimate demise in the nineteenth century.

1

CONTENTS

Volume II

Chapters:

2(f) The question of God's pennies.

2(g) Several examples of the struggles between lords and tenants over fines and leases from the upper Eden valley, Garsdale and Wensleydale.

(13) **The forest of Mallerstang**; its origin in the vaccarial system. By 1597 eleven primary farms are divided into 54 tenancies, and 61 in 1604.

(14) An examination of the division of farmholds in Mallerstang from 1582 to 1604; the division of ancient rents, and the succession of tenants. In the main the original families still occupy the primary though divided farms.

(15) The evidence from Mallerstang Wills and inventories of the economic results of dividing the primary farms before 1604. By then the number of tenancies had increased to 61. A table gives the grouping of farms according to partitioned rents, and the creation of uneconomic units.

The estates of George third earl of Cumberland.

(16) His early protestant education, and expensive sea voyages. The 1597 plague and bad harvests in the north. Long absence leads to estrangement from his wife; the estates are assured to his brother Francis, and his daughter is disinherited. His debts of over £40,000 at his death in 1605.

(17) The passing of the northern estates to earl Francis leads to a bitter feud between him and the dowager countess and her daughter Lady Anne. Court proceedings last from 1608 to 1616, and are unresolved due either to the interference of the King or Earl Francis. Lady Anne refuses a cash settlement.

(18) King James imposes his award March 1616/17 confirming the Clifford estates to earl Francis and his heirs male; failing these to lady Anne and her heirs etc. £17,000 is raised from the northern estates mostly by compositions by the tenants (a) to confirm tenant-right, (b) to raise Lady Anne's portion, and (c) to establish a 7d. fine certain. The consent of Lady Anne and the tenants not obtained.

(19) £3,000 was raised by sales in Craven, £15,000 from compositions in Westmorland. There was great hardship in the fellside manors of Mallerstang and the Stainmores, followed by the bad harvests and sickness of 1623.

The north

(20) Lady Anne's two marriages are no advantage.

An examination of the effect of Ship Money demands from 1635, and the two Scottish wars of 1639 and 1640 on the northern counties. The raising and quartering of troops cause discontent. Political dissent probably dates from 1635.

(21) The civil wars, and the north 1641-1649, mark the emergency of active political and religious dissent in Cumberland and Westmorland marked by the imposition of the Protestation Oath 1641. The emergence of the Presbyterian faction at Kirkby Lonsdale and Kendal from 1642 gives the core of the political opposition to the King; the quartering of the Scots army for two years 1644 to 1646 in Westmorland demanding supplies on credit destroyed any hope of the presbyterian faction obtaining much support.

Henry last earl of Cumberland died in December 1643 without heirs male, and his old Clifford estates returned to Lady Anne; the Civil Wars prevent her from leaving London till 1649.

The development of border tenant-right

(22) The development of the 17th C. law on fines on improved rents.

The compositions between three lords and their tenants converting arbitrary fines to fines certain. The effect of three important Chancery cases on fines on an improved valuation.

(23) The arrival of Lady Anne in the north in 1649 begins eight years' bitter struggle with her tenants. She is opposed by the leaders of the presbyterian faction in the upper Eden valley.

(24) The Chancery depositions of 1650 reveal the bitterness of the Westmorland tenants from the King's Award of 1617. Some of the early Quakers appear in the evidence. Her cases conclude in 1657.

(25) The tenantry in Mallerstang 1657. The final agreement with Lord Thanet 1740.

(26) The later history of northern customary tenant-right. The Board of Agriculture Survey of 1793, and the Third Report into the Law of Real Property 1832. Its ultimate demise.

Appendices.

I. MS sources for the reconstruction of the Ravenstonedale Indenture of 22 Eliz.

Chapter 1

One summer evening, about six years ago, my sister drove me up the dale of Mallerstang between Kirkby Stephen and Wensleydale. We approached the lane which leads up to the oldest farm, Southwaite. The evening light was casting long shadows across the fields, and, just as we passed the lane we could see the farmer walking across a nearby field. He was just a silhouette against the sky. He was walking as men have walked that land for hundreds of years; and if the soil could speak it would tell of winter snows, of the spring day when the curlew and plover return from their winter shore, of summer days when yellow rattle, ragged robin, woody cranesbill and Easterledges flower in the ancient meadows, and of autumn when bracken and seaves are cut for winter bedding, peat and wood were stored, and some Shorthorn cattle were killed and salted for winter months when fresh meat was scarce. That soil could tell of the joys of man and boy, of spell and nur played in the garth, of courtship, and the joyful day when a man-child was born who could inherit the customary farm. There were the days when harsh tidings came up the dale, when every man had to obey the call of the Lord Warden of the Marches, put on his war gear, his leather boots, steel cap and jacket, sling his bag of arrows on his back, and with bill, sword or bow set out with every man aged sixteen to sixty to defend the Borders against the raiding Scots. They had to serve on the Borders for fourteen days, with two to come and two to go. They were grim days when drove after drove of men and boys on horseback, from the middle dales, Garsdale, Dent, Wensleydale, Abbotside, Grisdale and Mallerstang rode past for some fateful encounter such as Flodden Field in 1513.[1] On that 9th of September, the day of English victory, the Scots lost an archbishop, a bishop, ten earls, nineteen barons and Masters, the Provost of Edinburgh, and over three hundred knights, gentlemen and lairds, and in all at least ten thousand dead. The English lost no more than one thousand seven hundred men, with about five or six English knights, and ten or more squires. Next day the corpse of King James of Scotland was found stripped among the slain. The fields and hills stank with blood and corpses for weeks, while the weary men, boys and horses from the dales slowly made for home. Long years after, by the light of the winter fires men would tell tales of courage and treachery, and remember the son or father who never saw home again, and the hundreds of tenants (as at Middleham) who lost all their horses. The bow, and bag of arrows hanging in the kitchen were reminder of the price every fellsider had to pay to preserve his home, wife, children and cattle against murder, fire, rape and theft.

Then came the later days of King Henry VIII when the ancient order began to change. The north had always been troubled by feuds between great lords, the Cliffords and Dacres, the Whartons and Musgraves and their dependant tenants.[2] So entrenched were these old hatreds that fights between the tenants of rival lords continued to the brink of the outbreak of the Pilgrimage of Grace, when the very fabric of the state was at the point of collapse. Indeed in all the Border counties deriving from the old Kingdom of Northumbria the great lords, the Percies, the Dacres, the Scropes and Cliffords were princes who commanded greater loyalty than the King of England; and this contributed a great deal to the instability of the Borders. It was far from an idyllic society. Though the great monastic houses drew rents and tithes far and wide the local lord often acted as their steward, so that a monastic tenant could not escape the grip of a local lord. At the time of the Pilgrimage of Grace the earl of Cumberland, and Sir Thomas Wharton of Wharton Hall were notorious for their grasping ways and screwing tenants of every penny, to the point that they were considered one of the chief causes of the rising.[3]

It was a hard world of strange opinions. The little chapel of St. Mary in Mallerstang, which still has its thirteenth century bell, saw the Mass on Sunday and school on weekdays. In 1526 one of the Gilbertine canons of Ravenstonedale had drawn a picture on parchment of a moon waxing, with a number of years growing as the moon did; when the moon was full a cardinal was painted, and beneath him as the moon waned there were two headless monks, and on either side stood a child with axes and butchers' knives and other revolutionary instruments about them.[4]

In April 1536 a wandering priest, Thomas Sowle of Penrith, was in an alehouse at Tewkesbury, and as he sat on a bench with his pot companions he had brought the King's money, 'and we be kept bare and smete under, yet we shall rise again, and 40,000 of us will rise upon a day.' This low boasting was reported to a magistrate, and Sowle found himself lodged in Gloucester gaol. He in turn reported it to Cromwell; Sowle's fate is not known, yet he spoke the common mind.[5]

By midsummer 1536 the smaller religious houses with an annual income of less than £200 were ordered for closure. Those which could offer redemption money were reprieved for a time. The sort of social problems created by these closures can be seen from the account of a small religious house to survive from what is now Cumbria. Cartmel priory had ten religious persons, and thirty-eight servants and others dependant on them for their livelihood. When these and more were thrown out of home and work a vast army of poor and discontented men started to walk the roads.[6]

By the beginning of October 1536, when the King's commissioners arrived in Lincolnshire to dissolve the smaller monasteries, collect the King's subsidy, and enquire into the moral and educational fitness of the clergy, opinion in the dales was already explosive. The Lincolnshire rising occurred between the 2nd and 18th of October. By the 5th October the men of Dent, Sedbergh, Wensleydale had risen, and Kendal was very uneasy. The rising in the dales preceded that in Yorkshire by about a fortnight. In all these dales the monasteries had large estates, either in manors, tithes or properties. In Kirkby Stephen the abbey of St Mary of York held the rectory and drew the greater tithes; in Wensleydale the abbeys of Easby, Coverham, and Jervaulx had extensive properties, and Easby and Coverham had properties in Garsdale and Sedbergh. In Ravenstonedale the Canons of Watton, Yorkshire had the Liberty, manor and rectory. By Sunday 15th October 20,000 men from all over Yorkshire camped before York, and as the Archbishop and his archdeacon had fled to Pontefract, the city of York capitulated to the summons of Robert Aske. By the 17th a further 10,000 men had arrived to join the host.[7]

Meanwhile only the two earls of Cumberland and Westmorland had refused to join the Rising. All the other gentlemen were sworn as Pilgrims, under threat of death and spoliation. The earl of Cumberland at Skipton was besieged by half the Durham host from the 19th to the 28th October. When he was approached by Sir Stephen Hammerton of Hellifield and Slaidburn to throw in his hand with the commons, the earl replied 'I defy you, and do your worst, for I will not meddle with you.' The earl was related to the King, and they had been companions in youth. His castle was not taken. His chief steward was Christopher Aske, the brother of Robert the leader of the Commons.[8]

While Hammerton supported the monks of Sawley, the men of Kendal barony, led by William Collyns, supported the monks of Conishead and Cartmel. The men of Dent, near Sedbergh, were led by George Willan and William Gaunt. The captains from the Sedbergh district were John Atkinson, James Cowper, John Middleton, John Hebblethwaite of Sedbergh, James Bushell of Middleton, and the vicar of Clapham. By the end of October the men of Craven led by Hammerton were camped on a hill near Whalley, preparing for an attack by the earl of Derby. Meanwhile, as the men of Dent, Sedbergh and Kendal were marching to the aid of the Craven men, Berwick Herald-at-Arms arrived at Preston to inform the earl of Derby of the truce between the duke of Norfolk and Robert Aske at their first meeting at Doncaster. The men of the dales returned home, having achieved nothing.[9]

When the duke of Norfolk arrived at Doncaster on the 26th October he and the earls of Shrewsbury and Surrey had about 8,000 men, while Aske had a host of about 30,000. On the following day there were two meetings on the bridge at Doncaster, the first with four on either side, the second with thirty. At the second the heads of complaint by the commons were taken down, and Norfolk promised to take them to the King, supported by two gentlemen from the commons, Sir Ralph Ellerker and Robert Bowes. Aske and Norfolk agreed to a truce to hold till Norfolk and the two gentlemen returned with the King's answer. Up till then Aske had the stronger hand, but many of his followers who had come from Wensleydale and the other Yorkshire dales were in no mood to accept disbanding. Their captains, lord Scrope of Bolton and Sir Christopher Danby were willing to accept Norfolk's word; but the dalesmen were embittered and trusted neither their gentry, nor Cromwell the King's principal minister. Eventually they agreed to go home, weary and empty handed. Between the declaration of the truce on the 27th October, and the second conference at Doncaster on the 6th December the north remained highly disturbed, with the King's forces holding the line of the river Trent, and the commons holding the line of the rivers Humber, Ouse and Aire.[10]

Meanwhile the Rising in the Eden valley took another road. On Sunday the 15th October Peter Bane the vicar of Kirkby Stephen at the bidding of the beads as Mass forgot or omitted to announce St. Luke's day in three days' time. The proclaiming of saints' days had already been forbidden by Cromwell, and for the vicar to ignore the order would have been risky. To the men in church that day it was a threat to their autumn Luke Fair, when they sold off their sheep to pay rents, and reduce their cattle stocks to survive the winter. There was uproar in church, and the vicar was not allowed to leave his place till he had proclaimed St. Luke's day. That was the spark which ignited the whole of the Eden valley, which in common with the dales believed the wildest rumours. They heard that their savings were to be taxed, that the churches were to be deprived of all their valuables, that all churches less than five miles apart were to be pulled down, and that all christenings and wheaten bread were to be taxed. Word was sent to all the surrounding parishes for the men to meet next day on Sandford Moor. There they chose the captains for each district. In the upper Eden valley Robert Pullen, and Nicholas Musgrave were chosen for Kirkby Stephen, Christopher Blenkinsop for Brough, and Robert Hilton for Burton. Pullen, Hilton and Blenkinsop were minor gentry. Robert Thomson, a native of Penrith and former fellow of Queens College, Oxford, the new vicar of Brough was chosen chaplain. A muster was appointed next day to meet at Lammerside Hall south of Wharton Hall, where they hoped to take Sir Thomas Wharton, but he had fled. On Wednesday the 18th October they met in the large close round Lammerside, where they chose the captains for the villages. They had to bring in all the gentlemen to be sworn, or their houses would be plundered. On Thursday the 19th the march down the Eden valley began, with Pullen taking the east side, and Musgrave the west. Pullen arrived at Penrith the same day, Musgrave the next. There they joined forces with the Penrith rebels, who had already chosen their captains, with titles copying those adopted in Lincolnshire. They were Anthony Hutton (charity), John Beck (faith), Gilbert Whelpdale (poverty) and Thomas Burbeck (pity). Robert Thomson, brother in law of Gilbert Whelpdale, was sworn in as chaplain and secretary. Two days were spent in swearing in the gentry and commons of the district, and on the 27th the abbot of Holm Cultram came with his tenants. On Monday the 30th October the gentlemen, and tenants of Cockermouth and the Eden valley met at Burford Oak near Carlisle, requesting the mayor and burgesses of Carlisle to come and take the Pilgrim Oath. The defences of Carlisle were weak; but a few days previously Sir Thomas Clifford, son of the earl of Cumberland, had taken refuge there on his way to Berwick, and when the city was about to capitulate to the commons he revealed his presence and persuaded the mayor and his followers to resist. The situation was precarious; but the city's resolve was stiffened when William Lord Dacre of Naworth, who had been in serious trouble with the King in 1534, and was not likely to risk his head or estate again, sent word to Clifford that he would support him if attacked.

On the same day, as the commons, numbering about 5,000, were approaching from Dalston, a priest brought news of the King's proclamation against unlawful assemblies. The host was in no mood to retire, and thought it a trick to gain time. The next day the leaders went to Carlisle, where they were shown the proclamation, which they took back to their followers. They were persuaded to disband until Friday 3rd November. They reassembled on that day, and a party from Carlisle including Sir Christopher Dacre came under safe conduct, and with the help of some priests persuaded the commons to accept the truce agreed at Doncaster. They then dispersed; and from that point Robert Thomson, the vicar of Brough, took no further part in the rising.

It is important, in view of the King's later moves, to have a clear view of the rising. The majority of the clergy remained aloof, except for the vicar of Brough, two chantry priests at Penrith, and the parsons of Melmerby and Edenhall. The abbot of Holm Cultram, and Chancellor Townley of Carlisle completed the number. With the exception of the bishop of Carlisle who was prudently in London, Sir Thomas Wharton, and the Cliffords, all the gentry took the Pilgrim oath under varying degrees of compulsion.

Apart from the wild rumours which had swept the fellsides, which have been noted, there are four sets of documents which give the thinking behind the revolt. The first was the short letter sent from York, after Aske had entered the minster on the 16th October and had nailed his proclamation to the church door. Copies were sent into the dales, similar to that which was read by Thomson in the upper Eden valley.

'Wellbeloved brethren in God, we greet you well, signifying unto you that we your brethren in Christ have assembled us together and put us in readiness for the maintenance of the faith of God, His Laws, and his church, and where abbeys were suppressed we have restored them again and put the religious men into their houses: wherefore we exhort you to do the same.'

While this protests at the sack of the abbeys, there was more at stake than the spiritual or educational work for which they stood. With their vast interest in sheep, the monasteries provided routes through which wool from the dales was sold. Between the declaration of the truce and the middle of December the north was highly disturbed; the gentlemen feared that they had too much to lose if the wild men of the dales gained the upper hand. Aske for his part had to deal with the Percys, the arming of several strategic places on the Lincolnshire coast by the earl of Suffolk, and the plight of the religious in Watton priory left destitute by their prior, Robert Holgate, who had fled to London on the outbreak of the rising. The King's reply was received in the north on the 11th November; it was so disdainful of the commons' demands, that when Christopher Aske read it the same day in Skipton market place it nearly caused a riot. Pardon was offered to all who sued for it; but Robert Aske, and nine others, were excluded.[11]

Westmorland drew up two proclamations; that from the barony of Kendal ran as follows:

'All commons stick ye together, rise with no great man to (till) ye know his intent. Keep your harness in your own hands and ye shall obtain your purpose in all this North land. Claim ye old customs and tenant-right to take your farms by God's penny, all gressumes and heythynges to be laid down, and then may we serve our sovereign lord King Henry VIII. God save his noble Grace. We shall serve our lands lords in every righteous cause with horse and harness as custom will demand. Gentle commons, have this in your mind, every man take his lands lord and ye have need, as we did in Kendalland, then shall ye speed. Make your writings, command them to seal to grant your petitions at your desire. Lords (spiritual) and temporal, have it in your mind, the world as it waveth, and to your tenants be kind, then may ye go on pilgrimage nothing to withstand, and commons to you be true through all Cristen land, to maintain the faith of Holy Church as ye have taken in hand. Adieu, gentle commons, thus I make an end.

Maker of this letter, pray Jesu be his speed. He shall be your captain when that ye have need.'[12]

This declaration was dated 27th or 28th October. The reference to God's penny is authentic; in the Richmond fee of the barony of Kendal 'at the exchange of lord or tenant, one silver penny, commonly called a God's penny, was paid to the lord of those lands or his deputy.' The phrase 'as we did in Kendalland' suggests that it was written by an outsider. There is also a poetic turn of phrase mindful of Piers Plowman. Perhaps the vicar of Clapham, who had come with the men of Dent and Sedbergh, was the author.

The demands of the Kirkby Stephen men were addressed to Lord Darcy of Templehurst on the 15th November, and make no mention of abbeys. It is agrarian, and is concerned with manorial fines, barony dues, and mistrust of the gentry:

'Ask him (Lord Darcy) to shew them some favour concerning the wealth of their country, by giving them advice 'concernynge the gyrsumes for power men to be laid aparte but only penny farm (?) penny gyrsum, with all tithes to remayn to every man his awne, doyinge therefor according to their dewtye, also taxes casten among the benefest men, as well as tham in abbett with in us as thai that is not incymbent.

Wish to know Darcy's pleasure, what they may do in these causes. Think that they may be put in their room to serve God others that would be glad to keep hospitality, for some of them are no priests that have the benefice in hand, and some are lord Cromwell's chaplains. Accept no gentleman of their counsel, because they are afraid of them as yet, 'and haffe nowte gyelt and sargeant corne layd downe, quyche we thynke war a great welthe for all the countrethe, and all intakes yt noysum for power men to be layd down.'

Kyrkby Stephen 15. Nov. (1536).

By your servandes, Robert Pullen to dethe, Nycolles Musgraffe, the Captaynes of Westmoreland, and ye commaunallyte of ye same.'[13]

The reform they aimed at was the reduction of gressoms, that is fines on the death of the lord, and change of tenant by death or alientation, to one year's annual rent of the farm, instead of as many times the rent the lord thought he could screw from the tenants. What the reader must remember is that the rent paid on all the customary farms in the north was an ancient rent, fixed as long ago as the reign of Henry II in lieu of rents in kind. It was not a rent fixed on the open market. The reference to Intacks points to a number of inclosures made by local landlords, which deprived the commoners of their grazing.

The northern Pilgrims met at a great council at York on Tuesday 21st November presided over by Robert Aske. Pullen and Musgrave went from Kirkby Stephen; there were representatives from Penrith and Kendal; all had to bring with them their list of grievances. The council proceeded to draw up a list under four main heads, Religious, Constitutional, Legal and Economic. Under the first head one of the points made was that the northern abbeys gave great succour to poor men and tenants in time of want, selling their corn at reduced price. Robert Aske in his confession in the Tower in April 1537 painted a moving picture of the usefulness of these northern houses:

> 'Several of these abbeys were in mountains and desert places, where the people be of rude conditions and not well taught the law of God, and when the abbeys stood the people not only had worldly refreshing in their bodies, but spiritual refuge . . . and many of their tenants were their fee'd servants, who now want refreshing both by meat, clothes and wages, and know not where to have any living, but also strangers and baggers of corn betwixt Yorkshire, Lancashire, Kendal, Westmorland and the Bishoprick was in their carriage of corn and merchandise succoured both horse and man by the said abbeys; for none was in those parts denied horse-meat nor man's meat, so that the people was greatly refreshed by the said abbeys where now they have no such succour.'[14]

Under the fourth head of agrarian grivances the dalesmen demanded:

> 'that lands in Westmorland, Cumberland, Kendall, Dent, Sedber, Fornes, and the abbey lands in Mashamshire, Krykbyshire, Netherdale may be by tenant right, and the lord to have at every change two years' rent for gressom, according to the grant made by the lords to the tenants there. This to be done by Act of Parliament.

In the latter of inclosures:

> 'that the statute for inclosures and intacks be put in execution, and all inclosures and intacks since 4 Henry VII to be pulled down, except mountains, forests and parks.'[15]

This was an old grievance which successive governments had failed to check. The wilder demands of the dalesmen were dropped by the gentry who had too much to lose. Those retained were knocked into respectable form. On the other hand the King had no intention of conceding anything, and ordered the duke of Norfolk to temporise in order to conceal the King's fury and desire for revenge. The King was determined to separate the gentry from the commons, and when they were leaderless wreak his revenge. At the conference at Doncaster on the 6th December Aske obtained three promises; a free parliament, a free pardon, and the provisional restoration of the abbeys. Aske returned to his 3,000 followers at Pontefract to report the agreement, which they first received with joy. When Aske returned to Doncaster to report this to Norfolk, Hallam and Pulleyn at Pontefract raised a near revolt on the ground that the gentlemen had looked after their own interest, and the commons had got nothing. They threatened to raise all Yorkshire again. Aske rushed back bringing the Lancaster Herald with them to prove the King's promise of Pardon. This was read to the commons on the 8th December, and thereafter they returned reluctantly to the dales, feeling that nothing had been granted them, and that the gentry had betrayed them. The heralds toured the north in the following days. The promised pardon was read at Skipton on the 16th December, Kendal on the 19th, Appleby on the 20th, and Penrith on the 21st. They visited all the border counties, and their tour ended at the end of the month. When the proclamation was read in Kendal church the opening lines nearly caused a riot:

> 'Albeit that you the King's Highness' subjects and commons . . . have now of late attempted and committed a manifest and open rebellion against his most royal majesty, whereby was like to have ensued the utter ruin and destruction of these whole countries, to the great comfort and advancement of your ancient enemies the Scots, which as his Highness is credibly informed do with great readiness watch upon the same, and to the high displeasure of God . . . .'[16]

He then went on to blame the designs of evil men who had fomented the trouble. The offer of pardon for all who sued for it infuriated the commons. Why should they seek for pardon for protesting against enclosures, tithes, high fines, and the threat to trade following the closing of the monasteries? The year closed on this ominous note.

Abbreviations used in the references.

C.R.O. The County Record Offices of Kendal or Carlisle.

C.U.L. Rare books in the Cambridge University Library.

C. & W. The transactions of the Cumberland & Westmorland Antiquarian Soc.

D.N.B. The Dictionary of National Biography.

Hist. MSS. Comm. The Historical Manuscripts Commission.

N. & B. The History of Cumberland & Westmorland by J. Nicolson & R. Burn, 1777.

P.R.O. The Public Record Office, Chancery Lane, London.

S.P. The Calendars of State Papers, domestic.

V.C.H. The Victoria County Histories.

Chapter 1. References

(1) Great Battles, Flodden. The Anglo-Scottish War 1513. Charles Kightly. Almark Publishing Co. 1975. Yorkshire Arch. Soc. Record Series. CIV, Three Yorkshire Surveys, T.S. Willan & E.W. Crossley. 1941. xvii. The loss of horses at Middleham.

(2) The Clifford Papers of the sixteenth century. A.G. Dickens. Surtees Soc. CLXXII, 1957. Introduction p. 23 et seq. The Clifford/Dacre quarrel.
    S.P. Henry VIII. 1534. Introduction by James Gairdner. xlii-xliv.
    S.P. Henry VIII. 1534. (1013) 27 July, Chapuys to Charles V. (p. 389)
    S.P. Henry VIII. 1534. (1217) 26 Aug. & 18 Sept. (7-9)
    S.P. Henry VIII. 1534. (676) 9 May. Twelve inventories of moveables of Lord Dacre.
    S.P. Henry VIII. 1534. (1217) 18 Sept. (p. 474). Henry earl of Cumberland appointed Lord Warden of Western Marches & Capt. of Carlisle, & to hold certain manors, and lordships.
    S.P. Henry VIII. 1534. (1549) 17 Dec. The composition of the quarrel between Dacre & Cumberland.
    S.P. Henry VIII. 1534. (1270) 17 Oct. Wm. Lord Dacre to Cromwell, and part payment of the sum of £10,000 for his composition.

(3) S.P. Henry VIII. 1535. (991) 5 July, Henry earl of Northumberland to Henry VIII.
    S.P. Henry VIII. 1535. (863) 13 June. Sir Ric. Tempest to Cromwell.
    S.P. Henry VIII. 1535. (893) 18 June. Cromwell to Henry earl of Cumberland to appoint justices to try the late rioters.
    S.P. Henry VIII. 1535. (970) 1 July. A correspondence to Henry VIII reports the indictment of 80 at Gisburn.
    S.P. Henry VIII. 1535. (991) 5 July. Henry earl of Northumberland reports in the same vein, & imprisonment of ringleaders.
    S.P. Henry VIII. 1537. (919) 12 April. Norfolk to Henry VIII.

(4) S.P. Henry VIII. 1537. (534) (Feb) p. 247. Examination of William Todde, prior of Malton, a dependance of Watton.

(5) S.P. Henry VIII. 1536. (693) 20 April. 2 papers. Examination of Jas. Tomekyns of Tewkesbury, painter et cl.

(6) S.P. Henry VIII. 1536. vol. I. p. xlvi & (1191) 24 June 1536. (p. 500) Conishead is also given.

(7) I am indebted greatly to 'The Pilgrimage of Grace & the Exeter Conspiracy' by M.H. & R. Dodds. Camb. 1915. 2 volts. Hereafter: Dodds. Dodds. I. 148 et seq.

(8) Dodds. I. 211, 209-210.

(9) Dodds. I. 216-217, 218-220.

(10) Dodds. I. 260-268, 270.

(11) Dodds. I. 220-225, and the following confessions in the Tower:
    S.P. 1537. (687) 28 March. Robert Thomson, clerk.
    S.P. 1537. (687) 20 March. Bernard Towneley, clerk.
    S.P. 1537. (914) 12 April. William Colyns, bailiff of Kendal.

(12) S.P. Henry VIII. 1536. (892) October, (3).

(13) S.P. Henry VIII. 1536. (1080) 15 Nov.

(14) S.P. Henry VIII. 1537. (901) 11 April (p. 405), (23)

(15) S.P. Henry VIII. 1536. (1246) 4 Dec. sects: (9) & (13). Instructions to Sir Thomas Hilton. Dodds. I. 346-373 (esp. p. 369.)

(16) Dodds. II. 28-30.

Chapter 2

The year 1537 opened with the Duke of Norfolk at Court awaiting instructions from the King, who did not take him fully into his confidence. The King proceeded to play a skilful and many-handed game. His aim was to detach the nobility and gentry of the north from the commons; to provoke such breaches of the truce that he could ignore Norfolk's concessions at Doncaster; to crush the leaderless tenants; to hang the principal leaders; to break the almost princely powers of the Percy family in Northumberland; and to devise new means of governing both the northern province and the Scottish borders. The following events can only be understood with these aims in mind.

In mid-December 1536 there were two brushes between Thomas Clifford a bastard son of the earl of Cumberland, his deputy at Carlisle Castle, and Richard Dacre in Carlisle. In Craven the earl of Cumberland's deer were being killed in his park at Rylston. At Kirkby Stephen there was a disturbance in the town when it was discovered that one of their leaders, Robert Pullen, seeing which way the wind was blowing quietly paid his neat-gelt dues to the earl of Cumberland. When the local commons heard of this they stormed his house, and threatened to give him a drubbing. He was rescued by some local gentry, who gave certain sureties to the commons.[1]

On the 6th January Thomas Clifford the bastard decided to deal with the disturbance by a bold initiative. On the 6th January he arrived at Kirkby Stephen from Carlisle to capture Nicholas Musgrave, and Thomas Tebay the new captain. Had he succeeded it would have been a fine stroke. But Musgrave and Tebay took refuge in the tower of the parish church, and could not be dislodged, much to the pleasure of the locals. Clifford was forced to retire.[2] On the 12th January the earl of Cumberland wrote to the King and mentioned that the Westmorland commons had turned against their late captains; that there had been risings in west Cumberland; that bills had been fixed to church doors in Craven, and that Carlisle was in urgent need of repair.[3] In Richmondshire there was talk of a new rising after Christmas; and when the King's collectors

went to Barnard Castle to collect the King's rents, they found no money and no prospect of getting it. As January slipped away there was no news of the promised Parliament at York, on which the gentry pinned their hopes. On the other hand the commons felt that if the Parliament did meet at York, they would get no relief from the gentry. Their anxieties increased when they heard that the King had secretly invited Aske under safe conduct to go to London and explain the causes of the Rising. Aske was flattered by the King's friendly welcome, and returned to Yorkshire on the 8th January persuaded by his fair words. On his return Aske had to face several disturbances, and convince the majority of the commons of the King's good intentions. But he was accused of betraying the cause. In Kirkbyshire, the country round Templehurst the seat of Lord Darcy, a local leader issued this call which summed up the common view:

> "Commons, keep well your harness. Trust you no gentleman. Rise all at once. God shall be your governor, and I shall be your captain."[4]

Ever since Flodden in 1513 Norfolk had been the idol of the North, and the commons pinned vain hopes on his sympathy.

While Norfolk's tour of the north was being planned by King and Council, a new event forced the King's hand, and made the commons more restless. In mid-January a new rising occurred, centred on Watton priory, engineered by Hallam and Bigod. Cromwell's nominee Robert Holgate the prior had taken refuge in London, and Hallam had an old score to play off against Holgate for being put out of a Priory farm. In vain did Aske issue a proclamation on the 18th January saying that 'Bigod intended to have destroyed the effects of our petitions', that they had been foolish in listening to him. A day or two later Bigod lost heart, fled from Beverley, and making his way through Swaledale, where he had some estate, took refuge in Cumberland. Richmondshire was now aflame, and proclamations were pinned to church doors ordering the commons to rise in every township on pain of death. The Mass, and the abbeys were to be restored, heretic bishops were to be removed, and landlords were to take nothing of their tenants but rents. All gentlemen were to be seized, and if they refused the Pilgrim Oath they were to be put to death. Their heirs were to be offered the Oath in turn, and sworn in their stead. A copy of this bill was taken by Sir Thomas Wharton and sent speedily to London.[5] Hallam was captured and sent to York, where he was hanged on the 4th February 1536/7. The sub-prior of Watton, and two canons of Warter were arrested with several of Hallam's followers, and held until Norfolk's arrival. The failure of Hallam and Bigod gave the Yorkshire gentlemen sufficient courage to round up Hallam's followers, and denounce their former comrades in the Pilgrimage; thereafter they supported the King.[6]

Norfolk received his instructions from the King on the 16th January, and was in Lincoln on the 30th. He was at Doncaster on the 1st February where he proceeded to swear in all the lords and gentlemen. They were made to understand that if they supported the commons they would lose their estates and be hanged. Norfolk arrived at York on the 5th February. On the same day the commons of Swaledale, Wensleydale, Dent and Sedbergh, and all the nearby dales met at the Grey Friars in Richmond, to decide how to treat with Norfolk over tithes. As the gentlemen were at York, and the Richmond townsmen refused to have anything to do with the incompetent leaders from the dales, the meeting ended in confusion.[7] At York all the gentlemen were sworn in, and ordered to furnish the names of the principal rebels from their districts. On the 10th February nine persons were arraigned for treason. One was reprieved at the desire of the gentlemen, but the remainder were hanged in their own districts. Two monks of Warter, and the sub-prior of Watton were hanged at their houses, one suffered at Richmond and the rest in their own districts.[8] On the same day that the nine were tried at York, Bigod was taken in a chapel in Cumberland, and held at Carlisle to await the duke's arrival.

Meanwhile Norfolk issued orders to Thomas Clifford at Carlisle to arrest Musgrave and Tebay at Kirkby Stephen. He took with him some of the Border moss-troopers from the 'waters of Esk and Line', and again the two took refuge in the church tower. Unable to flush them out, the troopers proceeded to plunder the town, an ancient sport at which they were adept. In the following fights two Kirkby Stephen men were killed. The commons rose in such fury that Clifford and his troops were pursued to the gates of Brougham castle.

When the coast was clear they retreated to Carlisle. Norfolk was very scornful of Clifford's efforts.[9] The second rising of the Pilgrimage of Grace then followed. An urgent appeal was sent to the men of Dent and Kendal to join them.[10] Carlisle was hastily garrisoned by a force of five hundred gentlemen and their servants, but it was ill-prepared for a siege. On the 16th February a force of 6,000 men from the Eden valley and Cockermouth assembled at Broadfield moor. None of the tenants of Holm Cultram joined them, as their abbot refused to support them. On Saturday 17th February the host appeared within bowshot of the city, and discharged most of their arrows over the walls. Not making any impression, when they retired to consider their next move, Sir Christopher Dacre appeared with a party of five hundred 'prickers from Gilsland', hardened border spearmen, who set upon the rebels and chased them for twelve miles, slaying about seven hundred men, and taking about three hundred prisoners. Tebay was among the captives, but Musgrave managed to escape over the border into Scotland, where he remained for many years watched by English spies. Thomas Clifford had joined the chase when it was in full flood, but Dacre was the hero of the hour.[11] It may have given him some satisfaction that a number of the victims were the tenants of his old enemy the earl of Cumberland. Though the whole episode had been sparked off by Thomas Clifford's ineptitude, it served the King very well; he was now free to wreak full vengeance.

Norfolk arrived in Carlisle on the 19th February from Barnard Castle, and he received the celebrated order from the King to act as the King's deputy over a conquered province placed under martial law:

> We approve of your proceedings in the displaying of our banner, which being now spread, till it is closed again, the course of our laws must give place to martial law; and before you close it up again you must cause such dreadful execution upon a good number of the inhabitants, hanging them in trees, quartering them, and setting their heads and quarters in every town, as shall be a fearful warning, where by shall ensue the preservation of a great multitude. That done ye shall close up our said banner both for the advancement and ordering of justice between parties and for the punishment of other malefactors, for which we also send you the commission for Westmorland and Cumberland.

He then ordered Bigod (in Carlisle castle), Chancellor Towneley, the vicar of Penrith and others in the north to be sent to him. It was the vicar of Brough under Stainmore, and not Penrith who was intended. On the outbreak of the second rising Robert Thomson had been compelled by Christopher Blenkinsop of Brough to pray in church for the Pope. That was treasonable. The King then gave his final order:

> Finally, as these troubles have been promoted by the monks and canons of those parts, at your repair to Salley, Hexham, Newminster, Lanercost, St Agatha (Easby), and such other places as have made resistance since the appointment at Doncaster, you shall without pity or circumstance, now that our banner is displayed, cause the monks to be tied up without delay or ceremony.[12]

First all the gentry had to take the Oath; then they had to name the ringleaders from every district. On Tuesday 20th February six thousand commons from the Eden valley, and Cockermouth came to Carlisle in dejected bands. They had lost all, horses, harness, and weapons; they were in fear of a traitor's death, and the plundering and firing of their homes, and poverty to their families. Norfolk waited until they had all come in. The named ringleaders were selected. Sir Ralph Ellerker was appointed Marshal, and Robert Bowes attorney. These two men had been Yorkshire leaders during the first rising; they had been sent by Aske and the commons with Norfolk to the King with the commons' demands. Now they had to prove their loyalty and save their skins by prosecuting the rebels. Henry was a ruthless master. Norfolk was assisted by the leading gentry, Sir Christopher Dacre, Sir Thomas Wharton, Sir Thomas Curwen, Sir John Lamplugh and others. Seventy-four men of the Eden valley and Cockermouth were condemned to hang by Martial Law.

With regard to the order against the monks, with the exception of the abbot of Sawley and one or two of his monks, there is no record that any others on Norfolk's list were hanged. Though the number who suffered seems large by our eyes, yet it was small compared with the slaughter after some of the border battles. Norfolk proceeded after this to close Hexham abbey, and do further justice in Northumberland, Yorkshire and Durham.

Sir Thomas Wharton was present at all the hangings in Cumberland and Westmorland. In Cumberland he went with the sheriff and in Westmorland, as the sheriff was the old earl of Cumberland, he took charge and reported to Cromwell on the 2nd of March that Cumberland and Westmorland were in good obedience. He also reported that in Westmorland the earl of Cumberland had seized goods worth 300 marks of those hanged. In Cumberland the sheriff had goods worth 100 marks. He ended his letter with the crisp remark: 'The West Borders are quiet.' [13]

References Chapter 2

(1) Dodds II, 42, 43 & 111-2. Distinguish between Thomas Clifford of Carlisle (the bastard) and Sir Thomas Clifford, captain of Berwick. Pullen seems to have come from the Pullens at Scotton in Yorkshire.

(2) Dodds II, 42, 43, 111-2.

(3) Dodds II, 44.
     S.P.Henry VIII, 1537 (72) 12 Jan. Earl of Cumberland to Henry VIII.

(4) Dodds II, 51.

(5) Dodds II. 73, 79-80.

(6) Dodds II. 79-82.

(7) S.P.Henry VIII, 1537 (336) 4 Feb. Norfolk to Cromwell.
     Dodds II, 105-6.
     S.P.Henry VIII, 1537 (163) (1). 19 Jan. Articles of the bill sent to the town of Richmond.
     S.P. Henry VIII, 1537 (362). 7 Feb. Norfolk to Henry VIII reports preventing the inhabitants of Richmond supporting the men of Dent, Wensleydale, Sedbergh and Mashamshire.

(8) Dodds II, 109-110.

(9) Dodds II, 111-2, 113-4.

(10) Dodds II, 113-4.

(11) Dodds II, 113-8. Opinions vary over the number killed and taken by Dacre. He was keen to prove the loyalty of his house against the ineffectiveness of the earl of Cumberland, even to the point of exaggeration.
     S.P. Henry VIII, 1537. (492). 23 Feb. John Husee to lord Lisle:
     'Sir Christopher Dacre, uncle to lord Dacres of the North, skirmished with certain rebels there, and

slew 700 of them, ... and took the rest prisoners and hung them upon every bush ... He has won his spurs.'

(12) S.P. Henry VIII, 1537 (479). 22 Feb. sect. (3) & (6). Henry VIII to Norfolk.
S.P. Henry VIII. 1537 (594). 7 Mar. Norfolk to Council: it was the vicar of Brough who was intended.

(13) Dodds II, 118-122.
S.P. Henry VIII, 1537. (641) 12 March. Sir Thomas Wharton to Cromwell.

NOTE:

In these first three chapters my prime source is 'The Pilgrimage of Grace and the Exeter Conspiracy' by M.H. & R. Godds, C.U.P. 1915.

There are a number of secondary north-country accounts, viz. C & W trans. O.S. XIV, 1897. p.335. Aske's Rebellion 1536-7 by George Watson.

*V.C.H. Cumberland 1968, Vol.II, from p.46 gives the religious changes in the diocese of Carlisle from 1521, and is particularly good on the changes in the three reigns of Edward VI, Mary and Elizabeth Tudor, not overlooking the work of John Bost and Christopher Robinson, seminary priests, both Cumbrians who exercised great influence before their martyrdom.

*For John Bost see also D.N.B.

*In these three chapters Lincolnshire, Yorkshire and Northumberland have been touched on lightly in order to concentrate on the upper dales, and the upper Eden valley.

Chapter 3

On the following day, when Sir Thomas Wharton and the others were taking the prisoners to be hanged in their several districts, Norfolk wrote a letter to Cromwell which, though he had obeyed implicitly the King's orders for hangings, is as damning an indictment of the principal gentry, and a statement of the distressing poverty of the tenantry as one could desire:

> 'The poor caitiffs who have returned home have departed without any promise of pardon but upon their good abearing. God knows they may be called poor caitiffs; for at their fleeing they lost horse, harness and all they had upon them, and what with the spoiling of them now and the gressing of them so marvellously sore in time past and with the increasing of lord's rents by inclosing, and for lack of the persons of such as shall suffer, this border is so weked and specially Westmorland, the more pity they should deserve; and also that they have been so sore handled in times past, which, as I and all other here think, was the only cause of this rebellion.'[1]

It was a cruel irony that Sir Thomas Wharton, who was present at all the hangings, was one of the offending landlords. When Robert Southwell came north in August 1537 to survey the Cumberland estates of the Crown as well as the Percy estates of Cockermouth and Egremont, which had come to the King on the death of Henry sixth earl of Northumberland, he had some acute remarks to make about the way Sir Thomas Wharton treated his tenants. Sir Thomas was steward of the honor of Cockermouth for the Percys, and had several other personal properties in the district. The King was now entitled to a general fine from the customary tenants on the Percy lands. Southwell stated that 'the chyff cause of our tracts ther it may further lyke you to undertande to be the gressomyng of the kyng's tenants in Cumberland according to the custome of the contre ther.' He found that his commission of survey in the border counties did not include setting a fine. But he proceeded to do so, and wrote to Cromwell asking him to rectify the omission retrospectively. He pointed out that the appointment of fresh commissioners would be a costly delay, and he had obtained the agreement of the tenants to a moderate fine, they only needing convenient time to pay. He then went on to say that Sir Thomas Wharton had certain lands reserved to him by Act of Parliament with which he did not meddle. Not being certain how to act over them, though he could have gressomed them, he had refrained. But 'I have therefor commandyde Sir Thomas Wharton in the King's behalf to defer the gressomyng of them till the King's pleasure be therein knowen, who wolde ells have wrestyde them high inowgh as doe the more part ther which my lorde I dare say with the approvement of comens accustomably usyde ther, and no place elles that I have ben yn hath done mych more hurte than good. We shoulde have in lyke maner gressomed the tenants in Northumberland and Yorkshire hadde not the Erle (of Northumberland) a lytile affore his death gressomyde them and made then owght dimissions for xxj yeres after which expiryde the King's highness shall have their gressoms iff such shall be his pleasure . . .' He then went on to say that the moderate fining of these tenants would make them more able to serve the King, when others had thought only of their profit and had stretched the tenants so high, that they had been reduced from little to nothing. Southwell appears to have been fair in his observations, and in agreement with Norfolk.[2]

By mid-January 1537, and therefore the second rising, the King had formed a new policy for governing the northern province, and the Borders. The old northern noblemen, so divided by feuds, were to be dropped, and the Borders ruled by deputy wardens acting under the King. The earl of Cumberland was dismissed as Lord Warden of the Western Marches and rewarded with the Garter.[3] Councils were established for the respective Marches, with officers paid for loyal service. Sir Thomas Wharton was made deputy warden for the Western Marches.[4] When Sir Anthony Browne arrived in Berwick at the beginning of February to set up the border councils, he ordered Sir Thomas Clifford, the earl of Cumberland and lord Dacre to be reconciled, 'to put away his ancient grudges.'[5]

The lists of those hanged in February 1537 can no longer be ignored in the study of the rise of political and religious dissent in the northern dales in the seventeenth century.

In Cumberland
Thos. Burtbecke (Thomas Burbeck, a captain of Pity.)
Edw. Whitelocke
John Stephenson
Robt. Stephenson
Michael Grey
Wm. Stephenson
Sir Edw. Perith, chaplain (Cross-bearer)
Edw. Stephenson of Penrith
    (These eight appear to be Penrith men)
Wm. Buntyng of Graystock
Robt. Goodale &
Lancelot Richardson of Newton (Reigny)
Robt. Fyssher
Thos Bell of Cockermouth.
John Nylson of Brygham, junr.
John Jackson of Emelton.
Ric. Cragge of Eglesfield.
Percival Hudson of Perdishaw. (Pardshaw was later a Quaker centre)
Chr. Smyth of Branthwayte.
John Bewley of Dereham.
John Peyrson of Talentyre.
Sander Banke of Wedoppe.
(Total for Cumberland 21.)

In Westmorland.
Thomas Tebay (A captain from January 1537) Kirkby Stephen.
Robert Rowlandson
Edmund Playce
Peter Johnson
Thos. Syll
W. Shaw of the ...ganlownd. (Hanging Lund, Mallerstang)
Hugh Dent
Lancelot Shawe
Edw. Bowsfell
Ric. Waller
John Bowsfell
Roger Gibson
Jenkyn Waller
John Rakestraw 'of the same'
Robert Smyth of Winton
Hen. Bowsfell
Hen. Gibson of Mallerstang

Chr. Blenkinsoppe (He forced the vicar to pray for the Pope) (Brough under Stainmore)
Wm. Wylkyne
Thos. Taylor of Sowerby (? Brough Sowerby)
Thos. Westale of the Newhall (Newhall next to Sandford Moor where the commons met)
Wm. Hodgeson of the Newhall
John Wylson of the Newhall
Ant. Taylour of the Newhall
John Spencer of the Newhall
Thos. Westale of Sowerby (? Brough Sowerby)
Rynian Wallour (The Waller family were prominent supports of the Commonwealth)
Robt. Patrick of Stainmore
Hen. Gibson of Stainmore
Ant. Wharton of Nateby (Kirkby Stephen parish)
Thos. Wray of Soulby (Kirkby Stephen parish)
Hen. Bursy of Soulby
Thos. Sutton of Little Musgrave (Detached manor of Parish of Crosby Garrett)
Ant. Edmontson of Little Musgrave
Edm. Sponer of Asby
John Smyth of Asby
Wm. Nelson of parish of St. Michael, Appleby
Rowland Raysbeck
John Hall
Hugh Bayle
Wm. Waterman
Launcelot Dragley
Hugh Stedeman
Robt. Hodgeson
Hugh Nutt of parish of St Lawrence in Appleby
Ric. Burrell of parish of St Lawrence in Appleby
Geo. Morland of parish of St lawrence in Appleby
Thos. Jackson St Michael in Appleby
John Bryan of King's Meaburn (Parish of Morland)
John Dobson of Dufton
Gilbert Dennyson of Smardale (Parish of Kirkby Stephen)
Thos. Hall of Hartley (Parish of Kirkby Stephen)

Wm. Waller of Hartley (Parish of Kirkby Stephen)

(Total for Westmorland 53)[6]

Looking at these lists there are pointers to
those families, whose men suffered, who in a
later age supported political or religious dissent.
Too much need not be made of this, but it
cannot be ignored.

Penrith. Thomas Burbeck was hanged. It is
probable that the other three captains, Anthony
Hutton, John Beck and Gilbert Whelpdale were
killed by Dacre's men as they fled from Carlisle.

Pardshaw in Cumberland. Percival Hudson
of Perdishaw suffered. Pardshaw became an
early Quaker stronghold.

Little Musgrave.

Anthony Edmontson was one who suffered.
He was an ancestor of William Edmundson
of Little Musgrave, the pioneer Quaker preacher
in Ireland.

Brough under Stainmore. Apart from the
vicar, who ended in the Tower, Christopher
Blenkinsop (of Brough) was hanged. His family
remained loyal catholics for over a century.[7]

Rynian Waller. He and Ric. and Jenkyn
Waller of Kirkby Stephen parish suffered. The
Waller family of Winton embraced the Pres-
byterian faith during the Commonwealth, and

served in the New Model Army, and profited
from sequestrated royalist estates. Two, Captain
Robert Waller of Mallerstang was hanged, and
his nephew John of Mallerstang fled, after the
abortive Kaber Rigg plot of 1663.[8]

Kirkby Stephen. Of the two first captains,
Robert Pullen had joined the gentlemen, and
paid his neatgelt dues. The second, Nicholas
Musgrave fled to Scotland; he was watched
by Sir Thomas Wharton's spies for several
years. On the 3rd December 1541 Wharton
reported to the Privy Council that 'Nicoles
Musgrave (was) reset in Deare Abbey beyonde
St. Johnstone. One Leche who and the said
Nicoles Musgrave hafe beyn at sundry tymes
at Edynburghe in the house of George Leche
surgyon to the Kyng of Scottis.'[9]

Gilbert Dennyson of Smardale: A Peter Dennison of Kirkby Stephen was an early member
of the Ravenstonedale Quaker Meeting and
died in 1683.[10]

William Shawe of Hanging Lund in Mallerstang: In 1677 one Richard Shaw of Hanging
Lunds gave direction in his Will that he was
to be buried among the Quakers, though he
does not seem to have been a member: 'I
bequeath my soule into ye handes of almightie
God in hope of a joyful resurrection at ye
last day and my body to be buryed amongst
my frinds.'[11]

Ric. and William Waller have been noted.

Thus of the 74 men who were hanged in
Cumberland and Westmorland, 23 came from
the parish of Kirkby Stephen. It is remarkable
that none are recorded for Ravenstonedale. In
addition 31 were hanged in the south, plus
the 700 killed by Dacre's pikemen after the
skirmish at Carlisle; and there were 111 condemned in the other northern counties, making
a total of over 916 men.

There are grounds for believing that there
are a number of men who were leaders in the
first rising in the dales, who were rounded
up, put in prison, examined, and left there
probably to die. William Colyns, the bailiff
of Kendal was examined in the Tower, and
though there is no record of his execution, he
was guilty of treason, and would have suffered.[12]

Among the other early leaders the following
should not be overlooked: George Willen and
William Gaunt were active in Dent: A Thomas
Willan, Quaker, was one of the administrators

of the Kendal Fund under Margaret Fell.[13] The
four captains from Sedbergh were John Atkinson, James Cowper, John Middleton, and
the vicar of Clapham: there were several At-
kinsons both of Side and Frostrow members
of Sedbergh Quaker Meeting in the later seventeenth century.[14] Of the men who went to
Pontefract for the meeting with the duke of
Norfolk 2nd December 1536 the following
attended from the barony (as distinct from the
town) of Kendal: Mr. Duckett (of Grayrigg),
Edward Manser, Mr. Strickland, Anthony Lang-
thorn, John Ayrey and Harry Bateman. In early
Quakerism Thomas Ayrey of Birkfield, Miles
Bateman of Underbarrow and William Mansergh came from the Kendal district. Quaker
historians have rightly questioned the assertion
that ancient agrarian wrongs were a prime
force behind the movement. On the other hand,
too many family names occur at the Pilgrimage
of Grace which recur in early Quakerism for
the coincidence to be accidental.

Finally, there remains Robert Thomson, the vicar of Brough under Stainmore from 1534. He was native of Penrith, and former Fellow of the Queen's College, Oxford. Brough was a college living, and drew the rectorial revenues of £22.6.8. On the other hand the stipend of the vicar was £6.18.7.,[15] out of which from the 1st January 1535 he had to pay a tenth to the Crown. It was the poorest benefice in the upper Eden valley. The rector of Crosby Garrett received £19.14.4.; the rector of Great Musgrave £16.8.10½.; the vicar of Orton £16.17.4.; the vicar of Warcop £9.5.1½. (But he was also master of the singing school at Brough at 100s. a year); and the vicar of Kirkby Stephen received £48.19.2., while the abbey of St. Mary of York received an equivalent sum from the rectory. Lastly the two Gilbertine canons at Ravenstonedale received the enormous stipend of £132.19.6½. in right of the rectory.[16] Thomson might have been forgiven for joining the Pilgrimage. In 1703 bishop William Nicolson of Carlisle described the old vicarage which stood at the north gate of the churchyard as 'low, moist and smoaky'.[17]

Thomson took part in the first rising; he was secretary to the commons when they assembled at Penrith; had taken a leading part in swearing in the host, and in the Captains' Mass in Penrith church. He had been present with the host before Carlisle, and had persuaded the commons to go home after the first truce at Doncaster. He had accepted the assurance of pardon in December, and apart from being compelled by Christopher Blenkinsop to pray for the Pope before the second rising, had taken no further part in the movement. He was arrested by the earl of Cumberland on the order of Norfolk, and was taken to London and lodged in the Tower. On the 20th March he was examined by Tregonwell, Layton and Lee and wrote out a qualified confession. He gave his account of the rising, beginning with the episode in Kirkby Stephen church. His confession can still be read in the Public Record Office.[18] It had one obvious weak point; that the clergy and gentry had been compelled to join the first rising under grave threats. It may have been true of the gentry; but as regards the clergy, they had remained aloof. Only the abbot of Holme Cultram, Chancellor Towneley, a chantry priest in Penrith, and two local parsons had joined them. As he had prayed for the Pope he was technically guilty of treason. He was left in the Tower for three months, and then transferred to the Fleet Prison. In the autumn of 1537 he composed a letter to Cromwell, written for him by a scrivener:

"To the most honourable Lord Cromwell.

Please it your most honourable lordship to be advertysed that your poor bedman Robert Thomson clerke was brought afoor you in Leynte last past for praying for the Bishop of Rome at the compulsion of hyse parishioners, when he durst not contrarye at that tyme; and upon the same was comytted to prison in the Tower and from thynse removed to ye King's Bench.

Hyse lodge in the mean tyme what with yernes, and what with corrupts styngynge smells, what with coulde and hunger, and so sore pynched that yff hope had not been, whyche he hath in your good lordshippe to be meane of your most tendre pytye and charite to the King's hyness for hym to be releved thereof, by all lyklyhode he had not been lyve nawe.

Wherfor good lorde your said bedman most humbly besycheth the same, that it so awnswor unto hise said hope conceved towards your goodnes, as he may have cause to pray continually to Almighty God for the preservacion of your properous estate.

Your mot humble Bedman

Robert Thomson, clerke."

The letter is endorsed NO. At this point he vanished from the story, together with Chancellor Towneley, and William Colyns of Kendal. Remembering the King's desire for vengeance it is probable that they were left to rot in prison. There is a suggestion that he was the Robert Thomson who on 8th April 1548 was made vicar of Long Benton, Northumberland. We know that the college appointed Lancelot Shawe vicar of Brough in 1545/6. But there is no explanation of what happened to our Thomson between 1537 to 1546, and 1546 to 1548. It leaves too many unanswered questions.[19]

With the closing of the monasteries the north lost the only great civilising influence that remained. Only the years could tell the tenants how they would fare at the hands of new lords, and speculators. James Gairdner the historian of the Public Records made this comment on the records of 1537: 'There was no longer any resistance to the King. Martial law had done its work in the North, and the country had been completely terrified into submission. Trees and gibbets along the highways bore pitiful burdens suspended in ropes or chains, and, however great the sympathy, it could not be safely expressed. Women, however, had ventured to sally forth at night to cut down their husband's bodies and bury them decently - where they could, in consecrated ground, for rectors and vicars durst not connive at such defiance of authority. All other expression of feeling seems to have been most effectually repressed.'[20]

The only full contemporary account to survive of the Pilgrimage is in the verse of Wilfred Holme, the Yorkshire poet, of which only two copies survive. Though is was composed in about 1537 it was not printed till 1572/3.[21]

"The Evill successe of Rebellion from time to time . . . written in old Englishe verse by Wilfred Holme." After describing the arrest of Bigod in a chapel in Cumberland he proceeds:

'The Duke then intending more justice to execute,
In Divers other places this Insurrection hering,
Gathered a great number these traitors to confute,
For Rychmondshire & Kendal came at short monishing
And there was of Yorkshire in the trayne following,
Divers gentlemen furnished to this battaile vigorous,
But at Barney Castle when they were there gathering,
The Commons had a brawle to them ignominious,
For at Carlisle they lost with shooting at the Citie,
Al their arrowes their artillerie most principall,
And then fled away from their villanous enormytie,
This perceyved by the citie and gentlemen patrimoniall,
They came forth with Speares v.C. substantiall,
Well horsed in aray following in a chase,
And had three hundred taken within a little space.
The other fled awaye as Sheepe with Wolves chased,
Some oppressed, some spoyled, some with lamentation,
Thus five thousand, by five hundred were utterly defaced.
Latrant like Dogs for their abomination,
But after these newes and this expiation,
The Duke of Norfolk was as a Prince not in hebitude,
Came swiftly to Carlyle to do ministration
of Justice for their faults to their great penitude.
There were hanged uppon their heades capitall,
Three score and sixteene unto their friends puderous,
On trees in their Gardens to record for memoriall,
Thus heere was the end of this acte periculous ...'

References Chapter 3

(1) S.P. Henry VII, 1537. (478) 21 Feb. Norfolk to Cromwell.

(2) P.R.O. original letter. SP1/124. Robert Southwell, solicitor to the Court of Augmentation, to Cromwell. 20th Aug. 1537. He was appointed to survey the Crown lands, the Percy lands, and the lands of the dissolved monasteries in the northern province.
N & B. II, 66 & 105 for two of Sir T. Wharton's properties.

(3) S.P. Henry VIII, 1537. (372) 8 Feb. Henry earl of Cumberland to the King, 'will obey with his whole heart.'
S.P. Henry VIII, 1537 (373) 8 Feb. Henry earl of Cumberland to Council.

(4) S.P. Henry VIII, 1537 (2), (154) 28 June. Commission to Sir Thomas Wharton as deputy Warden of Western Marches, with stewardships of Carlisle priory, Wetherall priory, & Holme Cultram abbey. With these and the honor of Penrith the office of Warden was financed.

(5) Dodds II, 230.
Dodds 1, 35, 52-3, 73, 192, 305. and II, 103, 252-3, 264 for the feuds between the Cliffords, the Dacres, the Whartons, and Musgraves.

(6) S.P. Henry VIII, 1537. (498) p. 235. 24 Feb. Norfolk to Henry VIII. It is evident from Wills in the C.R.O. Carlisle that until the division of farmholds in the manor of Mallerstang from 1580 the principal farm families remained in their ancient settlements as in time past. I have omitted the King's anger against those women who cut down their men, whom he desired to punish. Their lords decided to leave well alone. See footnote (20).

S.P. Henry VIII, 1537. (1257) 22 May. Cromwell to Norfolk. The King is not satisfied with the deposition of the women who cut down their dead.

(7) S.P. Dom. Eliz. 1597. p. 354. Jan. Presentments of churchwardens signed by Henry Dethick, chancellor to the bp. of Carlisle.
S.P. Dom. Eliz. 1599. p. 362. 26 Dec. Henry bp. of Carlisle to Sec. Cecil giving numbers of Popish recusants in diocese. The Christian names have been added from the first list.

(8) C & W trans. N.S. XI, 1909. The Kaber Rigg plot. Francis Nicholson. 212.

(9) Hamilton papers. 1532-43. ed. J. Bain 1890. p. 136.

(10) Burial reg. Ravenstonedale Quaker Meeting 1652-1838 by the author.

(11) C.R.O. Carlisle. Will of Richard Shaw of Hanging Lunds. 1 Aug. 1677. There are a number of 17th c. Quakers in Mallerstang whose names do not appear either in the parish register of Kirkby Stephen nor in any Quaker register. The presumption is that they lie in a forgotten burial ground.

(12) I have excluded chancellor Towneley from the narrative. See S.P. Henry VIII 1537. (687) (1) 20 Mar. Confession of Bernard Towneley.

(13) Margaret Fell, Mother of Quakerism. Isabel Ross. 1984 ed. York. 62 & 63.

(14) Beginning of Quakerism. W.C. Braithwaite. C.U.P. 1955 ed. See Christopher & Mary Atkinson passim.
Marriage reg. of Grisdale & Garsdale Quaker Meeting by the author 1652-1838: A marr. occurred 1670 at the house of Edward Atkinson of Frostray. In the Marr. reg. of Ravenstonedale Quaker Meeting by the author 1652-1838, in 1686 John s.o. Edward Atkinson of Side was marr. to Sarah Pinder of Wath at Brigflats.

(15) The Queen's College, Oxford: Long Rolls (2.p.123)
The Queen's College, Oxford: Valor of College Possessions Jan. 1545/6.
By courtesy of the Keeper of the Archives.
Valor Eccl. Henry VIII 1535. II, 1810 ed. p. 296.
Religious Orders in England. Dom. Davie Knowles III, 1959 p. 268-290, for transfer of annates to the Crown.

(16) Valor Eccl. Henry VIII, 1535 op. cit. 294-7.
N & B, I, 523.

(17) Miscellany accounts of dioceses of Carlisle. Bp. William Nicolson, Carlisle, 1877. p. 48, The visitation of Brough.

(18) S.P. Henry VIII, 1537. (687) (2) 20 Mar. Confession of Robert Thomson.
S.P. Henry VIII, 1537. (687) (1) 20 Mar. Confessions of Bernard Towneley.
S.P. Henry VIII, 1537. (914) 12 April. Confession of William Colyns, bailiff of Kendal.
S.P. Henry VIII, 1537. (2) (181) The list of persons admitted to the Tower at several times, and the charges for their maintenance, including Robert Thomson at 6s. 8d. for three months. There are many famous names on this list.
S.P. Henry VIII, 1537. (1339) N.D. Robert Thomson to Cromwell.

(19) The Queen's College Oxford, J.R. Magrath, 1921. I, 188. II, 294. Thomson was fellow 1531-2. His successor at Brough, Lancelot Schawe was provost 1563.
N & B, I 569 says Shawe occurs 1568.
Par. reg. Brough under Stainmore ed. H. Brierley, 1923, p. 155:
Bur. 9 Nov. 1596: Mr. Lancelot Shaw 'viccar', aged 85.

(20) S.P. Henry VIII, 1537 (2). Preface p.i. by James Gairdner, see refs. passim.

(21) British Lib. Cat. C.122.bb.20. Date 1572.
Henry Huntingdon Lib. Harvard, U.S.A. Mic.A.779.(5), dated 1573.
S.T.C. numbers are 13602 & 13603. There is micro-film copy in C.U.L.

Chapter 4

St. John's College, Cambridge (1)

These essays are an attempt to ask how the remote dalesman came to change his political and religious opinions after the Reformation. Each dale was a world to itself, with its close community, its leaders and its church. Even the finer differences in dialect between the dales were ascertainable. It was said that if one stood in Kendal market place on market day up to the first part of the last century one could tell from which dale a farmer came from the subtle difference in his dialect. Thus one would expect change of local opinion to be very slow, especially in the northern border counties, where agricultural practice was far behind the rest of the country. The monasteries had a predominance in the dales, almost greater than the nobility. In the triangle of dales with which these studies are concerned the Gilbertine canons of Watton, Yorkshire owned the liberty, manor and rectory of Ravenstonedale. They had a cell there of two or three canons. The abbey of St. Mary of York held the valuable rectory of Kirkby Stephen, though the predominant land lord was the earl of Cumberland. The abbeys of St. Agatha Easby, Coverham, and Jervaulx were predominant in Wensleydale. Coverham owned the rectory of Sedbergh, while St. Agatha's owned the manor of Garsdale where they had a cell for two or three canons serving the chapelry of St. John. Both abbeys had properties in Garsdale and Sedbergh, with stewards and receivers taken from the local gentry.[1] It was a close-knit society. Two factors were to be crucial in the development of education and new beliefs, though the Mass continued to be said till Henry's death.[2] The first was St. John's College, Cambridge which appointed the schoolmaster of Sedbergh, and the second was Robert Holgate the President of the Council of the North, and later archbishop of York who planted a protestant schoolmaster at Ravenstonedale.

Nowhere is the history of northern education more dramatically illustrated than in Sedbergh. Up till the dissolution of the chantries the local schoolmaster was a chantry priest appointed by St. John's College, Cambridge. In May 1527 Dr. Roger Lupton, a native of Sedbergh and provost of Eton endowed six scholarships at St. John's, and linked them to the chantry school at Sedbergh. Where possible the master at Sedbergh was to be appointed from among the Lupton scholars. St. John's together with Queen's and Christ's, was devoted to the New Learning, and as such much praised by Erasmus. A century later Milton wrote a glowing passage in which he said that in these colleges the Bible was sought out of the dusty corners where profane Falshood and Neglect had thrown it, the Schools opened, Divine and Humane Learning rak'd out of the Embers of Forgotten Tongues...scorning the fiery Rage of the old red Dragon.[3] In 1537 one Robert Heblethwaite, no doubt a local man, was admitted B.A. at St. John's, a fellow in 1538, and from 1538 to 1552 was master of the chantry school at Sedbergh. By the Chantries Act 1547 the lands belonging to the endowment were confiscated by the Crown, but a warrant was issued allowing Heblethwaite to continue as master. On the 16th June 1549 the chantry lands were sold to a syndicate for £226.3s.4d., and Heblethwaite lost his income. But he was allowed to occupy the school house. How he survived is not known, but he probably took in gentlemen's sons and kept going in this way. As the chaplaincy of Garsdale was not a chantry, future chaplains were paid by the receiver for Crown lands in Yorkshire. Such was the lamentable position of the disendowed chantry school at Sedbergh, that St. John's pleaded in vain for some restoration of endowment. King Edward's advisors who had controlled the sale of chantry lands were deaf to these appeals. It happened that Thomas Leaver the master of St. John's was appointed to preach twice in 1550 at Paul's Cross. It was an opportunity too good to miss, though there was some risk to the preacher. The young King was present, and in two very blunt sermons Leaver revealed the parlous state of the northern grammar schools, stripped of their meagre endowments, and on the verge of collapse. These sermons bypassed the rapacious courtiers who had benefited from the sale of chantry lands. As far as Sedbergh was concerned, the preacher succeeded, and on 14th May 1552 Sedbergh was re-endowed by Letters Patent with other lands. These were scattered all over the place, and the school had great difficulty in obtaining control of them. Thus by this pious fiction Edward VI is credited with the foundation of a number of northern Grammar Schools. Robert Heblethwaite was appointed master under the new foundation, and remained from 1552 till 1585, though he was still living in 1590. Thus through the long tenure of Heblethwaite, and the Lupton scholarships, Sedbergh school was linked with the New Learning of St. John's, and became a centre for Protestant learning in the Sedbergh district. Sedbergh school was four years senior to that at Kirkby Stephen.[4]

The northern link with St. John's was to have far-reaching effect. Sedbergh taught, not only local boys with an aptitude for books, but a number of gentlemen's sons who made their own way outside the usual channels of church and school.[5] Two men come to mind.

In about 1560 one John Knewstub of the parish of Kirkby Stephen entered Sedbergh school, and in 1561 qualified for a Lupton scholarship and entered St. John's. There was at that time a protestant master of the Kirkby Stephen grammar school by the name of Edward Mynese who had been placed first at Ravenstonedale by Robert Holgate, and in 1556 was made first headmaster of the new Kirkby Stephen grammar school by lord Wharton. Mynese seems to have taught Knewstub, and prudently moved him to Sedbergh to obtain the scholarship to St. John's. The Knewstub family was distributed in that parish in Mallerstang, Waitby, Soulby and Ravenstonedale. They were all small farmers. John Knewstub was born at Shorgill in Mallerstang, and his brother Henry was admitted tenant in 1582. Henry died prematurely in February 1586/7 making his brother *MR* John guardian to his children. The eldest son William inherited the Shorgill farm, and the second son John a farm at Outhgill.[6] The third Richard lived with his uncle at Cockfield rectory, Suffolk. When Knewstub entered St. John's in 1561 Dr. James Pilkington had just been promoted the first protestant bishop of Durham; that was the emphasis of the college. The lot of the undergraduates was severe, as can be seen from the history of the college:

'There be divers which rise daily betwixt four and five of the clock in the morning, and from five until six of the clock are (at) common prayer with an exhortation of God's word in the common chappel, and from six until ten of the clock use ever either private study, or common lectures. At ten of the clock they go to dinner, where as they be content with a penny piece of beef amongst four, having a porage made of the broth of the same beef, with salt and oatmeal, and nothing else.

After this slender dinner they be either teaching or learning until five of the clock in the evening, when as they have a supper not much better than their dinner. Immediately after which, they go either to reasoning in problems, or unto some other study, until nine or ten of the clock, and there being without fire, are fain to walk or run up and down half an hour, to get heat in their feet when they go to bed.'[7]

Knewstub would be no stranger to a hard life. Miss Mary Noble in her History of the Parish of Bampton, Westmorland told of the early hours of fellside farmers, rising between four and five in the morning to tend their cattle in the byres.[8] And from William Harrison of Radwinter who died in 1593 to Dr. Augustus Jessopp writing as a country vicar in 1887, their description of the conditions of the poor is virtually the same as that of scholars at St. John's. Four of them would sleep on straw pallets on the floor of a college, or a tutor's room, covered with rough mats, with a log for a pillow. Pillows were thought meet only for women in childbed.[9]

Knewstub was taught in a college dominated by men who had been exiled under Mary, had used the Genevan form of worship, and had returned to question the Elizabethan prayer book as containing too many reliques of Popery, the surplice, the sign of the Cross, and a liturgy with too many reminders of the old religion to suit a reformed faith.[10] In 1565 Thomas Cartwright the leader of the Cambridge puritans preached three sermons attacking the use of the surplice, with the result that soon after, the fellows and scholars of St. John's appeared in college chapel without their surplices. This demonstration was soon copied at Trinity.[11] The term puritan dates from this year, and as Heylin noted, because these men were 'pretending to greater purity in the service of God than was held forth unto them (as they gave it out) in the Common Prayer Book.'[12] Knewstub took his B.A. in 1564, his M.A. in 1568, and his B.D. in 1576. He was made a fellow in 1567. Thus he came to his fellowship just as St. John's had embarked on this marked protestant course. How far the puritan faction dominated the fellowship is not clear; but they became an exclusive clique within the college. In 1595 some of the fellows complained that the puritans 'in their private sermons (say) that we ought to choose our fellows and scholars *religious* and *godly* men (as they term them) that be unlearned, rather than our greatest scholars; and following this principle they have pestered this house with unlearned puritans, picked out of the whole University and schoolmasters out of the country, and drive away all the best and to-wardly scholars that be of our college.' This is in marked contrast to the outlook of Roger Ascham, a fellow of St. John's of an earlier generation, a great greek and latin scholar, and from 1548 tutor to Princess Elizabeth. He was devoted to archery, and in his book on the subject (published in 1545) he added this dedication under the royal arms of Henry VIII:

Rejoyce Englande, be gladde and merie,
TROTHE over commeth thyne enemyse all,
The Scot, the Frenchman, the Pope, and heresie,
OVERCOMMED by Trothe, have had a fall.
Sticke to the Trothe, and evermore thou shall
Through Christ, King Henry, the Boke and the BOWE
All manner of enemies, quite overthrowe.[13]

That was a robust creed, far different from the cant of the later puritan faction.

Knewstub established himself as a lecturer and writer of devotional books. When in 1565 Lady Mary Grey married the Queen's serjeant-porter Thomas Keys, without royal permission, the erring husband was confined to the Fleet, and Lady Mary was placed in private custody till the husband's death in prison in 1571. During her restraint, Lady Mary read many religious works, including Mr Knewstub's Readings.[14] He published: a sermon he preached at Paul's Cross in 1576; his lectures on the twentieth chapter of Exodus in 1577, dedicated to the countess of Warwick; A confutation of the monstrous and horrible heresies taught by Hendrick Niclaes, and embraced by a number who call themselves the Family of Love, in 1579; and finally An Answer to certain assertions, tending to maintain the Church of Rome to be the true Catholic Church, in 1579. The dedication of his lectures on Exodus to the countess of Warwick, maid of honour to the Queen was a calculated move. She was sister of Margaret countess of Cumberland, whose husband owned the manor in Westmorland where he had been born; and both were daughters of Francis Russell second earl of Bedford, a strong supporter of the reformed religion.

On 13 August 1579 Knewstub was appointed to the rectory of Cockfield in Suffolk, a living he was to hold for forty years. During that time he became leader of the puritan faction in East Anglia, especially in Suffolk. He and John More, minister of St. Andrew's in Norwich worked to build up the classical presbyterian system within the established church in East Anglia. On the 8th May 1582 he convened a meeting of sixty ministers from Essex, Cambridgeshire and Norfolk at Cockfield church to consider the Elizabethan prayer book, what to reject, and what to tolerate.

Two months later a further meeting was held at Cambridge, the fount of the puritan movement.[15] Knewstub became so powerful that when the chief congregation at Bury St. Edmunds wished to choose a minister they asked Dr. Still the master of St. John's or Trinity, and Knewstub to guide them in the choice of a godly divine. The congregation had claimed the right to choose their minister and curates since the dissolution of the monastery. The Genevan form of worship was followed, and unsatisfactory curates were dismissed by vote of the congregation.[16] Both Bury and Sudbury became a very paradise of puritan dominance.

In 1585 Robert Dudley earl of Essex, and the Queen's favourite, was appointed to command the English forces sent to support the United Provinces in the Netherlands in their war against Spain. He appointed two chaplains, Knewstub, and Humfrey Fenn former vicar of Holy Trinity, Coventry, but recently suspended for refusing to subscribe to Whitgift's Articles. He was a stiff opponent of episcopacy; was restored in 1585, suspended 1590, taken before Star Chamber in 1591, and released in 1592. He died in 1634 protesting in his Will against episcopacy.[17] It is therefore not surprising that when the mastership of St. John's fell vacant in 1595, and Knewstub was the candidate of the puritan faction, the fellowship was wary, and elected Dr. Richard Clayton, dean of Peterborough to the post. He was a benefactor to the college, and built the second court; he could afford to do so.

It is probable that Knewstub was one of the Puritan leaders who drew up the Millenary Petition signed by a thousand ministers, and presented to James I on his arrival in England after the death of Queen Elizabeth. They objected to many things in the old church order, the cross in baptism, confirmation, the surplice, the ring in marriage, the length of the service, the profanation of the Lord's day, bowing at the Name of Jesus, and use of the Apocrypha in the lessons. Knewstub was certainly one of the leaders at the Hampton Court Conference in January 1604. Thomas Cartwright had died the previous December; he would have been the most gifted and learned of the Puritan speakers, and would have pressed for the Presbytering system, from which King James had just escaped on coming to England.[18] It is said that when Knewstub presented some of the demands of the Petition he spoke so confusedly that his meaning could not be collected therefrom. On the other hand it was said that he spoke 'most affectionately'.[19] The Conference resulted in two main changes; the catechism was revised, and the Authorised Version of the Bible appeared in 1611. Knewstub was not married, but Richard Knewstub appears in Cockfield parish registers. Shortly before his death he founded two Scholarships at St. John's on a rentcharge of £11 on 40 acres of land called Squires in the parish of South Minster and Steeple in Essex. Out of the £11 one pound was to go annually to the college, and two sub-sizarships of £5 for poor scholars. One was to come from the parish of Cockfield, and the other from his native parish of Kirkby Stephen. It seems he had not forgotten the lack of such a scholarship when he sent to Sedbergh in 1560 to qualify for one of Dr. Lupton's scholarships. The terms applying to Kirkby Stephen were as follows: 'One of them, to be a scholar born and brought up in the parish of Kirkby Stephen, and of Mr. Knewstub's name and kindred, and for lack of such, any other that hath been one whole year in the school of Kirkby Stephen; and for lack of such, to be taken forth of the school at Appleby. The nomination of which scholar to be always by the vicar and schoolmaster of Kirkby Stephen, subscribed with both their hands, and sent to the master and fellows of the said collage. And the said £5 to be paid yearly, till the said scholars be of standing to take the degree of master of arts, and be capable of or have for their better maintenance a scholarship.'[20] Knewstub died at Cockfield, and was buried in the church on 31st May 1624. His monument has vanished, but his epitaph has been preserved.[21] It is a strange reflection on changing church fashions, that in a church which was once the centre of Suffolk puritanism Mass vestments are now worn. The present incumbency seems to be very successful and warm. Perhaps the reliques of Popery have lost their force!

Refs: Chapter 4

(1) Valor. Eccl. Henry VIII. 1535. (O.P. 1825.) vol. V. 235/6.

(2) Foure Sermons preached in Westmorland by Richard Leake, minister of the Gospel at Killington, 1599, mentioned that the abomination of the Mass is still observed. (C.U.L. Peterborough. H.2.37⁴.).

(3) Cambridge Retrospect. T.R. Glover, Cambridge 1943. 19.

(4) Sedbergh School register. vol. I. E. Wilson. 1909. pp. 4-11 & 63.
Hist. of the College of St. John the Evangelist, Cambridge. ed. J.E.B. Mayor, 1869, Vol. I. 132.
Alumn. Cantab. J.A. Venn, part I. vol. II 1922. Robert Heblethwaite. There are 19 men of this surname at Cambridge before 1700.
There is also the letter of Roger Asham of St. John's to Robert Holtage bp. of Llandaff, and President of the Council of the North, written shortly after 1537 about an intrigue which threatened the newly-appointed Heblethwaite. The latin original is given in The Hist. of Richmondshire. T.D. Whitaker 1823. See also Hist. of Parish & Grammar School of Sedbergh. A.E. Platt. Kendal. 1876, p. 46.

(5) Sedbergh School reg. op.cit. 83.
Grace Book of the University of Cambridge. 1542-1589. J. Venn, C.U.P. 1911 for John and Richard Knewstub.
Hist. of the College of St. John the Evangelist. op.cit. for John Knewstub.

(6) C.R.O. Carlisle. Will of Henrye Knewstub of Mallerstang. 12. Feb. 1586/7.
This work, vol. I. Chapt. 14. Shorgill & Outhgill.

(7) Hist. of the College of St. John the Evangelist. op.cit. I. 131.

(8) Hist. of the Parish of Bampton. N.E. Noble, Kendal. 1901, 192.

(9) Description of England. William Harrison, ed. Georges Edelen. Cornell U.P. 1968, 200.
Arcady. For better for worse. Augustus Jessopp, D.D. London. 1887. 28.

(10) Puritanism in England. H. Hensley Henson. 1912. chap. I. A good exposition of puritanism. c. 1565.

(11) D.N.B. Thomas Cartwright of St John's and Trinity colleges.

(12) Puritanism in England op.cit. 7-8.

The England of Elizabeth. A.L. Rowse. Reprint. Soc. ed. 1953, 518. An acute judgement on Puritanism.

(13) The English Works of Roger Ascham. W. Aldis-Wright. C.U. reprint 1970. vii, Dedicatory plate to Henry VIII, before the treatise Toxophilus.

(14) Queen Elizabeth's Maids of Honour. Violet A. Wilson. 1922. 66.

(15) D.N. B. John Knewstub & John More who came from Bentham, Westomorland.
The Godly Puritans of the Elizabethan Church. Irvonwy Morgan. Epworth press 1965. passim, & p. 28, & J. Knewstub.
The Elizabethan Puritan Movement. Patrick Collinson. 1967. for Humfrey Fenn & John Knewstub.

(16) Tudor Puritanism. M.M. Knappen. Chicago U.P. 1965. 259-61.

(17) The Elizabethan Puritan Movement, op.cit. 386.
D.N.B. Humfrey Fenn, vicar of Holy Trinity, Coventry.

(18) D.N.B. Thomas Cartwright.
Oxford dict. of Christian Church. F.L. Cross. 1957. 242.

(19) D.N.B. John Knewstub.

(20) N & B, I. 543. John Knewstub's bequest. These small trusts lost their identity in the reform of college finances in the later 19th cent. But the 40 acres were not sold till 1918.

(21) D.N. B. John Knewstub, quotes Peck's Desiderata Curiosa, p. 216.

Chapter 5

St. John's College, Cambridge.(2)

The second Sedbergh boy to go to St. John's and have a lasting effect in the north was John Corney, who entered the college at Michaelmas 1585. He took his B.A. in 1589/90, and his M.A. in 1553. He was ordained deacon and priest at Peterborough on 8th July 1595. A relative of his, another Sedbergh and St. John's boy, Robert Corney was vicar of Orton, Westmorland from 1573-1594. On his death another vicar was appointed, but died the same year. Though there is some debate as to the year of his appointment, John Corney was probably instituted vicar of Orton on the 22nd December 1595. His first wife Grace died in 1610. On the 24th July 1612 he married a widow, Mrs. Sarah Salkeld in Great Musgrave church. John Corney has two claims to notice in north-country history [1]

Until the dissolution of the monasteries, the rectory and advowson of Orton were owned by Conishead priory. They were retained at the dissolution by the Crown, and were held as part of the possessions of the Duchy of Lancaster. Thus John Corney was appointed by the Crown. In 1618, when King James was short of money he sold a number of rectories and advowsons to two London merchants, Francis Morice, and Francis Phelips, who hoped to make a profit by resale. The vicar, John Corney, Edmund Branthwaite and Philip Winster bought the rectory estate and advowson of Orton for £570, and they in turn transferred it to twelve feoffees in trust for the landowners of the parish. The trust specified that on the avoidance of the vicarage the feoffees had to convene a meeting of the landowners of the parish within three months for the purpose of electing a new vicar. This Genevan form of election has continued until recent years.[2] We will return to the patronage issue in a moment.

In the year 1620 King James issued a proclamation, without Parliamentary sanction, abolishing Border tenant-right, on the supposition that as the two kingdoms were now united in one monarch, there was no further need of military service on the Borders. He further asserted, that as tenant-right and border service had been held together, the abolition of one cancelled the other. He claimed that the tenants could no longer claim tenant-right succession to their lands, but that the lands were now the property of their land lords. The case came to a head in the Crown lands of the Richmond and Marquess fees of the Barony of Kendal, which King James had recently transferred to his son Prince Charles. Prince Charles, through his steward, informed the tenants that if they wished to retain tenant-right they could purchase it from the Crown to re-establish their old right. The tenants protested, and in turn they were prosecuted in Chancery for claiming tenant-right of inheritance. The matter was compromised in the sum of £2,700, and a decree was issued confirming all their old rights in at least forty-four manors or sub-manors in those two fees. The King then issued a further instruction to all the lords of Westmorland, and later in all the four Border counties to do the same. A number of lords took up the suggestion and proceeded to eject the tenants who could not submit. By this time the country of Westmorland was in an uproar, and in December 1620 a meeting was convened at Staveley near Kendal, where leaders were chosen and a common purse established to meet legal costs.

Another meeting was held in January 1621, and soon the authorities in London heard of these subversive meetings. They also heard that a paper was circulating claiming that ancient tenant-right did not depend on Border service. Anthony Wetherell, vicar of Kirkby Stephen, was supposed to be the author, and he and a number of leading tenants in the country were accused in Star Chamber of breaking the King's peace. Writs were issued by Sir Thomas Coventry, the Attorney-General, to the leading gentry to examine the culprits. During the years 1621 and 1622 long lists of questions and answers passed between London and Kendal. There is a large bundle of these in the Public Record Office in Chancery Lane. It was some time before they found out that it was not the vicar of Kirkby Stephen, but

John Corney vicar of Orton who had written the tract on tenant-right. He had not written it for the present emergency, but had been asked to do so twelve years earlier by Margaret countess dowager of Cumberland, then living at Brougham Castle, near Penrith, during her case against her tenants at King's Meaburn. The ground was removed from under the feet of the Attorney-General when Mr. Corney told him that he had submitted the work to Sir Thomas Chamberlaine kt. one of the judges of the King's Bench, on the recommendation of the Lord Keeper of the Great Seal. There was nothing underhand about it. The case drizzled on until King James died in 1625, and on 19 June the same year the judges in Star Chamber declared for the tenants. Apart from the many tenants and landowners who gave evidence, two men stand out in the depositions as being well informed in this dispute. John Corney, and Martin Gilpin steward of many manors in the Barony of Kendal.[3] Gilpin will be referred to later.

John Corney lived till 1643, and spanned some of the most important years in Westmorland history. In the mid 1630s, there were three northern tenant-right cases which mark a further stage in the development of land-law: Middleton v. Jackson, Monsier v. Ducket, and Popham v. Lancaster which will be referred to later.[4] In 1634 the tenants of the barony of Appleby resisted the claim of Francis earl of Cumberland to receive the barony dues of neatgelt, serjeant-oats or bailiff corn. There had been several irregularities in their collection, and the case was heard in Chancery before Lord Keeper Coventry, the same man who as Sir Thomas Coventry had prosecuted the Kendal barony tenants in 1621. Though the dues were confirmed, their method of collection was to be revised.[5] These minor incidents in petty serjeanty came under review in the proposed Great Contract of 1610; and though the major feudal dues to the Crown were abolished in the reign of Charles II, the lesser to the barons were not.[6]

It is possible to argue that the political temper of the remoter dale parishes began to change after 1635 when the Crown extended the levying of Ship Money to the non-maritime counties. Cumberland and Westmorland became involved in 1635 when Northumberland was charged with transporting 3,000 loads of timber for the building of a large ship. The Northumberland justices suggested that Durham should bear half the cost; in turn the bishop of Durham suggested that Cumberland, Westmorland and the North Riding of Yorkshire should also contribute.[7] In this way Cumberland and Westmorland had to raise £1,000[8] and later £1,400 between them during 1636 and 1637. But the counties were so poor that the money was raised with difficulty, the market towns rated separately, and the poorer clergy excused. Kendal paid £15, and Appleby £5.[9] [10] In the end the Westmorland justices became so restive that they did not attend the meetings to levy the rate.[11, 12] While the raising of ship-money continued until 1638/9 in the four border counties, the king's attempt from 1637 to impose the Prayer Book on the Scots Kirk increased the anxieties of the Border counties. In the autumn of 1638 the government ordered the calling out and exercising of the trained bands, and ordered that supplies of bullet and match should be sent to Hull and Newcastle.[13] Thus while the Scots were signing the National Covenant against episcopacy, the King was arming the borders, and the local gentry were calling out and exercising the trained bands.[14] Henry lord Clifford occupied Carlisle on the orders of the earl of Essex in April 1639, using not only some local levies, but some 500 of Strafford's Irish troops.[15] the King declared war on Scotland on the 16th May. But his troops were so unsatisfactory that he signed the Treaty of Berwick on the 18th June.

The Short Parliament which met on the 13th April 1640 refused to grant the King any subsidies unless their grievances were met. It was dissolved on the 5th of May, and the King proceeded to raise money by illegal means, and plan the second attack on Scotland. He ordered 29,000 trained bands to be at Newcastle by the 1st of June. The Scots Covenanters set out from Edinburgh on the 20th of July, and crossed the Tweed on the 20th of August.[16] The King arrived at York on the 24th of September, and the Scots occupied Newcastle and Durham. The peers insisted at once on opening negotiations with the Scots, who refused to come to York unless Strafford was removed. The young Philip lord Wharton was one of the English commissioners who met the Scots at Ripon on the 1st. of October. After some haggling the Scots agreed to a subsistence of £25,000 a month to maintain their army, to be raised out of the northern counties.[17] When the borough of Newcastle delayed in paying a debt of £1,400 to the Scots, the mayor and aldermen were imprisoned till it was paid. On hearing this the Westmorland gentry agreed that every three able men should support one man in arms to resist the advance of the Scots to Carlisle.[18] There is no proof that the Scots ever occupied Carlisle, though by the terms of the Treaty of Ripon its garrison was disbanded. Its arms were placed in the cathedral fratry, and the key held by the mayor.

The Long Parliament which met on the 3rd November 1640 was predominantly Puritan, and proceeded to impeach Laud and Strafford, and debate drastic changes in the church. Bishops and cathedral clergy were to be abolished and their estates used to support godly preachers. Though the Root and Branch Bill was not passed, the ideals of the presbyterian system were voiced. Lay commissioners were proposed to govern the church; five ministers in each country were to ordain ministers. From this date we can trace the emergence of the puritan factions in market towns such as Kendal and Richmond, which a few years later were to form the nucleus of the county committees, which operated during the civil wars and the Commonwealth.

These two sections on Ship Money and the two short Scottish wars have been inserted to show that by November 1640 the northern gentry were irritated and divided by illegal taxation, futile military exercises, and the incompetence of the King and his advisers. While the majority of the gentry and nobility remained loyal, a minority began to look for other political and religious solutions, and this divided opinion found voice in the parishes. This can be seen at Orton, when John Corney was still vicar. In 1637 one Edward Newburgh put in a caveat claiming the vicarage on the death or resignation of Corney. In 1639 a similar caveat was entered by Thomas Barlow, M.A., Edward Birkbeck and others representing a faction of the landowners claiming the right of presentation. The Birkbeck family were astute business men, and for several generations had a finger in many pies.

John Corney died in 1643, while the civil wars were raging, and at once the factions tried to appoint their own vicar. The royalists sought the help of the Marquess of Newcastle, commander of the King's northern forces, and he recommended a Mr Lowther, a minister serving in Ireland. The feoffees turned him down. Then the puritan group, led by Edward Birkbeck the elder, William Thomson of Cotflatt, and Robert Whitehead of the Park, obtained the presentation of Alexander Fetherstonhaugh, a chaplain in the Parliamentary army. He took his presentation to Archbishop Ussher the exiled archbishop of Armagh, who held the see of Carlisle in commendam 1642-3, who instituted him. At the same time the feoffees proposed a third man, George Fothergill a Ravenstonedale man, then vicar of Pontefract, and he was elected by a majority

of the landowners within the prescribed three months. He went to Ussher, presented the nomination of the feoffees, and was refused on the ground that Fetherstonhaugh was already instituted. The feoffees then went to law, won their right to present, and Ussher was forced to appoint him. But that was not the end of the contest. Fetherstonhaugh and his supporters tried to gain entry to the church, and for nine weeks Fothergill and the feoffees kept the church locked, while worship was held in the churchyard. Eventually his rival conceded defeat and withdrew.[19] Thus from 1643 Orton parish was deeply divided by three factions.

George Fothergill of Ravenstonedale entered St. John's College, Cambridge from Sedbergh school in 1625, took his B.A. in 1628, and his M.A. in 1631. He was vicar of Pontefract from 1641, and went to Orton in 1643, where he remained till 1663, having refused conformity under the Act of Uniformity of 1662. It is clear that he was a Ravenstonedale man from the fact that on 10th May 1655 a manor court of Ravenstonedale was held to levy a general fine on the death of Lady Philadelphia Wharton, the widow of Sir Thomas Wharton of Aske Hall near Richmond. George Fothergill, clerk paid a general fine of 18s.4d. for Trannahill, near Brownber, Ravenstonedale. He thus already owned the property, and it was not a new admission.[20] Fothergill did not have an easy time at Orton. In 1648 when the royal forces were in the north one Thomas Birkbecke the blacksmith of Orton joined them, did a bit of plundering with them, and bought some of the animals they had taken from supporters of Parliament at bargain prices. He took a horse of Thomas Dawson of Orton, and for 15s. bought a cow of Alexander Dixon worth £5. He plundered the house of Mr. Edward Birkbecke of Orton, and also that of Mr George Fothergill, minister of Orton, declaring that 'the said Mr Fothergill had gone to the enemy and did not deserve to have one groat's worth left.[21] The blacksmith seems to have been after quick pickings.

The late summer of 1652 was to witness the most astonishing visit of George Fox the Quaker preacher to Orton and Revenstonedale. He came to Sedbergh in Whitsun week, and in the course of his journey towards Swarthmore laid the ground of that movement which was to change the religious history of the north. On his return through Kendal he had a brush with the presbyterian clergy, who pursued him to Orton and Ravenstonedale. Fothergill of Orton, Dalton of Shap, Dodson of Ravenstonedale, and Higginson of Kirkby Stephen confronted him. He on his part declared

30

the Day of the Lord, that they were Liars, Deceivers, Hireling Priests, oppressors of the poor through tithes, and that the Lord's judgement would sweep them away. He proclaimed the Light of Christ in each man's heart, and that his church was pure and without earthly corruption, and its members would walk in innocency and honesty, without distinctions of rank or wealth. The theological argument was bitter and brisk. But such was Fox's dominance of mind, that after each encounter he said 'The Lord's Power was over all.' A fortnight later he was followed by James Nayler, who held a meeting at the house of Robert Shaw of Orton, where he was attacked by the same clergy. He then went to John Pinder of Wath in Ravenstonedale, and then to John Knewstub at Shorgill in Mallerstang,[22] where he and his companion Francis Howgill were arrested at the instigation of Fothergill and Higginson, examined at Kirkby Stephen and committed to gaol at Appleby. This is not the place to follow the Quaker story, except to say that Orton was the birthplace of George Whitehead the young schoolmaster who attended Orton church, was dissatisfied with Fothergill's preaching, embraced the Quaker faith, and on the death of Fox became the leader of the movement. He talked with Kings, and lived to see toleration after years of the most bitter persecution.[23]

When in March 1654 Parliament passed the Act for the Approbation of Public Preachers and Schoolmasters, and appointed Triers to look at the political and religious credentials of all in office, Fothergill was examined on the 11th May, and was supported by his usual friends Higginson, Dalton, Dodson and Wil-kinson. His appointment was confirmed on the 24th May at Whitehall.[24] By now Fothergill was regarded by the Quakers as a persecutor of Truth, and a fit subject for their venom. Dr. Burn the later vicar of Orton, and no lover of the movement, tells of the Sunday when Fothergill and John Dalton of Shap decided to exchange pulpits. It may have been a carefully laid trap. A behatted Quaker stalked into Orton church as Dalton was in mid-sermon. To the astonishment of the congregation the Quaker shouted at Dalton and said: 'Come down thou false Fothergill'. 'Who told thee that my name is Fothergill?' said Dalton. 'The Spirit' said the Quaker. 'Then that Spirit of thine is a lying spirit, for it is well known that I am not Fothergill, but one-eyed Dalton of Shap!'[25]

Under the Act of Uniformity of 1662 all clergy were required to subscribe to the Prayer Book, repudiate the National Covenant, and declare the illegality of taking up arms against the King. Under pressure from lord Wharton, Higginson, Dodson and Dalton conformed, but Fothergill, and Christopher Jackson the intruded rector of Crosby Garrett, were deprived. Jackson came to Ravenstonedale, and under the patronage of lord Wharton founded the Presbyterian chapel there. Fothergill went south, and the same year conformed and was appointed vicar of Warsop, Nottinghamshire. While he lived there an Orton friend lived with him, Edward Birkbecke, who died there in 1670. Fothergill died there on 23rd August 1683 aged 76.[26]

Through these two men, Corney and Fothergill, the Calvinist tradition of St. John's College was developed in one Westmorland parish.

References Chapter 5

(1) Ejected of 1662 in Cumberland & Westmorland. B. Nightingale, p. 1201. Nightingale first suggests 1609; but p. 1400 mentions the institution 22 Dec. 1595.
Sedbergh School reg. op. cit. I, 86.
Alumn. Cantab. J.A. & J. Venn, I.

(2) N & B, I. 483.

(3) N & B, I, 51 et seq.
C & W trans. N.S. LXII, (1962) 224. Mr Gilpin and manorial customs, by Isaac s.o. Martin Gilpin; by Mrs Annette Bagot.
P.R.O. Chancery Lane.. Star Chamber papers. Ref. STAC 8 (James I) Bundle 34, file 4. (Item 24) 10th Sept. 20 James I. Among many depositions those of Martin Gilpin of Strickland Roger aged 75, and John Corney vicar of Orton aged 58.
Hist. of Westmorland. R.S. Ferguson. 1884. 125-139.

(4) This work, vol. I chapt. 22, refs. 21, 22, 25.

(5) N & B, I 292-4. Decree 23rd May 1634. (10 Car. I.)

(6) Constitutional Documents of the Reign of James I. J.R. Tanner, C.U.P. 1952, p. 345 et seq.
English Constitutional Documents of the 17th Century. J.R. Tanner, C.U.P. 1960, 221.

(7) S.P. Chas. I. 1635. CCXCI, 156. (?27) June. Bp Morton of Durham to the Council.

(8) S.P. Chas. I. 1636. CCCXi, 144. (no. 14) 3 Jan. Report of Edward Nicholas clerk to the Council. The assessment of £1,000 was a joint one.
S.P. Chas. I. 1636. (Add. vol. 1625-1644.) DXXXVI, 525, (no. 14) 1st March. List of English counties paying ship money.

(9) S.P. Chas. I. 1636. CCCXXVII, 20. (no. 71) 24 June. Letter of Wm. Mansergh to the Council on the taxation of Westmorland for ship money.

(10) S.P. Chas. I. 1636. CCCXXXIII, 152 (no. 9) 3 Oct. Alteration of sums assessed for ship money. Northumberland was reduced from £3,700 to £2,100.
S.P. Chas. I. 1636. CCCXXXIII, 159. (nos. 41 & 45) Third writs for ship money.

(11) S.P. Chas. I. 1636/7. CCCXLIX, 492. (no. 76) Receipt of the Council to Wm. Lowther on behalf of Francis earl of Cumberland as sheriff of Westmorland of £700 on the writ of 12th August last.

(12) S.P. Chas. I. 1637. CCCLXIX, 461. (no. 12) 2 Oct. Privy Council to Francis earl of Cumberland concerning raising ship money.
S.P. Chas. I. 1637. CCCXIX, 469 (no. 47) 9 Oct. Council of the North to the Council reports difficulty of collecting ship money in Cumberland & Westmorland, and reluctance of some justices to submit.

(13) Hist. MSS Comm. Rep. XII, Pt. II, 1888, vol. II, Coke 190. 3 Aug. 1638. Henry lord Clifford to Sir John Coke: the horse & foot in Westmorland are soon to be exercised, and private arms bought in London.
S.P. Chas. I. 1638, CCCXCVII, 548. (no. 6) 3 Aug. Remembrance of Thomas earl of Arundel & Surrey, and the finding of men and arms for the defence of Carlisle & the Border shires.

(14) S.P. Chas. I. 1638, CCCI, 95 (no. 39) 9 Nov. The Council to Francis earl of Cumberland, sheriff of Westmorland; instructions for raising ship money.

(15) D.N.B. Henry 5th earl of Cumberland.

(16) Fairfax Corresp. G.W. Johnson, Vol. II, 1848, p.9.
D.N.B. Charles I.

(17) S.P. Chas. I. 1640. CCCCLXIX, 157 (no. 77 sect. II) 10th Oct. Leonard Pickering, commissary-general for victualling the army to Windebank (sects. 1, 2, 3,).
Strafford, by the earl of Birkenhead, 1938, 263.

(18) S.P. Chas. I. CCCCLXXI, 197. (no. 67) 26 Oct. Dr. Thos, Read to Windebank. See also ref: (17) above.
V.C.H. Cumberland II, 287.
Hist. of Cumberland, R.S. Ferguson. 1890, 256.

(19) N & B, I, 483 et seq.
Ejected of 1662. B. Nightingale. 1202-4, which states that G. Fothergill was presented to the vicarage 11 Nov. 1643.

(20) Ejected of 1662. op. cit. II, 1202-4, 1207.
Lonsdale MSS, C.R.O. Carlisle. Summary of manorial incidents in the manor of Ravenstonedale in the case of Fawcet v. Lowther 1751. D/Lons/L. Ravenstonedale 4.
English Law Reports, 2 Ves. Sen. 299. 15 June 1751.

(21) Ejected of 1662. op. cit. 1205. 5 April 1651. Information of Lancelot Thwaites of Orton, yeoman.
S.P. Committee for Compounding, 1643-1660, 521. Dec. 1651. Information that Thomas Birkbeck of Orton, a blacksmith rode with the enemy and bought plundered goods.

(22) C & W trans. N.S. LIV, 1954, 176.

(23) First Publishers of Truth. ed. Norman Penney, 1907, 248.
N & B, I. 536-9.
Fox's Journal, ed. J.L. Nickalls, 1975, 117, passim.

(24) Ejected of 1662, II, 1206.

(25) N & B, I, 537.

(26) Ejected of 1662, 1207-8. He left £10 towards the building of the third court at St. John's.
Hist. & traditions of Ravenstonedale. Rev. W. Nicholls, II, 1914. p. 105.

Chapter 6

Robert Holgate

We now retrace our steps to 1537, the year of the brutal crushing of the second rising of the Pilgrimage of Grace. The King set up two councils to govern the north; the Council for the Borders, and the Council of the North. The latter had jurisdiction over Cumberland, Westmorland, Northumberland, and Durham whose palatinate jurisdiction was to be reduced. The latter had wide powers over agriculture, to defend the poor against the rich, and to supervise the justices of the peace. It was empowered to inflict any penalty short of death, and cases of difficulty could be referred to the Privy Council. Both councils were courts under the Privy Council, and in effect were bodies established to administer a conquered province. The Council of the North was mainly staffed by new men, gentleman who had taken part in the Pilgrimage, who quickly changed sides early in 1537, and had proved their loyalty to the King by betraying, and in some cases supervising the hanging of, the commons whose cause they had espoused. Nearly all the old quarrelsome nobility were excluded, Dacre, Scrope and Cumberland, pending good behaviour. The first President was the duke of Norfolk until his departure south in October 1537. He was succeeded by Cuthbert Tunstall, bishop of Durham, at a salary of £800 a year. His assistant was Robert Holgate, prior of Watton, Master of the Gilbertines, and recently bishop of Llandaff. His salary was £20 a year 'giving continual attendance'. The lesser officers had smaller allowances, and the Council was given a permanent secretariat, and accommodated in the buildings of the dissolved St. Mary's Abbey. The estimated expenses of the two councils were £2,607.6.8d. a year.[1]

In the very long instructions drawn up by Henry VIII on 16th January 1537 for the administration of the Council of the North he made this important concession to the complaints of the commons:

'One ground of the late rebellion was that certain lords and gentlemen have enclosed commons and taken intolerably excessive fines. The Duke is to receive complaints touching this, enquire who have been most extreme, and moderate between them, so that gentlemen and yeoman may live together as they be joined in one body politic under the King.'[2]

This was a remarkable change of tone, while the King's demand of the gentry for complete submission under oath was ruthless.

Robert Holgate who played so important a part in northern history was born about the year 1481, and at an unknown date became a canon regular in the order of St. Gilbert of Sempringham, and was educated at the house of the Order in Cambridge. He took his B.D. in 1523/4, and was preacher before the university in 1524. In 1529 he was summoned to convocation as Prior of the Gilbertine house of St. Catherine's-without-the-walls in Lincoln. During his time at Lincoln he became vicar of Cadney near Brigg, north of Lincoln. It was during this time that he had a dispute with a local landowner Sir Francis Ayscough, and was forced to pursue his cause in London. It was while in London that he came to the notice of Cromwell, and was made a chaplain to Henry VIII. In after years he admitted that this chance visit to London led to fortune. In or before 1534 he was made Master of the Gilbertine order. He remained at Lincoln, but was over the whole order, and without him no legal actions could be received or undertaken. That Thomas Cromwell seems to have been behind his promotion is clearer in the next move, when by 1536 he became prior of the major house of Watton in East Yorkshire. His promotion was resented by the sub-prior and most of the brethren of Watton, who addressed a letter to Cromwell complaining that 'the late prior of St. Catherine's near Lincoln has taken upon himself to be their prior and Master of their religion.'[3]

On the outbreak of the Pilgrimage of Grace in the autumn of 1536 a number of churchmen prudently fled to London, including Cuthbert Tunstall, bishop of Durham, and Holgate. Bishop John Kytte of Carlisle and one time friend of Wolsey was also in London, while Archbishop Lee of York remained. He fled from York on the arrival of the commons, and together with many Yorkshire gentry half sided with the rebels till the collapse of the revolt. They then sided with the King, saved their skins, and were only restored to favour on proof of loyalty. It was while he was in London in 1536 that Holgate made the acquaintance of John Hilsey, former provincial of the Dominicans, and now active reforming bishop of Rochester. When the Spanish bishop George de Athequa of Llandaff resigned in 1536 after the death of Queen Catherine of Arragon, Henry VIII's first wife, bishop Hilsey wrote on the 10th August 1536 to Cromwell suggesting that Holgate might be considered for Llandaff.[4] Nothing came of the suggestion for six months; and on a further nudge from Hilsey, Holgate was offered Llandaff and was consecrated by Hilsey in the Lady Chapel of the Blackfriars church in London on the 25th March 1537.[5]

During his absence from Watton that house had been the centre of the Hallam and Bigod rising in January 1537. Hallam was hanged within a month, and Bigod later that year in London. Also the sub-prior of Watton, and two of the Warter canons suffered. Thus when Holgate returned to Watton after the main hangings ordered by Norfolk, Watton was a broken and terrified community, as was all the north. Though is was some time before the rents of the northern estates were restored, from October 1537 Holgate enjoyed the following nominal income. From the bishoprick of Llandaff £154.2.8.; from the Mastership of the Gilbertines £64.13.4.; and from the Council of the North £20. Out of the first two he had to pay his tenths of £15.9.5. and £6.9.4., leaving him with a net income from the three sources of £216.18.3.[6] On his consecration Holgate was given permission to hold Watton priory and Mastership 'in commendam'. There is no indication that he had a separate income as prior. After his consecration he was styled commendator of his two monastic offices. It has been suggested that because Holgate was in favour and serving on the Council of the North the remaining canons and cannonesses at Watton, and the canons at Old Malton and Warter were protected. It is more accurate to say that Holgate's work on the Council was financed in part from monastic sources, which might be abolished at a stroke. He was kept on a short string till he proved his worth.

On the 27th June 1538 the King wrote to the council of the North informing them that he required Tunstall's presence at Court, and Holgate was appointed President in his place,[7]

at a salary of £800 a year, with a house of residence at York with servants. There was also the permanent secretariat. He resided permanently at York, ruling the north through the Council. It was a bold stroke by the King, but much resented by the old nobility whom he supplanted. They had seen this shrewd 'monk' rise to supreme power in under two years.

At the time of his appointment as President, Holgate still ruled the Gilbertines and the priory of Watton as commendator. On the 9th December 1539 he surrendered the Mastership of the Order and the priory of Watton with all its manors and advowsons to the Crown. Two days later he surrendered Malton priory. They seem to have been surrendered on his signature alone.[8] They thus came under the control of the Court of Augmentations. As a reward for past and future services Holgate was on the 16th July 1541 given the priory of Watton, excluding the nun's church, the manor of Watton, and seven other manors including that of Ravenstonedale, together with nine rectories for life. In the Valor of 1535 Watton priory was valued at £453.7.8. gross, and £360.16.10½. clear. The grant also included the Master of Sempringham's House in London. On the 26th June 1540 Holgate bought for £276. the house and site of Malton priory, the church, steeple, the demesne lands in Old Malton, the fishery of Derwent, Sutton Grange, and certain lands in the parish of Kirkby Overkarr.[9] On the dissolution of his house he ceased to be a monk in name, though he had probably abandoned his habit before then.

There is no need to follow Holgate's career as President from 1538 to 1550, except to note that he served on the two northern commissions of 1545 and 1547 for the abolition of the chantries, and supervising the transporting of the silver resulting from the sales to London. Though some country curacies were saved, even those chantries whose priests taught local boys were abolished. Among these were the singing school at Brough-under-Stainmore, and the chantry school at Sedbergh. Though a number of schools were later re-endowed, an opportunity to maintain education in the remoter parts of the north was lost. On the 10th January 1545 Holgate was made Archbishop of York. He received the pallium from Cranmer at a special service designed for the occasion. By this promotion he became the wealthiest prelate in England. On the 24th October 1546 he obtained letters patent for the foundation of three grammar schools at York, Old Malton and Hemsworth.[10] By these foundations Holgate sought to offset some of the ills occasioned by the dissolution of the monasteries and the chantries. Each school was to be a separate corporation, with a master and usher. The statutes were framed according to the principles of the New Learning. The masters might be laymen, and married. Latin, Greek and Hebrew were to be taught free, while parents paid a quarterly sum for instruction in English, writing and arithmetic. His principle was that sound learning was the best corrective against ignorance and superstition. His standards were high; in August 1552 he issued thirty injunctions for York Minster, with the chief emphasis on education. The vicars choral had to attend regular lectures in divinity, undergo a monthly examination and memorise weekly a chapter of St. Paul's epistles in the Latin translation by Erasmus. They must possess a copy of the New Testament, reading one chapter after dinner, and another after supper. The Minster Library had to acquire the latest commentaries by Erasmus, Luther, and those of Calvin and Bullinger. He controlled the list of the Minster preachers, forbade the playing of the Minster organ during services, and all singing except plainsong. He was a severe ruler. He was more conservative in eucharistic doctrine that Ridley or Cranmer, and held that England should develop a sound educational system based on the vernacular scriptures.[11] Until the writings of Professor Dickens, Holgate had not received his due.

We need only mention his marriage in 1549, which scandalised many of his contemporaries. He was removed from the office of President in 1550. In May 1553 he was sent for to attend Edward VI on the visit of the Admiral of France. In 1553 he sent to Hampton Court with about seventy horse, and stayed there over the death of the King till Michaelmas, spending £1,000 on the occasion. Mary Tudor was proclaimed Queen on the 16th July 1553, and on the 4th October 1553 Holgate was arrested and sent to the Tower 'on pretence of treason or great crimes.' On the 16th March 1554 he was deprived of his see on the ground of his marriage. His rich stores of goods and valuables at Cawood and Battersea were seized. He was examined in the Tower by Sir Richard Southwell, a member of the Privy Council, most particularly about his marriage. By this time his wife seems to have died. He confessed that he had been persuaded to marry for fear of being called a papist. In December 1554 he wrote to Southwell urging that his case was different from that of other protestant bishops, that he had not gone so far amiss as they; he was willing to act in his vocation as

a Gilbertine canon, obey the laws of the Queen, and to make amends for his offences. As a sweetener he offered £1,000 for his release.[12] This diplomatic confession would not be lost on Southwell, who in his day was Cromwell's tool against the monasteries, a Privy Councillor under Edward VI, and Master of the Ordnance under Mary. Holgate obtained his release on 18th January 1555. He retired into the Gilbertine house in Cow Lane, where he died on the 15th November 1555. He was buried in the parish church of St. Sepulchre. He left all his estate to the founding of an almshouse in his native Hemsworth. With the exception of those Gilbertine estates held by Holgate for life, which had been sold by the Crown in reversion, the remainder which he held for life fell to the Crown.[13]

One of the Gilbertine properties which Holgate held for life was the liberty, manor and rectory of Ravenstonedale in Westmorland, together with two properties in Kirkby Stephen. He was thus, as prior of Watton, in nominal control of the manor of Ravenstonedale from about 1536 to the surrender on 9th December 1539. From 16th july 1541, when he received his life grant, until his death on 15th November 1555 he was also in control of the manor. Thus his tenure of Ravenstonedale covered about twenty years. Until the dissolution his steward was Sir Christopher Dacre. It is possible that we have the names of the remaining Canons who lost their house in 1539, and were provided for by Holgate; they were Cuthbert Swynebanke clerk, and John Paycocke, clerk. Their names appear among the tenants when the manor was sold by the Crown to Sir Thomas Wharton in 1546. It is possible that Holgate employed another former canon to act as curate after the dissolution. A Mr. Toppin was curate after 1547.[14]

We are fortunate that the rental of Ravenstonedale has survived for one year, probably during the time that Holgate was absentee landlord. The park and demesne of Ravenstonedale were rated at £100 a year, and the rectory (including profits from weddings, churchings, mortuaries and burials) at £132.19s.6½d. The outgoings were: To Edward Mynese schoolmaster his stipend £20; to Mr. Toppin the curate, with 10s. for an horse, his wages £8.16s.8d.; to the bishop of Carlisle synage money 4s. The rectory was thus a rich one, and for reasons which follow the year 1548 is suggested. Compared with the pensions given to the dispossessed canons of Watton who received £4. a year the allowance to the curate was adequate. More startling is the salary of £20 given to the schoolmaster Edward

Mynese. The difference in salary between him and the curate reveals Holgate's emphasis on education. It was through this man that protestant education appeared in the upper Eden valley so soon after the dissolution. Who was Edward Mynese (or Menzies)?

Edward Mynese was a Scottish schoolmaster born at Castlehill outside Edinburgh, a protestant who fled to England during the reign of Edward VI. According to the records of Kirkby Stephen grammar school[15] Mynese was 'eminent for knowledge in the Grammar and that he had great store of Gentlemen's sons. His schollers were out of Westmorland and the adjacent countryes whereof he tables at least XX in his own house.' How did Mynese come to Ravenstonedale? There are two possible solutions: the first is that if the rental just given relates to 1546 when Sir Thomas Wharton bought the reversion of Ravenstonedale from the Crown, then Menzies must have fled from Scotland before that date. The more probable answer lies in Scottish history. In 1546 George Wishart, a leading Scottish reformer, was arrested and tried by cardinal Beaton and the bishops, and burned at St. Andrew's. In the same year Beaton was murdered in revenge by John Leslie. After the battle of Pinkie on the 10th September 1547, when the French Queen Regent of Scotland captured St. Andrew's, the defenders including John Knox were transported to France and held indefinitely. Knox did not obtain his release until early in 1549, when the English government interceded on his behalf, and ap-pointed him a preacher in Berwick, where he lived for nearly two years.[16]

Another fugitive after the battle of Pinkie was the ex-Dominican John Rough, who came first to Carlisle, and thence to Protector Somerset, who gave him a stipend to preach at Carlisle, Berwick, and Newcastle. Later he married, and was given by Holgate a benefice near Hull, where he formed a strong protestant congregation. On the death of Edward VI he and his wife fled to Friesland. In 1557 he came secretly to London on business, and was persuaded to care for a secret society of protestants, was betrayed, and burned at Smithfield on 22 December 1557.[17] It is my submission that Edward Mynese came to England in or after 1547, and was similarly provided for by Holgate as schoolmaster at Ravenstonedale. There was no school at Ravenstonedale at that date, and it was clearly a charitable provision. Thus, when in 1566 Thomas lord Wharton founded Kirkby Stephen Grammar School, Edward Mynese became its first headmaster, at a salary of £12 a year, thus relieving Wharton of the charge of £20 on the rectory estate of Ravenstonedale. By this means Ravenstonedale, and then Kirkby Stephen, became centres of protestant teaching so soon after the reformation. As Sir Thomas, later lord, Wharton supported Holgate's educational ideals continuity was preserved, and the ground of seventeenth century dissent in the northern dales laid. In addition, that school and Sedbergh school supplied a constant stream of scholars to St. John's college, the centre of Puritan teaching.[18] Mynese died in 1605 at Kirkby Stephen.[19]

References Chapter 6

(1) S.P. Henry VIII, 1537, part 2. (249, 250). pp. 204-8. The commissions for the three Marches and the Council of the North with pensions and allowances.

(2) S.P. Henry VIII, 1537 (part 1) (98) 16 Jan. p. 51. The King's instructions to Norfolk.

(3) S.P. Henry VIII, 1537 (part 1) (65), (11th) Jan. Draft complaint of the sub-prior and convent of Watton (in the hand of Sir Francis Bigod) to Cromwell that 'the commons of the country have expelled the prior of St. Katherine's from Watton, and will not suffer them to receive their rents, nor will the tenants pay till they have a new prior; have elected A.B.C, prior, hoping that he will please God, the King, and the brethren of religion ... '

(4) S.P. Henry VIII, 1536 (part ii) 9260) 10 Aug. John Hilsey bp. of Rochester to Cromwell.

(5) S.P. Henry VIII, 1537 (part 1) Grants in March p. 349 et seq. (5), (30), (47). D.N.B. Holgate; for consecration 25 March 1537.

(6) Valor Eccl. Henry VIII. Vol. IV, 1821, p. 345. The income for Llandaff was certified by George de Athequa, bishop. The bishop had been confessor to Catherine of Arragon, and appears to have resigned soon after her death.
Ibid. Vol. V. 1825. p. 126. The accounts for Watton are missing; the income of the Master of the order is given under Watton, not with the priory of Sempringham in Lincs. (See ref. 14 of this chapter.)

(7) S.P. Henry VIII, 1538. (1268) 27 June. The King to the Council of the North.
Ibid. 1538, (1269) 27 June. Instructions to the Council of the North from the King; appoints the bishop of Llandaff President of the Council of the North, and requires others to be obedient to

him, namely the Earls of Westmorland, and Cumberland, Lord Dacres of the North and other named gentlemen.

(8) St. Gilbert of Sempringham. Rose Graham. 1901. 191-194 & 198.

(9) Ibid. p. 198.
S.P. Henry VIII, 1541. (1500). Enrolment of grants. p. 715. II, to Robt. bp. of Llandaff the priory of Watton (excluding the nuns church) & other properties.
S.P. Henry VIII, 1540 (831) (73). Grant of Malton priory to Holgate. The charters of Sempringham: The Genealogist. N.S. XV. 158-161; 221-227. N.S. XVI, 30-35; 76-83; 152-158; 223-228. N.S. XVII, 29-35; 164-168; 232-239.
The charter of Ravenstonedale in N & B, I. 518-522.
An History of the city of York. Charles B. Knight 2nd. ed. 1944. For Holgate 369-370, 376-7, 386-7. Not too accurate.
V.C.H. Yorkshire III, gives the Yorkshire houses. 251, Ellerton on Spalding moor; 253 Malton; 254 Watton near Beverley; 255 St. Andrew's, York.
V.C.H. Lincs. II, 179 et seq. Gilbertines of Sempringham, by Miss Rose Graham. St. Gilbert of Sempringham. Miss Rose Graham op. cit. 198/9.
The Religious Orders in England. D. Knowles, III, 1959, 317 is curiously silent on the life and doings of Holgate, with no. ref. in index, but noted as a former canon as bp. of Llandaff. Prof. Knowles does not appear to have taken the point that Watton was respited not for spiritual reasons, but to assure an income to Holgate as the King's officer.
D.N.B. Holgate. One or two inaccuracies.
S.P. Henry VIII, 1541. (1500). Enrollments of Grants by the Crown in the Augmentations in the year 32 Henry VIII, p. 715. Grant for life to Robert bp. of Llandaff of the priory and possessions of Watton; this is important as it gives details of the Watton properties missing from the Valor of 1535. Vol. V. 1825, p. 126 as those papers were lost.

(10) D.N.B. Holgate.
V.C.H. Cumberland, 1968. Vol. II, 54-58. The Abolition of the chantries in Cumberland.
Eng. Historical Review 52 (1937) 428-42. The Marriage and character of Abp. Holgate. Prof. A.G. Dickens.
Robert Holgate, Archbishop of York etc. A.G. Dickens. St. Anthony's Hall pub. no. 8, 1955.

(11) The English Reformation, A.G. Dickens. Fontana Lib. 1967, 336-7. I owe much to Prof. Dickens' later writings on Holgate.

(12) D.N.B. Holgate.

(13) Ibid. and refs.
Harrap's Guide to famous London graves. Conrad Bailey, 1975, p. 40. Grave of Robert Holgate in Holy Sepulchre, Holborn. The Rector tells me that the grave is unmarked and that Cow Lane where the Gilbertine house once stood is now part of Smithfield Street.
E.H.R. 52, (1937) op. cit. 437.
Robert Holgate by W.C. Boulter. Holgate Record Sec. no. 2. 1949.

(14) S.P. Henry VIII, 1546 (38 Henry VIII) (pt. 2.) (648) (no. 17) Grants in Dec. Grant 6th Dec. to Sir Thomas Wharton of the Liberty, Manor and rectory of Ravenstonedale. All the Ravenstonedale tenants are named. Both Swynebanke & Paycocke have the description 'clk' after their names; omitted in Hist. of Ravenstonedale vol. II, 1915, op. cit. 20-21.
The Grant is also given in N & B, I. 522, and is dated 5th Nov. 38 Henry VIII. The date in the state papers is probably the exemplification.
The important rental of Ravenstonedale about the same date, giving the name of Edward Mynese, schoolmaster, see N & B, I. 522-3.
In the Valor Eccl. 1535 the rectory of Kirkby Stephen held by the abbey of St. Mary of York was valued at £61.3.4½., and the vicarage held by Peter Bane at £48.19.6½., making a total of £110.2.6½. At first sight the rectory of Ravenstonedale valued (gross) at £132.19.6½. seems excessive; yet in 1592 it was valued at £116.13.4d. See Hist. of Ravenstonedale Vol. 1. Rev. W. Nicholls 1877. p. 41. Thus the first figure seems to have been confirmed, and marks it as rich a living as the combined rectory and vicarage of Kirkby Stephen.

(15) Kirkby Stephen Grammar School 1566-1966. By Alec Swales. Pub. J. Whitehead, Appleby, 1966. Courtesy of Mr. Brian Coates, former headmaster. The account is taken from the Machell MSS.111, 195. C.R.O. Carlisle.

(16) The English Reformation. A.G. Dickens. 323.

(17) The English Reformation. A.G. Dickens. 323, 374/5.

(18) N & B, I, 542.
Kirkby Stephen Grammar School op. cit.

(19) Inventory of Edward Mynese, 1605 at C.R.O. Carlisle.

Chapter 7

Ravenstonedale (1)

The next four chapters illustrate the long process whereby a monastic manor and liberty changed not only from clerical to lay ownership, but also from a Catholic to a Protestant society run very much on Genevan lines. Sir Thomas first lord Wharton was very much after the mould of Henry VIII, a tough border soldier who had hanged over seventy men after the Pilgrimage of Grace, a man not to be trifled with. He bought a large number of monastic estates, of which Ravenstonedale was one. In 1556 he recorded and signed the prevailing custumal of Ravenstonedale which had obtained in monastic times. In 1559/60 he undertook a building programme, rebuilt Wharton Hall, and the deerpark wall. In Ravenstonedale he squared up to the tenants, turned off a number of tenants squatting on the demesne, and compensated them with other lands taken from other tenants, and forced all his tenants to build a new deerpark wall, nine feet high.

His son Thomas second lord Wharton was a catholic, a member of the Privy Council of Queen Mary, lived at Newhall in Essex, and was an absentee landlord. It fell to his son Philip third lord Wharton who reached his majority in 1576 to try to bring order out of chaos. Chapter 8 deals with the agreement between him and the Ravenstonedale tenants adapting the custumal of 1556 to a manor and liberty now in lay ownership. Chapter 9 deals with the rules governing the manor court backed by stern penalties. Chapter 10 covers parish administration, incorporating a number of the old monastic rules. Thus by 1587 this former catholic monastic property was transformed into a self-governing protestant society, with many powers delegated by the lord to the manor court. All this was at a time of political and religious turmoil with catholic and protestant forces striving for the mastery. This was against the background of periodic bad harvests and disease, as from 1585-1587, and bubonic plague from 1596-1598 when at least a quarter of the population died.[1]

The details of manorial government must be mastered before the further question is faced; what were the additional factors which impelled members of a well regulated and self-governing society, which should have been ideal, to embrace both the Quaker and Presbyterian dissent of the later seventeenth century?

When Sir Thomas Lord Wharton bought the reversion of the liberty, manor and rectory of Ravenstonedale in 1546,[2] he and his two sons Sir Thomas and Sir Henry Wharton were fully occupied in the effective and aggressive defence of the Western Marches.[3] Henry VIII's choice of Sir Thomas Wharton as deputy Warden in 1537 met the King's wish to have a deputy as ruthless as himself in ordering the borders, who would not be weakened by the eternal feuds which had so divided the old nobility. Thus when Archbishop Holgate died in 1555, Ravenstonedale fell into the hands of a tough military man, who was too preoccupied with his border duties to attend minutely to the many monastic properties which he had acquired. In particular, sooner or later the custumals of these church properties would have to be altered to the terms of lay ownership.

In 1531 Sir Thomas bought the manors of Healaugh and Catterton near Tadcaster from the earl of Northumberland for £500. He was also steward to the earl of the Honor and castle of Cockermouth; and this continued when the earl's estates fell to the King in 1537. In 1537 he rented from the Crown the estate of New Healaugh in Swaledale. In 1541 he bought the estates of Shap abbey at an annual rent of £41.11s. from the Court of Augmentations. He also bought monastic estates of Gisburne and Rievaulx, and among other lands this brought in the manor of Muker in Swaledale. In 1560 he bought the house and site of the priory of Sinninthwaite, with lands at Walton, Buckerton and Bilton in Yorkshire. Many of these former monastic lands were sold by the Crown in reversion failing heirs male, to lord Wharton, and at an annual rent to the Crown. These reversions were finally extinguished by grant of James I, after the death of Sir George Wharton in 1609 when it was discovered that his debts almost ruined his father Phillip lord Wharton. Thereafter they were the sole property of the Wharton family. As far as Westmorland was concerned Lord Wharton owned the manors of Wharton, Kirkby Stephen (part), Nateby, Ravenstonedale, Tebay, Langdale, Bretherdale, Shap, and lands in Reagill, Sleagill, Long Marton, and Bampton Carhullan, Great Asby, Bolton, Brampton, and some properties in the barony of Kendal. Lastly he held the lands and site of the late hospital of St. Nicholas in Appleby.[4]

To anticipate later acquisitions; with the accession of Queen Mary in 1553, lord Wharton's heir Sir Thomas who had seen much border service attached himself solely to the Queen's political and religious interest. He was made Master of the Henchmen in the Queen's household, and a member of the Privy Council. From 1553 to 1558 he was in almost continuous attendance in the Council.[5] He was rewarded by the Queen with the grant of many properties. He received the grant of several manors in Essex, and the stewardship of many Crown manors in Yorkshire. Among the Essex manors was that of Newhall in Boreham, which became his principal residence for the rest of his life. He and his wife were convinced Catholics, and came under grave suspicion for hearing Mass after the accession of Elizabeth in 1558.[6]

As far as Ravenstonedale was concerned the manor came under the control of the following lords in turn:

Sir Thomas first lord Wharton 1555-1568.

Sir Thomas second lord Wharton 1568-1572.

Phillip the third lord Wharton 1572-1625. He was a minor, and reached his majority in 1576.

Philip the fourth lord, son of Sir Thomas of Aske Hall near Richmond, grandson of Phillip the third lord. 1626-1696. He was a minor and reached his majority in 1634.

This does not include two wardships, and at least two jointures.

The Manor of Ravenstonedale

Up till the Dissolution Ravenstonedale formed part of the possessions of the Gilbertine order at Watton near Beverley. Their estates were held in free alms, and their exemptions were extensive. They were to be "quit of all fines, and amerciaments, and forfeitures, and aids, and wapentac, and cities, and trithings, hundreds, and shires, and thenementale; and from

murder, and robbery, and conspiracies, and outlawry; and hamsoken, grithbreach, bloodwite, footwite, and forestal, and hengwite, and larwite. And they shall be free from scott and wardpenny, and bordeshalfpeny; and from all carriage, and sumage, and navage, and building, and all other kinds of work about the King's houses; and from all aids of sheriffs and their officers, and scutage, and assises, and gifts, and summonses, and tallages, and frankpledges, and from borthevenlig, and all pleas, and plaints, and occasions, and customs, and from their beasts to be taken by distress, and from all earthly service, and secular exaction. And their woods shall in no way be taken for the aforesaid works or any other. And *they shall have their own court and judicature*, with sak, and soke, and thol, and theam, and infangtheif, and outfangthief, and slemensfrith, and ordel, and oreste, within time and without, with all other free customs, and immunities, and liberties, and of all pleas, plaints, and quietances...''[7]

This is but a third of their exemptions, and is quoted as establishing a court of the Liberty as distinct from the Court Baron and customary court of the manor.

It is probable that during the life interest of Holgate one of his old canons, or their steward if they had one, continued to act for him. But there is evidence that things got out of hand, and some tenants, especially the Chamberlain family, took advantage of the state of affairs and enclosed some of the commons, and encroached upon the demesne by taking in some of the lord's park. It is clear from other records that the extent of the demesne lands, and the rectory estate were still known. Two things were done by the first lord. Those members of the Chamberlain family who had enclosed some portions of the waste, and taken in portions of the lord's park, were granted leases, to make the point that they were tenants of these new grounds at will only, and not by custom. These tenures were thus at risk. The second was to set down the customs of the manor as these had been received from monastic days.

Document I.[8] (1556)

THE ARTICLES of the customary Tenant right of the sole Lordshipp and parrishing of Ravenstonedaile in the Countie of Westmorland as hereafter at lardge apperethe which hath bene accustomed and used within the said Lordshipp tyme owte of mans memory All which Articles and customary Tenannte Right I the Lord Wharton Lorde Warden of the East and Middle Marches of England for anempst Skotland and Capten of the King and Queenes Majestes

Towne and castell of Barwik am well contented & pleased withall IN WITNESS WHEREOF I have subscribed my name the vjth day of Octobre in the iij:ᵈ and iiij:ᵗʰ yeares of the most fortunate reagns of our Soveraigne Lord and Ladie King Phillipp & Queens Marye et/

FFURSTE it haith bene and is accustomed within the said Lordshipp that at the exchange or entre of every tenant to pay unto the Lorde as muche fyne or gressome as the whole years rent of the same tenement extendeth unto and not above/

ITEM yt hath bene and is accustomed within the same Lordshipp that all manner of fellonyes murders forfatures petty mychery and all other trespasses Comitted and done within the precincts of the said lordship & liberties of Ravenstonedaile ayther by any of the Inhabytants or by any other forrende persone to be Inquered upon by an Indifferent Jury taiken and appointed by the lord or his officers within the said lordshipp in yt behalf/

ITEM yt haith bene and is Accustomed within the said Lordshipp that for all maner of contencons variannces debats demands titles Clames or tenannt rights of ffermeholdes which haith bene is or shal be depending in travarse Betweene Tenannt and tennant and partye and partye within the said Lordshipp to be fully ordered determined and ended by an indifferent Jurye and inquest taiken and appointed by the lord or his officers ther By the assents and consents of the said parties within the said lordshipp in that behalf/

ITEM yt haith bene and is accustomed within the same lordshipp that none o the tenannts or other persons shall improve Inclose or taike upp any of the common pasture ther withowte lycenc of the lord And appoinctment of the Jurye taken and elect in that behalf/

ITEM yt is ordered and agreed Betwixt the Lord of the same Lordshipp and the tennants that frome hensforthe they shall break or devide noo ffermehold/

ITEM yt haith bene and is accustomed that suche a sonne as the father shall appoint Being hable to sarve the King and the Lord shalbe sett tennant of his fathers tenement before his death or after agreing with the Lord after the custome ther/

ITEM yt haith bene & is accustomed within the same lordshipp that if the tennante have noo sone But doighters that such a doighter as the father shall appoint using herself honestly before her mariedge shall have his tenement agreing with the lord after the custome ther/

ITEM yt haith bene and is accustomed that where any tenant dieth without issue of his body lawfully begotten that then it shall be lawfull to the said tenannt to assigne or appoint his tenannt right of the same tenement to whome as shall please him agreing with the lord as therto apperteneth in that behalf/

(On the left margin of the MS is this addition.)

I am contended the Chamberlaines ffermeholds goo with this Custome delyvering in their Leace and paing such money as is promysed/
(Signed) Thomas Wharton.

This document is but a prelude to sterner things to come. In 1559 Lord Wharton embarked on a scheme of improvement. He rebuilt Wharton Hall, demolished Wharton village, and removed the occupants to Wharton Dykes. He also built a deer-park at Wharton, traces of which can still be seen. He also decided to restore one at Ravenstonedale. The Chamberlain tenants who had taken in some of the park were ordered to leave, and when they resisted they were imprisoned in lord Wharton's house. There was a fearful uproar, and the principal tenant Thomas Chamberlain (and others) appealed to the Court of Requests. The Court ordered lord Wharton to answer the complaints and he ignored it. In the end the Court issued an order that the Chamberlain tenants were to be restored until such time as lord Wharton and his heirs had proved their title so to act, either in the Court of Requests or Chancery.[9] This seems to have had a more drastic result. In the following year lord Wharton appointed a commission of local gentlemen Michael Wharton, Ambrose Lancaster, Charles Wharton, and Philip Machel to clear the Chamberlains off the lord's land and recompense them with other lands at the expense of existing tenants. The Commission sat from 11th October 1560 onwards. The Chamberlains were dealt with first. One entry will suffice:[10]

(1) The 11th of October, Thomas Chamberlain surrendered a parcel of land in Vincent Park, of the yearly rent of 3s.4d., and another parcel in Wheatfield, containing 8 acres, for the use of the lord for ever; and received in consideration for the same, 2 acres above Howbers in Scandaling; 2 acres upon Stowp Hill and Newcloase, in the possession of Lancelot Murthwaite; 5 acres 1 rood in Newbiggen field, in the possession of Martin Fothergill and John Robinson.

The next two entries concern Leonard and John Chamberlain who received the like treatment. The commissioners then proceeded to a wholesale adjustment of all the holdings in the parish until 69 cases had been dealt with, notwithstanding the belief of the tenants that their holdings were inviolable. It will be observed that the Articles of 1556 which lord Wharton had signed contained no such assurance. The position of the Chamberlains who had enclosed some of the lord's demesne was clearly untenable; but the rest is open to question. This was a difficult area. Tenants were not being evicted, nor the number of tenants reduced, nor the number of tenants available for border service reduced. But the fact that they were compensated with bits of land, some good and some bad, all over the place may not have been equitable.

In addition, lord Wharton demanded the feudal aid of 'love boons' and compelled the majority of tenants according to the size of their farms to build the enclosing walls of the deer-park, nine feet high. One entry will suffice:

> (6) The same day and year (6th Dec. 1560) Robert Shaw surrendered his land in New Park, under Ash Fell, and received 2½ acres of new improvement. Paid 40 wathers as a fine. Led stones, and walled 10 roods of park wall.[11]

One tenant had to build sixty roods of wall. It would be interesting to ask whether this adjustment of holdings prevented the division of farms which occurred in the other dales in the second half of the sixteenth century. This ruthless treatment of the tenants was remembered bitterly against the Wharton family for over two hundred years.[12] It will be noted how carefully lord Wharton played his hand. While his son Sir Thomas was a favourite at Court with Queen Mary supporting her Catholic interest, his father merely recorded the old monastic custumal and left it at that. Lord Wharton changed his policy briskly on her death, and was quite ruthless in changing the old order, establishing absolute control over his tenants. In two major points the old custumal was defective for lay control; it did not claim a general fine on the death of the last lord, nor did it deal with woods and underwoods, or greenhew. We ought also to remember that one of the causes of the Pilgrimage of Grace was the enclosure of wastes by lords, and the Catholic Blenkinsop family of Brough under Stainmore had been one of the local offenders in the matter. So with lord Wharton, his conduct was equally high-handed on this occasion, and sailed very near the wind. Tudor governments tried in vain to curb northern landowners in the harsh ways they treated their tenants.

The income of lord Wharton from Ravenstonedale at the end of the sixteenth century was thus:

Ravenstonedale Park and the Lord's grounds there,	£100.0.0.
Rectory and Vicarage of Ravenstonedale in profits by calves and broken tithes,	3.6.8.
In oblations and other duties collected at Easter	16.0.0.
Tythe lambs and odds thereof,	30.0.0.
Tythe corn at the Old Barn,	11.6.8.
Tythe wool,	40.0.0.
Tythe corn at the New Barn,	16.0.0.
	£216.13.4.[13]

Lord Wharton died at Healaugh near Tadcaster on 23rd August 1568. A monument of Derbyshire marble marks his burial there, and a similar altar tomb with effigies was erected in Kirkby Stephen church.[14] His son Sir Thomas of Newhall, Essex succeeded him as lord. Since the accession of Queen Elizabeth in 1558 he had been under a cloud for his catholic sympathies. He was removed from the Privy Council, and in 1561 was confined to the Tower after conviction at Brentwood for hearing Mass in his house at Newhall. After cooling his heels there for some months he made his submission to the Queen, and was released. His lease of Newhall came under threat, but he seems to have held it.[15] There is no evidence that the second lord supported the rising of the northern earls of Westmorland and Northumberland, and Leonard Dacre in 1569-70.[16]

Dr. A.L. Rowse makes the useful point that Northumberland was weak, and has been led by his wife; Westmorland was a waster, and though he had nothing to lose; while Dacre followed his own course out of revenge for being denied the Dacre barony. The Duke of Norfolk was beheaded for his involvement with Mary Queen of Scots, and Northumberland also lost his head. Westmorland and Dacre ended their lives as exiles and pensioners of Philip of Spain.[17] If northern tenants had followed their lords to revolt it was because they were princes in their own lands, riding to the hunt in goodly company, generous in hospitality to all who came to their houses, and above all wary of new men and new-fangled religion which came from the south. Thus when old Richard Norton aged 71, sheriff of Yorkshire and a member of the Council of the North, raised the old Pilgrim banner of the Five Wounds of Christ, five of his eleven sons rose with him, he lost all and ended his life as an exiled pensioner, and his estates were confiscated. He represented as much as any the ancient northern loyalties of faith and neighbourhood.[18]

One useful fact has emerged from the Crown survey of the confiscated estates of the earls of Westmorland in Cumberland. The surveyors Hall and Humberstone reported that in former years the tenants had been content enough, but of late years the greediness of the lords had been such that they had made frequent conveyances and devises of their lands that their tenants had been forced to pay frequent (general) fines every two, three or four years, that the tenants were so ransomed as to be unable to maintain their families.[19] As far back as 23rd July 1537 Robert Southwell surveying the now Crown estates of the late earl of Northumberland in Cumberland had reported to Cromwell his master that (the steward) Sir Thomas Wharton had been ruthless in gressing the tenants of the Honor of Cockermouth, and had been forbidden by Southwell in the name of the King to follow this extreme course. He 'wolde ells have wrestyde them high inowgh as doe the more part ther which my lords I dare say...hath done mych more hurte than good.'[20] In vain did Tudor governments try to curb the rapacity of northern lords. As late as 1569 there was no legal check on lords forcing general fines at the frequent change of lords by sale or alienation. It is against this that the Ravenstonedale case must be reviewed.

Sir Thomas the second lord Wharton died in his house in Canon Row, London on 14th July 1572, and was buried in Westminster Abbey. He would certainly not have been buried there if he had been involved in the 1569 rising.

References Chapter 7

(1) Bygone Penrith. A popular arrangement of Penrith Parish Registers. George Watson. 1893. 127-8.
Parish registers of the C & W, A & A Soc. Par. Reg. series:
Brough under Stainmore, 1556-1706. H. Brierley, 1923.
Crosby Garrett, 1559-1812. J.F. Haswell, 1945.
Crosby Ravensworth, 1570-1812. J.F. Haswell, 1937.
St. Andrew's Penrith part I. 1556-1604. J.F. Haswell, 1938.
St. Andrew's Penrith part II. 1605-1660. J.F. Haswell, 1939.
Morland part I. 1538-1742. (no name), 1957.

Parish Registers of Ravenstonedale part I. 1571-1710. R.W. Metcalfe, 1893.
Last years of a frontier. D.L.W. Tough 1928, 55-57 giving additional infections on the Borders, where diseases were endemic.

(2) N & B I, 522.

(3) Acts of the Privy Council. Edward VI, & Eliz. passim. (1891 edn.)
Calendars of State Papers Henry VIII & Edwards VI passim.
The Hamilton Papers.
N & B I, xlv passim.

(4) Saw-Pit Wharton, G.F. Trevallyn Jones. Sydney U.P. 1967. 13-14.
The Good Lord Wharton. Bryan Dale, 1901. 15.
D.N.B. Sir Thomas first lord Wharton, 1495-1568.
Sir Thomas second lord Wharton, 1520-1572.
N & B I. 473 et seq.
English law Reports, vol. I. 1900 edn. p. 1058. Robert Lowther v. Michael Raw & others 24 April 1735, which refers to several indentures of Aug. & Sept. 1613 between Philip lord Wharton and the tenants of his named Westmorland manors, which are named in the main text.
N & B I. 473 must be read with these, and it is possible that where the Law Report refers to manors it may be that they are tenancies within named manors, or sub-manors within larger ones. There is a conflict I have not resolved. Ravenstonedale and Wharton are not named in Lowther v. Raw.

(5) Acts of Privy Council, Philip & Mary passim. (1891 edn.)

(6) Saw-Pit Wharton op.cit. 14.
The Good lord Wharton op.cit. 14-15.

(7) N & B I. 519-20.

(8) From the original C.R.O. Kendal. The contractions in the text are given in full, but the antique spelling retained.

(9) Inspeximus of Court of Requests and Order dated 15th & 19th February I Eliz. 1558/9 from the original C.R.O. Kendal.
Also listed in Public Record Office, London. Lists & Indexes. Suppl. Series No. VII. Proc. of Courts of Requests vol. 2. Eliz. I. Bundles 137-203 p. 82. Thomas Chamberlain (Westmorland) 188/14. (Kraus edn.)

(10) Hist. & Traditions of Ravenstonedale. W. Nicholls, 1877. 24.

(11) Ibid. 26.

(12) Ibid. 24 & 26 refers to copies of 'The means by which Lord Wharton got the Parks of Ravenstonedale in 1560' dated 1689 & 1777.
In the Last Years of a Frontier. D.L.W. Tough 1928. p. 58 there is a ref. to Tynedale, where tenements were divided equally between sons on the death of the father. Was this a late 16th C. development?

(13) Hist. of Ravenstonedale op.cit. 42.

(14) The Good Lord Wharton. op.cit. 13.

(15) S.P. Eliz. 1560. April. p. 152. no. (13).
S.P. Eliz. 1561. 14 Feb. p. 171. nos. (18) & (19).
S.P. Eliz. 1561. 19 Ap. p. 173/4. no. (50).
S.P. Eliz. 1561. 3 June p. 176. no. (18). The names of such offenders convicted at Brentwood inc Sir Thomas & Lady Wharton.
S.P. Eliz. 1561. 4 July p. 1979. no. (7). Answers of Sir Thomas Wharton & others in the Tower and other prisons after certain questions put to them.
S.P. Eliz. 1561. 16 July p. 180. no. (19). Among others in the Tower "Sir Thos. Wharton submits".

(16) Prelates & People of the Lake Counties. C.M.L. Bouch, 1948. p. 204 says that lord Wharton was involved. If so he would not have been buried in Westminster Abbey in 1572.

(17) The England of Elizabeth. A.L. Rowse. Reprint Soc. ed. 1953. 100.
The Lake Counties 1500-1830. C.M.L. Bouch & G.P. Jones, 1960. 44-45.

(18) Queen Elizabeth. J.E. Neale. 1934. 188.
D.N.B. Richard Norton. (?1488-1588).
The Lake Counties 1500-1830, op. cit. 45 states that 500 of the poorer sort were executed after the 1569-70 rising, by martial law. Another 129 were indicted at York, Durham and Carlisle. In addition many were punished by fines - a figure comparable to that of the Pilgrimage of Grace.

(19) England of Elizabeth. A.L. Rowse, 100-101. An important bit of evidence given by Dr. Rowse from the Exchequer Records.

(20) S.P. Henry VIII 1537. vol. II, 20th August. p. 205. no. 548. Southwell to Cromwell.

Chapter 8

Ravenstonedale (2)

Philip lord Wharton succeeded to the title on the death of his father in 1572; he was then aged 17, and reached his majority in 1576. His wardship fell to the Crown, and came under the control of the Master of the Court of Wards lord Burghley. He and the earl of Sussex Lord President of the Council of the North became his guardians, and were anxious to wean Philip from the Catholic sympathies of his father. He was therefore brought up in the south as a Protestant. His estates and stewardships came under the Court of Wards, and there is no doubt that as far as Ravenstonedale was concerned an absentee landlord was the cause of disorder in the administration of the manor.

About the same time an even more important northern estate fell to the Court of Wards, that of the earl of Cumberland in Craven and Westmorland. Henry the second earl died at Brougham castle on 8th January 1569/70, in the middle of the crisis of the rebellion of the northern earls. His widow was lady Anne Dacre daughter of William lord Dacre of Gillsland; she was a Catholic, and received the Westmorland estates in jointure; but the Craven estates came to the Court of Wards. Their son George became the third earl, then aged 11 years and 5 months. He was therefore under the Court of Wards for ten years. It was vital to the government that the boy should be taken from northern Catholic influences, and Francis Russell the Protestant earl of Bedford was made his guardian, and earl George was brought up in the south either at Chenies or Woburn,[1] and later at Trinity College, Cambridge. The long term effect of these two wardships on the Clifford and Wharton estates should not be overlooked, but for different reasons.

Burghley's plans came to fruition in 1577 when on 24th June George third earl of Cumberland was married to Lady Frances Russell, third daughter of the earl of Bedford his guardian. George was then aged 19. The ceremony took place in the church of St. Mary, Ovaries, the now Southwark cathedral. At the same ceremony the young Philip lord Wharton was married to earl George's sister Lady Frances Clifford. So much importance was attached to these two marriages, as healing at least one Border feud, that Queen Elizabeth attended the ceremony in great state.[2]

The Manor of Ravenstonedale.

Philip the third Lord Wharton reached his majority in 1576, and it was soon evident that both from the point of view of the lord, whether as lord of the manor or lay rector of the parish, as well the tenants, the manor was in great disorder and required an efficient administration. This culminated in an agreement between lord and tenants dated 12 February 1579/80. As the original is at present missing the text has been constructed from several MS sources.[3] The only serious difference in sources occurs in one vital respect. In section (I) one source (the earliest) states that a fine was due to the lord on the change of tenant, while three others state that one was due at the change of every lord and every tenant. A fine had not been due on the death of a lord in monastic days; there was no suggestion in the earlier Articles of 1556 that a fine had been due on the death of a Prior of Watton, but only on the change of a tenant by death or alienation. Insofar as the new agreement reflected past custom it was inaccurate. The reference to the change of lord was a lawyer's insertion to establish the new rule.

The second point to be noted in the indenture is that the general fine was to be due 'at the change of every lord'. It does not say by death, that is by an Act of God; it could be a change by alienation, sale or other conveyance. By this device the tenants could have no protection against more frequent changes of lord, and the levying of a more frequent general fine. The courts do not seem to have established the rule at that date that a general fine could only be due by an Act of God, the death of the last admitting lord.

In one respect the new custumal established by this Indenture was good; on all ancient tenements, established time out of mind, the rents were ancient rents, or rents of assize. It is a question for historians to discover when the primitive rents of ancient farms and communities in the kingdom of Northumbria were converted from food renders, and services to fixed money payments. There was a move to rationalise these ancient forms of payment and services from the reign of Henry II. Until Henry II every barony in the old kingdom of Northumbria was held of the King by cornage or horngeld, and from his day was converted to knight service.[4] It is probable that the food rents and renders of ordinary tenants were assized and converted to money payments some time after that reign. Thus the ancient rents in Ravenstonedale had been fixed time out of men's memory, and were unchangeable. The difficulty which faced lords was that, as the value of money fell, so did the worth of these ancient rents; and the only way whereby lords could increase their return was to increase the level of fines when they became due. The confirming of the old rule in the new Indenture, that the fine on the change of lord or tenant was to be one year's ancient rent, was no great burden.

But the new rule that the tenant of every inclosure from the waste, called a new improvement, was to pay a fine of eight times the annual rent for a fine seems at first sight to be stiff. It was, but may have been a device to prevent large inclosures from the common. There is no clue as to how the improved rents on new grounds were assessed. On the other hand a fine of eight years annual rent, if on ancient rents, may have been nearer to the market value of the land. If the rent was an improved rent, then a fine of eight years was too high; two years would at that date have been high enough. Indeed a fine of eight years ancient rent was accepted as the norm during the Commonwealth.[5] It should be added, that in a number of manors in the district in the second half of the sixteenth century, where new inclosures are noted they are often of small acreage to accommodate new peat houses, barns and fire-houses to meet the needs of farms which had been divided between heirs. A sense of proportion should be observed in this matter.

In one respect the new custumal was stiff; where a tenant died without issue, he could bequeath his tenement to whom he wished. But the new tenant had to pay a fine of twenty years rent on admission. This was to be paid both on ancient and improved rents.

Finally, in order that the reader may understand the terms under which these tenants lived, a close study of the Indenture is necessary.

The Indenture betweens the Lord and the Tennants.[6]

THIS INDENTURE made the xijth day of ffebruary the xxijth yeare of the Reigne of our Sovereigne Lady Elizabeth by the Grace of God of England ffrance and Ireland Queene defender of the ffaith etc. Betweene the right honble Philipp Lord Wharton of the one parte And George Greene John Taylor Richard Taylor James Taylor Christopher Rogerson Richard Wilson Henry ffawcett John Robinson Cuthbert ffawcett Anthony Pinder John ffothergill Michael Shawe and Richard ffawcett of the other partye WITNESSETH THAT whereas strife and variance did arise betweene Thomas Lord Wharton decd grandfather unto Philipp now Lord Wharton and the Customary tennants and occupiers of the Manor of Ravenstonedale and of the lands and tenements within the parish of Ravenstonedale within the County of Westmorland for and concerninge certaine customs and usages of Tennantright And after that as well by the willing Assent and agrement of the said Thomas Lord Wharton as of all the tennants and occupiers of the said lands and tenements certaine customes usages and agrements were declared and sett downe in writeing as by certaine articles bearing the date the sixth day of October in the third and ffowerth yeares of the late King and Queene Philipp and Mary subscribed with the proper hand of the said Thomas Lord Wharton it doeth more plainly and more at large appeare NOW SO IT IS that certain doubts imperfections and Questions have been moved and stirred betwene the said Philipp Lord Wharton who is now Lord of the said Mannor and the tennants of the said Mannor for and concerning as well divers of the said Articles as alsoe for divers grounds improved from the Waste of the said Mannor and for some grounds beinge parcell of the demaynes of the said Manor and also for and concerninge diverse Customes usages and things impugned by the now Lord Wharton against the tennants of the said Mannor and challenged by the tennants against the now Lord Wharton for the explaining ending and fynall determininge of all which said doubts questions strifes and things as well the said Philipp Lord Wharton as also the said George Greene and the other persons before named haveinge authoritye for all the now tennants of the said Mannor are and (have been) fully concluded and agreed in such manner and forme as is hereafter in these presents expressed/

(1) IMPRIMIS it is first declared and agreed that it hath been and is accustomed within the said Mannor tyme whereof the memory of man is not to the contrary that all the tennants which hold lands or tenements of the said Mannor of anncient tyme by the Laudable Custome of Tennantright have possessed and enjoyed the same to them their heirs and assignes payinge at the change of every Lord of the said Mannor and at the change of every tennant one yeares rent for a ffyne and not above Besides the Rent which they pay to the Lord and (?which) fyne hath beene payed alwayes according to the rent they pay unto the Lord of the mannor for their tenements and not according to the worth or value of the tenement as the same is or may be letten AND for such grounds as were improved or taken in from the Waist of the Mannor before the purchase and haveing of the said Mannor by Thomas Lord Wharton Grandfather to the now Lord Wharton if any such be it is declared and the said Philipp Lord Wharton doeth therunto assent and agree that they shall be taken and used in all payments usages and Customs as of the nature of the said Anncient Tennant right and for all other groundes that have beene taken and improved from the waists of the said Mannor since the date of the Letters Pattents made of the said Mannor to the said Lord Wharton the Grandfather IT IS DECLARED and the said Philipp Lord Wharton doth thereunto assent and agree that they shall be taken and used in all Customes and usages of the nature of the Anncient Tennantright saveinge that at the change of every Lord of the said Mannor and at the change of every Tennant of the said grounds soe newly improved ther shall be payed unto the Lord of the said Mannor for the tyme beinge Eight yeares rent for a ffyne and not above besides the yearly rent payed to the Lord which shall be rated according to the rent they pay to the Lord for the new improved grounds and the said tennants to pay their fynes upon the change of the Lord and the tennant as well for the old as for the new upon their admittances/

AND that every persons to whom any Alienacion of any of the said Tenements shall be herafter made shall at the Court of the said Mannor next followinge the said Alienacion by himselfe or some other give notice and knowledge thereof in the said Court to him that shall keepe the same Court and then shall take order ther for the payment of his fyne accordynge to the rent (?rate) before expressed AND that every of the said tennants shall pay to the now Lord Wharton in respect of the change of the Lord by reason of the death of Thomas laite Lord Wharton his father at or before the ffeast of St. Peter ad Vincula and Martinmas equally to be divided now next cominge one yeares rent for every anncient Tenement and eight yeares rent for every new Improvement to be rated and taxed as is aforesaid And that all the said Anncient tenements and new improvements shall from hencefurth be subject used occupyed and enjoyed under such forfeitures and paynes as hertofore hath beene used for anncient Tennantright within the said Mannor other then such as are by these presents expressed declared granted agreed and assented unto And that all the Tennants of the said Mannor shall appear at the Court of the said Mannor upon lawful warninge from tyme to tyme as hath beene accustomed and doe such suite and service as hertofore hath beene[2] done used and accustomed AND

(2) it is fully Covenanted granted concluded and declared by the tennants aforesaid for themselves and the rest of the said Tennants That none of the Tennants of the said Mannor shall devide or sever their ancient and Customary tenements or the said New Improvements or any part of them charged with any rent at this day upon payne of foreiture of every such Tenement unless they doe first agre with the Lord of the said Mannor or with the Steward of the said Mannor for the tyme beinge or with some other haveinge authoritye from the Lord soe to doe in which agrement it shall not be lawfull for the Lord of the said Mannor to augment or increase any rent ether of the Old anncient customary tenements or of the new Improvements already charged with any rent that shall be soe devided but shall devide the rent wherwith the same tenement or ground shall be soe devided was charged with to the Lord before rateablly accordinge to the value of the land soe divided And every such division of such tenements and grounds and the rateinge of the rents of the same to be sett downe in a Coppy or warrant under the Lords hand or the Stewards hand to be made by the Lord to such person as shall take the same and that to be entered in the Court Rooles of the said Mannor and the Coppy or warrant soe to be subscribed to be dilivered to the party that shall have the Land and this shall not be expounded or taken to be a change of a Tennant soe as the Lord shall or may challenge or have any ffyne of him in that respect for the porcon soe devided/

(3) Item it is further declared and agreed That if any tennants which now be or heerafter

shall be of the said Mannor ether of the Anncient Customary tenements or of the said New Improvements doe depart this life without issue of his body lawfully begotten not haveinge in his life by his Will in writeinge or otherwise by any lawfull Act done in the presence of ffower of of the Tennants of the said Mannor at the least aliened or bestowed the same that what Lands such tennant shall die seized of shall Escheat to the Lord as though such a Tennant had beene dead without heire generall or speciall/

(4) And it is nevertheless declared and agreed that any of the Tennants of the said Mannor ether of the anncient & Customary tenements or of the said New Improvements haveinge noe issue of his body lawfully begotten and being of the age of Sixteene yeares may by his last Will in writeinge or by any other lawful Act done in the presence of ffower of the Tennants of the said Mannor as aforesaid give and bequeath his said tenement to whom he will soe that the party to whom it shall be so given pay upon his admittance to the Lord Twenty yeares rent for a ffyne and not above after the rate of the rent payed to the Lord for the said Tenement And the Lord nor his officers or Steward of the said Mannor for the tyme beinge shall not refuse to admitt him tennant payinge as is aforesaid so that the party to whom it shall be give or bequeathed be an able man to serve and not notoriously knowne to be an enemy to the Lord of the said Mannor/

(5) Item The said Philipp Lord Wharton is pleased agreed and doeth promise herafter not to take any advantage or benefitt of any forfeiture or cause of seizure hertofore growne comitted or done by any tennant of the said Mannor But doeth by these presents release and discharge the said tennants and every one of them of the same AND it is nevertheless agreed that every of the said Tennants that have made any Alienacion or devision of their severall tenements either of their anncient tenements or of their new Improvements since the death of Thomas late Lord Wharton father to the now Lord Wharton and which have not payed nor compounded with the Lord for the same shall pay one yeares rent for a fyne for every such alienation and severance and noe more according to the rate of the rent of the tenement payed to the Lord/

(6) Item whereas ther is within the parish of Ravenstonedale a certaine tenement called the Wayngarthes otherwise called Chamberlanes tenement part whereof is in the possession and occupacon of Widdow Chamberlane and the other part in the possession or occupacon of Richard Wharton gentleman Henry ffawcett and Willm Chamberlane which said tenement and the grounds therunto belonging doeth consist partlie of ground newly improved from the Waste and partly of ground beinge parcell of the demeasnes of the said Mannor and demised for yeares by the Grandfather of the now Lord Wharton unto one George Chamberlane AND is neverthelesse by the said Philipp now Lord Wharton fully promised and granted that the said tenements and all the grounds as well in the severall possessions of the said Widdow Chamberlane as Henry ffawcett William Chamberlane and Richard Wharton shall be possessed and enjoyed severally by the said Widdow Chamberlane dureinge her life or Widdowhood and after her death or Marriage by Mychaell Chamberlane his heires and assignes And the residue by the said Richard Wharton Willm Chamberlane and Henry ffawcett and by their severall heires and assignes as if the said tenements and grounds had beene anncient and Customary tenements of the said Mannor and soe shall be taken and used hereafter as well in all payments of change of Lord & tennant as in all other customes usages and charges within the said Mannor And that the said Philipp Lord Wharton and his heires being Lords of the said Mannor shall upon reasonable request to him or them to be made without any thinge to him or them to be given for the same convey and assure the tenements and grounds which be severally occupied by the said Richard Wharton Willm Chamberlane and Henry ffawcett (to them the said Richard Wharton, William Chamberlane & Henry ffawcett) and to their heires and assignes and ye tenement and grounds which be now occupyed by the said Widdow Chamberlane to be assured to the said Widdow Chamberlane duringe her life or Widdowhood and after her death or Marriage to the said Michaell Chamberlane his heires & assignes according to the Custome of tennantright within the said Mannor used and this to be assured at the severall costs and charges of the said parties soe demandinge the same and as shall be by every or any of them reasonablly devised/

(7) Item it is further agreed betweene the said Philipp Lord Wharton and the said George Greene and other the persons before named as well for themselves as for all the Residue of the tenants of the said Mannor that whereas Thomas laite Lord Wharton father unto the said Philipp now Lord Wharton is departed this life and that the said Mannour of Ravenstonedale after his death is comed unto the

said now Lord Wharton and soe thereby a change of the Lord of the said Mannour and therefore a fyne to be paid as well for the ancient customary tenements as for the new improvements that the fynes that shall be paid as well for the ancient customary tenements and for such as be by these presents declared to be ancient tenements as for the new improvements shall be paid as is before declared and to be raited after the rait before expressed and not otherwise/

(8) And yet the said Philipp now Lord Wharton is contented and agreed that the money which the said tenants have already payed shall be accompted and allowed as parcell of the money that they are to pay for the said fynes and that it shall be lawfull for the said tenants to default and rebait out of the money that they are to pay for the said fynes soe much money as they have already paid unto the now Lord Wharton or to any other for his use or for him the said Lord Wharton in Respect of the said change of the Lord and that such tenants to whome any of the customary tenements or new improvements be discended since the now Lord Wharton came to his full age of xxi yeares which have not paid theer fynes or satisfied the Lord or his officers for the same shall pay their fynes for their ancient and customary tenements and for the new improvements to be raited as is before expressed and not otherwise/

(9) Provided nevertheless and it is agreed and declared that if there shall be any lease made of the said Mannour for yeare or yeares or if any of (the tenants of) the said Mannor shall hereafter make any lease or Demise of there tenements or new improved grounds or of any part of them for the tearme of seaven yeares or under from the tyme of the makinge of every such lease the same shall not be said to be a change of the Lord or tenant whereby there shall be due or ought to be paid to the Lord any fyne for the same/

And yet it is agreed that every tenant may Lett the said tenements for the tearme of xxj yeares in possession and not above And every leased (lessee) to whom any such Lease shall be made for the Tearme of xxj yeares or under and above the number of xij yeares shall pay to the Lord as for a change of a tenant in such sort as before is declared/

And it is further agreed that every such leased shall give knowledge at the next Court of the said Mannor of every such Lease and of the number of yeares Demised by the said Lease And of the tenement Letten To them that shall keepe the Court for the said Mannor/

(10) Item the said Philipp now Lord Wharton for the true performing and fulfilling of all the Articles Agreements Sentences and promisses in these presents expressed which upon the party and behalfe of the said Lord Wharton his heires and assignes are and ought to be performed and kept accordinge unto the true intent and meaning of these presents doth covenant and grant for him his heires Executors and Administrators severally to and with the said George Greene John Tailor Richard Tailor James Tailor Christopher Rogerson Richard Wilson Henry Fawcett John Robinson Cuthbert Fawcett Anthony Pinder John Fothergill Michaell Shaw and Richard Fawcett And to and with the severall heires Executors and Administrators of every of them that the persons before named and all other the tenants and occupiers as well of the said ancient Customary tenements as of such as are declared by these presents to be of the said nature And alsoe of the new improved grounds and every part of them shall be occupied possessed and enjoyed by them their heires and assignes as Ancient Customary tenements Paying fullfilling performing and keeping the payments promisses articles and agreements in these presents expressed which of there partyes ought to be preformed and kept against the said Lord Wharton his heires and assignes and against all other person and persons claiming any thing in the said Manor by from or under the Estate Right title or intrust of the said Lord Wharton Discharged or savyed harmless of all incumbrances hadd made or done or hereafter to be had made or done by the now Lord Wharton his heires or assignes/

IN WITNESS whereof the partyes abovesaid to these present Indentures have severally and interchangably putt theire hands and seales the day and yeare first above written. (Robinson MS adds the date 1579.)
PHILIPP WHARTON.

(MS. D. endorsement.)

Recognitum coram me Johanne Gybsone in canc m̄ro (magistro) die (et) anno supradictis.
Sealed signed and delivered in the presence of
George Chamberlain.
Thomas Warcup.
George Salkeld.

Richard Perkins. Finis.
(MS. B. endorsement.)

Et memorandum, quod die et anno supradictis, praedĩus (praedictus) Philippus Dominus Wharton venit coram dicta d̄om Regina, in Cancellarĩa suā et recognovit Indenturam praedictum et omnia et singula in eadem confirmavit et spet̃ (spectavit) sicut in forma supradicta et irrotulavit 12mo. die Februarii Anno supradicta. Finis Indenturae.

There is no evidence that widows ever paid heriots. The agreement soon proved incomplete; it did not mention woods and underwoods. It seems that lord Wharton had claimed timber growing on the farms for his own use, and tenants from each other. It may be that tenants with no timber had claimed from the lord, for housebote and other works about the farm. This dispute resulted in an agreement of 24th August 1592, whereby in return for a sum of £80 paid by the tenants, it was agreed that the tenants owned the woods growing on their own land, for the purpose of housebote etc. (the repair of messuages, cottages, barns, stables, houses and buildings) and probably hedge and ploughbote. Every tenant was to have the right to cut his own timber, and not that of another. Any person entering the tenement of another tenant and removing timber without consent was liable to action in the manor court, both as to fine due to the lord, and damages due to the tenant. The lord was discharged of any liability for farm repairs, and in return each tenant had to pay 1d. yearly for greenhew, that is lesser timber.[7]

References Chapter 8

(1) George third earl of Cumberland. G.C. Williamson. C.U.P. 1920. pp. 2-6.
D.N.B. George Clifford 1558-1605, third earl of Cumberland.

(2) D.N.B. George Clifford op.cit.
George third earl of Cumberland. G.C. Williamson, op.cit. 11.

(3) See Appendix I.

(4) English Historical Rev. 1920, vol. 35. Barony & Thanage by Miss R.R. Reid, pp. 182-3.

(5) That a fine, tho' arbitrary must be reasonable. See Willowes case in English Reports, vol. 77, 1907, p. 1413. Mich. 6 Jac. I. It was adjudged that a fine of £5.6.8d on a rack rent of 53s. was unreasonable. The case was brought by Richard Stallon against Thomas Brayde for breaking his house & close at Fen Ditton, Cambridge. The defendant pleaded that the place was land and freehold of Thomas & Richard Willowes, and he a servant in the manor of Fen Ditton.
S.P. Committee for Compounding, 1652, p. 585, June 5th. County Committee for Westmorland at Kendal to Committee for Compounding, reporting the levying of fines on sequestrated royalist and papist estates; on Sir Francis Howard's an 8d. fine; in Betham manor (late of the earl of Derby) a 6d. general fine, and an 8d. particular fine etc. Signed by Gervase Benson, Roger Bateman and John Archer. (Gervase Benson was soon to become a leading Quaker.)

(6) See Appendix I.
See Appendix II, Complaint of 1581 to Philip lord Wharton by the Jury of Ravenstonedale that Henry Fawcett of Waingarths has taken a tenancy case outside the manor court.

(7) Appendix III, Summary of Indenture of 27 Aug. 34 Eliz. concerning woods and underwoods.

Chapter 9

Ravenstonedale (3)

Though the Indenture of 1580 provided the exact frame in which the ownership of land and its transfer was to continue for many years, it was virtually inoperative unless two grave abuses were stopped. The first was the contempt with which the manor court was treated both by litigants and jurors. Some jurors walked out before cases were decided, and litigants asked for cases to be adjourned to a further court, claiming that not sufficient evidence had been given in their behalf. The second was the taking of a land tenure case away from the absolute jurisdiction of the manor court to a London court, thus making the manor court useless, and the prey of every scheming attorney. The parish seems to have recognised the hopelessness of their situation, and in 1581 a Supplication was drawn up by the Officer or steward and subscribed by two juries, and all the tenants, and sent to Lord Wharton.[1]

Considerable thought seems to have been given to the powers with which the manor court was to be invested, and it is certain that the attorney (whose hand can be seen in all these documents) who had sat as Officer through many unfinished cases, persuaded Lord Wharton's attorneys to advise Lord Wharton to levy stiff fines on jurors and litigants who broke the rules of the manor court. Many of the powers of the jurors were delegated from the lord, especially in the Liberty and rectory, as distinct from the normal powers of court baron and leet. What emerges in the documents which follow is a close regulated society. The jury seemed normally to have numbered about sixteen, four principal men being chosen from the four Angles of the parish. In a number of the documents which follow the names of the jurors are given to point to certain family names which a hundred years later formed the principal supporters either of the Presbyterian or the Quaker dissenting congregations. At first it seems paradoxical that a protestant society which was virtually self-regulating should feel the need of dissent. It should have been an ideal community.

After long negotiation there emerged ten orders to which Lord Wharton had set his hand, and were passed by the jury on 28th January 1583. The reader is asked to study all the following documents in detail, for without this knowledge it is not possible to understand the world from which the political and religious dissent of the seventeenth century arose.

Hereafter foloweth a copey of the tenn Orders of triall set downe by the Jury. (The xxxviij day of Jan. 1583)[2]

Certaine Orders sett downe under penalties by the grand Jury of Ravinstondaile that is to say George Greene Anthony Pinder George Dent Richard Wilson Cuthbert Hunter George Hablethwaite Willm Adamthwaite Robert ffothergill Thomas ffawcett of Lockholme Symond Bousfeild Richard Wharton John ffawcett Richard Bousfeild Richard Bouell Thomas ffawcett of Murthwaite and Stephen Swinbanke with consent of the Right honorable Phillip L: Wharton our L:(ord) and M(ast)er for reformation of certaine foul and wicked abuses in the mannor of usage of our Customary triall Crept in amongst us to the great hindrance of ye good and peaceable estate of the Lordshipp of Ravinstondaile & the prophanation of ye most holy name of God through soe many othes had and taken so usually amongst us in trifles and matters of noe valewe the w(hi)ch your said Customary triall so yt and it may hereafter used in some better manner that it hath beene heretofore, Wee the said jurors accordinglie as wee are specially moved in our consciences thereunto by the charge now specially Laide upon us as this present tyme doe set downe such orders as hereafter foloweth this xxviij day of January the xxvj yeare of the Raigne of our Soveraigne Lady Elizabeth by the grace of God queene of England ffrance & Ireland etc 1583.

1. ffirst wee deeme and award that the Right honorable Phillip Lord Wharton shall before White Sunday next cause reparations to be maid of that his house w(hi)ch joyneth to the West side of our church, that it may be a place for all Jurers and Arbiters, parties and witnesses at al times hereafter to resort unto when and as they shall be Lawfully commanded by the Lord or his Officer/

2. Secondly we deeme and award that at all tymes hereafter all Jurers and arbiters or any appointed to be either Jurers or arbiters upon Lawfull commandement & warning given to them by the Lord or his officer shall resort & come unto the said house or other place appointed abrode in the parishe if the matter shall soe require att day and howre appointed them all excuses sett apart, God and the Prince there causes excepted and there to receive there charge as they shall be commanded and appointed by the Lords officer upon paine every one offending against any part of this Order to forfit to the Lord for every default xij^{d}.

3. Thirdlie wee deeme and award that all parties shall alwaies have lawfull warning given them by the Lord and his officer to tend upon ye Jurers or arbiters within the said house or other place abrode in ye parishe if ye matter shall soe require as the appointment shall be at day and howre appointed them and in like manner all such witnesses as either parties shall thinke needfull and requisite for theire cause to have lawfull warning given them by the L: or his officer upon sute and demand to the L: or his officer ffirst made by the partie or parties for the same and both all the same parties and witnesses to resort unto the said house or other place abrode in ye parish as they shall be appointed and theire to tend till the Juriers or Arbiters have dispatched or shall dismiss them.

Alwaies provided that if the partie complayning shall not come and tend upon the Jurers or arbiters in ye said house or other place appointed abrode in the parish at day and howre accordinglie as he hath had lawfull warning given him by the L: officer al excuses laid apart God and the Prince there causes excepted that the same plaintive shall fall in this plaint and sute for that tyme till a new Court/

But if the party defendant shall ether refuse deferre or delay to come and tend to he shalbe lawfully warned by the L: officer either upon the plaint Jurye or other Jurers or Arbiters whereunto he hath given his consent within the said house or other place appointed at day and houre as he shalbe lawfully warned to doe by ye L: or his officer Wee deo award that ye same party defendant shall forfitt to ye Lord for that default iij^{s} iiij^{d}. Alwaies provided that ye officer And Jurers or Arbiters shall then presently before they depart appoint a new day with all conveniant spede to meete on the decyde and endd the said cause And commandement shall then presently be given by the officer to the Jurers or Arbiters And to both the partyes and all other wittnesses to resort and come again to the said house or other place appointed within ye parish at the day and houre then agreede upon And the said penalty of iij^{s} iiij^{d} to be leived by the officer upon the goods and Cattles of ye said partyes defandant alwaies for every default till the matter be ended/

Provided alsoe that none of ye Jurers or Arbiters shall upon there partye and behalf breake or transgresse Any part of the third Article upon paine every one of them offending to forfitt to ye Lord for every default xij^{d}/

Furthermore we deme and award that neither tennant nor cottager neither any other person or persons remaining w(it)hin any mans house within this L:(ordship) of Ravinstondaile having had lawfull commandment and warning given him by ye Lord or his officer to come to any place appointed within this L:(ordship) to bear witnesse in any cause shall deny defer or delaie to come accordingly as he shall be commanded neither shall refuse or difer being come to the place appointed at day and houre appointed him for any cause God and the Prince there causes excepted upon paine to forfitt to ye Lord every one offending against any part hereof for every default xij^{d}.

(4) ffourthlie wee deme and awarde that all Jurers or arbiters being come together shall enter into the said house and there recive theire charge and remaine togither and shall also in publicke manner take the examinations of all there witnesses and eivedence yt shall be brought in unto the(m) and farthermore the officer shall keepe them closelie there soe as they do not depart before they give forth there ends and verdicts in writing in al such causes as they shall have caused the parties with there witnesses to be there for or at least in all such matters as they have examined and taken sworne witnesses or evidence in neither shall the Jurers or arbiters depart before they shall so have done upon paine of envy every one of them ofending against any part of this order to forfitt to ye Lord for every such default xij^{d}.

Provided alwaies in this behalfe yt if the Jurers or arbiters shall not agree in any matter but fall of two sorts or partyes the one being content to give forth there verdict upon ye witnesse or evidence they have the other sort deneying the same & alledging that they will not doe soe till they be further resolved by learned counsell in this case wee fully award that either partie of the Jurers or arbiters soe contending shall appoint out one of there sort and this two to go together to such counsell as both the parties shall then agre upon and whether side or partie of the said Jurers or arbiters as shall afterward be found to have standed (stood) in a wrong pley (plea) to beare all ye charges of seeking the said counsell but the other sort yt stand in ye right to be at noe charge at all for the same.

5. Fifthlie wee deme and award that for the better avoiding of that vaine and much swearing used soe commonlie in triall of trifles & matters of noe valewe yt at all tymes hereafter when any contreversie or variance hapneth betwene neighbour w(hi)ch doth not concerne the very title of tennant right either of the ground itselfe or of ye housing itselfe but w(hi)ch doth onlie concerned other small pettie causes as hedges ditches and highwaies gutters water races and such like things wherein there happeneth often contention and variance in neighbourhood that when the partie or parties shall come to com-plaine in such causes to the Lord or his officers for order in the same that if they will not bee content and advised to reefire and put the same either to friends or other honest Indifferent men chosen and elect by the assents and consents of both the parties to decyde and put away without oath as God shall put them in minde for ye best And as it shall seame unto them most Indifferent for both ye parties in conscience that then they shall withall convea-nient speide according to the Custome and Orders of this L:(ord)shipp have a sworne triall granted them to decyde the same and the partie that doth fall in the matter that is to say against whome the Tryall doth passe whether it be ye plaintive or defendant to forfitt xij^d the one halfe to the Lord and the other to the Balife and Jurers or Arbiters that travaile therein equally betweene them, And the partie forfiting xij^d to pay the same at the giving forth of ye verdict or else ye Balife after ward by force of ye same verdict to levye the same upon his goods and cattles and to distribute it ac-cording to this Order/

Provided in this behalfe that if the defendant grant any part without triall off yt w(hi)ch is in controversy, and that the plaintive recover

noe more by triall but yt w(hi)ch was granted without triall, that then in this case the plaintive to forfitt the said xij^d and not the defendant/

Alwaies provided that this our End and award shall not extend unto any matters or controver-syes w(hi)ch touch or concerne either ye Title or Clame of tennant right of either ground or houseing or any parcell thereof nather unto any manner of causes matters or controversyes wherin the Lord of this mannor shall be of ye one partie nather unto any such matters Causes or controversyes w(hi)ch sworn Jurers or Arbiters may lawfully decyde and set downe of themselves w(i)thout takeing any sworne witnesse at all/

but all such causes and controversyes to be fully ordered determined and ended by sworne Jurers or Arbiters without forfiting any thing at all by either partie/

Furthermore we deme and award that noe tennant or occupier cottager or other remaner (remainer) within any mans house within this Lordshipp of Ravinstondaile shall at any tyme hereafter in any cause or controversy withstand deny refuse or not yeild and submit himselfe to abide indifferent triall in the same according to the Custome of this Lordshipp at such tyme as it shall be lawfully according to the Custome and orders of this Lordshipp required and demanded of him, that is upon Authoritie (B. party) defendant by the Lord or his officer in the behalfe of any party complaineing within this Lordshipp upon paine to forfitt to the Lord for every default against this order vj^s viij^d./

6. Sextly we deme and award that all tymes hereafter the Jurers and Arbiters lawfully warned by the Lord or his officer to goe to any place abrode in ye parish after our Common manner to try and take order betwene neighbour and neighbour concerning bye waies hedges ditches gutters or watter races or other such like things dependinge in controversye betwene partie and party that they shall come and meite at ye place day and houre appointed them, And ther recive their charge as they shall be appointed/

And furthermore in all such causes as they shall that day take examanation and sworne witnesse or evidence in they shall give forth ther verdict in writing thereupon before they depart of ye ground upon paine every one of the Jurers or Arbiters offending against any part of this Order to forfit to the Lord for every default xij^d.

And alsoe wee deme and award that all parties and witnesses w(hi)ch have had lawfull warning given them by the Lord or his officer shall come and tend upon ye Jurers or arbiters upon the ground where the meting is as they shall be commanded and not to depart before the officer and Jurers or Arbiters shall licence and dismisse them upon pains to Incur the dangers and Penaltyes before mentioned concerning parties and witnesses Least that through there negligence ye Jurers or Arbiters have there metinge disappointed/

7. Seaventhly we deme and award that ye grand Jury whose especiall charge is and ought to be for ye Common wealth of this Lordshipp shall cause presently at the charge of ye parish A great paper Booke to be provided before Easter next wherin to write all Ends & Verdicts And also to appoint A sufficient man fearing God & tendring Common wealth A private man and noe officer for writing all Ends and verdicts within the said Booke and alsoe for the safe keeping of the said book within the Chist appointed for keeping All register Bookes within this Lordship, And alsoe that the same man at ye first court houlden hereafter in Ravinstondaile to be sworne in open court truly to register all ends and verdicts in the same ye w(hi)ch either Jurers or Arbiters shall bring to his hand & accordinglie as they shall deliver them unto him and also faithfully & well to kepe the same in each respect & for doing of ye same we are content and doe award that he shall have that iij^d given him at the giving forth of ye verdict at all tymes hereafter together with the verdict w(hi)ch hath alwaies heretofore bene due to ye Jurers or Arbiters themselves;

And futhermore we deme and award that the grand Jury for ye tyme being shall alwaies hereafter yearlie have a speciall regard that all verdicts according to the trewe meaning hereof be faithfully registered in ye said Booke and that it be kept in order abovesaid, And furthermore at the death of ye partie or at ye exchange if it soe shall happen to be for any default Justlie found and provided (? proved) against him touching the premisses that ye said Jury for ye tyme being shall take into ther owne hands the keping of ye said Booke: untill that (? they) shall have appointed another man for ye keeping of ye said Booke such an one (and) in such order as is before mentioned (B. and have caused him to be sworn for ye true registering and safe keeping of ye said book as is before mentioned) Provided allso that he shall subscribe his name to every verdict w(hi)ch he regestreth in in ye said

Booke Furthermore we deme and award that the said Phillip L: Wharton shall cause his Officer to keepe a like End Booke for ye better preserving of all Ends and orders set downe either for his own behoofe or ye common wealth of this L(ord)shipp Provided alwaies that all tymes hereafter all Jurers and Arbiters within this Lordshipp shall observe and keepe this forme and order in writing and giveing forthe ther verdicts that is to say they shall not difer (defer) nor delay them otherwise then in this order is prescribed/

Secondly before they give fourth there end or verdict they shall alwaies cause ye same to be written twise severally Indented & ye one to be perused & conserved (B. conferred) with the other soe as they agree together word by word.

Thirdly they shall alwaise set downe in the latter end of ther verdict plainly against wheather party the same triall doth pas and if it be against ye plaintive then shall they write thus, THUS wee find the said A.B. to fall in his (B.this) matter because he hath failed in proving his challeng and hath not recovered any more by this our verdict then ye said C.D. granted him without triall In Witness etc - -

but if the triall pas against the defendant then write Thus wee finde the said C.D. to fall in this matter because he stood in a wrong pley and deneyed ye trewth accordinglie as ye said A.B. hath sufficientlie proved in publik manner before us In Witnesse whereof etc and this being done they shall opnlie before ye officer and all other ther present Reid and give forth ther said verdict & then presentlie to deliver first ye one of ye two said verdicts severally indented to ye officer yt he may Regester ye same in his booke, And ye other verdict with the ijd. before mentioned to him yt keepeth the parish end Booke yt he may register the same therein And noe Jurers or Arbiters ever hereafter to breake any part vijth of this Order upon paine to forfitt to the Lord every one so offending for every default xijd. Provided also that at all tymes herafter yt after ye giving forth of verdicts Copies thereof shalbe delivered unto ye partie or parties demanding them by the one of ye other of them two yt keepe ye said two end books without either deferring or delaying them And also we deeme and award that all Copies wch shall be delivered by them shall passe subscribed under both ther hands that keepe ye two said End Bookes and wheather of them as shall pen Coppy or write the verdict out of this Booke to have a penny of the partye for ye same And yt done the said Coppie to passe to ye hand of him that keepeth the other End Booke And so he to examine the same if it be agreable with this (?his) Booke, And yt done to subscribe ye same under his hand and then presently to deliver it unto ye partie againe and to take a penney of the partye for doeing ye same And what Copyes soever shall passe otherwise hereafter them subscribed under both ther hands that keepe ye said two Bookes to be of none effect valewe or accompt before either Juryers or Arbiters before whome they shall come/

And for the keeping of ye one of ye said Bookes by the Officer it is partlye that wee have sett him ye one halfe of ye two halfe penaltyes mentioned in these Orders.

Furthermore we deme & award yt at all times hereafter at such tyme and place as there shall be appointment made and lawfull warning given by the L: or his officer for the meeting of any Jurers & Arbiters and of partyes wth there witnesses for dealing in any Causes at the said house or abroad in ye parish yt the officer at the day and houre and in the place appointed shall first call and take view of all Jurers and Arbiters parties & witnesses be accordinglie as they had lawfull warning to doe and then presentlie in the presence of such as be come he shall write all absents in such sort as he will present them for the same offence when tyme shall require that for (? soe) he may prosede against them according as the default shalbe against any of these Orders & not otherwise and what causes soe ever the Jurers or Arbiters and the parties with theire witnesses shall be come the officer shall proceed in giving them there charge openlie and there alsoe then presentlie shall all witnesses of both ye parties be sworne taken and examined publikelie before both ye parties and in the publike auidence of all other people ther present & not otherwise, & even in like manner shall both the parties bring in all there written evidence touching theire cause and ye same to be openlie read before all there present And all ye same being orderlie finished the officer shall apoint them to remaine alone in the said house or other convenient place if it be abroade in the parish where the said Jurers or Arbiters shall reamaine alone and not depart but by the means of the officer be keept there severall from all other people till they give forth there verdict in writing and in order before mentiobled (? mentioned) soe Jurers & Arbiters in that behaulfe even in all such causes as they shall soe have examined & taken witnesse and evidence in without further drifte or delaye according to ther witnesse & evidence as God shall direct there consciences to their knowledge

in hearing and examination of the same and noe Jurers or Arbiters upon there partie and behalfe to offend against any part of this order upon paine to forfitt to ye Lord every one offending for every default xijd.

8. Eighthlie we deme and award yt for the avoiding of such suts that arise rather upon desire of contention then any just cause wherewith all Jurers are and hath (have) beene soe greatlie troubled that at ye court holden when the plaints shall be entered ye clearke of the court or his deputie shall alwaies before he enter any plaintt in the court Call both the parties before him and set downs ffirst in the plaint how much the plaintive Challengith & secondlie how much ye defendant grantith thereof yt soe the Jurers neid to be troubled with noe more but that onelie which is denyed by the defendant allwaies provided yt if the defendant shall grant the whole debt that is claimed by the plaintive that then the clarke of the court shall give fourth his precept to the plaintive that he may at his pleasure deliver the same to the Bailife to disern and levie the debt with other expenses in the precept contained without troubleing the Jury therwith at all/

Provided alwaies that if any pla(i)nt shall proced and come to be tryed & iudged by the plaint Jurye that then the partie against whome the same triall doth passe whether it be the plaintive or defandant to forfitt xijd. the one halfe to ye Lord and the other halfe to the Balife and Jurers that travell therin equally betwixt them But that if the defendant grant any of the debt which the plaintive (B. chalangeth) And yet the plaintive will not yeild that that is the whole debtt which the defendant grantith nather will consent to take it without triall And iudgement of the Jurye our End and award is herein yt if the plaintive recover noe more by triall And Judgment of ye Jurye but that which the defendant granted without triall that in this behalfe the Plaintive shall forfitt the said penalty of xijd. the one halfe to the Lord and the other to the Balife and Jurers that travell therin But the defendant to goe free and forfitt nothing at all

Provided alsoe that all Juriers and Arbiters in all and all manner of causes either at the Court holden or other tyme that hereafter shall be presented or put unto them within this Lordship of Ravinstondaile according to the Custome and Orders of this Lordshipp that they shall give forth a Verdict in writing upon every severall offence so put in or presented unto them making it either a matter or noe matter a default or noe default without either swearing deading or letting fall any such thing soe put in and presented unto them upon paine to forfitt to ye Lord every one offending against any part of this order for every default xijd.

9. Ninthlye we deme and award that the grand Jury shall be charged with noe presentment of any offenders at any tyme hereafter but such only as are put in And presented unto them within twelve dayes next after that Court day wherein they received there charge And furthermore we deme and award that ye said Jurye shall make an end of all such causes soe put in & presented unto them and deliver up ther virdict in writing, concerning every severall cause and matter presented unto them within fourteen dayes next after that Cort day, on which they received there Charge upon paine to forfitt to the Lord for every default every one offending herein at any tyme hereafter xijd.

10. Tently we deme and award that at tymes hereafter the plaint Jurye shall made an end of all matters that be put after the Order of ye Court unto them, And give up their verdicts upon every severall Action put in unto them in writing within twelve dayes next after that court day whereon they recived there charge upon paine to forfitt to the Lord every one offending herein of the said Jury for every default xijd. And for the full Confirmatione hereof to these tenn Orders with all there provises (B. premises) wee the said Jurers have set to our hands the said Phillip Lord Wharton our Lord and master very honorably promising to cause the same to be put in execution according to the trewe meaning and that end for which they are set downe and not otherwise the day and yeare above written.

The L: his subscriptione

All these Orders I ratifie confirme and allowe of and will they shalbe executed at all times hereafter within that my Lordshipp accordinglie as they are set downe and not otherwise, And thereto I set my hand/

Phillip Wharton.

The Jury their Subscriptione
George Greene
Thomas ffawcett Loc (?kholme)
Anthony Pinder
Symond Bousfeild
George Dent
Richard Wharton
Richard Wilson
John ffawcett
Cuthbert Hunter
Richard Bousfeild
George Hablethwaite
Richard Bovell
Willm Adamthwaite
Thomas ffawcett
Robert ffothergill
Stephen Swinbancke

finis.

(Endorsed) scriptum per me
Phillip Greene
manus scriptoris benedic°
precor.

References Chapter 9
(1)   Appendix II, Hollett MS.
(2)   Hollett MS.

Chapter 10

Ravenstonedale (4)

Parish Administration.

Having obtained Lord Wharton's consent preventing the taking the ownership and descent of land to an external court, the jury had to address itself to establishing the rules of government of the parish. In 1583 the jury appealed to lord Wharton for permission to draw up rules, and he gave his consent.[1] The documents which follow give a clear account of the administration of the parish through the manor court, to which were delegated a number of powers derived from lord Wharton who held the liberty, the manor and the rectory. Among the antique privileges listed in Nicolson & Burn[2] the liberty had the right of sanctuary, and the lord the right to prove wills. From early times the curate, appointed during pleasure by lord Wharton, acted as his notary in proving and recording wills; and each year the record of wills and probate had to be submitted to the manor court.

Document 1. The most interesting item is no. 4. relating to border service. It was common form in the four border counties that every man aged 16 to 60 was liable for fourteen days border service at the request of the Lord Warden of his march. Each man had to serve ten days, with two to come and two to go at his own charges.[3] He had to provide his own war gear, horse if necessary, and food. Any additional service was a charge on the Crown. In Ravenstonedale each man doing border service was paid an allowance met out of parish taxes.

Document (1) (Hollett MS.) A summary of eight orders 'for taxes and accompts' set down by the Jury, George Greene, Anthony Pinder, George Dent, Richard Wilson, Cuthbert Hunter, George Hablethwaite, William Adamthwaite, Robert ffothergill, Thomas ffawcett of Lockholme, Symond Bousfeild, Richard Wharton, John ffawcett, Richard Bousfield, Richard Bovell, Thomas fawcett, of Murthwaite, and Stephen Swinbancke, 'concerning taxers and constables and other collectors or disbursers of ye parish money' and their accounts, dated 24th May 1584.

(1) The present constables shall deliver their accounts and taxes in a book which shall be delivered to the keeper of the Great End Book to be kept in the Register Chest.

(2) When any tax is cast in future the taxers shall write it down, and divide it into bills 'according to our common order', and deliver them to the constables and collectors to gather the tax. At the same time the taxers shall deliver the original document of taxation to the keeper of the parish End Book for the names of the taxers, the amount of tax, and the receipts to be entered into the Tax Book, upon pain for every taxer failing in any point 12d. from his own purse. (All forfeitures under these 8 orders are to the Lord.)

(3) Constables, collectors, or disbursers of parish money shall keep written accounts of all monies received and paid, not only for the avoidance of slander but to deliver up these accounts when called for, upon pain of 12d. for every default.

(4) After any day of March 'or such like roode or business' the constables must write the names of all who go to the same, how many days they be away, and what each man was owed a day. And within eight days after their return home the constables shall deliver to the keeper of the Tax Book in the Chest the names of those who went, for how long they were away, and what each man had allowed him a day, and all to be written in the Tax Book; upon pain for every default to forfeit to the lord 12d.

(5) When the constables come to deliver up their unspent monies to their successors, if there are any monies owing they may distrain for such sums still unpaid before the day of accounts; upon pain for every default from his own purse 12d.

(6) Yearly the Jury shall choose four men of the Jury, and the sixteen men who are sworn for the church shall choose four of their number, and these eight shall within eight days after the court day, when the constables shall be

changed call before them the constables of the past year, and other collectors or disbursers of the parish money and receive their accounts. If any shall have done untruly or fraudulently in their charge, they shall be presented to the Officer & the Grand Jury that the parish may have its rights, and the penalties due to the Lord may be seized, and they to receive reproof. If the eight sworn men shall find the accounts to be good and true, they shall cause him who keeps the Book of Taxes to write them in it, and they shall be read before 'the parishing' publicly within fourteen days after the said court day, when the constables shall be changed, so that the 'whole parishing' may known how much has been collected and spent, and how much is left to be handed to their successors, that they may be fully discharged and commended for their good dealing. Neither the Grand Jury nor the sixteen sworne men shall fail in their duty under this order, on pain every man out of his own purse to forfeit 12d.

(7) Neither shall the constables, collectors or disbursers of parish money refuse to submit their accounts to, or absent themselves from the eight men charged to receive their accounts, upon pain for every man defaulting of 3s. 4d. to the Lord.

(8) Because men in observing these orders may be at some charges in writing and settling down their accounts, the men in charge shall allow their reasonable charges.

Signed by the Jury   *and Officers.*
George Greene,   John Whar-
Anthony Pinder,   ton
George Dent,   John Rigg
Richard Bousfeild,   Richard
Richard Bovell,   Wharton
Robert ffothergill,   Leonard Cal-
Richard Wilson,   vert
Stephen Swinbanke,
John ffawcett,
Cuthbert Hunter,
Thomas ffawcett,
Richard Wharton,
William Adamthwaite,
George Hablethwaite,
Symond Busfeild,
Thomas ffawcett.

There follow,

(1) An admonition to the constables and other collectors.

(2) An admonition to the Grand Jury for keeping the End Book.

(3) The oath to him who keepeth the End Book.

(4) The election on the 14th May 1584 by the Grand Jury of Willyam Cooke to be the Keeper of the End Book, and the Book of Taxes and accounts of the Constables, having first taken the oath (3, above) submitted to him by the 'clarke of the Court.'

(5) Correction for misdemeanors of the tongue. Every person 'converted before the Grand Jury' and found to have slandered person or persons of this Lordship shall, upon such a Sabbath day before the celebration of the general Communion following his conviction, before the people assembled in church, as the Minister and all such men as be in charge of the church having dewe consideration of the quality of the synne shall appoint the said offender or offenders in penitent manner to confess their fault and to ask the party grieved forgiveness for the same. But if the offender or offenders shall obstinately denye or deferr to make their reconcilement to the party grieved etc as they shall be enjoyned by the Minister and all the whole assemblie of them who have the charge of this church of Ravinstonedaile he shall forfitt to the Lord 3s.8d. And if the men in charge of the church fail in their duty to execute this they shall each forfeit to the Lord 12d.

Given at the Court holden at Ravinstondaile 28th November 1584. 'This ancient order of Correction of the misdemeanors of the tongue by you the Jury now revived and fortified by penalties, I confirm' etc. etc.

    (Signed) Phillip Wharton.

Signed by the Jury:
Anthony Pinder,
Richard Pinder,
William Cooke,
George Hablethwaite,
Richard Wharton,
Robert ffothergill,
Michael Chamberlaine,
Richard Bousfeild,
Jenkyne Greene,
Richard Bovell,
Symond Bousfeild,
Richard Wilson,
William Peares,
Richard Mourthwaite.
John Adamthwaite,

Document 2. and the two following are a collection of orders taken out of old court rolls, some probably going back to Catholic days, adapted to the needs of a Calvinistic society in which every aspect of parish life is governed by pains and penalties. No. 6. is an echo of the Henrician statute against the use of handguns and crossbows. No. 13 relating to estovers, the cutting down of timber for repairs other than botes, points to the need to make good fencing arising from such felling, and to protect new growth till it be past eating by cattle.[4] No. 17 repeats the common order that the lord's mill must be used by tenants in the grinding of their corn. Nos. 19 to 21 cover weights and measures approved by the jury. Perhaps No. 25 is the most interesting in that the churchwardens were regarded as officers of the court, together with other officers, and in their duty to regulate the church. The church seems to have been regarded as just one part of parish life which the jury had to control.

Document (2) (Hollett MS.) *A Collection of Old Orders* under running penalties to the Lord set down heretofore by the Grand Jury concerning either the Lords Royalties, Church government, or Common Wealth of this Lordship collected out of all ancient and former Court Rolls unto this present day. (A summary). By, George Greene, George Heblethwaite, Willyam Cooke, Roger Wharton, Christopher Bousfeild, Willyam Shawe, Michell Chamberlaine, Jenkin Greene, Richard ffawcett, Ralph Aulderson, Stephen Dent, James ffawcett, and Symond ffawcett, disannulling all other orders within all the old court rolls as either inconvenient or unnecessary for our estate, with the consent of the Right Honorable Phillip Lord Wharton so that all Orders to be observed henceforth: the Ten Orders of Trial, the eight Orders of Account, the Order for the Correction of Misdemeanors of the Tongue, together with this present collection of old Orders, may be had in writing and certainly known unto all persons in the Lordship for their orderly keeping; Given forth at the Court holden at Ravinstondaile 31st January 1587.

Orders touching the Lords Royalties.

(1) At the entry of every new tenant the Officer shall take his consent to all Orders within the Lordship.

(2) Any tenant or householder who lodges or harbours in his house any person or persons for two nights after they be *notoriously* known to have offended against any order within this Lordship shall himself be answerable for the penalty of the offender.

(3) All Jurers & Arbiters in their verdicts and presentments shall set down the amerciaments against offenders according to the written Orders of this Lordship, neither more nor less upon pain for every Jurer or Arbiter offending to forfeit to the Lord 12d. (All pains under this section are to the Lord.)

(4) No person shall break the peace within the precincts of the Lordship after warning by the Officer, Constable or Constables upon pain of 5d.

(5) For making an affray a pain of 6s.8d.

For shedding blood violently a pain of 3s.4d,

For making any 'hublestone' a pain of 20d.

For making a contract a pain of 12d.

(6) No person, stranger, nor inhabitant shall shoot with crossbow, or handgun, nor keep any hounds, grewhounds, or spanielts or hunt within the Lordship at hare, more cooke, partridge or other game without special licence from the Lord or Officer for every default 20s.

(7) No person or persons shall hunt, take or kill with dogges, netts or other like means any of my Lords Conneys within Ravenstonedale Park or within 400 foot of the wall upon pain of 6s.8d. for every fault.

(8) Neither stranger nor inhabitant shall fish within Ravinstondaile Parke without licence of the Lord upon pain of 3s.4d.

(9) None shall take up any improvement without licence of the Lord 'according to the Custome, neither set forth any post feete upon unrented ground without licence upon pain' etc. of 6s.8d.

(10) No stranger nor foreigner shall get any peats, turves or ling, neither break any soil within the Lordship without licence etc. upon pain of 6s.8d.

(11) No inhabitant shall sell peats, turves or ling to any foreigner upon pain of 6s.8d.

(12) None shall cut down any great timber of Oak or Ash without licence upon pain for every fault, and every tree of 3s.4d.

None shall cut down any ash spires upon pain of 20d, nor any ash 'sipling' upon pain of 12d, nor any ash plant upon pain of 6d.

None shall cut down any birkes upon pain of 6d. for every fault.

(13) Every tenant within the Lordship out of whose tenement wood shall be delivered 'shall make every severall stoven thereof fenceable and soe preserve the same untill they be growne up past eating with cattle' upon pain for every default of 6d.

Also the person to whom the wood is delivered in any man's ground beside his owne shall pay to the tenant from whose ground the wood is cut for every tree 6d., and leave him also the bowes and withs of every tree toward making fence of every several stoven upon pain for every default 6d. And that done the tenant to stand chargeable with the said stovens till they be grown up upon pain of the said penalties.

(14) Every person to whom wood is delivered shall build the same within that year wherein it is delivered upon pain of 20s.

(15) No person within the Lordship shall without licence etc. take or keep any cottager in any part of his housing, the same being not proveable and known to be a dwelling house or cottage, neigher shall any person let a dwelling house or cottage to any person or persons but to only such as be born within the Lordship, or dwelt with us three years before the date of these Orders, 'soe as they cannot be avoyded but be accounted for our owne parish poore by statute' upon pain etc. of 6s.8d.

(16) There shall be none without licence etc. take any goods out of the punfold after they be put therein, nor rescue any goods from the Officer, or from any who by his appointment go and distrain the same, nor from any who may lawfully impound the same, 'for any default in barley lawe' upon pain etc. 3s. 4d.

(17) None shall go from Ravinstondaile Mill 'being by Custome of this Lordship bound unto the same without cause', upon pain etc. for every default 3s.8d.

(18) None shall brew to sell, or dress any meat to sell 'after the manner of a typeling or viteling house' without special licence etc. in writing upon pain of 20s.

(19) No tipler or brewer to sell any drink in their house or abroad in pots, pitchers, jugs or other vessels but such as are owed and marked by the Grand Jury according to the statute upon pain of 6s.8d.

(20) The Grand Jury shall at every court and the twelve days following review all pots, pitchers and jugs in which tiplers sell drink; and those pots which will not hold six ale Quartes, those pitchers which will not hold three ale Quartes, and jugs which will not hold one ale Quarte shall be broken, and presentment shall be made of the offenders that they may be ammerced. But all pots which contain six ale Quarts, pitchers which contain three ale Quarts, and jugs which contain one

ale Quart shall be marked and allowed; and thereafter a pot of ale shall be sold for 6d, a pitcher for 3d, and a jug for a penny; that is they shall always sell a Quarte of drink for a penny. If the price of malt arise they shall brew their ale or beer so much smaller, but not alter the price.

Neither the Grand Jury nor Brewers to sell to offend against any part of their order upon pain for every default 6s. 8d.

(21) None shall sell by weights or pecks, or other measures, which have not been allowed by the Grand Jury upon pain etc. 6s.8d.

(22) Every person within the Lordship owing any mowing boon work in the Lord's Park of Ravenstonedale, shall on lawful warning come themselves or sent sufficient mowers upon the day appointed by sunrise upon pain of 12d. which penalty shall serve for discharge of the boon day.

(23) Also all owing raking boons shall come themselves or send sufficient work-folke as they shall be appointed upon pain to forfeit 6d, which shall discharge for the said boon day.

(24) That every tenant and occupier shall on lawful warning come and answer at the place of trial of causes at times appointed and keep silence etc. upon pain of 12d.

(25) At every court the constables, churchwardens, frithmen, woodwardes, mooremen, the four appointed for mending his ways, and all others having special charge search and enquire in their charges and make presentments in writing of all defaults against the Orders of the Lordship, which they shall deliver to the Officer in writing, and he to the Jury, and none to fail in his special charge upon pain etc. 12d.

(26) Every tenant shall yearly after due warning, on the eighth day after Whitsunday, and the eighth day after Martinmas pay their several rents due at the place appointed and to forfeit for every default 12d. Also if they shall fail to pay on the appointed day, they shall forfeit 12d. for each day following the eighth day after Whitsunday or Martinmas. Also if the eighth day after Martinmas be a Sabbath, they shall pay their rents on the morrow, the ninth day after Martinmas, upon pain & the forfeitures before mentioned.

Document 3. reveals the regulation of the parish more on the Calvinistic lines of the Scots kirk-session, in which lord Wharton representing 'the godly magistrate' delegated his spiritual rights as lay rector to the 'godly assembly' of the jury, which regulated the collecting of tithes, and church dues for the lord. The jury dealt with breaches of the sabbath, seeing that the church floor was regularly covered with bent or seaves, and that the mothers of illegitimate children confess their fault, and probably the name of the putative father in order that he might bear his responsibility, and not make the child a charge on the parish rates.

Mortuary Fees, taken from the statute of 21 Henry VIII, were a strong bone of contention with Quakers at a later date.

Document (3) Orders Ecclesiastical. (Hollett MS.)

(1) "First forasmuch as the Lord of this mannor hath by speciall previlidge within this libertie of Ravinstondaile certaine Jurisdiction both Civell & ecclesiastical to that end ye same may be the better executed and ordered according to the good lawes of this realme and the ancient and laudable Custome of this Lordship The Grand Jury for ye time being shall alwaies at the court holden next after Easter call in before them all the register Bookes of this Lordshipp as the Lo(rd) his End Booke, the parish End Booke, the booke of weddings, Christenings and burials, the booke of Wills & Inventories, the booke of taxes and accompts, the booke of taxes and accounts of churchwardens And shall peruse the same to see they be clenelie keept & all things therein registered according to the orders of the Lo: and the orders already begun in the said Bookes and what fault soever they shall finde they shall present upon paine every one of the said Juriers faleing upon there partye and behalfe in any parte of this order at any tyme hereafter to forfit to the L: everyone of them for every default xijd."

(2) Every inhabitant within the lordship upon a week's warning openly given in church shall come reckon and pay at time and place appointed for their tithe 'lyne' to the proctor or his deputy by themselves or some other on their behalf on pain of 6d.

(3) Every inhabitant shall at Martinmas upon open warning be at their own house at day appointed to reckon with the proctor, or leave it in writing, or leave it with another person to give in the same, upon pain etc. of 6d.

(4) All inhabitants shall yearly at Easter come to make their reckonings with the proctor for themselves and their households upon Good Friday or Easter Eve so that the same shall be finished by Easter Day upon pain of 6d.

(5) No person shall slander any other to the hurt or danger of their life, goods or good name upon pain to the Lord of 6s.8d.

(6) The Grand Jury at every court held within sixteen days after the Court Day shall deliver a note in writing of all such as they shall condemn and amerce for slander against person or persons unto the Minister or churchwardens of the parish containing both the names of the parties and the slander for which they shall be amerced, either by their own confession or by the mouth of two or three witnesses, so that those in charge of the church may procure reconciliation between the parties according to the Order of this Lordship. The Grand Jury shall not fail etc. upon pain for every default of 12d.

(7) No person or persons shall chide or raile upon each other in the church or churchyard upon pain to the Lord of 3s.4d.

(8) No tipler or brewer may sell within the lordship, nor harbour persons in their houses, or serve them with meat and drink upon Sundays or Holy Days during the time of Common Prayer or Sermon morning or afternoon upon pain of 3s.4d. whereof 20d. to be delivered to the Lord, and 20d. to the Minister and churchwardens by the Officer. The Minister and churchwardens to deliver the same to the poor and render an account thereof to the Officer, who must levy and distribute the same before the next court day. And no tipler or brewer to sell within the lordship (or) to suffer anything in his house contrary to this order etc, upon pain of 3s.4d. aforesaid.

(9) No person or persons shall remain in any alehouse upon Sundays or holy days during the time of Common Prayer, Service, or Sermon forenoon or after upon pain of 12d. to be levied by the Officer and given to the churchwardens before the next court for the poor, to distribute in order abovesaid.

(10) Every householder within the parish, having in his house any unmarried woman between the ages of seven and fifty 'shall cause a burden of bent or reshes to come to the church when' they shall be required by the minister and churchwardens etc upon pain of 6d. And the churchwardens to stand and take note at either church stile, and of offenders they shall make presentment at the next court.

(11) No persons shall carry away any bent or reshes from the church 'for barwhames or any other like purpose' upon pain of 6d.

(12) No Jurer nor Arbiter shall deal on the Sabbath with any trial nor prophane or worldly

cause within any part of the church forenoon or after upon pain for every one of them of 12d.

(13) No inhabitant shall keep or harbour in any of his housing any women begotten with child out of lawful wedlock without the precincts of this lordship before that she be first delivered of the child, and have also satisfied the law for her offence, upon pain etc to forfeit to the Lord of this manor 6s.8d.

(14) Any persons or persons who hereafter shall 'inter to the goods of orphans or fatherless children by way of sequestration or administration' shall give a faithful account thereof when lawfully required so to do by such as have authority in this lordship, without fraud or delay upon pain etc. 6s.8d.

(15) All such as be nominated executors in any testament or Will, or who have entered into administration of the goods of a dead person, or who intend to challenge any such administration having as yet no authority in writing for the same shall come to the next court, either judicially to prove such Will, or take such administration, or judicially to refuse the same upon pain for every default 3s. 4d.

Mortuary fees.

At the end of the Hollett MS.A. is this list of mortuary fees taken from the statute 21 Henry 8, but dated 14th Nov. 1666 in this MS.

Noe person shall pay mortuarys in more places than one, that is to say in the place of his dwelling or habitation. Noe mortuary shall be taken or demanded whatsoever he be which at the tyme of his death hath in moveable goods under the valew of ten marks. 21 Henry 8. 6.

Noe parson, vicar, (or) curate nor any other shall for any person dying or being deade and beinge at the tyme of his death of the valew in moveable goods of ten marks or more (above his debts paid) and under the summe of xxx[1]. take for a mortuary above iijs. in the whole.

And for a person seized at the tyme of his death of the valew of xxx[1]. (above his debts paid) in moveable goods and under the valew of forty pounds there shall not more be taken for a mortuary then vjs. viijd. in the whole.

And for a person dyeing at the tyme of his death of the valew of in moveable goodes of forty poundes or above to any somme above (his debts paid) their shall noe more be taken

for a mortuary then ten shillings in the whole. 21. Hen: 8.6.

Noe vicar (or) curate shall take, demand or aske any mortuary or any other things by way of mortuary for any woman beinge under Court barron nor for any child nor for any person not keeping house, nor also for any wayfaringe man nor other that maketh not residence at the place there they shall happen to dye but where they had there most habitation or dwelling house. 21 Hen. 8.6.

(Note: The taking of mortuary fees on the moveable goods of the dead, points to the importance of the inventory which had to be attached to a Will before probate could be granted.)

Document 4. No. 4. Though the Privy Council abolished the use of the long bow as a weapon of war in 1595[5] every man and boy was trained in its use in Ravenstonedale up till that time. Archery was regarded with an almost religious fervour by men such as Roger Ascham. The statute of 33 Henry VIII said this of the benefit of archery: 'Whereas the use of archery not only hath been, but yet is by God's special gift to the English nation, a singular defence of this realm, and an occasion of many noble victories; both a wholesome exercise for the health and strength of men's bodies, and a maintenance of a great number of subjects and artificers, as bowyers, fletchers, arrow-head makers, and others of this realm; among the other causes of the decay of archery, one great cause is the excessive price of bow staves brought into this realm...'[6]

No. 7 reflects the Elizabethan attempt to deal with poverty, the aged, the unemployed, and the homeless. While the poor of the parish resident for the three previous years were allowed to beg by licence of the parish officers, sturdy beggars and cripples from other parts were ordered out, and children under 14 were either whipped or stocked to forcé them away. Inhabitants who fed them were fined. No. 17 refers to the parish corn-drying kiln in private ownership. Very few of these kilns remain today, one in Dent, and another in Hartsop near Patterdale.[7] They were once common in the border counties, and the lowlands of Scotland, where summers were short. When the Quaker Stephen Grellet visited Wensleydale in the 8th month (August) 1812 he noted the sufferings of the people through bad harvest and shortage of grain. Wheat sold for 21s to 22s, 'and oats their chief food, at 11s.6d. to 12s. per bushel. My horse had but poor fare, and I made as little do as I possibly could.'[8] The corn-drying kilns were an attempt to stave off some of the worst effects of wet on the crops. In the dreadful years of 1597-8 and 1623 many died of starvation and the consequent disease.

Document (4). Orders Touching Common Wealth. (Hollett MS.)

(1) First there shall neither man or woman within this lordship lye or harken in any mans doors or windows after the manner of an easing dropper upon pain to forfett for every default 6s. 8d.

(2) There shall none hereafter milk any kine but there owne without speciall licence of the owners within Ravinstondaile parke or severall (ie. Severalls) upon pain etc. 6s. 8d.

(3) There shall no person or persons within the precincts of this lordshipp play at cards or dice, the Irish game, at tables onlie excepted for a pott of drinke in a way of honest recreations at any tyme at all except onlie it be within the twelve dayes after Christmasse during which tyme alsoe there shall none play at either cards or dice within this lordshipp for any stake or wager at all except it be onlie for meate or drinke nuts or apples or as childeren play for pinns for passing ye tyme away of in honest recreations without any by bettes or like colerable shiftes by themselves or others for them that soever neither shall any play at that game of cards caled Swigg at any tyme at all upon paine every householder within this Lordshipp (B. in) whose houseing there shall be any play at cards or dice in any respect contrarie to anie part of this Order by any kind of persons to forfett for every default 6s. 8d. and every player at cards and dice within ye precincts of this lordshipp in any respect contrary to any part of this order to forfitt also etc 3s. 4d. And the same alsoe to be answered by the householder if soe be they be strangers or such as afterward absent themselves soe as it cannot be distreaned or levid upon them.

(4) Every one within this Lordshipp being neither lame decrepit maimed nor having anie other lawfull reasonable excuse, betwene seaven yeares of age and three score shall not be without but shall provide and have in his house a long bow and arrows and exercise the same according to the statute and shall bring up his children and servants in ye same exercises & not suffer any of them to want bow and arrowes by one month togither contrary to the statute upon pain etc. 6s. 8d.

(5) There shall noe person or persons etc play at football within ye precincts of the same upon pain for every plaier for every default 6s. 8d.

(6) There shall noe person or persons etc play at or haunt any other unlawful game forbidden or disalowed by statute upon pain etc 12d.

(7) There shall noe Inhabitant within this Lordshipp give any harboroaghe, money, Lodgeing or any other reliefe to any 'gangrelts vagabones roges or running beggars' within the precincts of this Lordshipp except only to suche poore people of this our parish as shall be licenced and admited from tyme to tyme to travell and goe for there relife and Lodgeing within this parish by the Offecer, Constables and Church-wardens etc, who shall not licence or allowe any for poore people of this parish but such only as have not whereupon to live and not able to labour and which have either beene borne amongst us, or else have had ther abode with us three years before the date of these Orders, And as for lame people and Criples of our owne alwaies Collection to be made for them by Constables & Churchwardens and admonition to be given to ye parish to showe ther Charitie weekely yt way. But as for lame people and Criples which come to us and be none of our owne the constables shall cause them to be conveid away toward their owne parish without suffering them in contrary wise to come through this parish they shall alsoe carry great vagabonds and sturdy beggars above fourteen years of age when any such shall come within this Lordshipp to before ye next Justice of Peace. And for such as be under fourteene years to cause them to be whipped or stocked and soe to be set away from amongst us, neither shall there any person or persons within this Lordshipp serve any beggars or poore folks whether they be strangers or our owne with corne or meale skilling or groots or any other kinde of graine at the mill or upon ye mill hill and neither any of the Inhabitants Officers Constables Churchwardens or other persons within this Lordshipp upon any of ther partyes and behalfes to offend against any part of this Order upon paine of every default 6s. 8d.

(8) Noe person or persons shall put ye water out of a right and ancient course within this Lordshipp for there owne use to the hurt of there neighbour upon every default 6s. 8d.

(9) Forasmuch as all mens goods are to goe quietlie horn by horne in all places of the common pasture within this Lordshipp therefore shall noe man staff herd his owne goods or bate (beat) or slate (B. staff) anie other mans upon the common pasture upon paine etc. 12d.

Neither shall any mowe any reshes upon the common pasture ether take anie geese to keepe in this lo: forth of anie other parish upon pain etc 12d.

(10) None from henceforth within this lo: shall make anie 'widdy tethers neither cut downe anie under wood' in any mans tenement without licence of the owner upon paine etc 6d.

(11) There shall none from henceforth within this lo: having any mans goods breaking into his ground put ye same into any mans ground where it ought not to goe but he shall onli either put the same into the ground where it ought to goe, or bring it to the owner or carry it into the punfold and not otherwise upon paine 12d.

(12) Every one graveing flaughts peats or under turfes within this lo: shall well and closelie brigg or bedd all the said his peate potts within one and thirty dayes next after he shall grave the said his peates flaughts or under turfes upon paine 6d. Neither shall any grave any toppings at all upon paine 6d.

(13) Noe Inhabitant shall keepe any swine unringed or unbowed or any scabed sheepe unfeed (B. unfetched) six days after they shall be required so to doe by anie within this lo: upon paine 6d.

(14) There shall be no tenant or occupier within this lo: suffer either piatts or midding crowes to build in his tenement and bring forth young ones and let the same escape without takeing or killing ye same upon paine 3d.

(15) Ye Grand Jury shall yearlie at the court holden next after Easter, appoint foure men to be sworne for amending of high waies within this lo: and deliver ther names in writing to ye Officer and those foure to appoint every person within this lo: to what portion of high way he with his familie shall amend and every one shall amend the same as ye said foure men shall appoint according to the statute And the said foure men to goe about the parish and to view all the said worke before the end of their charge and to present every default they shall finde therein & neither the Grand Jury ye said foure men or any inhabitant within this lo: upon any of there parties and behalfes to offend against anie part of (this) Order upon paine every one of them 3s.4d.

(16) When at any time hereafter any person within the lo: shall come to the Grand Jury at ye court holden by the officer make & demand to have a running penalty set down by ye Jury in any point of neighbourhood, the

Jury shall require 3d. of the said partie having heard the parties if so be they agre to set downe the same and if the partie denye to give the same they shall let the matter pas and not meddle there withall, but if he deliver the 3d. the jury shall procede to set downe the same according as the equitie of the cause shall require and ye said Jury shall have 1d. thereof for writting the same and they shall deliver a coppy thereof with a penny to the officer and another to him that keepeth the parish End Booke At ye giving forth of there verdict that soe the same and such like running pennalties may be regestered in both the End Books and the Grand Jury not to faile in any part of this order at any time hereafter upon paine every one of them 12d.

(17) All ye owners of Ravinstondaile kill (ie. kiln) shall from henceforth leave all there ashes at every drying upon an heap toward ye reparation of the same and all other that shall dry any corne there not having any title in the said kill shall leave both all there ashes and there strawe for the same end upon paine for every offender 6d.

(18) Every inhabitant within this Lordshipp that shall at any time hereafter watch the Beacons shall at such tyme as the watch shall case (cease) carry the clubbs to the two houses that must watch next after them, And alsoe with one of the Constables come to him that keepeth the Booke of Taxes and accounts of constables and certifie him how they two be the last that have watched at that time And how they have carried and left the clubbs with them yt must watch upon ye next warning, and who the same be & what be there names And the keeper of the said tax books shall note all ye same in the place of his Booke appointed for that purpose yt soe ye watch may begin ye next tyme in due corse where it left upon paine every one of the said parties offending against any part of this order to forfett for every default 12d.

Given forth in Ravinstondaile the day or yeare above written. (31 January 1587)

Document 5. is either supplanting an earlier schedule of tithing, or supplementary to one already in force. Nicholls in his first History of Ravenstondale refers to four law cases before Exchequer and Star Chamber concerning the tithing of hay in the first half of the seventeenth century.[9] Lyn or flax was also commonly grown at that time, and it therefore possible that the present schedule of tithing is a supplementary one. Looking again at the rental of Ravenstonedale at the end of the sixteenth century there is no reference to hay or lyne, though lyne appears in the later list.

Ravenstonedale Park and Lord's grounds there	£100. 0s. 0d.
Rectory and Vicarage of Ravenstonedale by the calves and broken tithes	3. 6s. 8d.
In oblations and other dues collected at Easter	16. 0s. 0d.
Tithe lambs and odds thereof	30. 0s. 0d.
Tithe corn at the old barn	11. 6s. 8d.
Tithe wool	40. 0s. 0d.
Tithe corn at the new barn	16. 0s. 0d.[10]

Comparing the Ravenstonedale system of tithing with that of Askham in 1723 written down by the Revd. William Milner, we are able to see that the strictures of George Fox the Quaker against tithes had great force, and contributed not a little to the rise of dissent.[11]

Though the Great End Book of the jury in the seventeenth century contained further rules, the five documents in this chapter conclude the transition of one manor from monastic to lay ownership, from a Catholic to a Calvinistic community in the sixteenth century.

Document (5). Customary Rules of Tithing at Easter. (Hollett MS.)

Of Quyes (ie. an heiffer till she has had a calf) among the other calves for soe the summe of tenn would have beene exceeded, yet they are as tithable as ye rest for it is but for order in ye table they be omitted, There is farther to be noted that where and in what hand a Cowe, a quye or meare Renuieth there and by him is the tith to be answered, If a cowe happen to renewe twise in one yeare she shall tith for two calves and but for one milk. If a man buy a cow without this lordshipp after Whit Sunday soe as he hath the summer milke of her whether she had calfe or noe calfe, if soe be she renewed not within this lordshipp there shall be paid noe more but jd. for her milk and noething for ye calfe, if soe be a strip milke cowe be not milked after Whitsunday she is to answere noe tith that yeare for such a cowe also as a man makes his beife of, Wheither he milke her also after Whitsunday or not there shall be paid noe tith for the same, Od farthings at Calves have beene used neither to be taken or given hereof it Comith that in the table one Calfe is $\overline{ob}$ a jd. $\overline{ob}$ (Half a 1$\frac{1}{2}$d.) And yt at six calves, there is iijd. returned & ijd. at seaven, The procter at five Calves foles or hives will alwaies cavill or cast lots at the best yet ye owner may set upon ye same what price he will and the partie that wins ye calfe must returne the one halfe of the price to the other at Easter, The procter also at six calfes, fooles or hives will have one whole tith Calfe, fole or hive, but the owner must first both at six and seaven take up one where he will for his Chose (choice) he will alsoe take up for his Chose two at eight two at nine & two at tenn And ye procter then must take his tith and returne according as is to be seen in the table but if any man have killed anie calfe, sold, given away or made any use thereof, or any part thereof the skin onlie expected, that shal stand him for his Choyse soe farr as it goeth and be tithable with the rest of his calves, But if he can cleare himself by witnesse, or his own oath according to the Order of the Lordshipp in yt behalfe that it dyed not by his default, meanes or procurement, nor yet of his family, and that he neither made any use thereof, to himselfe nor to others any way further then of ye skinn only he shall pay noe tith for the same, If a man have put away all his Calves and have none to showe or moe then the number of his Choise to take up extendeth unto, then it rests at the pleasure of the procter to set a reasonable price upon him for his tyth whether it be whole or halfe, Calfe, foole, or hive, Calves in the South End of the Parish above Ellergill, and Arkeldgarth have used alwaies to beare the greatest price, But in the west end beneath Tibbyheads and Tranwath hill they have used to bear a smaller price, yet between Ellergill, Arkeldgarth and Tranwath hill and Teileyheads being ye middle of the parish they have alwaies borne the least price, Tith hey must be paid after iijd an Acre of Solemeadowe, and ijd. an Acre of Leace, but when such grounds as is subject to this kind of tith is plowed and beareth Corne it paieth noe tith hey (Note. Across pp. 2 & 3 in the text is the legend 'Customary rule of tithing at midsummer' without marking the division between Easter and midsummer tithing in the text.) at all for that tyme/Commuin (Communion) raits pay jd $\overline{ob}$ (ie. 1$\frac{1}{2}$.) a pece except Novices which at ye tyme of their first Admittance to the holy Communion doe but pay an halfe penny for ther offering and noe more, Now ther be some other duties gathered at Easter within this Lordshipp but they be but uncertaine and therefore not placed in the Table of this sort, is pigs which pay tith like other things, but returne and recive but qr. for one/for goose and grise be farthings both, Secondly poore folks offerings which be jd. o͞b. (1½2d.) a pece after the Common rait. Thirdly occupations which beside ther offering are commonly ijd. a pece, Fourthly servants wages where such as be growne up to mans estate be ijd. a pece and boyes and maids jd. a pece yet in all of these the procter useth commonly to deale in such Charitable manner as in to answere tith woll for or according to the pasture where it goeth feedeth and tith lambe at ye place where it doth renewe at tyme of tithing A man should lye all his woll in a Cheste or Rownedell, or else cast it hand over backe togither, And the procter ought to beginn at what end or side he will, and soe procede orderly to take the tith for all the sheepe the man had at Martinmas next before, Whereof if any be dead, the tith must be answered in skynes, And if any be sold or put to any either out of the parish, or to any within the parish the man soe selling them must answere ther tith wooll in the wooll of the rest of his sheepe, But if any man have sould all his sheepe both old and young then it rests in the pleasure of the procter what reasonable price to sett downe both for his tith wooll and lambs, If any sheepe be gone astray and not be found there tith must be paid when they be found otherwise never found never paid/If any have above the number of foure sheepe in all he hath, when he puts them to winter with any man he must alwaies put above the number of foure to any man, which if he doe not it is at the pleasure of the procter when the tyme of tithing doth come to cause all his sheep (to) be gathered and tithed together./or else to be tithed with the mans owne with whome they where (were) wintered,

(Customary rules of tithing at midsummer).

But if he have but foure sheepe only or under ther is noe question he may put them as he will. But if a man winter any of his Childrens sheepe the same are alwaies to be tythed with his owne, whether there is just five fleces, or skynes, The best fleece and skyne are equally to be devided, & the procter must have thone (the one) halfe for tith. And at five lambes a Cavell must passe for the best, yet the owner may set what price he will upon the same, and the procter if he wyne the lambe must returne thone halfe for the price set, But if he loose the lambe by lot, then he must recive thone halfe of the price set upon ytt, when they beginn to tith the tennant if he ha͡ ͡ either eight lambes or above he shall take up first two for his coise (choice),/but if he have noe moe but six, or seaven he shall take up one for his choice and then the procter shall take one for tith now afterward the tennant shall still take up nyne, and then the procter one for tith untill his lambs be all tythed, but if there at last remaine five there is to be taken up by the tennant but a Cavell must passe upon the best of them the procter alsoe of favour and upon request maide to let the Tup lambe stand for the first tyme and noe more, soe the tennant shall take up for his Chose at six one, at seaven one, at eight two, at nyne two, and at ten two, and these rules holde must hold for the summe of fifty five, but fifty sex lambes and above must Ryne (?run).

Tith Lyne (flax) is paid for when it is demanded about Lammas, for a pecke of seede sowne ijd., for halfe a pecke jd., and for a fourt part./finis.

(Note: In the text there follow the oaths for swearing in Constables, taxers, overseers of the highways and so forth).

References, Chapter 10

(1) Appendix IV. Petition to lord Wharton for the reform of abuses, 1583.

(2) N. & B, I, 519.

(3) Treatise on Copyholds, Charles Watkins, 1821, vol. II, 247-263 Customs of Weardale; page 249. 14 days on the borders, with two to come and two to go.

(4) The planting of new saplings was a common provision in ancient tenures. A seventeenth century tenant of a house in Skipton had to 'pay three hens yearly, and eight loads of coal yearly, do suit of court and mill, and set ten young trees yearly.' History of Skipton, W.H. Dawson, 1882, p. 201.

(5) English Social History. G.M. Trevelyan, 1945 ed. 168.

(6) History of Richmond, Christopher Clarkson, 1821. p. CXI. app. xxxviii, Statute about Archery. 33 Hen. VIII.

(7) For corn-drying kilns in Scotland see, Trans. Dumfriesshire & Galloway Nat. Hist. and Antiquarian Soc. vol. LIII, 1977-8. p. 134. Excavations at Polmaddy, New Galloway, M.J. Yates, and refs. The 18th C. kiln is at Rashmill in Dent. That at Hartsop has been recorded by Dr. R.W. Brunskill.

(8) A Memoir of the Life and Gospel Labours of Stephen Grellet, by Benjamin Seebohm. 1860. vol. I. 203.

(9) Hist. & Traditions of Ravenstonedale, Rev. W. Nicholls 1877, p. 52. Has four cases concerning tithe hay.

(10) Hist. & Traditions of Ravenstonedale op.cit. 42.

(11) Registers of the parish of Askham, Mary E. Noble, 1904, p.x. C. & W. trans. N.S. LX, 1960. p. 131. Tithing Customs in West Cumberland in the eighteenth century. R.F. Dickenson.

Chapter 11

Ravenstonedale (5)

The later history of the manor.

In weaving our way through the many tenant-right cases of the dales' communities, and the odium attached to James I for attempting to break the financial inadequacies of tenant-right and ancient rents, it is necessary to make several points. The first is that before he came to the throne of England Elizabeth's advisers had been looking for ways of raising extra revenue to meet the shortfall of revenue from Crown estates and parliamentary grants. It is true that the position was not improved by James' lavish gifts to favourites. It is also asserted by many local historians that James, as his proclamations suggest, tried to break tenant-right. What he did was to declare that tenant-right which depended on border service was abolished. Having proclaimed this by personal decree he then declared that tenant-right could be re-established by purchase. And the cases which will be given in these pages prove the point beyond doubt. All that James did was to make the point, first on the Crown estates, and then on the manors of his subjects that every title to estate, whether customary, copyhold or freehold should be examined. As far as northern manors were concerned a claim to copyhold, leasehold copyhold, customary leasehold or any other form of tenure which could not be established beyond the memory of man must be confirmed by purchase. It was this lever of defective titles which enabled James on Crown estates, and other lords on their manors to force tenants to compound, either to raise their fines, or to establish fines certain. It is probable that in the majority of cases the lever of defective titles was the lords' more effective weapon in James' reign, while the levying of unreasonable arbitrary fines was the usual weapon after his day.[1]

The most judicious exposition of tenant-right history was written by Dr. G.H. Tupling in the Economic History of Rossendale in 1927.[2] It avoids political and legal theory, and yet understands the national policy of James; that he was fairer in the treatment of his tenants than many private landlords. A brief look at Crown policy in Rossendale will put Ravenstonedale and the other dales' manors in a clearer light.

In the Jacobean search for defective titles Sir John Brograve, attorney to the Duchy of Lancaster discovered that the copyholds of the Forest of Blackburnshire and parcels of the Honor of Clitheroe had from 1507 been leaseholds for various terms of years. For an hundred years these leasehold copyholders had been admitted by custom, and, owing to administrative slackness leases had not been renewed, and tenants had been admitted as customary tenants on the same footing as ancient customary tenants. For an hundred years houses and barns had been built by the tenants in the belief that their tenures were secure. In fact their holdings were newhold copyholds or assarts taken out of the royal forests. The Duchy was quick to point out that they had no secure title, and must compound for such a proof. On the 7th January 1608/9 the tenants offered £3762, or twelve years' rent for confirmation. The Crown Commissioners demanded twenty years, and for various reasons the tenants were unable to agree. In the following January the commissioners agreed to the tenants' figure as a basis for settlement. The contributions of the lessees was fixed as follows: For three lives, 6 years' rent; for two lives, 5 years' rent; for one life, if between 20 and 40 years of age, 4 years' rent; if between 40 and 60 years of age, 3 years' rent; if between 60 and 80 years of age, 2 years' rent; if over 80 years of age, 1 years' rent. Tenants for 21 years, 4 years' rent; for 14 years, 3 years' rent; for 7 years, 2 years' rent. Having dealt with the leasehold copyholders of the forest lands, the commissioners turned to the copyholders on the wastes and demesnes. Not only were those rights in peril, but also the additional rights to graze the commons, and any claim to fines certain. The dispute drizzled on till 1618, by which time the tenants realised their hopeless position, and agreed to pay forty years customary rent to confirm their title, obtain fines certain, and to divide the commons on which they had grazed their sheep and cattle. The composition came to £973.17s.6d. The first half was to be paid on the issue of the confirmation on 10th February 1618/19, and the second half within one month of the Act of Parliament confirming it. The registration of the divisions of the commons of Haslingden, Accrington, and Oswaldtwistle was not completed till 1623. Following this, and before the allotments were walled in, there were a number of sales and exchanges to make more convenient units.[3] Dr. Tupling's exposition of a complex situation indicates that neither Crown, lay or former monastic manors were exempt from this review, and the result of James' policy (apart from raising money) was to put tenant-right in an even more entrenched position than it was before, to bedevil agricultural progress for generations. It had the sanction of confirmation for which the tenants had paid dearly.

Ravenstonedale. We have already covered the development of this manor till the end of the sixteenth century. Philip third lord Wharton succeeded to the title on the death of his father in 1572. He was a minor and did not succeed to the estate till 1576. As we have seen, in 1577 he married lady Frances the daughter of Henry, second earl of Cumberland,[4] who bore him two children, George and Thomas. She died at Wharton hall in 1592. In 1597 he married Dame Dorothy Colby, widow of Sir Francis Willoughby, on whom lord Wharton settled jointure lands in Yorkshire, and all his Westmorland lands, with entail to his elder son George, and remainder to his younger son Thomas.[5] The second marriage was not a success, and Dame Dorothy chafed at her quiet life, and complained that her husband was a poor manager of his estates. He sat for more than forty years in the Lords, but took no part in public affairs.

His elder son Sir George married Anne, daughter of John Manners, earl of Rutland, but had no issue.[6] Sir George pursued a fast life at Court, and accumulated large debts. He had a quick temper, and was reckless in speech. He was killed in a duel in 1609 after a dispute at cards with his friend James Stuart, son of lord Blantyre; James Stuart was killed at the same time, and the King ordered them to be buried in the same grave.[7] When lord Wharton came to examine his son's estate he found that he was bankrupt, and all his Westmorland manors in the hands of George Birkbeck of Orton, and forty other creditors. In 1605 lord Wharton had had an income of £2,107 a year, but the debts were now so large that in 1611 he made Dame Dorothy a new allowance of only £300 a year.[8]

The course followed by lord Wharton, and his second son Sir Thomas of Aske Hall, near Richmond in Yorkshire, was as follows: Sir Thomas undertook to assume his father's debts in return for all his Westmoreland manors and property. Sir Thomas and his father then sued George Birkbeck and the other creditors in Chancery for the title deeds of the Wharton moiety of the manor of Orton on the assurance that Sir Thomas would repay the loan.[9] A second action in Chancery was taken by Sir Thomas and lord Wharton against George Birkbeck and the forty other creditors for the return of the deeds of the manors or lordships of Wharton, Ravenstonedale, Nateby, Kirkby Stephen, Orton, Shap, Tebay, Langdale, Slegill, Bretherdale and (Long) Marton, all in Westmorland, and also the manors or lordships of Caldebecke, Deane, Whynfield, Great Broughton, and Birteby in Cumberland.[10] Possession was obtained on the like assurance that all loans would be repaid by Sir Thomas. As we have not seen the terms of the several mortgages, it is not possible to say what was the standing of Birkbecke and the creditors on the death of Sir George.

Having regained possession, Sir Thomas and lord Wharton came to the following composition with the tenants of ten of his Westmorland manors excluding Ravenstonedale: That whereas these tenants since time out of mind had held their several customary lands according to the custom of tenant-right on payment of certain annual rents, suit of court and mill, and services for the said tenements respectively, and 'paying on the death of the lord only', and change of tenant by death or alienation a fine arbitrary and uncertain, agreed upon as reasonable, they the said Philip lord Wharton and Sir Thomas Wharton in consideration of the sum of £3,651.3.7. paid them by the several tenants, parties to the said Indentures respectively and for the better confirming and establishing their customary estates and interests of inheritance, and that from henceforth the fines might be certain, and that the laudable custom of tenant-right might be confirmed etc, the tenants doing their usual suit and services, That upon the change of every lord by death only, and upon the change of tenant by death or alienation a fine of ten (10) times one year's ancient annual rent should be payable by the tenants of the manors of Kirkby Stephen, Wharton, Nateby, Shap, Reagill, Sleagill, Long Marton and Bambton Carhullan, and eight (8) times the annual ancient rents in the manors of Tebay, Langdale (parish of Orton), and Bretherdale without any increase, And that any covenants and agreements should be executed at the charges of the tenants. The tenants of these respective manors agreed to pay the fines of ten and eight years respectively as they fall due in two equal portions at Martinmas and Pentecost following. The agreement also stated that no further general fine shall be due until the death of either lord Wharton or Sir Thomas Wharton and the longer liver of either of them, nor until the heir or survivor of either of them shall have reached the age of twenty-one years.[11] It is fairly clear from the vague wording of the text, that the money due at Martinmas and Pentecost was the composition money. There was no reference in the Bampton Carhullan document, and presumably the other nine, of a general fine being due on the transfer of the Westmorland estates to Sir Thomas Wharton.

As the manor of Ravenstonedale was excluded from these ten agreements, because its fines had been fixed by the Indenture of 1579/80, it did not escape the edict of James I that tenant-right was abolished and could be confirmed by composition. This was effected by an Indenture of 3rd August 11 Jas.I. (1613) between Philip lord Wharton and Sir Thomas Wharton and Rowland Taylor, William Adamthwaite, William Cooke, Stephen Dent, Vincent Fothergill, Henry Dent, and the rest of the customary tenants. It states that lord Wharton had granted the manor of Ravenstonedale to his son Sir Thomas, and therefore by change of lord a general fine was due, and that the tenants in order to manifest their good will towards lord Wharton 'their honourable good lord and maister' have agreed to pay a general fine due on this occasion, and that they are excused any further fine until the death of Philip lord Wharton and Sir Thomas Wharton and whoever should live the longer etc. The general fine was on the basis of the 1579/80 Indenture, one year's ancient rent on old grounds, and eight years' on new. The tenants are to be admitted at the next court after paying the general fine. Sir Thomas now acquits them of the general fines now paid, and confirms their ancient customs, and that no further general fine shall be due until the death of lord Wharton on Sir Thomas his son, and the longer liver of them two. The tenants shall continue to pay their dropping fines on the change of tenant by death or alienation.[12] It is probable that the like composition was made with the Cumberland tenants, But neither these, nor the sales of south-country properties covered all the debts. In 1617 lord Wharton made one last attempt to obtain help from the King, and entertained him at great cost at Wharton Hall when the King returned from Scotland, The clamouring of the Westmorland tenants at the gates of Brougham Castle and Wharton Hall against the King's 1617 Award in the Clifford dispute did not improve the occasion, and Wharton was left in greater debt. In 1618 his debts came to £16,713, and he had no alternative but to put his affairs in the hands of trustees, Humphrey Wharton his man of business and others. He reserved £500 a year for Sir Thomas, and £600 for himself. When lord Wharton died in 1625 his total income was £434.7.4d.[13]

The 1613 agreement with the Westmorland tenants was of short benefit. Sir Thomas Wharton died at Aske in 1622, and his father in 1625. He was succeeded in a ruined estate by his grandson Philip, than a boy of eleven or twelve. As he did not reach his majority till 1634, a general fine was not due till then. A year of two after his grandfather's death be entered Exeter College, Oxford, but did not emerge into public life until May 1640, when he signed the Yorkshire petition against billeting soldiers on the county. He was rebuked by the King, and threatened by Wentworth if he and his fellow signatories persisted in public opposition. In September 1640 he was one of the commissioners to treat with the Scots at Ripon. During the Long Parliament he supported the policy of the popular leaders, and accepted several commissions from Parliament. His regiment was routed at Edgehill in 1642, and after his ignominious defeat he refrained from army life, confining himself to parliamentary work.

In brief he was for some accommodation with the King, and disapproved of his execution. He was on excellent terms with Cromwell, who begged him to do the Lord's work in the Protectorate. Though he had been a lay member of the Westminster Assembly of Divines, he went over to the Independent minority. He supported the restoration of Charles II. In 1670 he opposed the second Conventicle Act, and in 1675 opposed the act to impose a non-resistance test on the whole nation. After the Bartholomew Act of 1662 he persuaded a number of clergy of Presbyterian views of conform to the Church of England, among them the vicars of Orton, Ravenstonedale and Kirkby Stephen. When Christopher Jackson, the intruded rector of Crosby Garrett was ejected in 1662 he found a home at Ravenstonedale, and protection from lord Wharton. It is not without point that both the Presbyterian chapel, and the Quaker Meeting were established in the parish during his life, Indeed it is significant that the churchwardens of Ravenstonedale were prosecuted for not informing against the Quakers to the magistrates; and when the Toleration Act of 1698 was passed it was written fully into the Court Book of the manor.[14] His moderate views are best summed up in the following account. When in 1690 a bill was proposed to impose a general oath abjuring the title of James II, lord Wharton 'said he was a very old man, and had taken a multitude of oaths in his time, and hoped God would forgive him if he had not kept them all; for truly they were more than he could pretend to remember; but should be very unwilling to charge himself with more at the end of his days.' He died in 1696 and was buried at Wooburn. In him the fortunes of his house were restored, while his Bible charity represented that moderate Puritanism which has remained the dominant culture of the dales.[15] The work of Edward Mynese the Calvinist schoolmaster of Ravenstonedale in the 1550s and headmaster of Kirkby Stephen from 1556, and the life's work of John Knewstub his scholar had come to fruition. The magic of the Mass was but a dim memory, while a severe Old Testament Christianity ruled in its place.

The life of his grandson Philip duke of Wharton (1698-1731) brought many changes to the Wharton estates. He was about 17 when his father died in 1715. He was 'a person of unbounded genius, eloquence and ambition; he had all the address and activity of his father, but without his steadiness; violent in parties, and expensive in cultivating the arts of popularity, who it is said expended £80,000 in elections ... by which the estate became encumbered.'[16] He set out in the world as a Whig, and for his services was created duke of Wharton in 1718. He was a patron of the turf, and president of the Hell Fire Club till its suppression. After he set up in opposition to the administration he became a Tory, and in 1726 adopted the Jacobite cause in Vienna, and became a Roman Catholic. In the same year 'James III' in Madrid created him Duke of Northumberland. In 1727 he accepted a commission in the Spanish army and served against Gibraltar. He was outlawed in 1729, and died in abject poverty in the monastery of Poblet in Catalonia on the 31st. May 1731.[17]

When in 1721 the young duke was unable to cover his debts, he conveyed all his Westmorland estates and manors, including Ravenstonedale, to trustees to be sold to meet his obligations. They were administered by them till 1729, when they were sold for £30,400 to Robert Lowther of Maud's Meaburn, ancestor to the earls of Lonsdale.[18] Following this, the manor, liberty and rectory of Ravenstonedale passed to the Lowther family, and all the court books and records were transferred to the new owner. They are now among the Lowther records at the Castle, Carlisle. In 1734 the tenants of Ravenstonedale purchased the tithes of the parish from Robert Lowther for the sum of £1,958.8s. in right of the rectory, though the advowson of the perpetual curacy remained with him.[19]

The 1729 sale of the Wharton manors to the Lowthers produced the inevitable question, to which I have often alluded. Robert Lowther proceeded in 1731 to summon all the tenants of the ten manors of the 1613 agreements to pay a general fine on the death of the duke of Wharton. It is possible that, as Ravenstonedale had a separate agreement in 1613, it was excluded from this action. There was also a subtle difference between the Ravenstonedale agreement of 1613 and those of the ten other manors. Both state that one of the benefits to the tenants would be that there should be no general fine till after the deaths of lord Wharton and his son and the longer liver of them, but only the Ravenstonedale one says that a general fine was due on the transfer of the manor to Sir Thomas Wharton. The latter may have been shaky at law, while the agreement of the ten manors gives the like relief from a general fine without making the claim that a general fine was paid to obtain that benefit. When in 1731 Robert Lowther demanded a general fine of the ten manors the tenants refused to pay the fine on the ground that it was due on the death of the lord in occupation, not on the death of the last admitting lord. The reader will recall that I have been at pains to record the variations in several earlier documents covering this point, variations which were bound to be at issue sooner or later.

(1) The monastic custumal of Ravenstonedale which was repeated in 1556 contained no reference to any general fine due on the death of a lord.[20]

(2) The Indenture of 1579/80 said that a fine was due 'at the change of every lord of the said manor'. Thus it might be by death or alienation.[21]

(3) The preambles of the 1613 Indentures stated that in the ten manors a fine was due

'on the death of the lord only.'[22] The final agreements stated that a general fine was due 'upon the change of the lord for the time being by death only.'[23]

In the northern customary manors, especially in Cumberland and Westmorland the position was far from uniform. In Sir Edward Coke's Commentary on Littleton it is stated that in 38 Elizabeth there was a cause depending in Chancery between the copyholders of the manor of Gilcrux in Cumberland and their lord, one Armstrong. The lord claimed an arbitrary fine upon every change of lord, be it by alienation, demise, death or otherwise. It was resisted by the tenants. The Lord Chief Justice Popham said that the custom to take fines upon every alienation of the lord was unreasonable and unlawful. The change ought to be by an Act of God, otherwise no fine can be due.[24] The point was underlined by Isaac Gilpin in his commentary on the manorial customs in the barony of Kendal, written about 1656. After making the point that a new lord by purchase could not receive a general fine as purchaser, nor could any heir or assignee in occupation after him, while the old lord who last received a general fine was still alive. 'A general fine becomes due only upon the death of the old Landlord which formerly received or might or ought to have had a general fine and not upon the death of every Landlord as I have said before.'[25] That this rule was not uniformly held can be seen in Ravenstonedale, where the tenants under the 1613 agreement held that a fine was due on the death of the lord in occupation. The 1613 agreement prompts the question as to whether the tenants' attorneys were not sharp enough to see that it was a breach of the Gilcrux ruling, or whether they thought that the King's declarations against tenant-right put that rule into abeyance.

The case was heard in the Chancery on 17th June 1734 by Lord Chancellor Talbot.

The plaintiff was Robert Lowther, and the defendant representing the tenants of the ten manors was Michael Raw. Lowther claimed that a fine was due on the death of the last admitting lord, whether he had alienated the manor in his life or not. The tenants claimed that the 1613 agreements stated that it was due 'on the death of the lord only'; that meant the lord in occupation. The plaintiff attempted to bring evidence of custom from other surrounding manors, supporting the view that a general fine was due on the death of the last admitting lord, and not otherwise. The Lord Chancellor refused to admit this supporting evidence of custom contemporary with the 1613 agreements, that 'he saw no cause to give the appellant any relief in equity; and therefore that the matter of the appellant's bill should, from henceforth, stand absolutely dismissed, but without costs.'[26] Robert Lowther took the case to the House of Lords on 24th April 1735, which reversed the Chancellor's decree, and stated that a general fine was due on the death of the Duke of Wharton, according to the rates specified in the agreements of August and September 1613. Thereafter the rule was established that a general fine was due on the death of the last admitting lord, whether in occupation or not at the time of his death. The tenants of the ten manors were therefore faced with costs in Chancery as well as in the House of Lords.[27]

Under the Will of William Viscount Lowther of 13 January 1798, confirmed by Act of Parliament in 1806, provision was made for the enfranchisement of all 36 of the Lowther manors in Westmorland and 14 in Cumberland. Ravenstonedale was among these, and the deed of enfranchisement of 1808 contains about half the tenants. But provision was made for the process to continue, and the last payment was made in 1871.[28]

References Chapter 11

(1)   The Kendal barony case 1620-25, which accepted that the abolition of Border service did not break tenant-right, is the point of divide between the two approaches. N & B, I, 56-59.

(2)   The Economic History of Rossendale, Dr. G.H. Tupling, Chetham Soc. trans. 1927.

(3)   Ibid. 127-160.

(4)   N & B, I. 289.

(5)   The Good lord Wharton, Bryan Dale, 1901. 15-16.

(6)   N & B, I. 559.

(7)   The Good lord Wharton. op.cit. 16.
       N & B, I. 473 states that after the death of Sir George the King granted to lord Wharton the reversion and remainder of all the Shap Abbey lands granted to Sir Thomas Wharton kt. in 36 Henry VIII.

(8)   The Good lord Wharton op.cit. 16.

(9)   Cal. of Proceedings in Chancery in the reign of Q. Elizabeth, III, 1832. p. 210. Philip lord Wharton
       & Sir Thomas Wharton v. George Birkbecke & others.
       (In this and the following ref. this vol. extends to James I.)

(10)   Cal. of Proceedings in Chancery in the reign of Q. Elizabeth op.cit. Vol. III, 221. There are 2
       other refs. on pp. 223 & 312 which may also refer to Sir George's debts.

(11)   English (Law) Reports. House of Lords vol. I, 1900. p. 1058. Robert Lowther v. Michael Raw and
       others, 24 April 1735.
       The Bamptom Carhullan agreement 9 Aug. 1613 is given in Hist. of Parish of Bampton, Mary E.
       Noble 1901. 29-35.

(12)   Indenture of 3rd Aug. 1613 between Philip lord Wharton & Sir Thomas Wharton and the Customary
       tenants of Ravenstonedale. C.R.O. Kendal.

(13)   Saw Pit Wharton. G.F. Trevallyn-Jones. Sydney U.P. 1967. 14-15.

(14)   James Bayliff's MS 1738. The property of Mr C. Hollett, Sedbergh.

(15)   For short refs. to the Duke of Wharton see:
       D.N.B. Philip fourth lord Wharton. 1613-1696.
       Saw-Pit Wharton (for his political career 1640-1691). G.F. Trevallyn-Jones Sydney U.P. 1967.

(16)   N & B, I. 560.
       Hell-Fire Duke. The life of the Duke of Wharton. Mark Blackett-Ord, 1982.
       D.N.B. Philip Duke of Wharton 1698-1731.
       He was elected Grand Master of the Masons in doubtful circumstances 24 June 1722, and was
       succeeded in 1723 by Francis earl of Dalkeith: The Craft, A History of English Freemasonry, John
       Hamill. 1986, 42, 159 & plate 4. According to Transactions of Quatuor Coronatorum Lodge no.
       2076, vol. 101 (1988), p. 257 he was Grand Master of French Masons 1728-31.

(17)   English (Law) Reports. House of Lords. Vol. I. 1900, p. 1058.
       Robert Lowther v. Michael Raw & others 24 April 1735, & on p. 1060 gives an incorrect date
       of death.
       Hell-Fire Duke, Mark Blackett-Ord, op. cit. 223.

(18)   Lowther v. Raw, p. 1060, sect. 454.

(19)   Hist. of Ravenstonedale, W. Nicholls, II, 1914. 37-39, for the enfranchisement of the manor by Act
       of Parl. 1808.

(20)   Chapter 7, ref. (8).

(21)   Chapter 8, ref. (6).

(22)   Lowther v. Raw sect. 452.

(23)   Ibid. sect 453.

(24)   Hist. of Cumberland, W. Hutchinson, Carlisle 1794, II, 347, footnote*.
       First part of the Institute of the Laws of England, or a Commentary upon Littleton, by Sir Edward
       Coke, revised by F. Hargrave & C. Butler 18th ed. 1823, sect 59b. The change of lord ought to
       be by an Act of God. The footnote (9) dates the case 39 Eliz, between the copiholders of the
       manor of Gilcruix & one Armstrong before Popham L.C.J. & other judges. If the change of lord
       be by the act of the party, by that means the copiholders may be oppressed by a multitude of
       fines.
       Transactions of the High Court of Chancery, both by Practise & Precedent. W. Tothill & R.O.
       Holborne. London 1820. p. 49, under the head 'Custom': 'Tenants de ... contra Armstrong. One
       year's value and not above.' 40 Eliz. li. B. fo. 595.

(25)   C & W trans. N.S. LXII, 1962. Mr Gilpin & Manorial Customs, by Mrs Annette Bagot, 224-245,
       p. 235. On p. 233 Gilpin refers to Mr Shippard's Epitome. William Sheppard's Epitome of the
       Common & Statute Laws was published 1658. (Copy. Camb. Univ. Lib. J. 14. 16.)

(26)   Lowther v. Raw. p. 1061. sect. 455.

(27)   Lowther v. Raw. p. 1062. sect. 456.
       Treatise on Copyholds. J. Scriven & A. Brown. 2nd. ed. 1896. 16, 180. Law of Copyholds &
       Customary Tenures. D.I. Elton & H.J.H. Mackay, 2nd. ed. 1898. 171, 343.
       There is also a case of mortgage from Ravenstonedale, (Chancery Rep. vol. 28, 193) relevant to
       tenant-right, and which got into the law books. Fawcet v. Lowther, 15 June 1751. A mortgagor
       died within the 3 years in which he had to redeem, without issue, & not having aliened the equity
       of redemption. Two issues were put to the lord Chancellor. (1) whether the mortgagee could claim
       admission, he paying the fine to the lord, or (2) whether the lord of the manor became entitled to
       the equity of redemption of such mortgage; or whether one Copeland and his wife (who claimed
       redemption as collateral heirs of the mortgagor) consenting to give up the right of redemption of
       the mortgaged premises could be admitted. The case was first heard 11 July 1750, where the motion
       made to vary the issues was refused. At the re-hearing 15 June 1751 it was determined that the

first issue should be put to a jury; and on the second issue of the equity of redemption the lord Chancellor refused to determine.

Note:

The reader will recall that if a tenant of Ravenstonedale died without lawful issue, and without bequeathing his tenement by will or other conveyance to whom he will within the rule of the indenture of 1579/80 his tenement escheated to the lord. It was for the manor jury to decide whether the lord or Copeland had the prior claim, and failing them the mortgagee. A nice question.

See lso Scriven op. cit. 77, 108, 176, 185, 314.

Elton & Mackay op. cit. 68, 139, 184.

(28) Hist. of Bampton. Mary E. Noble. 1901. 69-91.

Hist. of Ravenstonedale. W. Nicholls. II, 1914. 37-39.

Chapter 12

Customary Tenant-right.

In the sixteenth century the northern customary tenant was not concerned with the historian's niceties on the origins of his estate. On the other hand a short general review of those roots is a help to understanding the controversies between lords and tenants which occurred in nearly every northern dale.

Northern customary tenure was a mixture of those tenures which obtained in the old kingdom of Northumbria long before the Norman conquest, and Norman feudalism which never completely assimilated it. Long before the manor took root as a legal entity there were isolated old border communities in Northumbria bound by loyalty to their local lord, and the needs of border defence.[1] For centuries these lords were virtual princes in their own right, where local loyalty was stronger than that due to the king. These communities were fiercely independent, and it is from them that communal government by a jury of Four-and-Twenty was derived. Some tenants held their land of the lord by foot-tenure, some by nag-tenure, others by renders of food or service.[2] It was not till the reforms initiated by Henry II that many of these were commuted for fixed money payments, which in later years were called ancient rents, or rents of assize. There were also primitive forms of servitude bond-men, drengs, cottars, and others whose tenures were slowly assimilated into the broad mass of customary tenants in villenage, which by the sixteenth century was well established as customary tenant-right. Their base origin was undisputed, but somewhere down the years, perhaps from the later fourteenth century, the tenants won the right for their offspring to succeed to their farms without question by the lords, and to sell as they wished.[3] It was a slow growth.

The northern border counties of Cumberland, Westmorland, Northumberland, Durham, and the northern parts of Lancashire and Yorkshire were the most backward parts of the country, and this is reflected in manorial law. In the greater part of England copyhold was the principal form of tenure, whereby the tenant was entitled to a copy of the entry in the court rolls which recorded either his succession to the tenement from his father, or his purchase of the property, and admission by the lord's steward. In Cumberland and Westmorland the new tenant was admitted at the next court, and recorded on the court rolls, and that was the only evidence of his admission. He did not receive a copy, and had no deeds except what was written on the rolls. The distinction may seem academic; but the point is that a copyhold tenant was generally customary by copy of court roll; the broad mass of customary tenants in Cumberland and Westmorland enjoyed their tenant-right, but without copy. Lawyers and lords were loth to give copy, except where it was specially granted by the lord or King. In the manor of Ravenstonedale deeds of purchase only begin to be mentioned in 1696.[4] Where copyhold arises in Cumberland and Westmorland it usually records an alteration in the form of tenure, [5] or the taking in of waste land from the commons or forests and the creation of new tenements or assarts. Copyhold in the north usually records something new. In making this generalisation I have ignored the use of copy in northern boroughs.[6] Thus in Ravenstonedale, when lord Wharton dealt with the Chamberlain family who had squatted on the lord's demesne during the time of archbishop Holgate, in 1560 he forced the Chamberlains off, gave them some compensation at the expense of other tenants, and where they were given some land from the commons, these new improvements paid higher rents and fines and were by copy of court roll. This was incorporated into the Indenture of 1579/80. Thus in Ravenstonedale the majority of tenants were customary without copy, and the minority were copyhold on new improvements.[7] The historian will observe that for simplicity I have avoided other variations, customary leasehold, copyhold leaseholds, and so forth.[8D]

The next point which was the cause of much friction was over the money payments due to the lord of a manor, either from these ancient fixed rents, or the fines due on the death of a lord, or the change of tenant by death or alienation. With the fall in the value of money the return from these fines and rents became less economic, and the only redress for the lord was to raise the fines, which were so many times the ancient rents. This will be referred to often in the following pages. Thus by the second half of the sixteenth century two problems met to agitate lords and tenants; in most manors in lay ownership the fines were arbitrary, and had to be negotiated; where the manor had been in monastic ownership there was now a lay lord who would die, and his successor would demand a general fine of all his tenants, and often the fines taken by the monastery were so low that the new lord had great difficulty in raising them to a more realistic figure. Further, if an aggrieved tenant wished to take his lord to court over an excessive fine, he could not do so. But all the tenants acting through their representatives could do so. There were three avenues open to them. It will be recalled that Henry VIII on the establishing of the Council of the North in 1538 gave it power to adjudicate in the tenancy cases. Many cases were also taken to the Court of Requests in London. But neither of these courts, being under the Privy Council, had the power of Chancery, and it was Chancery which became the principal court in hearing tenant-right cases. When tenant-right cases were heard at York (which had its own staff of judges) they were increasingly transferred from London by order of Chancery. Tenant-right cases heard at York thus became cases in Chancery.

There were, however, a number of small manors, owned by petty gentry where the ancient services had not been commuted, and remained until the nineteenth century. In the manor of Crosby Garrett, near Kirkby Stephen, there were about six or seven mowings of an acre each which had to be mown for the lord by different tenants. If they were warned before sunset the grass had to be cut before the following sunset. The lord or his steward supplied three meals and three bottles of ale for each boon. The first meal had to be an ale posset. There were twelve or thirteen loads of coals to be carried by pack-horse from the pits on Stainmore or from Bainbridge in Wensleydale. The lord paid the current price for the coals at the pits, as well as giving a pint of ale. The pack-horse loads were of six packs each. Each tenant was paid for his day's boon labour in the fields. One tenant had his land on foot-catch tenure, which means that the lord could send him on an errand to Kirkby Stephen when required.[9] One of the necessary

duties was to fetch salt from the former monastic salt-pans on the west Cumberland coast.[10] In the manor of Great Musgrave near Kirkby Stephen the boons and services were compounded in the following quit rents:

A day's ploughing	8d.
A day's harrowing	3d.
A day's shearing	3d.
A day's mowing	4d.
A goose	6d.
A hen	4d.
A load of coals	4d.[11]

Added to these manorial dues were those due to the lord of the barony of Appleby, the neatgelt, castle-hens and sergeant corn which were not abolished by the Great Contract at the restoration of Charles II.[12] These petty dues, more irritating than onerous, are well illustrated in the following deed from Crosby Garrett:

> 30th June 1719. Richard Wilkinson and his wife Isabella of Carlisle sold to William Taylor of Crosby Garrett a house, barn, garth and gardens of one acre, with two acres in Oxcroft at an annual rent of 3s.10d. one hen, one day's shearing, with tithe of 1s., with one close called Haber of ... acres between Bullflatt and Town field, with arbitrary rent of 2s.4d. one peck and two quarts of serjeant corn, for the sum of £66.[13]

We will now look at the problem which vexed lords and tenants in the sixteenth to eighteenth centuries relating to rents and fines. (a) *The Custumal.* If a tenancy case came before Chancery one of the first questions a judge would ask was, 'What is the custom of this manor?' The custumal was therefore a vital document, attested by the manor jury, specifying the rules governing the descent of land, the rents, whether ancient or improved, and the fines, whether arbitrary or certain. Fines were usually *general* on the death of the lord, *dropping* on the change of tenant by death of alienation, and sometimes *running* as in old church land where there was no lord to die. Running fines took the place of general fines and were levied every so many years, say five, ten or more years. A good custumal would also cover the use of woods and underwoods. A typical custumal comes from the manor of Preston Patrick in the barony of Kendal which was sequestered from Sir John Preston by the Commissioners for Sequestrations for serving in the Royal Army in the Civil War. He did not receive the estate back till he had compounded for his delinquency. It is dated 26th December 1651, and was sent by the Westmorland County Commissioners to the Committee for Compounding in London. This document is interesting in that among the tenants are names John Camme, and John Audland the first Quakers in the parish.

The Custumal of Preston Patricke.

'We present the Custom of the manor of Preston Patricke which is that our estates are Customary estates of inheritance descendible from Ancestors to heir for ever according to the Custom, and that we pay to the very Lord of this manor a fine at the change of the tenant by death or alienation, which fine is to be assessed and agreed upon between the Lord and that tenant, and likewise a fine at the death of the Lord he being possessed of the freehold estate; and that fine compounded for and agreed upon and not otherwise, which said fine is in lieu and satisfaction of all other fines during the joint lives of that very Lord and the several tenants according to the Custom time out of mind used; and likewise the widow is to pay a harriott in lieu for her fine for her widow estate.

We present that we pay a rent at the usual rent daye which is the second Sunday after Trinity and Andrew's tide and for other things that hath been paid and done by the said tenants unto the Lord of the said manor we do not present them as Custom, but as things done of good will, for which said service we had a sufficient recompence paid us by the Lord or his officers; (the services were:) That every Ancient Tenant did give unto the Lord 'a bounde shearing', which was four shearers, and they received from the hands of the Lord or his officers four shillings for their pains, or two shillings and meat and drink; And every Ancient Tenant did give a day harrowing for which he had nine pence allowed him; And likewise every one a hen in the year in lieu of which the tenant and his wife were feasted at Christmas by the Lord; Besides we were to have straw at two pence five threave or cartful for so much as we paid tithe corn, and every one according to their quantity, and likewise a Bull free; which things are all detained by reason that all the lands and tithes are sequestered and upon lease; And therefore we conceive ourselves no more bound to do these services unless we have and receive the considerations we usually had in lieu of them. We present and verdict that all the woods growing upon our own grounds in fences, hedges, ditches or other places is our own, excepting Parks Coppies and holts, which hath formerly belonged unto the Lord of the manor though it grew upon our estates provided always

and it is the Custom of the manor that no widow shall sell, make waste or destroy in the minority of the heir any wood upon that heir's estate, but such as shall be needful for repairing of the houses and husbandry gear, and it is to be set forth and viewed by the house-lookers appointed and sworne for that use within the said manor for the year and not otherwise.'[14]

The ancient rents of manors were used as the basic unit of negotiating any composition between lord and tenant, and the following cases are given to illustrate problems dealt with, and the rate employed.

(b) On the 24th June 1687 Philip lord Wharton procured a charter for a market at Shap weekly on Wednesdays, and three fairs yearly. On the 14th December 1687 the same lord Wharton in consideration of one year's customary rent paid by the tenants of the manor, granted to them and their heirs to be free from all toll in the said market and fairs.[15]

(c) During the reign of James I, who encouraged all northern lords to force their tenants to compound for the confirmation of their tenant-right, Sir John Lowther of Lowther and his son John of Hackthorpe claimed that their tenants in Crosby Ravensworth who held their lands under certain rents, fines, boon days, works and other services must compound for confirmation. Eventually the tenants agreed to pay forty years ancient rent for the confirmation, together with the following benefits; That the estate shall descend according to common law, that is through eldest son etc, and failing heirs male to eldest daughter or sister in turn; that there shall be a fine certain of two years' rent, and the tenants released from all servings of ploughing, harrowing, shearing, raking, peat leading, farm hens, and salt. The Lord reserved suit of court and mill.[16] It is worth noting that if the last admitting lord died in the year of this agreement, or the tenancy changed, the tenant would be liable for an additional general fine, or dropping fine of two years' ancient rent above the composition money. On the other hand the agreement cleared away many vexatious incidents.

(d) One of the more interesting cases comes from the manor of Bleatarn in the parish of Warcop, near Kirkby Stephen. In the reign of Henry II it was granted to the Cistercian abbey of Byland in Yorkshire, and the monks had a grange at Bleatarn. Byland was surrendered to the Crown 30 Henry VIII, and eight years later Bleatarn was sold to the Bellasis family, and after several owners it came in 25 Charles II to George Fothergill of Tarnhouse, Ravenstonedale. During the course of these several ownerships it was let in the reign of Elizabeth for forty years to John Pulleine of Scotton near Knaresborough. In 44 Elizabeth he took the tenants of Bleatarn to the Court of the Council of the North. After reciting the usual terms of tenant-right and border service he claimed an arbitrary general fine, and a dropping fine of seven years ancient rent, 'according to the moiety of their several rents', which probably refers to his moiety of the manor. The tenants replied that they had no such custom, but that on the death of the lord or tenant, they were to pay a God's - penny only, and nothing on change of lord by alienation or lease. The tenants appear to have been in error if they were citing custom from monastic days, where the lord did not die. They replied that they would not accept arbitration, but depend on trial at common law. The court appointed Philip lord wharton to arbitrate, and if the tenants refused to accept him, then the case should proceed at common law. In the end Pulleine dropped the case.

This case does, however, open up the origin of God's - pennies in northern manors as an early currency between lord and tenant. The Oxford English Dictionary gives its origin either as a small sum paid as earnest money on striking a bargain, a rebate given on making a payment, a penny given in charity, or a broker's commission. A number of manorial historians regard it as a down-payment on a fine, with the full sum to be paid later. In Cumberland and Westmorland there are several types of God's - penny.

(1) In the Richmond fee of the barony of Kendal in 16th Elizabeth it was used for customary admittances and defined as: 'one penny of silver, commonly called a God's - penny.'

(2) In the rectory manor of Church town in the parish of Caldbeck where the rector had 24 tenants they paid customary rents, arbitrary fines on alienation, but a God's penny on change of tenant by death.

(3) In the manor of Kirkoswald the tenants paid customary rents, and a God's - penny only for a fine.

(4) In the parish of Stanwix, Carlisle, the customary tenants paid only a small silver coin at the change of tenant, and nothing on the death of the lords.

(5) The silver penny seems also to have been used as a rent or a quit-rent. The manors of Old Hutton and Holme in the barony of Kendal in 25 Edward I were granted to Patric de Culwene, reserving to the vendor 'one penny of silver yearly' at Christmas.

In the parish of Grasmere, part of the barony of Kendal there was forest silver, and walking silver. The first seems to have been for agistment of cattle in the forest, and the second for the officers whose business it was to perambulate the forest.

In 30 Henry VIII the abbot of Shap conveyed to Thomas Blenkinsop of Helbeck a water course and water mill at Slegill for two pence of silver yearly at the feast of Pentecost, if demanded.

At Graystock in 1777 there were 257 customary tenants, and 106 freeholders, and the customary tenants paid a 20d fine (twenty year ancient rent) upon the death of lord or tenant, and a 30d. fine on

alienation. Among the petty rents was peat silver, for the right to grave peats.[18]

Thus, looking at these examples of God's - penny and silver rent, it is the present writer's view that they represent not so much earnest money on striking a bargain, but a very old form of ancient rent deriving from the earliest days when renders were commuted to fixed money payments. That some of these were to the church would explain them as something given to God. Where there are God's - pennies and customary rent I suggest that the latter was added at a later date to supplement the inadequacy of the former. But I question an assumption that God's - pennies always represent a lawyer's contract, rather a composition.

The Bleatarn dispute was not settled until 18 Charles II when the judge of assize recommended that it should be settled by the arbitration of Sir John Lowther, who awarded a 7d. fine on the death of the lord, and change of tenant by death or alienation. In the case of the widow occupying her moiety her fine should not be paid till her death, marriage or miscarriage. At the date seven years' ancient rent was reasonable.[19]

It took 128 years to change the custumal from monastic to lay ownership.

(e) In 1636 Sir Philip Musgrave of Hartley castle, Kirkby Stephen, owned the manors of Crosby Garrett, part of Kirkby Stephen, Little and Great Musgrave, Soulby and part of Bleatarn. Sir Philip had demanded composition to confirm tenant-right, and had probably raised the fines to an unreasonable level to force the issue. The tenants took him to Chancery. The Chancery decree is dated 18th May 1636 and contained the following terms: In return for a twenty years fine their tenant-right was confirmed, together with an 8d. fine (or eight years' ancient rent) both for general and dropping fines. Suit of court, and mill, boons, customs and services were reserved to the lord. Not all the tenants agreed to or were able to compound, and for over two hundred years the tenants were divided between Indenture tenants paying an 8d. fine, and Arbitrary who had to bargain with the lord for their general and dropping fines. The latter appeared before Chancery on 13th April 1678 complaining of excessive fines. The outcome is not known.[20]

(f) The manor of Thornthwaite in the parishes of Shap and Bampton illustrates a further difficulty. It was sold by the Curwens in the seventeenth century to lord William Howard of Naworth, who gave it to his younger son Sir Francis Howard. The rents were ancient, and the general and dropping fines arbitrary. As Sir Francis Howard had been a delinquent, serving with the King, his estates were sequestered by the county Committee for Sequestrations. In 1650 the commissioners Roger Bateman, and Gervase Benson at Kendal levied an 8d. dropping fine on the tenants, who submitted. An 8d. fine was adopted by the Committee on all sequestered Royalist estates in Westmorland. On the restoration of Charles II the Howards regained control of Thornthwaite, and all the old issues revived, with this addition that the tenants claimed relief for the fines they had paid under compulsion to the Commonwealth. During a long and tortuous enquiry *the Howards* demanded twenty-eight years' ancient rent for all general fines due, and to make future (general) fines certain of ten years' rent. Also they claimed that the tenants should for dropping fines on descents or alienations pay sixteen years' for one fine, and twenty-eight years for two or more. And those tenants who paid fines to the Commonwealth should pay twenty-four years' ancient rent to make a general fine certain of ten years. *The tenants* claimed twenty-four years' rent to make a general fine certain of ten years; and where a dropping fine was due on descent or alienation the tenant should pay ten years for one fine, and twenty for two or more fines. And those tenants who had been admitted by the Commonwealth should pay eighteen years' rent to make a general fine certain of ten years. *The final arbitration* of 28th January 1659/60 awarded as follows: The tenants should pay twenty-six years' ancient rent for their general fines then due, and to establish a future general fine certain of ten years' rent. That for dropping fines upon descent or alienation the tenant should pay thirteen years' rent for one fine, and twenty-four where two or more were due. Therefore the tenants had to pay twenty-four years' rent to make general and dropping fines certain, and

an additional ten years' rent on the accession to estate of a new lord, making a total of thirty-four years' ancient rent. The total capital sum was to be paid by the tenants in three payments; the first in full; and in the second and third payments, those tenants who had been fined an 8d. fine by the Commonwealth could deduct three years' rent at each second and third payment in respect of the eight years' fine already paid.[21]

This case makes the point that in many of the royalist estates sequestered by the Commonwealth the same issue would arise. In this instance three issues are dealt with, making fines certain, levying a general fine, and making an adjustment for fines paid to the Commonwealth.

(g) To the south of Ravenstonedale between Sedbergh and upper Wensleydale are the manors of Garsdale and Grisdale. Grisdale was a manor of Rievaulx abbey, bought by Sir Thos. 1st lord Wharton.

Few records remain of Grisdale. The abbey of St. Agatha, Easby near Richmond held the manor of Garsdale in 1303, when Michael lord of Upsall owner of certain properties in Garsdale took the oath of fealty to the abbot in the chapel of St. John in Garsdale in the presence of certain brothers of the abbey.[22] At the dissolution of the abbeys the Crown on 10th December 29 Henry VIII let all the house and lands of the abbey to John lord Scrope of Bolton for thirty years at a rent of £283.13.11 Certain woods and advowsons were reserved to the Crown. The brother chaplain at Garsdale at the time was William Coke. During the course of this lease the Crown granted another lease in reversion whereby the buildings and certain properties of the abbey near Richmond were let to Edmund Boughton for twenty-one years.[23] The chaplain of Garsdale continued to be paid by the Receiver for Yorkshire. Garsdale remained with the Scrope family till is was sold in 1621 by the Crown to Sir William Garway a London merchant, who in addition to extensive trade through the port of London, made a quick profit in the buying and selling of Crown Properties. As the deeds of Garsdale are in private hands, and I have been unable to examine them, only a bare summary is possible. There is an Indenture of 1587 between lord Scrope and the tenants of Garsdale presumably settling their customs and fines. It would have been useful to compare it with the 1579/80 one of Ravenstonedale. In 1620 the tenants came to an agreement with Gilbert Nelson, James Nelson, Richard Garthwaite, John Guy and Richard Hobson to act on their behalf, and the sum of £1,347.5.10. was raised from the tenants to buy the manor, and certain other Easby lands in Garsdale.[24] The purchase was effected in 1621. But a difference soon arose. The purchasers proceeded to act as if they were the lords of the manor, and not the whole body of tenants which had raised the money. In 1626 the tenants took the five purchasers to Chancery, producing the 1620 agreement as proof of their raising the money. Chancery took so unfavorable a view of the five, that they were ordered to vest the manor in all the tenants, and pay the costs of the action. Chancery then issued a writ of execution to make sure that the five completed the bargain.

(h) The manors in upper Wensleydale had an equally troubled history. *The manor of Fors, Wensleydale, or Dale Grange* was part of the possessions of Jervaulx abbey, and on the attainder and hanging of the abbot, Henry VIII granted it in fee to Matthew earl of Lennox & Margaret his wife. It returned to the Crown in the person of James I, their grandson. He granted it to Ludowic Stewart duke of Lennox, who had great difficulty in getting himself accepted by the tenants. The cause was thus: Under the late countess of Lennox the tenants paid fines of 9 - 10 years' rent for leases of twenty-one years. Now, for leases of the same terms they were paying fines of thirty years' rent to the duke. Some 16 to 20 tenants took leases on the new terms, and paid their first installments. Early in 1606 the tenants who had taken the new leases met at Hardraw, and decided to ask Lennox to mitigate their fines. After many stormy meetings among the dalesfolk the story peters out, and it appears the tenants lost their case.[25] In the Crown lordships of Richmond and Middleham there were different troubles. In the reign of Queen Elizabeth the tenants of *the Lordship of Middleham* claimed the custom of tenant-right, but could produce no written evidences. In 1588 the tenants were either persuaded or compelled to take leases of forty years, renewable to the eldest son etc. as formerly, every tenant doing duty on the border, and yielding their ancient rents and service. Two years' ancient rent was to be paid as a general fine on the death of the Prince, one year's rent at every alienation, and two upon every renewal. At the end of every lease the eldest son of every tenant then living should have a new one like the former. Every lease should revert to the heir, and not to the executor, and the heir should pay the fine. The words 'eldest son' should extend to eldest daughter and to the next in blood in default of issue

of the body. This excellent agreement was thrown into question in 1608 when the Lord Treasurer, following the King's edict against tenant-right demanded composition of the tenants to confirm tenant-right. The Crown demanded four years' ancient rent; it was still resisted in 1611, but there is evidence that the tenants paid, to receive assurance of their forty years' leases.[26]

On 25th September 1628 the lordships of Middleham and Richmond (with certain forests and chases reserved to the Crown) were granted by Charles I to be the citizens of London in satisfaction of divers large sums of money lent by the City to James I. For the next 35 years all the tenants of these lordships came under the control of the City of London.[27] From 1654 to 1663 the City sold the lordship of Middleham in parcels, and on 9th November 1663 the manor of Bainbridge was sold to eleven principal tenants:

> George Norton of Worton,
> James Calvert of Bleane (alias Bleasings),
> Richard Robinson of Countersett,
> Mathew Metcalfe of Appersett,
> Anthony Fothergill of Burghill,
> Cuthbert Wynne of Gaell,
> James Fawcett of Buske,
> John Coulton of Buttersett,
> James Allen of Snaiseholme,
> Francis Lambert of Marsett, &
> Thomas Metcalf of Hawes.[28]

The last surviving trustee Anthony Fothergill conveyed the manor on 19 October 1705 to twenty-four trustees; the last survivor of these, William Whaley died in possession of the manor in 1760, leaving it to his nephew John son of Thomas Whaley, who died in 1763. In April 1767 his executors appointed twenty-four trustees to exercise the manorial rights, with power to fill vacancies as they occur. Their successors, 'The Lords Trustees of the Manor of Bainbridge' continue to exercise these rights.[29] Richard Robinson of Countersett, one of the first trustees became a convinced Quaker in 1652, and in October 1663, when in London to arrange the final details of the sale, was arrested and imprisoned. The Kaber Rigg or Farnely Wood plot had broken out in the north in October 1663. It collapsed quickly, but the government of Charles II was very suspicious of sectaries. As one or two of the plotters came from Wensleydale, Robinson was held, and closely questioned. As nothing could be found against him, he was released and allowed to return to the dale. The signing of the conveyance probably coincides with his release.

Reference Chapter 12.

(1) Life & Letters of Mandell Creighton, by his wife. 1906. I, 238/9. He was one of the first to point to the uniqueness of Border communities before the Norman conquest.
Archaeologia Aeliana. The Ancient Farms of Northumbria, by Earl Percy, F.S.A. read. 25 July 1894. Refers to Canon Creighton's paper of 1884.
E.H.R. Vol. V. no. XX. Oct. 1890. Northumbrian Tenures. F.W. Maitland.

(2) N & B, I. viii.
Craven & the North West Yorkshire Highlands. Robert Speight. 1892. 27-28.

(3) A Treatise on Copyholds. C.I. Elton & H.J.H. Mackay. 2nd. ed. 1898. 1-5.

(4) Summary extracts from the old court books of Ravenstonedale 1578-1725 from the Lowther papers for the case Fawcet v. Lowther 1751.
C.R.O. Carlisle. D./Lons/L. Ravenstonedale 4. p. 18.

(5) It is important to note the breaking of customary tenures in the Percy estates in Northumberland & Cumberland. The Estates of the Percy family, 1416-1537. J.W. Bean, O.U.P. 1959. I sometimes feel that the use of the term copyhold is too general. p. 56.

(6) C & W. trans. N.S. LXXXV. 1985. Art. XI. Medieval Kendal and the first Borough Charter and its connexions. J. Munby.
Hist. of Alnwick. G. Tate. 1866. I. 266 & 268.

(7) Chapters 7 & 8.

(8) For customary & copyhold tenures: Hist. & Topography of Harogate & the Forest of Knaresborough. Wm. Grainge. 1871. 83, 92, 94, 97-106.
For newhold copyhold for life or lives: Hist. of the parish of Whalley, & the Honor of Clitheroe & parish of Cartmel. T.D. Whitaker, 4th ed. by J.G. Nicholls & P.A. Lyons. 1872. I, 265, 268, 292-4.
By far the best explanation of the development of customary & copyhold tenures and the policy of the Crown in need of money is: The Economic Hist. of Rossendale. Dr. G.H. Tupling. Chetham Soc. 1927, 127-160.
Surtees Soc. 1886, ii. Durham Halmote Rolls. Vol. I. p. xxxvi. For the 1577 dispute between the Dean & Chapter of Durham & their customary tenants.
Treatise on Copyholds. Charles Watkins. 1821. II, 249 for copyholders at Wolsingham & Stanhope.
History of Furness. T. West. 1774. (Camb. Univ. Lib. L1, 13. 34.) p. 167.
Manor of Kirkby Ireleth, dropping fine of 20d. p. 168. Pennington, 6 year general fine, a 7 year running fine. p. 189. Lowick, a running fine of 1 year's rent every 7 years, etc.
Short hist. of the Manor & parish of Witherslack, to 1850. G.P. Jones. C & W, Ant. Soc. Tract Series. XVIII, 1971. Chapt. III, The Tenantry.

(9) Hist. of Crosby Garrett. J. Walker Nicholson. Kirkby Stephen. 1914. 36.

(10) Hist. of Cumberland. W. Hutchinson. op. cit. II, 339.
Prelates and People of the Lake Counties C.M.L.Bouch.1948,36.

(11) By courtesy of the late author. Kirkby Stephen & District. R.R. Sowerby. Kendal 1948. 21.

(12) N & B, I. 292-4.

(13) From a bundle of conveyances in Crosby Garrett church chest, which were burnt in the church stove a few years ago.

(14) P.R.O. S.P. 23/258. Court Rolls sent to London from the Committee for Sequestrations in Kendal 5 June, 1652, of those manors in WEstmorland whose owners were sequestered for delinquency.

(15) N & B, I. 477.

(16) N & B, I. 501.

(17) N & B, I. 616 et seq. For John Pullen the owner see: The Pulleynes of Yorkshire, Catherine Pullein, Leeds 1915.

(18) (1) N & B, I. 48, 52, 617.
(2) N & B, II, 136.
(3) N & B, II, 424.
(4) N & B, II. 454.
(5) N & B, I. 107. (Old Hutton)
N & B, I. 149. (Grasmere)
N & B, I. 453. (Slegill)
N & B, II, 361. (Graystock)
In an Epitome of the Common & Statute Laws of this Nation, by Wm. Sheppard, London 1656 (C.U.L. J. 14. 16) p. 574 is an interesting explanation of King's silver as a fine upon licenses.

(19) N & B, I. 617.

(20) Hist. of Crosby Garrett. J.W. Nicholson op. cit. 28 seqr.

N & B, I. 532.
From a MS copy formerly in Soulby Vicarage.

(21) Hist. of Parish of Bampton, Mary E. Noble, Kendal 1901, 44-48. The three arbitrations are difficult to follow, as none cover the incidents fully. The defects are remedied from the others.

(22) Hist. of the Parish & Grammar School of Sedbergh, A.E. Platt op. cit. 190. In The Hist. & Traditions of Mallerstang Forest etc. by Revd. W. Nicholls 1883, p. 78 it is clear that in 1865 Grisedale was still a distinct manor.

(23) Hist. of Richmondshire, T.D. Whitaker op. cit. II, 373.
Hist. of Richmond, C. Clarkson, 1821. 376, 379.
Whitaker I, (above) 43/44 gives the rental of St. Agatha's, Easby from the Valor of Henry VIII.

(24) Sedbergh, Garsdale & Dent. Rev. W. Thompson, 1910. 239.

(25) V.C.H. North Riding, Yorkshire 1968, I. 207 (col. 2.)
Yorkshire Archaeological Soc. Record Series, CIV, 1941. Three Seventeenth Century Yorkshire Surveys. T.S. Willan & C.W. Crossley, viii - x.

(26) Three Seventeenth Century Yorkshire Surveys, op. cit. xvii - xxx & p. 147. There were other leases for 21 years and for lives (p. 147-8) but the position remains that they were tenants by lease.

(27) Ibid. xxx - xxxi.

(28) Record Office, Corporation of the City of London. Deed 73. 6 of 9 Nov. 1663; by courtesy of the Deputy Keeper of the Records, 5 Aug. 1985.
V.C.H. North Riding of Yorkshire. 1968, vol. I. 206, 209.
Since writing this 'Richard Robinson of Countersett, 1628-1693' has been published by David S. Hall of Bainbridge, (York, 1989) pp. 4-5 has some new material covering the purchase of the manor of Bainbridge from the City of London.

(29) Hist. of Askrigg. C. Whaley, 1890, 64.
Additional note to page 154.
The best explanation of the status of the Court of Requests, and the Council of the North is in: The Tudor Constitution; Documents & Commentary. G.R. Elton. Cambridge 1960. 184, 196-198. For the power of Chancery p. 197.

Chapter 13

The Forest of Mallerstang to 1597. (1)

At the head of the Eden valley, and five miles south of Kirkby Stephen, there lies the dale or Forest of Mallerstang. It lies due north and south, and forms the east side of a rough triangle of manors, Ravenstonedale, Garsdale and Grisdale, and upper Wensleydale, which are at the heart of these studies. From the cases already cited from the Upper Eden valley it will be seen that there was scarcely a manor where the tenants did not have a struggle with their land lord. This probably applies to the whole of the north. The vale of Mallerstang gives another view of this struggle.

From early times the Forest of Mallerstang was a chase appended to the possessions of Appleby Castle, held in fee from the Crown. Its road from Wensleydale to the Eden valley was guarded by the small Pendragon Castle. In early times it was a forest of birch, alder, ash, rowan, holly, juniper, willow and hazel, and the harbour of deer. It remained thus until the middle of the thirteenth century, when on the death of John de Veteripont in about 1242 the wardship of his son Robert was committed to the Prior of Carlisle, when during this time many encroachments were permitted by him in the forest.[1] It is particularly stated that a multitude of vaccaries, and purprestures had been made. In 1315 the forest and castle were held by Andrew de Harcla with a vaccary called Southwayt and six other vaccaries. On his execution for treason in 1323 Southwayt was valued at 40s. a year.[2] Thus by 1315 there were seven vaccaries, or cow pastures in the dale let to cowmen whose task it was to raise cattle, and perhaps oxen. It was a system of lease of land and stock provided by Appleby castle. We do not know from the absence of estate records whether these seven vaccaries were managed (as in the case of Rossendale) by a stockman acting for the castle who determined the number of cattle on each vaccary, what were to be sold, killed, and retained, or whether they were separate lettings. But it appears that by 1328 the rent from the vaccaries, and the profits of herbage came to £30 a year.[3] In 1337 Edward Baliol king of

Scotland took refuge in England, and was entertained by Robert de Clifford at Pendragon castle, and in 1341 it was burned by the Scots in revenge.[4] Thus by 1315 the foundation of cattle-farming had been laid in the dale. By the beginning of the sixteenth century the number of customary farms had increased to eleven, and were Southwaite, Castlethwaite, Outhgill, Elmgill, Hanging Lunds, Aisgill, Angram, Hesleygill, Deepgill, Shorgill, and Sandpot. The demesne lands of the manor were the castle garth, and the Frith.

There are two surviving documents among the Appleby castle records which shed much light on the division of these eleven primary cattle farms in the second half of the sixteenth century.[5] The first is an undated bailiff's rental, which from the evidence of Wills, is almost certainly from 1597, the year of starvation and plague. The second is an estate Survey of 1604, the year before the death of George, earl of Cumberland, who at that time was heavily in debt. The 1604 survey is valuable in several respects. It recapitulates by name and in succession the tenants of every farm back to a previous survey of 1582. Thus the names of all the 1582 tenants are known. It places the groups of tenants under their respective primary farms. From this survey 1597 tenants can also be placed. Thirdly the effect of the 1597 plague and poverty can be seen in the unpaid fines still due in 1604.[6] The 1604 survey proves that the division of primary farms was already under way in 1582. The 1597 rental in giving the ancient rents of the divided farms, tell us which were halves, quarters, or thirds of the old primary farm. There are also a few halves held by custom by widows. There are also a few widows on small farms which were too poor to be divided, who shared part of the income and continued to live in the old home. The 1604 survey gives a number of additional inclosures from the waste, for the accommodation of new field-houses, fire houses and peat houses for the occupation of sons or daughters allotted part of the primary farm.

The *rental* *of* *Malerstang.* *c.1597.* (Farm names taken from the 1604 survey).

Old Rent.

		Old rents.
Southwaite.	John Birbecke. (Blewgrasse.)	vijs. jd.
	Hugh ffuthergill.	xjs.
	Vincent ffuthergill.	viijs.
	Cristofer ffuthergill.	ixs. iijd.
	Edward Guy.	viijs. vd. ob.
	Gabriell ffuthergill.	ixs. ijd. ob.
	Nicholas ffuthergill	vs. iiijd. qr.
	Thomas Waller.	xvs. xd.
	Edward ffuthergill.	xixs. xjd. (£4,14.1¼.)
Castlethwaite.	Thomas ffuthergill.	xijs. iijd. ob.
	William ffuthergill.	xjs.
	John ffuthergill j.	xxs. iijd. ob.
	Thomas Hoopes.	viijs. iiijd.
	John Goosedaile.	viijs. ixd. (See Sandpot 1604)
	Richard ffuthergill.	xixs. vjd. ob. qr. (£4.0.2¾.)
Outhgill.	Uxor William Dent.	xvs. iijd.
	Thomas Dent.	xvs. iijd.
	Thomas Gibson.	xvs. iijd.
	Thomas ffuthergill.	xxijs. xjd.
	Thomas Knewstopp.	xjs. vd. ob.
	John Knewstopp.	xjs. vd. ob. (£4.11.7.)
Almgill.	Ingrame Shawe.	xvjs. ixd.
	Miles Shawe.	viiijs. ivd.
	Richard Shawe &)	
	Hugh Shave)	viiijs. iiijd.
	Robert Shawe.	xjs. ijd. ob.
	Edmond Shawe.	xjs. vjd. ob. (£2.16.2.)
Hinging Lunds.	Edmond Shawe junr.	xxvijs. iiijd.
	Peter Shawe.	xiijs. viijd.
	Henry Shawe.	xiijs. viijd.
	Henry Hugginson.	xijs. (£3.6.8.)
Aisgill.	Richard Shawe.	xxvijs. iiijd.
	Henry Shawe &)	
	Thomas Whitfeld.)	xxvijs. iiijd. (£2.14.8.)
Angerholme.	Lionell Shawe.	xxiijs. iiijd.
(Angram.)	John Shawe.	xvs. iiijd. ob. qr.
	Lancelott Shawe.	vijs. vijd. ob. qr. (£2.6.4½.)
Hesleygill.	Thomas Birtle.	xjs. iiijd.
	John Parkin.	xjs. iijd.
	Hugh Shawe.	xvjs. xd. ob.
	John Shawe.	xvijs.
	John Shawe junr.	xvjs. xd. ob.
	(note. s.o. Gilbert)	
	William Shawe.	xvijs. (£4.10.4.)
Deepgill.	Rowland ffuthergill.	xs. jd.
	Thomas ffuthergill.	xs. jd.
	Lionell Birtle.	vijs. vjd.
	Uxor Barnabie Skafe &)	
	John Birkbecke.)	vijs. vjd. (£1.15.2.)
Shorgill.	William Gibson &)	
	Lionell Turner.)	xvijs. iiijd. ob.
	William Knewstopp.	xvs. ijd. ob. qr.
	Thomas Knewstopp.	xvs. ijd. ob. qr. (£2.7.10.)
Sandpott.	Michaell Wharton.	xixs. xjd.
	(note: father of Phillip)	
	Thomas Gibson	vjs. viijd. ob.
	(note: s.o. John)	
	Thomas Hutchinson.	xxijs.

(Sandpott, contd).	John Ewbanke.	xijs. xjd.
	Richard Wilson.	xijd.
	Michaell Dent.	vjs. jd. (£2.8.5½)
	(note: s.o. Thomas.)	

Malerstange ad huc.

Itm. paid yerely by the foresaid tenants of Malerstange for sheepp & Cattell which they take in of strangers xxxiijs. iiijd.

Itm. paid by all the tenants one yerely rent which they call a yerely gressome. 1s. ijd.

(At the foot of the page is this total for all rents etc.) £43.16.2.

Commentary.

(1) It will be seen that the full rent of a primary farm was about £4. The slight variations were probably due to small improvements, an inclosure, or a new building, for which a small rent was added to the original.

(2) Nowhere is the division of a primary farm into uneconomic units better illustrated than at Southwaite, where a farm of £4.14.1¼ rent is divided into nine holdings.

At Hanging Lunds, Edmund Shawe has half, and Peter and Henry Shawe have quarters of the old farm. While Henry Hugginson probably has a new inclosure at Hellgill. At Aisgill the old farm is divided into halves, while one half is in the joint ownership of Henry Shawe and Thomas Whitfeld. The same applies at Angerholme. There are a number of units under £4, Almgill, Hanging Lunds, Aisgill, Angerholme (Angram), Deepgill, Shorgill and Sandpott where it is not possible to state how they were divided, and what larger unit they represent. For example the starvation and infestation years of 1587 and 1597 causing many deaths, and debts undoubtedly accelerated division, sales and other changes in ownership.

(3) Thus by 1597 eleven primary farms had been divided into fifty-four tenancies, of which three are in joint ownership. Only two widows are enjoying a widow's right to half the husband's farm. But if the evidence of later court rolls is a fair guide there were usually about five widows in the dale in any year, and so it would appear that in 1597 there would be about three on farms too poor to be divided, and of whom there is no record.

We will now consider how the eleven primary farms were divided between 1582 and 1604.

References. Chapter 13.

(1) N & B, I. 562.
Hist. & Traditions of Mallerstang Forest. Rev. W. Nicholls 1883., 24/5.
Mallerstang Forest, and the Barony of Westmorland. Cornelius Nicholson, Kirkby Stephen, 1888.
Calender of Inquisitions, Miscellaneous, (Chancery) vol. I., 1916. p. 143. (no. 436) Inquisition of the waste committed in lands late of John de Veteripont during the minority of his heirs.
Sir Andrew de Harcla, a Personal episode in English history. Cornelius Nicholson. Kirkby Stephen, post 1888.

(2) Cal. of Inquisitions, Misc. (Chancery). vol. III, 1937. p. 139.

(3) The Economic History of Rossendale, G.H. Tupling, op.cit. 17-27.
N & B, I. 562

(4) Hist. of Mallerstang op.cit. 26/7.

(5) The 1597 rental, and the 1604 Survey are in C.R.O. Kendal. ref. WD/Hoth, (Box 34). Rental of lands of George earl of Cumberland 1604. 1. Mallerstang.

(6) Three works consider the effect of bad harvests on the economics of farming. Eng. Hist. Review, 1973. 2nd. Series. 26. p. 403. Disease or Famine, Mortality in Cumberland & Westmorland 1580-1640. Andrew B. Appleby. He distinguishes between plague, typhus and starvation, pp. 405, 406, 408, 419, 430.
Famine in Tudor & Stuart England. Andrew P. Appleby. Liverpool U.P. 1978-9. p. 93 et seq.
Agricultural Hist. Review. vol. XII, 1964. p. 28. Harvest Fluctuations & English Economic Hist. 1480-1619. W.G. Hoskins. p. 28 et seq.
Note:
I am not sure whether Dr. Appleby's distinction between plague being a warm weather disease, and typhus a winter one is entirely borne out by the parish registers of the upper Eden valley. Bad harvests and starvation seem to have spread both over summer and winter.

Chapter 14

At the time of the 1604 Survey the Clifford estates of the earl of Cumberland in Westmorland and Craven were in the hands of commissioners. The earl was heavily in debt from his old seafaring days; he was separated from his wife, and had failed to pay her maintenance; and he had a mistress at Grafton Regis. Thus the Survey was part of the process of examining every tenancy in every manor from 1582 to see that all the fines on descent or sale were properly paid, and to see that improvements and encroachments were recorded by the steward, the additional rent added to the old, and, where necessary a fine of admittance charged. The labour which faced the steward and his clerks must have been immense. If the earl had hoped to raise extra money from his estates he must have been disappointed; the majority of his customary tenants paid ancient rents, fixed time out of mind. There was no room for increase. There might have been some hope for small increase in rent on demesne lands; but stewards were local men who had to live with their neighbours, and in years after bad harvests.

The 1582 Survey shows that by then the eleven primary farms were already in process of division. Aisgill into 2, Angram 3, Hesleygill 6, Deepgill 3, Shorgill 3, Sandpott 6, Southwaite 9, Castlethwaite 4, Outhgill 6, Almgill 5, and Hinging Lunds with Helgill 4, thus making 51. The 1597 rental increased the number to 54 including 4 farms where moieties were not rented separately.[1] The 1604 Survey gives 60 holdings with four widows' moieties rented separately.[2] The 1582 Survey indicates from the number of admittances that courts had not been held for many years, when the estate was held in jointure by Anne countess dowager of Cumberland, who had died in 1581. The number of 1582 admittances must be viewed with caution for this reason. When the 1604 Survey records the division of a farm in or after 1582 the ownership of each division is recorded back to that of 1582. Thus the 1582 owner will be recorded for each section so divided, and thus in proportion to the number of divisions. The number of admittances recorded in 1604 are as follows: 1582 (58), 1584 (4), 1587 (7), 1588 (6), 1590 (9), 1592 (5), 1596 (5), and 1597 (15). Thus the 1582 figure represents two factors, long failure to hold courts, and the original owners of the farms being recorded for each division. The 1597 figure of 15 admissions appears about right, when it is remembered that the bad harvests and plague of that year trebled the number of deaths. In 1604 there were 13 widows with the right to a moiety (or half) the farm, but who were not rented separately owing to the smallness or poverty of the farm; there were only four widows who were rented separately and occupied their half. In later court rolls there was an average of 4 or 5 widows in any year. The large number of 17 widows in 1604 represents the deaths of husbands in 1597.

These abbreviations are used in the following tables:

(M) = moiety.   adm. = admitted.   ten. = tenet ie. holdeth.   ass. = by assignment or assigned.
Bond. = refers to the compositions made on the death of George earl of Cumberland in 1605, and due to his widow countess Margaret on receiving the Westmorland estates in jointure.

AISGILL.

1582 tenant	old rent	1604 tenant	1604 rent	Notes
John Shawe	27/4.	Thomas Whitfield assignee of Henry Shaw assignee of John Shaw of 1582. Henry Whitfeld adm. 1597. (M)	13/8	
		Henry Shaw adm. 1597 assignee of John Shaw. (M)	13/8	Henry owes £5 of his gressum and covers it by bond 1605.
Richard Shaw	27/4.	The same. But Arthur Richard's younger son has been given part of the farm, but not separately rented and thus not adm.	27/4.	Richard has a new house & garth.

Notes. John and Richard Shawe appear to be brothers 1582 dividing the primary farm.

John's farm descending to Henry is divided between Henry Shawe & Thos. Whitfeld. Whitfeld may be a tenant by marriage, or Henry may have been hard up and sold the farm, as he is in debt for £5 unpaid gressums from 1597.

Richard is is process of dividing his farm between sons; the younger has been handed half the farm, and an extra house has been built. Thus Aisgill has been divided into four farms.

Looking at the 1582 farms at Hinging Lunds where the halves of the primary farm came to 27/4 as at Aisgill one wonders if the total of 54/8d. represents the original rent of the early primary farms.

ANGERHOLME (Angram).

1582 tenant	old rent	1604 tenant	1604 rent	Notes
John Shaw.	15/4¾	Issabell widow of John, (M)	7/8¾	
		Issabell widow of Adam (adm.1587) son of John. (M)	7/8¾	
Lyonell Shawe	23/4.	The same. He buys land of John Parkine of Hesleygill and adm. 1597.	23/4.	
			–/1.	
John Shawe, (? same as above.)	7/7¾	Lancelott son of John who buys more land for Lancelott from	7/7¾	
		Thomas son of George Birkdale and Hugh Shawe both of Hesleygill.	2/-	
			2/.	

Notes. John & Lyonell Shawe of 1582 seem to be brothers.

John appears to divide his farm between Adam and Lancelott. He buys more land for Lancelott to make up a deficiency.

The widow's rights of Issabell widow of John (1582) and Issabell widow of Adam (1587) both enjoying their moiety may take long to resolve. As no child of Adam is mentioned, the widow could either sell or remarry.

In: Abbotside Wills, Yorks. Archaeological Soc. Trans. CXXX, 1968, Will no. 70. Thomas Shaw of Lunds, 9 Dec. 1637 leaves 'to Margaret Shaw wife of Lyonell Shaw of Maller-stang, all the money which she did owe him'. This Lyonell may be connected with or the tenant of 1582.

HESLEYGILL.

1582 tenant	old rent	1604 tenant	1604 rent	Notes
George Birkdale.	11/4.	Thomas son of George Birkdale adm. 1587 & 1590. He has sold lands of 5/3 to Wm. Shaw, John Shaw, and Lancelott Shaw.	6/1.	See Angerholme.
William Shawe	17/- (M)	The same. He bought land of 3/2 of Thos. Birkdale above. He has passed his tenement to Richard his bastard son, not having other issue, but not yet adm.	17/-. 3/2.	See the Will of Wm. Shawe 22 Dec. 1608. [3]
Mabell Shawe widow of Richard Shawe.	17/-. (M)	John son of Richard Shawe adm. 1584. Plus land bought of Thos. Birkdale above, and adm. 1597. John has alineated half his farm to Richard his son 'sans licence'.	17/-. -/1.	John Shawe owed half of £13.6.8. fine of 1584 in 1604. His 14d. fine may represent half for his mother the tenant of 1582. On the -/1 rent his 10d. gressum of 1597 was still owing 1604. Covered by bond 1605.
Hugh Shawe.	16/10½	The same adm. 1 (M) 1582; 1 (M) 1597. Hugh Shawe sold land of 2/- to John father of Lancelott Shawe of Angerholme.	14/10½	Hugh owes 26/8 of the 1597 gressum. He has built a house on the waste.
Roland Shawe	11/4.	John Parkine adm. 1597. He has sold land of 1d. to Lyonell Shawe of Angerholme.	11/3.	
Gilbert Shawe. (s.o. Hew Shawe: Will of 31.Jan.1580.)	16/10½.	John his son.	16/10½	Part of Gilbert's gressum 26/8 (1582) still owing 1604. Covered by bond 1605.

Notes. William and Mabel Shaw occupy moieties totalling 34/- old rent.

Gilbert and Hugh Shawe occupy moieties totalling 33/9.

George Birkdale and Roland Shawe occupy moieties totalling 22/8.

Thus Hesleygill was divided into three before 1582 and six by 1582.

The steward added this note on sheep-stealing against Wm. Shawe, in Norman French. 'Wm. Shaw est accuse de larcenie per emblier barbits per testes Hugh Birkdale, Ingram Shaw & Roland Shaw ac Thome Dent.'

DEEPGILL.

1582 tenant	old rent	1604 tenant	1604 rent	Notes
John Fothergill	20/2.	John Fothergill infant s.o. Roland adm. 1590, s.o. John tenant of 1582. Agnes widow of John occupies her (M). Thomas the second son of John & adm. 1584.	10/1. 10/1.	Agnes' moiety is not rented apart. A house on the waste.
Lyonell Birkdale.	7/6.	The same.	7/6.	
Henry Birkdale, alias Birtle.	7/6.	John Birkbecke assignee of Humfrey Blenkarne formerly in tenure of Barnabie Skaif (forisfecit. adm. 1592.) assignee of Henry Birkdale. The widow of Barnabie Skaif occupies her (M).	7/6.	John Birkbecke bought the farm from Humfrey Blenkarne for £46.13.4d. Not rented apart.

Notes. John Fothergill of 1582 divided his farm between his sons Roland & Thomas. The rent roll shows that these moieties were rented at 7/9 each. Additions from several improvements brought the rent up to 10/1 each.

The rents of Lyonell & Henry Birkdale were 7/6 each. Thus the primary farm was split into four.

Dr. R.T. Spence of Leeds informs me that among the Clifford papers there is the report of a court case over the ownership of Barnabie Skaif's farm.

John Birkbeck of Bluegrass (Will 6 Aug. 1619.) [3] bought this fourth part of Deepgill for his second son Geoffrey. He in turn was the ancestor of William Birkbeck who left Deepgill for Settle on his father William's death in 1697. William of Settle married Sarah Armistead of Settle the 11th of the 9th month 1703. They were both Quakers, and founders of the famous Quaker family of that place.

SHORGILL.

1582 tenant	old rent	1604 tenant	1604 rent	Notes
Henry Knewstubb (of Shorgill & Nettlehole)	15/2¾	William eldest s.o. Henry Knewstubb adm. to (M) 1587.	15/3¾	A house on the waste. (Henry Knewstubb's Will, 12.Feb.1586.) [3]
John Knewstubb.	15/2¾	Thomas s.o. John Knewstubb adm. to (M) 1590 & (M) 1597.	15/3¾	
Robert Gibson.	17/4½	Lyonell Turner by assignment of Thomas Gibson, assignee of his bro. William who adm. 1587. assignee of his elder bro. Phillip assignee of Robert Gibson their father. (M).	9/3¼	
		Elizabeth widow of William Gibson (M).	9/1¾	

Notes. This is a clear example of the primary farm being divided into three by 1582.

Henry Knewstub the 1582 tenant died prematurely in February 1586/7. He made his brother Mr John Knewstub fellow of St. John's College Cambridge his executor. The eldest son William inherited the Shorgill farm. Henry's widow went to live at Henry's second farm at Outhgill, q.v. When she died the second son John took her moiety. When Mr John Knewstubb was appointed to Cockfield rectory, Suffolk in 1579 Henry's third son Richard went to live with him. Mr John was rector of Cockfield for forty years, and a leader of East Anglian puritanism.

Will of Henry Knewsubb of Shorgill, (notes above) proved 3, Feb. 1588. [3]

SANDPOTT

1582 tenant	old rent	1604 tenant	1604 rent	Notes
John Ewbanke.	12/11.	Thomas Ewbanke s.o. Nicholas Ewbanke adm. 1597 assignee of John Ewbanke adm. 1582. Margaret wid. of Nicholas 'ten' ie. holdeth.	11/6.	(On the last page of the 1604 survey is this note: 'John Ewbanke holdeth a peat house, a fyer house stead & half a rood of ground on the waste since the Survey 1582'.)
		John Fothergill of Castlethwaite by assignment of John Ewbanke adm. 1582 & 1597. (Steward's note: 5d. is still due of John Ewbanke's rent; but see John Fothergill below.)	1/-	John Ewbanke's 1582 gressum 26/8d. owing. Nicolas' 1597 gressum 66/8 owing. The bailiff distrained
			-/5.	Thomas for 11/11½d. in 1617, (after the King's Award in the Clifford dispute).

John Wharton.	22/0½.	Phillip Wharton, nephew of John adm. 1588, assignee of John Wharton. (M)	11/0¼.		John Wharton by his Will 30 Nov. 1587 gave his farm to Phillip his nephew, a minor.
		Cristian Wharton wid. of John. (M)	11/0¼.		His father Michael held the farm during his
		John Grosdale of Catlethwaite adm. 1587 assignee of Henry Warde adm. 1584, assignee of John Wharton, (M)	7/6 + 1/3.		minority, and in 1597 paid a rent of 19/11.[3] & [4].
		John Fothergill of Castlethwaite adm. 1597 s.o. Thomas Fothergill adm. (M) 1588, assignee of John Fothergill (1597) assignee of Richard s.o. Thomas Fothergill (1588) assignee of John Wharton. (M).	7/6 + 1/5.		Thomas F. owed 26/8 of 1588 gressum. John F. owed £3.10.0. of 1597 gressum. Thus about an 8d. fine on a rent of 8/11d.
Thomas Dent.	6/1.	Michael s.o. Thomas Dent adm. 1588. (M) Isabell wid. of Thomas Dent.	6/1.		A fyer house and a peat house.
John Gibson.	6/8.	Thomas s.o. John Gibson (n.d.) late in tenure of Roland Ewbanke.	6/8.		
Jenkin Ewbanke. (of Cocklacke)	1/-.	Richard Wilson n.d. assignee of Anthony Mason s.o. Henry Mason adm. 1597 assignee of John Fothergill adm. 1590 assignee of Michael Fothergill assignee of Phillip Fothergill assignee of Jenkin Ewbanke adm. 1582.	1/-		Henry Mason adm. 1597 fined 20s. on a 1/- rent. Thus a 20d. fine; still owed by the purchaser Richard Wilson 1604.
Thomas Hastwhitle.	1/10.	Thomas Hutchinson n.d. by assignment of Hugh Hastwhitle adm. 1597, formerly in tenure of his mother, formerly in the tenure of his father Thomas Hastwhitle adm. 1582.	1/10.		A house on the waste.

Notes. Looking at the 1582 rents: John Ewbanke 12/11, John Wharton 22/0½, Thomas Dent & John Gibson 12/9, we have two quarters and one half of the primary farm. The year of bad harvest and plague 1597 is the key to debts and several small sales of land. A number of 1597 gressums are still unpaid in 1604.

John Wharton the 1582 tenant by his Will of 30th November 1587 left his farm to Philip a minor, the son of Michael Wharton his brother. Michael occupied the farm during his minority and paid the rent in 1597. As John Wharton's widow was alive in 1597 she enjoyed half the profits of the old farm in her widow's right. But Michael paid the rent.

John Wharton added a condition to the gift of the farm to his nephew, that he should marry one of the daughters of his wife's brothers or sisters. If he did not, he had to find £20 to be divided equally between those daughters. Despite these money difficulties, the Wharton family survived on the farm for many generations.

Dr. R.T. Spence of Leeds who has studied the accounts of the Clifford estates has re-minded me that during the widowhood of Lady Anne Dacre countess of Cumberland from the death of her husband in 1570 the Westmorland estates were held in jointure until 1582. During her time they were much neglected and few courts were held. As she was a Catholic her son was for ten years placed in ward to the Protestant duke of Bedford, so that from either point of view the estate was at the mercy of inefficient stewards. The 1582 Survey was an attempt to bring some order into the estate.

SOUTHWAITE.

1582 tenant	old rent	1604 tenant	1604 rent	Notes
Alexander Birkbeck, (of Bluegrass).	6/-.	John s.o. Alexander Birkbeck. Alex. adm. to (M) 1582 and the other (M) 1588.	6/-.	Bluegrass was part of the Southwaite primary farm. Alex. Birkbeck's 1582 total gressum of 18/- still unpaid 1604, ie. a 3d. fine.
		Also an improvement assigned by Christofer Fothergill adm. 1592 s.o. Hugh Fothergill adm. 1582, also a piece of ground assigned by Gabriell bro. to Henry Fothergill of Castlethwaite decd. (q.v.) a 1582 tenant. John Birkbeck has 'married' part of his tenement to Wm. his son.	1/- -/1.	
Hugh Fothergill.	12/-.	The same (M) Cristofer Fothergill adm. 1592 s.o. Hugh less 1/- land assigned to John Birkbeck above. (M) (*Note:* This land at 11/- is in Hugh's name in the 1597 list.)	6/-. 5/-.	Since the 1604 Survey this C. Fothergill has assigned to another Crist. Fothergill s.o. Thomas a meadow called Scalerigg, rent 11d. See below.
Vincent Fothergill.	10/11½	The same. Less land of 3/4 sold to Wm. Fothergill of Castlethwaite (q.v.).	7/7½.	
Cristofer s.o. Thomas Fothergill.	9/5. (9/3.)	The same.	9/5.	(*Note:* It would appear from the above that this Fothergill should also pay 11d. for Scalerigg, above.)
Thomas Waller. (Gale House.)	15/10.	John s.o. Thomas Waller, who was still tenant 1597. Elizabeth wid. of Thomas Waller. (M)	16/-.	The difference in rent referred to the jury.

John Fothergill.	8/5½ (1597)	Edward s.o. Edmond Guy adm. 1587 by assignment of John Fothergill adm. 1582 Agnes wid. of Edmond Guy. (M)	8/3½.	(*Note:* 'He hath sued over his interest to Robt. Knewstupp.')
Henry Fothergill.	9/5½. (9/2½. 1597)	Gabriell bro. to Henry Fothergill. Gabriell adm. 1592. Henry died 'sans fitz' and presumably intestate c.1587. The farm was let for 3 years at 40s., as it had lapsed to the lord. The earl of Cumberland's servant Thos. Walles was adm. 1590. He seems to have sold to gabriell bro. to Henry who was adm. 1592. Gabriell also rented the moat about Pendragon Castle for 20s. a year. Gabriell also sold land at 1d. to John Birkbeck of Bluegrass (q.v.).	9/4½.	
Edward Fothergill.	half of 19/11.	The same, and adm. to the other (M) 1590.	19/11.	Edward F. owed 17/6. of 1590 gressum, & bond taken 1605.
Nicholas Fothergill.	5/4¼. (1597)	The same. He has 'married' part of his tenement to his son William.	5/3.	(The steward questions the difference.)

Notes. It is not possible with any conviction to group old rents which were divisions of the primary farm.

Southwaite was the ancient settlement of the Fothergill family.

Bluegrass was a small division of Southwaite.

The death of Henry Fothergill without issue (or Will) escheats the farm to the lord, who appoints Thos. Walles his servant. Two years later he sold the farm to Gabriel Fothergill, the late Henry's brother; one would like to know the inducement!

CASTLETHWAITE.

1582 tenant	old rent	1604 tenant	1604 rent	Notes
John Fothergill.	20/3½.	Thomas s.o. John Fothergill adm. 1596, excepting land he sells to Wm. his brother at 8/-.	12/3½	Thomas owed £4. of 1596 gressum; covered by bond 1605. (Steward's note of 1604: 'He Thos. hath aliened thes tenements to (?John) Fothergill of Nateby'.) (11/4d.) Steward's note:
		William Fothergill his bro. n.d. holds the 8/- land from Thos. his bro. and also the 3/4 land acquired from Vincent Fothergill of Southwaite (above).	8/- + 3/4	'8s. of this R(ent) is reassigned to Adam Fothergill ante & 3/4. to John Fothergill s.o. Richard 1617.'[3]
Richard Fothergill.	20/3½.	John s.o. Richard Fothergill. John adm. 1597. Jennet wid. of Richard. (M)	20/3½.	Richard Fothergill's Will 4 Jan. 1596/7. (3)
Thomas Hopes.	8/4.	Anthony Wharton by assignment of Thos. Hopes adm. 1582 & 1588. (M) Elizabeth the wid. of Thos. Hopes. (M)	8/4.	A. Wharton married the dau. of Thos. Hopes. Anthony's adm. was part of her portion.
Thomas Fothergill. (the elder)	19/6¾. (1597)	Richard s.o. Thos. Fothergill. Agnes wid. of Thos. Fothergill. (M)	12/0¾.	The missing 7/6 of Richard's rent will be found under Sandpott in the sale by John Wharton to Thos. Fothergill of this land and adm. 1582. The 1597 rental gives Richard F's rent as 19/6¾.

Notes. John, Richard & Thomas Fothergill, tenants in 1582 were the three sons of John & Elin Fothergill of Castlethwaite; they divide the primary farm into three. (Elin d. 1570; see Will[3])

John's farm is divided between two sons Thomas & William. The other two remain entire. It is possible that, as Thomas Hopes rent of 8/4 is near Wm. Fothergill's 8/- rent, Thos. Hopes' wife Elizabeth was a Fothergill.

OUTHGILL.

1582 tenant	old rent	1604 tenant	1604 rent	Notes
Leonard Dent.	15/3.	Leonard Dent, infant s.o. Wm. Dent dec'd adm. 1596, s.o. Leonard Dent adm. 1582. Cristabel wid. of Wm. Dent 'ten'.	15/3.	Wm. Dent's 1596 gressum £4.11s. owing in 1604.
Thomas Fothergill.	22/11.	The same.	22/11.	
Thomas Knewstubb.	11/5½.	The same. (M). Richard s.o. Thomas Knewstubb adm. 1590. (M).	5/8¾. 5/8¾.	A house on the waste.
Thomas Dent.	15/3.	The same. (M).	15/3½.	Thomas Dent refused to compound for the other (M) 5 Oct.1596. T. Dent owed 33/4d. of 1582 gressum, but paid 1604.
John Dent.	15/3.	Thomas Gibson n.d. assignee of James Fawcett adm. 1590, assignee of Henry Fawcett adm. 1588, assignee of John Ingram adm. 1584, assignee of John Dent. (M).		Part of John Dent's 1582 gressum 23/4d. owing, 1604. Note in Norman French that Gibson is accused of sheep-stealing.
Henry Knewstubb.	11/5½.	John second s.o. Henry Knewstubb (of Shorgill) adm. 1582, lately in the tenure of Eliz. wid. of Henry (who d. 1587).	11/5½.	

Notes. The holdings of Leonard, Thomas and John Dent at a rent of 15/3 show that they were thirds of a large farm.

The holdings of Thomas and Henry Knewstubb at 11/5½ in 1582 show that their farms were halves of a moiety of which Thomas Fothergill held the other at a rent of 22/11.

The sum of the three Dent farms comes to 45/9; and the sum of the farms of Thomas Fothergill and Henry & Thomas Knewstubb comes to 45/10.

These two groups are ancient moieties of the primary farm.

ALMGILL. (Elmgill).

1582 tenant	old rent	1604 tenant	1604 rent	Notes
Richard Shawe. (M) Gabriell Shawe. (M)	16/9.	Ingram s.o. Richard Shawe adm. 1582 s.o. Gabriell Shawe also adm. 1582.	16/9½.	40/- behind of Richard Shawe's 1582 gressum.
Miles Shawe.	8/4.	The same, with land assigned by Richard Shawe adm. 1582 & 1596, and Miles was adm. 1597.	8/4½. + -/8.	
Richard Shawe. (M) 1582. (M) 1596.	8/4.	Hugh Shawe adm. 1597. Sold by Richard Shawe for £40 'for his pretended tenant - right', with one (M) in possession and the other (M) in reversion on the d. of Richard and after the widowhood of his wid. Elizabeth. (*Note:* the sale of the 8d. land to Miles Shawe above.)	7/8½.	All Richard Shawe's 1596 gressum of 33/4d. unpaid. Bond taken for 16/8. 1605.
Robert Shawe.	11/2½.	Abraham s.o. Robert Shawe. (Abraham n.d. but Robert a tenant in 1597.) (M) Margaret wid. of Robert Shawe. (M)	11/2½.	
Edmond Shawe.	11/6½.	Symond, infant s.o. Edmond Shaw. Symond adm. 1597. (M) Jane wid. of Edmond. (M).	11/6½.	

Notes. In general terms the 1582 farms of Gabriel 16/9; Miles & Richard 16/8 appear to be one half and two quarters of an original.

The farms of Robert and Edmond appear to be old moieties totalling 22/9d.

How the primary farm was divided is not clear. With the admission of Gabriel's son Richard to half the farm (disregarding widows) the primary farm had been divided into six by 1582.

HINGING LUNDS & Helgill Close.

1582 tenant	old rent	1604 tenant	1604 rent	Notes
Robert Shawe.	27/4.	Edmond s.o. Robert Shawe.	27/4.	
Peter Shawe.	13/8.	William Knewstubb by assignment of Peter Shawe one (M) in possession and the other (M) in reversion on death of Peter and after the widowhood of Eliz. Shawe his wife. W. Knewstubb adm. 1592.	13/8.	
Henry Shawe.	13/8.	The same.	13/8.	
James Warcop. Helgill Close.)	12/.	Henry Hugginson adm. 1590, by assignment of Francis Cowper by assignment of James Warcop.	12/-.	(*Author's note:* Henry Hugginson may be the s.o. John Hugginson of Soulby.) £10 behind of James Warcop's 1582 gressum. A note says that the sale to Francis Cowper was concealed; his fine was 66/8d. Bond taken for both fines 24 Aug.1605. Until Cowper's fine has been paid 'Hugginson hath no title'.

Notes. Disregarding Helgill Close, which may have been an inclosure on the fell, and not carved out of Hinging Lunds, it is clear that the 1582 holdings of Peter and Henry Shawe are divisions of a moiety which equalled the rent of Robert Shawe, and thus divisions of the primary farm.

As Hinging Lunds and Almgill are populated almost entirely by the Shawe family one wonders if at least part of Almgill was once part of Hinging Lunds, while the other part of Almgill may derive from Hesleygill.

On the last page of the 1604 Survey is a list of additional charges due to the lord. Every tenant paid 1/2 yearly for some unspecified right; the tenants jointly paid 33/4d. for the right to graze foreign cattle on the moors; the Frith at Sandpott was demesne land, and let at £4.; there was a quarry for stone on Wild Boar Fell, and a coal mine at Fell End (dues not known); the lord had a beast walk & sheep walk on the fells in right of Pendragon Castle. but not lately exercised; and the rights to fishing in the Eden, and turbary and stone rest in the lord, for which no recent rent has been taken.

There are only six admissions in the Survey which give the full fines on their ancient rents, and from which we can assess the rate:

1582. Alexander Birkbeck of Bluegrass was fined 18/- on an ancient rent of 6/-, that is a 3d. rate. This would be a fine by descent from father to son.

1584. John Shawe of Hesleygill (adm. 1584 on the death of his mother) was fined £13.6.8. on a rent of 17/-, that is a 7d. fine. As heriots are never mentioned in Mallerstang it is probable that half the fine related to the admission of his mother on the death of his father.

1596 or 1597. Hugh Shawe of Almgill purchased two (M)s one in possession and the other in reversion on the death of the vendor and widowhood or death of his wife for £40. The court book does not say whether Hugh was related to the vendor Richard Shawe. The fine was £1.13.4. on a rent of 7/8½, that is a 4d. rate.

1597. John Shawe of Hesleygill (see above) bought a parcel of ground from Thomas Birkdale of Hesleygill and was admitted 1597. He was fined 20d. on a penny rent, that is a 20d. rate.

*1597.*John Fothergill of Castlethwaite bought a parcel of ground from Richard s.o. Thomas Fothergill assignee of John Wharton of Sandpott 1597 (q.v.) The fine (1597) was £3.10.0. on a rent of 8/11d, that is an 8d rate.

1597. Henry Mason of Cocklacke in the Sandpott group was adm. to this small cottage/tenement in 1597 and was charged 20s. on a 1s. rent, thus a 20d. rate. This cottage changed hands six times after 1582, and the 1604 owner was liable (as often happened) for the unpaid gressums of previous purchasers. The 1604 owner Richard Wilson was liable for the 1597 fine. This is obviously a fine on purchase by a stranger.

While it is not possible to be more specific about the rates of fine in particular years, the general pattern emerges from these few examples. Fines on descent appear to be between a 3d. and 7d. rate. The fine on alienation to a stranger seem to be in the 20d. bracket, which is similar to the rule in the adjacent manor of Ravenstonedale under their 1579/80 Indenture. Two points need clarification, the fine on widows occupying a farm during a minority, and widow's fine on her moiety, and when these fines were paid and by whom. For example there are a few wills in which the farmer bequeaths his farm to his widow during the minority of the eldest son (or daughter failing a son), and on his reaching his majority he receives his moiety, and the widow her's. Then there is the son/tenant who has to buy out the child's portions of brothers and sisters. There is also the fine due from a tenant who was permitted to take on the farm, where the previous owner had no children and left no will, but to whom he was related. But the broad rule would appear to be that a fine to a relative was moderate, and that to a stranger stiff.

Refs. Chapter 14.

(1) The bailiff's rental of Mallerstang c. 1597. C.R.O. Kendal, WD/Hoth. Box 34.)

(2) Survey of Appleby Castle estates for George earl of Cumberland 1604. C.R.O. Kendal, WD/Hoth. (Box. 34.)

(3) All Wills are in C.R.O. Carlisle.

(4) Chapter 13, rental of 1597.

Chapter 15

Mallerstang (3)

An understanding of the two preceding chapters is essential to a clear view of the effect of the division of farms in the late sixteenth century, and the creation of a poor tenantry unable to resist bad harvests and infections. This above all was the seed ground of dissentient opinion, which was to come to full fruit in the struggles of the mid-seventeenth century. Among the many Mallerstang Wills to have survived from 1570 there are few in sequence, with the exception of those of the Shawe family of Hanging (or Hinging) Lunds. The Shawe wills illustrate perfectly the effect of the division of farms.

Hew Shawe of Hinging Lunds died in January 1576/7.[1] He was tenant of the largest farm of 27/4d. old rent. He gave Agnes his wife her widow's right of his farmhold for the rest of her natural life, and after her death his farm was to go to his son Robert, 'with licence of my ladie (Anne countess dowager of Cumberland) and her officers'. His goods and chattels were given to his widow and daughter Agnes, who were made executors. The Will is in the hand of Sir John Swinbanke vicar of Kirkby Stephen, who seems to have drawn up three quarters of the Wills of his parishioners. His inventory dated 14th January 1576/7 lists the stock of a fellside farmer:

ffirst viij kie	ix$^{li.}$ vj$^{s.}$ viij$^{d.}$
Item. a stirke	vj$^{s.}$ viij$^{d.}$
Item. a meare	xl$^{s.}$
Item. xxij wedders	iiij$^{li.}$ viij$^{s.}$
Item. xxiiij yews	iij$^{li.}$ xij$^{s.}$
Item. xiij hoggs	xxxiij$^{s.}$ viij$^{d.}$
Item. a cocke & iij hens	xij$^{d.}$
Item. in hay	xl$^{s.}$
Item. in bedding	xij$^{s.}$
Item. in fire vessell	xij$^{s.}$
Item. in wood vessell with two chists and an arke	viij$^{s.}$
Item. in cheese	xx$^{s.}$
Item. in butter	ij$^{s.}$
Item. in meaill ij bz(bushels)	viij$^{s.}$
Item. fleshe	x$^{s.}$
Item. in bordes & wood gere	iiij$^{s.}$ iiij$^{d.}$
Item. in yron gere	iij$^{s.}$ iiij$^{d.}$
Item. in wooll ix stones	iij$^{li.}$ iij$^{s.}$
Item. in his raments	ij$^{s.}$
Item. in golde & silver	liij$^{s.}$ iiij$^{d.}$
Some xxxiiij$^{li.}$ v$^{s.}$ [1]	

My farmer godson, Mr. Bernard Braithwaite of Milburn, near Appleby has pointed out that the number of sheep in this inventory would follow this cycle: The life of breeding sheep is five to six years, producing four lots of lambs. The 22 wedders follow a two year cycle, with ten being used for food etc. each year, and ten gelded male lambs being added yearly. As Hew Shawe's old rent was 27/4d. a year, if he sold 13 ewes a year at the valuation in this inventory he would more or less cover his rent, with the 13 hoggs replacing what he has sold. His sheep were of course an heaf-going flock remaining on the farm and fell. The small number of poultry is a common feature of contemporary Wills. As there was no arable in Mallerstang there were no oxen.

Hew Shawe's widow Agnes died about the 1st September 1577, and she left half of her goods 'now being at the house' to Agnes her daughter 'which I taike to be her own portion', and the other half to Robert her son who inherited the farm. The inventory dated the 1st September 1577 is instructive as it shows how a widow's interest was preserved in a farm, where she was entitled to half during her widowhood. Apart from the cattle there were:

Item. xx$^{te.}$ wedders	iij$^{li.}$
Item. ten wedders and rames	xxvj$^{s.}$ viiij$^{d.}$
Item. xx$^{te.}$ ewes	iij$^{li.}$
	(MS.torn)
Item. ten ewes	xx^{s}
Item. xiij lames	xxxvj$^{s.}$
She also had a swyne	vj$^{s.}$ viij$^{d.}$

And there was still £5. remaining in gold and silver, in an estate of £37.8.4d.[2]

98

It appears that Agnes the widow had her own small flock of sheep which in this case was half the flock of her inheriting son Robert.

The son Robert Shawe made his Will 17th October 1601, and the inventory is dated 28th November 1601. He left the farm to be divided equally between his two sons, Edmonde and Robert, 'with the lycence of my lord (the earl of Cumberland) and his commissioners'. It would appear from the 1604 Survey that Edmonde bought out his brother, for Exmonde is the only tenant in 1604. There were a number of small bequests of 'a yowe and a lambe' to the children of his son in law Thomas Wharton, and the same to his daughter Margreat and her daughter Jayne. It seems that his sister Agnes Shawe was still alive and single; she was to have 'hir finding upon my tenement during hir life naturall'. That there might be difficulty between the sons Edmonde and Robert appears in the provision, that if Edmonde will not suffer Robert to live on the farm, then Robert is to be sole executor. Edmonde's wife appears to be dead by 1601, as she is not mentioned.[3] Apart from cattle, the inventory lists the following sheep:

Item. xlvij weathers	xj^{li} x^{s}
Item. xlviij yowes	viij^{li} xiij^{s} iiij^{d}
Item. xl hoggs	iiij^{li} xiij^{s} iiij^{d}

It would appear that Robert had doubled the flock to provide for both sons. He left an estate of £72.4.4d., but the gold was reduced to six shillings.

Edmonde Shawe of Hanging Lunds made his Will on 20th April 1615, and his Inventory is dated 27th April 1615, and was proved at Appleby on 21st February 1615/16.[4] First he states that as his wife (Phillis) is now with child, if that child shall be a son, then he is to have the farm; but if it is a daughter, then Isabell Shawe his eldest daughter is to inherit, while the two younger daughters are to share £13.6.8d. between them. After his debts are paid the two younger daughters are to share the residue of his estate. No mention is made of his wife, who would be entitled to a half-share of the farm during widowhood. All his 81 sheep are lumped together, and valued at £22.5.0. As his father had left 134 sheep, the flock is down by about fifty sheep. His assets came to £70.0.2d. and his debts were £36.11.0.

His widow Phillis made her Will a month later on the 20th May 1615,[5] and her Inventory dated 1st June 1615. The number of sheep is not given, but they are valued at 36s.8d. Her assets came to £17.2.3d., and her debts (some of them due on her husband's estate) £10.18.10d. It appears from the Will that she did not have a son. She left two kine to her mother to bring up her youngest child Phillis. She gave a cupboard to her eldest daughter Isabell, and her bedding to her mother. The two youngest daughters Elsabeth and Phillis were made joint executrices, and given a fifth part of a tenement at Satteron in Swaledale. Both Wills were proved by her brother-in-law Thomas Wharton at Appleby on 21st February 1615/16. As Isabell Shawe the eldest daughter inherited under her father's Will, the main flock of sheep went with the farm. The small flock left by the widow was her widow's right. With her death this sequence of Wills comes to an end on the largest farm of the group, being half the primary farm.

The Will of Hew Shawe of Heslegill[6] dated 31st January 1580/81 with the Inventory of 16th July 1581 is on a farm of 16/10½d. old rent which was a sixth of the primary farm. The farm was left to Gilbert his son, whose son John was tenant in 1604. He left 3s.4d. to the repair of Heslegill bridge, and 2d. to every householder attending his funeral at Kirkby Stephen church. He left Agnes Grene his servant two lambs, and a stone of his best wool.

His Inventory contained:

Imprimis. vj kye	vj^{li} xiij^{s} iiij^{d}
It. ij stirkes	xvj^{s}
It. ij horses	iij^{li} xiij^{s} iiij^{d}
It. xxiij sheppe & a lam	iij^{li} iiij^{s}
It. in wooll	xxvj^{s} viij^{d}
It. in hay and grasses of the gronde	vij^{li}

The remainder concerns his goods, chattels and debts due to him, and by him. His net estate came to £30.18.0.

The Will of William Shawe of Hesleygill of 22nd December 1608 is on another sixth of the primary farm.[7] He was admitted tenant in 1582 at a rent of 17s, and his farm was a moiety of a larger farm already divided by his father with William's brother Richard. The Inventory is dated 1st July 1609. The 1604 Survey tells us that William had transferred his farm to his bastard son Richard, who was made his sole executor. The 1604 Survey says that Richard had not been admitted, and from the inventory William seems to have kept the stock in his own hands.

Imprimis. Twelve kine	xviij$^{li.}$
It. xx$^{te.}$ sheepe	iij$^{li.}$ vj$^{s.}$ viij$^{d.}$
It. vij whyes	vij$^{li.}$
It. iij stirkes	xxx$^{s.}$
It. ffower callves	xxvj$^{s.}$ vij$^{d.}$
It. thre stone of woll	xviij$^{s.}$
It. his apparrell	vj$^{s.}$ viij$^{d.}$
It. all impliments	iij$^{s.}$ iiij$^{d.}$
Sum bonorum	xxxij$^{li.}$ xj$^{s.}$ viij$^{d.}$

Neither of these two tenants owed unpaid
gressums in 1604, while the other four owners
of land there did.

John Fothergill of Deepgill was tenant in
1582 at an old rent of 20/2d. He divided his
tenement between his two sons, and the second,
Thomas was admitted in 1584 at a rent of
10/1d. The elder son Roland was admitted in
1590, at a rent of 10/1d. His parents seem to
have reserved their interest in some way and
lived with Roland. Roland died in 1595 leaving
a wife Alles, with two sons John (tenant) and
Thomas, and two daughters Agnes and Isabell.
Alles should have had her widow's moiety.
But John Fothergill and his wife Agnes are
both alive. John died about the first of February
1603/4 and Agnes had her widow's right to
half. Thus this farm of 10/1d. rent had to
support two widows, and four children. The
other two farms at Deepgill were rented at
7/6d. each, and hardly form quarters of the
primary farm. But by 1604 there were two
farms at 10/1d. and two at 7/6d.

*Roland Fothergill's Will is dated 27 No-
vember 1595*, and his Inventory 30th November
1695.[8]

His stock was as follows:

Imprimis. five kye & a calfe	vj$^{li.}$
a stoite ij stirks & half of a bull	xlvij$^{s.}$ viij$^{d.}$
Shepe xix wedders & a ram	iiij$^{li.}$
vij hogg shepe	xiiij$^{s.}$
iij ewes	vj$^{s.}$
in hay	v$^{li.}$

The remainder is goods and chattels. But
among the debts owing to him was 21s. owed
by James Waistdaill of Stanemore for ewes,
and 24s. for a stott, 9s. for money lent, and
15s. 10d. for more ewes. For some reason he
sold off his ewes before he died. Among his
debts out was 8s. to the chapel, where the
curate acted as schoolmaster. Roland's clear
estate came to £31.17.5d.

*His father John Fothergill's Will is dated
3rd January 1603/4*, and his Inventory the day
of his death 1st February 1603/4.[9] His cattle,
sheep, hay and a horse came to £18.13.4d.,
while his total estate came to £49.10.8d. In
that sum was £39 which he had lent to his
son Thomas on the second farm, and this he
left to his widow Agnes, with orders that his
supervisors shall from this pay Agnes her
maintenance from time to time. These sets of
Wills from Hanging Lunds, Hesleygill and
Deepgill establish the point that the better
farms ran a flock of at least twenty ewes,
twenty wethers, and about ten hogs; that at
death the estate was valued at above £30, and
that after the deduction of livestock (which
was their main livelihood) there was little else
to live on. This can be illustrated finally in
the farms of the Knewstub family of Shorgill.
The primary farm had been split into thirds
before 1582, and had probably all belonged
to the Knewstubs. But by 1582 Robert Gibson
had one third at 17/4½d old rent; Henry and
John Knewstub had the other thirds at 15/2¾d.
old rent each. They were probably brothers,
as their holdings are described as moieties.
Henry Knewstub of Shorgill's Will is dated
12th February 1586/7.[10] The Inventory is undated, but the probate is 3rd. February 1588/9.
Henry had two properties at Shorgill and Outhgill. He left the farm at Shorgill to his eldest
son William, then a minor. The other farm at
Outhgill was left to the disposition of his
brother Mr. John Knewstub, former fellow of
St. John's College, Cambridge and at that time
rector of Cockfield in Suffolk. Mr. John seems
to have had a claim on the farm, but Henry
while expressing a preference for Thomas, left
it to Mr. John to decide which of the remaining
younger sons was to have the Outhgill farm.
From the 1604 Survey we see that John got
the farm, and that Henry's widow Elizabeth
went to live there as her widow's right. Henry
made this provision for the two middle sons:
'I give my two sons John and Richard to my
brother Mr. John yf he be soe content, trusting
yt he will be a good father unto them, even
as my trust is in him, yf my brother will not
take them, I will yt my sonne John shall have
my tenement at Uthgill, and my sonne Rychard
to be executor with my wyfe, and my younger
sonne Thomas.' In the event at least Richard
went to live at Cockfield with his uncle as
his name appears in the parish register. But
it is possible that Thomas also went there. In
this way Henry provided as best he could for
his four boys.

Henry's Inventory dated about January
1588/9 gives his farm stock as follows:

| Imprimis. ten kyne | xiij$^{li.}$ vj$^{s.}$ viij$^{d.}$ |

It. five young calves	xlvj$^{s.}$ viij$^{d.}$
It. one horse	xlvi$^{s.}$ viij$^{d.}$
It. one meare and one foole	xxx$^{s.}$
It. fortie ewes	vj$^{li.}$ vj$^{s.}$ viij$^{d.}$
It. two tupes	v$^{s.}$ iiij$^{d.}$
It. xxvj$^{th.}$ hodgs	iij$^{li.}$
It. in hay	xlvj$^{s.}$ viij$^{d.}$

Among his debts was £3.3.4d. 'to our chappell', which as has been noted was for the curate schoolmaster. His clear estate came to £29.3.10d., which by the time one takes off the value of the farm stock (as with the other wills) does not leave much reserve. This left the mother Elizabeth with two farms to run for two boys under age, and two boys to be taken on by their uncle Mr. John. It may be that Richard was the Richard Knewstub who matriculated from St. John's College in 1598, got his B.A. in 1902, and M.A. in 1606.[11]

The bailiff's rental of 1597 and the Survey of 1604, giving the number of tenants and their old rents, provide a valuable guide to the number of tenancies created out of the eleven primary farms, and the drift to smaller units in the space of seven years. While we do not know the customary acreage of each farm, there is no doubt that rent was related to acreage. In the following table farms are divided into three rent brackets, and the number of tenants in their respective locations.

| Group | under 10s | | over 10s | | over 20s | |
	1597	1604	1597	1604	1597	1604
Aisgill	0	0	0	2	2	1
Angerholme	1	2	1	1	1	1
Hesleygill	0	1	6	4	0	1
Deepgill	2	2	2	2	0	0
Shorgill	0	2	3	2	0	0
Sandpott	2	6	3	3	1	0
Southwaite	6	8	3	2	0	0
Castlethwaite	2	1	3	3	1	1
Outhgill	0	2	5	4	1	1
Almgill	2	2	3	3	0	0
Hanging Lunds	0	0	3	3	1	1
Totals	15	26	32	29	7	6

Thus between 1597 and 1604 the number of tenements increased from 54 to 61; and while the Wills already quoted come from the middle to upper range of rent and acreage it is obvious that the lower range of tenant would not often be represented by Will. Two survive which are interesting:

John Fothergill (? Southwaite) made his Will on 13th January 1591/2, and his inventory is dated 17th January 1591/2. Again, it is in the hand of the vicar.[12] In 1582 his rent was 8/5½ a year. According to the 1604 Survey he conveyed it in 1587 to Edmond Guy, whose son Edward was admitted 1604. Thus when John Fothergill died in 1592 the farm belonged to Edmund Guy, while John farmed it. 'I geve and bequeathe to Christian Gye my handfest wife a meare and xlix shepps. Item: I geve vj ewes to my furthbringing (his funeral) and xijd. to every one of my godbarnes out of the price of the said sex ewes'. After several small bequests he left the residue to Christobell Gye, who was made sole executrix. The custom of handfasting and living together before marriage was explained by Sir Walter Scott as due to the paucity of clergy visiting their remote flocks. A better view is that a tenant had to establish that his wife could produce a child who could inherit the farm, before he married her. It is probable that Christian and Christobel Gye were daughters of Edmond. John Fothergill's assets were valued at £27.6s., and his debts at £16.19.2d., leaving a clear estate of £10.6.0. At 4s. each his handfast wife's legacy of 49 sheep comes to £9.8s., and Christobel Gye was thus left with 8s. Two odd things remain from his list of debts; his father Thomas Fothergill was alive and was owed 9s.6d., and Edmond Gye arranged his funeral which cost 7s. There is a fellside story behind this inventory!

John's chief interest is that he was a visitor to other markets than Kirkby Stephen. He owed 32s. to John Holme of Sedbergh, and was owed £6 by William Robinson of Wensley, and 13s 4d. by Richard & Leonard Hamonde of Wensley.[13]

The Will of Lanclote Shawe dated 27 January 1579/80,[14] though its place is not given is clearly from Mallerstang, as both his supervisors, and prisors are all Mallerstang men. His widow Elizabeth shall have the farm during her widowhood, and then his son Richard. In 1579/80 the rent was 5s. There were three Richard Shawes tenants in 1582, and he probably came from Almgill where in 1582 there was a small tenancy of 8/4d. divided into moieties. Lanclote had 5 kye, one mare, 4 young whies, and five sheep. He seems to have been a webster, for his 'webster looms and implements which he wrought withal' were valued at 10s. He owed 5s. rent, and 8s. to the chapel. His clear estate came fo £10.1.10d.

Looking back to the list of unpaid gressums in 1604, given in Chapter 14, we see that thirteen came from the rents over 10s., and 9 came from the under 10s. group.

As a post-script, there is one inventory which shows that even a fellside farmer had his lighter evenings. The inventory of Bartholomew Shawe of 3rd December 1579 probably from Angram has two wine tones, and a harpe, a lute, and a gittern. A gittern was a five stringed instrument for accompanying singing. They were still being made in England up till the middle of the eighteenth century. But his assets came to £17.14.1d., and his debts to £37.13.0.[15]

References Chapter 15.

All Wills and Inventories are from the C.R.O., Carlisle.

(1) Will of Hew Shawe of Hinging Lunds. 21 May 1576.
Inventory 14 Jan. 1576/77.

(2) Will of Agnes Shawe of Hinging Lunds 1 Aug. 1577.
Inventory 1 Sept. 1577.

(3) Will of Robert Shaw of Hangand Lounds, of Mallerstang, 17 Oct. 1601.
Inventory 28 Nov. 1601.

(4) Will of Edmunds Shawe of Hanging Lunds 20 April 1615.
Inventory of 27 April 1615.

(5) Will of Phillis Shawe of Hanging Lunds 20 May 1615.
Inventory 1 June 1615.

(6) Will of Hew Shawe of Heslegill, 31 Jan. 1580/81.
Inventory 16 July 1581.

(7) Will of William Shawe of Hesleygill 22 Dec. 1608.
Inventory 1 July 1609.

(8) Will of Roland Fothergill of Deepgill, 27 Nov. 1595.
Inventory 30 Nov. 1595.

(9) Will of John Fothergill of Deepgill 3 Jan. 1603/4.
Inventory 1 Feb. 1603/4.

(10) Will of Henry Knewstub. 12 Feb. 1586/7.
Inventory undated. Probate 3 Feb. 1588/9.

(11) Alunn.Cantab. J. Venn. Part I. up to 1751. Richard Knewstub. matric.pens. from St John's, Michaelmas 1598. B.A. 1602, M.A. 1606.

(12) Will of John Futhergill 13 Jan. 1591/2.
Inventory 17 Jan. 1591/2.

(13) Yorkshire Archaeological Soc. CXXX, 1968. Abbotside Wills, for refs. to the Hamonde family of Wensley. And p. 129 the bequest by Richard Blyth of Low Helm 4 Dec. 1678 to Elizabeth Fothergill of Castlethwaite of one whye about the price of £2.10.0.

(14) Will of Lanclote Shawe 27 Jan. 1579/80.
Inventory 14 Feb. 1579/80.

(15) Inventory only of Bartholomew Shawe. 3 Dec. 1579.
Note:
Two studies covering the division of farmholds and the creation of small units:
A short Hist. of the Manor and Parish of Witherslack. G.P. Jones. C & W, tract series, 1971.
Waste Land reclamation in the sixteenth and seventeenth centuries: The case of South-Eastern Bowland. 1550/1630. John Porter. Trans. Historic Soc. of Lancashire and Cheshire, vol. 127, 1978.

Chapter 16

George third earl of Cumberland.

When Henry second earl of Cumberland died in 1570 he was the owner or tenant of vast estates, comparable with those of the Percies in Northumberland, Cumberland and Yorkshire. In Westmorland the Cliffords had the habitable castles of Brougham and Appleby, and the ruined Brough and Pendragon, together with four forests of Whinfell, Mallerstang, Hieland and Stainmore, and 18 manors. They also had the patronage to eight parish churches and two chapels.[1] In Craven they had an even larger estate in four main blocks. The Skipton fee contained some 34 manors, the Percy fee about 20,[2] they held 10 manors and two advowsons of the dissolved Bolton priory,[3] while 6 manors of the Norton family were to come to them later on.[4] The Craven lands were dominated by Skipton castle, and Barden Tower in upper Wharfedale. In all, the Cliffords held some 80 manors and three castle with all their tenants who owed service to the baron and the King on the Borders, and their lord in the manors. Upon the death of the second earl the estate was probably as prosperous as it had even been. When earl Henry died in 1570 his widow Lady Ann Dacre received the Westmorland estates as her jointure, and she continued to live at Skipton and Barden. But she remained a Catholic and did not attend the parish church.[5]

When earl George became the third earl he was only twelve, and by prior arrangement he became the ward of Francis earl of Bedford and went to live in the Russell houses at Woburn, Chenies and London. In 1571 he entered Trinity College, Cambridge. In about 1574 he went for a short time to Oxford, and it is possible that while there he may have met Richard Hakluyt at Christ Church, who was later to chronicle the voyages of many famous Englishmen, including those of earl George.[6] We have already noted that George was married to lady Margaret Russell the daughter of his guardian on 24th June 1577 in St. Mary Overies, Southwark. The young Philip lord Wharton was married to earl George's sister lady Frances Clifford at the same service. George was then 19, and his bride 17. The next seven years were spent largely at Skipton, while the old countess retired to Barden Tower. But her influence was dominant over the young couple. The young wife was later to record her loneliness:

"I was separated from all I knew, one servant rather for trust, than wit, about me, only acquainted with me, in a country contrary to my religion, his mother and friends all separate in that opinion, himself not settled but carried away, with young man's opinions: Oh! God, where was I then, Not one to comfort me."[7]

The old countess died in 1581, and it was seven years from the marriage before their first child was born. Francis was born at Skipton on 10th April 1584, and Robert at Northall on 21st September 1585. This period marks earl George's gradual break with the north, and introduction to the Court circle. He had been made a member of the Council of the North in 1582, and was present at the execution of Mary Queen of Scots at Fotheringay on the 8th February 1587.

For ten years before 1587 Drake and his friends had been making their private sorties against Spanish ships, while Catholic and Protestant forces fought in Flanders. After the execution of Mary Queen of Scots both Spain and England prepared for a decisive encounter. In 1586 earl George fitted out his own small fleet at his own charge, which sailed from Gravesend in June. Clifford did not go with the fleet which went as far as Brazil. It took a few small prizes, but was not very profitable.[8] In 1588 Clifford placed himself under the command of captain George Raymond in the Bonaventure during the defeat of the Armada. The same year saw his launching on his sea career with the support of the Queen. She issued a commission under the Great Seal giving him leave to arm a fleet, including the royal ship Golden Lion, to raid shipping on the Spanish coast. They took only one small prize. The next year established his name, when in his third voyage, including one royal ship, they took thirteen prizes of French, Dutch, Portuguese and Spanish ships. Clifford landed at Falmouth on 30th December 1589. The voyage was very profitable, cleared his debts, and spurred him on to larger ventures. The Queen having lent one ship demanded more than her share of the profits. He spent the winter of 1589-90 meeting the claims of his seamen, and making what profit he could against the Queen's demands. In the middle of this he heard of the birth of his daughter lady Anne on the 30th January 1589/90 at Skipton. She was baptised in Skipton church on the 20th February.[9] So pressing were the claims of seamen, and those whom Clifford had plundered that he rode swiftly to Skipton, ordered his wife to pack, and within two days they were on the road to London.

The following events were to colour the development of the Clifford estates. His eldest son Francis died on 11th December 1589; the younger Robert on 24th May 1591. In 1590/91 (33 Eliz.) earl George drew up a settlement which barred certain remainders in his father's will, that if he should die without an heir male the estates should go to his brother Francis and his heirs male; failing these the estates should revert to his heirs, in this case his infant daughter lady Anne. The settlement was kept secret until his death in 1605, and was to have serious consequences for the tenants, and will be dealt with shortly.[10]

Between 1586 and 1598 earl George organised some twelve large and small voyages. After the defeat of the Armada none could sail without commission from the Queen. It is not necessary to record them in detail. His greatest triumph was the capture in August 1592 of the great Spanish carrack, the Madre de Dios near the Azores. He was not present, but the fleet was his, which joined with that of Raleigh. Before the carrack docked at Dartmouth on the 23rd August a pandemonium of looting broke out. Raleigh in the Tower for his marriage, was released, and it was said that £100,000 of goods were stolen. About £141,000 was saved, and Raleigh and Hawkins, who between them had spent £34,000 got £36,000. Clifford who spent £19,000 got £36,000. The city of London which spent £6,000 got £12,000. Merchants, shopkeepers, and goldsmiths flocked to the ports to pick up bargains from the seamen. When Cecil arrived to try to stop the rot he lamented that 'sailors' fingers are like limed twigs' and examining men on their oath was 'lost labour, and offence to God.' One result of the bickering was a coolness between Clifford and Raleigh.

While the stakes were high, so were the risks. This was proved in 1594 when his eighth fleet captured an even more valuable carrack,

the Cinque Llagas, which caught fire with the loss of 1,100 Spanish men. One result of the 1592 prize was that on February 19th 1592/3 an Act of Parliament was passed giving Margaret countess of Cumberland the Westmorland estates in jointure on the basis of the settlement in 1591.[11] Most of 1597 was spent provisioning and building up a fleet of twenty ships to sail against the Spanish ships coming from the West Indies passing the Azores. Thousands of pounds were spent; it was the gambler's last throw. While he was preparing, the price of corn rose steeply due to bad harvests, and the fleet did not sail from Portsmouth till 6th March 1598. It was largely a failure, due in the main to warnings which had been received by the people of the Azores who removed all their valuables before he took the islands. The fleet returned to Portsmouth on the 23rd September, and the economic results were best described in a letter dated 3rd October of Dudley Carleton to his friend John Chamberlain:

> '...All they have done is to take the town and castle of Porto Rico; the Spaniards knowing of their coming, the property had been removed, All the earl has brought (chiefly sugar and ginger) is worth but £15,000 or £16,000 not half the charge of setting out besides the waste of shipping and loss of 600 men. Some find great fault with the earl, saying he neglected present profit in hopes of greater matter.'[12]

Clifford lost 16 men of his household. So great were the debts that in 1598 the manor Essheton in Craven was sold for £2,000 to Robert Bindloss of Borwick Hall, with the provision that if it was not redeemed within five years the sale was to be absolute.[13] It was not recovered. The second and more drastic step was that on 20th December 1598 Clifford conveyed all his Craven estates to three local gentlemen William Ingleby, Lawrence Lister and William fferand for the term of 140 years, reserving to Clifford the right to recover under certain conditions. It was recalled in 1605, shortly before his death.[14] It seems that the Westmorland estates had also been put in commission, because, in the Will of Robert Shawe of Hanging Lunds, 17th October 1601 he left his farm to be divided equally between the two sons' with lycence of my lord and his commissioners'.[15]

These were not the only losses of land. In 1591 he had borrowed heavily from Gilbert Talbot earl of Shrewsbury, and through these loans was forced to sell much of his land at Malton and Rotherham in Yorkshire.[16] On 21st September 1596 Clifford granted the manors of Wellan and Sutton to W. Ingilby and M. Grimston.[17] These are small straws leading up to the surrender of his estates to trustees in 1598.

Mention has been made several times of the bad harvests and infections which spread over Europe from 1594 until 1597. In some English counties there were food riots, especially in Oxfordshire. The failure of the wheat harvest drove up all other food prices. There was an average harvest in 1595.[18] The year 1596 was a disaster. Bubonic plague broke out in Carlisle on 29th September 1597,[19] and lasted for a year. About a third of the population died. Fifty-one people died in the country parish of Kirkoswald, and over 2,000 in the deanery of Penrith. In Penrith town in the fifteen months before the outbreak of plague in October 1597, the mortality was 200 per cent above average.[20] This gives force to Dr. Hoskins' figures for the years of bad harvests. A quarter of the parishioners of Edenhall died. The pest spread slowly into Yorkshire, and on the 25th April 1598 the magistrates "ordered that the statute against rogues and vagrant persons shall be proclaimed in the market towns of the West Riding as followeth: that is to say on Friday next in Wakefield, on Saturday next in Halifax and Skipton, on Monday next in Leeds, Rotherham and Selby, on Thursday next in Bradford and Wetherby, on Wednesday in Barnsley and Knaresborough, on Tuesday next in Sheffield and Settle."[21] Plague broke out in Appleby on the 1st August 1598, and 128 people died there within 8 months. In the nearby parish of Warcop Richard and Jennet Lancaster of Bleatarn were buried on 25th May 1598 in the garth of their farm, and the place is still pointed out.[22] The Clifford estates were at the heart of this distress of poverty and disease, and we cannot avoid the charge that Clifford was loading his estate with huge debts to pay for his voyage, at a time when his tenants were faced with disaster.

From 1590 earl George's wife lady Margaret lived mostly around London, mixing with the Court circle. Her sister Anne countess of Warwick was a maid of honour to the Queen, and lady Margaret lived for a time at her house in Austin Friars. While earl George spent more and more time at sea, his wife returned to the world of writers and poets which she had known before her marriage. After each return from a voyage earl George saw less of her. In 1595 the child lady Anne became so ill that she was sent for the next five years to Lilford in Northamptonshire. In 1596 Lady Margaret Clifford countess of Derby, and half sister to earl George, left her home on Clerkenwell Green to lady Margaret, and from that point she had her own home, dividing her time between Austin Friars and Clerkenwell. The portrait of lady Warwick at Woburn shows a disciplined and courtly lady, who belonged to a generation of literary women who flourished at Elizabeth's court. That of the countess of Cumberland at the Bodleian shows a duller woman. In 1599 Clifford acquired a mistress, and took from the Crown a country house at Grafton Regis in Northamptonshire at a rent of £500 a year. On the 8th April 1601 formal articles of separation were signed between Clifford and his wife in the presence of Sir Drew Drury, Sir John Peyton and a Mr. Beale.[23]

From 1600 lady Anne returned to her mother's house in London, and for the next few years came under the tuition of the poet Samuel Daniel. That she was in London in August 1600 is proved by the account book which was last seen by Dr. T.D. Whitaker which contained a verse which was thought to be by Daniel:

> "To wish and will it is my part,
> To yow, good lady, from my hart,
> The yeares of Nestor God yow send,
> With hapynes to your life's end."[24]

This period of tuition is important in that at a time when Spenser and other writers inhabited a dream world of Arthurian legends and antique chivalry,[25] Daniel so filled lady Anne's mind with high notions of ancestry and nobility, that when after a lifetime of standing for her 'rights' she inherited the Clifford estates, she spent more money on restoring useless castles, than improving the lot of her tenants.

In 1602 Clifford was so pressed by debt that he spent most of the year at Skipton looking for money. But there was little chance of movement. Most of his tenants were on fixed ancient rents, and except when dropping fines became due on change of tenant by death or alienation could any slight adjustment be made by raising the level of fine. But as many of them had not recovered from the bad harvests and deaths in the 1596-98 disaster there was little hope of early recovery. Rents could be raised on demesne lands but with money so scarce there was little hope there. In addition Clifford failed to pay his wife any maintenance. On the 7th November 1602 she wrote to Sir Robert Cecil, Secretary of State, asking for his help. She was so in debt that she asked that the trustees of her Deed of Separation should be empowered to cover them by bond to the sum of £900. She wrote again in January 1603 in the same strain. She also sent a pious letter of rebuke to Clifford 'seeking a Christian reconciliation'. Cecil showed the correspondence to Clifford who wrote a furious reply to his wife: 'When I have of my own you shall not want. Till then, reason would you should have patience, and not run courses to my discredit...'[26] Though Clifford had an ally in Cecil, lady Margaret had an equally strong one in her sister the faithful countess of Warwick at Court. On the 27th January 1603 the trustees wrote to Clifford pointing out that he had not only failed to supply the linen, brass, pewter, and bedding which he had undertaken in the articles of separation, but also ready money. Clifford was summoned to appear before the Lord Treasurer; but the outcome is not known.[27]

When Queen Elizabeth died on the 24th March 1603, 'as the most resplendent sun setteth at last in a western cloud', the unseemly scramble for places in the new Court had begun. Earl George was assured of some sympathy under the new reign, for his ally Sir Robert Cecil had already secured his place as Secretary of State to James I. But lady Margaret's sister the Countess of Warwick was replaced at Court, and retired into private life. She died on 24/25th March 1605, and was buried at Chenies.[28] Clifford carried the Sword of State when James entered York on the 16th April. The lady Margaret and the countess of Warwick were in the Queen's funeral procession in London on the 28th April. When James reached Burleigh Harrington on the 23rd May, Samuel Daniel made his appearance and delivered his Panegyrike Congratulatory.[29] When it was printed later it contained four dedications in verse, three of which were to the countesses of Warwick and Cumberland, and to Lady Anne. The dedication to Lady Margaret was not very tactful, for it contained a clear reference to earl George's infidelities:

'And whereas none rejoice more in revenge
Than women used to do; yet you well know,
That wrong is better checked, by being condemned
Than being persued; leaving him t'avenge
To whom it appertaines; wherein you show
How worthily you clearness hath condemned
Base malediction, living in the dark,
That at the rays of goodness still doth bark.'

The King met the Queen at Grafton Regis on the 27th June, when Clifford entertained them. It was particularly galling to lady Margaret that though she was present, she was not honoured as the mistress of the house.[30] King James was crowned at Westminster on the 25th July 1603. Earl George carried the Cap of Maintenance, and lady Margaret was also present.[31]

On the death of the Queen in March 1603, and before James arrived in England an event occurred on the borders which was to have serious consequences. The borderers in the debateable lands got it into their heads that for a brief period the border laws were suspended, and that raiding would be unpunished. During 'the ill week' border clans rose against old enemies, and plundered, burned and killed far and wide. Between two and three hundred, mostly Grahams of Eskdale, swept unchecked over large tracts of Cumberland as far as Penrith.[32] It proved disastrous to the Grahams, for it gave James I an ideal excuse to pay off old scores, and make a radical change in border government. On the 8th June 1603 Clifford was made Governor of the Scottish borders, and of the castles of Carlisle, and Harbottle, and Custos Rotulorum of Cumberland.[33] He was given full power from Berwick to Carlisle. Up till that time border misdeeds had been dealt with by the Lords Warden of their respective marches meeting on the day of march with their Scottish counterparts to minister border justice. But in 1603 there was no-one able to deal with the perpetrators of 'the ill week'. The Grahams had been pushed into the lands between Esk, Sark and Leven by their enemies the Armstrongs; and since the division of the debateable lands in 1552 between England and Scotland they had lived largely in what is now the parish of Kirkandrews on Esk, watched over by the fortified towers of Sark, Kirkandrews, Netherby, and Liddle Strength.[34]

Clifford received his first instructions on the 29th September 1603 to reduce the expense of the garrison at Berwick.[35] He was in Carlisle on the 11th October, when he acknowledged his orders to proceed to Berwick, and to try certain cases with the assistance of a judge.[36] On the next day he issued his commission of Oyer and Terminer, and expressing the King's desire to reduce the borders to civil obedience. Privately he said that he would make an example of a few than make the north swim in blood. On the 4th December 1603 James sent further instructions for the repair of Berwick and for the appointment of a minister.[37]

106

On the same day, while at Wilton, he issued a proclamation sealing the fate of the Grahams:

'Forasmuch as all our subjects in the north parts, who have felt the smart of the spoils and outrages done upon them at our first entry into this kingdom, by diverse borderers, but especially by the Grames, cannot be ignorant what care we have had, that punishment should be done upon the offenders, having for that purpose to our charge maintained our forces to apprehend them and commissioners to try them according to law; by whose travail, namely, of our cousin the earl of Cumberland our lieutenant ther, with the assistance of other commissioners, things are brought to that point, that the offenders are all in our mercy, and do all (but specially the Grames) confess themselves to be no meet persons to live in those countries, and therefore have humbly besought us that they might be removed to some other parts, where with our gracious favour they hope to live to become new men, and to deserve our mercy...'[38]

He further said that rather than execute the full force of law against them they would be transported, and the leaders held in prison to guarantee good behaviour. It is obvious that the Grahams had confessed nothing, nor sought removal. Clifford spend many weary weeks reducing the garrison at Berwick, and repairing the town. But the King, in order to create a vested interest in removing the Grahams, on the 7th February 1603/4 issued two warrants; the first for the survey of the debateable lands, and the second granting the lease of those lands between Esk, Sark, and Leven to Clifford.[39] The grant was not as valuable as a later writer would have us believe:

'The only apparent reason why immediate and merciless destruction fell upon the Grahams on the accession of King James, was their possession of those valuable acres which the King had been persuaded to confer as a free gift upon one of this worthless favourites, who chanced to be a personage of importance in the north country.'[40]

This is the sort of slant taken in border history, when in fact the desolate debateable lands were not transformed until the mid-eighteenth century, when the great agriculturist Dr. Robert Graham of Netherby took them in hand. On the 19th February 1604 Clifford received a further grant of those parts of the border omitted from the first: of Nicholforest, and the manors of Arthuret, Lyddale and Radlinton, with the fishing on the Esk.[41] The lands of the two grants extended some 20 miles from

the Solway up the border to Kersope Foot. Clifford was so short of money that he immediately let these lands to farm. If what his brother said seven years later is true, they produced no real return for some years, and cannot have relieved his debts. Clifford was in London for the opening of Parliament on the 19th March 1604. On the same day James wrote to the Lord Treasurer about Clifford's application for the renewal of his licence for the export of undressed cloth; James decided to cut it by half.[42] On the 22nd June James wrote to Clifford asking him to stay proceedings against those who had taken part in the 'ill week'.[43] On the 18th July Clifford heard from Arthur Gray that the Scots had been raiding English cattle.[44] By August he was in Skipton preparing to go to the assizes at Newcastle.[45] But he was not well, and this may have prompted the King to make a change on the border, and on the 19th August his commission of Governor of the Borders was revoked,[46] and the removal of some Grahams, and the conviction of those guilty of murder passed to other hands.

During the spring of 1605 Clifford sat four times as a Privy Councilor on Star Chamber cases, and in the summer when James went on Progress to Oxford Clifford entertained him four nights at Grafton Regis. By then he was very ill, and returned to take lodgings in the old Palace of the Savoy. On the 12th October he terminated the lease of the Craven lands which he had arranged in 1598.[47] On the 19th October he made his Will.[48] He made his confession to Lancelot Andrewes, and as a result of his advice he sent for his wife and child who came to his bedside, and sought their forgiveness. News of his illness stirred hopes of pickings. The King wanted a higher rent for the debateable lands, and he wanted Grafton for the duke of Lennox. Cecil, now earl of Salisbury was sent to sound out Clifford. He agreed to Grafton, but begged that his debts to the late Queen should be paid. He told Cecil that his estates were so in debt that his brother who was to succeed him ought to be helped. Cecil gave some courtly assurances.[49] Clifford died in the Savoy on 30th October 1605. He was buried at Skipton on the 29th December. The funeral took place on the 13th March following. His debts to the Crown came to over £4,000 and these were cancelled by the King. His current debts and funeral expenses came to £700 and were paid by his brother Francis who became the fourth earl of Cumberland. Among the Devonshire MSS from Bolton Priory are five documents of 1620 which give other debts due for the victualling of ships still unpaid at that date. They came to £3,400.[50] In all earl George owed over £40,000 at the time of his death, and the sum may be as large as £80,000. He was aged 47.

References Chapter 16.

(1) Lady Anne Clifford. Dr. G.C. Williamson. Kendal. 1922. 465/6.

(2) Hist. of Craven. Dr. T.D. Whitaker. 2nd ed. 1812. p. 11. It is possible that a few Skipton & Percy manors occur in both lists. They are left in case they were divided between the fees.

(3) Hist. of Craven. T.D. Whitaker. 415.

(4) Hist. of Craven op.cit. 446. but compare with:
Hist of Skipton. W.H. Dawson 1882. 116 & 197 (sect. 3.) The Crown confiscated the Norton lands on the attainder of 'old John Norton' after the rebellion of the earls 1568. The Cliffords purchased the Norton lands 1605/6.

(5) Chapters in the Hist. of Yorkshire. J.J. Cartwright, Wakefield. 1872. 148/9.

(6) D.N.B. Richard Hakluyt (1552?-1610).
American Geographical Soc. Special Publication no. 10. Richard Hakluyt & the English Voyagers. Dr. G.B. Parks & Dr. J.A. Williamson. New York. 1928. 67.

(7) George third earl of Cumberland. Dr. G.C. Williamson, C.U.P. 1920. 286.

(8) Prime sources for Clifford's voyages:
Hakluytus Posthumus, or Purchas his Pilgrimages etc. by Samuel Purchas. Glasgow ed. 1905. vol. XVI.
Hist. of Skipton. W.H. Dawson, 230-236.
Hist. MSS Comm. Earl Cowper's MSS, rep. XII, pt. I. (1888) 16/17. The Coke MS containing a list of his voyages.
Appleby Castle MSS. Nine of earl George's voyages were written by Richard Robinson, citizen of London, Ap. 20, 1599.
Navigantium atque Itinerantium Bibliotheca; or a Compleat Collection of Voyages & Travels etc. John Harris. AM., F.R.S. London, MDCCV. Vol. I. Lib. V. Cap. I. 685.
George third earl of Cumberland, G.V. Williamson, C.U.P. 1920, Chap. 2. is confused and unreliable.
D.N.B. George Clifford third earl of Cumberland.

(9) Lady Anne Clifford, G.C. Williamson. 56.
Typescript diary of Lady Anne Clifford transcribed by G.C. Williamson, at Tullie House, Carlisle. p. 1/2. Courtesy the late Mr. T. Gray.

(10) Lady Anne Clifford. G.C. Williamson. 456. Summary of Clifford's Will.
Hist. of Craven, T.D. Whitaker, 275/6.
N & B, I, 290.

(11) Hist. of Craven. T.D. Whitaker. 307.
C. & W Record series. Records of the Barony of Kendal, W. Farrer, 1923, IV, 103.
Hothfield. MSS at Dawson & Bennett's, London 1916. In Dr. Williamson's list at Tullie House, Carlisle.

(12) George Clifford third earl of Cumberland. G.C. Williamson. C.U.P. 1920. 205.

(13) Hist. of Craven. T.D. Whitaker. 184.

(14) Hist. of Skipton. W.H. Dawson. 197.

(15) Chapt. 17 following.

(16) George third earl of Cumberland. G.C. Williamson. 236 (2).

(17) MSS from Bolton Priory (now at Chatsworth) from copies by Dr. G.C. Williamson at Tullie House, Carlisle.

(18) Agric. Hist. Review vol XII, 1964. Harvest fluctuations & English Economic Hist. 1480-1619. G.W. Hoskins, pp. 28, 32, 46.

(19) N & B. II, 234.
Great Salkeld, Its Rectors & history. A.G. Loftie, 1900, 52.

(20) Bygone Penrith. A popular arrangement of Penrith Parish Registers. George Watson, 1893. p. 127/8.

(21) Hist. of Skipton. W.H. Dawson 289. West Riding sessions rolls.

(22) From Warcop parish registers, Cumbria.

(23) Hist. MSS. Comm. Hatfield. XII, 617.

(24) Hist. of Craven. T.D. Whitaker. 313. This counters the belief that Daniel taught at Skipton. For major refs. to S. Daniel see:
Complete Works of Samuel Daniel. A.B. Grosart 1885. 5 vols.

The English Poets. ed. T. Humphrey Ward. London 1883, vol. I. 467 for an excellent article by G. Saintsbury.

D.N.B. Samuel Daniel, 1562-1619.

Encyclopedia Britannica.

Archaeological Journal. Sept. 1899. Vol. LVI, 187.

Samuel Daniel and Anne Clifford, countess of Pembroke etc. A. Hartshorne, F.S.A. Elizabethan Bibliographies, No. 25. Samuel Daniel (A concise bibliography) by Samuel Tannenbaum, New York 1942 & pp. VII-VIII for critique.

Oxford Bibliographical Soc. Proc. and papers 1930. vol. 2, 31. Bibliography of H. Sellers. (I am obliged to Mrs. Joan Rees of the Dept. of English at Birmingham Univ. for this ref.)

General Biographical Dict. ed. Alexander Chalmers. London 1813. vol. XI., 263; summary of Daniel from the notes of Henry Headley (see D.N.B.).

(25) See dedication, among others, of Spencer's Faerie Queene to the Right Honourable the earl of Cumberland.

(26) George third earl of Cumberland. G.C. Williamson. 300/1 & 299.

(27) H.M.C. Hatfield, XII, 617. The Articles of Separation.
George third earl of Cumberland, Williamson. 299, for letter 6th April 601 of Clifford to Lady Warwick.

(28) Lady Anne Clifford. Williamson. 492.

(29) Progresses of James I. J. Nichols, 1829, I, 93, 121, XXXVIII.

(30) Diary of Lady Anne Clifford. V. Sackville-West. 1924, 10.

(31) Progresses of James I. J. Nichols. I. 25 & 228.
George third earl of Cumberland. Williamson. 261.
Diary of Lady Anne Clifford. V. Sackville-West. 12.
On and along the Thames, 1603-1625. W.C. Gaze, 1913. 122.
Coronation of James I. J. Wickham-Legg 1902.

(32) N & B, I. cxv.
V.C.H. Cumberland. II, 282 et seq.
Condition of the Border at the Union. J. Graham. 1907. 105 et seq, and 130-139, is a partial account against Clifford.
Great Salkeld and its rectors. A.G. Loftie. 1900, 55.
Prog. of James I. Nicholls op.cit. I, 47 for Sir Robert Carey's letter on the rising.

(33) C.S.P. dom Jas. I. 1603. II, 13, 8th June.
Complete Peerage. III, 568.
George Clifford third earl of Cumberland. Williamson. 260.

(34) Major works on the Cumbrian side of the border:
Trans. Dumfriesshire & Galloway Nat. Hist. & Antiq. Soc. vol. XVIII, 1934, 49. Kinmont Willie in History. W.T. McIntire.
Hist. of Cumberland. R.S. Ferguson. 1890, 242.
The Public Career of Sir James Graham, Arvel B. Erickson. Oxford 1952.
The last years of a frontier. A Hist. of the Borders during the reign of Elizabeth. D.L.W. Touch. Oxford. 1928.
Condition of the Border at the Union. J. Graham, op. cit.
N & B, I, CXXXIV.
Hist. & Antiq. of Cumberland. W. Hutchinson & F. Jollie. Carlisle 1794. esp. footnotes in Vol. I. 22-31.
Survey of the Debateable and Border Lands adjoining the realm of Scotland an belonging to the Crown of England, taken 1604. ed. Roundell Palmer Sanderson. Alnwick 1891.
Hist. of Liddesdale, Eskdale, Ewesdale, Wauchopedale and the Debateable Land, Robert Bruce Armstrong, Edinburgh, 1883.
V.H.C. Cumberland.
English Social Hist. G.M. Trevelyan, London 1945, 153.

(35) C.S.P. Dom. Jas. I. 1603, III, 41. 29th Sept.

(36) Hist. MSS Comm. Hatfield XV, 257/8.

(37) C.S.P. Dom. Jas. I. 1603. IV, 56. 4th Dec.

(38) N & B, I. XCVII.

(39) C.S.P. Dom. Jas. I. 1603/4, VI, 75.
H.M.C. Hatfield. XVI, 25.

(40) Condition of the Border at the Union. J. Graham. X.

(41) C.S.P. Dom. Jas. I. 1603/4. VI, 78.

(42) C.S.P. Dom. Jas. I. 1603/4. VI, 88.

(43) C.S.P. Dom. Jas. I. 1604, VIII, 123.

(44) H.M.C. Hatfield. XVI, 176.

(45) H.M.C. Hatfield, XVI, 200.

(46) H.M.C. Hatfield, XVI, 269, 291, 393 & 398.
George third earl of Cumberland. Williamson. 260.

(47) Hist. of Skipton. W.H. Dawson. 198.

(48) Hothfield MS (Williamson copy of Tullie House, Carlisle), now C.R.O. Carlisle.
Lady Anne Clifford, Williamson. 456/7.

(49) H.M.C. Hatfield. XVII, 459, 21 Oct. 1605. Cecil to James I.
C.S.P. Dom. Jas. I. 1605. XV, 237. John Chamberlain to Dudley Carleton.

(50) The figure in D.N.B. of the debts of earl George is too low.
H.M.C. Hatfield, XVII, 585.
Hist. of Craven. T.D. Whitaker. 308/9.
Dr. G.C. Williamson's lists of the Bolton priory MSS at Tullie House, Carlisle.

Note:

I am advised by Dr. R.T. Spence of Leeds that earl George's debts in 1597 amounted to £40,000, that his mistress was still in receipt of a pension from earl Francis for over twenty years after earl George's death. Dr. Spence also believes that earl George's debts in 1605 may have been as great as £80,000.

Chapter 17

Francis fourth earl of Cumberland

Sir Francis Clifford who became the fourth earl was a man of country, literary and musical pursuits, who had rarely been to London. He had one surviving son, and two daughters. When countess Margaret received a copy of her husband's Will from Sir Robert Cecil, now earl of Salisbury, she learned of the settlement of 1591, and now reaffirmed in the Will.[1] She was to receive the Westmorland estates in jointure without the sheriffwick; her daughter lady Anne was to receive a portion of £15,000, and apart from certain personal legacies, all the old Clifford lands in Westmorland and Craven and the new properties were to go to earl Francis and his heirs male. Only if earl George and his brother Francis were to die without heirs male would the old Clifford lands revert to lady Anne and her heirs, or failing these to the daughters of earl Francis. Thus at first sight it appeared that lady Anne had been disinherited except for her portion of £15,000. It must be admitted from the point of view of the Crown there was a need of effective lords to assist in governing the borders. In addition a minority often meant the running down of an estate, slackness and peculation. Despite this, countess Margaret was not pacified; she proceeded to pursue earl Francis and his son with unbated vigour for the rest of her life.

As soon as she grasped the legal position she wrote to the chief executor of earl George's Will, the earl of Salisbury, asking for a commission to appraise her husband's assets.[2] She was owed money under the separation agreement, and a mistress had to be provided for. At the time Salisbury was fully engaged in the Guy Fawkes scare. Yet he supported earl Francis, and in 1605 issued a warrant to the Attorney-General asking him to allow earl Francis to compound for any defective title in the lands he had received from his brother.[3] But the matter was not so easily resolved; countess Margaret proceeded to claim for her daughter the sheriffwick of Westmorland, and the castle, manor and honor of Skipton.

When the lawyers began to examine earl George's Will they saw that despite all the precautions he had taken, the settlement of 33 Eliz., and his Will based on that settlement, were founded on certain entails in the Will of his father. As Sir Matthew Hale put it: 'as is the use of persons of plentiful estates, looking no higher than the will of his father, and finding an entayle there limited of these manors'.[4] earl George proceeded to bar those entails by fine and recovery, and to convey his estates old and new to his brother Francis, and his heirs male. The fine cost earl George £1,250.[5] What earl George and his counsel-at-law Sir Richard Hutton had not realised was that the old Veteripont estates in Westmorland which had come to the Cliffords, and the old Clifford lands in Craven were held of the Crown in capite. The Westmorland estates were granted in 5th King John to Robert de Veteripont *and his heirs*; the Craven estates were granted in 5th Edward II to Robert de Clifford *and the heirs of his body*.[6] Not only were these estates entailed to heirs of the body (not just heirs male), but on the descent of the estate to the heir the Crown had the right of livery and primer seisin. The right of primer seisin required that the heir of full age pay a whole year's profits on succeeding to his (or her) ancestor's estate to the Crown. If the heir was a minor, he had to sue out his livery on coming of age, and half a year's profits for taking possession.[7] Failing heirs the estates reverted to the Crown. According to the statute 34 Henry VIII the original entails could not be barred by fine and recovery, unless first the reversion were taken out of the Crown.[8] That was the case which now faced earl Francis and countess Margaret.

Earl Francis occupied Skipton castle immediately, and during 1606 was fully occupied in catching fugitive Grahams from his border lands, and taking forcible possession of their wretched hovels. The Council decided to prosecute none for murder, but to reserve all the Grahams for transportation to Ireland, A tax was laid on Cumberland and Westmorland to cover costs, and in April and September 1606, and in April 1607 they were rounded up in three batches, marched to Workington, shipped to Ireland, and marched to Roscommon in the centre of Ireland and left there. Only the very aged and decrepit were spared.[9]

Meanwhile countess Margaret decided to take further action. She persuaded lady Anne to make her her guardian, and then sued in the Court of Wards for the livery of all the Cliffords lands. In Westmorland this included the Veteripont estates and the sheriffwick; some more recent lands in Cumberland; and in Craven the castle, manor and honor of Skipton, which included all the old Clifford lands, and also the new properties of Bolton priory, the Percy fee, and the Norton lands. There were also some London and other properties. A commission of enquiry into the evidence was established by lord Salisbury before March 1607. During the summer countess Margaret and lady Anne went north and stayed at Appleby castle till the beginning of October, and on their way home decided to visit Skipton castle. Earl Francis' servants shut them out 'in an uncivil and disdainful manner', and they had to seek shelter in the town.[10] They reached London on the 23rd October.

Lord Salisbury as president of the Court of Wards, and chief executor was in a strong position and firmly supported earl Francis, and on 25th May 1607 he wrote to Sir Thomas Lake, the keeper of the records at Whitehall thus:

'The Earl of Cumberland has been a suitor to his Majesty, to admit him to compound in some reasonable sort for the manors, castles etc. whereof his Majesty has not only the remainder but a pretence of title, in respect of some imperfections in his grants long since made to his ancestors. His Majesty is informed that there be so many in remainder between the Earl and the Crown, as the possibility thereof is of little value.

Although we are not informed whether there be any great number of heirs in remainder now living, nor what these lands are, nor at what value they were passed from the Crown in former times, nevertheless because his Majesty in the general is resolved to grant his request, we require you to inform yourself of those particulars, and to draw up a book for his Majesty's signature, whereby the Earl may have a grant to him and his heirs, of all his Majesty's remainder and other rights and titles, in such sort as is usual; from Whitehall 25 May 1607.'[11]

A competent counsel could point out that the King's rights were neither pretended nor unclear. The money arising from primer seisin

on large estates was not of little value; and confusing the remainder in the Crown with the remainders under the Will of earl George's father was throwing dust in the air. It was a foxy letter of a minister of the Crown seeking to oblige a friend, and in the hope that the King would not see through it. It succeeded. On the 4th of June 1607 the King granted earl Francis and his heirs reversion of all the Clifford lands in Westmorland and Craven.[12] Sir Matthew Hale added this: 'though it passed nothing in possession, yet it passed the reversion out of the Crowne, though it came too late'. It was partly with this in mind that bishop Burnet made this comment:

'The Crown had great estate all over England, which was let out upon leases for years, and a small rent reserved. By this means most great families were tenants to the Crown, and many small boroughs depended on the estates so held. The renewal of these leases brought in fines, and the fear of being denied such renewal kept all in dependance on the Crown. The King obtained of his parliament a power of granting, i.e. of selling those estates for ever, with a reserve of the old quit rent; so was the Crown stripped of its authority, and the money raised by this means profusely squandered away'.[13]

There are four main sources of information on the actions followed by earl Francis and countess Margaret during the following years: the law reports, the diary of lady Anne, lord Salisbury's papers, and the summary of the case drawn up by Sir Matthew Hale. None is fully satisfactory. For example the summary of the cases in the Court of Wards in the modern English Law Reports is too concise when compared with the fuller 17th. C. reports of these two cases, though the point of law at issue is stated clearly. The following is an outline of the steps taken during the following years:

(1) The case opened in the Court of Wards and Liveries on the 18th April 1608.[14] lady Anne claimed the Westmorland estates by virtue of the grant of the 5th King John to Robert de Veteripont and his heirs, and in 5th Edwards II to Robert lord Clifford; and the Craven estates by virtue of the grant of 5th Edward II to Robert de Clifford and the heirs of his body. These estates were held of the Crown in capite, with reversion in the Crown failing heirs. Earl Francis claimed all the estates by virtue of the settlement of 33 Eliz. and his brother's Will. The Court appears to have decided to call for evidence. Writs were issued

to commissioners, and interrogatories submitted to the parties to produce evidence.[15]

(2) On the 21st December 1608 (6 Jas. I.) by force of a mandamus from the Court of Wards an Inquisition was held at Kendal to examine the title deeds of the Westmorland estates, together with the Wills of Henry second earl, and George the third earl of Cumberland, and the settlement of 33 Eliz. The Westmorland case was heard in the Trinity term of 1609. It was found that earl George had held those estates in tail to him and his heirs male, with certain remainders, by force of the Will of his father Henry the second earl. It also found that in 33 Eliz. earl George had by fine and recovery conveyed the Westmorland estates (except the sheriffwick) to himself and his wife for their lives, and to countess Margaret as her jointure, and afterwards to the heirs male of his body, and failing these to his brother Sir Francis and his heirs male, and failing these to earl George's heirs. At a later date earl George by an Indenture conveyed these estates in fee simple to his brother. Earl George died on the 30th October 1605, and countess Margaret occupied the Westmorland estates and enjoyed their profits from that date.

The Court also found that originally the estates had been held in capite of the Crown; that the reversion in the Crown had not been bought out; that the Crown was entitled to livery and primer seisin; that the provisions of the statutes of 32 & 34 Henry VIII governing estates held in capite were binding, and that the provisions of the settlement of 33 Eliz. were flawed as the reversion in the Crown had not been bought out. Thus the estate should have come to lady Anne as direct heir.[16]

(3) In the middle of these enquiries lady Anne was married at the age of 18 on the 21st February 1609 to Richard Sackville lord Buckhurst in her mother's house in Austin Friars.[17] Within four days his father Thomas Sackville earl of Dorset, the Lord Treasurer, died and the young couple became earl and countess of Dorset, inheriting Knole, and Dorset House in London. Sackville was a friend of Prince Henry, and spent much time and money at Court. He was a friend of scholars and a gambler, and, as John Aubrey put it 'lived in the greatest splendour of any nobleman in England. Among other pleasures he enjoyed, Venus was not the least'. Aubrey reported that he captured the favours of the two most sought-after courtesans of the day, Bess Broughton and Dame Venetia Stanley. Lady Anne's Knole diary is full of hints of the storms caused by these affairs, while Sackville's miniature in

the Victoria & Albert Museum by Isaac Oliver shows him in his most expensive dress.[18] Countess Margaret hoped that this alliance would strengthen her daughter's cause at Court. She was soon undeceived, and found that the itch for ready money was Dorset's ruling passion. Often he tried to persuade his wife to compound her Clifford claims for cash, but she refused. Her portion of £15,000 was now due under her father's Will, to be raised from the northern estates.

(4) The Skipton inquisition was held on the 24th April 1609 (7th Jas. I.)[19] at which the Letters Patent of Edward II granting the castle, manor and honor of Skipton to Robert de Clifford and the heirs of his body were produced. If the record of the Court, and the statement of Sir Matthew Hale are correct earl Francis' attorney stated that King Henry VI had granted the estate to Thomas lord Clifford 'as cousin and heir of the body of Robert de Clifford' either in possession or in reversion in fee simple. If that had been true, then the dispositions of earl George and his father were in order for that estate. The alleged grant was not produced, nor has been found.

The Skipton case was heard in Michaelmas term 1609 (7 Jas. I.), and though the report has been truncated, it seems that the case proceeded on the assumption that the grant of Henry VI existed. The argument was on the point whether Henry VI's form of grant in reversion or possession in fee simple was good at law. The three judges held that it was, though in newer form which did not recite the first grants by Edward II.[20] Lord Salisbury presided, assisted by three judges.

There seems to have been a resumption of the Skipton case in the Hilary term 7. James I, which following the old law terms would be from January 1610.[21] This hearing has not been reported except in the words of Sir Matthew Hale, who said that exception was taken to the findings of the inquisition of 24th April of 7th James I. But it was agreed that the new purchases, the Bolton priory estate, and the Norton estate were fully covered by the settlement of 33 Eliz. and were held in fee simply by earl Francis.[22] The lands of the Percy fee at a rent of £250 a year were different and required separate appraisal. The court ordered that the question of the supposed grant of Henry VI which was disputed by countess Margaret should be tried in the Common Pleas. In addition earl Francis claimed that by several Acts of Parliament the tenure of the estate had been converted to fee simple. This was resisted by counsel for countess Margaret.

If countess Margaret had hoped that lady Anne's marriage to Dorset would have strengthened her case against earl Francis, she was disabused when on the 25th July 1610 Francis' son Henry married lady Frances Cecil, the daughter of his trustee lord Salisbury.[23] Dorset's willingness to settle for cash, and his open criticism of countess Margaret made her even more determined to resist, and claim the whole estate. Francis' claims and Dorset's consent united against one woman and her daughter. It is one of the tragic ironies of the whole story that the Clifford tenants in Westmorland became the chief sufferers in the contest.

The years 1611 to 1615 will be noted briefly. Earl Francis and his son spent much time watching the borders, Henry doing most of the work. When in 1610 lady Arbella Stuart married William Seymour without the King's consent, and they were confined in the Tower, there was a rumour at one point that she would be placed in the custody of earl Francis at Londesborough. Then there was a dispute between earl Francis and countess Margaret that her servants were felling too much timber in Whinfell forest, and wasting the Appleby estate.[24] In October 1611 Henry lord Clifford's sister Margaret was married at Londesborough to a rising star Sir Thomas Wentworth, the Yorkshireman who became earl of Strafford. Clifford and Wentworth had been schoolboys together, and though lady Margaret died in 1622, they remained firm friends until Strafford died on the scaffold in 1641. Indeed, it was Strafford who persuaded Charles I to pay off some of earl Francis' debts, many of them going back to those of his brother earl George. Lady Anne's first daughter Margaret was born on the 2nd July 1614, and on the 4th of August her mother left London for ever, and went to live at Brougham castle in Westmorland. There she spent her last days in many prayers, distilling herbs, writing letters to her daughter, and stoking the fires of the family feud.

(5) The next hearing was in the Common Pleas in Westminster Hall on the 16th June 1615.[25] Lord Hobart presided. He had been attorney-general in the Court of Wards and Liveries, was well aware of the earlier Clifford cases, and recorded some of them in his Reports. It is said that he was a modest and learned lawyer and escaped the charge of subservience to the Crown. He was made Chief Justice of the Common Pleas in 1613. Earl Francis pursued the claim that Henry VI had granted the estates to Thomas lord Clifford in fee simple. Though the alleged grant was not produced earl Francis' counsel endeavoured to prove its existence because of Thomas lord Clifford's eminent services to Henry VI. Lady Anne's counsel replied that it was a dangerous precedent to prove a matter of record by such presumption. 'After the evidence on both sides, a reference was made by the Court, and a juror withdrawn.'[26] Though the grants of Edward II were clearly in lady Anne's favour, it is inescapable that Hobart and the other judges were pressed, either by the King or earl Francis, to delay judgement. They suggested that the family should compose the quarrel by compromise, lady Anne renouncing her claim in return for an increased portion. When the four judges asked the two women to accept their solution they complained that as the King by his patent of 1607 had awarded the reversion of all the Clifford lands to Francis in fee simple, he seemed to regard himself above the law, and free to alter it as he thought fit. They were at impasse, and two attempts were made to make the ladies change their minds. Earl Francis got Sir John Bowyer of Barwise Hall near Appleby to go to Brougham and try to soften the old lady's heart. He failed. Then on 17th January 1616 a great company of courtiers and relatives came to Dorset House to persuade lady Anne to accept a cash settlement. George Abbot archbishop of Canterbury was brought in. She told them that she would not decide without consulting her mother. They signed a declaration to the judges that she should be allowed to do this. Her reply had to be given by 22nd March 1616.[27]

On the 21st January lady Anne and her husband (he going part of the way) set out in the Dorset coach from London for the north.

Travelling as fast as snow would allow through Manchester, Chorley and Kendal she arrived at Brougham on the 5th of March. On the 20th March, lord William Howard, who had been at the Dorset House meeting, came with several witnesses to Brougham to hear the formal reply of the two ladies to the judges' request for a settlement. The old lady gave a flat refusal, and angry words passed. The answer was sent post haste to London, and when Dorset heard it he was so angry that he sent word that the carriage, the horses, and his men were to return to London immediately, ordering lady Anne to stay with her mother. When the messenger came to Brougham he had to face the old lady's anger, but the servants and the coach left. The case was resumed in the Common Pleas in Westminster Hall on the 2nd of April 1616, but no conclusion is recorded as deadlock had been reached.[28] After a few days' talk with her mother lady Anne decided to come south. As she had no coach, she rode horseback behind a servant nearly all the way; but Dorset sent a coach to meet her at Ware. She spent one night at Dorset House, and the next day went down to Knole to receive a very frosty reception from her husband. When on the following day she told him that the papers the judges had given for her and her mother to sign had been left in the north, his anger was unbounded, and on the following day he stormed off to London. On the 18th April Dorset sent a final letter asking for her consent, and she gave a flat refusal. On the first of May Dorset wrote to her that for the future she could live neither at Knole nor Bollbrook, the two great Sackville houses. On the 3rd of May the child Margaret and her servants were ordered away to London. Dorset came to Knole on the 15th to make a last attempt, but so failed that they slept in separate rooms. Dorset thought of a new plan to get lady Margaret to make over her jointure lands to him. Her manservant Christopher Marsh was sent north to gain her consent, but he was too late. The old lady died at Brougham on the 24th May 1616, and was wrapped in lead to await burial.

Lady Anne set out from London on the 1st July, and arrived at Brougham on the 11th. Her mother had been unburied for over a month, and she was immediately buried the following midnight in St. Lawrence Church, Appleby. In her Will dated 27th April 1616 she made provision for her tenants on the Westmorland estates. If she died within a year of making her Will, her tenants were to be spare a third of their fines; if she died within two years their whole fines were to be received,

and a third handed back to them. As a general fine was now due to earl Francis, presumably the third was to come out of lady Margaret's estate. I have seen no evidence that this was done, though it may have been.

In June Dorset told his wife that he intended to take possession of Brougham castle on her behalf. But he was shrewd enough to attach a condition, that she should assure the Westmorland estates to him and their children. Eventually she signed. Though he got an order from the Council that Appleby and Brougham castles were not to be disturbed, earl Francis occupied Appleby before the order came north. The servants of both parties met one day in Whinfell Park, and there was a fight, which threatened to become an assize matter. Then on the 12th August the Council, weary of these endless quarrels, sequestered the Westmorland estates, giving Appleby castle to earl Francis, and Brougham to Dorset for the time being. Dorset arrived at Brougham on the 22nd of August, and left for York on the 13th September. The case came up for hearing before lord Sheffield in the Council for the North on the 19th September. Nothing came of it,[29] and the case was returned to London.

By now the King decided to settle the case himself. He believed that he could over-rule the decisions of superior courts. Sir Edward Coke, whom he dismissed in September that year, had resisted that claim. Earl Francis, his son Henry lord Clifford, and the Dorsets were ordered to be in or near London by the end of December to await the King's pleasure.[30] Christmas was spent by lady Anne in social calls, and with her child whom she had not seen for seven months.

References Chapter 17.

(1) H.M.C. Hatfield. XIII, 586.
   Life of Lady Anne, Williamson, 456.

(2) H.M.C. Hatfield. XVII, 586.

(3) H.M.C. Hatfield. XVII, 586.

(4) Hist. of Craven, T.D., Whitaker, 1812. 276.
   Hothfield MSS. Williamson List. Countess Margaret's jointure settlement of 33 Eliz. confirmed by Act. of Parl. 35 Eliz.

(5) H.M.C. Hatfield, XIX, 75.

(6) N & B, I. 267 et seq. for Westmorland.
   N & B, I, 276 for Skipton.
   English Reports (Law) 1907 ed. vol. 77. Court of Wards 726/7.
   Reports of Sir Edward Coke, 1680 ed. part VIII, sect. 167.
   History of Craven, Whitaker, 275 et seq.

(7) Law of Real Property, Joshua Williams. 24th ed. 1926, p. 35, n. (h).

(8) Hist. of Craven, Whitaker. 276.

(9) Condition of the Border at the Union. J. Graham. 1907, 186.
   For the settlement in Roscommon:

Northern History, XIII (1977). 59-160. The pacification of the Cumberland border 1593-1628. Dr. R.T. Spence.

Post Roman Carlisle and the Kingdoms of the north-west. R. Cunliffe Shaw, Preston 1964, 55. N & B, I. cxvii - cxxix.

(10) H.M.C. Hatfield. XIX, 74/5; before 5th March 1607. Preliminary hearing of evidences. Diary of Lady Anne, Williamson MS, 7.

(11) H.M.C. Hatfield XIX, 138. 25th May 1607. Earl of Salisbury to Sir Thomas Lake. Ibid. 142. May 1607. The terms of the grant to earl Francis.

(12) Hist. of Craven. Whitaker 276. 4th June 5th Jac. I. Diary of lady Anne, Williamson MS, 7, says 9th June 1607. N & B, I. 291.

(13) Hist. of own Times. Bishop Burnet, Everyman ed. 4/5.

(14) Diary of Lady Anne, 9/10.

(15) Hothfield MS, Williamson list. 23 Nov. 1608. Exam. of Francis earl of Cumberland upon interrogatories.

(16) English Reports (Law) vol. 77. 1907. K.B. p. 1459. Reports of Divers Resolutions in Law arising upon cases in the Court of Wards and other Courts etc. in the reigns of James I & Charles I, by Sir James Ley, earl of Marlborough. 1659, 3/4. Sir James was attorney of the Court of Wards from 1608.

(17) Diary of Lady Anne, 11. Stowe MSS. Brit. Mus. cat. 449.

(18) Brief Lives, John Aubrey. Penguin ed. 1972, 258-261. Elizabethan Miniatures, Carl Winter. Penguin Book repr. 1955, xv.

(19) Hist. of Craven op. cit. 276.

(20) English Reports (Law) 1907 ed. vol. 77. K.B. 726. The earl of Cumberland's case. A better version: Reports of Sir Edward Coke, 1658 or 1680. vol. VIII, sect. 167.

(21) Hist. of Craven op. cit. 276 last line.

(22) Hist. of Craven op. cit. 276/7.

(23) Diary of Lady Anne, op. cit. 11. Progresses of James I. J. Nichols, II, 363. History of Skipton. W.H. Dawson, 43.

(24) C.S.P. Jas. I. 1611. LXIV, 38. 2nd June. Francis earl of Cumberland to E. of Salisbury concerning border Grahams, and countess Margaret's wastage of the woods. Reports of Sir Henry Hobart, judge of the Common Pleas, 5th ed. 1724, 37 & 85. D.N.B. Sir Henry Hobart who d. 1625. Hist. of Craven, op. cit. 281.

(25) Diary of Lady Anne, 12/13.

(26) Hist. of Craven, op. cit. 276/7; & 289. Letter 13 Mar. 1615, Cumberland to Pickering.

(27) Diary of lady Anne Clifford, V. Sackville-West, 1924, 19/20. Hist. of Craven, op. cit. 289/90. Aug. 25, 1615, Sir J. Bowyer to Cumberland. Lady Anne Clifford, Williamson, 273.

(28) Diary of lady Anne, William MS, 13.

(29) H.M.C. Le Fleming rep. XII, pt. 7., 14. Acts of Privy Council 1615-1616, 567, 577. Diary of lady Anne, Williamson MS, 14. Diary of lady Anne Clifford, V. Sackville-West, 39/40. It is probable that the events recorded for Sept. should be Oct., as Dorset left Brougham on 13th Sept.

(30) Prog. James I. J. Nichols, III, 226. Diary of lady Anne Clifford, V. Sackville-West, 43/4. Hist. of Craven, Whitaker, 289/90. An interesting record of countess Margaret's refusal. H.M.C. Le Fleming, rep. XII, pt. VII, 1890, p. 15. Letter 12 Nov. 1616. John Dudley to his bro. Thomas. 'The cause between the earls of Cumberland and Dorset is taken up by the King.'

Chapter 18

The King's Award. (1)

Lady Anne arrived in London from the north on the 18th December 1616. On the 5th January Dorset carried the Sword of State at the creation of George Villiers as Duke of Buckingham.[1] Three days later the Dorsets went down to Knole. On the 16th January 1616/17 Lady Anne was summoned to London, where Dorset had already gone a few days before. On the 18th the Dorsets were brought before the King at Whitehall, and the King asked if they would leave the decision to him. Dorset agreed, except Lady Anne, who begged his pardon, and declared 'that I would never part from Westmorland while I lived upon any condition whatsoever.'[2] Her ground seems to have shifted, that she would be prepared to let the rest go in return for the Westmorland estate. Despite some argument she refused to move, and the Dorsets were sent home. Two days later they were summoned for a full hearing before the King. Earl Francis, his son Henry lord Clifford, and the Dorsets were there in addition to the Lord Chief Justice Montague, Hobart, Yelverton the King's solicitor, Sir Randall Crew Dorset's solicitor, and a number of lords. Again both sides were asked to place the decision in the King's hands; all agreed except Lady Anne. The King was so angry, that she was taken out, while various attempts were made to change her mind. She was then told that the King would make an award without her, and she was sent down to Knole. On the 14th March 1616/17 the Award was signed by the King, and on the following day he set out for Scotland.[3]

The Award is complicated, but has been simplified for this review. For the purposes of brevity the principal names are given thus: Francis earl of Cumberland (F.C.), Henry lord Clifford (H.C.), Richard earl of Dorset (R.S.), Anne countess of Dorset (A.C.)

The Award is make by King James to determine matters at issue for some years between F.C., and H.C. on the one part and R.S. and A.C. of the other part.

(1) R.S. shall bind his estate in the repayment of any sums awarded should A.C. commence any suit involving this award.

(2) If R.S. and A.C. agree the Award shall be as follows:

(a) The castle, honor and manor of Skipton etc and the manors of Silsden, Barden, Sturton, Thorleby, and Crookrise and all properties in Skipton held by the late George earl of Cumberland,

(b) and the manors, farms, cottages etc. in Skipton, Silsden, Gillgrange, Holden, Barden, Sturton, Thorleby, Crookrise, Holme, Elsoe, and Skibden held by earl George, F.C. and H.C.

which were granted by Edward II to Robert de Clifford together with them, the cottages, rectories, advowsons, fishing, liberties and courts belonging to them.

(c) and the castles and manors of Brougham, Appleby, Brough and Pendragon, and the manors of Kirkby Stephen, Sowerby juxta Brough, Wynton, Kings Meaburn, Mallerstang and Knock; and the forests of Whinfield alias Whinfell, Stainesmore, and Mallerstang in Westmorland

(d) and the manors and tithings of Brougham, Appleby, Brough, Stainmore, King Meaburn, Langton, Winton, Kirkby Stephen, Sowerby juxta Brough, Mallerstang, Knock, Temple Sowerby, Kirkby Thore, Whinfell, Woodside, Moorhouses, Sandford, Cilburn, Brampton, Hornby, Bolton, Burrells, Clifton, Flakebridge, Southfield, Bongate, Burton, Helton, Milburn Fell, Kendal (sic) and Marton all in Westmorland (note: these were the old Veteripont lands) held by earl George, F.C., or H.C. and were lately held in jointure by the late Margaret Countess of Cumberland

(e) and the high Sheriffwick of Westmorland shall be estated upon F.C. and H.C. and their heirs male, and failing these upon R.S. and A.C. and their heirs male, and failing these upon the latter's heirs female.

(3) To F.C. and his heirs the townships and hamlets etc of Gargrave, Embsay, Eastby, Malham, Malham Moor, Halton, Flasby, Sutton, Carleton, Broughton, Scosthorpe, Hawkeswick, and Ulcet all in Yorks, and the patronage of Keighly church (these were lands of the Percy fee)

(4) Also to F.C. and his heirs the forest of Nicholl, and the manors of Arthuret, Liddell, Randelevington, Skelton, Lamonby, and Carleton and Penrith all in Cumberland, and the fishing on the Esk.

(5) Also to F.C. and his heirs Cliffords Inn in London, and

(6) on the lands limited in reversion to R.S. and A.C. (sects. 2a, b, c, d and e, above, i.e. the prime grants in Craven and Westmorland) it shall be lawful for F.C. and H.C. during the following four years to grant lease or leases for one, two or three lives in possession, or for the term of two lives in reversion (there being one in possession) or for the term of one life in reversion (there being two lives in possession) or for the term of fourscore and nineteen years or other years in possession determinable upon one two or three lives whereupon the usual accustomed rents and services or more shall be reserved and payable from time to time to all and every such person and persons to whom the immediate reversion or remainer shall appertain of all or any the said messuages farms lands tenements hereditaments and other the premises herein before in or by these presents (are) limited to the said F.C. and H.C. or either of them for life which for the space of twenty years last past were in lease or held by warrant or grant for one two or three lives or for years determinable upon one two or three lives to any person or persons as now hold for life or lives or for whose life or lives any such lands are holden shall not be altered but upon the death of such person or persons And that it shall and may be lawful to and for the said F.C. and H.C. or either of them and all and every the said sons and issues males of them and either of them and to and for the said R.S. and A.C. his wife and all and every the said sons and issues males or daughters of the said countess and their issues being tenants in possession of the freehold of the premises from time to time and at all times so long as they shall be tenants of the freehold of the premises to demise or grant all or any the said manors messuages lands and premises which for the space of twenty years now last past have been usually letten for lives or years to any person or persons whatsoever for the term of one and twenty years in possession whereupon the usual and accustomed rents and services or more shall be reserved and payable from time to time to all and every such person and persons to whom the immediate reversion and remainder shall appertain EXCEPT and other than all parks now used as parks and demesnes of any manors at any time within twenty years

last past as demesnes upon which there are convenient and fit houses of access and residence for the said F.C. That is to say within the county of York the Castle of Skipton and Barden Tower and within the county of Westmorland the castles of Appleby and Browham and that all such lease or leases for life lives or years so as to be made as aforesaid shall be good and effectual to all and every such lessee or lessees their executors and assigns respectively for and during such estates or terms for life lives or years as shall be to them or any of them granted as aforesaid under the limitations and reservations aforesaid

(7) Provided that annual rent charges of 1,000 marks shall be reserved out of the Yorkshire lands limited in reversion to R.S. and A.C. (sects 2a, and b above) for each wife or widow for life marrying F.C., H.C. and their heirs male and the heirs male of R.S. and A.C.

(8) 'Provided also and we do further award and decree that it shall and may be lawful for the said F.C. and H.C. or either of them or any issue of their several bodies to whom the said manors and lands are limited as aforesaid or any of them being tenant of the freehold of the premises in possession by the limitations aforesaid at any time hereafter to make or grant any estate of or in the said manors lands and premises or any part thereof whereof the remainder is limited and appointed to the said R.S. and A.C. his wife to any person or persons whatsoever for the term of three lives or one and twenty years or for the term of fourscore and nineteen years or other years determinable upon one two or three lives reserving such rent or rents as they shall think fit and that all estates or leases so had or made for three lives or one and twenty years or fourscore and nineteen years or other years determinable upon one two or three lives as aforesaid shall be adjudged esteemed held and taken to be good and effectual to all intent and purposes only as against the issues of the body of F.C. and H.C. and after their issue spent then to cease and be void and not in any wise extend to be good or effectual against any other person or persons...'

(9) the like power to grant leases for 3 lives, 21 or 99 years is given to R.S. and A.C. on the manors and lands which are limited to them in reversion (i.e. 2a, b, c, d, and e above); this also to apply to A.C.'s children.

(10) "And to the intent that the said F.C. may be the better inabled to raise some part of the money which by this our Award we set down and appoint by him to be paid to the said R.S. We do further award order decree

nd declare that it shall and may be lawful
o and for the said F.C. and H.C. or either
of them from time to time and at all times
hereafter to grant convey or assure all or any
he said messuages lands tenements and heredi-
aments situate lying and being within the said
county of Westmorland which are now claimed
or holden by force or colour of a custom or
pretended custom of Tenantright to the several
enants or occupiers thereof and to their heirs
and assigns or to any other their heirs and
assigns to be holden according to the Custom
of Tenantright and in the nature of Tenantright
reserving the ancient and accustomed yearly
ents duties and services and also reserving
into the lord or lords of the said manors and
ands for the time being a fine certain of seven
years rent to be reserved upon their several
grants the same fine in certain to be paid
upon the death of every lord or lords of the
said manors and lands for the time being and
upon the death of every tenant dying seized
of the said premises and upon every alienation
of the said lands and premises or any part
hereof by any tenant thereof for the time
being to any person or persons whatsoever
And this to be done by establishing ratifying
confirming and allowing of the said Customary
messuages lands and tenements to them and
heir heirs in such manner and form and by
such security as the tenants for the time being
hen shall by their counsel reasonably devise
and require and at their costs and charges in
he law And that the said R.S. and A.C. his
wife shall give their consents by joining in
one or more decree or in any other convenient
assurance to be made for the better establishing
and confirmation of the said Custom and that
all and every such grants conveyances and
assurances so to be had and made under the
reservations aforesaid and according to the true
ntent and true meaning of this our Award
shall at all times then after be holden accounted
esteemed and adjudged to be good and effectual
against all and every the lord and lords of
he said manors and lands for the time being
so as the same shall remain still Customary
and and the freehold be not thereby severed
or aliened from the said manors or any of
hem..."

(11) In the manor of Silsden, Yorks (in
sec. 2a above) F.C. and may grant leases up
to three lives on lands which for 20 years last
past have not been let for more than £20 per
annum.

(12) If by fine and recovery A.C. shall not
agree to the Award it shall be confirmed by
Act of the next Parliament.

(13) Neither R.S. nor A.C. shall dispute the
Award.

(14) In regard to the portion bequeathed by
earl George to his daughter A.C., F.C. and
H.C. shall pay £20,000 to R.S. in the following
portions: £5,000 at the following Michaelmas;
£6,000 on St. Baptist's day 1618; and £6,000
on the same day 1619. The final £3,000 due
at Michaelmas 1619 shall only be paid if
before that date A.C. has given her written
assent to the Award, or if before that date it
has been confirmed by Act of Parliament.

(15) If F.C. and H.C. should die without
male issue and the estates limited in reversion
to R.S. and A.C. (2a, b, c, d & e above)
should come to R.S. and A.C. before Michaelmas 1619 then all outstanding payments shall
cease, and any assurance in estate given by
R.S. shall be released.

(16) In order to prevent A.C. starting an
action for the recovery of the estates from F.
C. and H.C. etc., R.S. shall bind his estates
in the sum of £25,000 to assure A.C.'s good
behaviour.

(17) If A.C. should begin an action after
the death of R.S. then F.C. and H.C. may
claim £20,000 from his exors.

(18) If the exors of R.S. do not pay the
£20,000 after the commencement of the action
then F.C. and H.C. may enter any of the
castles, manors, lands, tenements, and hereditaments limited in reversion upon R.S. and
A.C. (Sect. 2a, b, c, d and e, above) and
alien, sell or dispose of them as they think
fit, and not in any way to be bound by the
Award.

(19) If the Award shall be confirmed by
Act of Parliament then F.C. and R.S. shall
share the cost equally. F.C. and R.S. are to
do their best to implement the Award, and
the King shall resolve doubtful questions in
its application.

In short, earl Francis and his son were given
powers to grant leases outside the old Clifford
lands in Craven. The Bolton priory lands and
the Norton lands, which were more recent
purchases, were not mentioned, and could be
disposed of as they thought best. Section (10)
which concerned the customary tenant-right
lands in Westmorland was omitted by Dr. G.C.
Williamson in his Life of Lady Anne, and is
the most important provision as far as these
studies are concerned.[4] Remembering Chancery
practice, where the consent of both lord and
tenants to accept the decision of the court was
a prerequisite to a hearing of a land tenure
dispute, the Westmorland tenants were neither
consulted, nor agreed to the Award. It was
imposed on them. As the Award was not

119

confirmed by Act of Parliament, nor signed by Lady Anne (with her interest in remainder) the tenants did not get her written assurance of a 7d. fine certain, for which they were forced to pay so dearly. Finally, lady Anne was treated as a litigious person, and Sackville's estate bound in the enormous sum of £25,000 to force her to keep the peace. The Award gave to earl Francis all that his brother intended by the settlement of 33 Eliz., with the additional provisions for the Westmorland tenant-right lands.

The King entered York on his way to Scotland on 11th April, and returned through Cumberland in August. In April lady Anne wrote 33 letters to the Westmorland tenants explaining the contents of the Award, and copies were sent out in July.[5] The King was entertained by earl Francis in some style at Brougham castle in August.[6] lady Anne's letters, and the news that £17,000 had to be raised from northern estates, so alarmed the tenants that they were waiting for the King when he came to Brougham.

We are fortunate that the events of these days were recalled over 40 years later when, after lady Anne had come to the Clifford estates, she engaged in long and bitter lawsuits with her tenants. On the death of Henry the last earl of Cumberland without heirs male in 1643 lady Anne was unable to come north until 1649 after the execution of the King. For six years courts had not been held, and rents were in arrears. On her arrival in the north lady Anne demanded an 8d. general fine, despite the provisions of the King's Award which had attempted to establish a 7d. fine certain. We will follow the law suits in a later chapter. Among the depositions taken between 6th December 1650 and 25th September 1651 is a series of depositions taken at the house of John Washington at Docker, Westmorland on the 25th Sept. 1651. Robert Spencley of Winton, bailiff to earls Francis and Henry, and to lady Anne, after saying that the fines paid to earl Francis and Henry lord Clifford were excessive and unreasonable and above what other lords in Westmorland had taken, referred to King James' visit to Brougham:

'The late King James coming (on) his progress into the north (August 1617) the said tenants of the said Earls then petitioned him when he was at Brougham for some relief in the premises and followed him down to Holme Park near Burton in Westmorland aforesaid for an answer to their said petition, and this deponent saith that the said King James answered the said tenants in this manner as this deponent now remembereth:

Ye that are tenants to the Lord Clifford they say that you hold your tenements by Custom and my service 'doinge' (?going) to Carlisle; there is no service to be make but gine I will make war against myself. I command you to lie down your swords and put your hands to plough, for there is an award made between Lord Clifford and Lord Dorset. I command you that are tenants to your Lord that you do agree with him for your fines and come not to me with your petitions if your discourses shall be no better; and I will give my son command that he perform this award or he shall have my malediction.'

William Waller of Winton gave similar evidence, adding that 'The late King gave them threatening speeches and commanded them to return home and agree with their lord, for if they petitioned him they should be no better.'

In November 1617 lady Anne asked to see the King, and he sent her to his attorney to explain the legal side of the Award, but got no further.[8] Earl Francis had now to face the task of raising £17,000; and as it would be a long time before fines, leases and sales could raise the full sum, he borrowed heavily from Sir William Craven in 1623 and 1624.[9] In 1637 Wentworth persuaded the King to compensate earl Francis out of the public exchequer for his losses on the cloth licence during the Cockayne experiment, 1614-1618.[10] Francis sold part of the manor of Silsden in Craven, and part he let on long lease. He also sold or let the manors of Rilstone, Threshfield, Cracoe and Linton, and the Norton lands. He also let, and ten years later sold, all the Debateable Lands on the Scottish borders to Sir Richard son of Fergus Graham of Netherby.[11] Francis also sold Clifford's Inn in London which for many years had been an Inn of Chancery.[12] These sales in London, Yorkshire and Cumberland raised £2,000, leaving the remaining £15,000 to come from Westmorland. I am informed by Dr. R.T. Spence of Leeds, who has done extensive work on the Clifford estate accounts, that it took six years from 1617 to 1623 to raise the fines and compositions from the Westmorland estates, when the final sum of £15,275.8s.5d. was brough in - a little above lady Anne's portion of £15,000. The tenants paid in instalments with difficulty. Loans by the London money-lenders cost Francis £1,700 a year in interest, a debt from which he never escaped. It has not been established whether the provisions of countess Margaret's Will, for the amelioration of the fines of the Westmorland tenants to Francis were given effect. Nor must it be forgotten that in 1623 bad harvest and a severe outbreak of typhus crushed many of the poorer tenants, and the annual figure for burials multiplied by four.

References Chapter 18.

(1) Prog. Jas. I. J. Nichols. III, 233

(2) Diary of Lady Anne Clifford. V. Sackville-West. 48.

(3) C.S. P. Dom. Jas. I. 1617/17. XC, 446.
Hothfield MS. Williamson list.
P.R.O. Pat. Roll. C.66/2102. Photocopy sent by me to C.R.O. Carlisle.
Note: though the lands of the Percy fee are included in the Award, they were not part of the grants of Edward II. For an explanation of the fee: Hist. of Craven. op.cit. 288. By 1614 the rent to the Percys of £250 was 20 years in arrear.
Lady Anne Clifford, G.C. Williamson. 223.
Prog. Jas. I. J. Nichols, III, 255.

(4) Lady Anne Clifford, G.C. Williamson, 473. His summary is too brief to be accurate; he omits sect. (10) entirely saying that its terms were the same as for the Yorkshire lands. He did not understand the tenant-right provisions. The spelling of place-names is from the P.R.O. copy, not Williamson.

(5) Diary of Lady Anne Clifford. V. Sackville-West. 64 & 73.

(6) The King's visit to Carlisle: V.C.H. Cumberland. II, 285.
Hist. of Cumberland. R.S. Ferguson, 1890, 254.
Visit to Brougham: Prog. of Jas. I., J. Nichols. III, 391.
Lady Anne Clifford. G.C. Williamson. 121-2 It was noted by Bp. William Nicholson of Carlisle in the (now missing) parish regs. of Clifton. Misc. Accounts 1703. ed. R.S. Ferguson, 1877, 68.
Visit to Kendal: Annals of Kendal, C. Nicholson. 1835, 106.
Local Chronology, Kendal, 1865. VII.

(7) P.R.O. London. SP/C.21/p.25/1. Anne Countess dowager of Pembroke v. Robert Atkinson & others. Depositions taken 6 Dec. 1650-25 Sept. 1651. Depositions of Robert Spencley of Winton; & William Waller of Winton.

(8) Diary of Lady Anne Clifford. V. Sackville-West. 80/81.

(9) P.R.O. SP/C.21./p.25/1. Deposition of Christopher Pettie of Orton, taken 25 Sept. 1651. For some years he was servant to John Taylor Esqre, agent and commissioner to F.C. and H.C. in all their affairs in London, who procured and borrowed the £17,000 of Sir William Craven & others.

(10) D.N.B. Henry Clifford, 5th earl of Cumberland. 1591-1643
Information from Dr. R.T. Spence of Leeds.

(11) Hist. of Craven. W.H. Dawson, 197, is not quite accurate that the border lands were sold in 1618. They were then let, and sold to Sir Richard Graham of Netherby in 1628. See: The Public Career of Sir James Graham, Arvel B. Erickson, Oxford. 1952. The conveyance is dated 21 May. 1628. C.S.P. Dom. Jas. I. 1622. CXXVII, p. 339, 27 Jan. The King to the Bp. of Durham, 'As Sir James Graham is endeavouring to reform vice in Cumberland, where he lives, by building a church, educating the young, he is to have the benefit of presenting to the church at Kirkandrews (on Esk), the King's right to which is good.'

(12) Lady Anne Clifford. Williamson. 454.
The Deed of Sale of Silsden lands is among the Hailstone MSS in the Dean and Chapter Library, York.
The Deed of Sale of certain lands at Winton, Westmorland is dated 17 Jan. 1619/20 and was among the MSS of the late Miss Marcia Mason, of Eden Place, Kirkby Stephen.

Chapter 19

The King's Award (2)

In raising £17,000 several issues now faced earl Francis and his son; (a) the level of general fine due to him on the death of countess Margaret from the Westmorland estates; (b) the feudal aid which he could impose to raise lady Anne's portion under the Will of her father; [1] (c) the compositions which would purchase tenant-right to the tenants, and establish a 7d. fine certain for general and dropping fines, or seven times the ancient rent on each tenant-right property. In addition to these three main groups there were any dropping fines due from the accession of earl Francis on the change of tenants by death or alienation.

Formerly the setting of a general and dropping fine was 'as the tenant could agree with his lord'. The raising of an aid was so rare an event, that the rate is not known. The rate of composition for making fines certain was variable as readers of chapter 12 will recall. But twenty years' purchase would have been customary. Readers of chapter 14 will recall that of the five fines still unpaid in whole in Mallerstang in 1604 fines on descent appear to vary between a 3d. and a 7d. rate; while the fine on alienation was in the 20d. bracket. This tallies with the Ravenstonedale Indenture of 1579/80.

The 1650-51 Chancery depositions in the case between lady Anne and her Westmorland tenants contain startling accusations of the severity of the demands of earl Francis and his son on their tenants, and their disastrous effects.[2] Of the nineteen who gave evidence on behalf of the tenants Thomas Johnson came from Stainmore, and four others from Mallerstang. Unfortunately the MS is defective where one figure is given. His evidence will be given fairly fully:

Thomas Johnson: The tenants of earl Francis did pay unto him 'very excessive and unreasonable fines for their several estates so that many tenants were greatly impoverished and utterly ruined and undone and were constrained to sell their estates for raising and payment of the same', and he for his part did pay for his fine on a tenement rented at 16/10d. a year 'the sum of twenty pounds in money and he had all his quick goods as beasts and sheep driven and carried away for the rest, his whole fine being between ... (MS defective) and four score pounds, besides himself imprisoned six weeks, which fines the said earl's officers affirmed was but after seven years rate: and deponent saith that the same was as much as the estate was worth to be sold; and he saith that the said fines were raised and paid ... for the confirmation of their future fines to be paid after the rate of seven-penny fine, that is seven years rent for a fine.'

He heard that it was to pay (lady Anne's) portion.

At least twenty tenants were utterly beggared; several were imprisoned and two died there, Lancelot Johnson, and Christopher Carter.

As Thomas Johnson's fines did not exceed £80 it is possible to come to an approximate rate for his fines. Taking the top figure of £80 with the rent of 16/10d. the fine seems to have seen between an 80d. and a 90d. fine, with the ultimate assurance of a 7d. fine certain for the future.

Phillip Gibson aged 64, of Grisedale, Yorks: The fines paid to earl Francis were excessive. His fine was so great he sold his tenement (of 7/- rent) for 40/- and left it, leaving the purchaser to pay the fine. In lady Margaret's time after the death of earl George (1605) he paid a 30/- fine on his 7/- rent ... 'other tenants compounded with her for their fines after an easy rate, and some more, and some less.'

Phillip Gibson probably came from Sandpot in Mallerstang, where in 1604 Thomas son of John Gibson was tenant of a small farm of 6/8d. rent. The fine paid to lady Margaret in 1605 was therefore a 4d. one.

John Blenkarne aged 68, of Wensleydale, Yorks; Earl Francis' fines were excessive. His rent was four nobles (a noble = 6/8d.), and the tenement worth about £80. As the worth would not discharge the fine, he was so molested for payment, he with his wife and family were forced to leave and go and live in another county.

There was no farm of 26/6d. rent in Mallertang, and he may have come from another Clifford manor; though it must be remembered that improvements, sales or purchases can alter the rent of a farm from the figures given in chapter 14. But the rate of fine is about 60p.

Nicholas Fothergill aged 44, of Swaledale, Yorks: His father died before his fine was paid. His other and eldest son paid £16.4.0, but not being enough, she and seven children were driven off the farm by earl Francis' agents, who held it for seven years, when they were allowed to return. Meanwhile she and the children went a-begging. Twelve tenants out of a total of 52 in the dale were thus turned off for seven years.

As family christian names are fairly constant, it is possible that Nicholas was the son or grandson of Nicholas Fothergill of Southwaite, Mallerstang. Nicholas Fothergill was the tenant of a small farm of 5/3d. rent in 1582 and 1604. In 1604 he transferred part of his farm to his son William, and it is possible that William was the tenant who died before his fine was paid.

Geoffrey Birkbeck aged 71, of (Deepgill), Mallerstang: After the King's award, £17,000 was paid to Richard earl of Dorset. £26,000 was raised out of the tenants for the confirmation of their customary tenures, and for a 7 years fine certain on every change of lord or tenant.

In the raising of the £26,000 many tenants were utterly ruined, and forced to fly and leave their estates, and with their families go a-begging. When lady Margaret came to her (jointure) estate on the death of earl George (in 1605) he paid a two years fine, but others 3 or 4. Thomas Fothergill paid three years; on a rent of 11/3d. he paid 35s. George Birkdale paid 10s. on a rent of 3/1d.

Geoffrey Birkbeck was the second son of John Birkbeck of Bluegrass.

Geoffrey seems to have misread the £25,000 penal clause in the Award. There was a Thomas Fothergill admitted tenant at Deepgill at a rent of 10/1d. in 1604. The only surviving Birkdale family was at Hesleygill, Mallerstang. George Birkdale was tenant at 11/4d. in 1582, and his son Thomas tenant of the much reduced farm at 6/1d. in 1604. It is probable that more land had been sold by 1617. Geoffrey Birkbeck was speaking of his neighbour, where fines of 2 to 4 years rent were paid in 1605. Birkbeck seems to have been an ageing and inaccurate witness.

Though the evidence of the four Mallerstang witnesses, and of Thomas Johnson probably of Stainmore needs corroboration, it suggests

(a) that the general fine in 1605 when lady Margaret inherited her jointure estates was a 4d. one;

(b) that the fines levied after the King's Award were in the 60d. range, that is sixty times the ancient rent;

(c) and that the Award, inrolled in Chancery, was intended to establish a 7d. fine certain both general and dropping.

Three men gave evidence on behalf of the tenants' sufferings:

John Addison, aged 60, shoemaker of Appleby: The fines levied by force of the King's Award were very oppressive. many tenants were ruined, and took refuge in the country. In customary Tenant-right the tenants can alienate their tenements without licence of their lord. Before the 'Confirmation' fines were arbitrary, but afterwards fixed at 4 years rent. (sic)

Lancelot Blenkinsop aged 66, of Helbeck, gent: The fines under the Award were very oppressive; and many were ruined and forced 'to sell some all and some half or most of their real and personal estates as he knows in particular; John Rudd sold half his tenement at Brough; William Walter (?Waller) most part of his estate; Henry Rudd most part of his estate; Robert Wardell a great part of his estate; Matthew Smith the like; Thomas ...'s estate was in the said earl Francis' hands for 14 years and afterwards sold it for paying his fine; John ... was forced to fly the country and leave his tenement for the space of 9 years, and the said earl Francis took the profits thereof all that time; Thomas Rudd sold all his tenement after the said earl Francis had taken all the profits thereof for eight or nine years; Christopher Dalmaine sold half of his tenement; Christopher Hodgson sold all his tenement of 25s. rent and reserved of the price but £12 from discharging his fine; for Michael Shaw the said earl had his tenement for the space of 8 years in lieu of his fine albeit he had paid £20 of the said fine; Richard Ayray sold most part of his tenement; Anthony Salkeld and Anthony Appleby did the like; All the said persons before named being the said earl's tenants; they were constrained for payment of their fines to convey and part with their estates as aforesaid, which fines were so raised to pay (lady Anne's) portion.

Customary estates can be aliened without the will of the lord.

Ever since the Pilgrimage of Grace, when Christopher Blenkinsop of Brough was hanged in 1538, the family had remained loyal Catholics, being reported regularly to the government for refusing to attend the parish church, and suffered much under the penal laws.[3] Part of the manor of Helbeck was sold in 1638, and the remainder in 1657, while the Hall and demesne was sold in major Skaife of Winton one of Cromwell's sequestrators.

Thomas Laidman aged 60 of Stainmore: mentioned the heavy and oppressive fines, which ruined many tenants; some died in prison, and some sold a great part of their estates and went a-begging in the country; 'as Lanclott Johnson died in prison; William Gills, Henry Johnson, James Waller, Richard Dickinson, James Wastall, George Wastall, Matthew Smith, Henry Smith, Matthew Wharton, William Johnson, Robert Wastall, James Devis, Lanclott Midleton, Robert Hunter, and William Wastall all of these either lost their estates and were not able to pay their fines, or sold their estates both real and personal and so died for (lack of) maintenance having nothing left to live on; and he further saith that James Johnson, Michael Wastall, Leonard Aiskell, William Aiskell, Cuthbert Aiskell, Henry Johnson, Thomas Johnson, Thomas Dawson, Matthew Wharton, Robert Wastall, William Ewebank, William Nichilson, Regnold Whitfield, Henry Whitfield, Leonard Whitfield, Christopher Grainger, Thomas Cumpston, Thomas Waller, William Waller, Michael Brunskell, Robert Hunter, George Wastall, William Johnson, William Gills, James Waller, William Waller, and Peter Wardell, all these being tenants within Stainmore sold all or most part of their estates for payment of their fines; and he further saith that many of the tenants of (Brough) Sowerby sold either all or most part of their real and personal estates for payment of the said grievous and excessive fines imposed by the said earls of Cumberland Francis and Henry, as Miles Brunskell, Robert Smith, Richard Smith, and John his son, Richard Wharton, William Collin, Lanclott Waller, Thomas Wilkin, Thomas Jackson, Robert Jackson, John his son, Cuthbert Laidman, Richard Wardell, Cuthbert Key, Robert Waller, Thomas Laidman, and Henry Laidman his son, and Henry Cumpston.' Thomas Laidman of Stainmore also gave evidence on behalf of lady Anne in 1651, and said that he was a tenant at £8. per annum. He was therefore on a large farm, and in a better position to survive the fines and lean years 1622/3 when bad harvests and disease decimated the population, and the number of burials multiplied by four. In Brough parish, which included the Stainmores, and

Brough Sowerby there were 109 burials from March to December 1623, and 45 from January to July 1624.[4] The vicar of Brough, David Heckstetter S.T.B. of Queens College, Oxford, died of the infection. He was a descendant of the mining family which settled in the Crosthwaite area of Cumberland in Elizabethan times.

If we take this evidence from four manors, Mallerstang, Brough, Brough Sowerby and Stainmore it is a fair assumption that the like story could be told of the purely pastoral of the other 14 Clifford manors in Westmorland. There is yet a great deal to be uncovered from this period of Westmorland history. The little revealed in these 1651 depositions points to the strains following the King's Award, and the suffering caused by the bad harvest and diseases of 1623. It is not pleasant to record lady Anne's diary of 10th February 1619: 'Wat. Coniston began to read St. Austin of The City of God to me, and I received a letter from Mr. Davis with another enclosed in it of Ralph Coniston (they had been in lady Margaret's household at Brougham), whereby I perceived things went in Westmorland as I would have them.' This refers to some Clifford tenants at King's Meaburn who were resisting earl Francis' demands. Through two representative tenants John and Richard Dent they were taken before Chancery and lost.[5] All this was taking place at the same time as the Kendal barony tenant-right case referred to in Chapter 5, when the vicars of Kirkby Stephen and Orton were questioned by commission from Star Chamber over a tract supporting tenant-right, that it did not depend on border service.

The 1651 deposition contained two final bits of evidence:

Christopher Pettie of Orton, gentlemen aged 55 said that he was present in London when the final £17,000 was paid to the earl of Dorset's privy gentlemen. The money was taken to London by Mr. Elton and Mr. Guy. Pettie was one of the tellers who counted out the £17,000, and he received his share of £5 as a gratuity to drink.

John Pettie of Sowerby, yeoman aged 55 was in London about 32 years ago, and going to Westminster he met John Atkinson, then servant to earl Francis, who told him to come and see the money to be paid to the earl of Dorset, which had come out of Westmorland. He did so, and saw thirteen porters and their carriages carry it away.

References Chapter 19

(1) The provision of aids for the marriage portion of a son or daughter of the lord. An Epitome of all the Common & Statute Laws of this Nation now in force; by William Sheppard, serjeant at law. London, 1656, p. 706. Aid.
C. & W. trans. N.S. LXXXV, 1985. Medieval Kendal; the first borough charter, John Munby, p. 191 (10). Contribution to aids.
The Popular Movement for Law Reform 1640-1660. Donald Veall. Oxford, 1970. 51 et seq.
Principles of the Law of Real Property, Joshua A. Williams. 24th ed. 1926, 34.

(2) P.R.O. SP/C.21/P.25/1. Anne countess of Pembroke v. Robert Atkinson & others Writs, Interrogatories, and depositions. The first depositions taken at Appleby, 18th January 1650/51; the second taken at the house of John Washington at Docker, Kendal, (?25th) September 1651.
The Chancery writs were dated: 6th December 1650 and 3rd July 1651.

(3) N & B, I. 586.

(4) Par. Register of Brough under Stainmore, ed. Colonel F. Haswell, 1923. C. & W. par. reg. series.

(5) Diary of lady Anne Clifford, V. Sackville-West. 87, 96, 97, 99, 102.
NOTE:
I am advised by Dr. R.T. Spence of Leeds, who has done a great deal of work on the accounts of the later earls of Cumberland both at Skipton, Appleby and Londesborough, that earl Francis did much to temper the severity of the fines levied after the King's Award, among his poorer tenants.
I agree with his point that the evidence of the tenants given in 1650/51 of the suffering of the Mallerstang and Brough under Stainmore tenants after 1617 does not mention the far more severe effect of the bad harvests, and heavy mortality in 1623.
I am grateful for Dr. Spence's observation that the estate accounts give a better view of earl Francis than the tenants. On the other hand the Stainmores and Mallerstang were the poorest parts of the Appleby castle estates, and should be viewed in that light.

Chapter 20

(The north; 1619-1641)

The earl of Dorset received the last payment of the £17,000 on 24th June 1619,[1] and thereafter lady Anne had no further contact with earl Francis or his son Henry. Henry's wife bore several children, but only one daughter survived. Of the several born to lady Anne only two daughters survived, Margaret and Isabella. During the next four years lady Anne spent most of her time in dreary seclusion, while Dorset enjoyed himself at court. Ill health overtook him in 1623, and on the 10th July 1623 he signed lady Anne's jointure deeds.[2] He was in the House of Lords in the early months of 1624 for the debates on the war with Spain, and last appeared there on 24th March. Two days later he made his Will, and on the 26th March he died aged 35.[3] Lady Anne was ill at Knole at the time, and did not attend the funeral. Laud made a typical remark upon the event:

> "March 28 (Anno 1624) Easter Day, Richard Earl of Dorset died, being well and merry in the Parliament House on Wednesday the 24th. Quam nihil est vita hominis? Miserere nostri Dominis. His grandfather, Thomas Earl of Dorset died suddenly at the Council table. His grandfather rose well, and was dead before dinner. His father Robert lay not above two days. And now this man."[4]

According to the Court gossip John Chamberlain he left debts of £60,000.[5] He also left two illegitimate daughters, one of whom died young; the other married a clergyman. Lady Anne gave her a portion, and presented the cleric to a living worth £140 a year.[6] Lady Anne received Bollbrook House and a handsome estate in jointure. As part of that estate had already been set aside by Dorset's father to found the college for aged men and women at East Grinstead it was the subject of litigation for the next forty years.[7] Lady Anne spent the next quiet years between Sussex and London, paying regular visits to Chenies and Woburn. She also settled a pension of £40 a year on each of Dorset's chaplains: Dr. King, later bishop of Chichester, and Dr. Duppa, later bishop of Winchester. In all, previous obligations were decently wound up as she retired into private life.

Francis earl of Cumberland remained nominal head of affairs in three border counties, but Henry his son did most of the work. Henry Clifford and others were made joint lieutenants of Cumberland, Westmorland and Northumberland in 1626.[8] There are a number of letters from Henry Clifford among the State Papers of their time covering the exercising of the trained bands, the poverty of the north, and the unwillingness of many country squires to pay forced loans on the proclamation of the King, and without parliamentary sanction. When in 1627 Wentworth refused to pay his assessment, it was his friend and old schoolfellow Henry Clifford who persuaded him.[9] After a short period of opposition in Parliament culminating in the Petition of Right, Wentworth was converted to the Court party in 1628, and in the same year was created baron Wentworth, President of the Council of the North, and in 1629 Privy Councillor. These promotions occurred after the death of Buckingham. Lord Scrope, now earl of Sunderland was removed for incompetence from the Presidency of the Council of the North, and Sir John (now lord) Savile was removed from all his offices for taking bribes from catholic recusants refusing to attend church. Wentworth's sudden rise at the expense of these two men signalled the beginning of those resentments of the northern gentry who chafed not only at being forced to obey the edicts of the King governing without parliament, but also at the greater efficiency with which the Council of the North conducted its business.

As far as the northern tenants were concerned Wentworth's rule was of great benefit. He restored the effectiveness of the Court at York, which it will be recalled had been empowered by Henry VIII to hear cases between lords and tenants. This had largely lapsed, and many lords had crushed their tenants by taking tenancy cases to London courts, whether Requests, Chancery or Star Chamber. Wentworth stopped that, to the fury of the northern landlords and the London lawyers.[10] Many northern tenants benefited from their cases being heard at York at less expense. It was at York that the three most important tenancy cases were heard, which will be dealt with shortly: Middleton v. Jackson 1630, Popham v. Lancaster 1637, and Monsier v. Ducket 1639. Through his energy the Yorkshire cloth trade was regulated, and commerce flourished. The poor were better cared for. The clothiers disliked the fixing of wages, and the gentry the collecting of poor rates. Wentworth's policy of 'thorough' earned him the ill-will of the wealthy.

During the early days of 1628 Charles, wanting to pack the Lords with supporters, summoned Henry Clifford to the Lords under the title of Baron de Clifford. This raised the wrath of lady Anne, who claimed the barony direct from her father. She petitioned the Lords against it, but Clifford was admitted without prejudice to her claim.[11] The Committee of Privileges presented its report; but it was never debated, as Parliament proceeded to attack Laud and Buckingham, and to debate the Petition of Right, and was eventually dissolved. Clifford continued to sit as baron de Clifford, while lady Anne assumed the titles of baroness Clifford, Westmorland and Vescie.[12]

During 1629 a rumour began to circulate that lady Anne was considering another marriage, this time with Philip Herbert earl of Pembroke and Montgomery. As Lord Chamberlain he was one of the inner circle of Court favourites whom it was dangerous to cross. He was attractive, of courtly manners, not bookish, but keen on horses and dogs. At times he could be coarse, with a constant itch for women, and could be easily provoked to violence at the races or in Parliament. Lady Anne hoped that this marriage would restore her fortunes. From the date of the wedding on 3rd June 1630 she endured him for the next four and a half years, and then left him. She sought the advice of Laud when Pembroke treated her badly, hoping through his mediation to obtain relief from his severity.[13] They finally parted on 18th December 1634; she left Whitehall and went to live at Wilton and Ramsbury, then settled permanently at Baynards Castle by the Thames.[14] Hartley Coleridge made this unctuous comment: 'Had she loved either of her lords she could not have found her genius so potently happy to sustain their unkindness She considered marriage as a necessary evil, a penalty of womanhood, and, expecting no felicity, suffered no disappointment.'[15] During their marriage Pembroke took all her Dorset jointure; there were two sons to the marriage, but neither survived. Pembroke signed her jointure deeds on the 1st June 1635 setting

aside his lands on the Isle of Sheppey for the purpose. On the other hand he exacted £5,000 out of the Craven estates, should they ever come to her, as a portion for her second unmarried daughter Isabella Sackville.[16]

As the levying of Ship Money has already been dealt with in chapter 5 covering the years 1635 to 1639 in Cumberland and Westmorland there is no need to repeat it, except that it increased the distrust growing between the King and his advisors on one side, and the gentry on the other who were predominantly represented in the House of Commons, when that body met. This irritation is well illustrated by the story of Roger Moore of Middleton, near Kirkby Lonsdale.

On the 4th November 1638 Mr. Place, usher of Kirkby Lonsdale, William Smyth junior, and Thomas Layfield of Fellgarth met at Smyth's house for Sunday dinner. Afterwards they retired to the oasthouse for a gossip, and their discussion turned upon conformity to the church. It is interesting that Laudian policy was being discussed in a north-country market town. Smyth informed his friends that he had heard from another source 'that Roger Moore of Middleton having a question propounded to him what he would do if the King should command him to turn Papist, or do a thing contrary to his conscience, he replied that he would rise up against him and kill him.' It seems that Layfield had long borne a grudge against Moore, and this gave him a chance to pay off an old score. He reported the words to the deputy sheriff, and eventually through earl Francis they came to the notice of Windebanke, secretary to the Council.[17] On the 6th December 1638 Henry lord Clifford, acting in his father's name, ordered Moore's arrest, and witnesses were ordered to appear before a judge. On the 13th December Layfield wrote to his brother saying that he had reported Moore out of subjection to his Majesty, and expressed the hope that he would be spared a winter's journey to London. Sir Jacob Astley visited earl Francis at Londesborough on the 6th January 1639, carrying two letters to him from London. One concerned the raising of the trained bands for the Scottish wars, and the other ordered the magistrates to examine Moore. He appeared before Sir Philip Musgrave and Sir George Dalston at Appleby on 16th January 1639 and three facts emerged: in April 1636 Moore had come from the Low Countries, and had said that people might lawfully take up arms against their prince in matters of conscience or religion. When the justices asked him what he would do if the King asked him to change his religion he was silent. But

Thomas Layfield asserted that Moore had said in Middleton that he would rise and kill the King if ordered to turn papist. Moore was described as very rich, a great oppressor, and an indirect dealer, so that no poor man dare speak the truth against him, for fear of an ill turn of him or his sons, 'who are the rudest, most drunken, desperate young men in the whole county.' However, the justices found that the real bone of contention between Moore and Layfield was that there has been some bargains and mortgages between them. By now Layfield began to feel frightened, and wrote to Windebanke through Clifford, saying that as a result of the information he has laid against Moore he is now threatened by him and his sons, not only with a suit in Star Chamber but also with death. Grave preparations for the Scottish wars were now in full swing, and after the justices had examined more witnesses the matter was laid aside till peace had been signed. In March 1640 Sir Phillip Musgrave and Sir Henry Bellingham took final depositions from three people at Orton. In their report to Clifford they said that the witnesses were afraid to say too much, and it seemed useless to follow the matter further; the affair petered out.

The contrast between the brilliance and frivolity of the Court, the ineptitude of Charles' rule in England and Scotland, and the irritation of the northern gentry at Wentworth's more efficient rule in the raising of loans and the training of the militia, especially for the two Bishops' wars in Scotland, gives point to the remark of Wenceslas Hollar the engraver who came to England in 1635. He supported the King in the civil war, but escaped to Antwerp. After his return to England in 1652 he made this observation: 'When he first came into England (which was a serene time of peace) that the people, both poore and rich, did looke cheerfully, but at his returne, he found the countenances of the people all changed, melancholy, spightfull, as if bewitched.'[18]

(1) *The first Scottish war*. By the summer of 1638 Clifford was at Skipton supervising the trained bands in Craven and Westmorland. His inability for the task is best surmised in a letter to him from the earl of Arundel and Surrey dated 31st July 1638. He is sorry that the 'three poore northern shires' are so ill provided for defence. He recommends that the men be fitted with light arms such as they have been accustomed to bear, rather than load them with heavier; and also that archery should be kept alive. He suggests that local blacksmiths be encouraged to make simple firearms, with rests for muskets, and that lead may be had

from Derbyshire, and powder from Hull.[19] Clifford was on excellent terms with the local gentry of Westmorland and Yorkshire but unfitted for military administration. The final explosion between Charles and the Scots occurred in November 1638 when the General Assembly at Edinburgh was dissolved after an eight day debate in which they decreed the end of the Bishops and the Prayer Book which Charles and Laud had tried to force on the kirk. It seems that Clifford had very largely left military matters in Northumberland to others, who in turn had done nothing.[20] He was ordered to Newcastle on the 6th February 1639 in order to accelerate its defence.[21] Two days later Colonel Francis Trafford was placed in command of the troops in Cumberland, Westmorland, and Northumberland.[22] The King reached York on the 30th March,[23] and Clifford was hurriedly sent by way of Westmorland to occupy Carlisle.[24] This he did with some local levies, supplemented with five hundred of Wentworth's Irish troops.[25] On the 16th May war was declared against the Scots, and on the 23rd Sir Ferdinando Fairfax was ordered from Yorkshire to Carlisle to make good Clifford's deficiencies.[26] He marched by way of Knaresborough and Richmond and arrived at Penrith by the 11th June to find that Clifford had provided neither arms, powder, match nor wages, and very little food.[27] Upon sight of the Scots army at Berwick the King's inferior forces had to withdraw, and the King was forced to concede all for which the Scots had rebelled, and terms were agreed in June. This miserable venture was summed up by Sir Ferdinando Fairfax, writing from Penrith to his father Thomas lord Fairfax at Denton on 18th June 1639: They have little news; they exercise the regiment daily; snow fell last Thursday, and there may be more; strong winds have blown down many of their tents. Except for £500 advance money they brought from Ripon with them, which has now been spent, they have had no supplies. If supplies do not arrive before Saturday they must disband. Despite promises of supply they are in a miserable plight, and the next day he will write for money, or seek leave to disband.28

Clifford remained in Carlisle until late July, when to his surprise his command at Carlisle was taken from him, and given to William lord Howard. But he remained loyal in his service to the King, though he complained of ill usage.[29] On the 31st August Clifford was dismissed as one of the joint lieutenants of the three border counties.

Hardly had the King returned to London, than he recalled Wentworth from Ireland to aid and advise him. This gave the Scots every fear that strong measures would be directed at them. Charles was persuaded to call a new Parliament. Both earl Francis and Henry received their summons. Though the King made a few concessions, the opposition refused to grant subsidies until their grievances had been met. The City population was angry, and Pym led the opposition. Though Wentworth tried to infuse life into the Council, the King was in a weak position between two extremes. After a session of twenty-two days Parliament was dissolved, and the King looked for money from the City companies.[30]

(2) If the first Scottish war was ill planned, *the second* was more so. The Scots were prepared, and knew that many English gentry and their people viewed the coming clash with apprehension. It is clear that by 1640 the borders dreaded a Scottish invasion, and disagreed strongly with the King's policy. The first indication of this is seen when the young Philip lord Wharton of Wharton Hall signed the petition of the Yorkshire gentry to the King on 28th May 1640, urging compromise.[31] Charles' reply was that 'it was not lawful for them to meet in this manner upon petitions, and charged them never more to do so; and if they meddled with it any more he would hang them.' The Scots army marched towards the border, and Charles reached York on the 23rd August, to be followed shortly by Wentworth. They found the Yorkshire gentry hostile, and the troops almost mutinous. In spite of Wentworth's attempt to induce some discipline into local forces, he was unable to prevent the Scots from crossing the border and occupying Newcastle. By September they had advanced to Durham, plundered Darlington and demanded £800,000, and the right to occupy the four border counties until the money was paid.[32] In desperation the King summoned a council of peers to meet at York on the 24th of September, at which the majority was hostile to Wentworth. No matter how high the policy of Wentworth, the troops were useless without pay, and the exchequer was empty. Charles was persuaded to summon a Parliament for November. Philip earl of Pembroke, lady Anne's husband, like many more of his class, ventured much for the King, advanced £20,000 and raised a regiment of 600 horse, of which George Sedgewick his secretary was paymaster.[33] Outside private and noble patronage the trained bands were without food and money. Pembroke was one of the five peers who went to London at the beginning of October to get £200,000 from the City companies.[34] Lord Wharton was one of the commission who

treated with the Scots at Ripon. The Scots refused to come near to Wentworth at York, and demanded a subsistence of £25,000 a month for their army. They imprisoned the mayor of Newcastle till an arrears of £1,400 were paid.[35] The English had no alternative but to agree, and the fateful Long Parliament which met on the 3rd November proceeded to arrest and impeach Wentworth, and do the like to Laud in the new Year. While this was proceeding Clifford had his own worries. His old father died at Skipton on the 21st January 1640/41. The Londesborough accounts contain these entries:

Jan. 14th. For opening the vault, and for frankincense, 5s.

Jan. 20th. Doctor Padua, who came to my ould Lord in his sickness, £4.

Jan. 22nd. To the ringers at my Lord's burial, £1.[35]

The impeachment of Wentworth does not concern us here, nor the Act of Attainder. But Henry, now earl of Cumberland, followed the trial, visited him in the Tower, and stood by his side on the scaffold. In July he did not forget archbishop Ussher who had also been on the scaffold, and had lost his estates; he paid him a benevolence of £5.[37] Archbishop Laud was the second victim in the puritan attack. On the 25th June 1641 he resigned the chancellorship of Oxford, and Philip earl of Pembroke was elected in his place. Laud, in the Tower, made this comment: 'The truth is, I suffered so much by the clamour of the Earl of Pembroke, who thought it long, till he had the place, which he had long gaped for.'[38] Eighteen days after his Oxford election, on the 19th July there was a debate in the Lords where lord Mowbray and Maltravers called him a liar, and Pembroke retorted by striking him over the head with his chamberlain's staff, and Maltravers in turn threw an inkstand at him. Both were committed to the Tower for eight days and had to apologise. The King who had long been irritated by Pembroke's vulgarities dismissed him, and Essex became Lord Chamberlain.[39] From this point Pembroke supported the Parliamentary party either from pique, or to save his estates. This change of front had an unforeseen sequence. When on the death of earl Henry in 1643 the northern estates came to lady Anne, they enjoyed Parliamentary protection through Pembroke, though she was a royalist. His secretary George Sedgewick summed up his master thus: he could scarce read or write, being less fond of books than sport. When he paid his first visit to Oxford as Chancellor he was received with great contempt, and LORD, WE ARE VISITED, was found scribbled on some doors. He was very temperate in eating and drinking, but much given to women. He was fond of hunting in the New Forest, and he was an excellent bowler. He always kept 2 or 3 servants who were expert bowlers. And for wagers of up to £500 he would challenge the best, and mostly win. He had an income of over £18,000 a year, but was deeply in debt.[40] He had much to lose if he backed the wrong side.

References Chapter 20.

(1) Diary of Lady Anne Clifford. V. Sackville-West. 104.

(2) Diary of Lady Anne Clifford. Williamson MS. 16.
Lady Anne Clifford. G.C. Williamson. 142.
N & B, I. 299 for Sedgewick's figures of £3,500 income.

(3) Lady Anne Clifford. G.C. Williamson. 143.

(4) Hist. of the Troubles and Tryal of the Most Reverend Father in God, and Blessed Martyr, William Laud, etc. wrote by himself to which is affixed the diary of his whole life. Henry Wharton, London. 1695, 11.

(5) C.S.P. Dom. Jas. I. 1624. CLXII, 212, Apr. 10. John Chamberlain to Dudley Carleton.

(6) Lady Anne Clifford. G.C. Williamson. 144.
Dairy of Lady Anne Clifford. V. Sackville-West, 106 & 110 may have a ref. to the mother of the children, in the footnote.

(7) Lady Anne Clifford, G.C. Williamson. 449.

(8) C.S.P. Dom. Chas. I. 1626, 578, Nov. 6.

(9) D.N.B. Henry Clifford (1591-1643).
Strafford. Earl of Birkenhead. 1938, 78.

(10) Strafford. op.cit. 139.
D.N.B. Sir Thomas Strafford. 1593-1641.

(11) D.N.B. Henry Clifford.
Complete Peerage, III, 569.

(12) Lady Anne Clifford. G.C. Williamson. 484, for history of the barony.
Hothfield MSS. Williamson lists Tullie House, Carlisle, 11 Aug. 1628. Power of Attorney by Anne countess of Pembroke to Mr. Christopher Marsh concerning her claims. There were others: 27 Jan. 1629 and in 1632.
C.S.P. Dom. Chas. I. 1628. CII, 95, April. Claim of Anne countess of Pembroke.

(13) William Laud. W.H. Hutton. 3rd edn. 1905, 56.
D.N.B. Philip Herbert earl of Pembroke. 1584-1650.
Strafford. Earl of Birkenhead, 130.
Brief Lives, John Aubrey. Penguin Edn. 1972, 304.
In recent years a memorial to Philip 4th earl of Pembroke has been erected in Salisbury Cathedral.

(14) Diary of Lady Anne Clifford, Williamson MS. 23. She lived in Baynards Castle for 15 years.
Lady Anne Clifford. Williamson. 177.

(15) From, Some Craven Worthies, W.A. Shuffrey, Leeds, 1903. 6.
Diary of Lady Anne Clifford. Williamson MS. 21.

(16) Diary of Lady Anne Clifford. Williamson MS. 23.
Hothfield MSS. Williamson list. 1646. Power of Attorney for receiving £5,000 out of lands in Skipton in favour of Isabella the daughter of the countess of Pembroke.

(17) The following are the refs. in C.S.P. Dom. Chas. I. 1638 onwards to this episode:
1638. CCCCIV, 151. 6 Dec. Henry lord Clifford to Sec. Windebanke.
1638. CCCCIV, 167. 13 Dec. Thomas Layfield to his bro. Edward.
1638/9. CCCCIX, 311/12. 11th Jan. Henry lord Clifford to Windebanke.
1638/9. CCCCIX, 321. 16th Jan. Sir Philip Musgrave & Sir George Dalston to Henry lord Clifford.
1638/9. CCCCX, 360. 24th Jan. The information of Thomas Layfield of Felgarth.
1639/40, CCCCXLVIII, 585. 25th Mar. Sir Philip Musgrave and Sir Henry Bellingham have examined John Bayliff, John Moore, William Ward, Richard Foster & William Baylye of Middleton, who were present when the words were spoken.

(18) Brief Lives, John Aubrey, op.cit. 324. Wenceslas Hollar.

(19) Hist. of Craven T.D. Whitaker. 299. 31 July 1638. Earl of Arundel & Surrey to Henry lord Clifford.
Hist. MSS. Comm. Rep. XII, App. II, Coke MSS 190, 3 Aug. 1638. Clifford to Sir John Coke on raising troops in Cumberland & Westmorland.

C.S.P. Dom. Chas. I. 1638. CCCXCVII, 584. 3 Aug. Memo of Earl of Arundel & Surrey on raising men and arms for the defence of Carlisle and 3 border counties. Recommends archery for lack of suitable firearms.

C.S.P. Dom. Chas. I. 1638. CCCXCIX, 38, 30th Sept. Council to lords lieut. of three border counties. The King has placed bullet, powder & match in Newcastle & Hull, where they may be purchased.

(20) C.S.P. Dom. Chas. I. 1639, CCCCIX, 310. 11th Jan. Sir Jacob Astley to Clifford.

(21) C.S.P. Dom. Chas. I. 1639, CCCCXII, 430.

(22) C.S.P. Dom. Chas. I. 1639, CCCCXIV, 544.

(23) Drake's Eboracum (1735 edn.). 135.
Fairfax Corresp. G.W. Johnson, 1848, I. 345.

(24) D.N.B. Henry lord Clifford.

(25) C.S.P. Dom. Chas. I. 1639. CCCCXVI, 11, 12. 3 April. Sec. Coke to Sec. Windebanke.
Hist. of Skipton. W.H. Dawson, 45.

(26) Fairfax Corresp. I. 366.

(27) Fairfax Corresp. I. 363, 366, 369.
Hist. of Skipton, Dawson. 45.

(28) Fairfax Corresp. I. 372.

(29) C.S.P. Dom. Chas. I. 1639. CCCCXXVI, 409. 21 July. Henry de Vic to Windebanke.
D.N.B. Henry lord Clifford.
Strafford. Birkenhead. 215, 6.

(30) London during the Great Rebellion. A Memoir of Sir Abraham Raynardson, Kt., Lord Mayor, 1646, dismissed 1649, re-elected 1660. C.M. Clode, London 1892. 4.

(31) The Good Lord Wharton. Bryan Dale, 36.

(32) C.S.P. Dom. Chas. I. 1640, CCCCLXVIII, 127. Note of Sec. Vane.

(33) N. & B, I. 296. from memoirs of George Sedgewick.
The original MS was among the Lowther records, Le-Fleming MS.D.: prob. now P.R.O. Carlisle.

(34) London during the Great Rebellion, C.M. Clode op.cit. 6/7.

(35) Fairfax Corresp. II. 22.
C.S.P. Dom. Chas. I. 1640. CCCCLXIX, 157.
C.S.P. Dom. Chas. I. 1640. CCCCLXIV, 604. For most of this period Clifford seems to have been in Westmorland, whither he had been sent to raise troops on 19 Aug. 1640.
V.C.H. Cumberland. II. 287. 3 Oct. 1640. He ordered the mustering of troops at Carlisle.
Hist. of Craven. Whitaker. 412. 8 Oct. Clifford paid George Dent for dressing carbines and petterills at Appleby castle.
C.S.P. Dom. Chas. I. 1640. CCCCLXIX, 157. 10th Oct. News that Westmorland has agreed to arm itself against the Scots at its own charge.
C. & W. trans. N.S. XXXVI, 144. Letters from the garrison at Carlisle. 1640-41.
C.S.P. Dom. Chas. I. 1640. CCCCLXX, 197. 26 Nov. Dr. Thomas Read to his bro. Robert: Cumberland & Westmorland, notwithstanding the late order for defence, are by this time in the Scots possession.

(36) Hist. of Craven. Whitaker. 277.
Complete Peerage. III. 569.
Diary of Lady Anne Clifford. Williamson MS. 24.
Hist. of Craven, Whitaker. 356. A description of coffin.
Lady Anne Clifford. G.C. Williamson. 49, 179/80.
Hist. of Skipton. W.H. Dawson. 43.

(37) Hist. of Craven, Whitaker. 279.

(38) Hist. of the Troubles & Trials of...William Laud, and his diary. op.cit. (1695)...61, 181.

(39) D.N.B. Philip Herbert earl of Pembroke. 1584-1650.
Lady Anne Clifford. G.C. Williamson. 170.
Hist. MSS. Comm. Rep. X., App. 6. Braye, 143, for the original report.
A Selection from the Harl. Misc. London 1793, 159.

(40) N & B, I. 297.
Le-Fleming MS, D. Lowther records. Now in C.R.O. Carlisle. George Sedgewick's figures do not tally, thus I have taken the first figure.

Chapter 21

The Civil Wars and the North (1642-1649).

The year 1642 marks the point of parting between the King and his shifting policies, and Parliament which was straining to extend its powers to control the policy of the King in the field of foreign affairs, the militia, the church, and raising taxes without parliamentary sanction. Strafford had been executed, and Laud was confined to the Tower. The early months of 1642 were occupied by manoeuvres between the King and Parliament to gain possession of the military forces of the kingdom and to place themselves legally in the right before the nation. In September 1641 the King had agreed in Scotland to the abolition of bishops, and to the distribution of church lands among the aristocracy.[1] He returned to London in November, and after his attempt to impeach the five members in early January he left Whitehall on the 10th January for Hampton Court to avoid the triumphal return of the five to Westminster from the Tower. On the 2nd March, Parliament failing any agreement with the King proceeded to try to assume control over the militia, and nominated lords lieutenant for the English counties. Hoping to obtain his support they named Henry earl of Cumberland for Westmorland.[2] On the 15th March the King sent a message to Parliament declaring his intention to remove to York, urging them not to be slow in pacifying Ireland, and warning his subjects not to accept ordinances for the militia without his warrant. He arrived at York on the 18th March.[3] Parliament retorted by declaring itself the supreme judicature of the realm.[4]

Two sets of documents brought to the notice of ordinary people in the counties what was at stake. In July 1641 Parliament ordered that the Protestation Oath should be taken by all men over the age of 18. The oath promised to defend the Reformed Protestant Religion expressed in the Doctrine of the Church of England against all Popery and Popish innovations, to defend the King, the power and privileges of Parliament, the Liberties of the Subjects, and to oppose by all means those who conspired against these rights. The Protestation was promulgated by the magistrates at Appleby on the 3rd March 1641/2, and conveyed to parish officers to be read on or after 6th March after evening prayer in the parish church. Non-attendance at church and refusal to sign, was regarded as proof of recusancy. At least one parish misunderstood the purpose of the swearing in, that it was to obtain a list of able men for army service. Three points may be made. It was to identify the number of papists. Few parishes had any except Brough under Stainmore which had 20 under the patronage of the Blenkinsops of Helbeck. It was the first time since the Pilgrimage of Grace that popular concern could be expressed without prosecution by the Crown. More important, and for the first time, it conveyed to the smallest fellside farmer the political and religious points the puritan party wished him to follow. Though the majority of Cumberland and Westmorland manors were dominated by royalist gentry, there must have been many places where dissenting opinion was given an airing by this declaration. In Westmorland the lead was given by Kendal men, some of whose families had been involved in the Kendal barony tenant-right case of 1620-25.[5]

The second series of documents followed the arrival of the King at York on 19th March 1641/2.[6] The Humble Petition of the gentry and commons of Yorkshire urging the King to return to Parliament was adopted at the York assizes on the 5th of April, and presented to him on the 22nd.[7] Henry earl of Cumberland with 35 other peers left London in May to join the King, and on the 3rd of June between 80,000 and 100,000 Yorkshire freeholders assembled on Heyworth Moor to hear his reasons for raising a guard. Sir Thomas Fairfax led a counter move, and from the pommel of his horse he presented a petition for the King's removal from the county, and a compromise with Parliament.[8] The Lancashire petition in the same vein was presented on the 6th of June.[9] Earl Henry and his fellow peers signed their engagement to support the King, without desiring a war with Parliament on the 13th and 15th June.[10] On the 22nd June earl Henry promised to raise a troop of 50 horse for three months, at a rate of 2/6d. a day, and the defence of York was put in hand.[11] At the request of the Yorkshire gentlemen he was made colonel of the regiment raised by them, and the King appointed him commander-in-chief of Yorkshire, including York, with Sir Thomas Glemham as his lieutenant.

The Humble Petition of the gentry, ministers and others of Cumberland and Westmorland was presented to the King on the 5th July, and a rival one from the gentry, ministers and commonalty of the barony of Kendal was presented to the House of Commons on the 6th August. The latter appears to have been organised by James Moore, a minister, Jeremias Banes and others of the parish of Kirkby Lonsdale, a small puritan clique who were working to intrude puritan lecturers into south Westmorland. Banes appears to have organised the petition to instal two preachers Henry Masy of Kendal and William Ellison to lecture in Kirkby Lonsdale church on market days. They were appointed by the House of Commons on the 6th August; the vicar Mr. Buchanan was ordered to accommodate them in the church. On the same day "Master Bayns" presented 'The Humble Petition of the Gentry, Ministers and Commonalty of the Barony of Kendal' to the House. It was largely religious in tone, praising the labours of the House of Commons in preserving the Protestant religion, against the subtle innovators who laboured to suppress many worthy and powerful preachers. There was also a plea on behalf of distressed Protestants in Ireland. There was the usual flourish embracing the defence of his Majesty, the privileges of Parliament, and the liberties of the subject. Bayns was called before the House when the Speaker thanked him for the loyal message of the barony, promising that the House would have a special care of them.[12] It is stretching the point to claim that this Petition represented more than a minority opinion in South Westmorland; it was the first move of a small faction to get a toe in the church door. Two years later Henry Masy was elected vicar of Kendal by the master and fellows of Trinity College, and he became the leading Calvinist minister in south Westmorland.[13] Though the Westmorland Petition was limited in origin, it had a wider sequence. When the civil war broke out, on the 18th November 1642 Parliament issued a declaration ordering the inhabitants of the northern counties to raise horse and foot against the Popish and Malignant Party in the northern parts and the City of York.[14]

In Yorkshire earl Henry's declaration of loyalty to the King was issued on the 20th August, and appointed to be read in churches.[15] The earl was ill and unfit for military command. He was besieged in York from October; but the defences were inadequate, and, but for the timely arrival of the earl of Newcastle on the 30th November the city would have fallen to Parliament. On his arrival earl Henry resigned his command, and he was replaced by Sir John Mallory of Studley castle near Ripon. He proceeded at once to Skipton castle, and from December 1642 for the next three years it became an effective garrison, harassing the small dissident groups in the dales, and guarding the Aire gap in the Pennines.[16] There are many references during the next three years of soldiers being buried in Craven, both from these forays as well as from the siege of the castle.[17] By the autumn of 1642 Philip lord Wharton, aged 30, had sided with Parliament and commanded a regiment at the battle of Edgehill on 23rd October. That and three other regiments were routed; and though Parliament fawned on him for supporting their cause, he was not a military man, and until the end of the Commonwealth confined himself to committee work in Parliament. Though it has been claimed that his northern tenants fought under him at Edgehill, that is probably not true. His regiment was largely drawn from his southern estates.[18]

There is no need to follow the course of the Civil War, but until the fall of York after the battle of Marston Moor on the 1st July 1644 the castles of Carlisle, Appleby and Skipton were in the hands of the royalists. Sir John Lowther used Brougham castle for the storage of grain, and Appleby was of little military consequence. Sir John Lowther and Sir Philip Musgrave effectively controlled the two counties, though Kendal seems to have been strongly in favour of Parliament. In June 1643 the borough council ordered a watch to be kept at nights, and all strangers were to be scrutinised. And on the 9th June it ordered that no-one was to leave the borough without leave on pain of 40s.[19]

Henry earl of Cumberland died in one of the prebendal houses in York on 11th December 1643 after a sickness of six days. He was only 52 years old. Despite the war the funeral was arranged in some style. Coats of Arms were painted; the minster bell was rung at double fees for a nobleman; the body was embalmed, and the death chamber was painted black. The oak coffin was lined with lead and covered with leather.[20] Ferdinando lord Fairfax issued a pass for the body to go to Skipton in a special chariot. The journey cost £28, and £15 was spent on wine for the mourners, and the soldiers of the garrison received £10, and £3 was given to the poor at the gate.[21] Thus unexpectedly lady Anne became mistress of all the old Clifford estates in Westmorland and Craven, though it was seven years before she was able to come north to occupy them. Earl Henry bequeathed all the later Clifford lands of Bolton Priory, Barden Tower, and the remaining Cumberland lands to his only daughter Elizabeth countess of Cork.

The year 1644 saw much fighting in Yorkshire and Craven. Both before and after the siege of York in the summer twelve soldiers were buried at Skipton. After Marston Moor on the 2nd July and the surrender of York on the 16th July there were more. Some of these were rebels, but probably the majority were of Prince Rupert's army as it retreated through Craven.[22] After Marston Moor Sir Thomas Fairfax ordered his men to spare unnecessary carnage among the deluded countrymen, adding that 'an honest man that overlooked the dead reported later that he thought there were two gentlemen to one ordinary soldier that was slain.'[23] There were two consequences of the royalist defeat in Yorkshire. Parliamentary forces entered Westmorland and plundered Sir Philip Musgrave's estate to the value of £3,000.[24] and sequestered his estate at Edenhall and Hartley. On the approach of the Scots commander David Lesley from Newcastle with 4,000 horse and foot, Sir Philip and Sir Thomas Glemham with other gentlemen took refuge in Carlisle which was invested from October 1644 until 25 June 1645. The garrison was reduced to eating horseflesh (without salt or bread), hempseed, dogs and rats. They capitulated on honourable terms on the 25th June, and the city was taken over by the Scots.[25] Sir Philip went and joined the King at Cardiff; he was taken prisoner at Rowtenmore, was eventually released and conducted some of the King's negotiations with the Scots. Carlisle was not relinquished by the Scots until December 1646. In July 1645 Parliament ordered the blocking up of the castles of Skipton, Sandall and Bolton. After the fall of Sandall and Sherborne in October some 600 royalists took refuge in Skipton, as the rest of Yorkshire was in Parliament's hands. With all hope gone, Skipton surrendered on the 21st December 1645.[26]

The articles of the surrender of Skipton contained an important clause that 'all the evidences and writings whatever belonging to the Countess of Pembroke or the Countess of Cork in any of the evidence houses of this Castle, shall not be looked into by any, until both the Countesses be acquainted therewith, and for that end that two months time for notice to be given them, and the Kayes to be delivered to Col. Thornton, who is intrusted with them in the meantime.' It is probable that the earl of Pembroke had obtained this provision through his support of Parliament. As soon as news of the surrender reached London lady Anne, with the support of her husband, sent a warrant north to the celebrated antiquary Roger Dodsworth of Hutton Grange near Preston, and to his pupil Charles Fairfax of Menston to proceed with all speed to catalogue the Skipton evidences. They prepared to leave Menston on the morning of the 4th February 1646, when Fairfax received a note from the agent of the countess of Cork asking him to do the same for her. This he could not do. Off they set, and as Dodsworth and Fairfax rode towards Skipton they met lady Cork's agent on the same quest. They entered the castle together, and though Fairfax had every respect for lady Cork and would have allowed him to see the evidences, Dodsworth flatly refused. He would not allow him to enter the muniment room in the round tower when he examined the documents. The agent appealed to the Parliamentary commander in charge of the castle, but Dodsworth was so firm that he carried the day, and the agent reported his reverse to lady Cork the same day. This was the beginning of Dodsworth's great work of research into the Clifford records, which was condensed into the three great volumes commissioned by lady Anne.

For the three years that Skipton castle was under the command of Sir John Mallory the Craven rents were collected under his supervision.[27] The Westmorland rents were collected under the supervision of Sir John Lowther.[28] The old receiver of the Westmorland rents under earl Henry had been Edmund Guy an alderman of Appleby.[29]

The Scots army entered Cumberland in September 1644, and the border counties were occupied until December 1646. Their arrival was welcomed by the puritan faction in the Kendal area, who expected under Parliament's agreement with the Scots to establish a Gospel magistracy and ministry in the borders. In October 1644 the House of Commons ordered Sir Thomas Widdrington to introduce well-affected ministers in Cumberland and Westmorland. On the 23rd April 1645 it ordered a preaching minister to be appointed for Appleby at the large salary of £150 a year out of the revenue of the Dean and chapter of Carlisle. There is no proof that a man was appointed.[30]

In August 1645 Parliament passed an ordinance intending that each parish should be organised on the lines of the Scots kirk, with a minister and lay elders, with parishes grouped in classes, and classes into synods. A letter was sent by Speaker Lenthall on the 22nd September to the mayor of Kendal and others supportive of Parliament there to take the advice of godly ministers with a view to convening a meeting to establing the presbyterian system in Westmorland.[31] The letter was not received in Kendal till 3rd February 1645/6. A committee was formed of which the composition is instructive. The core was a number of aldermen of the borough, *Richard Prissoe*, mayor; *Allan Gilpin*, mayor 1646/7; *Thomas Sandes*, mayor 1647/8, and founder of the Blue-Coat school; *John Archer*, mayor 1648/9, and a candidate for Parliament in 1656; *Thomas Sleddall* and *Rowland Dawson*, local names; and *Gervase Benson*, who had been captured by the royalists and imprisoned in Skipton castle until exchanged; mayor 1644; notary for the proving of wills in the deanery of Kendal in the diocese of Chester; was also responsible for paying the Westmorland assessment for the Scots army in 1644; by 1645 he was colonel of militia for Parliament in Westmorland; in 1646 he was made a justice of the peace, as well as being an alderman and chamberlain of the borough of Kendal. Benson was a very busy man in the county, and through Henry Masy vicar of Kendal kept lord Wharton fully informed on the political and religious events in the county. The other two members of the committee informed him on the state of affairs in north Westmorland; *Richard Branthwaite* of Ravenstonedale was lord Wharton's steward, and made a lieutenant-colonel of militia. *Edmund Guy* alderman of Appleby, had until 1643 been receiver and agent to Henry earl of Cumberland. Having had the control of the Westmorland Clifford estates he was able to inform on all the supporters of the King in the upper Eden valley. He became a member of the county committee and receiver for sequestrations in the upper Eden valley. He was replaced as receiver for lady Anne's rents by Mr. Edmund Pollard in September 1645. But as he is one of the aldermen trustees named by lady Anne in 1656 in the trust for the repairs to Appleby church, the school and moot hall he had not lost his credit in the town, nor with her. By 1654 he had been replaced as county receiver by Edmund Branthwaite of Newbiggin near Ravenstonedale, who operated as receiver for all sequestrations in Cumberland and Westmorland until 1660. In the recommendations of March 1645/6 Guy

was suggested as an elder of Appleby church.[32] On the whole it is probable that Guy was one of those men prepared to serve the new order in order to keep his grip on local affairs.

It was this committee in Kendal which was used by Parliament to try to introduce the new order. Their report to Speaker Lenthall of 10th March 1645/6 listed every Westmorland parish, noting particularly those clergy who had not subscribed the Covenant, those who had served with the King, were disaffected or were pluralists. By 1646 the following parishes had their clergy removed by this committee; Hevershaw 1644, Kirkby Lonsdale 1646, Kirkby Thore 1646, Crosby Garrett 1644, and Brougham 1646.[33] Westmorland was divided into two Classes, but the system never got going for two reasons. Though the presbyterian system was the law of the land from 1645 to 1660 too many clergy in Westmorland were indifferent, and a number were royalist. In particular north Westmorland was owned largely by the royalist Lady Anne, whose husband the earl of Pembroke had thrown in his lot with Parliament, and by this means her estates enjoyed political protection through her husband. The second and more fatal cause of failure was the presence of the Scots army in Cumberland and Westmorland demanding constant supplies on credit from September 1644 till December 1646. The Scots were the old border enemy, and any hope that the Scots system of religion would take root in Westmorland was dashed by their presence. On the 20th February 1644/5 Parliament passed an ordinance to raise £21,000 monthly from the six northern counties for the payment of the Scots army.[34] By April 1645 Cumberland and Westmorland were seething with discontent, and on the 16th The Committee for both Kingdoms wrote to the committee at Newcastle that the Westmorland people were to be warned not to irritate the Scots. At the same time they wrote to the Scots that they must try to pacify Westmorland people. The Scots replied to the local commanders in the two counties to keep their own people in order.[35] Lesley also added this remark:

'The distempers of the people in Westmorland have been so notorious we need say nothing of them, but those in Carlisle have by sundry papers, some of which we have seen, endeavoured to stir up the humours of the discontended people in Westmorland, and we have taken in to consideration their grounds and reasons, as they pretend, for the commotion amongst them, to which answer is returned, that they ought to give them satisfaction if they be our friends, but if this should not content them, we trust that you and all honest men will join with us to suppress such intolerable insolences.'

The occupation was not without grim humour. On the 29th May 1645, when the Scots were preparing to move into Yorkshire Lesley wrote to Richard Barwise of Ilekirk demanding draught horses and provisions for the move. The old soldier must have enjoyed the next remark: 'You will therefore consider, if we be not timely provided, that the burden may be the longer and heavier on the county, and we cannot be to blame therefore.'[36] Barwise sent a growling reply. He promised to find food for four to five days by the next weekend, at the rate of 18,000 lbs. a day, and 75 draught cattle. This he promised to transport from Penrith to Appleby, all to be provided on credit. Both Cumberland and Westmorland sent bitter complaints to Parliament on the 8th June, and their justice was admitted.[37] The total amounts of money, draught-horses and provisions which the border counties had to raise for two years must have been a heavy burden. On the 12th July the Committee of both Houses ordered a commission under the Great Seal to deal with the Scots commissioners over the unpaid debts. The meeting with the Scots commissioners had not taken place by 5th September. Parliament was crippled for want of money, and it must have been some time before some or all of the debts were paid.[38] When the castles of Skipton, Appleby and Carlisle had been taken the squires of the two counties who had sided with the Kings were fined by Major-General Lambert and had to compound for their estates.[39] During the following months Westmorland came under the general supervision of the Lancashire forces of Parliament; but this was fitful. In August 1647 the godly committee sitting in Kendal were rounded up by local dissidents and held prisoners for two days, and with the presbyterian vicar of Kendal subjected to much abuse. The new order was not popular.[40]

The national course of the second Civil War need not detain us, except to note the principal events which affected Westmorland, and the tenants.

On the 3rd January 1647/8 the Commons resolved that they would no longer treat with the King, and the Lords agreed on the 15th. On the 26th December 1647 the Scots commissioners had signed a secret treaty with the King, that they would send an army to restore him to the throne in return for agreeing to the establishment of presbyterianism for three years, and the crushing of all sects. Towards the end of 1647 an attempt was made to release the King from imprisonment, and Sir

Marmaduke Langdale received a commission from the Prince of Wales as Colonel-General of the five northern counties. He appointed Sir Philip Musgrave as commander-in-chief of Cumberland and Westmorland, and governor of Carlisle. Sir Philip captured Carlisle by surprise in April 1648, and Sir Marmaduke proceeded to raise a force of 800 horse and 5,000 foot from the two counties, with the help of the squires who had recently compounded for their estates.[41] On the 13th May there was a skirmish on Kendal Heath between these forces and those of Parliament, when the Royalists were defeated.[42] By 16th June Major-General John Lambert arrived with 3,000 Parliamentary forces in Penrith, and Sir Marmaduke and his supports retreated into Carlisle. The Scots army of 20,000 men under the duke of Hamilton crossed the border on the 10th July, and Sir Philip Musgrave handed over Carlisle to him. On the arrival of the Scots Lambert retreated through the dales to Ripon, leaving a token force at Appleby.[43] While Sir Philip Musgrave retook Appleby, the duke of Hamilton made for Kendal, and was in Lancaster by the 10th August. Meanwhile Cromwell and Lambert and their forces passed through Skipton on the 14th August, and two days later held a council of war at Hodder Bridge. At the running battle of Preston on the 17th to the 19th August the royalist Scots forces were defeated, and many Scots seem to have fled by way of Skipton, for in the following days a number were buried there.[44] The Scots surrendered Carlisle to Cromwell on the 1st October and Carlisle and Appleby were strongly garrisoned by him for many years to come. Appleby castle surrendered on the 16th October,[45] and on the same day the committee at York ordered the slighting of Skipton castle. The old part with flat lead roofs which could mount canon was disroofed, and the battlements thrown down. The roof timbers were sold.

On the 27th November the Committee for both Kingdoms in London received a petition from the commanders of their forces in Westmorland that the county was so wasted, and their forces in such want they must have speedy relief. The committee replied that no harm was to be done to Appleby castle, nor spoiling of the countryside when they departed. Only sufficient force was to be left to prevent the castle being surprised. The King's trial opened in Westminster Hall on the 20th January 1648/9, and on the 30th he was executed. On the following day Sir Philip Musgrave escaped to the continent. Cromwell's hand fell heavily on Cumberland and Westmorland; heavy taxes were levied for the maintenance of his garrisons; leading royalists like Sir Philip Musgrave lost their estates, while others had to pay heavy fines to the Committee for Compounding to redeem their delinquency. Any lesser men from the dales who had followed their squires in the King's forces were also caught and had to compound. From the upper Eden valley the following had served for the King, and were fined;

Robert Atkinson of Kirkby Stephen	£45.
William Spencely of Kirkby Stephen	£6.
John Petty of Soulby	£6.17.6.
John Fothergill of Ravenstonedale	£17.10.0.[46]

It was the day of the informer and new men looking for pickings.

References Chapter 21.

(1) The Fairfax Correspondence. G.W. Johnson. London. 1848. II, 260.

(2) D.N.B. Henry earl of Cumberland.
Complete Peerage. London 1913, III, 569.
Fairfax Correspondence. II, 355.

(3) Fairfax Correspondence. II, 360.
Drake's Eboracum. 142.

(4) Fairfax Correspondence. II, 361.

(5) Westmorland Protestation Returns 1641-2. M.A. Faraday. C & W Trans. Tract Ser. XVII, 1971. passim. The value of these returns is that they give the complete male population over 18 in the Bottom of Westmorland.

(6) Drake's Eboracum. 142. 18th March.
Fairfax Correspondence. II, 389. 19th March.

(7) Fairfax Correspondence. II, 396.

(8) Fairfax Correspondence. II, 406/7.

(9) Drake's Eboracum. 153/4.

(10) Drake's Eboracum. 154/5.
D.N.B. Henry earl of Cumberland.
Hist. of Great Rebellion and Civil Wars. Clarendon. 1819 ed. Oxford. Vol. I. pt. II, p. 879.
Copy in Cambs Univ. Lib. (Peterborough. K.5.10.)

(11) C.S.P. Chas. I. 1642. CCCCXCI, 344. List of lords and others willing to contribute.

(12) Copies in Dean and Chapter Lib. York, and Cambs. Univ. Lib.
C & W trans. O.S. V, 159.
Older Nonconformity in Kendal. F. Nicholson & E. Axon. Kendal 1915, 4.

(13) Ejected of 1662 in Cumberland and Westmorland. B. Nighingale. 1911, II, 877/8.

(14) Older Nonconformity in Kendal, op.cit. 6.

(15) Drake's Eboracum. 160.
Hist. of Skipton, Dawson. 120.

(16) Drake's Eboracum. 161.
Hist. of Rebellion etc. Clarendon, op.cit. IV, Book. VIII, 668.

(17) Hist. of Skipton. Dawson. 123, 126, 130.
Hist of Craven. Whitaker. 354.

(18) Saw-Pit Wharton. G.F. Trevallyn Jones. Sydney U.P. 1967, 62/3.
Hist. of Crosby Garrett, J. Walker-Nicholson. Kirkby Stephen 1914. 58.

(19) Kendal. Local Chronology, being notes of principal events pub. in Kendal papers. 1865. 109.

(20) Hist. of Craven. Witaker. 279, 356.
Hist. of Skipton. Dawson. 47. 167.
Lady Anne Clifford. Williamson. 180.
The countess of Cumberland died two months later and was buried in the Minster. Whitaker. 269.
Drake's Eboracum 505, dates her death on the 4th Feb. 1643/4. Whitaker 269 the 14th. Her table tomb vanished in the great minster fire. Drake gives the place and inscription.
M.S. of James Toori in the Dean & Chapter Lib. York.

(21) Hist. of Skipton. Dawson. 328, 332 for his charitable bequests.
Hist. of Craven, Whitaker. 279.

(22) Hist. of Skipton. Dawson. 130/31.

(23) The Lord General. A life of Thomas Fairfax. M.A. Gibb. London. 1938, 79.

(24) Hist. of Westmorland. R.S. Ferguson. 212.

(25) N & B, II, 234-6.
V.C.H. Cumberland. II, 289.
Prelates and People of the Lake Counties. C.M.L. Bouch. 262-7.

(26) Hist. of Craven. Whitaker. 341 says 22nd Dec.
Hist. of Skipton. Dawson. 134/5 says 21 Dec.

(27) Hist. of Skipton. Dawson. 135.
Bolton Priory MSS, Williamson list. 30 Mar. 1645. Warrant to Sir John Mallory to collect arrears of Bolton rents for the Skipton garrison.
Hist. of Craven. Whitaker. 341.

(28) Lady Anne Clifford. Williamson. 190 & plate.
Appleby MSS. Williamson list. 21 June 1644. Lady Anne to Sir John Lowther regarding care of her estates as she cannot yet come north.

(29) For Edmund Guy;
Northern History. no. 5. 1970. 34. County Committees & Local Government 1642-1660. C.S. Phillips. 43. Edmund Guy combined his county committee work with the treasureship of sequestrations in the Bottom of Westmorland; and had been receiver and agent to the earl of Cumberland.
C & W trans. Tract series. no. XVII. 1971. Faraday op.cit. p. 3. Edmund Guy signed the Protestation return 3 May 1641, as alderman of Appleby. He may have been related to Edward Guy, vicar, or Edward Guy an alderman.

(30) Older nonconformity in Kendal. Nicholson & Axon. 8/9.

(31) Ejected of 1662. B. Nighingale. I. 108.
Older nonconformity in Kendal op.cit. 9/10.

(32) Older nonconformity in Kendal op.cit. 10/14.
Ejected of 1662 in Cumberland & Westmorland. op.cit. passim for Edward Guy.
Lady Anne Clifford. Williamson. 190/1 with plate.
N & B, I, 327.

(33) Walker Revised. A.G. Matthews. 1948. 367-369.

(34) C.S.P. 1644/5. DVI, 315 (51) Ordinance of Parl.

(35) C.S.P. 1645. DVII, 411/12, 413, 431/2. (The county committees of Cumberland & Westmorland warn Parliament of the disturbed state of Westmorland.)

(36) C.S.P. 1645. DVII, 537/8, 542. Alexander earl of Leven to Richard Barwise.

(37) C.S.P. 1645. DVII, 574, 8th June. Two papers; the complaints of the committees of Cumberland and Westmorland. The Scots demanded £3,800 of Cumberland in Nov. 1644, and proceed to demand the same in Dec. without Parliamentary sanction.

(36) C.S.P. 1645. DX, 16-17. 13 July. Instruction to commissioners going to Scotland (8) That a commission be granted under the Great Seal as in 1641 to adjust accounts and claims in the 4 northern counties and Yorkshire.
C.S.P. 1645. DX, 144/5. 5th Sept. Papers intended to be given to the Scots commissioners for adjusting accounts in the northern counties.

(39) Hist. of Westmorland. R.S. Ferguson. 215.

(40) Older Nonconformity in Kendal. Nicholson & Axon. 17/18.

(41) Hist. of Westmorland. R.S. Ferguson. 213.

(42) Kendal. Local Chronology. Extracts from local newspapers. 1865. XVIII.

(43) C.S.P. 1648. DXVI, 130. Newsletter from Penrith signed R.S.
Hist. of Cumberland. R.S. Ferguson. 262.
Some Craven Worthies. W.A. Shuffrey. 1903. p. 31. John Lambert.
Hist. of Skipton. Dawson. 137.

(44) Hist. of Skipton. Dawson. 138.

(45) N & B, I. 310.
V.C.H. Cumberland. 290.
Lady Anne Clifford. Williamson. 425/6.
Later Records of North Westmorland. J.F. Curwen. 60.
(For the slighting of Skipton castle:)
Lady Anne Clifford, Williamson. 419.
Hist. of Skipton. Dawson. 139. Hist. of Craven, Whitaker, 339.

(46) C.S.P. Committee for the Advance of Money. II, 652, 834, 835. III, 1381. 1389 (3) & also 1121, 1435, 1444.
Hist. of Westmorland. Ferguson. 215. This list is selective and inaccurate. Dorothy Cardenas, and John Duncomb belong to Westminster, not Westmorland.

C.S.P. Committee for Compounding. 99, April 13. 1648. The list for the Bottom of Westmorland. p. 176. 22 Feb. 1650. The Barony of Kendal.
Same. 203. list of 25 April 1650.
Same. 520/1. list of Dec. 1651 for those of the Upper Eden Valley. It is possible from the lists of the Committee for Compounding and from N & B. I. 163 to discern only some of the men who followed the royalists in the Civil wars.

Chapter 22

The development of fines in border tenant-right.

In order to follow the development of the law and practice in the levying of fines on customary and improved tenant-right lands, the evidence in this chapter is submitted in the following sequence:

(A) The development of 17th century law on fines on improved rents.

(B) Compositions between lords and tenants converting arbitrary fines into fines certain, by
  (a) a Parliamentarian.
  (b) a Royalist.
  (c) a Recusant.

(C) The influence of Chancery in three cases, which while leaving ancient rents untouched, assessed fines on an improved valuation bringing them within the protection of fines on improved rents.

Tenant-right cases.

We return to the development of tenant-right in Cumberland Westmorland.[1] On his accession to the English throne, King James had declared that border service was obsolete, and that tenant-right which went with it was abolished. He stated that the tenants had no right of inheritance, and that they were henceforth tenants-at-will. The Kendal barony case which came before Star Chamber 1620-25 was on this issue, after Prince Charles had forced his tenants to compound to re-establish their tenant-right. After the death of King James in 1625 judges confirmed tenant-right of succession, and added that border service was not mentioned on their admittance to their tenements, but was part of that duty laid on all to obey the call of the lord warden of the Western Marches to defend the border in time of need.[2] Tenant-right was 'absolutely ratified, confirmed and for ever settled', though border service was abolished by personal decree of the King.

Though I have said that after 1625 tenants were no longer forced to repurchase their tenant-right of succession, there is some evidence that confirmation of tenant-right was mentioned in later settlements between lords and tenants when arbitrary fines were abandoned, and fines certain purchased by composition. It may have been formality on the part of lawyers to establish the title of tenant-right lands which would now bear fines certain.

As we have seen tenant-right lands were liable to two kinds of rent, ancient rents on customary lands and improved rents on improvements taken out of the wastes and forests. The latter were often by copy of court roll. The law books are a minefield of case-law covering the issue of fines. Not only are there conflicting verdicts in different courts,[3] but the reports are not always clear whether they refer to improved rents, as the land could be let in the open market, or ancient rents of assize which were fixed time out of mind.

(A) *Improved rents.* In the seventeenth century those customary and copyhold estates which paid improved rents fell under three cases:

(1) *Willowes Case.* 1608 (Mich.6 Jas.I.) It was held that a fine though uncertain must be reasonable. It was held that a fine of £5.6.8. on a cottage and one acre of copyhold land at Fenditton near Cambridge rackrented at £2.13.0. per annum was excessive. Thus a fine of two years rent was excessive.[4]

(2) *In Dow & others v. Golding*, 1630 (Hil.5 Chas.I.rot.125) the lord demanded 2½ years value of copyhold land on a rack rent for a fine upon surrender and admittance, and for non-payment to enter for a forfeiture. All the court conceived that one year and a half rent is high enough, and that the defendant assessing 2½ years is unreasonable. Therefore the plaintiff might well refuse payment thereof, and consequently the entry of the defendant for a forfeiture not justifiable.[5]

(3) *Morgan v. Scudamore*, 1677, was a case wherein a bill was brought by copyholders of a manor against the defendant lord of the manor, desiring to be admitted to their tenements, they paying a reasonable fine. The court decreed two years value of their respective tenements to be a reasonable fine, and that they be admitted accordingly, they paying their fine. This rule was followed till this century.[6] Thus in those manors where fines were

paid on improved rents, the general and dropping fines developed in this way: Willowes case 1608, one year's improved rent; Dow v. Golding 1630, one and a half year's improved rent; and in Morgan v. Scudamore 1677 two years. But in the majority of Cumberland and Westmorland manors where fines were arbitrary on ancient rents there was no such protection, except in those cases to be mentioned.

(B) *Ancient rents*. Two courses were open to lords owning manors where fines were arbitrary on ancient rents. They could either come to an agreement with the tenants, and in return for composition money grant fines certain; or they could demand an excessively high arbitrary fine, which would force the tenant to sue their lord in Chancery, with all the attendant expense.

(a) *Local agreements*. Richard Barwise of Hildkirk (Ilekirk) Cumberland came to prominence during the Civil War; in 1643 he joined General David Lesley in his attack on the Royalist garrison in Carlisle, having joined the Parliamentary cause. He was burgess for the city of Carlisle in 1640 and 1641. He acted for Parliament during the Scots occupation of the borders 1644 to 1646, and had the invidious task of raising money and provisions for the Scots. Mercifully he died in 1648/9 and was buried in Westward church, thus being spared sequestration and arrest at the Restoration.[7] He came to an agreement with two groups of his tenants. In 1633 his tenants in his moiety of the manor of Deerham, Cumberland compounded with him (sum unknown) to obtain a fourpenny fine certain.[8] On the 26th June 1635 Richard Barwise lord of the manor of Blencogo, Cumberland granted to his 18 tenants for 40 years ancient rent that they shall hold to them and their heirs their customary estates of inheritance, paying the yearly ancient rent, and two years ancient rent (and no other fine,) after the change of lord by death, and change of tenant by death or alienation, doing suit of court as before. Every alienation to be entered at the next court, paying for the entry 12d. and no more. He granted to them also all trees, woods and underwoods on their respective tenements; with power to get freestone and limestone in their several grounds, or in any waste ground within the townfields or commons, for their own use, but not to give or sell the same to any other. It was a moderate agreement. It is probable that 20 years ancient rent bought the fines certain, and 20 bought the rights to timber and stone.[9]

(b) Sir Philip Musgrave of Edenhall and Hartley castle was one of three landlords who held the manors of the upper Eden valley.

The earl of Cumberland of Appleby Castle.	Sir Philip Musgrave of Edenhall & Hartley	Lord Wharton Wharton Hall.
Murton,	Hartley,	Wharton,
Appleby,	Kirkby Stephen (part),	Nateby,
Brough,	Little Musgrave,	Ravenstonedale,
The Stainmores,	Great Musgrave,	Kirkby Stephen (part).
Brough Sowerby,	Crosby Garrett,	
Winton,	Soulby,	
Kirkby Stephen (part),		
Mallerstang.		

Sir Philip Musgrave of Hartley castle was an ardent royalist, and took his part in the Civil War against Parliament. He fled abroad on the execution of the King, and returned to his homeland in 1660. He was M.P. for Westmorland in Charles II's long parliament. At the Restoration he was made governor of Carlisle, and came down (to use his own words) as 'State physician to purge the corporations of Carlisle, Kendal and Appleby'.[10] He died in 1678.

In 1635 the tenants of Sir Philip in the manor of Soulby obtained the confirmation of their tenures without settling their fines. The purchase price is not given.[11] In 1636 the tenants of his six manors filed a bill in Chancery against Sir Philip, and in return for a composition of twenty years ancient rent obtained fines certain of eight years ancient rent, both for general and dropping fines.[12] The sums paid by the tenants of each manor were as follows:

Hartley	£403.10.0.
Kirkby Stephen	58. 3.4.
Soulby	313.10.0.
Crosby Garrett	397. 1.8.
	(The two Musgraves are not mentioned)

But this does not tell the whole story; there were a number of tenants who either refused or were too poor to pay. When Sir Philip's estates were sequestered after his flight abroad, the county commissioners for sequestrations held courts for the four manors just mentioned. That of Crosby Garrett was held on the 21st June 1650, and the names of all the tenants were recorded on the roll. There were four free tenants, 38 who had compounded for fixed fines and were called Indenture Tenants, 18 who remained customary tenants paying arbitrary fines, and one cottager.[13] The same division between those tenants who paid or did not can be seen in the other rolls. Widows enjoyed a third of their husbands' estates. Richard Richardson, one of the Crosby Indenture Tenants rose to be a colonel in the Parliamentary forces in the Commonwealth . Another indenture tenant was Will Grainger who had a son William in 1645. The son went to Sedbergh School, later to St. John's college, Cambridge, and finally became a vicar of Waberthwaite, Cumberland in 1677.[14]

During the early days after the execution of the King there arose the question of the disposition of sequestered royalist estates. In the Kirkby Stephen district there was great competition to rent Sir Philip Musgrave's lands. Mr. Edmund Branthwaite, one of that family from Carlingill, Orton was made receiver for all sequestrations in Cumberland and Westmorland. When Richard Crackenthorpe of Little Strickland, one of the commissioners for sequestrations came to view Sir Philip Musgrave's estates he found that they had already been taken at a moderate rent by Major Arthur Skaife of Winton Hall. When Crackenthorpe proceeded to try to re-let the lands 'by the candle' and at a better price, Skaife interposed with the threat that whoever took the land must have a longer sword than he, and thereby win it. Thomas Buster the major's trumpeter threatened with an oath that if anyone grazed horses on the land, he would run his sword through their guts.[15] This was not all; as the Blenkinsops of Brough were Catholics and delinquent, they were liable to sequestration. In 1651 they let the Helbeck estate to William Mawson of Penrith for six years. Eventually they were bought out by Major Arthur Skaife of Winton.[16] Finally the Musgrave estates in the Eden valley were sold off by the Committee for Compounding in London as follows:

(a) on the 24th May 1650 Lady Musgrave was granted a fifth of her husband's income to be paid by the Treasurer for Sequestrations in Westmorland.[17]

(b) The manor of Soulby. On the 14th June Richard Burton of Dufton clerk claimed that in 1639 Sir Philip Musgrave had mortgaged the manor to him for £1,000 and had not redeemed it. Burton was allowed to retain it with arrears of rent.

(c) The remaining Musgrave estates were sold through their London lawyer Thomas Wharton. He acted for a number of Royalists whose estates had been confiscated, in Cumberland, Westmorland, Lancashire, Yorkshire and Somerset enabling another member of the family to buy them back, in this case Richard Musgrave, Sir Philip's son. The legal process was not by the modern method of bargain and sale, but as Blackstone put it: 'That bargains and sales shall not endure to pass a freehold, unless the same be by Indenture, and enrolled within six months in one of the Courts in Westminster Hall, or with the Custos Rotulorum of the county'. In this case an Indenture was drawn up dated 10th October 1653, and enrolled in Chancery the 10th November following, between the following three parties: (1) Sir Philip Musgrave and his son Richard in consideration of the sum of 20s. paid them by (2) Edward Huish of the Inner Temple and John Pomeroy of London, gent conveyed to Huish and Pomeroy and to their heirs etc in fee simple barring all entails and remainders the following estates; the castle and manor of Hartley, the manors of Crosby Garrett, Great Musgrave, Little Musgrave, with all the messuages, tenements and hereditaments therein, and also in ffletholme, Langrigg and Kirkby Stephen, all within Westmorland; and in Cumberland, and on the same terms, the manors of Edenhall, Dolphonby and Bramary, with the messuages etc. therein, and in Penrith and the Forest of Inglewood. Following this (3) Thomas Wharton of Grays Inn gent and Richard Edmondson of London tailor were empowered before the end of the following Michaelmas term to prosecute a writ in Chancery returnable in the Common Pleas to sue for the recovery of the said lands from Huish and Pomeroy "according to the usual course of Common Recoveries for assurance in lands in such cases used". It was agreed by the three parties that these recoveries and assurances were to assure the use of all these manors and lands etc. to Richard Musgrave and his heirs for ever.[18] Huish and Pomeroy were the intermediaries; and in due time Richard Musgrave bought back the estates from Wharton as he could afford to do so.

(c) The third type of case dealing with ancient rents and fines comes from the recusant family of Middleton of Leighton within the

Duchy of Lancaster. They owned the three manors of Yealand Redman, Yealand Conyers and Yealand Storrs. In Easter term 1642 the tenants of the three manors laid a complaint in the Duchy Court of Lancaster against George Middleton alleging that Thomas his father had levied a general fine of 7 years ancient rent, and very heavy particular (dropping) fines, namely ten, sixteen and even thirty years ancient rent. The complaint is confirmed in an admittance of April 1624 in which he exacted a fine of £3. In respect of a tenement rented at 3s.4d, that is a fine of 18 years rent. The tenants in their plea claimed that the general fine on the death of the lord was arbitrary, sometimes 2 years, sometimes 3 and 4 years ancient rent. But this last was considered grievous because of the poverty of the country and barrenness of the land. Widows also enjoyed their widows rights without fine, but were liable for heriots. The tenants made the particular complaint that when Thomas Middleton levied a 7d. general fine the tenants paid, because they were too poor to defend themselves. On the death of a tenant he would demand ten, sixteen and even thirty years ancient rent, and from some of the poorer tenants he extorted the whole of their tenements. He would also enter into the inheritance of an heir under age, and take the profits for himself, and when the heir came of age he would demand an unreasonable fine as if he had not enjoyed such profits. If the heir were a daughter he would sometimes seize half and sometimes the two parts of the tenement, and keep the same to himself and his heirs for ever, pretending this to be in satisfaction for his particular fine. He would never admit an heir to his inheritance unless he agreed to such unreasonable provisions, conditions and covenants as would quite overthrow the ancient customary estate of inheritance. They also accused him of overstocking his parks with deer so that they fed on the crops and grass of his tenants. They also claimed that he had enclosed certain commons for which the tenants paid a quit rent to the King, and stopped up certain wells, and rights of way to church and market. Since the death of Thomas Middleton his son George has demanded general fines of 12 and 14 years ancient rent, being twice as much as his father extorted. He has also demanded an heriot of every tenant dying seized of his tenement, whether widow or not. He had demanded particular (dropping) fines of sixteen, twenty or thirty years rent, and threatened forfeiture if they refuse to pay. He also threatened to treat all heirs and heiresses under age as his father treated them. Even allowing for

over-statement it is a grim picture. The complaint was referred to the arbitration of Alexander Rigby of Preston esq., William West of Middleton (in Lancs.) esq., Ralph Baines of Meweth (in Yorks) esq., and George Pigot of Preston, gentleman. If they did not agree, then Rigby and West had to make the final award, which was dated 18th September 1658. All actions between the parties had to be withdrawn. George Middleton was awarded certain monies due from Thomas Hobkin. The tenants had their ancient tenant-rights confirmed, they paying their ancient rents and services as before. Their claim to arbitrary fines of not more than four years ancient rent was rejected. They were awarded fines certain, both for general and dropping fines of eight years ancient rent. The general fine on the death of the lord was to be paid within one year; the particular fine within three months of the change of tenant by death or alienation. The award went on to regulate boons, heriots, timber for housebote, ploughbots, wainbote, cartbote, and hedgebote. Rules for obtaining stone for building and repairs, and regulations for turves, bracken and pasture were included.

There was one additional award which the tenants did not dispute. They had paid to the lord every ten years a running fine, or 'Town Tack', of double the annual rent. They were also bound to use the lord's mill as customary.[19]

A great deal of heat has been generated by writers on the subject of fines, and the writer of the article from which these details were taken states that an arbitrary fine of eight years ancient rent was excessive at that date. This is questionable. The problem was how to relate fines based on ancient rents to the annual rent of a farm let on the open market. At that date eight years ancient seems to approximate to one year's improved rent on the open market. It will be remembered that the county committee for sequestrations in Westmorland levied an 8d. fine on ancient rents in manors sequestered from royalists. When lady Anne Clifford came north in 1649 to claim her estates in Westmorland and Craven she demanded an 8d. fine.[20]

(C) *Three Chancery Awards.* The second device used by three lords of manors was to claim so high an arbitrary fine that the tenants as a whole were forced to take their lords to Chancery and seek relief there. Both sides had to agree to accept the award of the court.

Midleton v. Jackson. 1639-30.[21]

(This case also concerns the Middletons of Leighton, who were allied by marriage to the Duckets of Grayrigg, the Bellinghams of Levens, the Musgraves of Hartley and Edenhall, the Riggs of Strickland, and the Hebblethwaites of Dent.) The law reports put it thus:

'A moderate Year's Value, a reasonable Fine in Case of Tenant-Right.'

The Plaintiffs and Defendants were to produce Precedents for Fines, in Cases of Tenant-Right, in what Manner they had been assessed formerly by this Court; the Defendant now offering to give the Plaintiffs a moderate Year's Value for a Fine; this Court in Case of Tenant-Right conceiving the said Offer to be fair and reasonable, decreed the Defendants to pay the Plaintiffs for the present, one whole year's value of their lands for a Fine, and as the land riseth or falleth upon every Alienation or Death of the Tenant, or Death of the Lord, a moderate Year's Value; and the Defendants to give notice of every Alienation of the Lord's Court; and the Fine now assessed is not to be taken as a Fine certain; and the Master of his Court to set the said Fine.

The said Master assessed the defendants to pay for a Fine to the plaintiff for every Acre of Land, according to the usual Measure in those parts, which in a Tenant-Right they shall hold of the Plaintiff's Manor, the sum of 7s., except it be a Land called Moss Land, which is rateth at 12s. the Acre, which the Defendant submitted unto, which this Court decreed accordingly.

Popham v. Lancaster. 1636-37.[22]

'Chancery decrees a moderate Fine certain between the Lord and his Tenant'

The Defendants being Tenants of the Manor of Newby in the County of Westmorland held of the Plaintiff, complain that the Steward of the said Manor sets too high a Rate on their Lands and Tenements, and insists, that their Fines ought to be assessed according to the ancient Rent after such Proportion as had been used, as the Lord and Tenants could agree, and submit to this honourable Court for their Fines.

This Court finding there hath been a Variation of the Fines, so as the same were not certain, and upon Perusal of Precedents by the Defendants produced, and especially the Case between Middleton and Jackson, 5 Car. I, before-mentioned, decreed, that an improved Year's Value in a moderate Way shall be given and accepted from the Tenant to the Lord for a Fine.

Notes: (1) These two cases do not in any way alter the paying of ancient rents and services, but substitute an improved year's value for a fine, as the land riseth or falleth on every alienation or death of a tenant. By this means it appears to fall under the protection of Willowes case mentioned at the beginning of this chapter, which covered fines on improved rents.

(2) The Popham mentioned as plaintiff was John Popham of Littlecote, esq, in the county of Wilts. He was the grandson of Sir John Popham, lord chief justice; and John Aubrey describes the grandson as a great waster.[23] How he came to hold the manor of Newbystones in the parish of Morland at this time is a mystery.

(3) The reporter of this case has misread the names of the defendants. It is not Lancaster, but Lowther. They were Sir John Lowther, John Lowther esq, Richard Rigg, and Richard Crackenthropp.[24]

(4) These two cases give the clue to the system of recording rents in tenant-right manors which developed at a later date. The stewards recorded (a) the ancient rent on a particular tenement, (b) the improved rents on improvements, (c) hens and boons, and items covered by quit rents, and (d) the rent of the land at current valuation for the purpose of these two cases and others which followed the rule.

Both Middleton v. Jackson, and Popham v. Lancaster were heard at York under the firm rule of Strafford, who compelled northern lords to have their cases heard there instead of in London.

Monsier v. Ducket[25] 1635/6 (11 Chas.I.)

This third Chancery case was also heard at York. Though it preceded Popham v. Lancaster, and because it did not add to that case and Middleton v. Jackson, it was not reported in later law books. As in the previous case the reporter has mistaken the tenants; their names are recoverable from the documents. Monsier should read Moser. They were Roger Moser, Henry Warde, Issabell Robertson widow, Edward Rowlandson, John Becke, Marie Tarne, Henry Jobson and Richard Newby, representative tenants of the manors of Grayrigg, Lambrigg, and Docker; and their lord was Anthony Ducket esq, of Grayrigg. In 1636 the tenants obtained a decree at York changing their fines to one year's moderate value both for general and special (dropping) fines. Widows were to pay the general fine, but no fine on their admission but only the best beast. When Anthony was succeeded by his son James in 1661, the son refused to accept the Decree on the ground that he came in by entail, and not by descent. The tenants took him to court in 1662 and won. Again, in 1670 when James was succeeded by his son Anthony the story was repeated; the tenants obtained the decree that they should pay for a fine one

clear value (i.e. improved value) that the tenement would let for, above the lord's rent and
other reprises. It is not without force that one
of the tenants was Captain Henry Ward of
Sunnybank, Grayrigg, who was converted to
Quakerism in 1652, and became one of the
leading Quakers in south Westmorland. It was
at his house that George Whithead of Sunbiggin
near Orton was convinced.

References Chapter 22

(1) See Chapter 5.

(2) N & B, I, 56-59.

(3) A treatise on the Law of Copyholds and Customary Tenures of Land, C.I. Elton & H.J.H. Mackay,
     2nd. ed. 1898, (1) Hobart v. Hammond, 4 Rep. 27. b.; Jackman v. Hoddesdon, Cro. Eliz. 351.
     A Treatise on the Law of Copyholds etc. J. Scriven & A. Brown. 7th ed. 1896., 182, 198. Willowes
     case. These works are used in finding two cases quoted below; and in Morgan v. Scudamore, Elton
     & Mackay are more informative.

(4) English Law Reports, K.B. vol.77. (1907 ed.) (from the 13th Part of Reps. of Sir Edward Coke,
     kt.) p. 1413. *Willowes case*. Mich. 6 Jac. I. In Common Pleas. The lords of the manor of Fenditton
     were Thomas Willowes & Richard Willowes, and the case was Richard Stallon v. Thomas Brayde.
     Stallon an attorney accused Brayde of entering and breaking Stallon's cottage and one acre of land
     at Fenditton, Cambs. which was held by Stallon of the Willowes by copy of court roll in fee
     simple. The court resolved sec.(2) that a fine though uncertain and arbitrary, must be reasonable;
     and if unreasonable, a refusal to pay is justified. Sect. (4) A fine of £5.6.8. was considered
     unreasonable on a rack rent of £2.13.0. Brayde appears to have been the lessee or agent of the
     Willowes.

(5) Reports of Sir George Croke, revised by Sir Harbottle Grimston. 1683, Vol. III, p. 196.
     (C.U.Lib.J.14.65.)
     Dow & others v. Golding. 1640.

(6) English Law Reports vol. 21, Chancery (1902 ed.) p. 638. *Morgan v. Scudamore* 29 Car. 2. f. 658
     (1677-78). The plaintiffs were tenants of a manor by copy for 99 years, yielding a rent and paying
     a heriot. The lords upon expiry of every estate ought to renew upon reasonable fines, which estates
     by custom of the manor descent from ancestor to heir. The tenants claimed that the lord ought to
     renew upon two years' value.
     The lord insisted that the fines were at the will of the lord, as the tenants could agree with him,
     and they were arbitrary. The lord had demanded 10 to 12 years for a fine which was extravagant.
     The Court declared that the Will of the Lord ought to be limited, and the plaintiffs to pay two
     years' value and the plaintiffs to renew within one year. Minors or tenants beyond the seas to
     renew within one year of attaining the age of 21 or return from beyond the seas.

(7) Hist. of Cumberland. Ferguson. 257.
     C.S.P. Chas. I. 1645. DVII, 537/8. 29 May. Alexander earl of Leven to Richard Barwise.
     C.S.P.Chas. I. 1645. DVII, 542. 30 May. Barwise to earl of Leven.
     N & B, II, 583. The burgesses for Carlisle, for Barwick read Barwise.
     N & B, II, 143. His monument.

(8) N & B, II, 113.

(9) N & B, II, 189.

(10) Hist. of Cumberland. Ferguson, 265.
     D.N.B. Sir Philip Musgrave. 1607-1678.

(11) Original Deed dated 30 May 1636 in the Hartley chest of the Hartley trustees at Kirkby Stephen.
     In 1950 there was a 19th C. copy by Capt. T. Grimshaw of Soulby in the Soulby vicarage papers.

(12) Hist. of Crosby Garrett, J.W. Nicholson. p. 26 dates the deed 18 May 1636 and p. 31.

(13) P.R.O. S.P.23/258. Court Roll of Crosby Garrett, and those of Hartley, Brough, Thornthwaite, Kirkby
     Stephen, Little and Great Musgrave sent to London 5 June 1952 to Committee for Compounding.
     C.S.P. Committee for Compounding 1652. GCCLVIII, p. 585 (55 & 55i) 5 June. Letter of Roger
     Bateman, Gervase Benson and John Archer the Kendal Committee, to the Committee for Compounding
     in London, enclosing the Court Rolls.

(14) Ejected of 1662 in Cumberland & Westmorland. op. cit. 852.
     Hist. of Crosby Garrett. Nicholson, op. cit. 58.

(15) C.S.P. Committee for Compounding. 195. 7 April 1650, five papers.

(16) Hist. of Westmorland. Revd. John Hodgson, 1820. p. 162.

Hodgson's account of the disposal of Helbeck may be wrong. According to the minutes of the Committee for Compounding (S.P. Committee for Compounding, 3024) March 1651, Thomas Blenkinsop of Helbeck let his lands 1651 for 6 years to Wm. Mawson of Penrith.

(17) C.S.P. Committee for Compounding. 24 May 1650. 2308.
Ejected of 1662 in Cumberland & Westmorland. 1154.

(18) MSS of the late Capt. R.P. Hewetson of Stobars Hall, Kirkby Stephen, in the Bird MSS. Now C.R.O. Kendal. WDX/595.
Commentaries on the Laws of England. Wm. Blackstone. 1770. II, 338, (13)(14).

(19) C & W Trans. N.S. IX, 1909. 147. The Customary tenant-right of the manors of Yealand. J. Rawlinson Ford. A 'town term' was also paid in the manor of Dent. See: The Sedbergh Historian, vol. 2 p. 37. The Dent Survey of 1602, by Richard Hoyle.

(20) N & B. I, 301.

(21) English Reports. 1 Chan. Rep. 33, p. 499. Middleton v. Jackson.
Hil. 5 Car. I. fol. 353, 397. (1629-30)

(22) English Reports. 1 Chan. Rep. 96, p. 518. Popham v. Lancaster.
Trin. 12 Car. I. fol. 477 (1636/7)

(23) Brief Lives. John Aubrey op. cit. under Sir John Popham, 408.

(24) P.R.O. London. C2 Chas. I. 68/12. The writs, depositions & award.

(25) Transactions of the High Court of Chancery both by practice & precedent.
W. Tothill, London. 1671, p. 164.
Also the same, ed. by R.O. Holborne, London 1820, p. 100. There is a discrepancy between the date of two cases reported by Tothill and the present English Reports. Popham v. Larcesse (sic) Trin. 13. Car. I. and Monsier v. Ducket. Mich. 14 Car. I. Tothill adds after the three cases, 'These after a decree at York'. Tothill adds Fox v. Huddleston 4. Jac. Li. B. fo. 204, a year's value in tenant-right.
See also N & B, I. 113.
P.R.O. C2. Chas. I. 41/53.
Note:
For an explanation of how tenant-right cases heard at York were cases in Chancery see: The Tudor Constitution; Documents & Commentary. G.R. Elton. C.U.P. 1960. 197/8.

In dating law cases by law terms I have used: Handbook of dates for students of English History. C.R. Cheney. Royal Historical Soc. Guides and handbooks. No. 4. 1978.

Chapter 23

The countess of Pembroke and her tenants (1).

King Charles was executed in January 1649. In the same month lady Anne prepared to leave Baynards Castle by the Thames, to assume control of her northern estates which she inherited in 1644 and had not seen. With Parliament in dire straits for money and combing the country for revenue by fines and sequestrations, it was imperative that she should go north. She was short of money and had to borrow. Apart from any income assured by her husband, her Dorset jointure had been taken by Pembroke whom she saw for the last time on 3rd June 1649.[1] On the 10th July Roger Dodsworth the antiquary came to see her, and shewed her the copies of the Clifford evidences he had already gathered in the north, and in the Tower.[2] The next day she left London for ever, and arrived in Skipton on the 18th. She lodged in the town, as the castle had been slighted by order of Parliament, and was half wrecked. She spent ten days interviewing those officers who had managed to administer the estate during the troubles. On the 29th she went to see Barden Tower which, though earl Henry had willed it to his daughter the countess of Cork, Lady Anne promptly claimed, and held for the rest of her life. She found that the Craven tenants had been forced to pay some years' rents to the Skipton garrison. Because of this the Yorkshire commissioners for sequestrations jumped on the tenants and distrained their cattle by way of fines. In a letter, probably from Skipton, of 27 May 1650 a correspondent wrote:

> 'The sequestrators came on Thursday last, and they and their soldiers lay here till Monday. I never saw so great distraction in hous and towne in my life; little rest taken by any but children neither night nor day; the soldiers came into the house to carry Doctor prisoner to London, because he would not be bound to pay £300 in two daies, and threatened to sequester him too; which they had done, if he had not his discharge to shew out of Goldsmith's Hall. All the tenants are so frightened, that they will keep theire rents in their hands to loose their owne cattle when they are (dis)trained...'[3]

On the 7th August lady Anne left Skipton, travelling by way of Kirkby Lonsdale, arriving at Appleby on the 9th, which was her only habitable house. On the 15th she rode to see the ruins of Brough and Pendragon Castles. On the 18th she rode to Brougham Castle, which she had not seen since her mother died there over 30 years before. It was damp and rat-ridden since its use as a grain store. She found the nearby Whinfell Park plundered of timber and broken down. In all, the estate bore the scars of long neglect. She spent the winter of 1649-50 at Appleby.

Her first step was to summon her tenants in Craven and Westmorland to their respective manor courts. The second was to make an accurate survey of all her lands, to contest encroachments, and to ride all her manor boundaries. The third was to examine all the alienations which had been made by earls Francis and Henry which might have contravened the limitations of the Award of 1617. Everything, past and present, had to pass her scrutiny and that of her lawyers. As a result of Roger Dodsworth's investigations all the major Clifford charters were written into three great books, which were in the hands of her lawyers by December 1650.[4] Years of adversity in the south, and deprived of what she believed to be her rightful inheritance, drove her to try to restore her estates to an ideal Elizabethan grandeur they had never known before. This was at a time when unemployment and poverty were high, when the new Parliamentary men in the county were riding high. They were the minor gentry, major Arthur Skaife of Winton, Colonel Richard Richardson of Crosby Garrett, and their followers who saw service at the battle of Preston, the siege of Carlisle, and the battle of Dunbar on 3rd September 1650. Skaife, Richardson and John Waller of Winton saw service before the battle of Preston. Thereafter they formed the nucleus of military rule and local government with the county committee in north Westmorland, and were bitterly opposed to lady Anne.

While she was in the middle of these preparations she received the unexpected news of the death of her husband at Whitehall on the 23rd January 1650. He was a councillor of state, whose tacit support of the new order was much valued. As far as the north was concerned his position on the Council of State gave lady Anne immunity from sequestration. As in life so to the grave he was followed by the scribblers who wrote to the underworld to expect him: "He's come from England. His name was Pembroke, one of our chief champions. For damning, stinking, swearing, and cursing, all the inhabitants of Hell can hardly equal him."[5] On his death she received her two jointure incomes which brought in about £3,400 a year, of which £1,800 came from the Dorset estate. Pembroke died £55,000 in debt, all of which was paid off in four years.[6] Thus at a stroke lady Anne became a person of wealth, no longer dependant on her northern rents.

When reviewing the policy followed by lady Anne in bringing her estates into order, it is necessary to remember the world which raged around her. Carlisle was heavily garrisoned by Cromwell; and it is probable that Appleby had a token garrison. England had been declared a free commonwealth on the 29th May 1649. On the 1st March 1649/50 the House of Commons passed a bill to establish committee to govern the four northern counties and to examine all the clergy, and establish a gospel ministry. The Committee was headed by lord Wharton, Edward lord Howard, Sir Henry Vane senior, Sir Arthur Haslerigg and others. Among the Cumberland commissioners were Thomas Lamplugh, John Stoddart, Robert Hutton, Cuthbert Studholme, Thomas Craister, Thomas Cholmley, Edward Winter (appointed receiver for sequestrations in the four counties), John Crosthwaite, William Mawson, Thomas Langhorne (whom John Musgrave the pamphleteer describes as a petty shopkeeper),[7] and Thomas Garth (though not on the commission) was appointed solicitor and agent for sequestrations in Cumberland.[8] In Westmorland Gervase Benson, John Archer, Roger Bateman, Edward Briggs, Richard Branthwaite, and Richard Crackenthorpe represented the two parts of the county.[9] Apart from reports which were sent by the Westmorland committee led by Gervase Benson to London, lord Wharton kept himself fully informed of events in the county through Richard Branthwaite his steward, and the recently appointed vicar of Kirkby Stephen, Francis Higginson. These names have been given to point to the fact that in making her future dispositions lady Anne was guided by Philip lord Wharton, who was better acquainted with the district than she.

In the autumn of 1649 lady Anne ordered her steward John Thwaites to hold courts in all her Westmorland manors. He had been steward for the past twenty years, for earls Francis and Henry, and took office some time after the King's Award of 1617. Despite the fact that the Award had granted the tenants fines certain of seven years' ancient rent, both for general and dropping fines, lady Anne ordered Thwaites 'not to do anything which might seem to confirm or assent to the late King James his award.'[10] Only admissions and alienations were inrolled at the first courts; the general fine was not then demanded. But in some way Thwaites intimated that he disagreed with lady Anne's refusal to accept the award on which the tenants rested their case for fines certain, though she had received the estate by virtue of its provisions. She called for the court rolls, and dismissed Thwaites. She decided to demand an 8d. fine, both general and dropping, on the ground that the award had been imposed on the tenants, and she had never given her sanction. The tenants had paid their composition, Dorset had received the money, and lady Anne proceeded to act as if no money had been paid, nor assurance given by earls Francis and Henry. The fatal loophole was this: the Award stated that if lady Anne and Dorset her husband had agreed to it, they were to confirm the same in legal instruments to be devised by their counsel, confirming the tenant-right estates of their Westmorland tenants. Lady Anne had refused to accept the Award, and the tenants lost the written assurance. That was her case, and she refused to alter her opinion; their fines were arbitrary.

Her dispositions were as follows: The Skipton estates were placed under the supervision of Richard Clapham of Skipton Castle aged 33/4; the Westmorland estates under the supervision of Thomas Garth of Newhall in the parish of Warcop aged 39/40. He was up till then the solicitor and agent to the Cumberland Committee for sequestrations. Christopher Marsh who had worked in the Dorset household since 1613 was appointed to administer her Dorset and Pembroke jointure estates, and to pay her London lawyers during her many law cases. Her first two courts were held in September 1649, and May 1650. She gave strict orders to Thwaites who kept the first and Garth who kept the second in Westmorland that neither was to do anything which might assent to the King's Award. Commissioners were appointed to treat with the tenants in both estates.

The Craven commissioners were: Sir Henry Cholmondely, Mr. Charles Fairfax the antiquary, Mr. Christopher Clapham her lawyer (distinct from Richard Clapham of Skipton Castle), Mr. Peter Jennings, and Mr. Robert Hiche. The Westmorland ones were Sir John Lowther, Mr. Hilton, Colonel Robert Briggs, Mr. Crackenthorpe, Mr. Clapham her lawyer, and a Mr. Teasdale. It is possible that both Briggs and Crackenthorpe were members of the Westmorland County Committee. Richard Branthwaite (lord Wharton's steward) of Ravenstonedale kept her audits for her. It is probable that the Craven commissioners were similarly balanced. It can be seen that lord Wharton's influence was paramount. As the Westmorland committee had levied an 8d. fine on sequestered estates, lady Anne's position was strong if her claim to arbitrary fines were secure. The Craven commissioners started work with the tenants in March 1649/50.12 She appointed her Westmorland commissioners on the 6th February 1649/50.13 The Committee for Public Revenue claimed the Skipton rents on the 8th February,14 and the situation seemed to have been so uncertain that lady Anne left Appleby and arrived at Skipton on the 14th February. During the coming weeks she often sat with her commissioners, and most of the tenants settled their general and dropping fines with her, but not without protest. In a letter to Marsh dated 25th March 1650 she mentioned that the Westmorland tenants were refractory.15 The Craven tenants paid £150 to the Committee for Sequestrations at York on the 27th May, 1650.[16]

The situation in Westmorland was stormy in the Brough and Kirkby Stephen area. As far back as 1645 when Mr. Edmund Pollard of Lancashire collected the Westmorland rents

for lady Anne he wrote to Marsh (who had acted for her ever since she was countess of Dorset) that: 'by violence the tenants of Kirkby Stephen stand obstinately out, and will not pay any (rents) but by compulsion; every other graveship and bailiffwick have expressed their willingness and paid something.'[17] So the present difficulties were not new. When in February lady Anne appointed her Westmorland commissioners they gave notice to the tenants to attend their courts in May. The tenants counter-attacked by presenting a petition on the 25th February 1649/50 to the national Committee for Indemnity.[18] It was from the tenants of lady Anne countess of Pembroke etc...in the manors of Stainmore, Brough Sowerby, Winton, Kirkby Stephen, Mallerstang, Burrells, Scattergate, Bongate, Brampton, Knock, King's Meaburn, Cogglebridge (?Flakebridge), and Woodside in the county of Westmorland, Shewing that neither the countess nor her agents had demanded their rents for several years, whereby they have become in arrears, and now she strictly demands full payment of all the rents in arrears (which the tenants are willing to pay), but claim relief out of their rents for the monthly assessment laid upon them by Parliamentary Ordinance, which the countess refuses to allow; also her stewards do 'daily distrain and drive away your petitioners' cattle whereby your petitioners are utterly disabled to maintain their families, and to make tillage of their tenements, their stock being wholly taken away...'

They pleaded the poverty of the north, being the seat of two recent wars, and the burden of assessments; they alleged that lady Anne had imprisoned John Wardell (of Brough) one of her rent collectors for not executing her oppressive demands. The petition was signed by

Capt. Thomas Ewebanke (elder of Brough 1645),
Tho: Jackson,
John Jackson,
John Wilson,
Robert Wardell,
Michael Waller,
John Waller,
Geo. Pinder (Not a Brough name),
Tho. Williamson,
Robt. Wardell,
John Wardell,
Wm. Wilkin,
John Munckhouse,

John Swyer,

John Wilkin,
Lancelot Wilkin,
Rowland Kay,
Robt. Cumston jun.,
John Laidman,
Cuth. Wharton,
John Wharton,
John Coulson,
Mich. Hodgson,
Tho. Monkister,
Robt. Shenton,
Tho. Glenton.

Lan. Wesitall (Waistall),
Edward Wardell,
Henry Robinson,
Tho. Bowsell (Busfeld, Bousfell),
Ric. Sumner,
Robt. Cumston,
Geo. Shawe,
J. Aisted (Aiskell),
Michael Shaw,
Humf. Williamson (?Kirkby
   Stephen).

Vera cop: et exacta: Ste. Kirke, Clarke
to the said Committee.

'I lye at Mr Juces over agt. the sugar loafe
in Cursiter Alley neere Chancery Lane,
London.

Gilbert Croucher'

Comparing the names with the Protestation returns for 1641 all but two of them belong to the Brough and Stainmore manors, and cannot be said to represent other manors. Comparing them with those who either lost all or part of their estates after the King's Award of 1617 in the same manors,[19] these family names recur in this petition: Laidman, Waller, Wharton, Aiskell, Ewebank, Cumpston, Jackson, Wilkin, and Wardell.

On the other hand the 1649/50 petition did not make clear that the tenants were paying ancient, not rack rents. Given a good harvest an 8d. fine was a fair return. When lady Anne wrote to Marsh on the 11th December 1649 she mentioned that if her tenants would not compound for their fines, the only course would be to sue them in Chancery; 'Wherefore good Mr. Marsh for God's sake hasten it all you can, that so the Bill may be put into Chancery at the beginning of the next term, which if it be done it may then be, they will come to offer me some reasonable condition of Peace...'[20] She then mentioned the recent discovery of a decree in Chancery by which her mother 'was to have two years full value of her tenants which they tell me is more than twenty penny fine.' The Chancery case was probably heard at York. The important point is that a two year improved rent exceeded a twenty year ancient rent before 1616. The clearest confirmation of this evaluation comes in the tract of 1654 issued by John Musgrave of Catterlen, the scurrilous pamphleteer, entitled "A True Representation of the State of the Bordering Customary Tenants" against lord William Howard of Naworth.[21] He stated that two twenty pence fines equalled four years' (improved) rents. This is proof by an adversary.

In May 1650 Thomas Garth held the second manor courts in Westmorland, but the tenants refused to pay rents or fines. Following this, three commissioners, Messrs. Garth, Hilton and Christopher Clapham her steward held a meeting at Appleby in June with representatives of the Westmorland manors. The tenants admitted that all had agreed that unless lady Anne allowed one sixth off her free and ancient rents for taxes, they would not pay. The commissioners said they had no authority to grant this, but that if the tenants could produce evidence of custom in Westmorland to this effect, or an order from the Westmorland County Committee ordering it, they would grant it. The tenants were given three weeks to produce this evidence, and proof that the one sixth demanded bore any relation to the taxes they had paid.[22] It was not produced. Deadlock had been reached. The tenants made another frantic appeal to the Committee of Indemnity on the 16th July 1650, and the matter was postponed till November.[23]

Meanwhile Cromwell was in York, preparing for his expedition against the Scots, which terminated in the Battle of Dunbar on the 3rd September. Hearing of these Westmorland disputes he issued a commission to several gentlemen of the barony of Kendal to meet lady Anne at Appleby, to try to reach a compromise... On their arrival, 'she used them with all kindness and courtesy, but told them plainly she would never refer any of her concerns in that kind to the Protector or any person living, but leave it wholly to the discretion of the law; adding further that she that had refused to submit to king James on the like account, would never do it to the Protector, whatever hazard or danger she incurred thereby.' The Committee of Indemnity heard the tenants' appeal for allowances for taxes out of their rents on 26th November, which was dismissed. Lady Anne was left to follow her own course at law.[24]

Two footnotes are relevant here; In 1651 when the government of the four northern counties was placed under Sir Arthur Hazlerigg, Appleby was garrisoned by Major General Thomas Harrison and was full of soldiers for the most part of the summer.[25] It was during this time that lesser men in the upper Eden Valley came to prominence. The military rule, and opposition to lady Anne centred on the hamlet of Winton in the parish of Kirkby Stephen. Winton hall was held by the Skaife family of some antiquity,[26] and in 1641 Robert Skaife was probably the owner. His younger brother was major Arthur Skaife a parliamentary sequestrator. They in turn were related to the Atkinson family of Winton and Kirkby Stephen, and the Sanderson family of Kirkby Stephen.[27] Apart from major Arthur Skaife who was the principal speculator in sequestered lands, cornet Lancelot Skaife, lieutenant (later captain) Robert Atkinson of Kirkby Stephen, captain Robert Waller of Mallerstang (Atkinson's brother-in-law) and John Waller of Mallerstang (nephew of Atkinson and Waller) were the principal adventurers at this time. Lieutenant Robert Atkinson was placed in charge of a small company at Appleby castle after Harrison's departure.[28] Lieutenant Robert Atkinson's troop was disbanded by order of the Council of State on May 10th 1652.[29] That the Skaifes led the opposition to lady Anne is indicated by the case of one Skaife of Stainmore. He resisted some claim of lady Anne, and the case was tried in the Common Pleas in London on 9th November 1653 before three judges and a jury, and won by Skaife 'against the evidence and direction of the courts' as lady Anne ruefully noted in her diary.[30] She did not have all her own way.

The second footnote relates to Francis Higginson who was appointed to the vicarage of Kirkby Stephen by lord Wharton in October 1648. He was the son of Francis Higginson an M.A. of Cambridge and till 1629 a puritan preacher in Leicester. He left England in 1629, following an attempt of archbishop Laud to discipline him, and settled at Salem, Massachusetts. He died in the following year, leaving a widow and two sons, John and Francis. John eventually succeeded to his father's ministry at Salem. Francis first became a schoolmaster at Cambridge, Massachusetts, and then was befriended by some merchants who paid for his education at Leyden. He was befriended by lord Wharton who appointed him to Kirkby Stephen. The vicarage house had been occupied by some Scotch and Irish soldiers during their march towards Preston, and his bedstead and wood in the house had been burnt by the soldiers. Eventually he married Isabell the sister of Edmund Branthwaite. He was a scholar, and a presbyterian. With Thomas Walker vicar of Kendal from 1653, and Gervase Benson, Higginson became one of lord Wharton's informants on the needs of the district, soliciting

his aid when poor boys needed help in schooling. One of his most interesting comments to Wharton concerns tenant-right, in a letter of 1655/6:

> 'The inhabitants of our parish are yet stiffe in retaining their old though groundless Customes; and they have I think the worse opinion of me reporting me to be an Independent because I endeavour sometimes when a necessity lyes upon me to persuade them to forsake them. But they are not words that will persuade them, that have not reason or witt to understand them. It must be Authority; that only will be a convincing argument to refractory men.'[31]

Higginson, the vicar of Kendal, and Richard Gilpin rector of Greystoke were the three leading presbyterian ministers of the two counties. Though neither the classis system, nor the Association movement gained a foothold in Westmorland, they maintained the Calvinist opinion in the counties. Higginson with Dodson of Ravenstonedale, Fothergill of Orton, and Jackson of Crosby Garrett did the same in the upper Eden valley.

The next move against lady Anne was an attempt to outflank her in religion. One of the standing committees of the county, more lay than clerical, composed of 'godly men', was empowered to examine all persons whom they suspected of error. During June 1651 they came to Appleby to examine her. She received them very courteously, but firmly replied to their questions:

> "That her faith was build upon the foundation of the Prophets and Apostles; that is upon the Holy Scriptures, the Word of God, as delivered and expounded by the Church of England, whose doctrine, discipline, and worship, as by law established, she was bred in, and had embraced; and by God's Grace would persist in it to her life's end."[32]

These firm answers impressed the Committee, that they left in some admiration, and she was left in peace. She did not attend the parish church during the Commonwealth, but observed the full rule of the Church of England at home, having the psalms of the day read daily with three or four chapters of Scripture. She had the church services in her chapel on Sundays, with the sacrament celebrated there four times a year. They threatened her with sequestration, but she never wavered.[33]

References Chapter 23.

(1) Diary of Lady Anne Clifford. Williamson MS, 27.
Lady Anne Clifford. Williamson. 196/7. She borrowed £100 from lady Kent, which was repaid. Jan. 1650.

(2) Appleby Castle MS. Williamson lists.

(3) Hist. of Craven. Whitaker. 304, 473.

(4) Appleby Castle MS. now C.R.O. Carlisle.

(5) Lady Anne Clifford. Williamson. 185.

(6) Hist. of Westmorland. W. Sayer. Kendal & London 1847. I. 433.
N. & B. I, 299.
Deposition of Richard Clapham of Skipton, in Chapt. 24 following.

(7) Ejected of 1662, Nightingale. I. 633.

(8) Ejected of 1662, Nightingale. I. 620.

(9) Older nonconformity in Kendal. Nicholson & Axon. 20.

(10) P.R.O. Chancery depositions. C.21/p.25/1. Anne Countess of Pembroke v. Robert Atkindon & others. Depositions taken at Appleby 18th Jan. 1650/51. Deposition of Richard Clapham of Skipton castle on behalf of Lady Anne.

(11) The Levellers. H.N. Brailsford ed. Christopher Hill. Spokesman Books, 1976, p. 467, 319.

(12) Lady Anne Clifford. Williamson. 214.

(13) Lady Anne Clifford. Williamson. 192.

(14) Hist. of Craven. Whitaker. 473.
Hist. of Skipton. Dawson. 136.
The Bolton Priory MSS, Williamson lists. Contain several undated MSS which prove that it was many months before the Craven tenants were clear of the sequestrators.

(15) Appleby Castle MS. Now C.R.O. Carlisle.
Lady Anne Clifford. Williamson. 214/15 & plate opp. p. 215.

(16) Hist. of Craven. Whitaker. 303. Letter of S. Ball concerning some tenants paying £150 to the committee for sequestrations at York.

(17) Appleby Castle MS. 3 Mar. 1645. Mr. Edmund Pollard to Mr. Marsh.

(18) Appleby Castle MS. C.R.O. Carlisle.
Lady Anne Clifford. Williamson. 207.
There is a petition from the Craven tenants among the Bolton priory MSS of 1650 to the Committee for Public Revenue in London, which may refer to their sequestrations.

(19) Cp. Chapt. 19. The King's Award.
The Parish registers of Brough under Stainmore. Henry Brierley, 1923.

(20) Appleby Castle MS. 11th Dec. 1649. Lady Anne to Marsh.
Lady Anne Clifford. Williamson. 213.

(21) Brit. Mus. catalogue, formerly catalogued under R. Muncaster, p. 5.

(22) See Ref. (10). Anne countess dowager of Pembroke v. Robert Atkinson.
Evidence of Richard Clapham of Skipton Castle.

(23) Lady Anne Clifford. Williamson. 207/8.
N & B, I. 300/1.
Lowther muniments (now C.R.O. Carlisle), le Fleming MSS. Memoirs of George Sedgewick of Collinfield. p. 75.

(24) N & B, I. 301.
Lady Anne Clifford. Williamson. 208.

(25) C.S.P. Commonwealth, 1651. XV, 261. (2) June 20. Major-General Harrison at Appleby.
Lady Anne Clifford. Williamson. 199.
Diary of Lady Anne Clifford. Williamson MS. 35.

(26) N & B, I. 548, 586.
C & W, Tract series. XVII, 1971. op.cit. Protestation Returns. Parish of Kirkby Stephen, Winton. p. 15.

(27) C.R.O. Carlisle. Probate records. 1 Oct. 1667. Will and Inventory of Jane Atkinson of Kirkby Stephen, widow, mother of 3 children, minors, Robert Skaife, Arthur Skaife, & Isabell Atkinson. Will of Francis (Frances) Atkinson, 4 May 1666, of Kirkby Stephen, seamster, sister of Arthur & Robert Skaife; mentions cousins Phillip and ffrancis Sanderson. The Sandersons were examined after the Kaber Rigg Plot of 1663.

(28) C & W trans. N.S. XI, 1911, 212 et seq. The Kaber Rigg Plot.

Protestation Returns 1641. op.cit. Robert Atkinson of Kirkby Stephen, p. 15, may have been the son of William of Winton p. 14. In Ejected of 1662 op.cit., II, 1072, in the petition of the inhabs. of Kirkby Stephen for a new vicar 1646, Robert Atkinson signs immediately after the schoolmaster William Willis.

N & B, I. 101n. When in 1656 Cromwell appointed commissioners in the English counties to raise £600,000 monthly, the Westmorland commissioners included Philip lord Wharton, Thomas Burton, Robert Branthwaite, Francis Sisson, Edward Briggs, John Archer, and Roger Bateman esquires; and Edmund Branthwaite, Robert Atkinson, James Cock, William Garnet, Richard Burton, Robert Skaife, gentlemen etc. Thomas Langhorne the shopkeeper of Penrith figures among the Cumberland commissioners. Thus by 1656 the dissident group in the upper Eden valley had standing.

C.S.P. Committee for Compounding. 1650. GCCL, 195. Five papers sent by Capt. Rich. Crackenthorpe to the Committee for Compounding mainly relating to the letting of the Hartley demesne. (2) Gives the cert. of Francis Blenkinsop to the Westmorland Committee of the activities of Major Arthur Skaife, Robert Wardell, Cornet Lancelot Skaife in acquiring the demesne of Helbeck. (5) gives the challenge of Edward Morley to John Thompson: "You being a double officer, and accorded with the Levellers, and I being one of the meanest of Major Skaife's troop, set you at defiance, and desire you will vindicate yourself according to your profession, by meeting me in Gramskey by 8 o'clock tomorrow with back swords; otherwise send me an answer".

The Regimental History of Cromwell's Army. C. Firth & G. Davis. 1940. I, 264 ref. to Capt. Richard Birbeck, Sept. 1645. II. 553. ref. to Lieut. Waller 1653. II 554. ref. to Capt. Waller 1656. Marston Moore, Peter Young, 1970. p. 1150 refers to Lieut. Bryan Richardson, & troop commander John Richardson.

(29) Northern History. vol. V. 1970. p. 61. County Committees in Cumberland & Westmorland. C.B. Philips. Lieut. Robt. Atkinson raised his troop in 1651. A member of the Westmorland county committee 1656.

C.S.P. Commonwealth. 1652. XXIV, 236. Council of State to Commissioners for Cumberland to raise their proportion of the assessment of £90,000 a month, & pay Lieut. Robt. Atkinson for his troop on being disbanded.

(30) Diary of Lady Anne Clifford. Williamson MS. 43/4.
There are no Skaifes in the Protestation Returns of 1641; the presumption is that they were tenants by purchase or sequestration.

(31) D.N.B. Francis Higginson sen. 1587-1630.
The New England Hist. & General register. vol. 50. 1896. p. 79. Vol. 52, 1898, pp. 348, 353 and others for refs. to the family.
Orthodoxy in Massachusetts 1630-1656. Perry Miller, Cambs. Mass. 1933, 137.
Short Title Catalogue of Books printed in England, Scotland & Ireland 1475-1640, A.W. Pollard & G.R. Redgrave. London 1926. p. 299. Francis Higginson.
S.T.C. 1641-1700. See: Francis Higginson of Kirkby Stephen. 1653.
John Higginson of Salem 1663, 1686.
The Winthrop Papers. Vol. II, 1623. 1630. Massachusetts Hist. Soc. 1931. Letter of John Winthrop to his wife 9 Sept. 1630. Vol. III, April 1631 John Winthrop writes about Mrs Anne Higginson, widow, and her future.
Calamy Revised, A.G. Mathews. 1934. Francis Higginson jun. of Kirkby Stephen.
The Puritan as Colonist & Reformer. E.H. Byington, London, 1899. pp. 73, 76, 77/80. Refs. to Francis Higginson, sen.
Sedbergh School Reg. op.cit. Refs. to Francis s.o. John Higginson of New England (nephew of Francis of Kirkby Stephen), who ent. St. John's Coll., Cambridge 1678. B.A. 1681.
Alumn. Cantab. Venn. for Francis Higginson sen. of Salem, and his grandson John.
Ejected of 1662 in Cumberland & Westmorland. op.cit. 1075.
The Will of Francis Higginson of Kirkby Stephen, dated 14th May 1673 is in C.R.O. Carlisle. He bequeathed his property at Kaber to his nephew Francis, a minor who later went to Sedbergh School, above.

(32) Sermon preached at the funeral of Anne Countess of Pembroke etc. by Bp. Edward Rainbow of Carlisle. 1675/6. Reprinted in Carlisle Tracts. 1839, p. 56. Both in Cambs. Univ. Lib.

(33) N & B, I. 302.

Chapter 24

The countess of Pembroke and her tenants (2).

Proceedings in Chancery against the Westmorland tenants were started in December 1650. A Chancery warrant was issued on the 6th December to certain Westmorland gentlemen, Richard Barrow, Thomas Sandes, Jo. Preston, and Robert Harrison to take depositions of witnesses both for the countess, and the tenants.[1] The interrogatories submitted for both parties are long and have been summarised, except where extracts are important. The following key is used to identify names used in the text:

George third earl of Cumberland	= G.C.
Margaret countess of Cumberland	= M.C.
Francis earl of Cumberland	= F.C.
Henry earl of Cumberland	= H.C.
Anne countess of Pembroke	= A.C.
Richard earl of Dorset	= R.S.
Philip earl of Pembroke	= P.H.

The following are the names, places, ages, quality or professions of witnesses;

(1) For the countess of Pembroke.
John Thwaites of Appleby, esq. 72.
Thomas Garth of Newhall, gent. 40.
Thomas Johnson of Appleby, gent. and servant to A.C. 58.
John Powley of Appleby, gent. 60.
George Bainbridge of Appleby, gent. 50.
John Midleton of Appleby, gent. 65.
Leonard Smith of Appleby, grocer. 22.
Robert Parcveel of Scattergait, Appleby, tailor. 72.
John Richardson of Marton (Long Marton), weaver. 66.
John Atkinson of Knock, husbandman. 40.
Richard Clapham of Skipton Castle, gent. 34.
Thomas Webster of Browham, yeoman and servant to A.C. 63.

(2) For the tenants.
George Shepherd of Long Sleddall, yeoman. 68.
George Jackson of same, yeoman. 60.
Christopher Powson of Nateby, yeoman. 67.
(Note: of Ravenstonedale 1641)

Philip Gibson of Grisedale, yeoman. 64.
John Blenkarne of Wensleydale, yeoman. 68.
Nicholas Fothergill of Swaledale, yeoman. 44.
Geoffrey Birkbeck of Mallerstang, yeoman. 71.
John Addison of Appleby, shoemaker. 60.
(Note: prob. of Crosby Ravensworth 1641)
Lancelot Blenkinsop of Helbeck, gent. 66.
Henry Ward of Grayrigg, gent. 63.
James Tarne of Lambrigg, yeoman. 40.
William Cartmell of Preston Patrick, yeoman. 48.
Robert Johnson of Holme, yeoman. 76.
Richard Coulstone of Morland, yeoman. 70.
Thomas Laidman of Stainmore, yeoman. 60.
(3) Additional witnesses heard at Docker, Westmorland (?25th Sept.) 1651.
Robert Spencley of Winton, yeoman, 80.
William Waller of Winton, yeoman. 54.
Christopher Pettie of Orton, gent. 55.
John Pettie of Soulby, yeoman. 55.

Interrogatories submitted on behalf of Anne countess of Pembroke

(1) Do you know the plaintiff and Robert Atkinson and the other defendants?
(2) Are the records and pedigrees submitted to you correct?
(3) How did G.C. and M.C. grant estates to their customary tenants; were fines certain or arbitrary; did the tenants compound with the lord as they could agree; were those fines on the death of the lord, and on change of tenant by death or alienation?
(4) What is the custom of Tenant-Right; how far does it extend over Westmorland?
(5) Did the late P.H. and the complainant subscribe an Indenture in your presence, now shown to you?
(6) When did R.S. and P.H. die? Were you steward of A.C.'s Westmorland manors before the death of P.H. How many courts were held after the death of H.C. In whose name were they held. What was the business conducted at them. Had you 'directions to forbear to do anything in affirmance of the late King James' Award.' Were you as stewart reproved by A.C. for making such affirmance?

(7) What assessments or taxes have been laid by ordinance of parliament since the death of H.C. on the tenants; what were they, and for how long?

(8) Did any of the tenants demand allowances for taxes. When they paid rent did they offer any receipt for taxes paid, with a demand for allowance. Did A.C.'s agents ever refuse to make any such abatement?

(9) Were rents of assize, free rents and quit rents ever charged with taxes in Westmorland. Have any other lords in the county given any such abatement?

(10) Did A.C. or her agents offer to allow taxes out of their estate according to the usage of the country and ordinance of Parliament, so that she might receive the overplus as other landlords did. Did the tenants refuse to pay their rents alleging that they were swallowed up in taxes and free quarter?

(11) Has A.C. always paid taxes on all her demesne lands, rack rents, and improved rents?

(12) Have the tenants combined and made collections of money to oppose A.C.'s claims?

(13) Have you an interest in the issue of this suit. Are you a tenant in Tenant-Right of land in Westmorland. Have you contributed to the cost of the suit?

(14) Do you know the messuages and tenements held by the defendants; what are their yearly value?

(15) Have you anything further to say of the matters at issue?

Ex parte complainant.

John Thwaites of Appleby. He knew G.C., F.C. and H.C. In the time of G.C. fines were arbitrary. Most manors in Westmorland are the same.

Thomas Garth of Newhall. He knows not that the tenants have demanded allowance for taxes on their rents of assize; nor have they submitted an acquittance from the collector of taxes, when they have paid rent and demanded allowances.

He with Mr. Hilton and Mr. Richard Clapham A.C.'s commissioners had a conference with certain tenants at Appleby in June last about the payment of rents. They admitted that they had order from the rest of the tenants not to pay rent unless A.C. agreed to allow about a sixth part of rent for taxes. The 3 commissioners said they had no authority to grant this, unless it was ordered by the county commissioners for Westmorland, or unless it was the custom of the country. The commissioners for A.C. offered the tenants 14 days to procure this order; but the tenants asked for 3 weeks, and this was granted. The tenants produced no such order, and several have retained all or part of their rents upon pretence of taxes.

Thomas Johnson of Appleby. He has heard from old men that fines in the time of G.C. were arbitrary.

John Powley of Appleby. Has heard from old men that in the time of G.C. and M.C. fines were arbitrary.

George Bainbridge of Appleby. The tenants have agreed to band together for the maintenance of the suit, and have demanded a year's rent from him for the same.

John Midleton of Appleby. A.C. was not assessed in taxes on her free rents or rents of assize in the manors of Appleby, Skattergait, and Burrells, nor in any of her Westmorland manors before this suit, nor F.C. nor H.C. But she has always paid on her demesne lands, or allowed the same in the rents of the tenants of those lands.

Leonard Smith of Appleby. The tenants have agreed to band together. The constable of Skattergait has been to him and asked for a contribution, as the other tenants had agreed to do.

Geoffrey Birkbeck of Mallerstang. 'The custom of tenant-right is that the tenants shall enjoy their estates, paying their fines, and that there are some that in part of custom or service pay boon coals and some hens and some carry loads from Bainbridge to Westmorland, and other such like boons and services', but how far the custom extends he does not know.

He is not now a tenant of the manor of Mallerstang, having passed his tenement to his son, but reserving part of it to himself and his wife for their lives. He has contributed a proportional part of his rent towards the tenants' costs.

Robert Parcveel of Skattergait. Fines were arbitrary in the times of G.C. and M.C.

John Addison of Appleby. On the death of G.C. they paid a 4d. fine, i.e. 4 years' rent to M.C.

John Richardson of Marton. 'About the beginning of this suit Thomas Walton the bailiff of Knock came to (him) being a tenant of A.C. and demanded of him half a year's rent for the maintenance of the suit against A.C. touching the customs and fines in question which (he) not being willing but refusing to do the said bailiff wished him to go and speak with the neighbours of Knock about it, which he did, and they then read a note or writing to him, which they said was sent from Robert Pattison and Robert Atkinson the defendants employed by the tenants of the several manors of Westmorland in this business, and that the same was to be subscribed by the said tenants as their agreement to stand together and contribute equally towards the charge of this suit, and the differences between them and A.C. And (he) saith that he refused to subscribe any such writing, or contribute anything thereto; whereupon and divers times afterwards the said Walton, and divers others of the said tenants threatened to serve a writ upon him, and as he hath heard sayd, they would have his lands from him for it.'

John Atkinson of Knock. Thomas Walton came to him at the beginning of this suit, and to other tenants of Knock asking them to meet at his house, where a paper was sent by Roger Pattison and read to the effect that they should stand together and contribute equally. Most of them subscribed including this deponent. But afterwards he thought better if it, and refused to contribute anything. Since then Walton has come to him and threatened to distrain his crop unless he contributes.

Lancelot Blenkinsop of Helbecke, gave general evidence on Tenant-Right.

Richard Clapham of Skipton Castle. Two courts have been kept since the death of H.C. in September 1649, and May 1650. Before the keeping of these courts he 'heard A.C. give special order to Mr. Thwaites who kept the first, and the Mr. Garth who kept the latter, not to do anything which might seem to confirm or assent to the late King James his award.' He has been A.C.'s receiver or commissioner since she came north about 1½ years since, and that till Candlemass last the tenants of Westmorland never demanded any assessments for any of her free rents or rents of assize, and then some petitioned and demanded allowance, but no particular sum. She said that if other lords in Tenant-Right gave this she would do the same. The tenants have not tendered any acquittance from the collectors of assessments for part of their rents. But last summer when he, Mr. Hilton and Mr. Garth summoned the tenants to Appleby to pay their rents and arrears, they demanded an abatement of one sixth out of her free rents and rents of assize, without shewing whether the sum related to the assessments demanded. Some tenants came from every manor of A.C. in Westmorland. The commissioners offered to allow the abatement if the tenants could produce an order from the Westmorland County Committee by virtue of an ordinance of Parliament compelling this. They offered 14 days' grace to the tenants to procure the order, and the tenants demanded three weeks, and this was granted. No order was ever produced. Many of the tenants have since paid their rents.

Since he became agent for A.C. she has always paid and allowed all assessments and taxes for quarter imposed upon her demesne lands, or lands rented at rack in Westmorland. On lands now rented at £500 per annum she did not receive in one year, after the deductions for assessments and free quarter, above £60 clear. In the manor of Brougham the tenants retained the £100 rent of 1648, and £60 in arrears from 1647 for the assessments of 1648.

Thomas Webster of Browham is a customary tenant in Westmorland under a Mr. Wright, and Sir John Lowther, both of whom receive arbitrary fines. He has paid Mr. Wright a fine of 20 years' rent, and Sir John 10 years'. Other tenants have paid some 16 years' and others 18 years', and some more or less.

A.C. has always paid taxes on demesne lands, and allowed this when tenants have paid on her behalf.

Thomas Laidman of Stainmore. A.C. was never assessed before the beginning of this suit on her free rents in Stainmore where he lives. He is a tenant of A.C. at £8. per annum, and pays his share towards the tenants' costs of the suit.

Interrogatories submitted on behalf of Robert Atkinson and others.

(1) Do you know the plaintiff A.C. and the defendants Robert Atkinson, William Barnett, John Fothergill, Robert Shaw, George Rudd, John Waller, John Munkas, George Fothergill, Christ: (ms. torn), John Aiskell alias Rose, Robert Pattinson, John Dent, Tho: Cleasby, Thomas Ewebancke?

(2) Do you know the manors of Appleby, Brougham, Brough under Stainmore, Pendragon, Kirkby Stephen, Sowerby juxta Brough, Winton, and Mallerstang, Knock alias Shalcocke, Stainmore, King's Meaburn, Langton, Augleburgh alias Whinfell, Kirkby Thure, Woodside, Moorhouse, Bongate, Burrells, Scattergate, Branton, Woodend all in Westmorland; do you know the defendants and how many are customary tenants in Tenant-Right, and of which manors?

(3) Did you know G.C., F.C., and H.C. late earls of Cumberland and for how long each were seized in turn of the manors in question?

(4) What was the nature of the estate of G.C.; was it a good estate in fee simple. Did he assure or convey it to F.C. and H.C. and upon what terms. Is the Will of G.C., a copy of which is shewn to you subscribed by the commissioners' names, a true copy, and where is the original?

(5) Do you know that after the death of G.C., the Crown escheators made an inquisition of the estate of G.C. Was it recorded in

Chancery, and did they find that the estate was held in fee simple, and that it was settled upon F.C.?

(6) Did F.C. and H.C. after the death of G.C. enjoy the estates and receive the rents. Do you know that King James made an award settling the differences concerning the settling of the estate. What were the terms of the award. Was not A.C. given her portion out of that award. How was the money raised, and were not F.C. and H.C. empowered to confirm the custom of Tenant-Right, and to reduce fines to a certainty. Is this a copy of the award subscribed by the names of the commissioners?

(7) Were not the fines set by F.C. and H.C. persuant to the award 'very excessive, high and far above what other lords of the said lordships or their ancestors had formerly had, received, and accepted of them or their ancestors, and whether did not the said tenants yield obedience thereto howbeit the same tended to the utter impoverishment and ruin of some of them and their several families, and whether were not many and what families forced to sell all their personal estate for the payment of those great fines that there might be for all times after a certainty of fine (vizt.) of seven years' rent; and was not all this done upon pretence to raise money for the plaintiff's said portion'...and by what means?

(8) Did R.S. or P.H. receive any of the portion mentioned in the award; were receipts given, and who holds them?

(9) Is there in Westmorland a custom called Tenant-Right whereby a customary estate descends from ancestor to heir. Has this held in the manors in question, and what fines have been paid. What was paid on the deaths of F.C. and H.C. Have the tenants enjoyed their customary estates according to Tenant-Right doing suit of court etc.?

(10) Do all the Westmorland manors hold to the Custom of Tenant-Right; and in how many are fines certain. Has not a moderate year's value been decreed in Chancery for a reasonable fine. What lords have received fines from 2, 3, 4 to 5 years' rent. What were the fines before and during the time of G.C.?

(11) Do you know the defendants, their manors in which they are tenants, what rents and services are due from them. Are you a Commissioner, steward, bailiff, receiver, attorney or solicitor to the plaintiff, or were you to R.S. or P.H., or to F.C. and H.C.?

(12) Have not Parliamentary taxes and assessments been levied upon the manors in Westmorland in question for the past 7 years. How have they been rated; have they been assessed on the improved yearly value of the tenements, or have the assessors made any abatement to the tenants in regard to the rent payable to the lord of the manor. Which lords have been assessed in taxes on their rents; have they paid or allowed these taxes. Has A.C. refused to make any allowance for taxes on rents received?

(13) Did A.C. or R.S. receive the £20,000 mentioned in the award, or how much. Does A.C. receive a jointure from the estate of R.S. and how much?

(14) Did you know that G.C. by fine and recovery assured his estates to F.C.

(15) Did you know or hear that after the death of G.C. the tenants of the Westmorland manors in question paid £26,000 to F.C. and H.C. for the confirmation of their customary tenures in Tenant-Right. Was this established by deed, and for the establishing of fines certain?

Ex parte defendants.

John Thwaites. The tenants of the manors in question are customary tenants. During the time of G.C. they paid arbitrary fines. On the entrance of F.C. and H.C. they paid a 7 years' rent for a fine. He was clerk and kept the courts for 20 years. The tenants were called customary tenants, and 'he conceives they were so called and held their estates by force of the late King James his award, by indenture and decree in Chancery.'

George Sheppard of Long Sleddall. Several manors in Westmorland have fines certain, as Kentmire, Gressmire, and Windermere; with a 2 year rent for a fine on the death of the lord, and 3 years' on change of tenant by death or alienation; except in Kentmire where the fine is always a 2 year one. A moderate year's value is taken by several lords for an arbitrary fine, as has been decreed in Chancery in the cases between Mr. Anthony Ducket and his tenants, and Mr. Midleton and his tenants at Burton.

Tenants of most manors in Westmorland for the past years have been assessed in taxes on the improved value of their lands; and several lords have been assessed on their free rents, as Sir Henry Bellingham, and Mr. Harrington.

George Jackson of Long Sleddall. There are fines certain in Kentmire, Grassmire, and Windermere (as above). Several lords accept an improved year's rent in a moderate way, as Mr. Ducket and Mr. Midleton (as above). Several lords, where there are arbitrary fines have taken 'some two, some three, some four, and some five years' rent, and that when they have been paid after four or five years' rent for their fine the same hath been more than a moderate year's value of their estates would have amounted unto'.

Thomas Johnson (1641 in Stainmore). His extract is given in Chapter 19 on the King's award, concluding with: 'At least 20 tenants were utterly beggared; several were imprisoned and two died there, Lancelot Johnson, and Christopher Carter'.

Christopher Powson of Nateby is a customary tenant in Tenant-Right of Lord Wharton.

Philip Gibson of Grisedale, Yorks. His extract is given in Chapter 19.

John Blenkarne of Wensleydale, Yorks. His extract is given in Chapter 19.

Nicholas Fothergill of Swaledale, Yorks. His extract is given in Chapter 19.

Geoffrey Birkbeck of (Deepgill) Mallerstang. His extract is given in Chapter 19.

John Addison of Appleby. His extract is given in Chapter 19.

Lancelot Blenkinsop of Helbeck (Brough). His extract is given in Chapter 19.

Richard Clapham. A.C.'s portion from R.S. is about £1,800 per annum, but she did not enjoy this during her marriage to P.H. who took it himself.

Henry Ward of Grayrigg says that according to the judgement of a high court of justice at Westminster the tenants have a customary estate in Tenant-Right descendable from ancestor to heir according to the nature of copyhold estates. Fines are certain in the Richmond and Marquess fees of the barony of Kendal. The tenants of Whinfell (one of the manors in the large parish of Kendal), and of Justice Hutton at Lupton and Farleton pay a 2 year fine. Several Westmorland manors pay from 2 to 4 years' fine. He mentions the cases of Mr. Midleton at Burton, Mr. Popham at Newbystones (parish of Morland), and Mr. Duckett at Grayrigg, Docker and Lambrigg.

James Tarne of Lambrigg, is a customary tenant in Tenant-Right of Mr. Duckett, and mentions the Duckett, Popham and Midleton cases. (Chapt. 22. sect. (C)).

Williams Cartmell of Preston Patrick; for two years has been constable of P.P. of which Mr. Preston, Mr. Wharton and Mr. Hutton are lords. The free rent of P.P. is about £32 per annum; they have been assessed in taxes on this, and have paid £9.17.8. for the said two years.

Robert Johnson of Holme, for two years has been constable of Holme, of which Mr. Preston is lord. On his free rents of £11.10.0. he has been assessed and paid his taxes, and for 7 past years.

Richard Coulstone of Morland. The tenants of Morland hold of the Dean and Chapter of Carlisle in Tenant-Right; they pay a 3 year fine on change of tenant, but nothing on death of lord. There are 4 tenements of the like in Bowlton and Bongate.

Thomas Laidman of Stainmore. His extract is given in Chapter 19.

The second writ of Chancery was dated 3rd July 1651 and issued to the same gentlemen.

Depositions taken at the house of John Washington in Docker, Westmorland (?25th) Sept. 1651.

Robert Spencley of Winton, bailiff to F.C., H.C., and A.C. at Winton. Fines paid to F.C. and H.C. were excessive and unreasonable, above what other lords in Westmorland had taken. (His extract is given in Chapter 18, and relates to King James' visit to Brougham Castle on 6th August 1617, Appleby Castle the 7th, Wharton Hall the 8th, and Kendal the 9th.)[2]

William Waller of Winton. (Referred to in part in Chapter 18). The tenants of F.C. and H.C. petitioned King James when he came on his progress into the north about their excessive fines imposed by the award, and asking for relief. The late King 'gave them threatening speeches and commanded them to return home and agree with their lord, for if they petitioned him they should be no better,' with other such hasty speeches.

Christopher Pettie of Orton. (Referred to in part in Chapter 19). He was servant to John Taylor esq., for the space of...years. Mr. Taylor was prime agent and commissioner for F.C. and H.C. in all their affairs both in London and the country. 'He well remembers about the years 1623 and 1624 there was £17,000 procured and borrowed in London by his Master's means of Sir William Craven and others which was paid at several times to R.S., his agents or servants namely to Mr. Lin...and Mr. Granengr (Edward Lane, scrivener, and Mr. Gravener, gentleman usher in R.S.'s household. Diary of Lady Anne Clifford, V. Sackville West. 1924. lviii/lix.) two of his privy gentlemen, but where the acquittances or discharges for the same are, it being so long, he doth not know where or in whose custody they remain, or now are'; the £17,000 was raised out of F.C.'s tenants in Westmorland and taken to London by Mr. Elton, and Mr. Guy their agents there; it was for A.C.'s portion. He has reason to remember these, being used by his Master; and at the last payment R.S. by his agents gave £5. to the tellers of the £17,000 as a gratuity to drink, of which this deponent had his share.

John Pettie of Soulbie. His extract is given in Chapter 19.

Note: Robert Spencley of Winton, William Waller of Winton, and Christopher Pettie of Orton were cross-examined on behalf of A.C. Nothing new was elicited, except that *William Waller* said that he was a tenant of A.C. at Winton at a yearly rent of 20s. and that he paid taxes with the rest of his neighbours, which as they told him were for the maintenance of the suite between 'A.C. and the tenants.'

Notes: The origins of Christopher Powson of Nateby, and John Addison of Appleby are suggested from the Protestation Returns of 1641.[3] The distinction between Richard Clapham of Skipton castle in these depositions, and Christopher Clapham steward of Lady Anne's Westmorland estates is not clear.[4] The Mallerstang contingent led by Geoffrey Birkbeck of Deepgill (referred to in Chapter 19) included John Blenkarne of Wensleydale, Nicholas Fothergill of Swaledale, and John Gibson of Grisedale, all three of whom were driven off their small farms after the award.

The presence of Capt. Henry Ward of Sunnybank, Grayrigg aged 63, James Tarne of Lambrigg, and William Cartmell of Preston Patrick are significant among the witnesses for the tenants. Ward was one of the leading tenants in the Moser v. Ducket tenancy case of 11 Charles I. Marie Tarne was another, and James Tarne was probably connected. More significant is the recurrence of names from the 1621 Kendal barony tenant-right case, Edward Tarne who took part in the meeting at Staveley Bridge; Henry Ward, Thomas Duckett and Richard Helme or Holme who took part in the 'stage-play' acted in Kendal castle in July 1621 representing local land lords to be in Hell; and John Cartmele of Wathsudden (Preston Patrick) aged 48 who had also taken part in the Staveley meeting. The presence of these family names in early Quakerism is significant.[5]

By July 1650 Marsh her agent in the south was thoroughly alarmed by the number of legal wasps' nests lady Anne was determined to stir up. She wrote to him on the 18th as a result of his warning, and admitted that she was meeting with strange oppositions, but that if she did not attend to her worldly fortunes the estates would fall back into their wonted ill habit.[6] Though money was very short, any Westmorland or Craven tenant who refused to

pay rents in specie or kind, or fines had warrants signed against him, and taken to court. In Craven in 1653 William Atkinson of Otterburne (Kirkby by Malhamdale), with Samuel Waddington, and Anthony Feston had refused to pay their rents and castle-hens for the past four years. The court rolls which recorded these things had been destroyed in the Civil wars, and the tenants were elated. As with the Murgatroyd case, they probably lost.[7] Eight hundred hens were paid yearly to Skipton castle. On the 29th November 1654 she obtained her verdict against several Craven tenants.[8]

In Westmorland the position was even more serious, with the Stainmore, Brough and Winton tenants taking the lead. On the 3rd June 1653 the Milburn tenants appealed to the Council of State against lady Anne's threat to sue them. The Council referred the matter to Colonel Briggs, and Major Arthur Skaife for a report. The Council replied on the 8th that the tenants must pay up or shew cause to the contrary.[9] Lady Anne's diary mentions a number of cases heard in the coming years without specifying whether they refer to one or all of the Westmorland manors. One came before the Appleby assizes on 17th August 1653, but was put back because lady Anne's counsel objected to many jurors.[10] We have already noted that the case against Skaife of Stainmore was heard in the Common Pleas on 9th November 1653, and given in favour of the tenant. On the 12th August 1654 the case covering all her Westmorland manors came up before judge Richard Newdigate at the Appleby Assizes. Though she won her case it was quite unsuccessful in quelling the tenants.[11] Again they were taken to court before the Common Pleas in Westminster Hall on the 16th and 17th May 1656. This was a full dress occasion heard before three judges Windham, Atkins and Matthew Hale. Counsel for lady Anne were serjeants Maynard, Newdigate and Barnard, and for the tenants serjeants Earle and Evers. She had to produce many proofs, but the jury gave her her verdict in the first case, and she won the second by default, as the tenants refused to plead. She also won her costs at £250 and the verdict exemplified under the seal of the court.[12] There was another case on the 17th November 1656 in the Common Pleas before four judges, Oliver St. John (C.J.), Atkins, Windham and Hale in which she won her verdict against her tenant James Walker of Nether Brough. The defendant did not appear and was non-suited, and she recovered costs of £100 from him. His farm was awarded to Lady Anne.[13] James Walker was dispossessed by the deputy sheriff Thomas Gabetis and other officers of the West Ward on 3rd February 1656/7. The land was let to John Salkeld of Brough on a 21 year lease on a plain rack rent, not a fineable rent.[14] There was a final case in Common Pleas before the same four judges on the 23rd April 1657, where she was victorious against the remaining tenants.[15] Her secretary George Sedgewick recorded in his memoirs that these long law suits cost £4,000 on either side, an immense sum for those days.[16] Looking at the story as far back as the revolt of 1537 when eight or nine men were hanged from the Winton, Brough and Stainmore manors one cannot avoid the conclusion that the Cliffords were blind to the poverty of the fellside farms in those manors, as well as in Mallerstang. The tedious details of these many chapters prove beyond doubt that the tenants on marginal lands should have received more consideration. Though lady Anne won her cases at law, it was a poor triumph against men who had paid for fines certain under the 1617 Award, and had lost because of a loophole in its provisions. The attack on this injustice was led by Robert Atkinson, first a lieutenant and then a captain, of Kirkby Stephen and later of Mallerstang.

References Chapter 24.

(1) P.R.O. S.P./C.21/P.25/1. Anne countess of Pembroke v. Robert Atkinson & others. 1650-51.

(2) Progresses of James I. J. Nichols. 1828, III, 391, 393/4.
C & W trans. N.S. III, 364. Refers to James I's visit in the Brougham registers.
Lady Anne Clifford. Williamson, 121/2.
Kendal, Local Chronology from Kendal newspapers. 1865. vii.
Annals of Kendal, Cornelius Nicholson. 1835, 106.

(3) The Westmorland Protestation Returns. M.A. Faraday, op.cit. 28/30; 46/47.

(4) Lady Anne Clifford. Williamson. passim.
There was also a letter of 28 Oct. 1656 from Richard Clapham to Lady Anne among the Appleby MSS (Williamson lists). Neither Whitaker's Craven or Dawson's Skipton throw light on these men.

(5) Taken from the depositions in P.R.O. of Star Chamber: STAC/James I. Bundle 34, file 4. Writs, Interrogatories, and depositions in the Kendal Tenant-Right case 1621-5.

(6) 18th July 1650. Lady Anne to Mr. Marsh. Appleby MS. now C.R.O. Carlisle. Lady Anne Clifford. Williamson, 216/7.

(7) P.R.O. Chancery Proc. circa 1653. Chas. I. B & A Digest. p. 87. no. 22.
N & B, I. 301.

(8) Hothfield MS, in 1916 at Messrs Dawson & Bennett in London (Williamson list) 29 Nov. 1654. Statement of claim against tenants in Craven, with warrants to agents to make entrances.

(9) C.S.P. Commonwealth. 1653. xxxvii, 377 & 393.

(10) Diary of Lady Anne, (Williamson text) 42.

(11) Diary of Lady Anne, (Williamson text) 47.

(12) Diary of Lady Anne, (Williamson text) 53.

(13) Diary of Lady Anne, (Williamson text) 57.

(14) Diary of Lady Anne, (Williamson text) 58.

(15) Diary of Lady Anne, (Williamson text) 60 (which she called her fourth verdict against her tenants)

(16) N & B, I. 301.

Chapter 25

Tenant-Right in Mallerstang from 1657.

This chapter is concerned with development of tenant-right in Mallerstang from lady Anne's last case against her tenants in 1657 until the final settlement of fines between Sackville earl of Thanet and his tenants in 1737-9. This will conclude the survey of the triangle of dales, Ravenstonedale, Garsdale and Grisdale, upper Wensleydale and Mallerstang. This will be followed by a chapter on the surveys of the Board of Agriculture and Internal Improvement in Cumberland 1789/9 and Westmorland in 1793. The table provided by the Royal Commission on Agriculture of 1895 is also instructive illustrating the gradual decay of customary tenant-right until it was abolished by the Law of Property Act 1922.

(A) Perhaps the most remarkable feature of the struggle of lady Anne against her tenants was that she won most of her cases in Commonwealth courts against men who were supporters of the new political and religious orthodoxy, and bitterly opposed to her. On the conclusion of her last case lady Anne ordered her courts to be held in all her Westmorland manors. An immense task faced her officers; they had to record and levy an 8d. fine on every change of tenant by death or alienation from 1644 to 1657. In the manor of Mallerstang the average admittances for any year were about four. In 1657 there were about 49 major admittances. Compared with the survey of 1604 recorded in Chapter 14 there are so many sales of separate fields that the original quarterings, thirds and halves of the primary farms are unrecognisable; the exception is the purchase of one quarter of the original farm of Hanging Lunds by Rowland ffothergill from Thomas Shaw at an ancient rent of 13s.8d.[1] In the 1657 admittances there are 18 by descent, and 31 by purchase. This ignores four later entries of changed ownership. In 1659 there were 3 descents and 5 purchases; in 1660 one descent and 3 purchases; and in 1661 no descents and 3 purchases. By then the droving of cattle from Scotland through the northern dales to fairs and markets had started in force;

that and the rapid spread of the knitting industry in the dales' farms transformed the economy of the district,[2] with the result that the majority of old cruck-framed farm houses were pulled down, and new long houses built with mullioned windows. Servants and children no longer slept under the unventilated thatch, but in bedrooms with small mullioned windows. The survival of two such new buildings at East and West Scale in Grisdale next to Garsdale is an indication of how far the new prosperity penetrated.

In the following list of admissions in Mallerstang several points should be observed:

(1) Captain Robert Atkinson of Kirkby Stephen bought five properties based on Bluegrass with a combined ancient rent of 22s.10d. In the survey of 1604 this farm was a subsidiary of Southwaite at an ancient rent of 7s.1d. Thus these purchases trebled its size to a medium dale farm.

(2) Several of the early Quakers are here recorded. There are two Thomas Knewstubs, one the son of John, and the other of Robert. One was Thomas of Shorgill who received James Nayler and Francis Howgill in the autumn of 1652 and became Quaker. Agnes Grosedale of Castlethwaite was an early convert. Her father John made his Will on 30th August 1656, and one of his overseers was Captain Atkinson to 'see thay my wife and children be not wronged'. She seems to have sold land worth 1s. ancient rent to her neighbour John ffothergill of Castlethwaite to pay her dropping fine of £3.10.0. John Shaw of Castlethwaite was another early Quaker, living until 1691. He may be the John in the admissions next to the two above, who bought a fire house and two garths. Henry Whitfeild of Aisgill has another Quaker who bought another messuage and tenement of 10s.3d. ancient rent. William Shaw of Cocklake was another early Quaker.

(3) There are a number of entries where the elder son who inherits a farm buys out the shares of his brothers or sisters to preserve the unity of the farm. The most interesting entry comes from the admissions of 1659. William Birkbeck of Deepgill bought out his

father Geoffrey and brother James in lands of 3s. ancient rent. William's Will is dated 19th January 1697. His second son William migrated to Settle soon after, and became a member of Settle Quaker Meeting in 1698 and became the founder of famous Birkbeck family, merchants, bankers, and philanthropists.

Manor of Mallerstang. Book of Admissions 1657

Ancient Rent	New Tenant; by descent (D) by purchase (P) From, & Description of property	Fine L.S.D.	Receipts L.S.D.
12s.	John Bousfield (D) fr. Henry his father; messuage & tenement.	4.16.0	2.8.0. 2.8.0.
8/1d.	Christoffer ffothergill (D) fr. Symon his father; mess. & temnt.	3.4.8.	
	(Later note: This is now in ye possession of Ro: Atkinson of Mallerstang: gr.		
6/9½d.	Thomas Knewstubb (D) John his father, mess. & tenmt.	2.13.8.	
4/6d.	Robert Atkinson (P) John ffothergill. Parcels of ground.	1.16.0.	1.16.0.
23d.	Robert Atkinson (P) Edward ffothergill. Parcel of ground.	0.15.4.	0.15.4.
8/1d.	Robert Atkinson (P) Chrer. ffothergill. Parcels of ground.	3.4.8.	3.4.8.
3d.	John Dixon (D) Thomas his father. House & Garth.	0.2.0.	
	(Later note: Capt. Atkinson bought this & is to pay ye fine.)		
4/2d.	Rowland Shaw (P) William Wharton. Parcel of ground.	1.13.4.	0.16.8. 0.16.8.
6d.	Cuthbert Shaw. (P) John Shaw. House & parcel of ground.	0.4.0.	0.4.0.
12/6.	Bryan Hugginson (D) Henry his father. Parcels of ground.	5.0.0.	2.10.0. 2.10.0.
9/5d. & / 3 part of 1d.	Elizabeth Wilson (P) Lancelott Wilson. Mess. & Tenmt.	3.15.6.	3.15.6.
21d.	Thomas Knewstubb (P) John Norland. Parcels of ground.	0.14.0.	0.14.0.
11/-	Nicholas ffothergill, heir to Eliza. ffothergill. Parcel of ground.	4.8.0.	2.4.0.
11/-	Thomas Ward (P) of Nicholas ffothergill above, for same tenmt.	4.8.0.	4.8.0.
8/9d.	Agnes Grosdall (D) John (note: her father) Mess. & Tenmt.	3.10.0	1.15.0. 1.15.0.
12d.	John ffothergill (P) of Agnes Grosdall. part of above.	0.8.0.	0.8.0.
4d.	John Shaw (P) John Morland. A ffyre house & two garths.	0.2.8.	
12/6d.	John ffothergill (D) Adam his father, Mess. & tenmt.	5.0.0.	2.10.0. 2.10.0.
4/8d.	John ffothergill (P) Michaell Birkedale. Parcel of ground.	1.17.4.	1.17.4.
4/8d.	Thomas Shaw (d) Henry his brother. Mess. & tenmt.	5.9.0.	5.9.0.
4/8d.	Rowland ffothergill [?P] for the same tnmt.	5.9.0.	5.9.0.
7/6d.	Henry Higginson [?Hugginson] (P) Charles Hastwhitle. Parcels of ground.	3.0.0.	
	(Later note: Bought by Cuthbert Shaw, and by him sold to Thomas Tunstall the elder.)		
7/4¾.	John Hugginson (P) Charles Hastwhitle. Parcel of ground.	2.19.0.	2.19.0.
2/-	Michaell Wharton. (P) Phillipp Wharton. Parcel of ground.	0.16.0.	0.16.0.
2/-	Michaell Wharton (same) (P) Michaell Wharton of Sandpotts. Parcel of ground.	0.16.0.	0.16.0.
15/11d.	Henry Shaw (D) Thomas his father. Mess. & tenmt.	6.7.4.	6.7.4.
10/3d.	Henry Whitfeild (P) Chrer. Wharton & Gyles Hall. Mess. & Tenmt.	4.2.0.	4.2.0.
2/10½d.	John Atkinson (P) his father John. Mess. & parcel of ground.	1.3.0.	1.3.0.
11/-	Hugh Shaw (D) his father Thomas. Mess. & tenmt.	4.8.0.	4.8.0.
10/10d.	William Birkbeck (P) John Birkbeck. Part of mess. & tenmt.	4.6.8.	4.1.4.
(10/2d.)	(Later note: 8d. rent of this bought by Jo: ffothergill.)		0.5.4.
5/6d.	Thomas Tunstall (P) Cuthbt Shaw. Parcel of ground.	2.4.0.	2.4.0.
7/7½d.	Jeoffrey Wharton (D) his father William. Mess. & tenmt.	3.1.0.	3.1.0.
19½d.	Michaell Wharton (P) Charles Gibson. Parcel of ground.	0.13.0.	0.13.0.
8/8d.	Thomas Kn stubb (D) his father Robert. Mess. & tenmt.	3.9.4.	3.9.4.
8/6½d.	Thomas ffothergill (D) Thomas his father, Tenmt.	3.8.4.	1.14.2.

4/4d.	Richard Tailor which he claymes by (D) from Margarett Airay who was aunt to Richard Bell that dyed possessed thereof. Mess. & tenmt.	1.14.4.	0.17.2.
2/2d.	William Shaw (P) Thomas Shaw. Parcel of ground.	0.17.4.	0.17.4.
5/6d.	Cuthbert Shaw (P) Henry Hugginson. Parcel of ground.	2.4.0.	2.4.0.
4/4d.	Abraham Bell (D) Richard his father. Mess. & temt.	1.13.8.	

(Separate list, same year.)

4d.	Michaell Wharton (P) John Morland. House & parcel of ground.	0.2.8.	0.2.8.
7/-	Rowland Shaw (P) Jeffery Wharton. House & parcel of ground.	2.16.0.	2.16.0.
4/4d.	John Shaw (D) which he had after the death of Richard Bell & his two sons. A tenmt.	1.14.8.	1.14.8.

(Separate list, same year.)

3/4d.	Henry Shaw (P) Gyles Hall. Parcel of ground.	1.6.8.	1.6.8.
13d.	Thomas Harrison (P) John Morland. Parcel of ground.	0.8.8.	0.8.8.
9/-	Robert Shaw (P) Edmond Shaw. Parcel of ground.	3.12.0.	3.12.0.
8/2½d.	John Shaw (D) Edmond his father. Part of tnmt.	3.5.8.	3.5.8.
2/6d.	Mary Shaw & Sarah Shaw (P) Rowland Shaw. Several houses & parcels of ground.	1.0.0.	1.0.0.
29/13¾d.	Henry Shaw (D) Rowland his father. Tnmt.	11.13.2.	5.16.0.
			5.16.0.
9d.	(Later note: And for a parcel of ground bought of Tho: Shaw, rent 9d.)	0.6.0.	0.6.0.
4d.	James Walker (P) Thomas ffothergill. House & garth.	0.2.8.	0.2.8.
2/-	Robert Shaw (P) Richard Shaw. Parcels of ground & three houses.	0.16.0.	0.16.0.

(From book of admissions, Sept. 1659.)

10/10¾d.	Paule Knewstub (D) Thomas his father. Tnmt. (Note: Mich. Wharton is to pay this ffyne, hee being Guardian of the child.)	4.7.2.	
11/3½d.	Geoffrey ffothergill (D) John his father. Tnmt.	4.10.2.	4.10.2.
3/2d.	Richard Tunstall & Lyonell Turner (P) John ffothergill. Parcel of ground.	1.5.4.	1.5.4.
3/-.	William Birkbeck (P) Geoffrey & James Birkbeck. Parcels of ground.	1.4.0.	1.4.0.
16d.	Thomas ffothergill (P) John ffothergill. Parcels of ground.	0.10.8.	0.10.8.
6/7½d.	Gabriell ffothergill (P) Thomas Shaw. Parcels of ground & houses.	2.13.0.	2.13.0.
9d.	Henry Shaw (P) of same Thomas Shaw. Parcel of ground.	0.6.0.	0.6.0.
5d.	Same Henry Shaw (D) ... Shaw his father. Tnmt.	0.3.4.	0.3.4.

(From book of admissions: April 1660.)

2/-	William Shaw (P) Cutbert Shaw. Parcel of ground.	0.16.0.	0.16.0.
12/-	John Wharton (D) Philip Wharton. Tnmt.	4.16.0.	2.8.0.
			2.8.0.
3/1d.	John ffothergill (P) Elizabeth Wilson. Parcels of ground.	1.4.8.	
6/4d. & a ⅓ of 1d.	James Morland (P) Elizabeth Wilson. Parcels of ground.	2.10.10.	2.10.10.

(From book of admissions: 8th April 1661.)

5/4d.	James ffothergill (P) James Weatherhead. Tnmt.	2.2.8.	2.2.8.
2/-	William Shaw (P) Edmond Shaw. Parcel of ground.	0.16.0.	0.16.0.
8/4d.	Thomas Whitfeild. (P) Henry Whitfeild. Tnmt.	3.6.8.	3.6.8.

The same admissions book of 8th April 1661 contains three later endorsements relating to two further disputes over fines heard in Chancery in 1678 and 1737.

'This book was showne to Richard Clapham gent att the time of his examination taken in Chancery on the parte & behalfe of John Tufton Esqre defendant to the bill of complaint of Michael Hopes & others Complainants.
Thomas Estcourt.

'January ye nynth 1678.
Shewed and deposed unto by George Sedgwick & Thomas Gabetis Esqres at the tyme of there (their) examinations at the execution of a Commission between Michael Hopes and others Complnts & John Tufton Esqre defdt at Kendall in ye County of Westmorland the day and yeare above written.
(Signed) Phill: Sanderson
Lancelott Machell

John Jackman
Tho: Simpson.

'In the High Court of Chancery between:
The Right Honble Sackville Earle of Thanet and the Honble Sackville Tufton Esqre commonly called Lord Tufton Complnts &
Thomas Pattison Esqre & others Defdts.
Memorandum. 9th May 1737. This book was produced and shewn unto Thomas Wycliffe Esqre a witnesse produced sworn and examined on the Complnts part at the time of his examination before us.
Tho: Rudd
Jno. Air...
Geo: Foster.
Jo: H...

Perhaps the best way to assess the worth of these fines is to compare them with the yearly servants' wages at the time. In the Naworth castle accounts of 1648 the following are a good comparison: a dairy wench was paid £1. a year; a kitchen boy and a swine boy £1.6.8d; a miller, a washmaid, and a coachman £2; a carter from £2.10s. to £3; a nursery maid £3, and a bailiff £8. Thus the fine was by no means negligible. They represent working wages on a large estate.[5] They were probably better than those on the fellside farms. As Dr. Spence has remarked lady Anne was tough and uncompromising over estate matters, generous only when she had her way[4] Apart from the issue of fines during the turmoil of the Commonwealth, when there was great hardship, it can hardly be said that after 1660 when trade revived an 8d. fine was excessive. Apart from demesne lands and a few lands let at rack where rents could be raised, it is not appreciated that there was no room for manoeuvre on customary lands which paid ancient rents. Take for example the manor of Mallerstang; in the year 1667-8 the sum of £32.6.6. was received from ancient rents. When it is remembered that in 1328 the ancient rents on vaccaries and the profits of herbage came to £30 there was no variation. There were a number of encroachments recorded and rented in the Survey of 1604, which accounts for a slight increase in the total figure. On the other hand Bluegrass was forfeit to lady Anne on the execution of Captain Robert Atkinson on 1st Sept. 1664. His rent of 22s.10d. ancient rent was changed, and his widow Jane Atkinson an initial rent of £12.18.9. in 1667.[5] This of course excluded general and dropping fines and all other dues. Bluegrass became part of the demesne.

The receipts on the Appleby castle estate in 1667-8 are instructive.[6]

Manor of Winton (Joint Graves: John Bracken & Thomas Ubancke)	£ 32. 5. 4½.
Manor of Brampton (Bailiff: Robert Richardson)	8. 2. 6.
Manor of King's Meaburn (Grave: Rowland Dent)	28.12. 6½.
Forest of Stainmore (Bailiff: Edward Thornbrowe)	136. 1. 0.
Manor of Brough (Grave: William Jackson)	31.19. 0½.
Manor of Brough Sowerby (Grave: John Laidman)	16. 9. 0.
Forest of Mallerstang (Grave: Thomas Knewstubb)	32. 6. 6.
Out of Appleby, Scattergate & Burrels (Lancelot Robinson)	20. 5. 8.
Manor of Bongate & Langton (Robert Bolton)	18. 0. 0.
Manor of Knock (Bailiff: Robert Thornbrowe)	8.18. 0.
Forest of Oglebrige (Woodside & Moorhouses)(William Spedding)	19. 0. 0.
Manor of Kirkby Stephen (Graves: John Barnett & William Fawcett)	28.17. 5.
Total	£380.17. 0½.
Demesne rents with some arrears	476. 5. 7.
Total	£857. 2. 7½.

Assuming that an 8d. rate was equal to one year's improved rent, the total income of £380.17.0½. on ancient rents should be multiplied by 8 to arrive at the real value of the farms let on the open market. This would have brought it to over £3,000. This does not take into account the difference in profit between the marginal fellside farm, and one in the lower valley with arable land. Mallerstang had no arable land, and the Stainmores very little.

This is not the place to follow lady Anne's extensive restoration of castles, churches, mills, walls, bridges and woods, except to note that they cost about £40,000. This could not have been achieved without her jointure rents. As soon as the houses were completed she went on tour for the rest of her life, staying usually about three months in each place. All her groceries, spices and stuffs, her wines, malt, hay, corn and straw were brought locally for ready money. Wherever she stayed she distributed 10s. every Monday morning to 20 of the poor householders of the place, besides the daily alms she gave to all who came to her gate. She seldom had any goods from London, being determined that her northern tenants should benefit fully from her presence.[7] Despite the pain of early years, and the wrongs suffered by her tenants in the past, she did more than any of her family to support the economy of her tenants. She died aged 86 on 22nd March 1675/6 full of honour and respect, a legend at least to the gentry of her day.

(B) The three endorsements after the 1661 admissions[8] shew that the tenancy troubles had not been quelled by lady Anne. In 1678 there was a case between Michael Hopes, probably of Stainmore, and others against the new lord the earl of Thanet. This may have adjusted the general fine at 10d. and a dropping fine at 17d. on ancient rents. It has not yet been found.

The second[9] was between Sackville earl of Thanet and Paterson and others representatives of the manors of Brougham, Appleby, Brough under Stainmore, Pendragon, Kirkby Stephen, Brough Sowerby, Winton, King's Meaburn, Langton, Mallerstang, Knock, Sowerby, East Stainmore, South Stainmore, Scattergate and Burrells, Woodside, Moorhouses, Bongate, Burgh Over and Burgh Nether (Church Brough and Market Brough). The Bill was filed in Chancery on 11th July 1738, and covered all the plaintiff's customary tenants in Westmorland. The plaintiff sought two years' improved value for a general fine; and on the change of tenant by death or alienation a reasonable fine to be assessed by the lord, but not exceeding two years' improved value. There were two hearings, one in London in 1739, in which the defendants claimed that the daughters of the late earl who died in 1729 had claimed the manor in tail; but the court decided that as the daughters had not entered upon the manors, nor held courts the cross bill failed. The court decided that the case be heard in Westmorland before a Middlesex jury. When it came to be heard at bar in K.B. in Westmorland there was confusion as to the issue being tried. A new trial was sought, granted and fixed for 7th February 1740. However, the jury found that fines according to the yearly value were not payable, but that on the death of the last general admitting lord a 10d. fine on every penny old rent was due. On the change of tenant by death or alienation a reasonable fine be assessed at the will of the lord not exceeding 17d. for every 1d. old rent was due. When the case came up on the 7th February 1740 it was announced that the earl

of Thanet had accepted the tenants's plea that on the death of the last admitting lord a 10d. fine, or 10 years' ancient rent was due as a general fine. He also accepted that a 17d. fine was due as a dropping fine on the change of tenant by death or alienation, subject to certain adjustments which were left to the arbitration of three commissioners. They determined that: on the admittance of a tenant, where the ancient rent exceeds 1s. then 3s. and no more is payable to the steward for every single admittance; where the tenant has several admittances at the same court, and the ancient rents of any one of them exceeds 1s. then 3s. is payable for the first admittance and 6d. for every other. Where the ancient rent does not exceed 1s, then only a 1s. is payable for every single admittance; and where one tenant has several admittances and the ancient rent of one of them exceeds 1s., then 1s. is payable for the first, and 6d. for every other admittance.

Further rights included the right of the tenant to quarry stone on his own lands for repairs for houses and fences; but licence had to be obtained to get stone from the lord's quarries. The tenants may cut turves, peats, heath, furze and bracken on the wastes for fuel and thatching, without licence. They may plow their lands without licence. Tenants are to have the right to lease their lands for not more than three years. All absolute sales must be by deed poll or indenture, and presented at the next court for admittance and payment of the dropping fine. Tenants may mortgage for three years without licence or fine; when the mortgagee is admitted he shall pay a dropping fine. Tenants may exchange lands of equal value in the common fields with the approval of the lord's steward. They may cut underwood growing on their tenements, and may cut other wood or timber for the repair of their tenements, and for hedge boot, plough boot, cart boot, estovers and other necessary uses, the same to be set out by the steward without fee within 20 days of written request; if it is not set out in that time the tenant may proceed to cut down and use. The lord may fell timber provided he leave sufficient for repairs, boots and estovers.

Lord Thanet only obtained ten years' ancient rent (one year's improved value) for a general fine, and only 17 years' instead of 20 years' (under 2 years' improved value) for dropping fines. The scale of steward's fees for inrollment is interesting. Thereafter copies of admittances on the court roll were issued on printed forms, and were used in land sales. Thus they might be called copyholds!

References Chapter 25.

(1) Chapter 4. passim.

(2) The Drovers. K.J. Bonsor. County Book Club 1970 ed. 20-21.
Hist. & Traditions of Ravenstonedale. W. Nicholls. vol. II, 1914. 179.
Description of Westmorland, Sir Daniel Fleming. Ed. Sir G.F. Duckett, 1882. p. 18.
Hist. of Westmorland. R.S. Ferguson, 1894. 166-7. The Kendal wool and cloth trade.
Hist. of Cumberland. R.S. Ferguson, 1890. 264. Between 1st. Aug. 1662 and 1st. Aug. 1663 no less than 26,000 Scottish & Irish cattle passed thro' Cumberland.

(3) C.R.O. Kendal. WD/Hoth. (Box 20). Book of fines 1657-1661.
Surtees Soc. CLXVIII, 1958. Naworth accounts 1648-1660. C.R. Hudleston. 21/2.

(4) Northern History. XV. 1979. 43. R.T. Spence. Lady Anne Clifford Countess of Dorset Pembroke & Montgomery (1590-1676). A reappraisal. pp. 50 & 58. Dr. Spence's view of Lady Anne's harsh maternalism has force.

(5) It is possible that Jane Atkinson's initial rent of £12.18.9. was an admission of some sort. Her rent after 1667 was £6.10.0. Her son Richard's rent in 1699/1700 was £8. C.R.O. Kendal. ED/Hoth. Box 19. Westmorland rental 1697-1732.

(6) C.R.O. Kendal. WDI Hoth. Box 23. Lady Anne's estate accounts 1667-68.

(7) N & B, I. 300 & 302.

(8) C.R.O. Kendal. Book of admissions & fines 1657-61, ref. 3. above. A grandson Michael Hopes may be Michaell s.o. *Michaell Houpes* bapt. at Brough Church 13 Sept. 1698. Par. reg.

(9) N & B, I..306-308.
Hist. & Trads. of Mallerstang Forest. W. Nicholls. 1883. 49-52.
English Law Reports. Vol. XXVII, Chancery VII, 632-635. 11 July 1738. Sackville earl of Thanet v. Paterson & others.
The copy of the Award dated 3 July 1741 was among lord Hothfield's evidence at Messers Dawson & Bennett in 1916. Williamson lists.

Chapter 26

The decay of customary tenant-right

The reader will recall that the division of the ancient farms in the later 16th century, and their even greater disintegration in the mid-seventeenth century created a small tenantry unable to resist years of bad harvest. The parish registers of the upper Eden valley, and especially of Brough, Ravenstonedale and Kirkby Stephen, in the mid-eighteenth century repeatedly record the burial of 'a poor man' or 'a poor woman'. Even a remote dale such as Mallerstang had a small poor house. The poverty seems to have been acute. We can certainly date the decay of the Quaker meetings in the dales from that period, and the drift into the market towns to find work.

The famous agricultural writer Arthur Young travelled through the north (in 1770) twenty years before his appointment as secretary to the newly created Board of Agriculture. He rode from Brough to Askrigg through Kirkby Stephen and Mallerstang to upper Wensleydale, and thus describes his journey. 'The road if I may give it that name, to Askrigg, lies over one continued range of mountains, here called Moors. The uncultivated vallies are too inconsiderable to deserve a mention. Most of these fifteen miles, however dreadful the road, are tracts of very improveable land; if a good turnpike road was made from Askrigg to Brough, the first great step to cultivation would be over; for it is almost impossible to improve a country with spirit, the roads of which are impassable. It is extremely melancholy to view such tracts that are indisputably capable of yielding many beneficial crops, remaining totally waste; while in many parts of the kingdom farms are so scarce & difficult to be procured, that one is no sooner vacant, that twenty applications are immediately made for it.' He then went on to say that farms let at so trifling a rent give no inducement to the landlord to improve. He also pointed to the lack of good drainage and manuring.[1]

An anonymous clerical writer in the Monthly Magazine of 1802 mentions two obstacles to enclosure of wastes to improve agriculture.

First the lords of manors with their strong remains of feudalism take good care to demand ample satisfaction for their mineral and other rights. Secondly, 'as for the clergy, their eagerness and rapacity is proverbial. And if their claims, however unfair or exorbitant, are opposed, they have a number of vigilant and powerful friends who can lay a dead weight upon a proposed enclosure.' The procuring of an Act of enclosure is a very lucrative job to the solicitors and others concerned. Thus the freeholders seeing or meeting with what they believe to be unfair claims are intimidated or disgusted, and prefer to leave uncultivated land as they found it.[2]

(C) When Sir John Sinclair appointed Arthur Young secretary to the newly created Board of Agriculture and Internal Improvement in 1793, surveyors were appointed to report on the state of agriculture in all the English counties. Most of the surveys were conducted during the winter of 1793-4, when there was no chance to see active agriculture. The Cumberland survey was conducted by J. Bailey, and G. Culley; the Westmorland by A. Pringle in October and November 1793. In the lower valleys they were dealing with arable lands ploughed in the immemorial fashion by oxen; on the fellsides there was little or no ploughing, with the tenant dependent upon his few cattle and sheep, his weaving and knitting, and butter and cheese sold at the local market. As Wordsworth wrote of the dale communities of 1760 'there was no communication between these vales by carriage roads; all bulky articles were transported on packhorses...the valleys themselves were intersected as now by innumerable lanes and pathways, leading from house to house, and field to field.'[3] The comments of the surveyors on the plight of the innumerable small tenants in the dales are interesting for two different reasons.

The Cumberland: 'The greatest part of this county is held under lords of manors by that species of vassalage called customary tenure; subject to the payment of fines and heriots, on alienation, death of lord, or death of tenant, and the payment of certain annual rents, and performance of various services, called boon days; such as getting and leading of the lord's peats, ploughing and harrowing his land, reaping his corn, haymaking, carrying letters etc, whenever summoned by the lord. We cannot pretend to be accurate, but believe, that two thirds of the county are held by this kind of tenure, principally in those small tenements described in the last chapter. The remaining part is mostly freehold, which has increased with the closure of commons; and sometimes whole parishes, or manors, have been enfranchised on those occasions. Copyhold and leasehold are rarely met with.[4]

The second and more important section is in Chapter XVI: 'One great obstacle to improvement, seems to arise from a laudable anxiety in the customary tenants to have their little patrimony descend to their children. These small properties (loaded with fines, heriots and boon days, joined to the necessary expense of bringing up and educating a numerous family) can only be handed down, from father to son, by the utmost thrift, hard labour, and penurious living; and every little saving being hoarded up for the payment of the eventual fine, leaves nothing for the expense of travelling to see improved modes of culture, and to gain a knowledge of the management of different breeds of stock, and be convinced, by ocular proofs, that their own situations are capable of producing similar advantages; and even should they be half inclined to adopt a new practice, prudence whispers, that, should the experiment fail, it would require the savings of many years to make good the deficiency. The customary tenure is allowed on all hands to be a great grievance, and check to improvement. Would not this be best done away with on the division of commons as was the case at Brampton etc, where lord Carlisle had one twelfth for his consent, as lord of the soil, and for enfranchising the allotments? There are other lords who ask one fourth for their consent and enfranchising. The yearly value of customs, fines, etc might be easily settled by commissioners, and twenty-five years' purchase on this value be the price of this enfranchisement, which might be allowed out of the allotment, upon the division of a common; or paid in money at the option of the tenant.'[5] On the topic of leases and letting and surveyors said: 'Where the tenant cannot enfranchise under 40 years' purchase, it would be a humane act of the Legislature to relieve these bondagers by law etc.' They added that short leases will not induce a tenant to improve. But long leases (say) of 21 years would induce a prospect of gain, and induce the tenant to improve.[6]

Arthur Young's rival William Marshall in his review of these reports in 1808 made the point that in abolishing these customary tenures 'twenty five years' purchase is but a moderate offer...From thirty to thirty three years' produce appears to me to be a more reasonable and fair price for the whole.'[7]

The Westmorland surveyor pointed to a change beginning to appear in the dales: 'The customary tenants, as distinct to farmers or those who hire the land they occupy, are usually denominated statesmen. They live poorly, and labour hard; and some of them, particularly in the vicinity of Kendal, in the intervals of labour from agricultural avocations, busy themselves in weaving stuffs for the manufacturers of that town. The consciousness of their independence renders them impatient of oppression or insult, but they are gentle and obliging when treated by their superiors with kindness and respect. This class of men is daily decreasing. The turnpike roads have brought the manners of the capital to this extremity of the kingdom. The simplicity of ancient times is gone. Finer clothes, better dwellings, and more expensive viands, are now sought after by all. This change of manners, combined with other circumstances which have taken place within the last forty years, has compelled many a statesman to sell his property, and reduced him to the necessity of working as a labourer in those fields, which, perhaps, he and his ancestors had for many generations cultivated as their own.'[8] This last observation is probably the most acute of all in pointing to the drift from the smaller uneconomic fellside farms.

Marshall, quoting from Pringle, was unable to resist a reference to the uncivil treatment of female servants in Westmorland. 'It is painful to one, who has in his composition the smallest spark of knight-errantry, to behold the beautiful servant maids of this county toiling in the severe labours of the fields. They drive the harrows, or the ploughs, when they are drawn by three or four horses; nay, it is not uncommon to see, sweating at the dunghill, a girl, whose elegant features, and delicately proportioned limbs, seemingly but ill accord with such rough employment.'[9]

(D) There is one further case covering northern land law to which we now refer. It was presided over by Edward Law, lord Ellenborough L.C.J. Edward Law was the second son of Edmund Law bishop of Carlisle 1768-1787. Edward was leading counsel for Warren Hastings in 1788, and made Lord Chief Justice in 1802. On 14th November 1803 he heard the case in King's Bench of: Doe, on the demise of Robert Reay v. Huntington & others. It concerned the manor of Cardue in the parish of Dalston, Cumberland next to Rose Castle where his father had lived as bishop.

(a) On the 30th August 24 Car. II, C. Denton of Cardue, Cumberland, lord of the customary manor of Parton, Mickelwhaite, Neelehouse and Cardulees in the parish of Dalston by Indenture made since the Statute Quia Emptores granted to his customary tenant T. Donnald, who held by payment of certain customary rents and other services, that in consideration of a 61 penny fine (or 61 years' rent) he the lord ratified and confirmed to the tenant and his heirs all his customary tenant-right estate etc, and that the tenant and his heirs etc should be freed and excepted from the payment of all rents, fines, heriots, carriages, boons, dues, duties, customs, services and demands whatsoever, and at any time hereafter happening to become due in respect of the tenancy, granting to him full liberty to cut timer without licence, but reserving to the lord an annual 1d. rent payable on the 11th November, suit of court and service incident thereto; saving also to the lord all royalties, escheats and forfeitures and all other advantages and emoluments belonging to the seignory, so as not to prejudice the immunities thereby granted to the tenant.

The tenement had passed through several ownerships by sale and demise, and at one time the accession to estate of a new owner had not been inrolled on the court roll, though the tenant's name was on a later roll.

(b) The lord was claiming the tenement on two grounds: reversion by custom of the manor in that it was not deviseable by will; and because the accession of the new owner had not been inrolled in the first instance, though noted as a tenant on a later roll.

In the main the issues at law were: Had the original Indenture of 24 Car. II extinguished it as a customary estate, and made it one held in free and common socage; and under what description was it deviseable under the Statute of Wills?

(c) The report covers $8\frac{1}{2}$ pages, and the most interesting part of lord Ellenborough's judgement is as follows:

'These customary estates, known by the denomination of tenant-right, are peculiar to the Northern parts of England, in which border-service against Scotland were anciently performed, before the union of England and Scotland under the same Sovereign. And although these appear to have many qualities and incidents which do not properly and ordinarily belong to villenage tenure either pure or privileged, (and out of one or other of these species of villenage all copyhold is derived) and also have some which savour more of military tenure by escuage uncertain, which according to Littleton, sect. 99, is knight's service; and although they seem to want some of the characteristic qualities and circumstances which are considered as distinguishing this species of tenure, viz. the being holden at the will of the lord, and also the usual evidence of title by copy of court roll, and are alienable also, contrary to the usual mode by which copyholds are alienable, viz. by deed and admittance thereon (if indeed they could be immemorially aliened at all by the particular species of deed stated in the case, viz. a bargain and sale, which at common law could only have transferred the use); I say, notwithstanding all these anomalous circumstances, it seems to be now so far settled in Courts of Law that these customary tenant-right estates are not freehold, but that they in effect fall within the same consideration as copyholds, that the quality of their tenure in this respect cannot properly any longer be drawn into question. In the case of Stephenson v. Hall 3 Burr. 1278 Lord Mansfield and Mr. Justice Dennison considered it to be a settled point that in the case of customary estates 'the freehold was in the lord'. And in the very late case of Burrell v. Dodd, 3 Bos. & Pull. 378 the Court of Common Pleas expressly held these customary tenant-right estates not to be freeholds. Assuming therefore that these estates were prior to the execution of the Indenture of the 24 Car. 2. holden by copy of court roll within the enlarged sense of those words as they occur in the Stat. of 12 Car. 2. (and the contrary has not been even insinuated in argument by the counsel on either side), we are of the opinion that by virtue of the Indenture of the 24 Car. 2. operating upon that species of tenure, the tenement in question has become frank free; or in other words, land holden in free and common soccage, and of course, under that description and character, deviseable by the Statute of Wills.'[10]

(E) This review of the development of northern customary tenure from 1537 concludes with two reports:

(a) The Third Report by the Commissioners to enquire into the Law of England respecting Real Property. House of Commons 24 May, 1832.

Customary freehold. 'A tenure called Customary Freehold, exists in many parts of the kingdom, especially in Cumberland, Westmorland, a part of Lancashire called Oversands, the south-western parts of the counties of

Durham and Northumberland, and the northern parts of Yorkshire.

It is a base tenure, partaking, to a considerable degree, of the nature of copyhold; but the holding is, generally, declared to be according to the custom of the manor, without being at the will of the lord; and, not infrequently, instead of a surrender in court by the tenant in person, or by attorney, alienation is allowed by a common law conveyance, which is presented at the lord's court, and inrolled, whereupon the grantee is admitted, and becomes the tenant on the roll; but it is in the tenant on the roll, or his heir, that the legal estate always resides.

The customs in these manors vary considerably. Generally the fine upon admittance is certain. Among females of equal degree, the whole estate sometimes descends to the eldest, instead of being divided in coparcenary.'[11]

(b) In 1895 the Royal Commission on Agriculture submitted its report to Parliament, and the Cumberland report was written by Mr. Fox Wilson, assistant commissioner. He took evidence from the agents of the principal estates in Cumberland and Westmorland, and particularly reflected on the agricultural depressions in the 1820s, the 1840s, and at the time of the Commission.'[12]

Mr. Fox Wilson made this observation: 'I must allude to the position of the freeholders or "statesmen" as they are called in this county. This class of men has been gradually diminishing in numbers for many years, and the position of some of them is now worse than that of tenants, owing chiefly to charges which they or their ancestors have put on the land. It is difficult to say whether the larger proportion of them are mortgaged to such an extent that they are paying more in the shape of interest than neighbouring tenants are in rent. I am inclined to think that, generally speaking, the statesmen are in worse position than that of tenants, especially where the property has been in their families for generations, and consequently subject of family charges.'[13]

An agent on one of the large estates said: 'My experience is that, in consequence of the legacies and annuities with which many of the estates are saddled, statesmen have heavier burdens to bear than the ordinary farmer.'

The best evidence came from Mr. F. Grainger who owned 168 acres at Holme Abbey, which had been held by his family since 1605. He listed the difficulties which had faced the 'statesman', and added this point: 'Where statesmen sell their land to a large owner, and remain on the farm as tenants, they do not as a rule make good ones, for they live as they did before and forget that they have a rent to pay.' Mr. Grainger's most effective evidence is a table showing the gradual extinction of the statesmen in the parish of Abbey Quarter in the Wigton Union. 'It will be observed that agricultural depression is not the cause of the decrease in their numbers':-

Year	Number of Statesmen	Number of Leaseholders	Average size of holdings
1604	83	none	42 acres
1648	81	6	54
1780	51	9	58
1812	38	18	58
1837	30	20	100
1864	21	29	100
1894	9	41	100

References Chapter 26.

(1) Six Months' Tour through the North of England, 1770. 2nd. ed. 1771, vol. II, p. 187-189. Young also gives useful information on the price of labour, implements, provisions, building materials, and the economy of small farms, which compares interestingly with Pringle's survey of Westmorland 1793.

(2) Monthly Magazine, 1802 (No. 83) vol. XIII, p. 1-3.
Monthly Magazine, 1801 Part II, vol. XII, 393 has a description of the parish of Asby, & vol. XIII, 112-116 (same vol.) 419 of Crosby Ravensworth.
Monthly Magazine Aug. 1804 No. 118 (I of vol. 18). 103 has an unfinished account of the parish of Kirkby Stephen. The M. Mag. of Feb. 1805 vol. 19, 213-215 has an unfinished article on Mallerstang.

(3) Guide to the Lakes. W. Wordsworth. 1970 reprint. 64.

(4) A General View of the Agriculture of Northumberland, Cumberland and Westmorland by J. Bailey & G. Cullen, and A. Pringle, 1st. ed. 1794. This ed. 1972, with introd. by D.J. Rowe, p. 205 Cumberland sect. (See also Pringle's observations for Westmorland, p. 302 in the 1805 ed.)

(5) Ibid. 263, chapt. XVI.

(6) Ibid. 264.

(7) A Review of the Reports of the Board of Agriculture, Northern Department. W. Marshall, 1818, 174.

(8) A General View of the Agriculture of Northumberland, Cumberland and Westmorland. J. Bailey & G. Cullen, and A. Pringle 3rd. ed. 1805, 302.

(9) A Review of the Reports of the Board of Agriculture, Northern Dept. W. Marshall op.cit. 234.

(10) English (Law) Reports 1910 ed. Vol. 102, K.B. XXXI, pp. 834-843. Doe. on the demise of Robert Reay v. Huntington & others. Monday 14 Nov. 1803.
From the evidence of Wills in Ravenstonedale, Kirkby Stephen and Mallerstang from 1570 onwards many tenants demised their tenements by Will.
N & B, II. 317 notes that this manor was formerly part of the Forest of Inglewood. p. 318 refers to the sale in 1672 by Geo. Denton to the tenants of their tenant-right dues referred to in this case.
Law of Copyholds and Customary Tenures. Elton & Mackay op.cit. Doe. Reay v. Huntingdon. pp. 6, 51, 324 and 353. This case introduces a question: On the Clifford manors in Westmorland tenements seem to have been deviseable by Will, on the evidence of Wills in the C.R.O. Carlisle. Why this should have been questioned in this case is not clear.

(11) Third Report by the Commissioners to enquire into the Law of England respecting Real Property. House of Commons 24 May, 1832. p. 20. Sect. 8. Customary Freehold.

(12) The Royal Commission on Agriculture. England Report, by Mr. Fox Wilson (Assistant Commissioner) on the county of Cumberland. 1895. pp. 32-3. P. 34 refers to Pringle's Report of 1797 (sic).

(13) Ibid. p. 32. Sec. 51. et seq.

APPENDICES

Appendix I. (**Manuscript sources**).

Ravenstonedale manor. The indentured agreement between Philip third lord Wharton and the customary tenants of the manor is dated 12th February 22 Eliz. 1579/80. Neither of the original Indentures has yet been found. The parish copy was last seen by me about thirty years ago at the Vicarage, Ravenstonedale, and was then in the care of Miss Ann Metcalfe-Gibson of Ravenstonedale. The text has been reconstructed from the following MS sources:

MS.A. is the eighteenth century copy made for the Lowther steward after the purchase of the Wharton estates from the last duke of Wharton in 1729. The duke died in poverty in Spain in 1731. The Lowther copy is in the C.R.O. in Carlisle among the Lonsdale MSS, and was dictated from lord Wharton's original. There were two clerks employed, in sections 1-6 and 7-10, and their slight differences in spelling can be seen. This is used as the base text, with corrections from the others.

MS.B. is that of John Robinson schoolmaster of Ravenstonedale dated 1775 and copied from the parish original, and is in the C.R.O. Kendal. It has very few mistakes and in section (6) has a phrase omitted from the Lowther copy above. It has also the latin Chancery endorsement which is not in the other principal versions. *MSS. A & B* agree in one vital respect: In the devolution of former monastic property to lay ownership the custumal had to provide for each new lord by death or alienation. In Ravenstonedale there does not appear to have been a running fine levied by the Gilbertine canons every so many years in place of a general fine due on the death of the lay lord. Thus in section (1) of the text these two versions agree (with the legal fiction) that the tenants paid 'at the change of every lord of the said manor and at the change of every tenant one year's rent for a fine and not above.' Whereas the Articles of Customary tenant right agreed between Thomas the second lord Wharton and the customary tenants of Ravenstonedale dated 6th October 3 & 4 Phillip & Mary made no such mention; the first article states that at the exchange or entry of every new tenant a fine of one year's rent was to be paid and not more. There is no mention of a fine due on the change of lord. This was the old monastic custumal. The second lord Wharton was a Catholic, and supporter of Mary Tudor.

MS.C. is a battered 17th C. volume in the possession of Mr.C. Hollett of Sedbergh, and was copied by Philip Greene of Ravenstonedale from the Great End Book of the manor of 1586 in 1652. The chief attraction of this version, which is thus second hand from the original, is its phonetic and dialect spelling. It has two important features: (a) In section (1) it omits the key sentence referred to about the fine due on the change of the lord, and only mentions the fine due on the change of tenants; (b) It has a complete set of orders, partly culled from the old monastic court rolls, and partly new to meet the needs of a community no longer ruled by the Gilbertine canons, with the authority of the lord delegated to the manor jury. They cover three aspects, the church, titles to land and admittances, and the regulation of the parish by a court leet. There are two additional items covering the levying of certain (but not all) tithes, and church dues. From the social point of view it is the most important document of them all; it gives the ethos of a parish run on Genevan lines with the godly lord and the godly jury predominant, and the curate appointed by the lord very much under the thumb of the jury.

MS.D. is another small volume in the possession of Mr. C. Hollett and is dated 1738, and belonged to James Bayliff of Ravenstonedale. He may have been the clerk or 'Register' to the jury. He married a Quakeress, who was expelled from that society, but was reconciled before her death. She was buried at Cat-Keld, and he was buried there thirty years later in 1766. His version contains some textual errors, but may have been taken from the parish copy of the Indenture. His copy contains the endorsement of the Court of Chancery, not in the other versions.

MS.E. was in the possession of Mr. A.M. Fell, solicitor of Hallam & Son solicitors of Kirkby Stephen. It was part of a small volume of custumals of the surrounding manors in the upper Eden valley, such as would be compiled by a country solicitor for his professional use. A similar volume was destroyed some years ago at Sedbergh. The Kirkby Stephen volume was compiled by Mr. T.H. Preston solicitor, and is late 19th C. but contains material up to 1923. This volume is probably now in the collection of old material deposited in the C.R.O. Kendal, as yet unclassified. This version omits about five sentences in the main text and all of sections 6, 7 and 8, being of no later use. The Preston text is, however, useful in confirming the point made in *MSS. A & B* that a fine was due on the change of the lord. The lawyer will observe that the Indenture did not state that a fine was due on the death of the last admitting lord, an omission which was to cause endless trouble at a later date. The full text cannot be reconstructed from the Preston text.

MS.F. There is a short version printed in The History of Cumberland and Westmorland by Joseph Nicolson & Richard Burn, 1777, vol. I. 526.

Here after followeth A Supplication maid by the Tennants and Occupiers of this Lordshipp of Ravenstondaile unto the Right Honorable Phillip Lord Wharton for the Maintenance of the Customary Tryall there. 1581.

Humbly sheweth and in earnest manor compleneth unto your good L: your dayly orators your L: power teneants & occupiers most part in generall within your whole Lordshipp of Ravenstonedaile WHEREAS Henery ffawcett of ye Wainegarthes your L: teneant within ye said manner late attempted a Sute to ye utter overthrowe if it be not prevented of one of the severall previlages of ye said your Lordshipps liberties theire and to ye utter undoeing and disquieting of all your L: tennants and occupiers there being a thing flatt against the third Article of our Ancient Custome and ancient usage that any man shall either refuse indiferent triall when it might be had within ye said Lordshipp according to the ancient Custome thereof or yet to goe to Lawe with the tenants or occupiers within the said Lordshippp so long as Indiffrent trial might be had within ye said Lordshipp according to ye custome thereof for ye said Henry not withstanding your Lordship granted him & commanded him to bide Indiffrent triall within the said Lordshipp yet hath he wilfully neglected the same and hath atempted sute at London notwithstanding the other partie being a whole Jury was contented to have bidden any indifferent triall within the said Lordshipp according to the ancient Custome thereof Wherefore such a gapp as this being opned both to the utter overthrow of your L: liberties and the Custome of the Manner And the good and peaceable estate of us all your L: tennants ther WE your L: Jury there now in charge have thought ourselves many ways & specially bound in conscience to give your L:shipp warning hereof And furthermore we and ye rest of your L:ps tenants there doe in the behaulf of our & your neighbours now put to troble And also in our behalfe doe hereafter earnestly becech your good L: with speciall consideration to examine this matter And to forse and prevent whatsoever shall be espied not onlie against your L: but also against ye good peaceable estate of your L: tennants there wch thing that it may be ye better accomplished and brought to passe we both tending our L: & common wealth of us all your L: tennants there have undertaken this humble sute unto your L: that is to say, to beecech your good L: to be soe good as to joyne by consent with us your L: Jure to set downe a speciall verdict & order under penaltye

to your L: that none at all within the said L:(ordship) shall when they may have triall according to the Custome of ye Manner attempt or take suite upon any person within the said L:(ordship) to any forraine Lawe without or not within the said Liberties but that he or they, whosoever they be Inhabiting within the said parish of Ravinstonesaile which shall at any tyme hereafter take suite at any forrayne corte without and not within the said Lordshipp upon any person or persons at any tyme ever after that ye said Order be sett downe by your L: and we your Jurye ther contrary (to) the treue meaning of the said Award to forfit some speciall Penalty of good valewe unto your L: And in thus doing you binde us and every of us to pray unto ye everlasting God to blesse your good L: for ever.

Hereunto subscribed two severall Jures with the rest of the parish accordingly as is to seend (sic) at large in the End Booke-This sute was also granted by ye Lord And soe returned againe from him to ye grand Jury who sett downe the orders as foloweth.

Ravinstondaile.

Anne Dom 1581 the xxiij yeare of the Raigne of our soceraigne Lady Elizabeth queene of England etc this xij day of Aprill

A true coppy of ye third Article of ye Custome of Ravinstonedaile

It has beene and is accustomed within ye said Lordshipp that for all manner of Contintions variances debats demands Tytles Clames or Tennentright of farmehoulde which hath beene is or shall be depending in Traiuce (Travarse) between tennant and Tennant party & partis within the said L:(ordship) to be full ordered determined and ended by an Indifferent Jury and Inquest taken And appointed by ye Lord or his officers thereby the assents and consents of ye said partyes within the said Lordshippe in that behalfe.

The names of the Lords Jurye now in charge Stephen Bousfeild George Greene James Taylor Anthony Pinder Christopher Rogerson Richard Wilson Wilyam Adamthwaite John ffothergill Edward ffawcett Thomas ffawcett John Ubanke Vincent Cautley/

Memorandum that it is fully and absolutely Concluded agred And set downe the day and yeare abovesaid betwixt the Right Honorable Phillip L. Wharton and his L: Tennants within his L: Liberties of Ravinstonedaile and also his L: Jurye there abovenamed by the mutuall Assents and Consents of ye said his L: and the said his L: tennants And Jurye there THAT for the more strengthening fortifying And the better maintenance of the abovesaid Articles of ye Customary triall of the Liberties and Lordshipp of Ravinstondaile both for the better safty of that priviledge of triall within the said his L: Liberties and also for ye better Quietnesse of ye said his L: tennants ther that from the day of ye date hereof there shall noe person or persons within the said Lordshipp attempt or take suite at or to any forrayne Corte that is to say without and not within the said Liberties of Ravenstonedaile neither by any colourable means as apounting or making of any factors (ie. agent or deputy) or Atturneyes to Attemspt or take any such sute against any person or persons within the said Lordshipp for any Manner of contentienions (sic) variences debats demands titles or Tennantright of farmeholds at any tyme hereafter depending in travise betwixt tennant & tennant party & party within the said Lordshipp so long as triall may be had within ye said Lordshipp according to the true meanieng of the abovesaid Articles upon paine of every default of every one within the said Lordshipp offending therein at any tyme hereafter Contrary to the true meaneing hereof to forfit to the Lord xxxixs. xid. ob. given forth by us the said Juryes in open Court holden next after the daite hereof/

Appendix III.

(Concerning woods and underwoods)

Between Philip lord Wharton of the one part
& the named tenants of the manor of R. to
resolve certain doubts and questions arising
between P. 1d. W. and the named tenants of
the manor concerning woods & underwoods
growing upon the tenements of the respective
tenants for the taking of wood for housebote
for the repair of messuages, cottages, barns,
stables, houses & buildings of the sd. persons
& tenants; That daily destructions have been
made of wood & underwoods And trouble
between Ld W. and his servants on one part
and the tenants on their part over the taking
of timber for housebote etc and for the deter-
mination & perpetual quiet and preservation
of the sd woods etc it is agreed between
themselves and their heirs

THAT the woods & under-woods upon the
several tenements belong to the several tenants
and their heirs respectively as part & parcel
of their customary lands, and not to be used
otherwise... AND NOT TO THE LORD OF
THE MANOR or any other tenant of the same
manor or to any other person, And every
tenant shall have the right to cut down his
own woods & underwoods on his own land,
and not on the land of any other tenants

And that 1d W. his heirs and assigns shall
receive yearly from every tenant for every
tenement ONE PENNY for GREENHEW and
no more in consideration of the sd woods &
underwoods

AND that 1d W. in consideration of four score
pounds of lawful Eng. money paid by the sd
tenants and now acknowledged and received
& discharged and for the accomplishment of
the good order & agreement of the Lady
Frances the late wife of the sd P. 1d W. doth
confirm & allow the sd custom & usage of
the sd woods & underwoods in manner afsd
for ever and the sd P.1d. W. doth confirm to
the sd tenants all his right & title in the sd
woods & underwoods afsd according to the
custom of the sd manor as part of the sd
customary lands, they paying yearly one penny
as greenhew

And the sd P.1d. W. doth grant that from
time to time the sd tenants may cut down

woods or underwoods at their free will and
pleasure according to the sd custom without
let or trouble or vexation of the sd P. 1d W.

And that the sd tenants disclaim to pretend
to have any claim for timber for housebote
hereafter from P. 1d W. his heirs & asigns
upon their several tenements and the sd tenants
promise to pay each of them 1 penny yearly
for each tenement for greenhew for the sd
woods, and the sd tenants shall not pretend
to demand any timber or housebote to be
bestowed upon their premises other than the
sd woods & underwoods growing upon their
several tenements

And that they shall not cut down timber on
tenements of other tenants afsd their heirs &
assigns or enter into each other's customary
lands & tenements & cut down woods &
underwoods without consent first obtained from
the owner of the same lands & tenants woods
& underwoods and for each offence the sum
of three shillings and fourpence to be paid to
the sd P.1d W. his heirs & assigns and Also
another 3^s4^d to the owner of the sd woods &
underwoods which shall be wrongfully cut
down to be reckoned by the party grieved
tenant of the sd manor by action within the
court of the sd manor in addition to damage
to be recovered for the value of the same
woods & underwoods so cut down, And it
shall be lawful for the L. or his officers to
enter the customary lands of the offender to
distrain and levy such sum or sums as may
be forfeited and the distress there taken to
lead drive carry away appraise & sell to satisfy
the sd P. 1d W. his heirs & assigns & every
party grieved for such forfeiture according to
custom & usage for levying of debts recovered
within the sd manor

LASTLY it is agreed between P. 1d W. his
heirs & assigns & the tenants & their heirs
& assigns that they the tenants shall not at
any time in future sell, bestow convey or give
woods or underwoods outside the manor or
parish without first obtaining the licence of
the sd P. 1d W. upon pain for every felling
or aliening or giving of sustenance for every
offence 20^s to the sd P. 1d W. his heirs &
assigns to be levied as afsd. 1592.

(MS. C.R.O. Kendal)

Hereafter followeth a supplication made to the Right Honorable Phillip L: Wharton for Reformation of Certaine Abuses in our daly trialls And alsoe that some perfect orders may be set downe for ye better usage hereafter

Hombleye besechith your good L:shipp that Whereas ther is within your L. Liberties of Ravinstondaille soo many troubles variances and other inconveniences arising amongst us your L: tenneants ther wich also can not be staied or brought to any good end And that cheiflie by reason of ye foule and shamfull abuses growne to such fullnesse in ye mannor of usage of our Customary triall Wich although it ought to be ye stay of our quietnesse is notwithstanding as it is used And hath beene a long tyme the very Mother of disorder contention & varence and that (in) many ways / as first by trobling the church there withall upon ye sabath day. And by differing and delaying of verdicts And long continuance of Masters (i.e. matters) without makeing end thereof, after that they be notwithstanding put to order by ye officer the cause & defaulte whereof experience hath taught us to be not only in ye parties w(hi)ch doe use as a common practice when they perseive matters like to goe against them by one means or other to stay and differe (defer) the verdict till a new day makeing aledgement to bring in better profe (proof) or other subtill excuses, but alsoe in ye Jeurye or arbiters themselves, W(hi)ch when they weare assembled togither and had throughly examined ye causes have not used before they departed they (sic) presently to procede in Judgement and to give forth theire verdict as they ought to doe although they had taken all ye evidence and witnesses that ye parties could make but every man at his pleasure to depart home and to differ (defer) there full conclusions or giving forth theire verdict tell a new day and soe leave the parties at as full varience or worse then before Whereupon it hath to(o) often happened amongst us that either great Inconveniences have happened and fallen out in the meane tyme betweene the parties or else that the parties have beene made privise (privy) & by such may have gott knowledge of all that ye Jurers or Arbiters had done & how far they had proceeded in ye matter they had in hand before that the Jurers or arbiters did meete againe, Whereby malice & contentions hath greatlie increased And matters have become more heinous than before,

first therefore that our Church ye place of God's worship may be purged and clearelye

ridd and avoided of all such propheine matters with handling whereof therein we have abeused it a verey long tyme noe otherwise than it had beene a common muite hale (moot hall) To that end alsoe that the Jurers & arbiters may hereafter be ye better kept togither and others barred and keept from trobling them till they come to give forth ther verdicts and that all ye aforesaid mischeifes may be the better be prevented and roted out from amongst us Wee the said Juerers now presently in charge with others tendring the common Welth of that L:shipp doe in humble manner and most Intirelie beseeche your good L: that by your L: meanes a convenient house may be provided & knowne whereunto at all tymes hereafter all Jurers and Arbiters parties & Witnesses according as they shall have lawfull warning by your L: or your officers may commonly resort unto and theire by the good meanes of the officer be closely kept togither, several and apart from all other people soe as they depart not before they give forth the verdict in writing and furthermore wee pray your good L: that for the better executione heereof and bringing the same more fully to passe to Joyne by consent with us the said Jurers to set downe playne orders under convenent (convenient) penalties to your L: that from henceforth all Jurers arbiters parties and witnesses at days and hours appowinted them by lawfull comandment of your L: offecer shall come & make their repaire unto ye said house when it shall be beulded or other convenient place abrode in ye parish if ye matter shall soe require and theire ye Jurers & arbiters to abide and remaine togither untill they doe give forth their verdict in writing as God shall direct there conscances according to ye witnesse & evidence that shall be brought in unto them and alsoe that neither ye parties not witnesses shall depart or goe away but tende untill such tyme as ye offecers and Jurers and arbiters have dispatched with them and shall licence them to go away farthermore alsoe because there are soe many trifling causes amongst us and daly complaynts in matters of noe valewe w(hi)ch notwithstanding the willfullnes of parties canot at any tyme be perswaded to have descided except it be by Jurers or sworne men not considering what great token and firgament (Argument) if ye want of the true feare of God there is in such dealing And how shamefull a thing and unworthy a good Christian it is for every exebiting Cause, by soe many solemne othes to call the most holy name of God in Question and (in) such manner to prophaine the same through swearing of Jurers or arbiters parties & witnesses & in effect all aboute nothing the common usage whereof with grefe wee doe speake it hath brought aboute as wee doubt in our conscience this day that Conscience of any oth is but very smale in many hands This prophanation therefore of ye name of God: And the shipwracke of conscience w(hi)ch we see daly ensewe thereupon moveth us in humble and moste ernest mannor to beseach your good L: that an order may be set downe thereby both all such matters as be worthy of a sworne triall may at all tymes by sworne Jurers or arbiters be spedely tried and that alsoe all other pelting (?petty) trifles wherein men stand rather upon their wills for most part, then upon the matters themselvs may without oath be decyded and put away by some godly and Cristiane manner referring such like theire controversies unto such honest Indifferent neighbours within ye parish as both ye parties shall agree upon when they come to

1. complaine in such things before your L: or your officers for the bringing of which thing to passe wee doe not see a more conveneant or better ways then this yt is to say yt (that) when any partie or parties shall come before your L: or your L: officer to compleaine in any causes or controversie w(hi)ch concernith

2. not ye title of Tennant right of house or tenement, or, wherein the Lord of ye Manner shall not be of the one partie or Quch (which) may now lawfully be

3. decided by sworne Jurers or arbiters without takeing any sworn witnesses upon either partie of w(hi)ch sorte are the aggrements for farme holds paied unto younger brethren for ye most part that if they will not be content

to put all other smaler causes to Indefrent men unsworne to put away as God shall put them in minde for ye best that then an order may be set downe that they shall have a sworne triall indeede but yet soe as the partie Against whom the same triall doth passe shall forfitt a penaltie of xij^d. the one halfe to ye lord and ye other to ye baliffe And Jurers or arbiters that travell (travail) therin ffurthermore wee pray your good Lordshipp that some good order may be taken for better keping (of) all ends and verdicts after they be given further then hath beene used heretofore These things wee are fully perswaded if it please your L: to grant and that there (they) be orderly set downe and by your L: means and procurement well executed shall doe much good (&) avoide great troble and contention many wayes and make much quietnesse amongst your good L: tenneants there and all they that feare God & tennder the good and peaseable estaite of that L:(ordship) shall pray unto God to blesse your good L; for ever/

Your humble and dalie orators the said Jurers that is to saie/

George Greene Anthony Pinder George Dent Richard Wilson Cuthbert Hunter George Hablthwaite Willm Adamthwaite Robert ffothergill Thomas Fawcett John ffawcett Richard Bousfeild Simond Bousfeild Richard Wharton Richard Bouell Thomas ffawcett Stephen Swinbanke,

(endorsed in margin) Phillip Wharton 1583.

All this was granted by the Lord And subscribed unto, And soe returned againe unto the Grant Jurye who sett downe the orders afterwards in such manner as hereafter followeth/

Appendix V. **Summary of Manorial incidents of Ravenstonedale 1578-1725.**

After the Duke of Wharton sold the Wharton properties in Westmorland to Robert Lowther of Maulds Meaburn in 1729, the Lowther steward made an analysis of the court books of the manor of Ravenstonedale from 1578 until 1725 which had been transferred to the new owner. This summary provided the precedents which would guide him in administering the manor by the rules of the Indenture of 1580. The summary is also a valuable guide to the manorial historian wanting to know the frequency of the several incidents. The final summary makes these points: Deeds of purchase begin to be mentioned from the court of 5th August 1696.

(1) There were 9 instances of mortgage.

(2) There were 9 escheats.

(3) There were 7 licences granted.

(4) There were 7 instances where the devisee by Will was not the child of the devisor, and a 20d. fine was due.

(5) There were 19 cases where a common fine was charged where the devisee by Will was a child.

(6) There were 11 cases of admittances with special provisos, where it is mentioned that it should be no prejudice to the Lord in respect of Rent, Fine, or otherwise.

The following examples are selected under these six heads, mainly with the view of mentioning surnames which appear in the early history of Quakerism.

(1) 8th October 1585, George Whitehead by his writing dated 28th June 1584 mortgaged unto John son of Thomas Robinson of Newbiggin two named parcels of ground at a yearly rent of 20d. in condition that G. Whitehead pay to J. Robinson £13.10s.0d. at midsummer 1586. If the sum is paid, then Whitehead to repossess, but if not, Robinson to be admitted on paying 26s.8d. for a fine on the 20d. rent (The fine is thus 20+d.)

(2) 20th April 1597. (The year of the plague). John Fawcett of Ravenstonedale town aged 8 years siezed of a tenement of 6s.8d. ancient rent, and 2s. 5d. new rent died without issue or Will. His tenement escheated to the Lord, saving the widows's right (one third) of Margaret Fawcett the mother.

(3) 19th June 1623. (The year of bad harvests and (?) typhus epidemic). Christopher Fawcett upon the surrender of Henry Fawcett is admitted a tenant of a tenement late in the tenure of the said Henry lying at Wandall Bank of the yearly ancient rent of 2s. paid for a fine 2s. 4d. and for licence of alienation 46s. 8d. (Thus a fine of 20d.)

(4) 17th October 1721. A fine of 20d. was taken of James Bayliff under the Will of Jo: Bayliff.

(5) 23rd October 1711. A common fine taken of Stephen Dent (a child) under the Will of his father Stephen Dent. 1d. old rent, 8d. new rent.

(6) 23rd October 1708. Anthony Pinder purchased by Deed several parcels of land upon a common fine. Memorandum: there is due upon the land for the above Anthony Fothergill his licence for parcelling the premises above said.[1]

There is an important note in the Wharton estate court books of 1711(G) which refers to a court held of Kirkby Stephen by Humphrey Wharton, Roger Gower, Richard Riggs, Esq. and Edmund Branthwaite gent. 10th April 1621: 'Kirkby Stephen - Fynes assessed at the Courts of Wharton, Nateby, and Kirkby Stephen - none in respect that the King's Majesty's Proclamation is against it.'

At the Court of Ravenstonedale holden there the 12th of April 1621 by the Commission aforesaid - no entries.'[2]

This refers to the Proclamation against tenant-right issued by James I on 28th July 1620, that tenant-right had ceased with the union of the two kingdoms in one king, and that henceforth tenancies ought to be by lease only. Anthony Wetherell, vicar of Kirkby Stephen was accused of writing a libel in favour of tenant-right, and was charged before Star Chamber. John Corney vicar of Orton was the author of the tract. The King's case was primarily against tenants in the barony of Kendal, but he extended his proclamation to the four border counties. The case was finally decided in favour of the tenants and tenant-right after the death of the King, on the 19th June 1625. The judges decided that tenant-right did not cease with the end of border service. But the whole of Westmorland was in an uproar from 1621 to 1625.[3]

References:

(1) Summary of manorial incidents in Ravenstonedale 1578-1725. From papers of Fawcett v. Lowther 1751. C.R.O.Carlisle. D/Lons/L.Ravenstonedale 4.

(2) Ibid. & N & B, I. 55 & 536.

(3) N & B, I, 55-59. And Chapt. 5 ante.

Acknowledgments.

To the memory of the late Mr. T. Barnes of Carlisle, archivist to the late Hugh Cecil Earl of Lonsdale, who from 1942-1944 introduced me to the 16th and 17th century documents at Lowther.

To the staff of the Cambridge University Library, especially the Rare Books department, and the Seeley Law Library who have been so helpful.

To Miss S. MacPherson, B.A. and the staff of the Record Offices at Kendal and Carlisle for invaluable help.

To the Librarian of Trinity College, Cambridge for permission to read the Higginson pamphlets.

To Mr. Gordon Dent of Dent whose research at the Kendal and Carlisle record offices has contributed much to this work.

To the late Mr. T. Gray, librarian of Tullie House, Carlisle who allowed me to make full use of Dr. G.C. Williamson's transcripts of the Clifford records.

To the late Chancellor Harrison, Librarian of York Minster who allowed me to examine Sir Edward Hailstone's MSS. and the MS. of James Toori.

To Mr. A.M. Fell of Hallam & Son, solicitors of Kirkby Stephen; Mr. G.B. Harker of Hewitson & Harker, solicitors of Kirkby Stephen; and the late Capt. R.P. Hewetson of Stobars Hall, and the friends of over forty years who have allowed me to consult MSS. in their care.

To Mr. C. Hollett, bookseller of Sedbergh, whose generous permission to use the valuable records of Ravenstonedale in his possession has enabled me to reconstruct the transformation of that parish from a Catholic to a Calvinist society.

To Dr. R.T. Spence of Leeds whose wide knowledge of the Clifford records has enabled me to correct two serious errors. His perceptions have been much appreciated.

To His Honour Judge J. Blackett - Ord of Helbeck Hall for expert criticism of my interpretation of certain land transactions relating to north Westmorland.

To Miss Rena Beech of Ickleton, Cambridge whose patience in typing has been invaluable.

Carlisle Cathedral; Dean & Chapter Library. The Machell MS.

County Record Office, Carlisle.
Lord Lonsdale's MSS. Steward's copy of the Indenture of 12.Feb.1579/80. between Philip lord Wharton and the customary tenants of Ravenstonedale from the Wharton records transferred to Lowther 1729.
Lord Lonsdale's MSS. Summary of manorial incidents of Ravenstonedale 1578-1725 prepared for the case Fawcett v. Lowther 1751. D/Lons/L. Ravenstonedale 4.
Bishop's transcripts of Kirkby Stephen parish registers 1700-1.
Will of Richard Shaw of Hanging Lunds, Mallerstang, 1 Aug. 1677.
Will of Francis Higginson vicar of Kirkby Stephen 14 May 1673.
Lord Lonsdale's MSS. Memoirs of George Sedgewick of Collin Field, Kendal, from the Le-Fleming MSS (MS.D.)
Will & inventory of Jane Atkinson of Kirkby Stephen widow, 1 Oct. 1667.
Will of Francis (Frances) Atkinson of Kirkby Stephen seamster, 4 May 1666.
Inventory of Edwards Mynese schoolmaster of Kirkby Stephen, 1605.
Will of John Wharton of Sandpott, Mallerstang 30 Nov. 1587.
Will of Henrye Knewstub of (Shorgill) Mallerstang, 12 Feb. 1586/7.
Many other wills & inventories of Mallerstang 1576 - 1615.

Crosby Garrett Church, Westmorland.
A bundle of 18th C. conveyances of glebe and other lands formerly in the church safe, but burned in the church stove a few years ago. The conveyance 30 June 1719 by Richard Wilkinson & Isabella his wife of Carlisle of certain lands in Crosby Garrett to William Taylor of Crosby Garrett.

Hallam & Son, solicitors Kirkby Stephen.
A MS volume of custumals from the upper Eden valley prepared by the late Mr. T.H. Preston, solicitor of Kirkby Stephen, late 19th C.

Hewitson & Harker, solicitors of Kirkby Stephen.
From the records of Hartley manor. Confirmation of tenant-right between Sir Philip Musgrave and his tenants of Soulby etc. 30 May 1636.

Hewitson, the late Capt. R.P. of Stobars Hall, Kirkby Stephen.
Sale 15 March 1652/3 of the estates of Sir Philip Musgrave of Hartley.

Agreement tripartite 10th Oct. 1653 between Sir Philip Musgrave, his son Richard, Richard Huish & others barring entails on his estates in Cumberland & Westmorland recently sold by the Committee for Compounding.

Hollett, Mr. C., bookseller of Sedbergh.
James Bayliff's copy of the Indenture of 1579/80 of Ravenstonedale, with the orders and rules of the manor court 1738.
Philip Greene's 1652 copy of the 1586 manor court book of Ravenstonedale containing the custumal of 1558, the Indenture of 1579/80, sundry petitions to lord Wharton, and the subsequent orders and rules covering the manor court, taxation, the manor, the church, tithing and mortuary fees etc.

County Record Office, Kendal.
Copy of the Ravenstonedale Indenture of 1579/80 by John Robinson, schoolmaster of Ravenstonedale 1775.
Appleby Castle estate rentals 1697-1732. WD/Hoth. Box 19.
Appleby Castle estate rentals & accounts 1667-68. WD/Hoth. Box 23.
Appleby Castle estate admittances & fines (Mallerstang) 1657-1661. WD/Hoth. Box 20.
Indenture 3 Aug. 1613 between Philip lord Wharton, his son Sir Thomas and the customary tenants of Ravenstonedale.
Appleby Castle MSS. The 1604 survey of the Clifford manors in Westmorland for George third earl of Cumberland; with the undated (c. 1597) bailiff's rental of Mallerstang. Both WD/Hoth. Box 23.
Indenture of 27 Aug. 34 Eliz. 1591-2, between Philip lord Wharton and the tenants of Ravenstonedale concerning woods & underwoods.
Inspeximus of the Court of Requests 15th & 19th Feb. 1558/9 (I.Eliz) on complaint of Thomas Chamberlain & others of Ravenstonedale for expulsion from their tenements by Thomas lord Wharton.
Articles of Customary Tenant-Right in the manor of Ravenstonedale 1556.

Mason, the late Miss Marcia, of Eden Place, Kirkby Stephen.
Conveyance 17 Jan. 1619/20 of certain lands at Winton.

Public Record Office, Chancery Lane, London.
S.P. 23/258. Court rolls of Crosby Garrett, Hartley, Brough, Thornthwaite, Kirkby Stephen, Little & Great Musgrave, & Preston Patrick sent from the Committee for Sequestrations, Kendal to the Committee for Compounding 5 June 1652.

SP/C,21/p.25/1. Anne countess of Pembroke v. Robert Arkinson & others tenants on the Countess' Westmorland estates. Writs, interrogatories and depositions taken 6 Dec. 1650 & 25 Sept. 1651.

C2 Chas.I. 68/12. Writs, depositions & award in Popham v. Lancaster (ie. Lowther) 1636/7.

C2 Chas.I. 41/53. Monsier (ie. Moser) v. Ducket, 11 Chas.I.Award.

STAC. 8. (James I.) Bundle 34, file 4 (Item 24) Kendal Barony tenant-right case. Information, writs by Sir Thomas Coventry attorney-general against certain tenants in the barony, interrogatories & depositions taken in Westmorland 1621-5.

C.66/2102. King James' Award in the Clifford disputes 14 March 1616/17. Patent Roll.

SP1/124. 20 Aug. 1537. Report of Robert Southwell, solicitor to the Court of Augmentations to Cromwell on the estates of the late Henry sixth earl of Northumberland, esp. in Cumberland.

S.P. Henry VIII, 1537, vol. XII, pt. II, no. 1339. n.d. (but autumn 1537) Letter of Robert Thomson, clerk, in the Fleet to Cromwell.

E.36/119/7843. March 1537, confession of Robert Thomson in the Tower.

The Queen's College, Oxford. (By courtesy the Keeper of the Records) Valor of the college possessions January 1545/6.

Long Rolls 1531-38 (college accounts) Robert Thomson 1531-2. Lancelot Shawe 1535-1544.

Soulby Vicarage papers. Capt. T. Grimshaw's (of Soulby) 19th C. copy of the Chancery decree May 1636 between Sir Philip Musgrave and his customary tenants of Crosby Garrett, Kirkby Stephen (part), Little & Great Musgrave, Soulby, & part of Bleatarn settling fines certain.

The Library, Tullie House, Carlisle. (By courtesy the late Mr. T. Gray). Dr. G. C. Williamson's typescript copies of:
The Diary of Lady Anne Clifford,
Evidences at Appleby castle, 1920. Also at Skipton Castle, Bolton Priory (Chatsworth), Hothfield in Kent, and with Dawson & Bennett, solicitors in London 1916.

York Minster Library (Courtesy the late Chancellor Harrison). The records of Sir Edward Hailstone.

Deed of sale of the Silsden Lands in Craven, 1623/4.

MS. of James Toori relating to the death & burial of Henry earl of Cumberland 1643.

Bibliography.

Agriculture. The Royal Commission on; England Report, by Mr Fox Wilson, under Cumberland. 1895.

Appleby, Andrew B. English Historical Review. 1973. 2nd Series. Disease or famine; mortality in Cumberland & Westmorland, 1580 - 1640.

—. Famine in Tudor & Stuart England. 1978 - 9.

Armstrong, Robert Bruce. History of Liddesdale, Eskdale, Ewesdale, Wauchopdale & the Debateable Land. 1883.

Aubrey, John. Brief Lives. Penguin edn. 1972.

Bagot, Mrs Annette. Cumberland & Westmorland Antiq. Soc. NS. LXII, 1962. Mr Gilpin & the Manorial Customs of the Barony of Kendal.

Bailey, Conrad. Harrap's Guide to famous London graves. 1975.

Bailey, J. & Cullen, G. & Pringle, A. A general view of Agriculture in Northumberland, Cumberland & Westmorland. 1794 & 1972.

Bain, J. The Hamilton Papers. 1532 - 43. 1890.

Bean, J.W. The Estates of the Percy family, 1416 - 1537. 1959.

Birkenhead, the Earl of. Strafford. 1938.

Bonsor, K.J. The Drovers. Country Book Club edn. 1970.

Bouch, C.M.L. Prelates & People of the Lake Counties. 1948.

— & Jones, G.P. The Lake Countries, 1500 - 1830. 1960.

Boulter, W.C. Robert Holgate. Holgate Record Soc. no. 2. 1949.

Brailsford, H.N. The Levellers. ed. Christopher Hill. Spokesman Books 1976.

Braithwaite, Wm.C. The Beginnings of the Quakerism. 1955.

Brierly, H. The Parish Registers of Brough under Stainmore. 1923.

Burnet, bp, Gilbert. History of Own Times. Everyman edn. nd.

Byington, E.H. The Puritan as Colonist & Reformer. 1899.

Calendars of State Papers: Henry VIII, Edward VI, Mary, Elizabeth I, James I.

— Charles I, Commonwealth, & Charles II.

— Committee for the Advance of Money.

— Committee for Compounding.

Cartwright, J.J. Chapters in the History of Yorkshire. 1872.

Chancery. Calendar of Proceedings in the Reign of Q.Elizabeth, vol. III, 1832.

—. Calendar of Inquisitions (Misc.) vol. I. 1916.

Clarendon, Earl of. History of the Great Rebellion & Civil Wars. Oxford, 1819.

Clarkson, Christopher. History of Richmond, Yorks. 1821.

Coke, Sir Edward. Reports, 1658 & 1680.

—. First Park of the Institute of the Laws of England, or a Commentary upon Littleton. Revised by F. Hargrave & C. Butler. 18th ed. 1823.

Collinson, Patrick. The Elizabethan Puritan Movement. 1967.

Creighton, bp. Mandell. Life and Letters by his wife. 1906.

Croke, Sir George. Reports of, revised by Sir Harbottle Grimstone. 1683.

Cross, Dr. F.L. Oxford Dictionary of the Christian Church. 1957.

Cumberland & Westmorland Antiquarian Soc. Parish register series.

— Brough under Stainmore, 1923.

— Crosby Garrett, 1945.

— Crosby Ravensworth, 1937.

— St. Andrew's Penrith, part I, 1938. part II, 1939.

— Morland I, 1957.

Cumberland & Westmorland Antiq. Soc. OS. XIV, 1897. Aske's Rebellion 1536 - 1537, by Geo. Watson.

—. NS. XI, 1909. The Kaber Rigg Plot 1663. Francis Nicholson.

Curwen, J.F. Later Records of North Westmorland, and the Barony of Appleby. 1923.

Dale, Bryan. The Good Lord Wharton. 1901.

Dawson, W.H. The History of Skipton. 1882.

Dickens, A.G. English Historical Review, 52. (1937). The marriage and character of Abp. Holgate.

Dickens, Robert Holgate, Abp. of York. St. Anthony's Hall pub. 8. (1955)

Dickens, The English Reformation. Fontana Lib. 1967.

Dickenson, R.F. Cumberland & Westmorland Antiq. Soc. NS. LX, 1960. Tithing customs in West Cumberland in the 18th C.

Dictionary of National Biography:
  John Boste 1543? - 1594.
  Thomas Cartwright 1535 - 1603.
  King Charles I. 1600 - 1649.
  George Clifford third earl of Cumberland, 1558 - 1605.
  Henry Clifford fifth earl of Cumberland, 1591 - 1643.
  Samuel Daniel 1562 - 1619.
  Richard Hakluyt 1552? - 1610.
  Philip Herbert earl of Pembroke 1584 - 1650.
  Francis Higginson, sen. 1587 - 1630.
  Sir Henry Hobart, d. 1625.
  Robert Holgate 1481? - 1555.
  John Knewstub (of Mallerstang) 1544 - 1624.
  John More (of Bentham) d. 1592.
  Sir Philip Musgrave, 1607 - 1678.
  Richard Norton, 1488? - 1588.
  Sir Thomas Strafford, 1593 - 1641.
  Philip Duke of Wharton 1698 - 1731.
  Sir Thomas 1st lord Wharton, 1495 - 1568.
  Sir Thomas 2nd lord Wharton, 1520 - 1572.
  Sir Philip 4th lord Wharton 1613 - 1698.

Dodds, M.H. & R. The Pilgrimage of Grace & the Exeter Conspiracy, 1915.

Drake, Francis, Eboracum. 1736.

Elton, C.I. & Mackay, H.J.H. The Law of Copyholds & Customary Tenures, 2nd. ed. 1898.

Elton, G.R. Tudor Constitutional Documents. Documents & Commentary, 1960.

English Law Reports, 1911 ed.

—, 1907. ed.

Ericksen, Arvel B. The Public Career of Sir James Graham. 1952.

Faraday, M.A. Westmorland Protestation returns, 1641. Cumberland & West-morland Antiq. Soc. tract series XVII, 1971.

Farrer, W. Records relating to the Barony of Kendal, ed. J.F. Curwen, Cumb. & Westmorland Antiq. Soc. Record series, vols, 4 & 5, 1923.

Ferguson, R.S. Miscellany accounts of the diocese of Carlisle of bp. Wm. Nicholson. 1877.

Ferguson, History of Cumberland. 1890.

—, History of Westmorland. 1894.

Firth, C. & Davis, G. The Regimental History of Cromwell's Army. 1940.

Fleming, Sir Daniel le. Description of Westmorland, ed. Sir G.F. Duckett, 1882.

Ford, J. Rawlinson. Cumberland & Westmorland Antiq. Soc. NS. IX. 1909. Customary tenant-right in the manors of Yealand.

Gaze, W.C. On and Along the Thames 1603-1625. 1913.

Genealogist, The NS. XV, XVI, XVII. The Charters of Sempringham.

Gibbs, M.A. The Lord General. A Life of Thomas Fairfax. 1938.

Glover, T.R. Cambridge retrospect. 1943.

Graham, J. The Condition of the Border at the Union. 1907.

Graham, Rose. St. Gilbert of Sempringham. 1901.

Grainge, Wm. History & Topography of Harrogate & the Forest of Knaresborough. 1871.

Grellet, Stephen. Memoir of the Life & Gospel labours of, ed. Benjamin Seebohm. 1860.

Grosart, A.B. Complete Works of Samuel Daniel. 1885.

Hamill, John. The Craft; A History of English Freemasonry. 1986.

Hamilton Papers, The. ed. J. Bain, 1890.

Harleian Miscellany, The; a selection from. 1793.

Harris, John. Navigantium atque Itinerantium Bibliotheca; A Compleat Collection of Voyages & Travels. 1705.

Harrison, William. Description of England, ed. George Edelen. Cornell, 1968.

Hartshorne, A. Archaeological Journal, Sept. 1899. Vol. LVI. Samuel Daniel & Lady Anne Clifford.

Headley, Henry. General Biographical Dict. ed Alexander Chalmers, vol. XI. Notes on Samuel Daniel by H.H.

Henson, H. Hensley. Puritanism in England. 1912.

Historical Manuscripts Commission:
  Rep. X. App. 6. Braye.
  Rep. XII. Hatfield.
  Rep. XII. pt. II, 1888. Coke.
  Rep. XII. pt. 7. Le Fleming.
  Rep. XII. pt. I. 1888. Earl Cowper.
Hobart, Sir Henry. Reports 5th ed. 1724.
Hodgson, Rev. John. History of Westmorland 1820.
Holme, Wilfred. The Evill successe of Rebellion from time to time ... written in Old Englishe.
  1572/3. Brit. Lib. Cat. C. 122. bb. 20, dated 1572.
Hoskins, W.G. Agricultural Hist. Review XII. 1964. Harvest fluctuations & English Economic
  History 1480 - 1619.
Hudleston, C.R. Surtees Soc. CLXVIII, 1958. Naworth Accounts 1648 - 1660.
Hutchinson, W. History of Cumberland. 1794.
Hutton, W.H. William Laud. 3rd ed. 1905.
Jessopp, Dr. Augustus. Arcady; For better for worse, 1887.
Johnson, G.W. The Fairfax Correspondence. 1848.
Jones. G.F. Trevallyn. Saw-Pit Wharton. Sydney U.P. 1967.
Jones, G.P. Cumberland & Westmorland Antiq. Soc. Tract Series. XVIII, 1971. A short history
  of the manor & parish of Witherslack.
Kendal. Local Chronology. Extracts from Kendal newspapers. 1865.
Kightly, Charles. Great Battles (Flodden). The Anglo-Scottish War 1513. 1975.
Knappen, M.M. Tudor Puritanism. Chicago. 1965.
Knight, Charles B. History of the City of York. 1944.
Knowles, Prof. David. The Religious Orders in England, III, 1959.
Leake, Richard. Vicar of Killington, Westmorland. Foure Sermons preached in Westmorland.
  1599. (C.U.L.)
Loftie, A.G. Great Salkeld, its rectors and history. 1900.
Magrath, J.R. The Queens College, Oxford. 1921.
Maintland, F.W. English Historical Rev. Col. V. no. xx. Oct. 1890. Northumbrian tenures.
Marshall, Wm. A review of the Reports of the Board of Agriculture, Northern Department,
  1818.
Matthews, A.G. Calamy Revised. 1934.
—. Walker Revised. 1948.
Mayor, J.E.B. The History of the College of St. John the Evangelist, 1869.
Miller, Perry. Orthodoxy in Massachusetts, 1630 - 1656. Cambs. Mass. 1933.
Monthly Magasine, 1801, 1802, 1804, & 1805.
Morgan, Irvonwy. The Godly Puritans of the Elizabethan Church. 1965.
Munby, J. Cumberland & Westmorland Antiq. Soc. NS. LXXXV, 1985. Art. XI. Medieval
  Kendal & the first borough charter.
Neale, J.R. Queen Elizabeth. 1934.
The New England Historical & General Register. Art. 50. 1896. et seq.
Nicholls, Rev. W. (Minister of Ravenstonedale) History & Traditions of Ravenstonedale Vol. I.
  1877.
—. Vol. II. c. 1914.
—. History & Traditions of Mallerstang Forest & Pendragon Castle. 1883.
Nichols, J. The Progresses of James I. 1829.
Nicholson, Cornelius. The Annals of Kendal. 1835.
Nicholson, Sir Andrew de Harcla; A personal episode in English History, 1888.
Nicholson, Mallerstang Forest & the Barony of Westmorland. 1888.
Nicholson, F. & Axon, E. Older Nonconformity in Kendal. 1915.
Nicholson, J. Walker. History of Crosby Garrett. 1914.
Nickalls, J.L. The Journal of George Fox. 1975.
Nicolson, Joseph. & Burn, Richard. History of Cumberland & Westmorland. 1777.
Nicolson, William, bp. of Carlisle. Miscellany accounts of the diocese of Carlisle, 1877.
Nightingale, Benjamin. The Ejected of 1662 in Cumberland & Westmorland. 1911.
Noble, Miss Mary E. The History of the parish of Bampton. 1901.
—. The Registers of the parish of Askham, 1904.

Parks, Dr. G.B. & Williamson, Dr. J.A. American Geographical Soc. Special publications no. 10. Richard Hakluyt & the English Voyagers, 1928.

Peerage, The Complete, 1913.

Penney, Norman. The First Publishers of Truth. 1907.

Percy, earl. F.S.A. Archaeologia Aeliana, 25 July 1984. The ancient farms of Northumbria.

Phillips, C.B. Northern History no. 5. 1970. County Committees & Local Government 1642 - 1660.

Platt, A.E. History of the parish & grammar school of Sedbergh. 1876.

Porter, John. Transactions of the Historic Soc. of Lancashire and Cheshire, art. 127. 1978. Waste land reclamation in the sixteenth C.

Privy Council. Acts of, Edward VI, & Eliz. 1891.

—, Philip & Mary. 1891.

—, 1615 - 1616. 1925.

Public Record Office, Lists & Indexes. Court of Requests, vol. 2. Eliz. p. 82. 1964 ed. N. York.

Pullein, Catherine. The Pulleynes of Yorkshire, 1915.

Purchase, Samuel. Hakluytus Posthumus, or Purchas his Pilgrimes. 1905.

Rainbow, Edward, bp. of Carlisle. Sermon preached at the funeral of Anne Countess of Pembroke, 1675/6. Carlisle tracts. 1839.

Real Property. Third Report of the Commissioners to enquire into the Law of England respecting Real Property. 24 May. 1832. sect. 8. Customary freehold.

Reid, Miss R.R. English Historical Review, vol. 35. 1920. Barony & Thanage.

Reynardson, Sir Abraham. London during the Great Rebellion. ed. C.M. Clode. 1892.

Ross, Isabel, Margaret Fell, the Mother of Quakerism. ed. 1984.

Rowse, Dr. A.L. The England of Elizabeth. Repr. Soc. ed. 1953.

Sackville-West.V. The Diary of Lady Anne Clifford. 1924.

Sanderson, Roundell Palmer. A Survey of the Debateable & Border Lands adjoining the Realm of Scotland, 1604. 1891.

Sayer, W. History of Westmorland. 1847.

Scriven, J. & Brown, A. A Treatise on Copyholds, 2nd. ed. 1896.

Sellers, H. Oxford Bibliographical Soc. Proceedings & papers, vol. 2. 1930.

Shaw, R. Cunliffe. Post Roman Carlisle & the Kingdoms of the north-west. 1964.

Shuffrey, W.A. Some Craven Worthies. 1903.

Sowerby, R.R. Kirkby Stephen & district. 1948.

Speight, Robert. Craven & the North West Yorkshire Highlands. 1892.

Spence, Dr. R.T. Northern History XIII, 1977. The Pacification of the Cumberland Border 1593-1628.

—. Northern History, XV. 1979. Lady Anne Clifford, countess of Dorset, Pembroke & Montgomery, 1596-1676.

Spenser, Edmund. The Faerie Queene.

Surtees Soc. LXXXII, p. xxxvii, 1889. The Durham Halmote Rolls.

—. CLXXII, 1957. The Clifford papers of the 16th century, by Prof. A.G. Dickens.

Swales, Alec. Kirkby Stephen Grammer School, 1566-1966. Appleby 1966.

Tannenbaum, Samuel. Elizabethan Bibliographies, no. 25. Samuel Daniel, New York 1942.

Tanner. J.R. Constitutional Documents of the reign of James I. 1952.

—. English Constitutional Documents of the 17th C. 1960.

Tate, G. The History of Alnwick. 1866.

Thomason, George. The Thomason Tracts 1640 - 1661. 1908.

Thompson, Rev. W. (Of Mallerstang & Sedbergh) Sedbergh, Garsdale & Dent. 1910

Tothill, W. Transactions of the High Court of Chancery, both by Practice & Precedent. 1671, & 1820.

Tough, D.L.W. The Last Years of a Frontier. 1928.

Trevelyan, Dr. G.M. English Social History. 1945.

Tupling, Dr. G.H. The Economic History of Rossendale, Chetham Soc. 1927.

Valor Ecclesiasticus, Henry VIII. 1535. II, 1810 cd.

Veall, Donald. The Popular Movement for Law Reform, 1640 - 1660. 1970.

Venn, J.A. The Grace Book of the University of Cambridge, 1542-1589. 1910

—. Alumni Cantab. part I. Vol. II. 1922.

Victoria County Histories:
    Cumberland I & II 1968.
    Lincolnshire II, 1906.
    North Riding of Yorkshire, 1969.
    Yorkshire III, 1974.
Ward, T. Humphrey. The English Poets. 1883.
Watkins, Charles. Treatise on Copyholds. 1821.
Watson, George. Bygone Penrith. A popular arrangement of Penrith parish registers. 1893.
West, Thomas. (Jesuit mission priest). The History of Furness. 1774.
Whaley, Revd. C. A History of Askrigg. 1890.
Wharton, Henry. The History of the Troubles & Tryal of the Most Revd. Father in God...William
    Laud. 1695.
Whitaker, Dr. T.D. History of Craven. ed. 1812.
—. History of Richmondshire, 1823.
—. History of the parish of Whalley & the Honor of Clitheroe & the parish of Cartmel. 4th
    ed. 1872.
Wickham -Legg, J. The Coronation of James I. 1902.
Willan, T.S. & Crossley, C.W. Yorkshire Archaeological Soc. CIV, 1941. Three seventeenth
    century Yorkshire Surveys.
Williams, Joshua. The Principles of the Law of Real Property, 24th ed. 1926.
Williamson, Dr. G.C. George third earl of Cumberland. 1920.
—. Lady Anne Clifford. 1922.
Wilson, E. Sedbergh School Register vol. I. 1909.
Wilson, Violet A. Queen Elizabeth's Maids of Honour. 1922.
Winter, Carl. Elizabethan Miniatures. Penguin Book 1955.
Winthrop Papers, The. 1623 - 1630. Massachusetts Hist. Soc. 1931.
Wordsworth, Wm. A Guide to the Lakes. 1970 repr.
Wright, W. Aldis. The English Works of Roger Ascham. ed. 1970.
Yates, M.J. Dumfriesshire & Galloway, Nat. Hist. & Antiq. Soc. LIII, 1977-1978. Excavations
    at Polmaddy, New Galloway.
Young, Arthur. Six Months' Tour through the North of England. 1770, 2nd ed. 1771.

Select Index Vol. II

This index contains only key references to names and topics.

—, Manor. (Tenant-right) 67.
—, —. Compositions of 1613 68.
—, —. Sales of 1729 70.
—, Enfranchisement 1798. 71.
—, Summary of manorial incidents 1578-1725 179.
Real Property, Third Report into the Law of England respecting, 1832 169.
Rebellion, Northern of 1569-70 41.
Rents, Ancient 44–5.
—, Improved 45.
—, improved. (17th C. law) 140.
—, ancient. (17th C.) 141.
—, — compared with improved. 1667-8. 164.
—, quit. 75.
Requests, Court of. 40.
Richmond Grey Friars. 14.
Richmondshire. 13.
Robinson, John, schoolmaster of Ravenstonedale. 172.
Sackville, Richard earl of Dorset. 113, 114, 115, 117, 126.
Saint John's college, Cambridge. 23, 28.
Sandford Moor, 9.
Scottish War, the first, 1639 29, 128.
—, the second 1640 29, 129.
Scots army in Cumberland and Westmorland 1644-46 135.
Sedbergh. 8.
— chantry school 23.
Sedgwick, George of Collinfield. 129.
Sequestrators, Parliamentary, 1650 147.
Ship money. 29, 127.
Skaife, major Arthur of Winton. 147.
— family of Winton Hall, 151.
Skipton. 10, 133, 134.
— castle. 103, 105, 111, 112, 113, 117, 118, 119, 147.
— castle. 1645. 134.
Sowle, Thomas, a priest of Penrith. 8.
Spence, Dr. R. T. of Leeds. 110, 164.
Star Chamber, Court of. 28, 29, 124.
Strafford, Sir Thomas Wentworth earl of. 126.
Tenant-Right, customary. 28, 67, 74, 140, 151.
—, compositions for. 68, 76, 78, 79, 122, 144 et seq.
—, decay of. 167.
Tenants, Clifford in Westmorland 1653. 159.
—, cases against from 1650-1657. 159–60.
Tewkesbury. 8.
Thanet earl of v. Paterson, 1738-40. 164.
Thomson, Robert, vicar of Brough. 9, 15, 20.
Thwaites, John solicitor. 148.
Vaccaries. 82.
Walker, James of Brough. 159.
Warter priory. 14.
Watton priory. 13, 34, 39.
Wensleydale. 8, 14, 79.
Westmorland, Demands of Commons, 1536. 10.
—, Hangings 1537. 15, 18.
—, Clifford lands. 118–9.
Wetherall, Revd. Anthony, vicar of Kirkby Stephen. 28.
Wharton, Sir George. 68.
—, Philip 3rd lord. 44, 68, 69, 103.
—, — 4th lord. 69.
—, — duke of (The Jacobite). 70.
—, Sir Thomas. 14, 15, 17.
—, — 2nd lord. 38, 39, 42.
—, — of Aske. 68, 69.
Whitehead, George, Quaker of Sunbiggin. 31.
Willowes case, 1608. 140.
Wordsworth, William. 167.

Volume III

INTRODUCTION

This book was born by chance. A few years ago I enquired at the Library of Friends' House, Euston Road, London if they had any record of a handful of Quakers in Mallerstang, who do not appear in the Quaker registers of Ravenstonedale. A small volume was shown to me bearing on the cover the name of Ralph Alderson of Narthwaite. It was the earliest register of Ravenstonedale Quakers. But it is evident from the contents that it came from the early meeting at Dovengill, which was led by Anthony Robinson from about 1653. The register is far from complete, and these studies are the result of wider research in the Public Record Office, the County Record Office at Kendal, and the Cambridge University Library. A small heap of stones is all that remains of the Meeting House at Cat Keld in Ravenstonedale; that in Grisedale hard by the beck was swept away by a flood about an hundred years ago. The five burial-grounds covered by these registers are mostly merged into nearby farmland. Not a single stone marks the last resting-place of the early heroes of the movement. The small farm meeting rooms at Narthwaite and Grisedale are empty and broken. The glory has departed. Yet three hundred years ago the Meetings at Wath, Cat Keld and Dovengill, Grisedale and Garsdale were vibrant with faith, stern in discipline, and adamant in dissenting from the old order in church and chapel.

The English church, whether Catholic, Anglican or Protestant, has not found it easy to accommodate dissent. When Quakerism came to Westmorland and divided the dales' communities from 1652, Europe was engaged in bitter struggles between Catholic and Protestant communities. If the reader of the sufferings of early Quakers is shocked by the vigour with which the landowners and the clergy persecuted them, he must not overlook the vitriolic language used by the Quakers against them. Whether in England or Europe they were hard and unforgiving days.

Early Quaker writings are a compound of glorious faith in the Inner Light of Christ in each human heart surrounded by page upon page of opaque verbiage, from which comes the rare gleam of Truth, appeal and judgement.

Once it is understood that Quakerism was at the apex of Protestant belief that no priest should stand between man and his Maker, then the ideal of a purely spiritual church can be understood. Though whether it is possible for more than a few to live at these heights, rather than in the plain, is a matter for reflection.

George Fox must have been an able teacher, able to communicate the main points of his creed in a few meetings to a handful of converts in a farmhouse kitchen. He visited Grisedale twice in 1652, and laid the foundation of the Meeting at Scale, which, despite its remoteness was within fifty years to prove stronger than Garsdale or Ravenstonedale. From the earliest days Fox's mannerisms and terms were adopted as the distinctive soberness of the Society of Friends. The slightest levity in word or dress was frowned upon; words were few and savoured; innocency of life was the aim, and every word and action was carefully weighed. Indeed the consolations of marriage came under this scrutiny, and a number of early Quakers were concerned that marriage and the begetting of the usual large families might be yielding too much to 'carnality'. The first marriage register of the Richmond Monthly Meeting contains two records of marriage, prefaced by a long reflection that marriage is an ordinance based on Genesis I, 28 'be fruitful and multiply and replenish the earth'. From that assurance the marriage followed. Thus Fox gave an identity and assurance to many dalesmen who were far from the ministry of the market town church; they could worship God without all the legal and financial controls of squire and parson.

This writer has often been moved at the simple courage and obedience of the early Friends. Every Meeting produced one or more young men or women who obeyed the call to witness to the Light at home or overseas. The long journeys, the beatings, the imprisonments, the dangers, the loss of possessions, and the many deaths in the vilest prisons...all were embraced as the will of Christ, but not without great fear and trembling. The first Quakers will not be understood without their sense of obedience. Christopher Winn the Quaker schoolmaster of Frostrow, Sedbergh, put it thus:

> 'About ye year 1683, being watchful over my own Spirit and faithfull to the Lord's requirings I grew in favour with him, & waiting Diligently in Meetings for his divine power I had given me to believe I should ere long have a public Testimony to bear for him, and when ye Day came A terable one it was, ye word of ye Lord burned in me like a fire, saying this is the Day neglect it not, so that I was willing to speak a few words, and it has been my cheif care ever since to Minister in the ability that God gives...'

After mentioning his happy marriage in 1686 (to Margaret the daughter of John Thompson of Frostrow), he referred to his joining her brother Gilbert in 1694 in the management of his school at Penketh, Warrington. He undertook several journeys into Wales, Cheshire, Yorkshire and Cumberland. He mentioned his fear and horror of using plain Quaker speech, the Thee and Thou of equal address. 'But this would not do; Peace was not to be obtained without obedience; this kept me weak, but when I gave up, strength returned, and I had the answer of well done'. After mentioning his many travels he added: 'I mention this to Incouridge Gospell Ministers to Obedience.'[1] This sense of obedience is at the heart of early Quakerism, in the Light of which all its heroic service of Truth must be viewed.

Early Quakerism was not a pious middle-class eclectic group. It expressed in Christian terms the most radical view of church and community to appear in the dales. It won the hearts and minds of a whole generation of young men and women, who gave up all to follow their new creed. But it was not just a new faith; it was intended by Fox to be at the very apex of the Puritan rule of society. He wrote this in 1655:

> 'That there may be none idle, but that people in every Town where they are, may work and be maintained, and that every Constable in every town may have the law committed to him, and call all the people together, that they all may know it; and that no drunkard and swearer may bear office, for such cannot restrain others; and that there be no gaming, as carding, dicing, shovel-board, swearing in Ale-houses, drinking of healths, nor no Ale-house but such as keep Lodging for Travellers; for they nourish up young and old people to vanity, and also draw them unto uncleannesse, so the creation is devoured by such, for the people lust after such things, and that begets idleness, adultery, theft and murder; and that there be no cock-fighting, nor Bull-baiting, nor observing holy-dayes, as the times of Christmasse, Easter and Whitsontide, for these are times of sporting and wantonnesse, and filthy pleasures, driving the Creation upon their lusts. For the righteous Law of God is a limit to the Carnal mind.'[2]

Perhaps the desire to rule proved its undoing.

References

(1) The Testimony of Christopher Winn of Frostrow who died 1732. C.R.O. Kendal, WDFC. F.1. Testimonies of decreased ministers, 76.

(2) Newes coming up out of the North sounding towards the South etc. George Fox, 1655. 28/9. (C.U.L. Syn. 7.65.130.)

CONTENTS

Chapters

The Rise of Quakerism

(1) The poverty of the north from 1649, the return of the farmers' sons from Cromwell's army to poverty and a distressed countryside. The protestant teaching of Sedbergh and Kirkby Stephen grammar schools stemming from St. John's College, Cambridge had established the protestant ethic in the dales for an hundred years, despite the survival of pockets of catholicism. The arrival of Fox in Sedbergh in 1652 gathers together many strands of religious, and political opinion and completely changes the course of religious and political thought in the dales. Central to the understanding of Fox, and his followers, is his mystical experiences.

(2) An examination of Fox's creed, and his theology.

He gives an outline of his policy.

These two sections give us the gist of what he said on Firbank Fell, and the instruction he would give when settling meetings in the dales.

(3) The principal points of early Quakerism which would attract the dalesman, taken from contemporary writers, many from the dales.

(4) *The Lamb's War*. Quaker invective against the clergy and their churches; The opposition of the clergy, especially the presbyterian.

Fox's attack on tithes in 1652 is one of the most powerful against the old church order, and its oppression of the poor; he attacks the whole old church order and the presbyterian doctrine of the utter corruption of man.

(5) *The Lamb's War*. Quaker attack on the rich and powerful; their oppressing the poor; their worldly fashions; the worldliness of the clergy and their followers; pride in the partial use of the HAT; the covetousness of landlords and merchants. Early Quakers were wary of some of the Levellers, and did not support Edward Billing.

Fox's attack on forced conformity; and the baseness of church intolerance compared with the free spirit of Christ. Fox's attack on institutional Christianity is graphic and forceful, and in truth reiterates the point first made by the Puritans in Cambridge in 1565, that they claimed a greater holiness than the 'professors' of the established Elizabethan church.

(6) *The Lamb's War*. The early Quaker teaching on the Bible, the Lord's Prayer, Baptism, women Ministers, and the Lord's Supper. Fox's advices to Quakers as to how they should walk. Illustrations of Quaker discipline from Sedbergh, Ravenstonedale and Kendal Meetings.

(7) An examination of the question as to how far the rise of Quaker dissent had been coloured by tenant-right troubles in the Honor of Cockermouth, the upper Eden Valley, and in the barony of Kendal 1620-1625. John Boulton and Edward Guy of Appleby, and Francis Howgill a prisoner for six years in the gaol, set the tone of witness in the upper Eden valley.

(8) The distribution of Quakers in the upper Eden valley; their names. (8, Appendix) The Fothergills of Carr End, Wensleydale, and their links with Mallerstang.

(9) Cromwell's proclamation of 1655 against public disorders in religion encouraged protestant worship within the bounds of public order, and until 1660 persecution was moderate. From 1660 the rising of the Fifth Monarchy Men, and the Kaber Rigg Plot destroyed any hope of toleration.

(10) Persecution at Strickland Head 1664-1671.
  at Ravenstonedale 1673-1690.
  at Grisedale 1703-1708.

(11) Named Quakers and their witness:
  Richard & Katherine Wilson of Garsdale.
  Agnes the wife of Edmund Winn of Grisedale.
  John Close of Grisedale.
  Richard Pinder of Wath, Ravenstonedale.
  John Fothergill of Trannahill, Ravenstonedale.
  John Pinder, and
  Anthony Robinson of Ravenstonedale.
  Alice the wife of Ralph Alderson of Narthwaite.
  William Edmundson of Little Musgrave.

(12) *The Old Quaker Meeting.* Extracts from Edmundson, Francis Higginson, John Griffith of Radnor, and Stephen Grellet. The testimonies of Burrough and Howgill. The comments of Thomas Crosfield, and bishop Burnet. Ruskin on: *The House of God.*

ACKNOWLEDGEMENTS. Vol. III

To the memory of Carlton Milner the Quaker of Kendal, who in the years 1944-1948 sowed the seeds of this book.

To Mr. Gordon Dent of Dent, descended from Ravenstonedale Quakers, who by research and kindness has put me so much in his debt.

To Miss S. MacPherson, B.A., the archivist at the Kendal and Carlisle Record Offices, who has been unfailing in efficient help.

To the staff of the Cambridge University Library, particularly in the Rare Books Department, whose efficiency and help have been invaluable.

To the staff of the Public Record Office in Chancery Lane, London.

To the staff of the Library, Friends' House, Euston Road, London, for permission to use the early register of Ravenstonedale.

To Miss Rena Beech of Ickleton, Cambridge for patient and careful retyping.

MANUSCRIPT AND TRACT SOURCES

The Dean and Chapter Library, Carlisle. The Machell MS.

The County Record Office, the Castle, Carlisle.

The Consistory Court Books, DRC/3/4 & DRC/5/4/.1670-81.

Bishop's Transcripts, parish registers of Kirkby Stephen, 17th & 18th C.

Earl of Londsdale's MSS, D/Lons/L. A bundle of papers of Sir John Lowther relating to Westmorland Quakers.

Probate of Wills and Inventories of the 16th & 17th centuries relating to Kirkby Stephen and Mallerstang.

Mr. Gordon Dent of Dent for the use of several family papers from the Quakers of Ravenstonedale.

Mr. Arthur Duxbury, the Quaker of Hartley, for information of the receipt of 7.11.1689 by Anthony Pinder of Parrackmoor of £5 from Richard Murthwaite of Rigg End for the rent of Parrackmoor.

The Library of Friends' House, Euston Road, London.

The directive of the Westmorland Quarterly Meeting at Kendal to the Monthly Meeting at Sedbergh 6th or 12 mo. 1695 to clear the unpaid debt on the building of the Meeting House at Brigflats 1675.

The MS register of Ravenstonedale, MS. S.125.

Mr. Christopher Hollett the bookseller of Sedbergh has generously allowed me to make full use of the MSS copies of the customs, and court books of the manor of Ravenstonedale in his possession.

The County Record Office, Kendal.

Westmorland Quarterly Meeting book of accounts, memoranda and minutes 1658-1699. (93) ref: WDFC/F/1, p. 37.

Westmorland Quarterly Meeting, Book of Sufferings 1676-7 & 1703-8. Ref: WDFC/F/1 (51D)

Register of Quaker Wills & Contracts from Brigflats 17th & 18th centuries. WDX/515.

Demesne rents of Appleby Castle 1667/8. WDIH/box. 23.

Appleby Castle estate accounts 1667. fol. 4. WDIH/box. 23.

West Yorkshire Archives, Leeds District Archives. Wills of John Fothergill of Carr End, 1683 & Alexander Fothergill of Carr End, 1695.

Public Record Office, Chancery Lane, London.

Star Chamber Papers. STAC. 8 Jas. I. bundle 34, file 4. (Item 24).

Attorney-General v. certain defendants in the barony of Kendal 1620-25. (The Staveley case).

SP./C.21/p.25/1. Anne countess of Pembroke v. Robert Atkinson & others; depositions taken 18 Jan. 1650/51 & 25 Sept. 1651.

SP.29/94. & SP/29/98. The examinations of Robert Atkinson in the Tower 19. Mar. & 28 May 1664.

For the Quaker registers of Ravenstonedale, Grisdale & Garsdale, Dent Sedbergh, Wensleydale, Richmond, and the Westmorland Quarterly Meeting; also the presbyterian registers of Ravenstonedale and Birks, see the acknowledgements in the register section at the end of this volume.

The Library of Trinity College, Cambridge.

A Brief Relation of the Irreligion of the Northern Quakers, with A Brief Reply to some parts of a very scurrilous Lying Pamphlet called Saul's Errand to Damascus (by George Fox 1653) by Francis Higginson, minister of Kirkby Stephen. 1653. Two copies K.7.84.13. & K.4.1.3.

For accidental omissions I offer my apologies.

Explanation.

This volume is the second part of a wider study of: The Agrarian background to the rise of Political and Religious Dissent in the north-ern dales in the sixteenth and seventeenth centuries. The first volume is as yet unpublished. A few references are to that volume.

This Volume: General Abbreviations

C.R.O. = County Record Offices at Kendal and Carlisle.

C.U.L. = The Cambridge University Library.

C.U.P. = Cambridge University Press.

C. & W. trans. = The Transactions of the Cumberland & Westmorland Antiquarian Soc.

D.N.B. = The Dictionary of National Biography.

F.P.T. = The First Publishers of Truth, ed. Norman Penney, 1907.

Journal = The Journal of George Fox, 1891 ed.

N. & B. = The History of Cumberland & Westmorland by J. Nicolson & R. Burn, 1777.

P.R.O. = The Public Record Office, Chancery Lane, London.

V.C.H. = The Victoria County Histories.

Additional abbreviations used in Chapters 8 & 9 will be found with the references in Chapter 8.

CHAPTER 1

George Fox arrived at Sedbergh at Whitsuntide 1652. He had come through Wensleydale, Garsdale, Grisdale and Dent. The people of the dales were in great distress. They had been through two or three years of bad harvest and consequent poverty. From 1649 a large number of men and families had walked over the Pennines to Yorkshire, Durham and Northumberland seeking work. A writer in the London broadsheet The Moderate Intelligencer in March 1649 said in regard to poverty and work:

'those who choose rather to starve than beg, and truly both at this time swarm more than ever, the first by reason of the scarceness and deernesse of commodities, insomuch that the third part of the people of most parishes, stand in need of relief, who before did not recieve unless under some heavy affliction of sickness or losse, this might have been prevented, and hereafter may, and many kept alive, who are, and are like, before harvest to be at death's doore, or dead, for want of food: that this is probable; know that very many thousand families have no worke, and those who have, can hardly by their labour get bread only: For the others, viz. Beggars, they swarm through the neglect of the present Magistrates, who cannot spare time from Committee business to minde the good of the Country where they live, nay, is not this true, that many Justices, High Constables etc are kinde and favourable to Theeves, Rogues and Beggars, that so their own houses and goods may be safe, through their neighbours lose every week ...'[1]

Royalist squires and their retainers had been smartly fined for their part in the Civil Wars; commissioners for sequestrations were scouring every parish for any who could be caught in this net; and new men who had been the core of Puritan and Presbyterian local government during the Civil Wars were busy packing the county committees with their own kind, but not admitting too many who might upset their monopoly. Gervase Benson of Kendal, as notary for the proving of wills in the old archdeaconry of Richmond, as colonel of militia in the Civil Wars, and former mayor of Kendal

wielded great power in the barony of Kendal. In the north Edmund Branthwaite of Orton and Newbiggin, and soon to be deputy sheriff for the county, Richard Branthwaite steward to lord Wharton at Ravenstonedale, and major Arthur Skaife of Winton, these and others were riding high, and some out for pickings. In the middle of all this turmoil the countess of Pembroke was conducting a vigorous case in Chancery against all her Westmorland tenants, and one of the men to give evidence for customary tenant-right in the barony of Kendal was Captain Henry Ward of Sunnybank in Grayrigg.[2] In the nation parliamentary government was in a state of turmoil, the Levellers, the army, the residual members of the Long Parliament, the Presbyterians who had vainly tried to establish to classis system in the northern counties, the sectaries and more were working for political power in London. It was a time of great confusion. As far as the dalesmen were concerned, the young men who had served under Cromwell and Lambert at Dunbar, Preston and Worcester had returned home to the fellside farms to find great want, and no work. They also carried home what they had heard in the New Model Army, the new religious and political ideas of John Lilburne[3] and James Nayler, both of whom at a later date were to become Quakers. Thus when George Fox appeared at Sedbergh fair and hirings at Whitsuntide 1652 there were young men there with their fathers who already knew what Fox was preaching about. Also their fathers could from their experience add their memory of the way in which from the Pilgrimage of Grace, the clergy with the system of tithes, and the landlords in their attempt to break border-tenant-right had treated the poorer tenants in the dales. Fox was essentially the catalyst, who wittingly or not drew together many strands of history. In forming his Society of Friends he broke the old moulds of thought in politics and religion, stirred up incredible hatred, and founded a band of young men and women filled with an idealism which had not been seen since the coming of St Francis and the Friars Minor.

The registers of the Quakers of Ravenstonedale, Grisedale and Garsdale which follow are but a dry compendium if not read, either with the historical eye, or with some knowledge of the condition of the farms, not so much of the lower dales, but of the fellsides where life had always been harsh. There in their crude cruck-framed hovels men and women had brought up their large families round the peat fire. Life in the fields was never easy; a bad summer or cattle plague could within months reduce them to destitution. An occasional combination of bad harvests and consequent infections, as in 1586, 1597 and 1623, swept away at least a third of the population. On the backs of these men rode not one but two men, the landlord and the priest, both maintained out of the labours of poor men. It can be argued that the abolition of the monasteries substituted a more grasping society for a benevolent. It can also be said that the old system was a dead hand maintaining huge ecclesiastical corporations, resisting progress, and sitting on the backs of the poor. In the early centuries the monasteries were civilising agencies, in the latter a dead weight. As an Arab guide once said to the writer when going up the Lebanon coast from Beyrut to Biblos, 'plenty churches, plenty monasteries, plenty lunatic asylums; no progress!'

Yet from these primitive homes some great men had come. Nicholas Metcalfe of Bear Park in upper Wensleydale, became master of St John's college, Cambridge 1516 to 1537, and a supporter of the New Learning[4]. In 1537 one Robert Heblethwaite, no doubt a Sedbergh youth, was admitted B.A. at St John's college, Cambridge, a fellow in 1538; and from 1538 was master of the chantry school, Sedbergh.[5] He seems to have earned his keep after the confiscation of the chantries in 1547; but after the re-endowment of the school from 1552 he remained master until 1585. The regular supply of boys to study of St. John's was guarenteed through the six scholarships founded in 1527 by Dr. Roger Lupton, a native of Sedbergh, and friend of Nicholas Metcalfe. Thus through the Lupton foundations, and tenure of Hebblethwaite, a regular succession of local boys, and gentlemen's sons went to St. John's and became imbued with the new learning, and more particularly, the Genevan churchmanship which flourished at St. John's and Trinity from 1565. There was a second, but smaller supply of boys coming from Kirkby Stephen Grammar school. In 1547 after the battle of Pinkie in Scotland a number of Protestant refugees fled to England, the most notable being John Knox. Another was a young man called Edward

Mynese, a native of Castle Hill near Edinburgh.[6] Through the patronage of Archbishop Holgate who held the manor and rectory of Ravenstonedale for life, Mynese was made schoolmaster of Ravenstonedale.[7] When in 1566 Thomas lord Wharton founded Kirkby Stephen grammar school, Mynese was appointed its first headmaster. Kirkby Stephen had no scholarships, and Ravenstonedale had no school after the departure of Mynese. But occasionally Mynese persuaded the parents of a likely boy to transfer him to Sedbergh in order to qualify for a Lupton scholarship. Thus in 1560 one John Knewstub, a native of Shorgill in Mallerstang[8] transferred from Mynese at Ravenstonedale to Sedbergh, and a year later entered St. John's on a Lupton scholarship. He became a fellow in 1567, and a strong Calvinist within the university. In 1579 he was made rector of Cockfield in Suffolk. He became the leader of Puritanism in East Anglia. He took part in the Hampton Court Conference in 1604. Before he died at Cockfield in 1624 he left two subsizarships at St. John's of £5 each. One subsizar was to come from Cockfield, and the other from Kirkby Stephen.

This explains how, though the abbey of St. Mary of York had owned large interests in Kirkby Stephen parish, though the Gilbertine canons had held the manor and rectory of Ravenstonedale, Rievaulx, Coverham and Easby abbeys had large interests in Sedbergh, Garsdale and Grisedale, these three or four valleys became centres of Protestant learning so soon after the Reformation. The Puritan ethic had been established in Sedbergh and district for about a hundred years before the arrival of Fox. The ground was ready.

The essential ingredient of Fox's world was the Bible, the only book (where it could be afforded) which was owned and read in a fellside farm. From this period it begins to be mentioned in inventories of wills. Early Quakerism will not be understood unless it is remembered that the saints of the Old Testament had replaced those of the Catholic Church. When Robert Thomson became vicar of Brough in 1535 every window of his church was filled with the heroes of his faith; Our Lady, St. Michael, St. George, the angel Gabriel, St John Chrysostom, St. John of Beverley, the Gospel Saints and 'all the Holy Host of Heaven'.[9] When he stood at the altar and uttered the words 'Hoc enim corpus meum est', he believed with all Catholick Christendom that the wafer became the actual body of Christ. As John Mirk wrote in his Instructions for Parish Priests

10

'Teche them thenne wyth gode
entent, to be-leve on that sacrament;
that they receyve in forme of bred
ys Goddes body that soffered ded
up-on the hole rode tre,
to bye owre synnes and make us fre.'[10]

All that miracle or magic was smashed by the
New Learning. In 1529 Erasmus picked out
Queens', Christ's and St. John's colleges at
Cambridge, where 'the Sacred Bible was sought
out of the dusty corners where profane Falshood
and Neglect had thrown it'.[11] Even with the
return to the dales of men, as clergy and
schoolmasters, of the new Protestantism there
were pockets of Catholicism in Cumberland
and Westmorland which did not die out. Richard Leake, vicar of Killington near Sedbergh
published four sermons in 1599, and in the
dedication mentioned the great dearth and disease which swept the north in 1597. He added:
'those great and capitall sines, which rule and
reigne amongst us: as grosse Poperie, and
blinde superstition in very many places, in so
much, that I am afraide, that the abominable
Idoll of indignations the Masse is used in
diverse places about us, and that very boldly'.
He also mentioned 'the open prophanation of
the sabbath and unlawful pastimes'.[12] Catholicism was not just confined to the old families
such as the Blenkinsops of Brough, the Hiltons
of Burton, the Middletons of Leighton and the
Duckets of Grayrigg. After the foundation of
the English college at Louvain in 1568, later
transferred to Douay, and the excommunication
of Queen Elizabeth in 1570, there was a
constant stream of students from Oxford and
Cambridge. They returned as seminary priests
to call their homeland to the old faith. As
Canon Wilson wrote: 'none of the old priests
had anything to do with the new movement'.
Chief among the seminarists from Cumbria
was Father John Boste, the son of Nicholas
Boste of Well Inge in the parish of Dufton.
He was fellow of Queens College, Oxford in
1572, went to Douay in 1580, and returned
on the English mission in 1581. No more able
an agent could have been found for intellectual
gifts and family. With his knowledge of Cumberland and Westmorland he laid the foundation
of non-conformity and the Roman faith in
those counties, which the heirarchy of the
diocese of Carlisle were powerless to put down.
After capture he was racked in the Tower,
and went bent with a stick thereafter. He was
hanged at Durham in July 1594; he was cut
down and hacked to pieces while still alive.[13]
He, with Father Christopher Robinson, a native
of Wigton who was hanged at the same time,
laid the foundation of dissent from the established church. As Dr. A. L. Rowse has noted,
there were under 300 executions in the last
30 years of Elizabeth's reign, and an equal
number in the last three of Mary Tudor's
reign.[14] So eager were the Puritans to capture
the Church of England that they could not see
that the hated Papists were pioneer dissenters
in whose steps they trod.

In the following pages we will try to get
the gist of Fox's teaching which so impressed
the fellside farmers' sons and daughters, without compiling a compendium.

Having spent over three years studying the
primary Quaker books and pamphlets in the
Cambridge University Library, one is left with
several predominant impressions. (a) That Fox
will not be understood unless his mystical
experiences are recognised as a divine sanction
and driving force behind his early mental
Pilgrimage. (b) As Christ's references to the
Light predominate to the Johannine rather than
the synoptic gospels, so the bulk of Fox's
teaching is more Greek than Hebraic in emphasis. (c) As the Bible was the common book
of the nation the types and shadows, and the
Old Testament allusions would be understood
by a nation bred on over fifty years of Cal-
vinism. How far Fox would have got if he
had preached today to a nation largely ignorant
of the minutae of the Scriptures is another
question. (d) Whether Fox received any of the
chief points of Lutheran or Calvinistic doctrine
through his mother, the Levellers, or any of
the sects he visited during his pilgrimage before
his convincement will never be known. The
impression he gives in The Journal is that
every point of doctrine emerged through divine
guidance. But the historian is free to claim
that there was nothing new in Fox's teaching
which cannot be traced through the English
reformers, Colet, Erasmus, Tindale, Barnes,
Bilney, Latimer and many more, back to Luther,
Calvin, Zwingli and their followers. In addition
the demands of the commons at the Pilgrimage
of Grace to abolish manorial dues, and extortionate fines, the burden of tithes had received
a very recent airing in the Leveller writings
of John Lilburne during the civil wars. It does
not belittle the uniqueness of Fox to state that
he taught nothing which had not already been
aired during the past hundred years. His uniqueness was that with his mystical view of his
call, and of the spiritual church which he
founded, he was at the very apex of Protestant
belief that no man or priest should come
between man and his Maker. Fox was the
catalyst who drew together so many strands
of Protestant belief, and agrarian distress at a
time of great national confusion. (e) In the

tradition of the Judaeo-Christian religion he was a prophet recalling man to a primitive purity which man, in the person of Adam, had before the Fall. The Apostolic days were regarded by Fox in that light. The church which followed was regarded as corrupt or apostate, as the eighth century prophets regarded their nation as corrupted from the simple faith of the early nomadic tribes, before they settled to an agrarian life and its corrupt culture. The churches of Fox's day were regarded as corrupt and thus false, and to be destroyed. (f) Finally, following his convincement, and his mystical conversion to and by the Light, Fox's view of the Truth was absolute. It must be obeyed without question. It is at once the most noble as well as the most frightening part of his doctrine. It had to be obeyed at all cost. As Penn wrote 'No Cross, no Crown' - even if it meant leaving home, family, friends and employment. Thus John Fothergill (II) (1676-1744) of Carr End, who lost his first wife, and felt called to go to America on mission, left his children in the care of relatives and friends just at a time of adolescence when they most needed him, the Truth had to be obeyed. So he went; the farm was let and mortgaged, and he was abroad for two years. So obsessed was Fox with the absolute claim of Truth, that he regarded persecution, imprisonment and death as something to be embraced if it was the will of Christ. It never seems to have crossed his mind that he, Fox, was responsible for so much persecution, suffering and death as a result of his absolute teaching. He was merely obeying the Truth as he saw it.

Fox's Mysticism. In 1648 he travelled through the midland counties; coming to Nottinghamshire he had this experience:

> 'Now was I come up in Spirit through the flaming sword into the Paradise of God. All things were new; and all the creation gave another smell unto me than before, beyond what words can utter. I knew nothing but pureness, and innocency, and righteousness, being renewed into the image of God by Christ Jesus, to the state of Adam, which he was in before he fell. The creation was opened to me; and it was showed me how all things had their names given them, according to their nature and virtue. I was at a stand in my mind, whether I should practise physic for the good of mankind, seeing the nature and virtues of things were so opened to me by the Lord. But I was immediately taken up in the Spirit, to see another or more steadfast state than Adam's innocency, even into a state in Christ

Jesus, that should never fall. And the Lord showed me that such as were faithful to him, in the power and light of Christ, should come up into that state in which Adam was before he fell; in which the admirable works of creation, and virtues thereof, may be known, through the openings of that divine Word of wisdom and power, by which they were made. Great things did the Lord lead me into, beyond what can by words be declared; but as people come into subjection to the Spirit of God, and grow up in image and power of the Almighty, they may receive the Word of Wisdom, that opens all things, and come to know the hidden unity in the Eternal Being.'[15]

This passage is crucial to understanding the theology of Fox, and the convincement of those who followed him.

John Alderson of Nathwaite the son of Alice and Ralph Alderson, and a member of Ravenstonedale meeting, was born in 1721 and died in 1764 in London. He was a minister about 12 years, visiting Scotland and Ireland. In his youth he seems to have been a typical youth, full of fun, but too light and airy for his grave parents. 'After his disobedience he put out the candle of the Lord.' On his death-bed he gave this testimony:

> 'While he was in the employment of a shepherd, being alone, he was by the love of God so powerfully attracted to love him again, and all mankind that under the sacred influence and holy anointing thereof, he found, the gospel of Salvation flowed universally towards all, and the word of Life sprang and flowed in his soul as if he had been preaching to many people.'[16]

Samuel Bownas of Shap and Strickland meeting, was apprenticed in youth to a blacksmith at Brigflatts, where he had a very loving master and mistress. He had meat and work enough, but little thought of religion, slept through most meetings and was unmoved by sermons. He was convinced by the words of a young woman Anne Wilson. During meeting he fixed his eye on her 'and she with great zeal pointed her finger at (him) uttering these words with great power:'

> 'A traditional Quaker, thou comest to Meeting as thou went from it (the last time) and goes from it as thou came to it, but art no better for thy coming; what will thou do in the end?' This was so pat to my condition, that, like Saul, I was smitten to the ground, as it might be said, but turning my thoughts inward, in secret I cried, 'Lord what shall I do to help it?' And a voice as it were spoke in my Heart,

saying, 'Look unto me, and I will help thee;' and I found much comfort, that made me shed abundance of tears. Then I remembered what my Mother told me some years before, that when I grew up more to man's estate, I shall know the reason of that Tendernesse and Weeping.'[17]

John Fothergill (II) of Carr End, Wensleydale (1676-1744) was the son of Alexander who was imprisoned at York in 1695 for refusing to pay tithe, and died 6 months after his release. John became an eminent minister, visiting America three times. His early searchings for guidance at Meetings at Counterset were painful and laborious. Words would come to his mind, and he would be so fearful of offending God that he remained seated. When he was in his 20th year:

'For some months I could not either eat or sleep much, and was often alone in the Fields both day and night, mourning under a load of inward sorrow and deep fear, lest I should become a castaway; but by degrees I was brought to a desire after Stilness, and a patient waiting for the saving help of God to appear.

When the clear and evident Time and Requiring came, I then saw distinctly (and I have often considered it since) it was a Trial suffered to attend me ...'

'I am not without fear, that such a due attention for distinct Certainty of the immediate Call, or Requirings of the Word of Life, hath not always been practised; and for want hereof, some have appeared as Ministers before Ripe ...'[18]

Richard Robinson of Counterset (d. 1693) was convinced by Fox in 1652. Robinson was a tall, strong farmer who founded the Meeting at Counterset. He walked miles to attend Meetings, speak in market places, steeple-houses, and a few times walked naked as a sign (probably in his shirt) to prophesy the destruction of false churches. He was imprisoned three times covering at least 6 years over tithes or church rates. He was present between May and July 1670 when the magistrates fined every attender and leader at meetings. He was a man of clear and brave faith. He was also imprisoned a month in London after the Kaber Rigg Plot of 1663, just as he was about the sign the conveyance of the manorial rights of Bainbridge to the freeholders with the City of London. He died in 1693. His tribute to Fox was inserted in Fox's folio works 1706.

'This messenger of the Lord came into our parts in the 3rd Month 1652, who taught that every Man was enlightened, and had a Measure of Light and Grace from the Lord Jesus Christ, and that if it was to be obeyed and followed, it would lead to God, but being disobeyed, would become Man's Condemnation, which reached home to my understanding; and from that day and time I became affected to him; and that People that holds forth that Doctrine, and lived up to the same, altho' there were but few that then professed the Truth in these parts; I found him to be a man fearing God and living Righteousness, and endued with the Spirit of Judgment; and discerning, of a sound mind, and with Grifts and Graces becoming a true Minister of the Gospel, a Messenger of our Lord Jesus Christ; in a great measure, being learn'd in Christ's school, in the Things relating to God's Kingdom; he stood in the defence of the Truth against all opposition, and in all things he came to be tried with, he did approve himself as a Minister of God, in much Patience, in Afflictions, Imprisonments. Tumults, Sufferings and Travels; through whose Labour, diligent Testimony, and good Example, many have been turned to the Lord, and had occasion to rejoyce in the God of their Salvation; and being gone to rest ... it hath been sealed upon my Spirit, that his soul is with the Lord, to rest in the Paradise of his Pleasure for evermore.'[19]

Refs. Chapter 1

(1) Moderate Intelligencer. no. 207. Mar. 1 - Mar. 8. 1649
     no. 210. Mar. 22. - Mar. 29. 1649 (C.U.L.Sel.4.18.)
     The Levellers. H.N. Brailsford. Spokesman Books ed. 1976. 466-7.

(2) P.R.O. SP/C.21/p.25/1. Chancery Depositions in: Anne countess of Pembroke v. Robert Atkinson & others, taken 18th Jan. 1650/51, and 25 Sept. 1651. For the tenants: Henry Ward of Grayrigg, gent, aged 63, and William Cartmell of Preston Patrick, yeoman aged 48, gave evidence.

(3) Come out of her my people, OR An Answer to the Questions of a Gentlewoman (A Professor in the Anti-Christian Church of England) about hearing the Public Ministers; where it is largely discussed and proved to be sinfull and unlawfull etc. By mee John Lilburne, a close prisoner in the Fleete for the Cause of Christ. London 1639. (C.U.L. 9100.d.8207). pp. 3, 8 & 22.

'Oh! You (prelates) Night-Owles and Birds of Darknesse and uncleanness, that dare not come to show your crooked faces in the bright Sun - Shining light and cleare Crystall glasse of God's

Sacred and unspotted Truth.'

The Ordinance of Tithes Dismounted (by Richard Overton the Leveller) London 1646. (C.U.L. Peterborough. K.3.21[5].) p. 8 'The Bishops' Courts stript us of our clothes, but the Presbyters' Courts will strip us of coates, skinnes, lives & all, for anything I can discern.' pp 7 & 13.

'Oh, Martin, cannot forget the German proverbe, The Covetousness of Priests, and the Mercy of God endure for ever.'

The Declaration of John Lilburne & others in the Tower, 1st May 1649. (C.U.L. U*.5.118[6].) An Agreement of the Free People of England. Art. XXIII, It shall not be in their power to continue the Grievance of Tithes. Art. XXIV. It shall not be in their power to impose ministers upon parishes; but the parishes shall choose, and upon such terms as themselves shall contribute.

D.N.B. James Nayler (1617? - 1660). An officer who heard him preach said afterwards 'I was struck with more terror by the preaching of James Nayler than I was at the Battle of Dunbar' (3 Sept. 1650). Nayler was ploughing when he became convinced of a call to the Travelling Ministry. At first, not obeying it, he fell ill; recovering, he left home in 1652 and travelled north and met Fox and Margaret Fell at Swarthmore. Was present at Fox's trial at Lancaster 30 Oct. 1652; returned to Kendal, Orton and Mallerstang, where he was taken. He and Francis Howgill were committed to prison at Appleby, tried at the Sessions at Appleby (8) Jan. 1652/3, and acquitted. N. & B.I. 538/9. There are several accounts of the trial, not all complete.

(4)   D.N.B. Nicholas Metcalfe 1475? - 1539.

(5)   Sedbergh School Register I, E. Wilson, 1909. pp. 4-11 & 63

Hist. of the College of St John the Evangelist, Cambridge. ed. J.E.B. Mayor, 1869, I. 132.

Alumn. Cantab. from ancient times to 1751. J. & J.A. Venn, part I. vol. II, there are 19 men of the Leake family before 1700.

(6)   Dean and Chapter Lib. Carlisle. per. C.R.O. Carlisle. Machell MS, Vol. 3, p. 195. 'Borne at Castlehill near Eadenbrough in Scottland'.

(7)   N. & B.I. 522/3. Rental of Ravenstonedale temp. Edw. VI; among disbursements were 'To Edward Mynese schoolmaster his stipend £20.' The curate Mr. Toppin received £8.16.8. with 10s. for an horse.

N & B.I. 542 gives the salary of the Master of Kirkby Stephen Grammar School at £12 a year, with £1.6.8. to the usher. The Machell MS above gives Mynese as the first master.

(8)   C.R.O. Carlisle. Will of Henry Knewstub (of Shorgill) Malerstang. 12 Feb. 1586/7, mentions 'my brother Mr. John Knewstub'; one of Henry's sons went to live with John at Cockfield Rectory, Suffolk. See D.N.B. John Knewstub 1544-1624.

Sedbergh School reg. op.cit. 83.

Grace Book of the University of Cambridge 1542-1589. J. Venn. C.U.P. 1911 for John & Richard Knewstub.

Hist. of College of St. John the Evangelist, Cambridge op.cit. for John Knewstub.

N. & B.I., 543. The deed founding the Knewstub sub-sizarships at St. John's dated 7 Oct. 1623.

(9)   N. & B.I. 572/3

(10)   Lund Studies in English, vol. 49. p. 67. John Mirk's Instructions to Parish Priests. ed. Gillis Kristenson.

(11)   Cambridge Retrospect. T.R. Glover. 1943, 19, quoted from Milton.

(12)   Foure Sermons, preached & publicly taught by Richard Leake preacher of the Word of God at Killington, Westmorland. London 1599. (C.U.L.Peterborough. H.2.37[4]). The dedication to M. Thomas Strickland & H. James Bellingham Esquires.

Alumn. Cantab, earliest times to 1751. J. & J.A. Venn, op. cit. Richard Leake may have been Preacher of the Word of God at Lyeth in Cleveland. Walker Revised. A.G. Matthews, 1548, 19 & 395.

(13)   V.C.H. Cumberland II, 1968, p. 82. for John Boste, and p.87 for Christopher Robinson of Wigton, and George Swallowfield.

(14)   The England of Elizabeth. A.L. Rowse, Reprint Soc. ed. 1953, 498

(15)   For the purpose of this summary the Journal of George Fox, 1891 ed.1.28/9 has been followed. op. The Journal ed. by John L. Nickalls 1975, pub. by the Reglious Society of Friends p.27.

(16)   Piety Promoted ed. J. Kendal 1789 (C.U.L. Ddd.3.30). p. 191-194.

John Alderson of Narthwaite.

(17)   The Account of the Travels and Christian Experience in the Work of the Ministry of Samuel Bownas, London 1756. by J. Besse. 4-6

(18) An Account of the Life and Travels in the Work of the Ministry of John Fothergill. London 1754. pp. 13-14. (C.U.L. 7100.d.968).

Note: The Fothergills of Carr End occur thus:

John Fothergill (I) rebuilt or acquired Carr End in 1667. His origin not known, nor his wife. He died 1684; buried at Bainbridge.

His only child *Alexander's* birth unknown. He married Ann Langton at Brigflats 1673; was imprisoned twice for non-payment of tithes; died Sept. 1695, six months after release from prison.

His only son *John Fothergill (II)* born 1676, succeeded to Carr End, at the age of 19. He married twice, and went on three extensive tours of America. He died in 1744. Among his children was *John Fothergill (III)*. M.D. born 1712. He was the eminent doctor, botanist and philanthropist. He died 1780.

(19) Gospel Truth. The Collected Works of George Fox, 1706 ed. The Testimony of Richard Robinson of Counterset. Not to be confused with Richard Robinson of Brigflats.

CHAPTER 2

When Fox stood in Sedbergh churchyard at the Whitsun Fair 1652 he declared 'the everlasting truth of the Lord, and the word of life for several hours, showing that the Lord was come to teach his people himself, and to bring them off from all the world's ways and teachers, to Christ the true teacher, and the true way to God.'[1] It is worth noting how similar was his approach to that of John Wycklif in about 1384: 'This Gospel (St.Matth.IX,35) telleth of the office that should fall to Christ's disciples:

'Christ went to those uplandish towns as Bethphage and Cana not for winning of money; for he was not smit with pride or covetousness. He chose places to teach in that were most able, as Synagogues.

Christ was not only occupied with preaching but in healing sick men.

Christ telleth him the manner that should always keep in working God's work.

Christ preached not fables, but the Gospel of God.

Christ ordained his disciples to travel among men, because not all people travelled to hear his word. 'They were liggene as sheep without heerde.'

Christ bade them wend forth and preach to the people that the Kingdom of God shall come.

For Christ said thus: God gave freely, therefore give freely your traveil to the people, or else it is simony. And here is begging of preachers, since it is hid selling of preaching.'[2]

On the following Sunday afternoon Fox spoke to about a thousand people from the rock above the chapel on Firbank fell. His address of about three hours is one of the most memorable in the religious and political history of the north. It marks a watershed between the old established churches and chapels with their paid ministers, and the new spiritual church he came to found, which was embodied in the Society of Friends. Though Quakerism has vanished from the remote dales where at first

it had its strength, the principle of an unpaid lay preacher, and a congregation of free people outside the established church was continued first in the chapels of the Revd. Benjamin Ingham (1712-1772) with their Moravian background, and later in the chapels of the Methodist connexion. There were Inghamite chapels in Kendal, Dent, Kirkby Lonsdale, Kirkby Stephen and Bleatarn. They gathered a number of Quakers and old non-conformist Presbyterians into one; their evangelical successors still survive. Just as Fox gathered into the Society of Friends a body of dissenting belief circulating at the time, so in the eighteenth century a similar amalgam gathered a weakened Quakerism in the dales into the Inghamite and Methodist chapels. Ingham and Wesley were strongly influenced by the Moravian churches, and Zinzendorf (1700-1760), where pietism, or 'the religion of the heart' based on an intimate fellowship with the Saviour was a strong ingredient. The local lay preacher of the Inghamite and Methodist chapels was the successor to the itinerant Quaker minister travelling between meetings with the certificate of approval from his own meeting. Where a number of dales' chapels are less sacramental than preaching in outlook, this may be due to the part Quaker background of some of the dale communities.

Fox's sermon on Firbank Fell at Whitsuntide 1652 was a public declaration of convictions which had already matured four years before.[3] As Christ's Sermon on the Mount was his declaration of principles long considered, so Fox's was comparable. As another writer has put it, Westmorland became the Galilee of the new movement.[4] The purpose of these pages is to try to recall to the present reader the main points of that teaching which impressed a large number of men and women in the dales. Fox's sermons of three to six hours, his numerous booklets and pamphlets, his long pastoral letters, and the hundreds of pamphlets written in prison as testimonies by his followers are often couched in langauge of such pious obscurity as to defy the understanding. Many of Fox's tracts were involved, others were brilliant. Through the fog of obscurity there emerges the mystic, the prophet, the evangelist, the social reformer on puritan lines, the loving pastor, the fearless adversary, with all the marks of a Messenger of the stern judgment of God; this is summed up in his section on the church bell...as a market bell that the priest might sell his wares.

Fox's Creed.

J.L. Nickalls in his edition of Fox's Journal (Cambs. Univ. Press 1952) remarks in his introduction that the Journal was not written up daily, but dictated from time to time, often when he was in prison. Thus the initial events of 1652 were dictated when Fox was in Lancaster Gaol later that year. This account is general in parts and needs to be filled in with the details supplied by the separate Meetings of the 'First Publishers of Truth' (ed. Norman Penney (1907) called for by the Yearly Meeting in 1676. So also with Fox's creed, there is the outline in his Journal of 1648/9 which remained private till its publication at the end of the century. His public declarations were heard in the lengthy sermons, and in his many pamphlets. One of the first to alarm the Presbyterian leaders of Westmorland was his tract 'Saul's Errand to Damascus' issued about 1652. This raised the wrath of Francis Higginson vicar of Kirkby Stephen who wrote two tracts, the first against the newly arisen Quakers, and the second against Fox's tract, both in 1653. But the two by Fox which seem to have made the greatest impact were:

A Paper sent forth into the World From them that are scornfully called Quakers, Declaring the Grounds and Reasons why they deny the Teachers of the World, (who profess themselves to be Ministers) and Dissent from them. (By George Fox), London 1652.

The theme of this tract was repeated by many other Quakers, and issued several times.

Newes coming up out of the North, Sounding towards the South, or A Blast out of the North up into the South, and so to flie abroad into the World: And a Warning to all England, and Nations elsewhere, The Terrible Day of the Lord is appearing, that all your hearts must be ript up and laid naked and open before the mighty God, before him where nothing can be hid, and that no hiding place will be found for him. (by George Fox), London 1655.

The first tract is a blistering attack on the ministries of the established churches which he hoped to supplant by his new spiritual Society; and the second was an apocalyptic and prophetic declaration of God's imminent Day of Judgment, for the ripping up of all hearts, and the Salvation of Man through the Cross and Blood of Jesus, leading to a new life guided by the inner Light of Christ in every man's heart.[5]

The following is an attempt to examine the sequence of Fox's ideas in his Journal as distinct from any order followed in his public writing and utterances. (Journal; 1891 ed. Vol. I. page nos. given in turn). The period of writing is 1648-9.

28. (His mystical experience). *I was come up in the Spirit through the flaming sword into the Paradise of God*...beyond what words can utter. I knew nothing but pureness, and innocency, and righteousness, being renewed into the image of God by Christ Jesus, to the state of Adam, which he was in before he fell.

29. *The Lord opened to me three things*, relating to those three great professions in the world, physic, divinity, and law.

The physicians were out of the wisdom of God, by which the creatures were made; and knew not their virtue, because they were out of the Word of Wisdom.

The Priests were out of the true faith, which Christ is the author of; the faith which purifies and gives victory.

The lawyers were out of equity, and out of the true justice, and out of the Law of God, which went over the first transgression, and over all sin, and answered the Spirit of God...

That all three ruled the world out of wisdom, out of faith, and out of the equity and law of God: the one pretending to cure the body, the other the cure of the soul, and the third the property of the people.

I felt his power went forth over all, by which all might be reformed, if they would receive and bow unto it...that all might be reformed and brought into the Law of God.

30. *The Lord opened to me who the greatest deceivers were*, and how far they might come:

(a) *The followers of Cain* (who) hear the voice of God;

(b) *Such as came out of Egypt*, and through the Red Sea, and to praise God on the banks of the sea shore, who could speak of his miracles and wonders;

(c) *Such as were come as far as Korah and*

17

Dathan, and their company;

(d) *Such as were come as far as Balaam*, who could speak the Word of the Lord, who heard his voice and knew it, and knew his Spirit, and could see the star of Jacob, and godliness of Israel's tent, the second birth, which no enchantment could prevail against; these could speak so much of their experiences of God, and yet turned from the Spirit and the Word, and went into gainsaying. These were and would be the great deceivers, far beyond the priests.

31. *Likewise among Christians*, such as should preach in Christ's name, and should work miracles, cast out devils, and go as far as a Cain, a Korah, and a Balaam, in the Gospel times; these were and would be the great deceivers. They could speak of some experiences of Christ, but lived not in the life; these led the world with a form of Godliness, but denied the power. These followers of Cain etc. have brought the world, since the apostles days, to be like a sea...and might deceive now. But it is impossible for them to deceive the elect, which are chosen in Christ, who was before the world began, and before the deceiver was, ...not keeping their minds to the Lord Jesus.

This applies also to Christians, both priests and people, *in their reading the Scriptures*, who cry out against Cain, Esau, and Judas in the Scriptures, and yet see not the like in themselves. They came to see the nature of wild Ishmael in themselves, and the son of perdition in themselves...calling them fat bulls of Bashan etc...that it was they who hated the Light, and resisted the Holy Ghost.

(32) they were wells without water, clouds without rain. When they came to look into themselves, the cry could not be 'is it he, or they?' but 'I and we are found in these conditions'.

(32) I saw that *none could read the Scriptures without a right sense of them, and without applying it to themselves*. That the ministry of Moses, and all the prophets leading to John the Baptist, saw Christ, the great prophet that was to come to fulfil them. That none could understand John's words except by the divine Spirit by which John spoke, by his burning shining Light, which is sent from God.

(33) *All must know the voice crying in the wilderness*, in their hearts, which through transgression were become a wilderness.

(34) But as man comes through the Spirit and power of God, to *Christ, who fulfils the types,* figures, shadows, promises, and prophecies that were of him, and is led by the Holy Ghost into the truth and substance of the Scriptures, sitting down with him who is the author and end of them; then they are read and understood with profit and great delight.

(34) When I was brought up into his image in righteousness and holiness, and into the paradise of God (see p. 28 above) he let me see how Adam was made a living soul, *and also the stature of Christ*, the mystery that had been hid from ages and generations. For all sects in Christendon...could not bear to be told that any should come to Adam's perfection, into the image of God, that righteousness and holiness that Adam was in before he fell; to be clear and pure without sin, as he was. None could bear to be told that any should grow up to the measure of the fulness of the stature of Christ...that any should come, whilst on earth, into the same power and Spirit that the prophets and apostles were in. It is a certain truth that none can understand their writings, without the same Spirit by which they were written.

(34) *The Lord opened to me by his invisible power 'that every man was enlightened by the divine Light of Christ'* and I saw it shine through all, and that they that believed in it came out of condemnation to the light of life, and became children of it; but they that hated it, and did not believe in it, were condemned by it, though they made a profession of Christ. This I saw in the pure openings of the Light, without the help of any man; neither did I then know where to find it in the Scriptures, though afterwards, searching the Scriptures, I found it. For I saw in the Light and Spirit which was before the Scriptures were given forth, and which led the holy men of God to give them forth, that all must come to that Spirit, if they would know God, or Christ, or the Scriptures aright, which they that gave them forth were led and taught by.

(35) *I observed a dulness and drowsy heaviness upon people*...I saw death was to pass over this heavy sleepy state; and I told people they must come to witness death to that sleepy, heavy nature, and a cross to it in the power of God.

(35) Once when I was walking in the fields, the Lord said unto me *'Thy name is written in the Lamb's book of Life'*... and as the Lord spoke it, I believed, and saw in it the new birth. Then, some time after, the Lord commanded me to go abroad into the world, which was like a briery thorny wilderness; and when

I came in the Lord's mighty power, with the word of life...the world swelled, and made a noise like the raging waves of the sea. Priests, and professors, magistrates and people, were all like a sea, when I proclaimed the day of the Lord, and preached repentance to them.

(35) *I was sent to turn people from darkness to the Light*, that they might receive Jesus; for as many as should receive him in his light, I saw that he would give power to become the sons of God, which I had obtained by receiving Christ. I was to direct people to the Spirit, that gave forth the Scriptures, by which they might be led into all truth...I was to turn them to the grace of God, and to the truth in the heart, which came by Jesus, that by this grace they might be taught, which would bring them salvation.

(36) I saw that Christ died for all men...and enlightened all men with his divine and saving light...that none could be a true believer, but who believed in it. I saw that the grace of God, which bringeth salvation to all men hath appeared, and that the manifestation of the Spirit of God was given to every man.

These things I did not see by the help of man, nor by the letter, though they are written in the letter, but I saw them in the light of the Lord Jesus Christ, and by his immediate Spirit and power, as did the holy men of God, by whom the Holy Scriptures were written. Yet I had no slight esteem of the Holy Scriptures, but they were very precious to me, for I was in that Spirit by which they were given forth; and what the Lord opened in me, I afterwards found was agreeable to them.

...All would prove too short to set forth the infinite love, wisdom, and power of God, in preparing, fitting, and furnishing me for the service he had appointed me to.

(36) When the Lord God and his son Jesus Christ sent me forth to preach his everlasting Gospel, *I was glad...to turn the people to that inward Light*, Spirit and Grace, by which people might know their salvation and way to God; even that Divine Spirit which would lead them into all Truth, and *which I infallibly knew would never deceive any*.

(36) By the Light of Jesus I was to bring people off from all their own ways to Christ, the new and living way:

from their churches, which men had made, to the church in God, the general assembly written in heaven;

(37) *from the world's teachers*, made by men, to learn of Christ, who is the way, the Truth and the life...that they might worship the Father of Spirits; I was to bring people off *from the world's religions* which are vain; that they might know the pure religion, might visit the fatherless, the widows, and the strangers, and keep themselves unspotted from the world; *from the world's fellowships, and prayings and singings*, which stood in forms without power, that their fellowship might be in the Holy Ghost; that they might pray in the Holy Ghost, and sing in the Spirit, with the grace that comes from Jesus.

from Jewish ceremonies and from heathenish fables, from men's inventions and windy doctrines...from their beggarly rudiments, with their schools and colleges for making ministers of their own making, but not of Christ; *from all their images and crosses, and sprinkling of infants*, with all their holy days, and all their vain traditions, which they had instituted since the apostles' days...I was moved to declare against them all, and against all that preached not freely, as such that had not received freely from Christ.

(38) *The Lord forbade me to put off my hat to any, high or low; and I was required to Thee and Thou all men and women*, without any respect to rich or poor, great or small.

I was not to bid people Good morrow or Good evening; neither might I bow or scrape with my leg to any one. This made the sects and professions to rage. But the Lord's power carried me over all.

Oh! the rage of the priests, magistrates, professors, and people of all sorts. Though THOU, to a single person was according to their rules of grammar, and in the Bible, yet they could not bear to hear it.

And, because I would not put off my hat to them (in hat honour) it set them all in a rage...an honour invented by men in the fall. They would be looked upon as saints, church-members and great Christians......(yet) seek not the honour that cometh from God only...an honour which must be laid in the dust.

(39) Oh! the blows, punchings, beatings, and imprisonments...the bad language and evil usage we received for refusing to move our hats; sometimes we were in danger of losing our lives...and that by great professors of Christianity! But many came to see the vanity of putting off the hat, and felt the weight of Truth's Testimony against it.

(1) In going to their courts to cry for Justice, and in speaking and writing to judges and justices to do justly;

(2) In warning such as kept public houses for entertainment, that they should not let people have more drink than would do them good;

(3) In testifying against their wakes or feasts, may-games, sports, plays, and shows, which trained up people to vanity and looseness, and led them from the fear of God;

(4) And the days they had set forth for holy-days were usually the times where they most dishonoured God by these things.

(5) In fairs, also, and in markets, I was made to declare against their deceitful merchandise, cheating and cozening;

(6) Warning all to deal justly, and to speak the truth, to let their Yea be Yea.

(7) And their Nay be Nay; and to do unto others as they would have others do unto them; forewarning them of the great and terrible day of the Lord;

(8) I was moved also to cry against all sorts of music, and against the mountebanks playing tricks on their stages, for they burthened the pure life, and stirred up people's minds to vanity.

(9) I was much exercised, too, with school-masters and schoolmistresses, warning them to teach their children sobriety in the fear of the Lord, that they might not be nursed and trained up in lightness, vanity and wantonness.

(10) Likewise I was made to warn masters and mistresses, fathers and mothers in private families, to take care that their children and servants might be trained up in the fear of the Lord. For I saw that as the Jews teach their children and servants the law of God and the covenant, yea, even strangers were to keep the Sabbath, and be circumcised, before they might eat their sacrifices;

So all Christians, and all that made a profession of Christianity, ought to train up their children and servants in the new covenant of Light, who is God's salvation to the ends of the earth, that all may know their salvation;

And they ought to train them up in the law of life, the law of the Spirit, the law of love and faith, that they might be made free from the law of sin and death.

(11) And all Christians ought to be circumcised by the Spirit, which puts off the body of the sins of the flesh, that they may come to eat of the heavenly sacrifice, Christ Jesus, that true spiritual food, which none can rightly feed upon but they that are circumcised by the Spirit.

(12) Likewise I was exercised about the star-gazers, who drew people's minds from Christ, the bright and morning star... who is the wisdom of God, and from whom the right knowledge of all things is received.

The Church Bell

The earthly spirit of the priests wounded my life; and when I heard the bell toll to call people together to the steeple-house, it struck at my life; for it was just like a market-bell, to gather people together, that the priest might set forth his wares to sell. O! the vast sums of money that are gotten by the trade they make of selling the Scriptures, and by their preaching, from the highest bishop to the lowest priest! What one trade in the world is comparable to it? notwithstanding the Scriptures were given forth freely, and Christ commanded his ministers to preach freely, and the prophets and apostles denounced judgment against all covetous hirelings and diviners for money: but in this free Spirit of the Lord Jesus was I sent forth to declare the Word of life and reconciliation freely, that all might come to Christ, who gives freely, and who renews up into the image of God, which man and woman were in before they fell, that they might sit down in heavenly places in Christ Jesus.

(Journal, George Fox, 1891 Edn. I, 41.)

Refs: Chapter 2

(1) Journal I, 112.

(2) Select Works of John Wyclif, ed. T. Arnold, Oxford 1869, Vol. I extracts from pp. 197 & 199.

(3) Journal I, 29-41.

(4) Quoted: The Lake Counties, C.M.L. Bouch & G.P. Jones, 1961, 179.

(5) Apart from Fox's writings, there are several early summaries of Quaker belief:

The True Light shining in England etc. by William Smith, London 1660, pp. 13 to 23 (C.U.L. Sel. 9.44.53[16].)

The Everlasting Gospel of Repentance, by Edward Burrough, London, 1660 contains 'Certain Propositions of Faith which everyone must believe'. There are ten propositions.

A Testimony to the True & Spiritual Worship, and a Word of Consolation to the Children of Light etc. by Thomas Taylor, 1670 (C.U.L. Broughton 256[13]) pp. 1-11.

A Declaration to the World of our Faith, and what we believe who are called Quakers. Edward Burrough. 1659. (C.U.L. Syn. 7.65.68.)

Francis Bugg, woolcomber of Mildenhall, Suffolk was a Quaker from boyhood, but was thought to have informed against a Quaker Meeting in 1675. After a long quarrel he left the Society in 1680, and wrote violent pamphlets against the Society 1682-1724. In 1684 he wrote a summary of Quaker belief, which was thought sufficiently fair to be printed in the Catalogue of Friends Books, by Joseph Smith, 1867, I, 334. See also D.N.B. Francis Bugg, 1640-1724.

A Refutation of some of the Modern Misrepresentations of the Society of Friends, commonly called Quakers, with a Life of James Nayler, by Joseph Gurney Bevan, London 1800. It also contains pp. 109-124 an excellent exposition of the Doctrine and Discipline of Friends, well worth reading. (C.U.L. Ddd. 3.21[1].)

Chapter 3

In this chapter and the following three we will attempt to uncover the principal points of early Quakerism as it was seen by contemporaries who were responsible for nurturing the Seed already planted by Fox.

The Galilee of Quakerism

Edward Burrough. (1634-1663) was a native of Underbarrow. On his conversion in 1652 he was rejected by his father, who would not allow him to return home unless he forsook his new faith. He had been trained for the parish ministry, and in his eleven remaining years he became one of the clearest and most outspoken of the band of young people who travelled far, suffered persecution and imprisonment, and eventually died in Newgate prison in 1663.[1] He is one of the most readable of early Friends. He wrote a letter in Dublin in 1655 directed to 'The Camp of the Lord in England'.

'O thou North of England, who art counted as desolate and barren, and reckoned the least of the Nations, yet out of thee did the Branch Spring, and the Star arise which gives Light unto all the Regions round about; on thee the Son of Righteousness appeared with wounding and with healing; and out of thee the Terror of the Lord proceeded, which makes the earth to tremble and be removed; out of thee Kings, Princes, and Prophets did come forth in the Name and Power of the most High, which uttered their voices as thunder, and laid their swords on the necks of their Enemies and never returned empty from the Slaughter'.[2]

The Man, George Fox

William Penn (1644-1718) in his Preface to Fox's Journal, gave as clear a picture of Fox's character to be met anywhere. In nine paragraphs he noted Fox's understanding of man's inner spirit, his patient work to point man to the inner Light of Christ to be their only teacher, his extraordinary capacity to open the meaning of the Scriptures, his emphasis on the innocency of the first Adam to which man can return through complete submission to the Light of Christ, his excellence in prayer, the innocence of his life, his incredible labours in Britain, America, Holland and Germany, his attention and response to letters from friends and meetings, particularly those passing through suffering in many lands, and finally his 'behaviour at Derby, Lichfield, Appleby, before Oliver Cromwell, at Launceston, Scarborough, Worcester, and Westminster Hall, with many other places...' From all this we are left with the question, how did the dalesman see him? Two extracts give the answer:

> 'Above all he excelled in prayer. The inwardness and weight of his spirit, the reverence and solemnity of his address and behaviour, and the fewness and fulness of his words, have often struck, even strangers with admiration, as they used to reach others with consolation. The most awful, living, reverent frame I ever felt or beheld, I must say, was his prayer. And truly it was a testimony he knew and lived nearer to the Lord than other men; for they that know Him most, will see most reason to approach him with reverence and fear.'

> 'He was of an innocent life, no busy-body, nor self-seeker, neither touchy nor critical; what fell from him was very inoffensive, if not very edifying. So meek, contented, modest, easy, steady, tender, it was a pleasure to be in his company. He exercised no authority but over evil, and that everywhere and in all; but with love, compassion, and long-suffering. A most merciful man, as ready to forgive, as unapt to take or give an offence. Thousands can truly say he was of an excellent spirit and savour among them, and because thereof, the most excellent spirits loved him with an unfeigned and unfading love.'[3]

These words give life to his voluminous works, which contain hidden gems.

Howl Ye People

Thomas Taylor (1617-1682) from Carlton in Craven, with his brother Christopher (1620-1686) were independent preachers, and convinced in 1652. Thomas was educated at Oxford, and as a Quaker proved a powerful preacher, suffering many imprisonments, and at least two at Appleby.[4] It has been suggested that he had relations at Ravenstonedale. He gives a common example of the opening salvo of a Quaker preacher, thundering out the Imminent Judgement of God to farmer families on market day:

'Weep thou England, Houl, Houl ye People; for the Dreadful Day of the Lord God is at hand, it is at the Door, as an armed Man, coming swiftly upon you to break down and tread under thy feet thy Pomp, Glory and Strength. Thou hast exceeded in thy Sins, and art grown monstrous in thine Iniquities; so the Lord will be exceeding Terrible unto thee. Thou hast suffered the Wicked in thee to have Liberty, and to take their fill of Sin, when the Voice of the Righteous cannot be endured in thee; but he that departs from Iniquity, and would persuade others to do so, is even made a Prey of by Ungodly and Unreasonable Men; their Bodies imprisoned and banished, and estates spoiled, and all sorts of Injuries done them for God's Name and Truth's sake. And therefore will the Lord God arise to take Vengeance for these things; Yea his Soul will certainly be avenged on such a Nation as this, saith the Spirit of his Servant. (Taylor proceeded to attack the passing of the second Conventicle Act which came into force on 10th May 1670.) Assuredly great Wrath is gone out from the presence of the Eternal Majesty of Heaven and Earth against you; nothing can stay it, but your ceasing from Persecuting the Blessed Truth of God, which we, the People of God, in scorn called Quakers, do love and live in'.[5]

The Appeal

James Nayler (1617?-1660) had been a most effective preacher in the New Model Army; then he was convinced in 1652.[6] After he had witnessed Fox's trial at Lancaster in early October, he went through Kendal, Orton, Ravenstonedale and Mallerstang, where he was arrested, examined at Kirkby Stephen, and with Francis Howgill held in the gaoler's house at Appleby until his trial in January 1652/3.[7] He epitomises that warm evangelical appeal which was to become so marked a feature of the Inghamite and Methodist chapels in the dales in later centuries.

'All people everywhere who profess that you love God, and have a desire to walk in his ways, and are in this dark world wandering too and fro, enquiring the way how you may come out of this great City, which is Sodom and Egypt, where filthiness and darkness rules, and is black, wherein the Lord is crucified, and all the righteous blood hath been shed, and yourselves kept in bondage to sin and unrighteousness, blindness and thick darkness, and know not where you are, nor the way out of this condition, though many of you have been enquiring after the way so many years, seeking after your blinde guides, who are not the way, neither in the way themselves, and so have forsaken the fountain of Light, and have run after, and have been led by them who are in the same darkness with you, *now stand still a while* and see where you are, and what you have been doing; You pretend as to the Kingdom of God, but you are not seeking where it is; you have been seeking without, but it is within you, and there you must find it, if ever you finde it; It is not to be found in Forms and Customs, and outside Observations; but the Kingdom of God is within you, and the way to the Kingdom is within you, and the Light that guides into the way and keeps in the way is within; Christ is the way, and know ye not that Christ is in you, except ye be reprobates? And as he is the Way, so he is the Light.'

You poor scattered sheep

'And now to you poor scattered sheep, who have been scattered by these hirelings, in this cloudy, dark day, which hath been upon all flesh spred upon the face of the earth...you have been seeking the living among the dead; he is not to be found in the world, nor formal worships, nor in humane wisdom and learning, but he is only to be found as he reveals himself freely, to those who patiently wait for his spirit. Dear People, to you that love the Lord above all earthly things, and ye have not your minds directed where to wait for him, to you I speak to your souls that lie in death till they hear the voice of the Son of God;

He is near you, who is the way to the Father; look not out, he is within you; That which I know, I declare unto you, and the way I know, where I have found my beloved, my Saviour, my Redeemer, my Husband, my Maker, who hath set me above all the world, my sins, my fears, my sorrows, my tears, with his love, to live with him in Spirit for ever; but dying daily unto all visible things. Praises, Praises to my Father for ever.'[8]

Christ is our sufficient Teacher

George Fox's belief that the Light of Christ in each human heart ready to receive him, and purified from all earthly corruption and distraction, as our only sure Teacher, was the bedrock of his experience and practice. All the established churches and chapels were apostate, false and counterfeit. The purified life, *the silent heart* in the silent Meeting, waiting for the guidance of the Holy Spirit to reveal the Truth in Christ, was the sanctuary in which Christ made his infallible presence known. Christ's word 'The Kingdom of God is within you' spoke direct to each person, and was available to all freely, and without price. These words were written by Fox to the magistrates who had imprisoned him in Launceston gaol in 1656:

'Therefore is this Word of the Lord God to you, and a Charge to you all, in the presence of the living God of Heaven and Earth: Every man of you being enlightened with a Light, that cometh from Christ, the Saviour of People's souls, from whom the Light cometh, that enlightens you, To the Light take heed; that with it you may well all see Christ, from whom the Light cometh, you may all see Him to be your Saviour, by whom the World was made, who saith; Learn of me.

But if you hate this Light, which Christ hath enlightened you withal, ye hate Christ; who doth enlighten you all, that you all through him (who is the Light) might believe. But not believing in the Light, nor bringing your Deeds to the Light, which will make them manifest, and reprove them; this is your Condemnation, even the Light. Remember you are warned in your Lifetime; for this is your Way to Salvation, the Light if you walk in it: And this is your Condemnation, the Light, if you reject and hate it. And you can never come to Christ, the second Priest, unless you come to the Light...'[9]

Writing in 1654 to Quaker ministers, Fox made this theological point:

'There is no justification out of the Light, out of Christ; justification is in the Light in Christ; here is the door of the will of God, here is the entering into the Kingdom. He that believes in the Light, becomes a child of Light; and here the Wisdom is received that is justified of her children. Here believing in the Light, you shall not abide in Darkness, but shall have the Light of Life; and come every one to witness the Light that shines in your Hearts, which Light will give you the Light of the Glory of God, in the Face of Jesus Christ. With which Light you will see him reign, which is the Prince of Life and Peace; which Light turns from him, that is out of the Truth, and abode not in it; where true Peace is not.'[10]

Perfection

James Parnell (1637?-1656) as a boy of 16 walked from Essex to see Fox in Carlisle gaol in 1653. 'He was convinced and came to be a very fine minister of the Word of Life and turned many to Christ.' Thus Fox describes this young hero who was imprisoned in Cambridge in 1654, and was confined in Colchester Castle in 1655 and died there as a result of the severity with which he was treated. They kept him in a place called Little Ease, whence he had to climb up and down for his food. One day the rope he used broke, and he was so hurt that he died of his injuries.[11] The hatred of the Calvinist preachers of the Quaker creed stemmed from Fox's doctrine of Perfection; that it is possible for man to be so receptive and obedient to the Light, that he could attain that perfection which Adam had before the Fall. This thirst after righteousness was to be the obsession of the early Quakers; and their abhorrence of earthly ways, carnality, apostate churches, hireling priests, dishonest trading, youthful games and pastimes marked them as 'the serious people'.

'Therefore all you, who desire Salvation to your Souls, Try and Prove your Faith and Hope, which you do trust to...let him that thinks he stands, take heed lest he falleth. So everyone, whose desire is after Righteousness, hearken to that in your Consciences, which raiseth up Desires after Righteousness, and which sheweth you the Vainness of your Lives, and checks you when you do amiss, and troubles you and torments you in Conscience when you have been Drunk, and have done an evil Act; be willing to be guided by that, and that will lead you to Repentance, and Newness of Life, to forsake those things which it discovers to be contrary to the will of God;

And if you be willing to follow this, and be guided by it, you shall find a Teacher continually present, checking in the Conscience for vain Thoughts, and for Vain, and Idle, and Needless Works and Actions, and so will Crucifie the Lusts, which is the Ground of those things, and which will lead you out of the Pathes of Death, into the way of Life; out of the Traditions and Customs, and Fashions and opinions of the World, into the Assurance of Eternal Truth.

And thou that art willing to follow this, and be guided by this, shall need no man to teach thee; that it will be a Teacher unto thee, Teaching and Directing in Righteousness, Purity and Holiness; and if thou art diligent, keeping thy Mind within, with an Ear open to the pure Voice, thou shalt find it present with thee wheresoever thou art, in the Fields, in thy Bed, in Markets, in Company, or wheresoever thou art, when thy Outward Priest or Teacher is absent, it may be in the Ale-House, or at his Pleasures and Delights, or far off, it will be present with thee...It will purify thy Heart, and will make it a fit Temple for Purity to dwell in; and then thy Sacrifices will be pure, which come from a pure Heart, (and) the Lord will accept them.'[12]

Truth

There are three times as many references to Truth in the Johannine as distinct from the Synoptic writings in the New Testament. Truth was to become a key word in Quaker faith and service. When a minister went on tour from his Meeting, he went 'in Truth's Service'; the word occurs frequently in the records of Meetings.

'Every one must come to their own Grace, Light and Truth in their hearts, that's come by Jesus, and the Word of Faith in their Hearts, if that they come to this Heavenly and Spiritual Unity and Fellowship and Order that is among the Saints in Light.'[13]

'Be obedient to what you know, walk in the Truth in your measure made manifest by Jesus Christ; wrangle not, strike not one another, but walk together in the Vineyard in love; nor think your time long, nor your work hard, which you must obey and do when your Master commands you, neither murmur nor complain...that when your Lord and Master cometh you may receive your blessing'.[14]

Power

Another word oft used by Fox was the word Power, the Power of Christ to win the souls of men, through his Friends who were innocent in heart and life, and obedient to the Light. As with the previous extract from Nayler, this sermon by Fox was wrapped in mystical verbiage, not to the taste of a modern reader. Remove this, and one is left with a remarkably direct appeal to a thoughtful person, often outside the churches, to trust Christ.

Christ and his Fishermen

'A Testimony for all Masters of Ships, Seamen etc. (1677)

Jesus began to preach by the Sea-side, and there was gathered unto him a great multitude, so that he entered into the Ship, and there sat in the Sea, and the whole Multitude was by the Sea on the Land. Now would not many say, that it was not a Consecrated Place to teach the Word of God in; but I must tell you, Christ consecrates and makes all Things and Places holy.

Now, consider ye Seamen, and Fishermen, and others, that are not disciples of Christ; for sometimes in your Ships you have been in scarcity of Bread; and now here was Christ and his Disciples which had but one loaf in the Ship, and Christ convinceth them that they had enough, by his former Miracles.

And therefore it is good for everyone to see with the pure Eye, and hear with the pure Ear, so that they may perceive and understand with the pure Heart what Christ did and doth do, and what he is able to do in all necessities...

And you that call yourselves Fishers of Men, you may toil all the Night and catch not a Man in God's Net to him, except it be with the Power of Christ; and therefore know his Voice, and obey it, and follow him, by whom all things were made.

Now all ye Fisher-men, and Sea-men and

others, consider what kind of Disciples and Ministers of the Lord Jesus Christ chose; and you may see that Peter and the rest, though they had been Disciples of Christ Jesus for some years, and such that Christ had sent forth to Preach before he was Crucified, and after that he was risen, Christ appeared the third Time unto them; and Peter had his Fishers Coat, and the Disciples who were Fisher-men, and Seamen, they were partners together in a Ship. And now, was this a fit Coat think you to Preach the Gospel in, and to meet Christ in, and to dine with him in? I say, Yes, as good as any of the Canonical Garments. (And when Christ provided fish and a Fire by the Sea-side, when he sent them forth to Preach). So here you may all see, how the Disciples of Christ were encouraged to trust in him, and that their Minds might be carried over all Distrust of carnal Things and outward Victuals...And so you may see it is not the Seamens Skill, but the Lord's Power, which all are to have Faith in, and to obey him, by which they are saved and preserved.

Here you may see the Fisher-men, James and John, and Peter and Andrew were Fishermen...and Preachers of Christ Jesus, and catched a Multitude of outward Fish, and a Multitude of Men, which they fish'd out of the great Sea of the World, by the Command and Power of Christ...whom he sent forth, and gave Commission to Preach, and said Freely ye have received, freely give'.[15]

Silent worship

Just as the ground of Quaker worship lay in a full knowledge of the Scriptures, so the New Testament matched their experience of his Presence. Edward Burrough of Underbarrow spoke of the reality of Quaker worship, of Christ's Presence which they knew and felt, with a certainty as sure as that claimed by any Roman Catholic or Protestant:

'We found this Light to be a sufficient Teacher, to lead us to Christ, from whence this Light came, and thereby it gave us to receive Christ, and to witness Him to dwell in us; and through it the New Covenant we came to enter into, to be made Heirs of Life and Salvation; and in all things we found the Light which we were enlightened withal, and all Mankind (which is Christ) to be alone and only sufficient to bring to Life and eternal Salvation, and that all who did own the Light in them which Christ had enlightened every man withal, they needed no more to teach them, but the Lord was their Teacher, by his Light in their Consciences, and they received the Holy Anointing...

And so we ceased from the teachings of all men, and their words, and their Worships, and their Temples, and all their Baptisms, and Churches, and we ceased from our own Words, and Professions, and Practices in Religion, in times before zealously performed by us, through divers Forms, and we became fools for Christ's sake, that we might become truly wise; and by this Light of Christ in us we were led out of all false Wayes and false Preachings, and false Ministers, and we met together often, and waited upon the Lord in pure Silence, from our own Words, and all mens words, and hearkened to the Voice of the Lord, and felt his Word in our Hearts, to burn up and beat down all that was contrary to God, and we obeyed the Light of Christ in us, and we followed the Motions of the Lord's pure Spirit, and took up the Cross to all Earthly Glories, Crowns, and Ways, and denied ourselves, our Relations, and all that stood in the way betwixt us and the Lord, and we chose to suffer with and for the Name of Christ, rather than all the pleasures upon Earth, or all our former zealous Professions and Practices in Religion, without the Power and Spirit of God, which the World yet lives in.

'And while waiting upon the Lord in Silence, as often we did for many Hours together, with our minds and hearts towards him, being stayed in the Light of Christ within us, from all thoughts and fleshly Motions, and desires, in our diligent waiting and fear of his Name, and hearkening to his Word, we received often the pouring down of the Spirit upon us, and the Gift of God's holy eternal Spirit, as in the days of old, and our hearts were made glad, and our Tongues loosed, and our Mouthes opened, and we spake with new Tongues, as the Lord gave us utterance, and as his Spirit led us, which was poured down upon us, on Sons and Daughters; and to us hereby was (were) the deep things of God revealed...and the Glory of the Father was revealed...and the holy Anointing, the everlasting Comforter we received...We were raised from Death to Life, and are changed from Satan's Power to God, and gathered from all the dumb Shepherds, and off all the barren Mountains, into the Fold of eternal Peace and Rest; and mighty and wonderful things hath the Lord wrought for us, and by us, by his own outstretched Arm.

And we became followers of the Lamb whither- soever he goes...,[16]

We Tremble at the Word of the Lord

The jibe of Justice Bennett of Derby who in 1650 nick-named the early Friends the Quakers, because (as Fox said) 'we bid them tremble at the Word of God', did not more than point to the effect of high religious enthusiasm in overwrought minds. On the other hand religious excesses were commonplace among the sects of those days, and Fox pointed to the more sensitive response of Friends to divine blessings:

'We tremble at the Word of God, by which all things were made and created, so we work out our Salvation with Fear and Trembling; and we that fear God, speak often one to another, and unto us the Lord hath hearkened, and heard, and we forsake not the Assembling of ourselves together, as the manner of some is, but edifies one another so much the more, as the Light doth approach, and we build up one another in our most Holy Faith, Praying in the Holy Ghost, keeping ourselves in the Love of God, Singing in the Spirit, having no confidence in the Flesh, nor in the Arm thereof, but trust in the Arm of the Almighty God, which doth the valiant Acts, which brings Salvation, in which Arm we are Armed, in which we Sing and Rejoyce, and Triumph in Glory...'[17]

Refs: Chapter 3

The Galilee of Quakerism: The Lake Counties; 1500-1830. C.M.L. Bouch & G.P. Jones. 1961. p. 179.

(1) D.N.B. Edward Burrough, 1634-1663.

(2) The Memorable Works of a son of Thunder Edward Burrough, 1676, p. 66 (C.U.L. Syn. 4.67.4.)

(3) Journal, I, pp. xlvi-xlviii, sects. V. and VI.

(4) D.N.B. Thomas Taylor, 1618-1682.

(5) A Testimony of the True and Spiritual Worship, and a Word of Consolation to the Children of Light etc. By Thomas Taylor, London, 1670, pp. 20, 22 (C.U.L. Broughton 256).

(6) D.N.B. James Nayler, 1617?-1660.

    James Nayler the rebel saint 1618-1660, Emilia Fogelklou, 1931. trans. from the Swedish by Lajla Yapp.

    Friends Hist. Soc Journal, 1954. James Nayler, a fresh approach, Geoffrey F. Nuttall.

(7) A Brief Relation of the Irreligion of the Northern Quakers, together with a Brief Reply to some part of a very scurrilous lying pamphlet called Saul's Errand to Damascus (by George Fox, pub. 1653, 4, 5), (By Francis Higginson minister of Kirkby Stephen), London, printed by T.R. for H.R. at the Sign of The Three Pigeons in Paul's Churchyard 1653. (Two copies in Trinity College Library, Cambridge. K.7.84.1[3]. & K.4.1[3].)

    The joint pamphlets are referred to in N & B, I. 536.

    I acknowledge my indebtedness to Dr. Richard Baumann: 'Let your words be few', C.U.P. 1983, for a fairer assessment of Higginson's description of Quaker practice, esp. p. 80.

    Higginson's Brief Relation...68-9 notes the confinement of Nayler and Howgill in the gaoler's house, not the prison.

(8) The Power and the Glory of the Lord, Shining out of the North, or The Day of the Lord Dawning...James Nayler, London 1653, pp. 1. 2. 4. 23. 25. (C.U.L. Syn. 7.65,57.)

    The lines here given are taken out of a long and involved text.

(9) The Journal or Historical Account of the Work of the Ministry of that Ancient...Servant of Jesus Christ, George Fox. London 1694. Vol. I. 201-3. An Exhortation & Warning to Magistrates written in Launceston gaol by George Fox, 1656. (C.U.L. Lib. F.1.29.)

(10) Journal I, 192.

    Fox's use of the word Seed, meaning the Life and Power of God in the heart was explained: A Collection of Many and Select and Christian Epistles of George Fox, London 1698. From the Preface by George Whitehead. (C.U.L. Syn. 3.69.30.)

    A discovery of the First Wisdom from Beneath, and the Second Wisdom from Above, and the difference between the two Seeds etc. James Nayler 1653, repr. 1656. (C.U.L. Syn. 7.65.51[1].)

(11) D.N.B. James Parnell, 1637?-1656.

    Journal I, 172.

(12) The Writings of James Parnell, London 1675. A Trial of Faith p. 7. (C.U.L. F.4.33.)

(13) The Saints (or they that are born of the Spirit) their Heavenly & Spiritual Worship, Unity and Communion, and the Ministers of the Spirit in the New Testament. G.F(ox), London 1683. pp. 1 & 7. (C.U.L. Syn. 68.25.)

(14) Newes Coming up out of the North towards the South, George Fox, London 1655. p. 33 (C.U.L. 7.65.130^d.)

(15) Gospel Truth Demonstrated. A Collection of the Doctrinal Books given forth...by George Fox, London 1706. Note the order of extracts: pp. 574, 575, 576, 577, 576, 577. (C.U.L. S100.a.70.3.) Without this pruning of two thirds verbiage, these discourses are intolerable.

(16) The Memorable Works of a Son of Thunder & Consolation, Edward Burrough, who dyed a prisoner for the Word of God in the City of London the 15th of the 12th month, 1662. London 1672. fol. 8/9. The Epistle to the Reader was written by Burrough and prefixed to a book of George Fox, 'The Great Mystery of the Great Whore unfolded', 1659. (C.U.L. Syn. 4.67.4.)

(17) Gospel Truth Demonstrated. op.cit. 230. The Lord's Triumph in the Eternal Power 1661.

NOTE. These few extracts are intended as a brief introduction to a few positive points in early Quakerism, which spread so rapidly in the dales from 1652, and as a pointer to the thinking of those early Friends whose names are recorded in the registers of Gris dale, Garsdale, Mallerstang and Ravenstonedale. They do not dispense from a close study of the memorable works of William C. Braithwaite: The Beginnings of Quakerism, and, The Second Period of Quakerism, latterly reprinted by Wm. Sessions of York 1981 and 1979.

Chapter 4

The Lamb's War (1)

But ... there was another side to early Quakerism which gave grave offence. Fox in his summary of conclusions in 1648[1] pointed to the priests of all churches,and their church order as apostate, lacking the Power which Christ and the first Apostles had, mirroring the innocence which Adam had before the Fall. It was very similar to, but more extreme than, the claim of the Puritans from 1565 at Cambridge, who claimed a purer observance of religion than the current Elizabethan church.

To Fox the ministers were deceivers, their worship an empty shell, their maintenance by compulsory tithes put a price on the Gospel, and their sueing in the courts for tithe a denial of the free and loving spirit which was the mark of Christ. The uncompromising attack on the churches and chapels was intended to destroy them, and to replace them with the spiritual church which marked the days of Christ and his apostles. It was summed up as:

The Lamb's War

George Whitehead (1636? - 1723) of Sunbiggin in the parish of Orton was convinced at a Meeting at Sunnybank, Grayrigg, the home of Capt. Henry Ward. The year was 1652 and he aged 16. As a young schoolmaster he had 'heard the minister in the steeple-house at Orton in Westmorland, who had deceived me and other under his Ministry, though he had great estimation in the World, and other Priests, in the same nature with him, and I heard several times; but something in me was not satisfied.'[2] When he went to hear Fox and the other Messengers of the Lord 'the Witness of God in me did witness and answer to the same, which I did really believe, and my understanding was opened by the Word of Power ...'.[3] He first heard Fox at Capt. Ward's house: 'I saw that (Fox's) Testimony was weighty and deep, and that it proceeded from Life and Experience. His speech was not with affecting eloquence, or oratory, or human wisdom, but in the Simplicity of the Gospel.'[4] Whitehead attended meetings at Brigflatts, Borrett and Sunnybank. For the first twenty years most meetings were held either in farmhouses, on commons, or in some remote place on the fells. After two years attending meetings in Westmorland and Yorkshire, 'a weighty concern came upon me to leave my Father's House, and County of Westmorland and to travel Southward, which I acquainted some Friends withal, my dear Friend, Edward Edwards, (who then was a young Man and lived at Gervase Benson's, near Cautley Crag, above

Sedbergh, tho' he was not then called into the Ministry), gave up to travel with me, and to keep me Company to York, (above sixty Miles) it being after Harvest, the latter End of the Summer 1654. Both of us were given up to travel on Foot, and went directly to York, where we stayed two or three Nights, and were at Friends' Meeting there on the First Day, which was but small, and had a few Words given me lovingly to declare among them'.[5] Thus began a most excellent ministry which landed him in many troubles, mobbing, persecution, stockings, and imprisonments. He appeared before the House of Commons to plead against a bill (13 & 14 Chas.II) for the sup pression of Quakers as dangerous to the public peace. He became a friend of Charles II, and succeeded Fox as the leader of the movement, and lived to see the passing of the Toleration Act in the first year of William and Mary. This Act was then written into the manor court book of Ravenstonedale.[6] But the early years of Quakerism were far from pacific. The language employed by Quakers (many coming from the Ranters and other dissidents) was extremely violent. 'The Quakers' Prophesie of the Dreadful and Utter Destruction of all the Ministers of the Church of England,' c.1660 said this:

'Go to, Ye Merchants of Babylon; who are now in this Day bringing forth, and exposing for Sale, your old Cankered, Rusty, and Moth-eaten Ware. And though you gather some heat from the sun (King Charles II) that is newly arisen ... yet know, such are not Permanent; but the withdrawing of the Sun's heat from them, soon return to their holes, and soon to Perish.

For there is a Cup prepared for You, being mixed with Plagues, Woes, Miseries, Sorrows, Torments, and eternal Burnings, which you shall not pass. You are Antichrist, Deceivers, Sorcerers, and Ravening Wolves; FLAMES, FLAMES, FLAMES OF FIRE, is prepared by the Lord to consume you as dry stubble. It had been better if you had never been born ... BURNINGS, BURNINGS, BURNINGS with unquenchable Fire, is your Portion from the Lord God of Heaven and Earth.

Howl, Howl, Hireling Priests of all Orders; for the Winepress of the Wrath of God Almighty is EVEN NEAR to be trod; into which You are to be cast; for the Lord God hath spoken it.[7]

Even the saintly Francis Howgill writing from Ireland in 1655 to 'The Camp of the Lord in England' said this: 'Spare none, neither Ox nor Ass, neither old nor young; kill, cut off, destroy, bathe your Sword in the Blood of Amaleck, and all the Egyptians, and Philistines, and all the Uncircumcised, and hew Agag to pieces; break the Rocks, cut down the Cedars and strong Oaks; make the Devils subject; cast out the unclean Spirits; raise the Dead; shut up in Prison; bring out of Prison; cast in your Nets ... divide the Fish ... cast the Bad away ... stop the Lyons Mouthes; feed the fat and strong with Plagues and Judgements ...'[8]

This was strong stuff, echoed in many Quaker pamphlets. Fox writing in 1659 said this: 'Come, Priests, did not the Whore set up your Mass-Houses with the Cross atop of it, with their Pictures and Bells, and call it Holy Ground where it stands, and name them St. Paul's, and St. Peter's, and St. Michael's etc. Come, Priests have you not drunken the Whore's Cup here? Is not this the Whore's Cup? Guilty or not Guilty? If Guilty thou must drink the Cup of the Indignation of the Wrath of the Almighty.'[9] During the first two years 1652-4 Whitehead' was moved in the Dread and Fear of the Lord to bear public Testimony against their (the Magistrates' and Priests') Places of Worship in Westmorland before I travelled South; yet the Lord was pleased to preserve me from Harm'.[10] He wrote these words in the gaol at Bury St Edmunds in 1656. At that time, Bury and Sudbury were under the Calvinistic rule of Colonel John Fothergill of Sudbury:

'Fear, Fear and tremble, O all ye Inhabitants of the Earth, who are at enmity against the pure God, for your Leader will fail you, and you will not be able to stand before the Mighty God in his dreadful Presence; now is his Thunders uttering, and his Trumpet a sounding, and his Arrows are polished, and his Sword is furbished, and his Arm is strong, and his Wrath is waxing hot against the Persecutors, and his Host is Mighty ... and his Day is exceeding terrible ... All the Powers of the Earth will not be able to stand in the day of his Battel, he is coming with ten thousand of his Saints to execute Judgement upon the World, and to quit himself and all his Elect of all their Adversaries, and utterly overthrow all their Adversaries ... and Oppressors ... He will render his Wrath with Fury and his Rebukes with flames of Fire. Wo, Wo to you all that are set against Him; behold his Day cometh swiftly with Wrath and Fury, as a Destruction from on high upon the ungodly.'[11]

As a result of these many verbal attacks in Steeple-Houses, and verbal attacks on ministers in market places many Quakers were imprisoned, among whom Thomas Taylor was imprisoned twice during the Protectorate at Appleby. Apart from the system of tithes which Lilburne and Edward Billing wrote so strongly against, there was the custom of Going Naked as a Sign of the imminent destruction of the Church of England. Richard Holme of Kendal, and Richard Robinson of Countersett indulged in this prophetic gesture in Kirkby Stephen market place. Francis Higginson the minister of Kirkby Stephen observed in 1653:

'Of their Railings; they are also as horrible Railers as ever any Age brought forth, a Generation whose mouths are full of bitterness, whose throats are open Sepulchres etc. The Billingsgate Oister-Women are not comparable to them. It is ordinary with them to call them Fools, Sots, Hypocrites, vain men, Beasts, Blasphemers, Murtherers of the Just. It is a customary thing with this Gang of People in their discourse with others to tell them they are Dogs, Heathen etc. One of Kendal going to the Burial of a Minister his acquaintance, met a woman of this Sect by the way, and asked her if she had seen the Corps go by; I saw, saith she, a company of Heathen go by to bury a dead dog.'[12]

'One of their gang in Westmorland, on Friday the Eighth of April last, ran like a mad man naked, all but his shirt, through Kendall crying Repent, Repent, wo, wo, come out of Sodome, Remember Lot's wife, with other such stuffe. His principal Auditors were a company of Boyes that followed him through the Town. I almost wonder, what the Devil should mean in sending abroad such naked Bedlam - Speakers'.[13]

Tithes

The second point of attack by Fox was in the matter of tithes. His point was, like that of Wycliffe, that by the compulsory payment of tithes, for the maintenance of a Christian minister, a price had been put on the Gospel. They used the word of Christ, 'freely ye have received, freely give'. The Quaker refusal to pay tithes or church rates resulted in finings, imprisonments and confiscations of goods, leaving very many heavily in debt to the day of their death. Fox's attack on the system of tithes was a brilliant piece of invective, largely overlooked by historians. Coupled with this attack was his concern for the poor. In 1648 he wrote: 'I was to bring people off from all the world's religions, which are vain; that they might know the pure religion, might visit the fatherless, the widows, and the strangers, and to keep them from the spots of the world; then there would not be so many beggars, the sight of whom often grieved my heart, as it denoted so much hard-heartedness amongst them that professed the Name of Christ.'[14] Again in 1650 he wrote: 'Wo unto them that covetously join one house to another; and bring one field so nigh unto another that the poor can get no more ground, and that ye may dwell upon the earth alone'.[15] Thus the tithe question, and the need of social justice were combined in this momentous pamphlet, first produced in 1652. That it was widely read is proved by the number of quotations repeated in other Quaker writings.

'A Paper sent forth into the World from them that are scornfully called Quakers, Declaring the Grounds and Reasons why we deny the Teachers of the World, (who profess themselves to be Ministers) and Dissent from them.

First *they are such Shepherds* that seek for their gain from their Quarters, and can never have enough, which the Lord send Isaiah to cry out against, who bid all come freely, without money, and without price, and was not hired, but spake freely, and these make merchandise and a trade of words, and therefore we cry out against them, and deny them.

They are such Shepherds that seek after the Fleece, and cloath with the Wool, and feed with the fat.

They are such Prophets and Priests that divine for money, and preach for hire, which the Lord sent Micah to cry against.

They are such Priests as bear Rule by their means, which was a horrible and filthy thing committed in the land, which the Lord sent Jeremiah to cry out against.

They are such as are called of men Masters, and call men Masters, and have the chiefest place in the Assemblies, and stand Praying in the Synagogues, and lay heavy burthens upon the People.

They are such Teachers as have told us, The Steeplehouse hath been the Church, whenas the Scripture saith, The Church is in God.

They are such Teachers as have told us, the Letter was the Light, whenas the Letter saith, Christ is the Light.

They are such Teachers as sprinckle Infants calling it an Ordinance of Christ, and Baptising into the Faith, into the Church, whenas the Scripture saith no such things. But the Baptism by one Spirit into one Body we own.

They are such Teachers as tell the People of a Sacrament, for which there is not one Scripture, and so feed the People with their own inventions, and therefore we deny them; but the Table and Supper of the Lord we own.

They are such Ministers as go to Oxford and Cambridge, and call them the Well-heads of Divinity, and so deny the Fountain of Living Mercies; and there they study, and read books, and old Authors, and furnish themselves with Philosophy, and fine Words, and other men's matter, and when they come again, they sell it to poor people.

They are such Teachers, that with feigned words, and through covetousnesse, make merchandise of us, and do upon the people, who by oppression maintain themselves and wives in pride and idlenesse, in hoods, vails, and changeable suits of apparell, who go in the way of Cain, to envy, murder and persecute, and after the error of Balaam, who loved the wages of unrighteousnesse, following after gifts and rewards, which the Apostle cryed against, and therefore we deny them.

They are such Teachers as have told us, that the Steeple-house is the Temple, whenas the Apostle said, your bodies are the Temple of the Holy Ghost.

They are such Teachers that take Tythes, the tenth of man's Labours, and Estates, and those that will not give them, they sue at the Law, and hale before Courts, and Session, yea, even those they call their own People, their own Parishioners.

They are such Priests as, besides their Tythe corn, hay, beast, sheep, hens, pigs, giese, eggs, cheries, plumbs, take 10s. for Preaching a Funerall Sermon, more or less, as they can get it, and 10s. for the death of a man, and money out of Servants wages, and money for smoke passing up the Chimnies, and Easter Reckonings, and Midsummer dues, and money for Churching of women, and thus by every device get Money, and burthen poor People that labour very hard, and can scarce get food and rayment, to main tain them in idleness and pride.

They are such Priests as not only take Tythes and Money for many other things of their own hearers, and sue them at the Law for it, but take money of them they do no work for, but only rail against them, and say, 'They that wait upon the Altar are partakers at the Altar.'

These are they that Christ cryed WO against, who lay heavy burdens upon the People, who oppress tender consciences that own the everlasting High Priest.

They are such Preachers as take a text out of the Saint's Conditions and take a week's time to study what they can raise out of it, adding to it their own Wisdome, Inventions, Imaginations, and heathenish Authors, and then on the first day of the week go amongst the People, having an Hour-glass to limit themselves by, and say, 'Hear the Word of the Lord' and for money tell the people what they have scraped together.

They are such Teachers that gave us, and give David's conditions in Meeter (the metrical psalms), and when we had no understanding, we sung after them, as ignorant People do now, his tremblings, his quakings, his weepings, fastings, Prayers and Prophesies; and when we sung, we put off out Hatts, and when we read them, we kept them on, and so they caused us to worship the work of their own hands.

They are such Teachers as deny the Conditions that the Saints witnessed, viz. Trembling and Quaking, whenas we find the Holy Men of God that gave forth the Scriptures, witnessed such things.

They are such Teachers as tell the People, That Christ hath not enlightened every one that hath come into the World, whenas Christ saith He doth enlighten every one that comes into the World ... And we witness the Light wherewith Christ inlightened every one that comes into the World.

They are such Teachers as have told us, we should never be make free from sin while we are upon earth, when, as the Apostle saith, they were made free from sin he thanks God, and had put off the body of sin; so we find they told us lies contrary to the Scripture ... and therefore we deny them.

And they are such Teachers that have told us, none shall ever be perfect while they are upon the Earth, when as Christ saith, Be ye perfect, as your Father which in heaven is perfect ... The Ministry of Christ is for the perfecting of Saints, till they come to the measure of the stature of the fulness of Christ, to a perfect man; here we find them to deny the Scripture ... Such Ministers are not Members of the Body, nor can present any man perfect in Christ Jesus.

Therefore all People consider what you do, and hold up, and worship, for the Worship is but one, and the Word is but one, and the Baptism is but one, and the Church is but one, and the Way is but one, and the Light is but one, and the Power is but one; But they that are without have many Teachers, many ways, many opinions, and judgements, and many Sects; but we have but one Priest which is over the Household of God, and therefore we are all of one Heart and Soul.

Moved of the Lord, written from the Spirit of the Lord, for the cleansing of the Land of all false Teachers, Seducers, and Deceivers, and Witches who beguile the People ... for the good of all People that fear the Lord, and own Jesus Christ to be their teacher.

All People that read these things, never come ye more at the Steeple-House, nor pay your Priests more Tythes till they have answered them; for if ye do, ye uphold them in their sins, and must partake of their plagues.'[16]

That this paper enjoyed wide circulation is proved by the fact that it was printed in 1652, 1654, 1655, 1656, 1657 and 1659.

Refs. Chapter 4

(1) Journal I, 30-34.

(2) D.N.B. George Whitehead of Sunbiggin, 1636-1723.

The vicar was George Fothergill. Alumn. Cantab. From earliest times to 1751, J. & J.A. Venn, Part.I. Vol.II, 165. George Fothergill M.A. of St. John's.

Jacob found in a strange Land etc. by George Whitehead, London 1656 (written at Bury St. Edmunds), p. 4 (Trinity Coll. Library. K.7.84[4].)

(3) Ibid. p. 50

(4) The Christian Progress of that Ancient Servant & Minister of Jesus Christ George Whitehead etc. In Defence of the Truth, and God's persecuted People, commonly called Quakers. London 1725. pp. 4-5 (C.U.L.Ddd.3.24.)

(5) Ibid. 21/2.

(6) Manor Court Book Ravenstonedale. MS of Mr C. Hollett, Sedbergh.

(7) Selected from an anti-Quaker broadsheet of 1700 containing extracts from the wilder Quaker books, c.1660. (C.U.L. Broughton 569).

(8) Works of Francis Howgill 1676. The First General Epistle to the Camp of the Lord in England, London 1655, pp. 28 & 32. (C.U.L.Syn.4.67.3. The Dawning of the Gospel etc. 1676)

(9) Gospel Truth etc. op.cit p. 146/7, The Lamb's Officer, with the Lamb's Messenger, 1659.

(10) The Christian Progress of that Ancient Servant ... George Whitehead op.ci. 9/10.

(11) Jacob found in a Desert Land op.cit.18.

(12) A Brief Relation of the Irreligion of the Northern Quakers, Francis Higginson, 1653, op.cit. 21.

(13) Ibid. 30.

(14) Journal I, 37.

(15) Journal I, 66.

(16) A Paper sent forth into the World etc why we deny the Teachers of the World, (George Fox). Four copies in C.U.L. 16.., 56, 59 (2). (C.U.L. Syn. 7.65.54[8].) etc.

The Catalogues of Quaker books by John Whiting & Joseph Smith, and Wing give impressions in 1652, 1654, 1655, 1656 & 1657.

In this summary the long passages, and involved Biblical allusions have been omitted. In a few cases the long sentences have been punctuated, and the main topics have been underlined.

Anthony Pearson was a Cumbrian by birth, and from 1648 secretary to Sir Arthur Haslerigg, from Feb. 1651/2 a member of the Committee for Compounding in county Durham, and from 1650-1653 acquired bishops' lands. From January 1651/2 he was made a justice for three border counties including Westmorland. He was only 24 and seems to have presided at Quarter Sessions to see that justices were kept in order, and it was he who was presided at the trial of Nayler and Howgill at Appleby in 1652/3. He was convinced by Fox at Swarthmore in 1653 and wrote extensively against tithes.

D.N.B. Anthony Pearson 1628 - 1670?

C & W. trans. N.S. LXXXIV, 1984, 99. Art.IX, Anthony Pearson, An early Cumbrian Quaker, by A.R. Jabes-Smith.

N. & B.I. 536 et seq.

C.U.L. has two copies of; 'The Great Case of Tythes Truly stated, clearly opened, and fully resolved', by Anthony Pearson, London 1659, and 1730. It was first published in 1657, and went through three editions in two years, and became the handbook for Quakers.

Journal of Friends Historical Soc, vol. 51, 1965-7, pp. 77-90 has an article by Amy E. Wallis on Anthony Pearson.

Chapter 5

The Lamb's War (2)

While it is easy to understand Fox's belief that the established churches and chapels were false and apostate, because they lacked the Power possessed by Christ and the Apostles, to teach, heal, cast out spirits, and overcome spiritual evil by divine interventions, it is less easy to grasp his attack against lawyers and judges. Remembering the Calvinistic aim during the Civil Wars, and the Protectorate, to install a Gospel magistracy and ministry, Fox went further and said: 'the lawyers were out of equity, and out of the true justice, and out of the Law of God, which went over the first transgression, and over all sin, and answered the Spirit of God, that was grieved and transgressed in man'.[1] It seems that Fox held that only a judge in a state of innocency (of Adam before the Fall) could judge each case before him, as the Quaker was guided in his Meeting. A judge had no other rule by training except to refer to law, when faced with the Quaker claim of divine guidance to testify against tithes, attending the national worship, using the hat to mark social distinctions, and serving in the army. Fox raised his concept of the magistracy to an etherial height beyond the realm of practicality. There was no such confusion in his attack against the rich in defence of the poor. It was direct and dramatic:

The Day of the Lord. (1653)

'Oh ye Great Men, and Rich Men of the Earth! Weep and howl for your Misery is coming, who heap treasure up for the Last Day, your Gold and Silver shall eat you up as the Rust and the Canker; the Fire is kindled, the Day of the Lord is appearing...'.[2]

Give over oppressing the Poor. (1654)

'O ye earthly - minded Men! Give over oppressing the Poor; exalt not yourselves above your fellow - creatures, for ye are all of one Mould, and Blood; you that set your Nests on High, join House to House, Field to Field, 'till there be no place for the Poor; Woe is your Portion. The Earth is the Lord's and the Fulness thereof. And you that have not so much of the Earth, give over your Murmuring, and Reasoning, Fretting, and Grudging, for all your Want is the Want of God; the Righteous God is coming to give every one of you according to your Works; now the Works of you all must be tried; you that have appeared unto Men beautiful outwardly, will be found in the Generation of Murtherers...'[3]

To the High and Lofty Ones (1655)

'O how are you daubed with Silver Lace, and your Jewels, and your Spots on your Faces, and your Feathers, and your wearing of Gold, and through the Abundance of your Vanity and of your Superfluity! Ambition and Pride, Loftiness and Haughtiness stops the Ear from hearing the Lord, his Decree and Sentence against you...and stops your Ear from hearing the Cry of the Poor, the Blind and the Lame, that lay up and down your Streets; so that he that regards not the Poor, regards not his Maker; and turning his Ear from the Poor, turns his Ear from his Maker.'

'Bow you not more and oftner with the Hat and with the Knee to one another, than you do unto the Lord? People cannot tell how to please one another in their Bowing with the Hat, in curtching one to another, but they will be ready to think, that I bowed with my Hat oftner to him than he did to me, and I curtchied more to her than she did to me; and thus they are offended one at another; and such a one hath more Ribbons, and Gold and Silver on him that I have, and Spots on their Faces, and he powders his Hair and Curls it; and so when any is in another Fashion contrary to them, then they envy one another, which is among such that have lost Gravity.'[4]

The Fashions of the World. (1657)

'Likewise the Women having their Gold, or Spots on their Faces, and on their cheeks, and Foreheads, having their Rings on their Fingers, wearing Gold, having Cuffs double under and above, having their Ribbands tied about their Hands, and three or four Gold Laces about their Clothes, this is no Quaker they say...And Men, to get a pair of Breeches like a Coat, and hang them with points up to the Middle, and a pair of double Cuffs on his Hands, and a Feather in his Cap; here is a Gentleman, bow before him, put off your Hats, bow before him; gets a Company of Fiddlers, a Set of Musick, and Women to Dance, this is a brave Fellow, a Gentleman...A Company of them get a couple of Bowles in their Hands, or Tables, or Shovel-board, or a Horse with a Company of Ribbands on his Head, as he hath on his own, and a Ring in his Ear, and so go to a Horse-Racing to spoil the Creature; Oh! these are Gentlemen, these are brave Fellows, these are bred up Gentlemen, these are no Quakers.'[5]

'Dost thou not see thyself ill favoured with all these Ribbands, tashling about thy Hands, and flapping upon thy Hat, and great Bunches as big as a hand flapping at the Backs of Women like a Besome, and thy great things a top of thy Shooes staring; and if you say how should the Poor live if we do not wear that; Give them all that Money which you bestow upon all that Gorgeous Attire, and needless things, to nourish them, that they may live without making Vanities and needless things, and costly attire for you...

Where do you read in Scripture that the Apostles taught any one that they should scrape a Leg, and make a Courtesie, or put off their Hats, for great Men will stand with their Hats on one to another, and sometimes they will bow and stirr them, but they will seldom bow to the Poor, or scrape a Leg to a Beggar; so if he hath got a Feather in his Hat, and a few Ribbands on his Breeches, and Hair Powdered, and if she hath got a Bunch of ribbands on her Back, then there's your Servant Madam, your Servant Sir, your humble Servant Sir, and this pleaseth proud Flesh, but to say Thou Friend makes him or her Mad, which is a proper loving Word, and Scripture Order and Practice.'[6]

The Serious People's Reasoning. (1659)

'The Priest and Professors of the World say, These Fools the Quakers, cannot endure to see us with two or three Rings on our Fingers, nor Jewels in our Ears, nor Bracelets about our Necks, nor Cuffs, nor Double Cuffs, nor great Tashling Band-Strings, they cannot endure we should wear a laced Cap of twenty shillings price, or less or more, and a pair of double Cuffs up our Hands, and double-white Boot-hose-tops, these Novice Quakers cannot endure to see us with this Garb upon our Backs. And how should poor People live if we should not wear them?

Say the serious People, all your Gold Rings, your Cuffs, your great Band-Strings, your Lace, your Jewels, your Bracelets, your gorgeous Apparel, and Attire, turn it all into Money, and give it to the poor to buy them Bread, and I will warrant you, that they and you will have all enough, and there will be no Want among you, for you are always wanting Rings, or Ribbands, Gold Hat-Bands, Laces and Bracelets, you are always wanting one thing or another, if you see another Fashion, the other is old; and you want to get into it, and you envy others that are gotten into the Fashion before you...and so you are more like Fools, that are Slaves to the Devil...that leads you to destroy the Works and Creatures, and Creation of God, and all your Want is of God, for you want God and his Wisdom to order you.'[7]

Dives and Lazarus

'Remember how in your Lifetime you fared sumptuously every day, and received Good Things, and likewise the poor Lazaruses the evil things from you, who had no Comfort amongst you.

Do you not think that (Dives) was a jolly Fellow, while he was upon the Earth, with his Dogs and his Sumptuous Fare, and Apparel and fine Linen, and fared sumptuously every day...do you regard the poor Lazarus, the poor Beggers that lie in your Gates full of Sores? And do you consider whither ye must go when ye die? Abraham tells the rich Man that he is tormented in Hell; so there is no Purgatory, nor middle place, as some imagine: And they in Hell cannot pass to Abraham, nor Abraham to them, so there is no Prayers that will get them out of Hell-fire...so this parable may stand to them that profess themselves Christians, and do not the Works of Christianity.

Oh! Therefore be warned, and be serious, and consider your latter End, and now you have Time, prize it, lest you say, you had Time, when it is past.'[8]

The young James Parnell who died in Colchester castle in 1656 made these two points:

The Partiality of the Clergy

'If a poor labouring Man come before one that you call a Minister, though he be one of his Hearers, and one who helps to maintain him, according to his Ability, yet he must YOU the Priest, and the Priest THOU to him. And here the Heathen Lord it over one another by their corrupt Wills.'[9]

Putting off the Hat

'If a Poor Man comes before a Rich Man, it may be the Rich Man will move his Hat, that is called Courtesie and Humility, but the Poor Man must stand with his Hat off before him, and that is called Honour and Manners, and due Respect to him; but if the Rich Man do bid him put it on, it is counted a great Courtesie.'[10]

Edward Burrough of Underbarrow writing in Ireland in 1659 commented on the Irish landlord:

'Wo unto you Great and Rich Men, ye covetous and earthly Worldlings, ye that have made yourselves rich by Oppression and grinding the faces of the Poor; that have got gain by hard dealing, and added Land to Land and Field to Field, and that have over-reached the Ignorant, and oppressed the Widows and Fatherless, and that exercised Cruelty and hard dealing to your Tenants and Servants, and have laid heavy Yoaks upon such with whom you have dealt, and that have made yourselves great and rich in the Earth by such means; Wo unto you, Misery is coming upon you, weep and howl, ye earthly greedy covetous Wretches of this World, who have sought Riches more than the Lord...'[11]

Of the merchants he said this:

'Wo unto you Merchants, Traders, Buyers and Sellers, that have been double-dealers and double-tongued, and dealt deceitfully in your Commodities with your Neighbour; Wo unto you that have got Gain by double-dealing, and by feigned and flattering speeches, and have sought to outreach in your bargaining every man his Brother. Ye have robbed the Poor by your Craft...and flattering Tongues. It is your use to discommend a Commodity when you buy it, and to praise it when you sell it; and ye make a fair outside to please the eye, and ye use multitude of Words and fair speeches, and deceive the Simple, and get gain by Oppression, Craft and Deceit. We unto you, Repent, of this your Sin.'[12]

While it was one thing to denounce the oppression of the poor in the strain of the Old Testament prophets, the movement was wary of political theory. Thus when Edward Billing, who served at the battle of Dunbar and was convinced by Fox at Leith in 1657, left the army in 1658 he settled in Westminster as a brewer and leading Quaker. In 1659 he published a tract entitled 'A Mite of Affection manifested in Proposals, offered to all Sober and Free-Born People within this Commonwealth.'[13] It followed the political theme of Lilburn's 'The Agreement of the Free People of England' written in the Tower in 1649. Billing repeated Lilburn's points that the magistrate should have no coercive powers in matters of religion; that none be compelled to swear an oath against their conscience; and that all servile Tenures or Copyholds, being a badge of the Conquest, be thorowly considered.'[14] He went on to propose the reform of prisons, the removal of unjust gaolers, and the prohibition of card-playing, music, and gaming-houses.[15] But the Quakers would not support Billing, and the tract was issued without their approval, though it contained a number of their tenets. George Whitehead in his preface to Fox's Epistles described the severe conditions in which Quakers met for worship in 'O. Protector's Days'. They were driven by droves to the prisons for not attending the national worship, for not paying tithes, taking oaths, or removing the hat etc. Their horses were taken from them under pretence of breaking the Sabbath, though their oppressors would 'ride in their Coaches, and upon their fat Horses to the Steeple-Houses themselves, and yet punish others. And many Friends were turned out of their Copyholds and Customary tenements, because they could not Swear'.[16]

Thus to the early Quaker oppression and humbug was one thing; political activity was another.

The other side of Fox's attack was the force of his invective, which contained much common sense. Through the Kendal fund many of his pamphlets were circulated to and read at Meetings.

The Protestant Quaker a Sufferer by Popery (1680)

'Since the Apostles' Days, how many Ways, Religions, Worships, Faiths and Creeds have been made by Men, and Councils, unto which Conformity hath been required.

The Papists they cry, Conform, Conform to their Image of Mass etc. or else away with them to the Inquisition, or Rack, or Torture or the like.

The Turk, he cries, Conform, Conform to his Image which Mahomet hath set up. and to their Alcoran.

The Heathen Emperors cry Conform, Conform, and persecute the Christians, because they could not conform to their idol Images.

The Protestant, he crys, Conform, Conform, or else Persecute and Imprison, as many Goals do testify.

The Presbyterian, he cryed, Conform, Conform to his Image the Directory, or else he will hang them on his Gallows, and cut off the Ears, Banish, Whip, and spoil the Goods of all such as will not Conform, as witness the Presbyterian Priests and Magistrates in New England.

And the Independants they cry, Conform, Conform to their Image, their Church Faith they made at the Savoy in eleven days' time.

And the Anabaptists, they cry Conform, Conform to their Image, and be of their Church or else persecute.

So all these cry Conform, Conform. So everyone that gets uppermost, and gets the Staff of Authority, commands People to put into his Bag, and to feed their Priests with Tythes, and set Maintenance, And so the Priests cry, The Law of the Land requires it. But no Law or Command of Jesus requires it, who said, Freely you have received, freely give.'[17]

Come to Christ the Substance

In an Epistle to the People of Uxbridge, 1659, Fox with his belief in the doctrine of Perfection, pointed to the obvious defect in established church practice in the World's churches, in which compulsory attendance at church and participation in its sacraments forced many to conform who were not in a state of Grace, mouthing with words of Faith, and not practising its precepts. On the other hand Fox's Spiritual church peopled only by the converted and elect, which dispensed with the sacraments and formal worships, was liable to the like defect when the first generation of Convinced Quakers had passed away:

'Come, away with your Self-righteousness, and your feigned humility, and your Will-worship, and your Carnal Security, and take heed of Drunkenness, and Filthiness, and Profaneness, and Scoffing, Mocking, Scorning, and Derision, for such who live in such things, and act such things, shall not inherit the Kingdom of God; and away with that you call Sacraments, and your Sprinkling Infants, and come to Christ the Substance, and come to the Spirit, that you may be Baptised into one Body, that you may come to possess the things the Scripture speaks of.'[18]

37

We deny all Popery.

Truth's Triumph in the Eternal Power. (1661).

'In the Name and Power of the Lord Jesus Christ we deny all Popery, and the Pope's Supremacy, that holds up Popery...for all Things are to be done in the Name of the Lord Jesus Christ, who is King of Kings, who is the Judge of the World. In the name of Jesus Christ we deny all their Rails, their Altars, their Crosses, their Crucifixes, their Images, their Pictures, their Representations, their Purgatory, that they have invented; we deny their Mumeries, and their visiting Graves, and Tombs, and Sepulchres, and Praying for the Dead, and to the Dead.

...We deny all their Ordination of Ministers, Bishops and Cardinals, who are not made as they were in the Apostles days, who makes them by Oaths, so did not the Apostles.

...We deny all their Swearing, for (Jesus) commands to "Swear not at all."

...We deny their observing Days and Times, and observing Meats and Drinks, and their commands to abstain from the same.

...and all their several Orders of Beggars, and Begging Fryars, and Priests, that tolerate Begging by a Law.

...we deny all their Marrying with Rings, and Sprinkling Children with the Sign of the Cross, and bowing to Crosses, and bowing before Images, and Altars, and all their Fasts for Debate and Strife.

...we deny all their old Mass-houses, which they call Churches, and their Idols and Images there set up, and their Hallowing pieces of Ground, which they make Graveyards on.

...We deny all their Colleges, and their Universities in which they make Ministers, by Tongues, Arts, and Schools, contrary to the Apostles, who were not made Ministers of Man, nor by Man.

...we deny giving or receiving of Tythes, the Tenth of Men's Estates, which they do (of them) that be separated from them, who are Apostasised from the Apostles, who denied the Jews Priesthood, and the Law that made them.

...we deny all their compelling Maintenance of the People, and forcing it from them, and we deny all their persecuting about Church, and Religion, and Ministry, and all their carnal Weapons.

...we deny all their Organs, Pipes, Whistles, Singing Boys, Singing of Prayers, Mattens, Praying by Beads, and all their lying Prophecies, and going on Processions, and their White Sleeves, Surplices, Tippets, Hoods, Caps, Red Gowns, Mitres, and the Cardinal's Cap, and Pope's Tripple Crown, Excommunication, Cursing with Bell, Book, and Candle, for the Scripture saith, Bless and Curse not, and his Holy Water we deny, and we deny kissing his Feet, and all his Pardons to be of no effect.

...we deny the Pope's Supremacy, knowing it to be got up since the Apostles days, and not found in the Scriptures of Truth; and all their Inquisitions, and Racks, and doing Penance etc.

...we deny the Doctrine of such, that says Bread and Wine after Consecration is the Real Body and Blood of Christ, that it's Christ, knowing this is contrary to the Scriptures that saith, concerning Bread, and the Fruit of the Vine, that was taken in Remembrance of Him, to shew forth the Lord's death till he come.'[19]

Our Religion is not by forcing. (1661)

'We are of that Principle, and mind to hurt no Man upon Earth, but do good to all, but especially to them of the household of Faith, and to do all things in Bounty and Love.

Our Religion, Church and Worship is not by forcing with carnal weapons, but by Love, knowing that Christ had loved us first...and he is our Head.

Our Ministers are not made of Man, nor by Man, but by the Grace of God which is free, and his Gifts are perfect, by which we Minister one to another, by which the Body is edified, and the Saints perfected; and our Worship is in the Spirit, that mortifies sin and corruption, and in the Truth, which the Devil is out of, and his Worship, and all the Will-worshippers, in that do we Worship God, the God of all Truth. And we Tremble at the Word of God.'[20]

You are out of the Catholick Church. (1667)

'You Ministers of Christendom: You are not in the Faith that works by Love, nor in the Universal Love of God, therefore you cannot build up Christendom by the Love of God, nor in the Holy Faith that works by Love, for Love edifies, and buildeth up; but your Faith is a dead one, and the fruits of it are Wrath, and Strife, and Envy, and tearing one another to pieces with Persecution; which Persecution was always Blind, and the blind leadeth the blind into the Ditch: So you are out of the Catholick Faith, and the Catholick Church, and the Catholick Love, Fellowship and Worship, and Catholick Gospel, which is Everlasting for Catholick is Universal.'[21]

The Apostolical Succession

'The Primitive Ordination and Succession of Bishops (1675)

So you may see...how Christ ordained Babes and Sucklings to preach his Name Freely, as they had received freely; and you know that Babes and Sucklings are not fit to be sent to Schoole, but these were taught of Christ and ordained of him to speak and confess Christ Jesus freely, as they had received, and he or dained Strength out of the Mouths of Babes and Sucklings...

All that do succeed the Apostles, they must be sent of Christ in the same Power and Spirit, that the Apostles were sent from God and Christ, and freely give as they have received from him freely, and preach the same Word of Faith, which is nigh in Men and Women even in their Mouths and Hearts to obey it and do it; for if People go not in the same Power and Spirit as the Apostles were in, and preach the same, they are not successors of them in their Possession...'[22]

True and False Ministers.

For all Bishops and Priests in Christendom (1674)

'Tho' Christ sent forth his Ministers without Bag or Scrip, Silver or Gold, and commanded them they give freely as they had received freely of him, yet they wanted for nothing: Therefore consider all you that call yourselves Ministers, that say, we have not heard the Voice of Christ, are not you always in Want, though you have Bag and Scrip, Silver and Gold? and will you go to any place except there be a great Parsonage, or some Augmentation; therefore measure yourselves with such as Christ sent forth, and see how unlike you are with them? It is not you who make division, (who) deceive the Hearts of the Simple, who serve not the Lord Jesus Christ, but your own Bellies...with your great Parsonages, and Glebe-lands, and Augmentations, Easter-Reckonings, and Mid-summer dues? for if you did serve the Lord Jesus Christ, then you would obey his Command, which is, Freely you have received, freely give.'[23]

Refs. Chapter 5

(1)   Journal I, 29.

(2)   Gospel Truth etc. op.cit. 6. The Day of the Lord. 1653.

(3)   Ibid. 12. Give over oppressing the Poor. 1654.

(4)   Ibid. 30, 31.

(5)   Ibid. 110.

(6)   Ibid. 158.

(7)   Ibid. 159.

(8)   Ibid. 568/9.

(9)   A Collection of the Several Writings of that Servant of God, James Parnell, who died in Colchester Castle 1656, pub. 1675, pp. 93/4. (C.U.L.F. 4.33.)

(10)   Ibid. 95.

(11)   The Everlasting Gospel of Repentance and Remission of Sins...A Message of Reconciliation to all People...particularly the People of Ireland, Edward Burrough, 1659. pp. 8/9.

(12) Ibid. 9/10.

Gospel Truth op.cit. 73/4. A cry for Repentance, by Fox 1656 made the point that honest trading at moderate profit, done at a word, is better.

(13) A Mite of Affection manifested in Proposals, offered to all Sober and Free-Born people etc. by E(dward) B(illing), 1659. (C.U.L.Acton d.25.982[4].) Thomason Tracts. II, 261, dates the tract 25 Oct. 1659.

(14) A Mite of Affection op.cit. scts. 1, 2, & 6

(15) Ibid. 18, 21.

(16) A Collection of the Many Select Epistles to Friends etc. by G. Fox, 1698. Preface by G. Whitehead, sect (3).

(17) Gospel Truth op.cit. 790-91.

(18) Gospel Truth 161.

(19) Gospel Truth 227.

(20) Gospel Truth 229-30.

(21) Gospel Truth 278.

(22) Gospel Truth 485-491.

(23) Gospel Truth (368), 373, 376.

Chapter 6

The Lamb's War (3)

The third point of difference between Fox and the established churches and chapels, which caused distress to those bred in the old church ways, was his insistence that their use of old church forms was empty and without Power.

The Bible. To the Protestant world the Bible was the Word of God, the immutable standard of faith and order binding for all time; it was a divinely inspired book. This view is still held by the Church of England. In the New Alternative Service Book (1980) in the Eucharist, after the readings from the Old Testament or the Epistles, and from the Gospels the reader says 'This is the Word of the Lord' or 'This is the Gospel of Christ' whether the reading quotes directly from the words of God or Christ, or is plain narrative. The Bible is described as The Word of God. Fox differed; he said that it was a book of record, as God spake in the time past to holy men and women of God. It was a record of God's word to them; indeed a priceless record necessary for every pilgrim. But you cannot go to a shop and for money buy the Word of God; the Word is what God by the Spirit speaks in each person's heart. THAT is the Word. Fox in his Journal (1656) said that Christ is that Word:

> 'Do not the Ministers of God say, that the Scriptures are a declaration, which you call the Word? Do you not rob Christ of his title, and of his honour, and give it to the letter, and shew yourselves out of the doctrine of the ministers of God, who call the Scriptures by the name of writings and treatises, and declarations; and who said Christ's name is called the Word of God?'[1]

Fox insisted on that distinction, that much of the narratives or the opinions of the writers ought not to be called the Word of God. In 1669 Fox and Jo. Stubbs made this comment:

> 'Where doth the Scripture say, That it self is the Word of God? Do you not belye the Rule there? For, doth not the Scripture say, that Christ is the Word? And the Scriptures are Words: Read Exodus 20, and Revelation 22.

> The Scripture speaks plentifully concerning Christ being the Word of God; God is the Word, is not this the Scripture? And in the Beginning was the Word, and all things were made by the Word; and were all things made by the Scriptures?

> And we say that the Scriptures are a better Rule than your Directory; for if the Scriptures be the Rule, why do you set up a Directory to be your Rule?...Do you not set up your Imaginations and Meanings above the Scriptures? Come, People will not sell their Wits, Reason, and Understanding...'[2]

Fox put it quite plainly; the Papists have their infallible Pope, the Protestants their Infallible Book, and the Quakers have the infallible Light, Christ, the Word of God spoken in the heart of every man and woman open to receive Him.[3] The Bible is that indispensible book of record of how that Word was spoken in times past.

The Lord's Prayer. The old churches taught that the Lord's Prayer is the matchless pattern of prayer, belief, and service from which all our worship, faith and work should follow. To Fox it was a temporary provision in the apostles' days, before prayer was in the Spirit. It's formal use in the churches was an empty shell, without the Power of the Spirit. William Penn in his tribute to Fox says that his was 'the most awful, living, reverent frame I ever felt or beheld, I must say, in prayer...it was a testimony he knew and lived nearer to the Lord than other men'. This does not communicate in Fox's writings, nor can it. Very rare are references even to a phrase from the Lord's Prayer, in his or the writings of his followers, most of which are very rambling. The fervency of the moment is missing.

> 'Now that all may come to know the true Praying, which is with the Spirit and with the understanding, and here you may come to know the praying with sighs and groans which cannot utter words with a sigh and a groan, and lo as this Spirit comes to guide and lead, ye come to the Father of Spirits, when he hears, and he is nigh unto all that call upon

41

him in truth, who call upon him with their hearts, whose hearts are nigh unto him; these come to know the praying, and lifting up of holy hands without wrath and doubting...'[5]

As with Quaker utterances at Meetings, Fox's writings are best read as short utterances, each phrase separated by a pause for inspiration. That the abandonment of the formal use of the Lord's Prayer had not been fully explained was realised by Robert Barclay. In his 'Apology for the True Christian Divinity' (1701) he wrote: 'This was commanded to the Disciples, while yet weak, before they had received the Dispensation of the Gospel; not that they should only use it in Praying, but that he might shew them by one Example how that their prayers ought to be short, and not like the prayers of the Pharisees.' He then went on to say that the other recorded prayers in the New Testament did not repeat it, but were as the occasion required. It then led to the apostolic days when 'the Apostle saith, "We know not what we should pray for as we ought, but the Spirit itself maketh intercession for us etc." But if this Prayer had been such a prescribed Form of Prayer to the Church, that had not been true...neither should they have needed the help of the Spirit to teach them.'[6]

As with the Lord's Prayer, to the average christian the use of water baptism, and the Lord's Supper was mandatory, whatever the theology with which they were invested. As early as 1652 in 'A Paper sent Forth into the World from them that are scornfully called Quakers...' Fox said 'the Baptism and Supper of the Lord we own'. But he rejected the outward use of these ordinances, claiming that Baptism and communion must be in the Spirit. To many Roman Catholics spiritual communion is a familiar rule, but not to the exclusion of the sacraments. Fox attacked the manifest abuses of the times, the compulsory attendance at church of all inhabitants whether in Catholic, Calvinist or Anglican countries, and the forced use of the church ordinances. The churches were condemned on two counts, they were apostate, and upheld by state laws both in maintenance and worship. Fox's church was spiritual, in worship and order. Baptism and Communion were to be spiritual, and not formal.

Baptism

'Now all that are Baptised with the Baptism of Christ, with Fire, and with the Holy Ghost, they know their Floor to be throughly purged and their Chaff of Sin and Corruption burnt up with unquenchable Fire, and their Wheat to be gathered into God's Garner by Christ their Baptiser...There is no coming to be Children of the Light, but by believing in the Light, which is the Life of Christ the Word; and they that believe in the Light, are grafted into Jesus the Word, by which all things were made and created, and all that walk in the Light as he is in the Light, have fellowship with another...'[7]

Fox described baptism of the Spirit both as circumcision of the Spirit, Baptism of Fire, and casting off the works of the flesh in the Spirit of Acts 2, being blessed directly by the Holy Ghost. From this proceeded his belief that none were excluded from the Promise, women, blacks or prisoners; the Spirit is poured on all flesh willing to receive it. University learning, wealth or rank were not essential to the ministry in the Spirit. As John and Samuel Fothergill (from Carr End) wrote: 'perhaps this is the only Society in the World, that have allowed any share in the management of their affairs to the Female Sex; which they do upon the principle that 'Male and Female are all one in Christ'.[8] *Alice Burton* of Dent married Ralph Alderson of Narthwaite in 1717. She had been called to the ministry in 1706, and her work extended to Scotland, Ireland and particularly America. She was a minister about 60 years, and died at Narthwaite in 1766, and was buried at Cat-Keld, the Meeting House at Street in Ravenstonedale.

'In the ministry, though she had not much human learning, she was frequently furnished with copious expressions, well adapted to the matter she had to deliver, and enabled to speak feelingly to the state of the meetings and individuals. She was remarkably diligent in attending meetings when at home, even to old age, often signifying that she believed none would be injured thereby in their outward circumstances, as the blessing of divine Providence upon honest endeavour would be an ample recompense for all their labour and seeming loss of time.'[9]

Women ministers must have been a great shock to the old churches.

Fox was even more far seeing in his instruction to American Friends (1679):

'All Friends everywhere, that have Indians or

42

Blacks, you are to preach the Gospel to them and other servants, if you be true Christians; for the Gospel of Salvation was to be preached to every creature under Heaven. Christ commands it to his disciples, "Go and teach all nations, baptising them into the name of the Father, Son, and Holy Ghost". And this is the one Baptism with the Spirit into one body...Also you must instruct and teach your Indians and Negroes and all others how that Christ, by the Grace of God, tasted death for every man and gave himself a ransom for all men...Therefore you are to open the promises of God to the ignorant...a light to the gentiles...that He is God's salvation to the end of the earth.'[10]

The fourth point of difference was over *the Lord's Supper*. From his early days Fox owned the Supper of the Lord, as a heavenly and spiritual feast, not the external one practised by the churches. James Parnell put it thus:

'We are accused to deny the Supper of the Lord.

The Supper of the Lord we own, which is the Body and Blood of Christ, which the Saints feed upon; and this is Eternal Food, and Life: And here they all feed upon one, and are of one Heart and Mind: and here is pure and Eternal Union and Communion; and this is not carnal, but Spiritual; for the Saints are Spiritual, and the Communion is Spiritual and Eternal; and this we witness, who are of one Heart and Mind, who are in the New Covenant, and herein we discern the Lord's Body; and here all Drunkards, and Lyars, Adulterers and Unrighteous Persons are shut out.'[11]

One of the most heroic men to embrace the Quaker cause was *William Edmundson of Little Musgrave* in the parish of Crosby Garrett. His service as a Quaker will follow in a later chapter.[12] His explanation of the Quaker view of Baptism and the Lord's Supper is one of the best. Written in Jamaica in 1672, he understood the practice of the old churches better than many, and was able to use their symbolism in explaining the Quaker view of spiritual baptism and communion.

'Christ is Priest according to the promise of the Father, Minister and Bishop of the Soul, who ministers Life, Peace, and Comfort unto them, and renews his holy and heavenly Ordinances in the Church, baptising into one Spirit, and into the one Faith that works by Love, and purifies the heart, giving a white Stone, and in it a new Name, and the sinceer Milk of the Word, officiating the Priests offices, in the Church of the first Borne; prepareing the Alter, and spreading the Table with fine white Linnen, which is his Righteousness, and prepares the Bread for his Church, and fills their Cup with new Wine, that they may all drink of the Cup of Blessings, which is the communion of his Blood, and may all eat of the one Bread, which is the communion of his Body; and his body is Bread indeed, and his Blood is drink indeed, and this is that that gives Life; and without it they cannot have Life; and this is free without money, which the Lord's Table is furnished with, and is inviting the People, and gathering the Nations to it, from your chargeable Tables, for you have sold them Bread, Wine and Water at a dear rate, and he will feed them with all things necessary, as one Household, of one Faith, and as one Family, Christ Jesus, greater than Solomon to Rule them, as their Lord and Master, setting up and renewing family Duties among them, to stand upon their watch, and to resist every appearance of evil, and to Pray with the Spirit, and with Understanding, and to Sing with the Spirit and with understanding also; And he shall rule whose right it is, and the Government is upon his Shoulders, whose Kingdome is Everlasting and of whose Government there shall be no end, and the Lord will perform this, to reform the Nations, to bring them to Uniformity, and true Conformity to his dear Son.'[13]

This concludes a plain introduction to the main Quaker tenets which won the hearts and minds of so many dalesmen from 1652. The remarkable thing is that Fox was able to communicate so much of Quaker principle to the little groups of fellside farmers and cottagers in one or two visits. More notable was the fact that early Quakerism was essentially a young person's movement, though many older people were convinced. In 1668 he wrote a letter to all men's and women's Meetings containing the following advices:

'Friends, Keep at a Word in all
your Dealings, without Oppression,
And keep sound Language, Thou to
everyone.

And keep your Testimony against the World's vain Fashions.

And keep your Testimony against Hireling Priests, and their Tithes and Maintenance.

And against the old Mass-houses, and repairing of them.

And against Priests and the World's joyning in Marriages.

And your Testimony against Swearing, and the World's corrupt Manners.

And against all Loosness, Pleasures and Prophaness whatsoever.

And against all the World's evil Ways, vain Worships and Religions, and to stand up for God's.

And to see that Restitution be made by every one, that hath done wrong to any.

And that all Differences be made up speedily, that they do not fly abroad to corrupt People's Minds.

And that all Reports be stop'd that tend to the defaming of one another.

And Friends, Live all in the Power of the Lord God, and in his Truth, Light and Life, that with it you may all with one Heart, Soul and Mind keep Dominion: and in the Light, Life, Truth and Power of God do true judgement, Justice and Truth, Righteousness and Equity in all your Men and Women's Meetings, without favour or affection to Relations, Kindreds, and Acquaintance, or any Respect of Persons; for if you do not so, Judgement will come upon you from God, to put you down from your Places: For the Power of God, Light, Life and Truth respects not any, but Justice, Truth, Righteousness and Equity, etc.

Let Mercy overshadow the Judgement Seat, and let Mercy be mixt with Judgement.

Take heed of foolish Pity; and if you be not diligent against all Prophaness, Sin, Iniquity and Uncleanness, Looseness and Debauchery, and that which dishonoureth God, then you let those things come up upon you, which you should be a-top of, and subdue, and keep down with Righteousness, and the Truth, and the Power of God.

And in all your Men and Women's Meetings, let all things be done in Love, which doth edify the Body; and let nothing be done in Strife and vain Glory, but keep in the Unity of the Spirit, which is the Bond of Peace: and let all things be done in the Wisdom of God, which is pure and gentle from above, above the Earthly, which is below, sensual and devilish.

And take heed of hurting concerning Marriages, if the thing be right (through any earthly Reasoning) lest they do worse.

And so be diligent for the Lord God and his Truth upon the Earth, and the Inheritance of a Life that hath no end, that you may live in that Seed that is blessed for evermore.

And be diligent in all your Meetings, and see to the setting forth of Apprentices, all Fatherless and poor Friends Children; and that all the poor Widows be carefully look'd after, that nothing may be lacking among you; then all will be well.

And keep your Testimony against all the filthy Raggs of the old World; and for your fine Linnen, the Righteousness of Christ Jesus.

And keep your Testimony for your Liberty in Christ Jesus, and stand fast in it, against all the false Liberties in old Adam, and your Liberties in the Spirit of God, and in the gospel of Christ Jesus, against all the false and loose Liberties in the Flesh.

And train up all your children in the Fear of the Lord, and in his New Covenant, Christ Jesus; as the Jews did their Children and Servants in the old Covenant, and so do you admonish your Children and Servants: And let no man or any live to themselves, but in that Love that seeks not her own.

And have an eye over them that come to spy out your Liberty in Christ, and will report out of your Meetings things to make Advantage, and to the defaming of Persons.

And let every one seek the good of one another, and their Welfare in the Truth, and make others Condition their own; and this keeps as a Father and Mother to condescend to a Child. And all live in the Seed which hath the Blessings, and in the Wisdom, by which you may order all things to God's Glory, over the evil Seed, that is out of the Truth.

And if any one hath any things to say, in opposition to the matter of Marriages, propounded by any to the Meeting, such Friend or Friends to make it known (what they have against the Parties) to such as are appointed by the Meeting, to enquire into the Clearness of the Parties, who laid their Intentions before the Meeting. And such Friends, as have Intentions of Marriage, first to lay it before the Men and Women of the Monthly Meeting they belong to, and to see that things are Clear, before they are brought to the Two Weeks Meeting.

And if any Difference arise, either about Marriages, or any other Case, in the Two Weeks Meetings, that the Business be presently (i.e. immediately) referred to Six Friends, to have a hearing of the Matter another day, or else for them to go forth and determine it presently, and not to discourse it in open Meeting.

And if any Legacy be left by any deceased Friend, to a particular Use, as to putting forth Apprentices, and breeding up poor Friends Children; that the said Money be kept distinct in a Stock for the said Use, and a particular Account thereof to be kept. And the Quarterly or Six Weeks Meetings to see, that the said Monies be disposed of to the Uses as aforesaid. And if any principal Money so given, be at any time made Use of to any other Use, that it be again made up by the Meeting of Friends in General. And though the money be left or given to any particular Friend for the Use aforesaid; yet the same to be paid to Two or Three Persons, whom the Quarterly Meeting or Six Weeks Meeting shall appoint to receive such Money; that so the Meeting may have the Ordering and Disposing of the said Money to the best Advantage, and the Use intended.

And that Friends do keep in their Testimony against the vain Fashions of the World, and all Loosness and Uncleanness whatsoever; and against all Prophane, idle Tipling, and taking Tobacco in Coffee-Houses and Ale-Houses, which is an ill Savour: And against all Strife and Contention whatsoever.

And that some Friends be appointed at every Meeting to keep the Doors, to keep down rude Boys and unruly Spirits; that so the Meetings may be kept Civil and Quiet.

And if one Friend hath any thing against another, let him not treasure it up, till the time of his Marriage, and the cast it upon him publickly; but let him presently speak to the Friend, and also to them, that the Meeting hath appointed to see after his Clearness, etc. And that things may not be deferred too long at the Two Weeks Meeting concerning Marriages; but that they may be answered in a short time, lest they be put to a strait in the Matter.

And stop all bad Reports (for thou shalt not raise a false Report upon my People saith the Lord) and minister Justice upon it presently, so that no Man or Woman may be defiled or defamed with such things.

Read this in the Men and Women Meetings in the Fear of the Lord, as often as you see Occasion, and record it in your Book. G.F.'[14]

The discipline of the Society was strict. The following occur from the area of these registers.

---

(1) *The Record of the Sedbergh Monthly meeting in 1693.*

"At out next monthly meeting is friends Testimonyes Concerning Tythes to be observed and there faithfulness therein.

Att our monthly meeting the 30th of 3rd month did Thomas Donkin of Newby Stones in the parish of Morland intimate then to friends his purpose of takeing to wife Elianor Cowston daughter of...Cowston late of Sedberg meeting but removed from thence (and) now belongs to Strickland meeting unto which also the said Thomas belongs, and in ye foresaid County of Westmorland, Against their next proposal is expected from Strickland monthly meeting a certificate of ye mans clearness from others in that concern with his Relations consent And likewise a certificate from our monthly meeting to signify to Strickland friends her clearness from other men with respect of marriage is to be sent from us.

ffurther enquiry att our next meeting is (to) be made of James Harker and Michaell Dawson about John Clerk walking as becomes Truth.

Att our Monthly the 27th of 4th month 1693

(1) There was presented to the meeting a paper written by John Segar prisoner att Lancaster approved by friends to be read in Quarterly, monthly and particularly meetings.

(2) Att that time also sent to our monthly meeting from ye Quarterly meeting att York a paper to excite friends of Yorkshire appertaining to this meeting to adjoyne and adhere to them in there Quarterly meeting but it was left till further consideration.

(3) At our meeting last mentioned did Thomas Donkin the second time signifie to friends his purpose of mariage with Elianor Cowston a Certificate came from Strickland monthly meeting of his clearness from other women in that respect to friends satisfaction as also his Relations Consent, such clearness appearing

friends freely gave way and left to friends at Strickland meeting to see it decently accomplished if they find it meet for Admittance.

(4) Grisdale friends appointed to speake to John Clerk gave account att our foresaid meeting that he answered them, he would endeavour better for ye future.

Att our monthly meeting the 27th of 10th month (page torn) did John Airey signify his continued Intent of taking to wife Agnes ffawcett being the second time that friends (?wished) to enquire of ye mans clearness they find nothing, that he is clear from all other women in that concern; friends findeing nothing of obstruction freely gave their consent to their proceeduce (!) to ye accomplishment in their own time Only Tho: Blaykling & Edw: Raws were appoynted to see it decently solemnised.

Richard Robinson's yearly gift distributed the 10th month 92/3.

Att our monthly meeting the 31st of 11th month did John Makereth confess & acknowledge to friends that he was sorry for doeing Contrary to Truth in going to marry with an hireling Priest as also for marrying his own cousen who because hereof was willing to give forth a paper to Clear the truth of those Aspersions that thereby may fale (fall) out by ye same occasions.

Att our Monthly meeting the 28th of 12th month was it desired that friends should take care to give their sufferings to friends appointed thereunto As also to give an Account concerning there faithfulness about (torn: ?it).

In that day proposed Robert Dent of Clough in Garsdale his intent of mariage with Ann Richardson daughter of John Richardson of Carperby belonging to Richmond Monthly Meeting; Edmond Winn and Michaell Dawson was appointed to enquire of his clearness of all other women in relation to marriage, His parents consent is expected against (ie. on behalf of) the proposal. 1693.

Att our Monthly Meeting the 25th of 2 mo. did Robert Dent shew the second time his Intent of mariage with Ann Richardson; ye friends appointed to enquire of his clearness report no otherwise and also his parents consent and (?his) clearness was signified to ye meeting; and from friends of this Meeting was sent a certificate to friends of Richmond (viz) to there mo: meeting to intimate his clearness from all others in Relation to mariage and their further proceeding left to ye discretion of friends of Richmond Monthly Meeting unto which ye woman appertains.

A collection also was att ye time abovesaid ordered to be made only for the supply of friends that are prisoners for the Testimony of Truth.''[15]

There is an interesting MS directive from *the Quarterly Meeting at Kendal* of the 6th of the 2nd month 1695 among the records of the Library at Friends House, Euston Road, London, related to the building of the Meeting House at Brigflats in 1675. George Myers and Leonard ffell directed John Blaikling and John Holmes of the one part, and friends of Sedbergh Meeting of the other part touching the execution of the last Will of James Guy (of Garsdale) and what moneys they have layd out and expended in every way about the same; and if the said John Blaikling and John Holmes have no assets, then we agree and order that John Blaikling and John Holmes and the Sedbergh Meeting raise £20 between them which is remaining unpaid, or so much of the assets allowed towards the building of the Meeting House at Sedbergh, and to pay the money to John Holmes to discharge the same.[16]

From the *Preparative Meeting of Ravenstonedale* dated 28th of 10th month 1718.

'Some account is brought that Sarah Rogerson bears company with a young man of a differing Perswation Respecting Religion on ye account of marriage. This meeting appoints Ralph Alderson and Thomas Thornburrow to deal with her, and give account to ye next meeting.' 'Preparative Meeting 25th of 11th month 1718. Ralph Alderson and Thomas Thornburrow have had an opportunity with Sarah Rogerson and according to her account she is clear upon ye said account at present'.[17]

The outcome was otherwise. Her young man was James Bayliff of Murthwaite, who later became registrar to the manor court; he married her in the parish church on the 21st June 1721, and on the 30th of the same month she was baptised there. She was disowned by her Meeting for 'not walking according to Truth'.

About 8 years later she had other thoughts, and was reconciled to the Society and died of smallpox in 1730. Her husband survived her and was buried beside her at Cat-Keld in

1766.

(2) Another side of Quaker Discipline occurs in the education of children. John the son of Alice and Ralph Alderson of Narthwaite, Ravenstonedale, was born in 1721, and on 3rd of 11th month 1763 made his will, shortly before going to London as a minister. He was ill at the time, and died there in 1764. His father-in-law, Richard Thistlewaite of Spicegill, Dent, and his brother Simond Alderson were made executors to employ his estate to maintain his wife and children. After providing for the division of his goods between his children surviving to the age of 21 years, and the maintenance of his wife for life, he added this proviso:

'I do further Will and Declare that if my said wife Alice Alderson do marrey after my decease then and imeditly upon such marriage she shall by virtue hereof be devested, excluded, debarred and for ever cut off from all benifit profitt payment and advantage by and from this my last Will and from the Guardianship of my children, and in this case I give and divise the Custody of my Children to the said Richard Thistlethwaite and Simond Alderson and appoint them Guardians only'.[18]

Alice and John had only been married four years, she went to live with her father Richard Thistlethwaite in Dent, and remarried in 1770.

(3) There are a number of Quaker wills where the testator bequeathes a sum for the poor to be administered by the churchwardens of the parish, as well as a further sum to the Meeting for the benefit of poor Quakers. Anthony Robinson of Dovengill, Ravenstonedale died in 1711, and by his Will 7th March 1710 he gave a number of legacies to poor Quakers, and in addition he left £5 to be added to the poor stock of Ravenstonedale parish.[19] Ann Shaw of Amatholme, Sedbergh by her Will of 10th July 1699 left 20s. to the poor belonging to Brigflats Meeting, and 20s. to the poor resorting to Sedbergh parish church.[20] John Shaw of Spisers, Sedbergh by his Will of 1st May 1707 left 20s. to the poor attending Brigflats Meeting, and the same to the poor of Sedbergh parish.[21] It is an interesting comment on the times that on the 21st August 1700 the Governors (of Sedbergh school) held a meeting when it was unanimously agreed 'that no persons of the Church of England that are of scandalous or irregular lives, or that are not frequenters of the Church Service and Sacraments, shall for the future receive any part of, or have any share in the distribution of any charitable alms deposited with the governors for the use and benefit of the poor in the parish of Sedbergh.'[22]

Refs: Chapter 6

(1) Journal I, 306.

(2) The Divinity of Christ, and the Unity of those that bear Record in Heaven. George Fox and Jo. Stubbs, 1669. sect. 9. (C.U.L. Broughton, 265).

(3) Gospel Truth op.cit. 905. & p. 714-5. We are come to our own Prophet, Jesus Christ. The Pope is not the head of the church.

(4) Journal I. Preface xlvii/viii.

(5) A Declaration concerning Fasting and Prayer...and sheweth the Prayer that God accepts. G. Fox. 1656. (C.U.L. Syn. 7.65.130^1.)

(6) An Apology for the True Christian Divinity...as held by the People in Scorn called Quakers. R. Barclay. 1701, 4th ed. p. 364. Proposition XI, of Worship, sects. 2 & 3. (C.U.L. Peterborough, 10.7.)
     In The Friends Quarterly Examiner, 1867, Vol. I. 295, there is an excellent devotion on the opening words of the Lord's Prayer, by J.S. Sewell.

(7) Gospel Truth op.cit. 902.
     A Collection of the Writings of James Parnell 1675. The Shield of Truth p. 67, Baptism in the Spirit.
     A Brief Account of the People called Quakers, John & Samuel Fothergill. Dublin 1776, p. 14.

(8)   A Brief Account of the People called Quakers, John & Samuel Fothergill. Dublin 1776, p. 14.

(9) Piety Promoted. J. Kendal 1789, III, 213, Alice Alderson. (C.U.L. Ddd, 3.28.)
     Cat. of Friends Books, J. Smith, I, 7.

(10) A Collection of the Select Epistles of...George Fox, 1698, op.cit. Vol. II, Epistle 355, 1679. pp. 426/7.

(11) A Collection of the Writings of James Parnell, London 1675, The Shield of Faith, p. 68.
     A Testimony to the True & Spiritual Worship and a Word of Consolation to the Children of Light. Thomas Taylor, 1670, pp. 3-11, sect (j) 'Our Supper is with the Lord etc.'

(12) Chapter 11, refs. 30, 31, 32, 33, 34.

(13) A Letter of Examination to all you who have assumed the place of Shepherds, Herdsmen, and Overseers of the Flocks of People...by William Edmundson (of Little Musgrave) from Jamaica, pub. London 1672, pp. 7-8. (From the Library of Friends House, Euston Road, London.)

(14) A Coll. of the Epistles of George Fox, op.cit. 274-276. Epistle 263. On p. 276 there is a letter 264 with further advices.

(15) P.R.O. RG6/1285, Monthly Meeting of Sedbergh. Births, Marr. & Burials. p. 2.

(16) From Library of Friends House, Euston Rd., London. Directive of the Kendal Quarterly Meeting of 6th of 12. mo. 1695 to named persons of Sedbergh Meeting to clear an unpaid debt incurred from the building of the Meeting House, 1675, to which James Guy of Garsdale had bequeathed a sum by Will.

(17) Parish Regs. of Ravenstonedale, ed. Rev. R.W. Metcalfe, Kendal 1893, p. xxvii.

(18) C.R.O. Kendal. Book of Copy of Wills recorded at Brigflats 1698 ref. WDX/515. Will of John Alderson of Narthwaite, 3rd Nov. 1763.

(19) Ibid. Will of Anthony Robinson of Dovengill, 7 Mar. 1710.

(20) Ibid. Will of Ann Shaw of Amatholme, Sedbergh, 10 July 1699.

(21) Ibid. Will of John Shaw of Spisers, Sedbergh, 1 May 1707.

Note: With regard to these four Wills it is not clear whether the originals were dated in Quaker fashion, and were misread by the copier, or whether legal form was accepted to avoid dispute.

(22) Hist. of Parish and Grammar School of Sedbergh, A.E. Platt, 1876. p. 27.

CHAPTER 7

In my earlier work I have dealt with the development of northern customary tenures in law, and the division of farmholds in the later sixteenth century which created a small-holding tenantry unable to survive years of bad harvest and disease. We must now consider the particular question of the relation of agrarian troubles to the rise of political and religious dissent from the Pilgrimage of Grace 1537/8. Seventy-four men were hanged in February 1538 on the order of the earl of Norfolk; twenty-one came from Cumberland, and fifty-three came from the upper Eden valley, from Appleby to Mallerstang. They had been carefully named as leaders of the revolt by the gentry, who had to save their skins and estates by betrayal, for having taken part in the first uprising. As Wilfred Holme the Yorkshire poet wrote:

'There were hanged uppon heades capitall three score and sixteene ... on trees in their gardens to record for memoriall ... the end of this acte periculous.'[1]

Looking at the places from which 21 came from Cumberland an interesting fact emerges. Ten were taken from the Honor of Cockermouth, of which Sir Thomas Wharton (who witnessed the executions) was steward. In 1537 Henry sixth earl of Northumberland had bequeathed his estates to the King. Wharton like the earl of Cumberland was well known for his oppression of tenants by high fines. Wharton was still steward in the autumn of 1537 when Robert Southwell was sent by Cromwell to survey the estates on behalf of the King. As a general fine was now due to the King as the new lord, and as Wharton was too extortionate, Southwell wrote to Cromwell of the action he had taken, though he had no power in his warrant to levy fines. He hoped that Cromwell would sanction his action retrospectively. 'I have commanded Sir Thomas Wharton in the King's behalf to defer the gressomyng of them till the King's pleasure by therein knowen, who wolde ells have wrestyde them high inowgh as doe the more part ther, which my lorde I dare say with the approvement of comens accustomably usyde ther, and no place

elles that I have ben yn hath done mych more hurte than good...'[2] He agreed with the observation of the earl of Norfolk to Cromwell in February 1538 that the lords had been responsible for high gressing, and inclosing of common lands.[3] That the landlords were responsible for most of the trouble is proved by a remark of Edmund Grindal, the son of a well-to-do farmer of Hensingham, and Archbishop of Canterbury 1578-1583. He described that part of Cumberland as 'the ingorantist part in religion, and most oppressed of covetous landlords of any one part in this realm'.[4] Dr. Burn writing in 1777 mentioned that the customary tenants of the manor of Branthwaite near Dean purchased the freehold of their estates of Henry Skelton Esq. by paying eighty years' (ancient) rent for their enfranchisement.[5]

The places in which the leaders were hanged in the Cockermouth area were recorded and sent to London:

Cockermouth (a chapelry of Brigham) 2,
Brigham 1,
Emelton (a chapelry of Brigham) 1,
Eglesfield (in the parish of Brigham) 1,
Perdishaw (in the parish of Dean) 1,
Branthwayte (in the parish of Dean) 1,
Dereham (N.W. of Brigham) 1,
Talentyre (parish of Bridekirk, north of Cockermouth) 1,
Wedoppe (Wythop a chapelry of Lorton near Embleton) 1.

In view of later Quaker history the most emotive hanging is that of Percival Hudson of Perdishaw. As Dr. Burn noted: 'Many of the inhabitants here are Quakers, being so approximate neighbours to Pardshaw Cragg, a most famous place formerly for Quakers, being far from any church'.[6] Looking at the Quaker onslaught of 1653 (which was considerable) in the Brigham and Pardshaw area there can be no doubt that the poverty of the area, the ever present claims of rent and tithes, and remoteness from school and church made the people receptive of Fox and his First Publishers of Truth.[7]

It is possible that the eleven who were

hanged in the Penrith district might be the subject of a similar study. Shap, Penrith, Clifton, Morland, Heltondale, Strickland, King's Neaburn, Reagill and Appleby were embraced by the Meeting at Strickland Head.[8]

Turning to the 53 who came from the upper Eden valley from Appleby to Mallerstang the figures are as follows:

Kirkby Stephen town, hamlets, and Mallerstang 23,
Brough under Stainmore, with Brough Sowerby and the Stainmores 7,
Newhall (parish of Warcop) 5,
Little Musgrave (parish of Crosby Garrett) 2,
Asby 2,
Appleby St. Lawrence, and Bongate 12,
King's Meaburn (parish of Morland) 1, and
Dufton 1.

Looking at the upper Eden valley since 1537, the following events coloured the outlook of the tenants towards their lords:-

(a) The general complaint at the Pilgrimage of Grace against high fines and inclosures in the dales taken by Pullen and Musgrave to the meeting of the commons at York on 21st November 1537. There is evidence that inclosures had taken place in the Brough district.[9]

(b) The high fines, compositions, sales and evictions which followed the King's Award of 1617 in the dispute between Lady Anne, countess of Dorset, and her uncle Francis earl of Cumberland and his son Henry lord Clifford. The greatest suffering came from the manors of Mallerstang, Brough, Brough Sowerby and the Stainmores.[10] Some of the family names either as supporters of the Commonwealth or of Quakerism can be seen in the lists of sufferers in 1617–21.

(c) The difficulty which Mr. Edmund Pollard, lady Anne's agent had from 1645 in collecting her Westmorland rents, that 'by violence the tenants of Kirkby Stephen stand obstinately out, and will not pay any (rents) but by compulsion ...' When Lady Anne came north in 1649 and appointed her commissioners in February 1649/50 to treat with her tenants over rents and fines, the tenants counter-attacked by complaining to the Committee of Indemnity in London, and of the 36 names, 34 came from Brough and the Stainmores, 1 from Kirkby Stephen and 1 from Ravenstonedale. The family names Laidman, Waller, Wharton, Wastall, Aiskell, Ewebank, Cumpston, Jackson, Wilkin and Wardell in the 1649/50 petition also accur in 1617/18. They will all be found in the Protestation returns of 1641.[11]

(d) The Chancery case between lady Anne and her Westmorland tenants began in December 1650. The principal representative tenants from the Westmorland manors were Robert Atkinson, William Barnett, John Fothergill, Robert Shaw, George Rudd, John Waller, John Munkas, George Fothergill, Christ: (ms.torn), John Aiskell alias Rose, Robert Pattinson, John Dent, Tho: Cleasby, and Thomas Ewebancke. Half the petitioners came from Brough and the Stainmores, and half from Kirkby Stephen and Mallerstang, though they claimed to represent all the Westmorland Clifford manors. Thomas Ewebanke was a captain of militia, and an elder of Brough church. Thomas Cleasby was then in Brough parish, and shortly to become a Quaker. Robert Atkinson, then a lieutenant and later a captain of militia, together with his nephew John Waller, were later living in Mallerstang and were involved in the Kaber Rigg plot of 1663. Ewebanke and Atkinson, and perhaps William Barnett of Kirkby Stephen were the political leaders both of the puritan faction, as well as of the distressed tenantry.[12]

(e) There was an additional factor from the barony of Kendal. Like the Eden valley it (with Dent and Sedbergh) had taken part in the Pilgrimage of Grace. But the more immediate memory was of the Kendal tenant - right case (1620-25) in which King James abolished tenant-right by personal decree, and tried to force tenants to re-purchase their right in order to raise cash from the Crown manors of the barony, as well as those in private hands.[13] Though its centre was in Kendal a few north Westmorland people had been involved. According to the Star Chamber depositions Humphrey Bell, aged 50, and John Robertson aged 51 of Crosby Garrett, and John Corney, vicar of Orton, aged 58, and William Wharton a young schoolmaster of Orton had come under suspicion and were questioned under writ of Star Chamber. Among the other suspects were John Cartmele of Preston Patrick, clothworker, aged 48, James Smith, Thomas Prickett of Audland gent, aged 28, Thomas Lucas of Burton yeoman aged 62, Richard Holme of Whinfell aged 52. Other suspects included Samuel Knipe, John Becke, Rowland Harrison, Robert Mawson, ffrancis Washington, Edward Tarne, Thomas Anderley, William Whitwell, Sampson Tomlinson, Richard Barkas, Thomas Williamson, Edmund Becke, Nicholas Carns (or Tarne). In addition three young sparks had acted a stage play in Kendal castle in July 1622. They represented many lords of manors of the district 'to be in Hell, to great abuse of the said lords, by which they were provoked to have fallen into a rage, and to have broken (the King's) peace'. The culprits were, Richard Holme, Henry Ward and Thomas Duckett and other unknown persons. In view of later Quaker history the names Cartmell, Holme, Tarne and Ward are interesting.[14]

(f) Returning to the Chancery case between lady Anne and her Westmorland tenants from 1650, the following gave evidence of behalf of the tenants: Henry Ward of Grayrigg, gent, aged 63; James Tarne of Lambrigg yeoman aged 40; William Cartmell of Preston Patrick, yeoman aged 48; and Robert Johnson of Holme, yeoman aged 76. In addition, Richard Caulstone of Morland, yeoman aged 70 gave evidence. Though the gathering of these threads of history has been tedious, it can no longer be doubted that many families which had been deeply involved in tenant-right struggles embraced Quakerism after 1652.[15]

When William C. Braithwaite wrote his book 'The Beginnings of Quakerism' he remarked that there was a small Meeting at Ravenstonedale among many others.[16] This is not sufficient. It was central to a wide scattering of Quakers of the first generation in the upper Eden valley, stretching as far as Appleby Gaol. Though attendance at Meeting was difficult in dowly (dreary) weather, Ravenstonedale was central to small groups in Tebay, Orton, Warcop, Brough, Kirkby Stephen, Nateby, Mallerstang, Grisedale, and Cautley. It had a special concern to attend the many Friends who were incarcerated in Appleby gaol, and to support Edward Guy, and John Bolton of Appleby who did much to try to relieve their wants, when they also were not in prison. Similarly Brigflats was the centre for Lune valley, Cautley, Garsdale, Grisedale, Dent and upper Wensleydale when distance prevented regular attendance at Meetings.

Quakerism in the upper Eden valley owes its origin to four or five principal men, George Fox, James Nayler, Francis Howgill, Thomas and Christopher Taylor. Francis Higginson of Kirkby Stephen called them journeymen preachers; in truth they were men of remarkable ability, who at great personal risk, preached a revolution in political and religious thought. Fox and Howgill came to Orton and Ravenstonedale in the autumn of 1652. Nayler and Howgill arrived two weeks later and preached at Ravenstonedale and Shorgill in Mallerstang, at which they were arrested and later imprisoned at Appleby. At Orton Fox and Howgill were received by Robert Shaw, at Ravenstonedale by John Pinder of Wath, and James Clerkson of Weasdale. In Mallerstang Nayler and Howgill were received by Thomas and John Knewstub of Shorgill, where John ffuthergill and several relations were convinced.[17] A second meeting at Ravenstonedale was founded by Anthony Robinson of Dovengill. From early days there were secondary house Meetings at William Skaife's at Blacksyke, Warcop; at John Knewstubb's at Shorgill, Mallerstang; and at the homes of Thomas Winn of Scale in Grisdale, and Richard Wilson of Knowscale in Garsdale. For the first twenty or thirty years meetings were in farmhouses, and whenever possible they walked over the fells to one or other of the Ravenstonedale Meetings. The very small Meetings at Warcop and Mallerstang did not survive the first generation of Quakers. That at Warcop seems to have melted into the dissenting chapel at Birks in Bleatarn; that at Grisdale grew into that at Garsdale, which in the eighteenth century became the predominant Meeting. The Warcop Quakers seem latterly to have been buried in the Birks burial grounds; as the Mallerstang group burials are not recorded in any surviving Quaker register, nor in the parish registers of Kirkby Stephen it is probable that a small Quaker ground has been lost. There were three burial grounds at Ravenstonedale, at Wath, Dovengill lane head, and at Cat Keld; that at Grisdale lies behind the derelict farm at East Scale, between the house and the beck; that at Garsdale is at Dandragarth.

The Distribution of Quakers in the upper Eden valley from 1652

As there are a number of early Quakers who do not appear in the Ravenstonedale Quaker registers, or who lived in the district but were not members of that Meeting, the following lists are given to include them within the scope of a complete survey. First we will deal with Appleby and its gaol.[18]

Appleby St. Lawrence

Edward Guy was a shopkeeper, taxed at four hearths in the Hearth Tax of 1669/72. (Later Records 63). He was a member of Strickland Head Meeting, and was married at least twice; in 1655 to Isabell, daughter of William Aray of Shap at Strickland Head, and in 1665 to Margaret Garth of West Tickley, county Durham at the same place. There were at least two children by each marriage.[19] After the ill-fated Kaber Rigg plot of 1663 great persecution fell on the Quakers in the dales, who were regarded as sectaries with political motives. On the 22nd November 1663 he and others were taken at a Meeting. probably Strickland Head, and at the Quarter Sessions of 11th Jan. 1663/4 he was fined 100s., and had his goods distrained. (Besse 11, 13. & Later Records, 27.). He was fined again on 18th April 1664 in 120s., and had his goods distrained. (Later Records 28). There is a letter from 'Ned Guy the Quaker' to Sir John Lowther and Sir Philip Musgrave among the Lowther papers, defending himself against various charges. (Hist. MSS Comm. 13th Rep. part vii, Earl of Lonsdale's MSS, p. 90.) In 1671 he was fined £6.10s. as part of a larger sum, laid on the house where they met. For the first time they took house goods worth £9.15s., and for this latter they seized his shop goods, but

did not take them away. (Besse II,20). In 1677/8 he had a number of goods seized by Exchequer process (presumably in lieu of tithes) after a fine of £5.6.8. (Besse II, 24). From the available records he suffered spasmodic persecution, mainly as a result of the attention of informers and Sir John Lowther who persecuted the Strickland Head Meeting vigorously.

In 1665 he composed the preface to Francis Howgill's 'The Great Case of Tythes'. In 1670 he wrote 'A Funeral Verse' on the death of Francis Howgill in Appleby gaol. He and John Bolton of Bongate, Anthony Pinder of Ravenstonedale, Thomas Langhorne of Heltondale, Richard Pinder of Ravenstonedale, and Thomas Carlton of Cumberland witnessed Howgill's death in gaol on the 20th of the 12th month, 1668. Howgill's dying words were printed in 1717.[20]

Appleby, Bongate

John Boulton (or Bolton). His trade involved the use of leather; taxed on one hearth in 1669-72. (Later Records, 80).. A member of Strickland Head Meeting, he had at least three children.[21] Three leaders of that Meeting were arrested on 14th July 1662, and were ordered to appear the following day at the Appleby Quarter Sessions. The fines imposed and the value of goods taken illustrate the point that the goods taken always exceeded the fine.

William Hebson of Sleagill for a fine of £5, had two cows taken worth £7. John Boulton of Bongate for a fine of £5 had leather worth £6. taken. Michael Langhorne (prob. Askham) for a fine of £4.10.s. had 2 cows worth £5. taken. (Besse II, 10).

As with Edward Guy, he and others were taken in November 1663 after the Kaber Rigg plot. Twenty-five were fined, and nine were sent to gaol. As this was his second offence he was fined 120s. On the 7th August 1665 he was among twelve men and woman (arrested in July 1664) who were still in Appleby gaol two months after the expiration of their sentence, for not paying either the clerk's or gaoler's fees. There were a further six in the same gaol at the same time upon a second conviction for attending 'unlawful conventicles', making a total of 18.[22] This was part of a long attack on Strickland Head by Sir John Lowther and informers beginning in the second half of 1664; on the 7th August 1665 ten men and women were arrested; on 14th fourteen; on the 21st eighteen; and on the 4th September 16 were similarly taken, and prob-

ably bound over to the next sessions. In addition to the eighteen in prison on the 7th August 1665 there were others arrested in July 1664: Thomas Langhorne of Heltondale[23], who died in Pennsylvania in 1687, a John Robinson, and John Thompson and William Scaife of Warcop parish. There were also six Kendal Quakers in prison at the same time.

Thus when they were not in prison, or plying their trades, Edward Guy and John Bolton were central to what help could be given by Friends from Strickland Head and Ravenstonedale to the many Quakers in Appleby gaol. In 1777 Dr. Burn described it at the west end of the bridge as 'a little, mean, incommodious building; without one inch of ground out of doors, wherein the prisoners might receive fresh air.'[24] So bleak was the lot of poorer felons, that they were allowed into the town from time to time to beg for food.

At the heart of the Quaker movement in the upper Eden valley was one man above all others FRANCIS HOWGILL. If his writings are the best guide he was the saint of early Quakerism. The warmth of his devotion, his patient submission to the Will of Christ, his long imprisonment gave spur to the waverer, heart to the sufferer, and inspiration to the doubter. He was the Quaker at his best. There is no need to write his life. He was aged 38 when he met Fox at Firbank Fell in 1652. He was a tailor by trade from Todhorne in Grayrigg. Backhouse claims that he received an university education, and that he was for a

52

time a clergyman of the established church. When Fox arrived, Howgill was an adherent of the Revd. Thomas Taylor, the minister of the separate congregation at Preston Patrick made up of a group of most religious and zealous of Roundheads and Puritans covering a wide area from Richmond in Yorkshire, Wensleydale, to the nearer communities at Yealand, Kellett, Kendal, Underbarrow, Grayrigg, and Hutton in Westmorland.[25] Taylor would occasionally allow John Audland and Howgill to preach in his pulpit at Preston Patrick, and it was in this capacity that Howgill was present with him in the chapel on Firbank Fell when Fox preached from the rock there in 1652. The convincement of Taylor and Howgill, and many of the congregation at Preston Patrick gave Fox the nucleus of an organisation, based on Taylor's monthly meetings, from which later Quakerism developed. Howgill was part of the team of eight who preached so successfully in the Pardshaw and Brigham area in Cumberland in 1653.[26] With Anthony Pearson he held the first Quaker meeting in London. In 1654 he was in the Bristol area. In 1655 he and Edward Burrough went to Ireland, from which they were expelled by Henry Cromwell the Lord Deputy. There is little record of his work 1656 to 1661; in December 1662 he was in Reading, and after the death of his young friend Edward Burrough in 1663 he came home to Grayrigg. He

was arrested in July in Kendal market, taken before the justices in a tavern, who submitted the Oath of Allegiance to him. Being a Quaker he refused to swear, and was sent to Appleby gaol, where they kept him in a smoky hole from the sessions to the assizes. He was allowed to go home to Grayrigg for a short time to settle his affairs, and return to gaol. At the August assizes at Appleby he again refused the oath, but was allowed to prepare his defence, and remitted to a future assize. As he refused to abstain from public meetings he was kept in gaol, and came up before judge Twisden on the 22/23 August 1664. This was the assize at which Captain Robert Atkinson was condemned to be hanged as a traitor. It was not a propitious moment to be refusing oaths. He was declared to be guilty of praemunire, and sentenced to imprisonment for the rest of his life. After much patient suffering in vile conditions he died in the presence of five friends on the 20th January 1669, and was carried home on horseback for burial at Grayrigg. And the trumpets sounded on the other side. He was a great and heroic man.[27]

Shortly before he died he said: 'I have sought the way of the Lord from a child, and lived innocently as among men; and if any enquire concerning my latter end, let them know that I die in the faith which I have lived in, and suffered for.'

REFS: CHAPTER 7

Note: References to vol. I in this section are to: The Agrarian background to the rist of political and religious dissent in the Northern Dales in the 16th and 17th centuries. As this may not be publishable, the key references alluded to will be added to each reference to vol.I.

(1)   This work vol. I. Chap. 3. ref. (21) Brit. Library cat.C.122.bb.20. Dated 1572.

(2)   Ibid. Chap. 3. ref.(2).

P.R.O. original letter, SP1/124. Robert Southwell, solicitor to the Court of Augmentations, to Cromwell 20th Aug. 1537. He surveyed the Crown and Percy lands, and the estates of the dissolved monasteries in the northern province.

(3)   Ibid. Chap. 3. ref. (1) S.P. Henry VIII, 1537. (478), 21 Feb. 1537.

Norfolk to Cromwell.

(4)   D.N.B. Edmund Grindal (1519? - 1583).

(5)   N & B, II, 59.

(6)   Ibid. II, 65. There is a hist. of Pardshaw Meeting by Margaret Irwin which I have not seen.

(7)   First Publishers of Truth, ed. Norman Penney, 1902, 33-46.

(8)   Ibid. 271/2.

(9)   This work vol. I. chap. 1. ref. (15)

S.P. Henry VIII, 1537 (1246) 4 Dec. sects (9) & (13) Instructions to Sir T. Hilton.

(10)   This work vol. I. chap. 19. ref. (2)

P.R.O. SP/C.21/P.25/1. Anne countess of Pembroke v. Robert Atkinson & others. Depositions taken at Appleby 18th January 1650/51; also at the house of John Washington at Docker, Kendal (25?th) Sept. 1651. Evidence of Geoffrey Birkbeck of Mallerstang, Lancelot Blenkinsop of Helbeck, and Thomas Laidman of Stainmore.

(11) Appleby castle MS, now at C.R.O. Carlisle. 3 March 1645. Mr. Edmund Pollard to Mr. C. Marsh. Also Lady Anne Clifford. G.C. Williamson, 207. Appleby castle MS. now C.R.O. Carlisle. 25 Feb. 1649/50. Appeal of the tenants of the countess of Pembroke in Westmorland to the Committee of Indemnity.

(12) C & W trans. Tract series, XVII, 1971. The Westmorland Protestation Returns, 1641. M.A. Faraday. The manors of Brough etc., Kirkby Stephen and Mallerstang.

C & W trans. N.S.XI. art.xvi. The Kaber Rigg Plot 1663. F. Nicholson 228/9.

(13) N & B, I, 51 et seq.

(14) P.R.O. Star Chamber papers. STAC.8. James I. bundle 34, file 4, (Item 24) Informations, writs, interrogatories and depositions 1620-25. Attorney General v. certain defendants in the barony of Kendal & others claiming tenant-right against the personal decree of the King, and alleged misdemeanours of certain tenants.

(15) Richard Coulston of Morland gave evidence for the tenants against the countess of Pembroke January 1650/51. ref. (10) above.

This vol. chap. 6 ref. (15) for Elianor Cowston (i.e. Coulston) of Strickland-head Meeting.

(16) The Beginnings of Quakerism. Wm. C. Braithwaite, 1981 ed. 370.

(17) First Publishers of Truth, op. cit. 248, 272.

(18) Works relating to the incidence of Quakerism in the upper Eden valley: The First Publishers of Truth, N. Penney, op. cit.

The Beginnings of Quakerism, Wm. C. Braithwaite, 1981 ed.

The Second Period of Quakerism, Wm. C. Braithwaite, 1979 ed.

Early Cumberland and Westmorland Friends. R.S. Ferguson, 1871.

(19) P.R.O. RG6/1246. Registers of births, marriages and burials of the Westmorland Quarterly Meeting, Kendal, 1649/1778.

(20) The Great Case of Tythes, Francis Howgill 1665. (Written in Appleby gaol), in Howgill's Works: The Dawnings of the Gospel Day etc. 1676 p. 551.

See Ref. (27) below.

'A Funeral Verse' on the death of Francis Howgill by E(dward) G(uy) 1671. in Cat. of Friends Books, Joseph Smith I, 898.

The Tract giving the dying words of Francis Howgill dated 1717 as in the Library of Friends House, Euston Road, London, under John Bolton.

(21) P.R.O. RG6/1246. Reg. of births, marriages and burials of the Westmorland Quarterly Meeting, Kendal 1649-1778.

(22) Hist. MSS. Comm. Rep. XIII, part vii. Earl of Lonsdale's MSS. pp. 90-91.

(23) F.P.T. 271.

(24) N. & B, I. 319.

(25) The Beginnings of Quakerism, Wm. G. Braithwaite, op. cit. pp. 80/1

(26) F.P.T. 37.

(27) D.N.B. Francis Howgill, 1618-1669.

A Collection of the Sufferings of the People called Quakers, J. Besse, 1753, 2 vols. II, 11-12.

Memoirs of Francis Howgill, James Backhouse, York, 1828, 63-87. (C.U.L.Oo.9.30^2)

A Testimony concerning the Life, Death, Travels & Labours of Edward Burroughs, that worthy Prophet of the Lord ... who dyed in Newgate Prison the 14th of the 12th month 1662. London 1663. (C.U.L.Syn.5.65.2^{13}.) p. 5 The Testimony of F(rancis) H(owgill) contains the notable passage including the phrase 'The Kingdom of Heaven did gather us, and catch us all as in a net'.

The Dawnings of the Gospel Day and its Light and Glory discovered by Francis Howgill who dyed a prisoner for the Truth in Appleby gaol in the County of Westmorland, the twentieth day of the eleaventh month one thousand six hundred and sixty eight. London 1676 (C.U.L. Syn.4.67.3.)

CHAPTER 8

Quakers in the upper Eden valley.

Remembering the tenant-right agitations in the upper Eden valley up till 1650, it must be understood that dissent took two courses. The first was the presbyterian which was more powerful during the Protectorate than its numbers warranted. The moderate section of this group was led by Philip lord Wharton largely engaged in London committee work, but ably supported by Edmund Branthwaite, whom the countess of Pembroke appointed her deputy-sheriff. The more militant was that led by major Arthur Skaife of Winton, colonel Richard Richardson of Crosby Garrett, John Waller of Winton, and lieutenant Robert Atkinson of Kirkby Stephen. In south Westmorland Gervase Benson, John Archer, Roger Bateman, and Edward Briggs ruled in the Kendal area. Benson and Branthwaite regularly corresponded with Wharton who was kept informed of all that was going on. After 1662 these groups continued in the Presbyterian chapel in Kendal market place, the chapel at Ravenstonedale, and Birks chapel at Bleatarn in the parish of Warcop.

The seond course opened up in 1652 when Fox arrived in the dales, already in a state of political and religious ferment. The anger of the parliamentary group was roused when Benson and Ward became Quakers, and small groups of Quakers appeared all over Westmorland, thus 'betraying' the popular support which the Puritans should have had. Nor can the element of jealousy be overlooked, that men who had been nobodies till 1650, made enough money to buy estates and be addressed as 'Mr' in official letters. The fellsider has a long memory of a man's family origin, and can be very blunt if someone gets above himself. Thus when Fox and his followers denied being involved in plots, the presbyterians thought this humbug from a section of the population which should have supported them. Thus the northern communities were hopelessly fragmented between a few papists, royalists, perhaps some levellers, presbyterians, and quakers against the majority of gentry and clergy who submitted to the prevailing state of affairs, but were not persuaded by the 'phanatics'. The culture of the valleys was protestant, for which the grammar schools of Sedbergh and Kirkby Stephen were responsible.

The following pages will give the distribution of early Quakers in the upper Eden valley centred on Ravenstonedale and Grisdale, and will include some names which are not recorded in the registers of these Meetings, nor were members.

Ravenstonedale. The Meeting at Wath was founded by George Fox in the autumn of 1652.[1] John Pinder of Wath and James Clerkson of Weasdale were the first members. The second Meeting began shortly after at the house of Anthony Robinson of Dovengill. There were early burial grounds at Wath and Dovengill Lane Head. The Dovengill Meeting transferred to the new Meeting House at Cat Keld in 1705, on land given by Anthony Robinson. There was an attempt in 1713 to acquire a barn near the parish church for a Meeting House, but it was rejected by Quarter Sessions. The impression is that the Wath community was trying to retain a separate identity. The burial ground at Cat Keld continued till at least 1838. As with all the dale communities in the mid eighteenth century, there was serious poverty which left its mark on Quakerism. In 1793 the Meeting at Cat Keld was closed, and removed to Narthwaite. A small room was made over a byre in a barn. Occasional Meetings were held there till the end of the last century, when a Friend came up from Brigflats for the purpose. At other times the Narthwaite community went to the Methodist chapel at Cautley. The Dovengill-Cat Keld dissenting community also melted into the Primitive Methodist chapel near Dovenhill Lane foot.[2]

Grisdale and Garsdale. Fox visited Grisdale, Garsdale and Dent twice in 1652, and the first converts in Dent were Thomas and George Mason; and the first in Garsdale were James Guy, and his wife with others; in Grisdale Thomas Winn, and (Elizabeth) his wife with others.[3] From the Ravenstonedale registers Thomas was a young man, as with so many

Quakers. The Winns appear to have lived at East and West Scale at the top end of Grisdale, now desolate and forsaken. Another early convert was Richard Wilson of Knowscale, upper Garsdale. Both these families appear to have connections with Ravenstonedale, and attended the Meetings at Dovengill, as well as having one of their own at Scale. James Guy and his wife went to Brigflats, while the Masons had a small meeting at Stonehouse in Dent. The Garsdale burial ground at Dandra Garth was bought in 1699. The Garsdale Meeting house, created out of the farmhouse of John Fawcett at Birkrigg, was bought in 1703.

The Grisdale Meeting, which in the early days linked with Dovengill, was probably at Scale. According to David M. Butler it established an independent Meeting in 1690. This agrees with the early register of Grisdale, which records the birth of Richard the son of Robert and Ann Wilson on the 28th of the 1st month 1692 (i.e. March 1692) of 'Grisdale Meeting'. The burial ground at Scale was ealier; the register records the burial of Abraham Dent of Grisdale on the 11th of the 12th month 1679 (i.e. Feb. 1680) at 'Friends burial ground in Grisdale'. This is the ruined ground between East Scale and the beck.[4]

Mallerstang leaves us with unsolved questions. There were four Quaker households which attended Ravenstonedale Meeting. There were four or five which are not recorded in any Meeting, either Grisdale or Ravenstonedale. There seems to have been a Meeting from 1652 either at Shorgill (Thomas & Elizabeth Knewstub) or at Outhgill (Thomas & Dorothy Wright). They may have been disowned by the Society for conforming to the restrictions of the Conventicle Act 1664. They were certainly Quakers, but as their burial is not recorded in parish or Quaker registers, it appears that a small burial ground has been lost.[5]

Warcop. There was a small Meeting at the house of William and Isabell Skaife of Blackside (Blacksyke). In the early days they and others were members of Ravenstonedale Meeting. In 1703 his house was licensed by Quarter Sessions as a place of worship for Protestants 'defealing' from the Church of England. But the burials of a number of Warcop Quakers do not appear in the parish or Quaker registers, and it is probable that they were buried in the small presbyterian burial ground at Birks near Warcop. This was the centre of a small dissenting group operating under the Five Mile Act 1665, which left the established church in 1662. Members came from Crosby Garrett, Asby, Kirkby Stephen and as far as Swalesdale.[6]

Early Quakers in the upper Eden valley.

Ravenstonedale.

John Pinder, 1652. (F.P.T.248). Reported in Consistory Court, Carlisle, 10 Mar. 1674/5 for causing the burial of Richard Fawcett in a field. (D.R.C./5/4. Mar. 10. 1674/5. Richard Fawcett died 1673. (R. reg).

James Clerkson. 1652. (F.P.T.248) wife Isabel d. 1684. (R. reg.).

Richard Fawcett,)   Of late turned Quakers. (Ep. visit. 18. 29 Nov. 1670)
Jane Hall,   )   Jane not noted in R. reg.

James Rogerson, for not bring child to baptims. (D.R.C./5/4. 5 Jul. 1671.) Robert son of J.R. born 1669. (R. reg.)

Thomas Fawcett, for burying wife in a field and refusing to come to church. (D.R.C./5/4 Mar. 10. 1674/5.) Mary wife of Thomas bur. 1673. (R. reg.)

Jane Audley, for burying husband in a field. (D.R.C./5/4. Mar. 10. 1674/5.) No trace of Audley in parish registers. But John Handley of R. bur. 1674 (R. reg.)

Edward Newby, for burying and baptising contrary to the church. (D.R.C./5/4. Mar. 10, 1674/5.) Richard son of Edward Newby bur. 1674 (R. reg.)

Eliz. Bovell, for burying husband in a field. (D.R.C./5/4. Mar. 10. 1674/5.) Eliz. & Reynold Bovell marr. 1659. (R. reg.). She bur. 1682. (R. reg.)

Richard Adamthwaite, for burying his father William contrary to the rites of the Church of England. (Ep. visit. 18). William buried 1675. (R. reg).

Richard Adamthwaite, Reported for conducting (D.R.C./5/4. Ellen Adamthwaite bur. 1675
Richard Clerkson, illegal burials. 4 Jul. 1677) John s.o. Richard born 1677
Richard Pinder, Richard d. at Norwich. 1695
Robert Pinder, Robert not known.
James Dent, Maudlin d.o. James born 1677
(All from R. reg.)

(Note: Richard Pinder lived originally at Kirkby Stephen. In August 1673 this entry occurs in the accounts of the countess of Pembroke: 'Mrs Bridget Pinder, wife to Mr Richard Pinder of Kirkby Stephen £5.14.0 for making men's and women's gloves to give away'.)[7]

Orton

Robert Shaw, 1652. (F.P.T.248).

William Parkin & Elizabeth his wife, 1678.

Thomas Wharton, 1678. (? of Coatgill, Orton).

John Holm & Elizabeth his wife, 1678.

John Fawcett & Elizabeth his wife, 1678. (All Ep. visit. 18)

George Whitehead of Sunbiggin (? 1636-1723) D.N.B. Convinced at Capt. Ward's house, Sunnybank, Grayrigg, c. 1652. From 1652-54 attended local Meetings in Westmorland and Yorkshire. After harvest 1654 travelled to York with Edward Edwards from Gervase Benson's farm at Cautley Crag, and thus began his notable ministry.[8]

Thomas Pratt of Sunbiggin. Wife not named. He appears in the early register from Dovengill, with children Rachel 1679, Rebekah 1681, and

Elizabeth who died 1695. (R. reg). Probably the Thomas Pratt prosecuted for non-payment of tithes 1696.[9] In 1691 Anne daughter of Thomas Pratt married Robert son of Richard Wilson of Garsdale at Garsdale. (G & G reg.) Robert died 1702/3. His widow is mentioned in the wills of Richard Wilson of Knowscale 1705, and Thomas Pratt of Ellergillbeck 1704.[10]

Note: After the Kaber Rigg plot of 1663 Thomas Wharton and Reginald Fawcett both Quakers of Orton came under suspicion. They had conferred with Robert Atkinson in the early days of the plot. Wharton went with Arkinson to Harrogate to confer with Dr. Richardson one of the plotters, and then withdrew, and was still a Quaker in 1678. Fawcett a more unstable character, was disowned by the society, fled after the failure of the plot, and disappeared.[11]

Brough under Stainmore

Thomas Fairer, wife and daughter, 29 Nov. 1670. (Ep. visit. 18)

William Murthwaite, wife and son Thomas, (ibid) & son Robert (or Richard) 6 June 1677.

(Dorothy Alderson, dismissed for attending church.) (Ep. visit. 19)

Michael Aiskell (d. 1682. R. reg.) (ibid) and daughter. 9 Jul. 1673. (Ep. visit. 19) she omitted 10 March 1674/5

Isabell Aiskell presented by churchwardens 26 June 1667.[12]

John Hutchinson, 29 Nov. 1670 (Ep. visit. 19).

Thomas Airey, 6 June 1677. (Ep. visit 19).

Isabella Holliday, 24 July 1678. (Ep. visit 19).

Note: 1) It is probable that most of the Brough Quakers went to nearby Warcop.

Note: 2) In 1701 William Edmundson of Little Musgrave, the pioneer Quaker in Ireland, revisited England and held Meetings at Ravenstonedale, Kirkby Stephen, Little Musgrave, Bluegrass on Stainmore (twice), Crosby Garrett, Brough and Great Musgrave; then at Strickland Head and Pardsey Crag. It is probable that Bluegrass was the home of one of the Quakers in the above list.[13]

Kirkby Stephen.

Thomas Cleasby & Mary his wife of Stowgill. (Ep. visit. 20.)

Richard Pinder & Bridget his wife. See Ravenstonedale list. (Ep. visit. 20.)

Peter Dennison & Isabella his wife.[14] (Ep. visit. 20.)

Peter Dennison & Anna his wife. (Ep. visit. 20.) Peter died 1722 aged 105. (R. reg.)

Thomas Ewbanke (Ep. visit. 20.)

James Skaife of Nateby (Ep. visit. 20.) and of Ravenstonedale Meeting. A James Skaife marr. Agnes Harker (? Grisdale) 17.1.1676. She was bur. at Ravenstonedale 1.3.1677. A James Skaife marr. Mary daughter of John Pinder at Wath 11.3.1681. Five children recorded 1682-1687. (R. reg.)

The following were probably presbyterian dissenters:

Reginal Raickstray of Waitby. (Ep. visit. 20). Note: A John Rakestraw was hanged after the second rising of the Pilgrimage of Grace 1538.

The churchwardens' presentments of 1666 give additional dissenters.

Charles Gibson of Wharton.

Hugh Bailey of Kirkby Stephen.

Henry Waller, formerly excommunicated for contumacy.[15]

Mallerstang.

The churchwardens presentments of 1622/3 give the following:[16]

Elizabeth Grosedale of Castlethwaite, a member of Ravenstonedale Meeting. Her husband John died in about 1656 leaving a wife and three children. He made provision that 'Capptane Atkinson and Thomas Harison...be overseers for my wife and children that they be not wronged'. Agnes the eldest of the three daughters inherited the farm of 8s.9d. ancient rent on which she paid a fine of £3.10s. Her mother retained her widow's moiety for life, and died in January 1671/72 leaving a gross estate of £5.15.8. and debts of £6.9.0. She was probably buried at Dovengill.[17]

John Shaw & Agnes (Grosedale, above) his wife were members of Ravenstonedale Meeting, where their four children are registered 1669-1676. The burial of John & Agnes is not in the parish or Quaker registers and it is probable that they joined the Shorgill group for convenience, and were buried there. John died in November 1691 leaving assets of £28.3.4. and debts of £102.15.7. The inventory implies that he was fined heavily as a Quaker, and that both Friends and neighbours came to his rescue. Among the Quakers were Anthony Robinson of Dovengill £10.15.3., and John Knewstub first of Shorgill and then at Frostrow 6s. There are also 3s. due to 'Mr. Sam. Shaw' vicar of Kirkby Stephen.[18]

Thomas Wright & Dorothy his wife of Outhgill probably belonged to the Shorgill group. He may have been connected with the Rev. Rowland Wright who was at the same time chapel reader and schoolmaster. Thomas was taxed on one hearth in the Hearth Tax returns 1669-72.[19] In 1660 he in company with other Quakers (including Henry Ward of Grayrigg) was prosecuted in the Exchequer Court for refusing to pay tithes. At the same time John Fothergill, presumably of Mallerstang, was imprisoned for 14 months for the same offence.[20] Thomas is not to be confused with Thomas Wright who prosecuted Joseph Gregg of Milnthorpe in 1684.[21] His wife Dorothy is omitted from the presentments of the Carlisle Consistory Court of 6 June 1677, and was probably dead by then.[22] Thomas died in April 1678. His assets came to £11.12.2½d. and his debts to £157.5.10.[23] Among his principal creditors were Anthony ffothergill (of Ravenstonedale) £50, Mr. Robert Branthwaite, steward of Pendragon castle 17s, and acquaintances from Sedbergh, Ravenstonedale, Kirkby Stephen and Mallerstang. There were no Ravenstonedale Quakers among them.

Thomas Knewstub and Elizabeth his wife of Shorgill saw James Nayler and Francis Howgill in the autumn of 1652,[24] and among the first converts were John Fothergill and several relations of his. Thomas signed the Protestation returns of 1641[25], and was taxed at one hearth in 1669-72.[26] He was the Grave or collector of rents for the countess of Pembroke in 1667.[27] The countess made it her policy to employ men and women of differing political and religious views on her estate, such as Mrs Bridget Pinder, Mr. Robert Branthwaite at Pendragon castle, and Knewstub at Shorgill, as well as Edward Guy at Appleby. Thomas and Elizabeth Knewstub were still reported as Quakers in 1677.[28] The countess was probably rare for her time in employing any who wished to serve her, and did not intrude on their political and religious opinions. Under this shelter Thomas Knewstub seems to have kept a small Meeting at Shorgill.

John Knewstub his brother received Nayler and Howgill in 1652.[29] He was an active member of Ravenstonedale Meeting where in 1675 he married Sibil Shaw. She died in 1677, and their daughter Dorothy in 1678.[30] In 1681 he married Elizabeth Bousfield of Sedberg at Brigflats, and lived at Frostrow. She died in 1699, and he in 1712, and were buried at Brigflats. He sold his messuage at Spisers, Sedbergh to John Shaw of Spisers, who bequeathed it in 1707 to his son James. It is possible that John Shaw was a relative of Knewstub's first wife.[31] He was an active member of Brigflats Meeting.

William Shaw of Cocklaik was a member of Ravenstondale Meeting. As he does not appear in the Hearth Tax Returns of 1669-72 he may not have been a householder, or could have been a poor cottager exempt from the tax.[32] In 1700-1701 Anthony Metcalfe and Wm. Shaw of the parish of Kirkby Stephen were presented as Quakers.[33] In 1710 William Shaw was left 3s. in the Will of Anthony Robinson of Dovengill.[34] William died in 1711 and was buried either at Dovengill or Cat Keld.[35]

Henry Whitfeild junr. and his wife. The churchwardens presentments of 1677 name her as Isabella.[36] He lived at the Aisgill group of farms, and is mentioned in the 1672 assessments of households in the dale for the wages of the chapel reader-schoolmaster.[37] In 1670, contrary to the Act of 3 Charles II (which provided that no carrier with any horse or horses, nor wagon-men with any wagon or wagons, nor car-men (i.e. with small box carts on runners or wheels for carrying peat or dung) with any cart or carts, nor wain-men with any wain or wains, nor drovers with cattle or sheep shall travel upon the Lord's Day, commonly called Sunday under penalty of 20s. for every such offence,) Richard Shaw and Henry Whitfeild of Kirkby Stephen were presented at Quarter Sessions for driving sheep on that day. (Later Records: 145) They both came from the top of the dale, Henry from Aisgill and Richard probably from Hanging Lunds. They were probably standing for Quaker principle that no particular day was sacred, but that every day was a Lord's day.[38]

This concludes the churchwardens' list of Mallerstang Quakers in 1662/3. There are however two further inventories which add to our knowledge of the tenuous links with early Quakers.

(1) The Will and Inventory of Mathew Whitfeild of Aiskell dated 14th Dec. 1683 mentioned two sons, Henry and Richard. He directed that he be buried in Kirkby Stephen churchyard. He left a gross estate of £31.4s. and debts of £67.16. Among his creditors were Thomas Clemmey £3.10s., and Edmond Win £1.6s. both Quakers of Grisdale. There were eight creditors by bond ranging from Simon Cuningham £16.8s. to Christopher ffawcett £2.16s. Apart from local debts the other creditors range from Kirkby Stephen, Ravenstonedale, Grisdale and Lunds. The question remaining is: is the son Henry he who was prosecuted in 1670, and did the father bear his debts?[39]

(2) The Will and Inventory of Richard Shaw of Hinging Lunds in Mallerstang dated 1st August 1677 gives further information. The Shaw, Whitfeild and Fothergill families at the head of the dale were interrelated. It will be remembered that in 1538 Wm. Shawe of Hinging Lund was one of the Mallerstang men hanged after the Pilgrimage of Grace. Richard Shaw in his 1677 Inventory reveals links with the Fothergill Quakers of Carr End, Wensleydale. He was a bachelor, lived sparely, and had considerable monies out on loan. This is his inventory:

	L. S. D.
'Imprimus:: his purse and apparell	3. 18. 10
Itm. Books.	00. 10. 00
Itm. Linnen.	00. 5. 00
Itm. two boxes one chist.	00. 5. 00
Itm. Stockings and yarns.	00. 9. 06.
Summe	05. 00. 06
Debts owing to ye decd:	
It. by John Shaw of Molerstange	14. 10. 00
more by Jo. Shaw	03. 10. 00
It. By Sander ffothergill of Carr End in Wensadale	03. 03. 07½
It. By Tho. Whitfeild Hinging Lunds	01. 13. 03
It. By Sander Ffothergill de Carr	02. 13. 00
It. By Wm. Nealson de Gastill	19. 01. 07

It. By Jeffray Ffothergill

	02. 00. 00.
Sume	46. 01. 05
Sume in all	51. 01. 11½
ffunerall expenses	03. 00. 00
Sume declar in	48. 01. 11½

In his Will Richard requested 'my body to be buried amongst my frinds', which was unusual except he meant a Quaker burial. As there is no record of his burial in parish or Quaker registers it adds to the question whether Mal-lerstang has a lost Quaker burial ground. As this inventory may be the key to the origins of the Fothergills of Carr End, it will be dealt with separately.[40]

Warcop.

William Skaife & Isabella his wife (Ep. visit. 19. 1677)

James Skaife (Ep. visit. 19. 1670)

John Thompson

John Salkeld. (Ep. visit. 19. 1673.) His wife remained with the parish church.

Marian Skaife. (? wife or relative of James). (Ep. visit. 19. 1673).

As distinct from the York records given above, the Carlisle Consistory Court books give the following 9th July 1673. (DRC/5/4.)

John Salkeld (of Burton Par. reg. Warcop)

Wm. Skaife and wife. (in earlier records, of Bleatarn).

John Skaife

Michael Skaife

Marian Skaife.

In the returns of Quakers in Appleby gaol 1664/5 John Thompson and William Skaife were committed for not answering an indictment, or paying the fees of the Clerk of the Peace.[41] The deaths of Barbara 27.2.1686 and Mary 13.3.1686 the daughters of William and Isabell Skaife of Blackside (i.e. Blacksyke) are given in Piety Promoted.[42] As their burials do not appear in the Ravenstonedale Quaker registers, it is presumed they were buried at Birks.

William Skaife, John Skaife, Isabel Skaife, Agnes Thompson and John Thompson fined in the wholesale finings of 1684.[43]

Though in the early days the children of Michael Skaife (from 1661) and William Skaife (from 1670) appear in the Ravenstonedale Quaker births, and the burial of John Skaife of Blackside (Blacksyke) appears in 1659/60, these families do not recur in later Ravenstonedale Quaker records, and appear to have kept a separate small Meeting at Warcop.

Note: Since typing this, Mrs. Amy Fawcett of Sandford, Warcop has discovered the lintel of the old farmhouse at Blacksyke on the end of a building at the back of the present house. This stone bears the following date and initials of Isabel & William Skaife:

I.
W. S. 1667

REFERENCES CHAPTER 8

Additional abbreviations to Chapter 8 & Appendix

Besse = A collection of the Sufferings of the People called Quakers etc. J. Besse, 1753, 2 vols. Westmorland sect. vol. II, 1-36. (C.U.L. Syn.3.75. 1-)

C. & W. trans. = Cumberland & Westmorland Antiq. & Arch. Sec. N.S. XXIX, 1929, p. 1. A book of old Quaker Wills. W.C. Collingwood. Now in C.R.O. Kendal.

D.R.C. = Carlisle Consistory Court books, in C.R.O. Carlisle. D.R.C/3/4 Court Book. & DRC/5/4 Correction Book.

Ejected. = The ejected of 1662 in Cumberland & Westmorland. B. Nightingale, 2 vv. 1911.

Ep. visit. = Presentations at Episcopal Visitations in Cumberland & Westmorland. Journal of Friends Hist. Soc. ed. N. Penney, vol. VII, 1910, p. 18 eq seq.

F.P.T. = The First Publishers of Truth, ed. Morman Penney, 1907.

G & G reg. = The Quaker registers of Grisdale & Gars dale in this vol.

Later Records = The Later Records of North Westmorland or the Barony of Appleby, J.F. Curwen, Kendal 1932.

R. reg. = The Quaker registers of Ravenstonedale in this vol.

S.P. = The Calendars of State Papers, domestic,

Chas. II. 1663/4 and, P.R.O. SP. 29/98. The
examination of Robert Artinson in the Tower.

---

(1) F.P.T. 248.

(2) The Parish Registers of Ravenstonedale. Rev. R.W. Metcalfe, III, 1894. p. xxiii

The Quaker Meeting Houses of the Lake Counties, David M. Butler, Friends Hist. Soc. 1978, 158.

(3) F.P.T. 329, 333.

(4) *Garsdale*. F.P.T. 249, 254, 329, 330, 333.

Quaker Meeting houses of the Lake Counties. op.cit. 155.

Grisdale F.P.T. 249, 329, 330, 333.

Quaker Meeting Houses of the Lake Counties. op.cit. 157.

(5) F.P.T. 248.

Hist. & Trads. of Mallerstang Forest etc. op.cit. 39.

C & W trans. N.S. LIV, 176, Kirkby Stephen churchwardens' accounts 1658-1670, by J. Breay.

(6) Later Records, 30.

The first register of Birks chapel from the late 17th C. was in the possession of the late Mr. F.W. Parrott of Kirkby Stephen, and was missing at the time of his death. The copy of the second register in the P.R.O. was deposited by me in the C.R.O. Kendal.

(7) Lady Anne Clifford. G.C. Williamson op. cit. 2nd. ed. 1967, p. 509. Also on p. 508 there is an entry that Mr. Edward Guy and his wife looked after her 'garde' at Appleby, and also bought Virginia tobacco from him for her own use. She also em ployed Mr. John Thwaites and Mr. Edmund Branthwaite.

(8) The Christian Progress of that Ancient Servant and Minister of Jesus Christ, George Whitehead in defence of Truth. 1725. p. 21 (C.U.L. Ddd.3.24.)

(9) A brief Account of the many Prosecutions of the People called Quakers in the Exchequer & Ecclesiastical Courts etc. J. Besse, 1736. p. 147. (C.U.L. 8.39.11^1.)

(10) C & W trans. XXIX. 1. A Book of old Quaker Wills etc. 4 & 11.

(11) Besse II, 12. Mentions Fawcett at the trial of Francis Howgill 19. Mar. 1663/4.

MS. sources: P.R.O. (S.P. 29/94 & 29/98) Examinations of Robert Atkinson in the Tower 19 Mar, 1 May & 28 May 1664. Dr. Richardson c. 28 Mar. 1664. Surtees Soc. XL, 1861, p. 102. Depositions taken by Sir Philip Musgrave in Westmorland 1663/4 deposited in York Castle.

C & W trans. N.S. XI, 212-333. The Kaber Rigg plot 1663, a fair short summary.

C.S.P. Dom. Chas. II. 1663/4 passim gives corresp. but nothing from the depositions above.

(12) Par. reg. of Brought under Stainmore 1556-1706. H. Brierley, 1923, 218.

(13) Journal of the Life of William Edmundson. Friends Library 1833, vol. 4, 152-3.

(14) Ejected. 1091.

(15) Ibid. 1091.

C & W trans. N.S. LIV, op.cit. 176.

(16) C & W trans. N.S. LIV, op.cit. 176.

(17) Will of John Grosedale 30. Aug. 1656, proved at Appleby 4 Sept. 1661.

Inventory of Elizabeth Grosedale widow of Mallerstang, 16 Jan. 1671/2

Both in C.R.O. Carlisle.

This work vol. I. chapt. 25 ref. (3) The Mallerstang admissions 1657.

(18) For the placing of Mallerstang tenants in 1672 see: Hist. & Trads. of Mallerstang Forest etc. op.cit. 36/7.

Inventory of John Shaw of Castlethwaite, 4 Nov. 1691, C.R.O. Carlisle.

(19) Later Records. 145.

(20) Besse II, 8.

(21) Besse II, 29.

(22) D.R.C./5/4. 6 June 1677.

(23) Inventory of Thomas Wright of Outhgill 19. Apr. 1678. C.R.O. Carlisle.

(24) F.P.T. 248. He is bound to have been present when his brother John received them.

(25) Protestation Returns of N. Westmorland, op.cit. 17.

(26) Later Records 145.

(27) C.R.O. Kendal. Appleby castle estate accounts, 1667. fol. 4. WD1H/Box 23.

(28) DRC/5/4. 6 July 1677.

(29) Not to be confused with John Knewstub of Hinging Lunds. Hist. of Forest of Mallerstang. op.cit. 37, 95.

F.P.T. 248.

(30) All in R. reg.

(31) C & W trans. N.S. XXIX, 1929. Quaker Wills & Contracts. op.cit. no. 15. Will of John Shaw of Spisers, 1 May 1707. Now in C.R.O. Kendal.

R. Reg.; from regs. of Sedbergh M.M. & Westmorland Q.M. for details of Elizabeth & John Knewstub.

(32) Later Records. 145.

Hist. of Forest of Mallerstang op.cit 37. He does not appear in the list of households supporting the chapel Reader 1672.

(33) Kirkby Stephen parish regs.; bishop's transcripts 1700-1, C.R.O. Carlisle.

(34) C & W trans, N.S. XXIX, Quaker Wills etc. op.cit. no. 18. Will of Anthony Robinson of Dovengill 1710. and C.R.O. Kendal.

(35) R. reg.

(36) DRC/5/4. 6 June 1677.

(37) Hist. of Forest of Mallerstang. op.cit. 37.

(38) Ejected. II, 1358. 29 Nov. 1670.

(39) C.R.O. Carlisle. Will of Mathew Whitfeild of Aiskell. 14 Dec. 1683.

(40) C.R.O. Carlisle. Will of Richard Shaw of Hinging Lunds. 1 Aug. 1677. See appendix to this chapt. 8 for Fothergill of Carr End.

(41) His. MSS. Comm. Rep. XIII, part vii, Earl of Lonsdale's MSS. p. 92.

(42) Piety Promoted. 1789. I, 143 & 145.

(43) Besse II, 35.

APPENDIX TO CHAPTER 8.

The Fothergills of Carr End, Wensleydale.

One of the unsolved questions in Quaker history is the origin of John Fothergill (I) of Carr End, whose initials 'J.F. 1667' appear on the stone lintel of the garden door. As well as in other places, the principal settlements of the Fothergill family may be found by the sixteenth century in Settrington, York, Swaledale, Wensleydale, Mallerstang and Ravenstonedale. There have been several statements on the origin of John Fothergill of Carr End, none backed by evidence.[1] Indeed that even his family did not know the answer is proved by the letter of 1776 from Alexander Fothergill of Carr End to the Fothergills of Ravenstonedale seeking some clue.[2] The lack of proof in the assertions of writers can be illustrated by the following from James Hack Tuke:

> 'Suffice for us, for the purpose of this sketch, is the fact that a John Fothergill migrated thence (from Mallerstang) to Counterset in Wensleydale, and afterwards to Carr End soon after the year 1600.'[3]

(1) What are the facts? John Fothergill appears as the rebuilder of Carr End in 1667. He was then a widower with one child Alexander. He was probably a Quaker by 1667, and became a member of Wensleydale Meeting centred on Counterset. Richard Robinson and John Fothergill were imprisoned for the non-payment of church rates in 1678.[4] This lasted for two years at Richmond.[5] Fothergill does not seem to have been a preacher. He died in 1684. 'John Fothergill the elder of Carr End died the 30th of the 2d month 1684 and was buried the day following in the burying place of the people of God at Bainbridge.'[6] His Will was dated 30th May 1683, and proved at Richmond 22 May 1684. His goods and chattels were valued at £116.11.8d. His son Alexander was made sole executor and legatee.[7]

(2) What substance is there in James Hack Tuke's generalities?

(a) There is evidence that there were trading or family links between the Fothergills of Southwaite, Mallerstang and the Parkin and Hamond families of Wensley, and the Robinson family of Askrigg in the late sixteenth century. The Will of John Fothergill of 13th January 1591/2 (probably of Southwaite) and inventory of 17th January 1591/2 notes the joint debt of 'William Robinson of Askrige, Ric. Hamonde & Leonarde of Wensley jointly together of £6.13.4d.'[8] There was a fourth debtor Rolande Parkin of Helbecke Londs (Lunds) who

owed 25s. There were strong connections between families in Wensleydale, Lunds, Mallerstang and Kirkby Stephen as can be seen in the Abstracts of Abbotside wills (1552-1688).[9] They and the parish registers of Wensley support this point.[10]

(b) The lordships of Wensleydale, Middleham and Richmond were in the early seventeenth century the property of the Crown. The manor of Wensleydale was till the dissolution the property of Jervaulx Abbey. These lordships were surveyed in 1605, and in Counterset, part of the manor of Bainbridge, there were eleven named tenants, 7 Metcalfes, 3 Harisons and 1 Ingram.[11] This illustrates the point seen in Mallerstang that dales families were still concentrated on their ancient lands, though the old farms had been divided. There was no Fothergill in this list.

In 1628 the manor and forest of Wensleydale was granted by Charles I to the City of London in satisfaction of certain loans to the Crown. On the 9th November 1663 the manor of Bainbridge (including Counterset and the township of Hawes) was sold to the freeholders. The eleven principal inhabitants of the townships within the manor acted for all the tenants, and Richard Robinson signed for Counterset.[12] The Records Office of the Corporation of London has a large number of deeds relating to these land sales (1658-1663), and though there are a number of purchases involving Anthony Fothergill of Burghill, and Abraham Fothergill of Barnards Inn, London, jointly, Anthony Fothergill alone, and Abraham Fothergill alone, there is no reference to John Fothergill of Carr End.[13] The family at Burghill and that at Carr End were separate. No books of admittances have been found in the P.R.O., the Guildhall Records, in several Yorkshire record offices, nor with the local trustees.[14] Thus we are left with the presumption that John Fothergill came to Carr End by purchase or Marriage.[15]

(3) Two facts suggest a future line of enquiry:

(a) John Fothergill's only child was named Alexander. Up till then in the dales' communities Christian names were usually handed on from grandparents to grandchildren; it is a constant which is helpful (tho' not infallible) in tracing family lines. If John Fothergill (I) came from Deepgill in Mallerstang he would know the Birkbeck family which were the progenitors of the Birkbecks of Settle. John Birkbeck of Deepgill (1604) was the son of

Alexander Birkbeck of Bluegrass (1582). Whether the family came from Orton or Brough under Stainmore is not known, but the name Alexander was used by the Birkbecks of Brough. When John Fothergill and Jane Birkbeck, both of Deepgill, married in 1656 the families had a stronger link.[16]

(b) Another line of evidence comes from Counterset itself, where the Metcalfe family was very strong.[17] At the time of John Fothergill (I) there were Alexander Metcalfes senior and junior. If John Fothergill (I) had married a Metcalfe daughter whose family used that name, it would be quite usual to call his son Alexander, after his wife's family. Unfortunately as the parish registers for Aysgarth for that period are lost, the point cannot be proved. Yet there is a stronger point: When John Fothergill (I) made his will in 1683 he empowered his son Alexander to nominate one or more persons to administer his estate in his stead, should his son be deemed incapable of acting on his own. The letters of administration issued by the Archdeaconry Court of Richmond dated 22 May 1684 are signed not only by Alexander Fothergill but also by Alexander Metcalfe. If Metcalfe was not a Quaker it would ensure that John Fothergill's Will was not interfered with, say, by a rival member of the Metcalfe family, if Carr End had originally been a Metcalfe farm.[18] Alexander Metcalfe had also been a witness to the Will; he may have been uncle or cousin.

When Alexander Fothergill and Anne Langton were married at Brigflats on 8th of the 1st mo: 1673/4 (Q.S.), among the immediate family witnesses were Thomas and Alexander Metcalfe. Among the secondary witnesses were John and Francis Blaykling, Lawrence Routh of Hawes, James Guy of Garsdale and an unknown John Fothergill[19]

When Alexander Fothergill made his will 28th September 1695 (O.S.) he committed the guardianship of his son John Fothergill (II) 'to my cozen James Metcalfe' (of Counterset) and John Blaykling (of Sedbergh.)[20]

I submit that the Metcalfe connection is the stronger.

(c) Returning to the 1677 list of debtors to the estate of Richard Shaw of Hinging Lunds of Mallerstang we read as follows:

John Shaw of Mallerstang	£14.10.0.
John Shaw of Mallerstang	3.10.0.
Sander ffothergill of Carr End	3.3.7½.
	2.13.0.
Tho. Whitfeild Hinging Lunds	1.13.3.
Wm.Nealson of Gastill (Garsdale)	19.1.7.
Jeffray ffothergill	2.0.0.[21]

John Shaw of Castlethwaite, and Agnes Grosdale his wife were members of Ravenstonedale Meeting for many years. He died in 1691 leaving debts of £102.15.7.22

Alexander Fothergill: His father John was imprisoned at Richard 1678-80. Was this a farm or family debt?[23]

Thomas Whitfeild of Hinging Lunds was not a tenant in 1672. But he was one by 1681 when he and Richard ffothergill of Uthgill signed a bond on the 23rd Ju: (June or July) to repay £5.6.0. to Stephen Dent of Lithside, Ravenstonedale by the 11th November following.[24] Thomas Whitfeild, sen: of Hinging Lund Dikes died in February 1683/4. He owned four kine, and one old mare. His gross estate came to £10.13.4. and his debts to £10.14.4., leaving a debt of 1.4d. He owed James Skaife (the Quaker of Nateby) 4s., and Edmond Winn (the Quaker of Grisdale) 5.6d. Thomas Whitfeild's widow Isabell by a power of attorney dated 5 May 1684 (O.S.) placed the proving of her husband's Will in the hands of 'my trustie and welbeloved freind' Hugh Shaw of Molerstang. Isabell made her Will on 19th Nov. 1692 (O.S.) which was proved 20th June 1694. In it she left five legacies totalling 18s., with the residue to her daughters Margaret and Janet.[25]

William Nealson of Garsdale is not in the list of Garsdale Quakers, but there were members of that family of Brigflats Meeting.

Jeffray ffothergill was, with William Birkbeck, Thos. Wharton and Brian Hugginson one of the four tenants of the Deepgill farms.[26] John Fothergill of Deepgill died in 1661. His wife was Jane Birkbeck of Deepgill whom he married in 1656, and by whom he had five children, Jeffrey, Thomas, John, Isabell and Margaret. When Jeffrey inherited the farm he was just a child. Thus these four names are on the borders of Quakerism, and the link of Sander Fothergill with Richard Shaw at a distance of at least 15 miles point to a possible family link with Mallerstang. With the large number of Fothergills in the dale it is unwise to press the point further without evidence.

(4) When James Nayler and Francis Howgill preached at Shorgill in the late autumn of 1652 there was 'a very large Meeting, & many were convinced, & particularly John ffothergill & several relations of his'.[27]

There were two John Fothergill tenants in 1652, John of Castlethwaite and John of Deepgill. John of Castlethwaite has probably been the one who in 1663 was involved in the Kaber Rigg plot, tried for treason and acquitted in

1664. He was probably a Presbyterian supporter of Robert Atkinson.[28] As we have seen, John of Deepgill married a Birkbeck (progenitors of the Birkbecks of Settle) in 1656, and died in 1661. He may well have been the convert of 1652. This however does not remove the possible link of John Fothergill (I) of Carr End with Mallerstang. Given that Alexander would have been at least 21 in 1674, and born at least before 1653, we are looking for a John Fothergill born about 1630 or earlier, a period for which the parish registers of Kirkby Stephen are lost. Remembering that younger sons would not inherit a farm, and have to make their way in the world, we are looking for a John who left home, either as a shepherd, an apprentice, or a soldier during the civil wars. As there is a curious silence in the family and Quakers as to the origin of John (I) of Carr End one wonders why. He was not the Colonel John Fothergill of Sudbury an ardent Calvinist who ruled that part of Suffolk from 1650-1660; he was probably descended from the family at Tarn House, Ravenstonedale. Despite the uncertainties I look for some link between Deepgill and Carr End, bearing in mind the Birkbeck link. That John of Carr End could rebuild his farmhouse in 1667 points to some substance, perhaps through the swift growth of cattle-droving. His inventory mentions that he had 65 little Scots sheep. The drovers went past his house from Bainbridge over the Stake to Wharfedale. The question is open.

REFERENCES – APPENDIX to CHAPTER 8

(1) Principal refs:

Old Yorkshire, ed. William Smith, London 1883, vol. 4. 133-141.

Dr. John Fothergill F.R.S. by James Hack Tuke. He also quotes from Drake's Eboracum for the early hist. of the Fothergills.

Biographia Borealis, By Hartley Coleridge. London 1833, p. 694.

Dr. John Fothergill etc. Repeated in Northern Worthies by Coleridge Vol. III, 1852, 341.

Dr. John Fothergill & his friends, by Dr. R.H. Fox, 1919, 4-8

(2) The Fothergills of Ravenstonedale. C. Thornton 1905, 20.

(3) Old Yorkshire ed. Smith, above. 133-141.

(4) Besse II, 143.

(5) F.P.T. 313/14. says 3 years.

Reg. of Richmond Monthly Meeting in P.R.O. RG6/1281, p. 568. The imprisonment of Richard Robinson & John Fothergill of Carr end, 1678-80.

(6) P.R.O. RG6/1403. Reg. of Wensleydale Monthly Meeting 1653-1784. The same reg. has the death of Richard Robinson of Counterset 31 of 10 mo. 1693 (Q.S.) and burial the 2nd of the 11th mo. following.

(7) Will of John Fothergill of Carr End 30 May 1683 (O.S.) at West Yorkshire Archives, Leeds District Archives. The parish regs. of Aisgarth of this period are lost.

(8) C.R.O. Carlisle. Will of John Fothergill of Mallerstang (Southwaite or Castlethwaite) 13th Jan 1591/2. Fothergill left a handfast wife Christian Guy; and an Edmond Guy was admitted to a tenement of 8/3½d. old rent by assignment of a John Fothergill of Southwaite in 1587. See this work vol. I. chapt. 14. The 1604 survey under Southwaite.

(9) Yorkshire Arch. Soc. Record Series, vol. CXXX, 1967. "Abstracts of Abbotside Wills (1552-1688) ed. H. Thwaite. See Will of Richard Blyth of Low Helm, 4 Dec. 1678 where he leaves a whye worth £2.10s. to Elizabeth Fothergill of Castlethwaite.

(10) Yorkshire parish reg. Soc. vol. 108. Parish regs. of Wensley 1538-1700 pub. 1939. There was a John Fothergill who produced Christopher 1584 and Ralph 1586.

(11) Yorkshire Arch. Soc. Record Series vol. CIV, 1941.

Three Seventeenth Century Yorkshire Surveys, ed. T.S. Willan & & E.W. Crossley, p.109 (111) 3. Counterside.

(12) The Parish of Askrigg, co. Yorks including Low Abbotside & Bainbridge. Rev. C. Whaley, 1890, p. 64.

V.C.H. North Riding of Yorks. 1969 vol. I. 209 the sale of parcels of the Lordship of Middleham 1654-1663. p. 206 the sale of the manor of Bainbridge 1663.

(13) Letter of the Deputy Keeper of the Records, Records Office, Guildhall, London 7 Aug. 1985.

(14) Letter of Willan & Johnson, Solicitors of Hawes, (Mrs. J. Winston) 14 Oct. 1985.

(15) The parish regs. of Aisgarth for this period are lost.

(16) This work vol. I. chapt. 14. John Birkbeck of Bluegrass bought a fourth part of Deepgill for his second son Geoffrey, who admitted tenant 1604.

c.p. Parish regs. of Brough under Stainmore op. cit, passim.

(17) Ref: (11) above.

Alexander Metcalfe of Counterset married Margaret Langton of Height of Winder in the house of Francis Blaykling at Height of Winder, 3rd. of 5 mo. 1684 Q.S. (P.R.O. RG6/1246).

(18) Ref. (7) above, probate and admon. 1684.

(19) Journal Friends Hist. Soc. vol.XXXIII, 1936. p. 68. Marriage cert. of Alexander Fothergill & Ann Langton.

(20) West Yorkshire Archives, Leeds District Archives, Will & Admon. of Alexander Fothergill of Carr End, 28 Sept. 1695.

(21) This work vol. II, chapt. 8 ref. (40)

Hist. of Forest of Mallerstang op. cit. 36-7 for tenants of 1672.

(22) This work vol. II chapt. 8. ref. (18).

(23) This appendix, ref. (5)

(24) MS of Mr Gordon Dent of Flintergill, Dent 23 Ju: 1681. By permission.

(25) C.R.O. Carlisle.

7 Feb. 1683/4 Inventory of Thomas Whitfeild sen. late of Molerstang.

5. May 1684 Power of Attorney of Isabell Whitfeild appointing 'my trustie and welbeloved freind Hugh Shaw of Molerstang' in the proving of the Will of her late husband Thomas Whitfeild.

19. Nov. 1962 Will of Isabell Whitfeild of Hingand Lund dykes; probate 20 June 1694.

(26) Hist. of Mallerstang Forest op. cit. 37.

(27) F.P.T. 248.

(28) C & W trans. N.S. XI. The Kaber Rigg Plot 1663. p. 228/9.

CHAPTER 9

Persecution

England was declared a free commonwealth on the 29th May 1649, the Protectorate in December 1653. On the 1st March 1649/50 the House of Commons established a commission to govern the four northern counties under Sir Arthur Haslerigg. The Westmorland members were Gervase Benson, John Archer, Roger Bateman, Edward Briggs, Richard Branthwaite and Richard Crackenthorpe. Lord Wharton as a London member of the commission kept in touch with parts of the county both through the vicars of Kendal and Kirkby Stephen, and Benson and Branthwaite, the latter being his steward at Ravenstonedale. The Kendal committee based on the borough had existed during the civil wars; Branthwaite and Crackenthorpe represented the north of the county. In the upper Eden valley, which is our concern, major Arthur Skaife, lieutenant Robert Atkinson, and perhaps colonel Richardson of Crosby Garrett, became the military force behind the new order. Skaife was made a magistrate. Of the three Atkinson was the more variable character. Before the defeat of the royalists he had worked for them, and figures in a list of 25 April 1650, of local men being fined by the Committee for Compounding for their recent activities:

Rob. Atkinson, Kirkby Stephen	£45.
Ant. Knipe, Fairbank	£6.
Miles Halhead, Underbarrow	£4.10.0.
Wm. Spencely, Kirkby Stephen	£6.
John Petty, Soulby	£6.17.6.
John Fothergill, Ravenstonedale	£17.10.0.[1]

As Skaife was the chief sequestrator in the district, and as Atkinson was made a lieutenant of militia in about 1651 and placed in charge of the small garrison at Appleby castle 1651-2 there had been some quick re-thinking on his part.[2] At the same time Lady Anne countess of Pembroke was beginning her great Chancery case against all her tenants in north Westmorland in which her chief antagonist was Robert Atkinson; the case lasted till 1657.[3] Therefore, apart from national politics, and new men assuming control of the county in the name of Parliament, north Westmorland was in a state of high ferment, and it was an open question as to which way radical opinion in the dales would go, bearing in mind that the predominant culture was puritan and biblical, and that many sons of the dalesmen had learned new ideas in Cromwell's army.

The response of Cromwell as Protector to the rise of Quakers, Ranters, Seekers, Familists, Levellers and others with religious ideas was summed up in his proclamation of 15th February 1655 announcing his intention to enforce the law against disorders in religion. The vitriolic denunciation by the Quakers of ministers as hirelings, and deceivers, and their interruption of preachers in their churches had provoked disorder. As the free dispensation of the Gospel had been dearly bought at the price of much blood, the Protector felt himself obliged to protect that freedom, and that this freedom did not extend beyond the bounds of Christian love and moderation. He referred to the late disturbances by Quakers and Ranters, and strictly required that these should cease, and that magistrates should proceed against those breaking this peace. In addition the Quaker practice of refusing hat-honour, and for not finding sureties for good behaviour, and refusing to pay gaolers' and clerks' fees increased the irritation of local magistrates.[4] Cromwell aimed, therefore, at a moderate toleration of the protestant religion within the bounds of public order. But this moderation was something the Quaker could not accept, if he felt that Truth demanded a direct attack on deceivers and their steeple-houses.

During the Commonwealth about 3,173 Quakers suffered in prison up till 1660.[5] As far as the London authorities were concerned it was for causing public disorder, and not for religion. To the convinced Quaker there could be no temporising. William Penn put it thus before his committal to Newgate in 1670:

'I would have thee and all men know, that I scorn that Religion which is not worth suffering for, and able to sustain them that are afflicted for it; and whatsoever may be my Lot for my constant Profession of it, I am no ways careful, but resigned to answer the Will of God, by the Loss of Goods, Liberty and Life itself. When you have all, you can have no more, and then perhaps you will be contented, and by that you will be better informed of our Innocency. Thy religion persecutes, and mine forgives: And I desire my God to forgive you all that are concerned in my Committment, and I leave you in perfect Charity, willing your everlasting Salvation.'[6]

So convinced were the Quakers of their rectitude, that 32 died in gaol during the Commonwealth.[7] The educated response of a man like Penn was one thing; the effect on unstable characters was another. John Gilpin of Kendal attended a Quaker Meeting in the town in May 1653 led by Christopher Atkinson, who rejected all ministerial teaching, and worldly knowledge, and urged all to wait on the Inward Light of Christ. After a third Meeting where neither Light nor trembling occurred Gilpin retired home to his bedchamber to read a tract, which so affected him that he fell on his bed, trembling and quaking, howling and crying. He believed this to be the pangs of new birth, that he was now a fit messenger to attack all ministers as false prophets, and priests of Baal. After three days of this religious dementia he imagined this to be a spiritual marriage and union with Christ. After a fifth Meeting attended by John Audland he was persuaded to stay behind; he fell twisting and turning to the ground, and remained there all night. Next day, when two swallows came down the chimney he thought them to be angels until they flew away. He was forced by the same power to his knees in the street, where he licked the dust, and, watched by several of the brethren, he danced several capers. They urged him: 'Be lowly, mind thy condition, and harken to the voice within'. That night when he was taken home and was alone, he thought he heard a voice urging him to take a knife to bore a hole in his throat, that he might receive the Word of Life. Being frightened by this deluded instruction, he threw the knife away. Feeling that he had been tempted he called aloud to God to deliver him. His wife, being in bed, heard his call and persuaded him to go to bed. Next day, after a wakeful night, he went in his shirt through the streets followed by his wife who with the neighbours forced him home to bed. There he continued his topsy-turvy capers on the beds. Seeing two butterflies in the window he seized one and swallowed it. After more bedroom capers he lay down and began to reflect on the events of the past days, and persuaded himself that he had been deluded by devils. On this he turned to a quaker and accused him of possession by devils, who in turn began to quake and tremble. This bedlam scene continued awhile, and eventually he calmed down and was persuaded to announce that the devil had appeared to him as an angel of light, and the quaker madness subsided. His carefully written confession and warning against novelties contained the unlikely Latin text: Turpius ejicitur, quam non admittitur.[8] The quaker fraternity immediately issued a tract accusing him of drunkenness. Gilpin's tract was issued under the approval of the mayors, ministers, schoolmasters and alderman of Kendal and Carlisle, and was a useful weapon against the ranting element of Quakerism which Fox did so much to control. It helps us to understand Cromwell's proclamation of February 1655, and the sincere belief of the Puritans that the new movement was possessed by devils.

As far as Westmorland was concerned the principal ground of fining and imprisonment was refusing to pay tithes, speaking to a priest in public, and interrupting a church service.

In Westmorland, between 1652 and 1660, a number of Quakers fell foul of the church for refusing to pay tithes; on claims of £36.8.5. cattle, corn and other goods were distrained worth £140.12.4. This was to be an oft repeated tale that the goods taken far exceeded the sum required. Of the twelve named by Besse, William Hebson of Sleagill was imprisoned forty weeks, John Fothergill, probably of Mallerstang, fourteen months, in addition to William Cartmell of Warth Sadden, and Mabel Camm of Preston Patrick. Henry Ward of Grayrigg, and Thomas Wright of Mallerstang were sued in the Exchequer court for tithes, and had goods distrained. In 1653 Thomas Taylor was imprisoned at Appleby for speaking in church, and released in 1655. He was again imprisoned with his brother Christopher, and Anne Airey at Appleby from 1657-8 for speaking to a priest. Both Thomas and Christopher wrote tracts from gaol complaining of their treatment, and the bitter persecution by George Beck the gaoler.[9] Thomas Taylor is perhaps the most interesting and learned man, a student of the mystical writings of Jakob Boehme a number of whose disciples became Quakers. Before he became a Quaker Taylor avowed intense hatred of bells, bonfires, maypoles, dancing and other amusements. He endured further confinements at York, Leicester, Coventry and Stafford where he died in 1682.[10]

In 1656 Thomas Alexander, and Richard Hebson of Newby were gaoled at Appleby for speaking to a priest. 'They were cruelly beaten and abused by the unmerciful gaoler, insomuch that the said Richard Hebson, being put out of prison, in a few days after died of the hardships there received.'[11] Apart from the issue of tithes, prosecution followed the tenor of Cromwell's general instructions of 1655. Given the disturbed condition of the times, and the wildness of a few, these instructions seem to have contained Quakerism within due bounds.

Shortly before the Restoration there was a national move by Quakers to have some magistrates appointed who were not so oppressive of the movement. Four persecutors were named for Westmorland, among whom was Robert Branthwaite, a strong Calvinist related by marriage to Francis Higginson vicar of Kirkby Stephen.[12] When between 1660-61 the countess of Pembroke restored Pendragon castle in Mallerstang she installed Branthwaite in the castle as her steward, much to the fury of Sir Philip Musgrave, who wrote to Secretary Williamson complaining that Captain Branthwaite who had served Parliament had been placed there. There is a refreshing independence in many of lady Anne's appointments; she seems to have done her best to heal old wounds.[13] Branthwaite remained there until his wife threw herself off the castle roof, after which he lived at Castlethwaite, near a number of Quakers.[14] Henry Ward of Grayrigg was one of those proposed for the magistracy.[15] In the autumn and winter of 1659 the northern castles were occupied by Parliamentary forces, and lady Pembroke had to endure soldiers at Appleby, Skipton and Brougham.[16] Prior to the Restoration parliamentary elections were held in April 1660, and in August the same year there was a general meeting of northern Quakers at Skipton, mainly to deal with the supply of money.[17]

The Restoration.

Any chance that the Quakers would receive a measure of toleration after the return of the King in 1660 was blighted by the rising of the Fifth Monarchy Men in January 1661, when they proclaimed King Jesus in London and a few northern towns. This so alarmed the King and his ministers that a proclamation was issued to the constables of all parishes that 'there be no numerous meetings of Quakers, Sectaries or other disaffected persons', with the result that there was a general round-up of Quakers through the kingdom. In Westmorland the magistrates Sir John Lowther, Sir Philip Musgrave, and Sir Daniel Fleming acted speedily, and 52 were lodged in Appleby gaol, and 64 in Kendal. A few days later James Ducket of Grayrigg caught some more attending a Meeting at Captain Ward's. He and Peter Moser were among a further nine lodged at Appleby.[18] It is no coincidence that Henry Ward and a Roger Moser were tenants in the Monsier (i.e. Moser) v. Ducket Chancery case of 1636.[19] Also Peter Moser was sued by the vicar of Kendal for his Easter Offering in 1660. He was imprisoned until the vicar persuaded his mother to pay 40s. for his release.[20] It is claimed that there were about 4,000 Quakers in English gaols at this time.[21] It is certain that the leaders of every Westmorland Meeting, Preston Patrick, Kendal, Strickland Head and Ravenstonedale were removed to gaol during the period of this alarm.

The Kaber Rigg plot 1663.

In July 1663 an anabaptist under examination before lord Falconbridge told him that the next month there would be a rising of the old presbyterians in the north, combining the Quakers and Scots.[22] This was confirmed by an unsigned letter to Secretary Bennett in the same month, and that the Quakers to a man were wholly behind it, with other sects and disbanded soldiers.[23] It is possible that the presbyterian faction mentioned the Quakers to divert attention from themselves. Nevertheless the authorities had three months' warning of small dissident groups in Westmorland, Durham and Leeds, and were ready. On the 30th September 1663 the countess of Pembroke received a visit at Skipton from Philip lord Wharton and his three daughters. They stayed two nights, and left for Helaugh near Tadcaster on the 2nd October. The information he gave her seems to have alarmed her to the extent that within four days she packed her trunks and on the 6th she drove in her coach from Skipton to Kilnsey, and on the following day over Buckden Rakes to her cousin Mr. Thomas Metcalfe at Nappa. On the 8th she drove past Hawes, up Cotterdale, over the fell road to Hellgill Bridge, and down the old Roman road into Mallerstang to Pendragon Castle.[24] It must have been a very uncomfortable coach ride. She was within half a mile of Robert Atkinson at Bluegrass.

The object of the plot was to capture Hull and Appleby castle, and the local royalist magistrates, and restore a gospel magistracy and ministry. On the night of the 12th October Atkinson left Bluegrass, and going by way of the Scotch alehouse at Ravenstonedale, through Smardale, and probably through Soulby and Beckfoot, arrived at Birka near Duckintree at Kaber Rigg late at night. The large force which he had been half promised from Yorkshire and Westmorland never materialised, and with only 30 supporters Atkinson and Captain John Waller of Mallerstang saw that their position was hopeless, and ordered everyone home, hoping that they had not been seen. By the 26th Sir Philip Musgrave had rounded up all the plotters and lodged them in Appleby gaol, from which Atkinson escaped a few days later. Francis Howgill was in gaol at the same time. So convinced were the magistrates that the Quakers were involved that by the 12th November 12 were in Appleby gaol, out of 463 arrested in other parts of the country, with 27 under sentence of praemunire.[25] Thomas Wright the Quaker of Mallerstang was one of the suspects; and Richard Robinson of Counterset in Wensleydale, who was in London at the time that the City was selling the manor of Bainbridge to the tenants, was held for a month and closely examined.[26] In the barony of Kendal 50 more were arrested and committed to the assizes at Lancaster.[27] George Fox first heard of the plot at York, and after service in Yorkshire and Durham he rode over Stainmore to Sedbergh and Swarthmore.[28] In order to bear some of the fury directed against the Quakers he allowed himself to be arrested and committed to the sessions at Lancaster.[20] He also wrote a tract 'to stop all forward, foolish spirits from running into such things. I sent copies of it into Westmorland, Cumberland, Durham and Yorkshire', and to magistrates and the King.[30] They were bitter days for Quakers. The principal attack came from Sir John Lowther against Strickland Head Meeting. Between the 8th November and 13th March 1663/4 Strickland Head Meeting was raided

by Sir John six times, and the leaders fined at the sessions. Thomas Langhorne senior and junior of Heltondale, Edward Guy, and John Bolton of Appleby, and John Salkeld of Warcop were among them.[31] Sir Philip Musgrave wrote to Secretary Bennett in January 1664 and said: 'Many suspected persons were bound and are continued; many Quakers are indicted for their meetings. They are a very dangerous people and I hope will not have encouragement as formerly. I find so many rogues among them as they expect no kindness from me.'[32]

At least three Kaber Rigg men were convicted at the Appleby assizes in March 1664, and hanged. John Fothergill of Mallerstang was acquitted; five fled; two turned King's evidence; three others were acquitted, while Atkinson ended up in the Tower, where he was examined several times. He was returned to the north in August, and was condemned at the Appleby assizes opening on the 20th August. The countess of Pembroke made this entry in her diary: 'Robert Atkinson one of my Tenants in Mallerstang, and that had been my great Enemy, was condemned to be Hanged, Drawn and quartered, as a Traitor to the King for having had a hand in the late Plot and Conspiracy; so as he was executed accordingly the first day of the Month followinge.'[33] His farm at Bluegrass was forfeit to the countess for treason; but his widow Jane Atkinson and their children remained, and paid a rack rent of £6.10.0. thereafter.[34] His son became butler to lord Tufton. As Mallerstang and Ravenstonedale had been at the centre of the rising, the Quakers had to ride out the storm as best they could. They were bitter days, when any hope of toleration was dashed by these events. An example comes from the churchwardens' accounts of Kirkby Stephen. With the exclusion of some puritan ministers who would not subscribe the Act of Uniformity 1662, there was a number who reduced to beggary. In 1667 the wardens gave 2s. 'To a poor minister'.[35]

REFERENCES CHAPTER 9

(1) C.S.P. Committee for Compounding. 1650. vol. GCCL. p. 203. 25 April. nos. 30, 31, 32, 33, 34, 35, 42, 43, 44, 45, 48, 49, 54, 55.

(2) This work vol. I. Chapt. 23 Refs: 26-29; and Lady Anne Clifford, G.C. Williamson, 199.

(3) Ibid. vol. I. chapt. 24. P.R.O. S.P./C.21/P.25/1. Anne countess of Pembroke v. Robert Atkinson & others 1650-51.

(4) F.P.T. 350.

(5) Fox's Journal op.cit. I, 522.

(6) Besse II, 435.

(7) Fox, Journal I, 522.

(8) The Quaker Shaken, or a Warning against Quaking. A tract of five parts, the first concerning the conversion and recovery of John Gilpin. London 1655. (C.U.L. Dd^x.3.26^9(E)).

See also the Thomason Tracts.

In the same vein, the delusion of Martha Simmonds and James Nayler: George Fox and the Valiant Sixty. Elfrida Vipond, 1975. 85 et seq.

(9) Besse II, 6-8. Christopher Taylor was also imprisoned at Appleby in 1654.

(10) D.N.B. Thomas Taylor 1618-1682.

F.P.T. 253 etc.

The Beginnings of Quakerism, Wm. C. Braithwaite op.cit. 360 et passim. Persecution Expounded in some Memoirs relating to the Sufferings of John Whiting & other Quakers. 2nd ed. 1791. 352 (C.U.L. Ddd.3.17).

(11) Besse II, 6.

(12) Extracts from the State Papers, ed Norman Penney & R.A. Roberts, 1913. 112. (Hereafter: Extracts.)

(13) Hist. of Mallerstang Forest op.cit. 37.

Later Records. 140.

(14) Hist. of Mallerstang Forest. 31.

(15) Extracts 111.

(16) Diary of Lady Anne, Williamson MS. 71.

(17) Extracts 118. The meeting at Skipton 11th of 8 mo. 1660. Q.S.

(18) Besse II, 8/9 & 9/10.

(19) This work vol. I. chapt. 22. ref. (25). Transactions of the High Court of Chancery both by practice and precedent. W. Tothill 1671. p. 164.

(20) Besse II, 10.

(21) V.C.H. Yorkshire III, 66.

Second Period of Quakerism. Wm. C. Braithwaite, 1979. ed. 9.

King Charles II, Arthur Bryant 1932, 132.

(22) Extracts, 150.

(23) Extracts, 171.

(24) Diary of Lady Anne Clifford. Williamson MS 102.

(25) C & W trans. NS. XI, 212. The Kaber Rigg plot.

C.S.P. Dom. Chas. II. 1663. p. 347. LXXXIV, 23 Nov. Sir P. Musgrave to Williamson.

Surtees Soc. XL, 1861. 102 Depositions from York Castle.

Second Period of Quakerism. Wm. C. Braithwaite. 29.

Extracts 165. Information dated 1st of 11 mo. 1662/3 Q.S.

This work vol. II, chapt. 8, ref. (11).

(26) Thomas Wright: Surtees Soc. XL, 1861. Depositions in York Castle. p. 107.

Richard Robinson: C.S.P. Chas. II. 1663. p. 338. LXXXIII, 13 Nov. His Examination.

(27) Extracts 177 & 185/6. C.S.P. Chas. II, 1663/4. p. 433. XC, 7 Jan.

Sir Daniel Fleming to Sec. Williamson.

(28) Journal II, 14.

Journal. ed. J. Nickals 1975. 452/3.

(29) Journal II, 18-22. Extracts 186.

(30) Ibid. II, 20.

(31) Besse II, 13.

(32) Extracts 186. Sir P. Musgrave to Sec. Williamson 13. Dec. 1663.

C.S.P. Dom. Chas. II, 1663/4. XC, 441, 14 Jan. Sir Philip Musgrave to Secretary Williamson.

C & W trans. NS. XI. The Kaber Rigg plot, 220.

(33) Diary of lady Anne Clifford. Williamson MS. 110.

(34) C.R.O. Kendal. Demesne rents of Appleby castle 1667/8. WDIH Box. 23.

(35) C & W trans. NS. LIV, 1954. Kirkby Stephen churchwardens' accounts 1658-1670. J. Breay 181.

CHAPTER 10

Persecution.

The two events of 1661 and 1663 recorded in the previous chapter were to colour the treatment of the Quakers for the next twenty-five years. Besse has recorded the many acts under which they were prosecuted.1 The Kaber Rigg plot of 1663 had links in Durham, Yorkshire, Bristol and other parts. Apart from the few hanged at Appleby 21 suffered in Yorkshire.2 Francis Howgill in Appleby gaol remarked that so many of his acquaintances were inclined to it, whom he could not support, neither reject as friends.3 Before we list the vicious attacks made on the Quaker communities, it should be remembered that it was a time of reviving trade; between 1st August 1662 and 1st August 1663 no less than 26,440 Scottish and Irish beasts crossed the border into Cumberland alone. Sir Philip Musgrave who had the grant of the tolls calculated that, at 8d. a head, he was able to put £882 into his pocket.4 On the strength of this increased prosperity many of the fellside farmers pulled down their old cruck-framed farmhouses, and built new homes with stone mullioned windows with glass to the upper floors. Most of them were probably still thatched with seaves; slabs and slates did not come into use till the nineteenth century. The Quakers took advantage of this prosperity, as witness the homes of Richard Robinson at Counterset, the Winns at Scale in Grisdale, and the Fawcetts at Dovengill. It is therefore worth remarking that the majority of the fellside farmers were too busy repairing their damaged economy after the disasters of the Common-wealth to be too concerned with plots.

The chief result of the 1663 rising was the Conventicle Act of 1664 which came into force on 1st July, and was to last three years. It abrogated some of the provisions of the Quaker Act 1662, reduced the powers of juries, and gave more to two justices acting without a jury. In the new act any person over the age of sixteen who attended a conventicle under colour of religion of more than five persons than the household was guilty of an offence. Now two justices could convict and imprison on a first and second offence for three and six months. For a third offence Quarter Sessions or Assizes could impose transportation for seven years. The Act could be extended for a further three years till March 1669.5 The chief persecutor in north Westmorland was Sir John Lowther. In May 1664 he had obtained the conviction of 16 Quakers at Appleby; and two Kendal Quakers, suspects after the Kaber Rigg episode were arrested and gaoled at Appleby.6 In this year 1664 ' the Mayor of Kendal caused the goods of many inhabitants of that town to be distrained for their absence from public worship; but when their goods were exposed to sale, the neighbours would not buy them, nor could the justices get them sold at any rate, till by bidding for them themselves, they animated some mean people to buy them at a very low price. About the same time William Cartmell and his wife, Edward Burroughs, Robert Atkinson, Rowland Warriner, William Mansergh, and Dorothy Lorimer were committed to prison.'7 Three were still in gaol on 18th March 1664/5.8

(A) Sir John Lowther was not slow in attacking the Meeting at *Strickland Head.* On the 24th July 1664 Anne Whinfell of Shap, Issabell Whitehead of Shap, Elizabeth Gibson of Shap, Anne Arey of Taylbert, and Mary Robinson of Cliburn were arrested under the new act and imprisoned at Appleby.9 Within a short time a further thirty-two were rounded up at Strickland Head and fined for the first offence. Among them was John Bolton of Appleby.10

By March 1664/5 the following were in Appleby gaol:

John Bolton (Bongate) Committed by order of Sessions upon the third offence.
Anthony Bownass (Shap)
Thomas Langhorne (Helton)
Robert Bowman (Bampton)
Elizabeth Holme (Sleagill)

72

Richard Barrick (Shap) Edmund Robinson (Newby) Robert Winter (Morland Edward Winter (Morland)	Committed for five months upon ye second offence, and remayned 2 monthes more then there tyme for the Clerk of ye Peace fees.
John Robinson (Cliburn or Newby) John Thompson (Warcop) William Skaife (Sandford, Warcop)	Committed upon a Sessions Utlawry and refused to submit or traverse to ye Indictment & pay the Clerk of ye peace fees.

Kendal Quakers:

William Cartmell (Preston Patrick) Elizabeth his wife Edward Burrow (Burrough. Underbarrow) William Mansergh Robert Atkinson (Middleton) Rowland Warriner	Committed by Allan Bellingham, Dan. ffleminge. James Duckett & Nicholas ffisher Esqrs. for refusing either to submit or traverse to the Indictments.
Michaell Langhorne (Askham)	Committed by Sir John Lowther Barron. for refusing to find security for his appearance and good behaviour.

ffrancis Howgill (Grayrigg)
& Wm. Hebson (Sleagill)
upon another account.[11]

The majority of the prisoners are from Strickland Head Meeting. The two, Skaife and Thompson from Warcop is the first notice of prosecution of that community and may mark the establishment of a separate meeting by that date. Of John Robinson Besse says that he was committed on false information, not having been at the meeting he was accused of.[12] Michael Langhorne wrote a long letter of 28th November 1664 to Sir John Lowther saying that he was taken to prison on the 8th June, and during his absence Guy Coperthwaite and John Jackson had come to his house, taken away his goods and threatened the people of Askham with their staves. They claimed a warrant of the justices for removing his goods. At a later meeting Coperthwaite confessed that Jackson an informer was the prime mover. Langhorne asked Sir John if a writ of distraint had ever been issued by the justices, and if not seeking redress.[13] He was still in gaol the following March.

There are two pieces of evidence illustrating the severe persecution suffered by the Strickland Head Quakers.

(1) Samuel Bownas was born at Great Strickland in 1676, and was placed on the register of that Meeting. His father died before he was one month old. He had suffered imprisonment, and had his goods distrained as some Meetings had been kept at his house. Samuel's mother was left with a cottage, two children and £4.10s. a year. At the age of 13 he was put to the trade of a blacksmith, with an uncle who used him hardly. Later he went to be apprenticed to a Quaker at Brigflats, Samuel Parat, where he was kindly treated, and from whence he eventually was called to be a travelling preacher. But he recalled that while still a child at Strickland:

> 'Persecutions being still very hot, and Friends lock'd out of our Meeting-house at Strickland, we met at the Door; and I remember at two several times when I was a child, and came to Meeting with my Mother, that the Informers came; the first Time the Meeting had been over about half an hour, the second Time not quite so much, so that we escaped their Hands both Times; but sundry Friends were in Prison at Appleby for attending that Meeting, whom my dear Mother went to visit, taking me along with her, and we had a Meeting with the Prisoners, several Friends from other Places being likewise there by Appointment. What I observed was, though very young, how tender and broken they were; and I was very Inquisitive of my Mother, why they cried so much (which we call Greeting) and 'thee greet too, (I said) why did Thee?' She told me that I could not understand the reason of it then, but when I grew up more to Man's Estate I might.'[14]

(2) After the passing of the second Conventicle Act of 1670 some of the severities of the 1664 Act were reduced, but greater powers were given to those suppressing conventicles. It resulted in dozens of Quakers being fined for attending meetings, and their goods being distrained regardless of poverty. One of the

leading informers against the Strickland flock was John Jackson, who appeared in the case of Michael Langhorne. According to Besse over twenty Quakers were fined on the word of informers. A few will suffice:

Anthony Bownas of Shap was fined £2.15s. for himself and others; they took two kine, one steer, and a little heifer worth about £7. At several other times for fines of £2.15s. they took goods worth £3.6.4d.

John Bolton of Bongate, Appleby was at several times fined 45s. for himself and others. His son, not being a Quaker, paid the fine, being unwilling as constable to take his father's goods away.

Thomas Langhorne sen. of Helton was fined 30s. for himself and others, and had a cow worth 40s. taken.

From Thomas Langhorne jun. of Helton; they took three stone of wool, and two brass pots worth £1.6.8.

Edward Guy of Appleby was fined several times for being at Meetings, £5.5s. And for part of a fine on the house where they met he was further charged £6.10s. For the former fine they took household goods worth £9.15s. and for the latter they seized his shop goods, but forgot to carry them away.

The more vicious side of these persecutions can be seen in the fate of Richard Simpson of Bampton Scar; for his fine of 10s. they took away his working tools as a plasterer. John Brown a carpenter of Askham had his working tools taken away several times.[15] There were more serious cases in other parts where a sick man, or a woman with child had most of the bedding and furniture removed. Besse added this remark about the informer:

'There was one John Jackson who acted the part of an Informer on every Act against the Quakers; it was observed, that notwithstanding his ill-gotten Gain that way, he was reduced to such extream Poverty as to beg his Bread.'[16]

So great was the suffering in the northern counties that in 1671 the London Quakers collected £80 and sent it north by the hands of James Moore. £30 was allocated to Westmorland and the same to Cumberland. The Quarterly Meeting at Kendal allocated it thus:

Strickland Head Meeting	£14.
Sedbergh Meeting	£6.
Underbarrow Meeting	£6.
Newton & Powbanke Meeting	£4.[17]

That gives the measure of the attack against the Strickland Head Meeting.

(B). Ravenstonedale Meeting. Ravenstonedale being a liberty derived from monastic days, and under the independent jurisdiction of lord Wharton, it is an open question as to whether the early Quakers had an immunity from attack. Wharton owned the impropriate tithes, appointed and paid the curate. In general, Quakers objected to paying tithes to impropriators as well as ministers. It is possible that the Ravenstonedale leaders were rounded up in 1660, and after the Kaber Rigg episode of 1663. There is no reference to any Ravenstonedale Quaker in the early pages of Besse, though in 1664 John Thompson, Michael and William Skaife of Warcop, members of Ravenstonedale Meeting, were imprisoned at Appleby. But they lived outside lord Wharton's jurisdiction, and by then may have had their own Meeting. As lord Wharton had given shelter to Christopher Jackson the Calvinist rector of Crosby Garrett after his ejection in 1662, and allowed him to erect a chapel at Ravenstonedale it is probable that he sheltered both the Quaker and the Presbyterian dissents provided they lived peaceably with their neighbours. The answer to our question probably lies in the career of the Revd. Thomas Dodson who was curate of Ravenstonedale from 1628 to 1673. Ordained episcopally, he accepted presbyterianism during the Commonwealth, and subscribed the Act of Uniformity in 1662. Though he took part in the attack on Fox in 1652, he was not in a position after 1662 to attack the Presbyterians or Quakers who differed from him.[18] On his death, and the appointment of a new curate the atmosphere changed.

On the 9th July 1673 William Fothergill of Adamthwaite, and Richard Clerkson (both of Ravenstonedale) were presented to Quarter Sessions for not bringing their children to church for baptism. On the 10th March 1674/5 Edmund (Edward) Newby was presented for burying and baptising contrary to the rites of the Church of England. On the 14th April 1675 Thomas Fawcet was presented for burying his wife in a field. On the 10th November 1675 Richard Adamthwaite was presented for burying his father William contrary to the rites of the Church of England.[19] Readers of chapter 8 of this volume 2 will find that they had already been presented in the Carlisle Consistory Court for these offences. These five belonged to the Ravenstonedale Meeting. In 1676 twelve members of Strickland Head were fined and distrained for refusing to go to church. In addition Thomas Cleasby and William Moorthwaite of Brough, and James Skaife of Nateby were fined similarly.[20] Moorthwaite and Skaife belonged to Ravenstonedale Meeting.

But the churchwardens of Ravenstonedale did not support these presentments:

> On the 21st April 1676 the Quarter Sessions ordered that the constable of Ravenstonedale should attach Robert Shaw, Henry Bousfield, Richard Alderson and Christopher Todd, the former churchwardens of Ravenstonedale, and bring them before the next Justice of the Peace to enter recognisance for their appearance at the next Quarter Sessions to be held at Appleby on the 8th May next. They were indicted for failing to deliver a list of all such persons who neglected to attend their parish church.[21]

In 1678 thirty-six Westmorland Quakers were fined under the Elizabethan statutes (23 & 28 Eliz.) against Popish recusants. For total fines of £22.12.2½. goods to the value of £43.5.5. were taken. James Clerkson, John Pinder, and Anthony Robinson, leaders of the Wath and Dovengill Meetings were fined £1.19.4., and had goods worth £4.12.0. taken.[22] Peter Moser of Grayrigg, and Thomas Langhorn of Heltondale were of the number.

In the same year a further forty-one Quakers had goods seized through Exchequer process, either for failing to pay tithes or church dues, to the value of £27.12.6½. Among them were Thomas Langhorne of Helton, William Cartmell of Preston Patrick, Richard Clerkson, Anthony Pinder, and Thomas Fawcett of Ravenstonedale, Michael Aiskell of Brough, John Thompson and William Skaife of Warcop, Edward Guy and John Bolton of Appleby.[23] In addition, twenty Quakers who attended a meeting at Bowness on the 15th November 1678 had goods and cattle worth £96.1.8. taken. A Meeting of fifteen who met at Heversham on the 13th October had goods and cattle worth £68.5.6. taken.[24] Besse gives more names. It is sufficient to say that every magistrate in the county attacked each Meeting nearest to him with harsh cruelty during this bitter year 1678. So it went on in greater or lesser degree year by year. In May 1682 Joseph Gregg of Milnthorpe was imprisoned five years in Appleby gaol for refusing to pay tithes. In 1684 Elizabeth Braithwaite a girl of 17 was imprisoned for eleven weeks and died there.[25] Perhaps the most astonishing direction came from the warrant of Edward Wilson, a Westmorland magistrate, against nine Quakers who had met on the 1st October 1684 in the parish of Beetham. After ordering the constables and churchwardens of each parish from which the offenders had come to levy the fines on goods and chattels, 'In case you cannot, by reason of Poverty, levy all the fines as before directed,

you are authorised to levy such in Arrear by Distress and Sale of the Goods and Chattels of any other Offender or Offenders above mentioned, provided you levy not above ten Pounds of any Person aforesaid for another's Offence.'[26] There was another wholesale fining of all Quakers in 1684; in a list of 57 fined under the Elizabethan Acts against Popish recusants the following names recur: John Bolton (Appleby), James Clerkson, Richard Clerkson, Thomas Fawcett, William Fothergill (Ravenstonedale), Michael Eskill (Brough), Edward Guy, Katherine Guy (Appleby), Isaac Handley, Anthony Pinder, Anthony Robinson (Ravenstonedale), Thomas Langhorne (Heltondale), John Skaife, Isabel Skaife, William Skaife, Agnes and John Thompson (Warcop). Besse concludes his list of sufferers in Westmorland with a list of all those farmers who had corn, hay and goods taken out of their fields in lieu of tithes between 1681 and 1690 to the tune of £359.16.5.[27]

The most moving manuscript remaining from this period is the 18th century copy of the customs and rules of the manor of Ravenstonedale dating from 1586, with later additions. It was written out by James Bayliff in 1738. He had married a Quakeress who died in 1730. He concluded his copy with the full text of the Toleration Act of May 24 1689.[28]

(C) Though the Toleration Act of 1689 gave freedom of worship to dissenters on certain conditions, it excluded Roman Catholics and disbelievers in the Trinity. Dissenters who took the Oaths of Allegiance and Supremacy, and Quakers who made their Affirmations instead of the Oaths, were relieved of the statutes against conventicles. Though dissenters were barred from civil office till 1828, their ministers were relieved of religious disabilities provided they signed the Thirty-nine Articles except the two requiring infant baptism.[29] But the issue of tithes remained. From 1652 *Grisdale* Quakers were closely linked with Ravenstonedale. The Book of Sufferings from the Westmorland Quarterly Meeting at Kendal records that on the 4th of 9th month 1703 Q.S. the principal Quakers of Grisdale, Garsdale and Dent were summoned by the tithe farmers of those three places before the justices of the peace for Yorkshire sitting at Thornton in Wensleydale for refusing to pay tithes, and church dues. The tithe farmers were Richard Trotter, Jonathan Rose and Anthony Ward. We will deal with the Grisdale and Garsdale Quakers only. The justices issued warrants for the recovery of tithes to the farmers, and church dues to the vicar of Sedbergh, by distress together with costs. The following table summarises the evidence:

Date Q.S.	Name	sum charged	costs granted	value taken
4.11 mo. 1703	*James Harker* of Grisedale for tithe & Easter reckonings etc for the farmers.	2.3.5.	10s.	
	And 1 year's tithe & reckoning	1.2.11½	10s.	
	And for communicants (money) for ye priest,	0.0.6.	. . .	
	was taken from him by Richard Nelson ye informer, Edw. Guy constable, John Blads & James Tenant warden,			
	Two cows & two young bease to ye value . . .			7.10.0.
Ibid	*Edmond Win* (as above)	1.18.3½	10s.	
		0.16.11	10s.	
		0.0.9.	10s.	
	Two cows worth . . .			5.10.0.
Ibid	*Robert Aikrigge* (as above)	1.10.9.	10s.	
		0.13.10½	10s.	
			10s.	
		0.0.6.		
	Two cows & one heffer worth . . .			6.15.0.
Ibid	*John Win* (Tithes)	0.1.9.	10s.	
	Money in the house . . .			1.2.6.
Ibid	*Thomas Clemey* (as above)	1.10.9	10s.	
		0.16.10½	10s.	
	Two cows & one heffer worth . . .			6.0.0.
Ibid	*Thomas Win* (as above)	0.1.3.	10s.	
		0.10.1½	10s.	
		0.0.6.	10s.	
	One cow & some wool.			3.8.0
4.11 mo. 1703	*John Hodgson* of Grisedall. (Tithes)	0.13.3.	10s.	
		0.5.10½	10s.	
	One cow worth . . .			2.14.0
Ibid	*Elinor Dawson widow* (as above)	1.2.3.	10s.	
		0.15.7½	10s.	
		0.0.10½	10s.	
	Two cows worth . . .			5.5.0.
Ibid	*Michaell Dawson*	1.3.1.	10s.	
		0.10.0½	10s.	
		0.0.6.	10s.	
	A cow worth . . .			2.10.0.
Ibid	*William Lambert* (place not given) (as above)	0.11.7.	10s.	
		0.4.6.	10s.	
		0.1.4.	. . .	

	Two cows worth . . .			3.15.0.
4.11.1703	*Robert Dent of Garsdall.* (as above)	1.18.3.	10s.	
		0.19.10½	10s.	
			10s.	
		0.0.9.		

One cow & one mare worth . . .   6.10.0.
Ibid   *Richard Wilson or Garsdall* (priest's dues).   0.0.6.   10s.

Pewter & bedding worth . . .   0.11.0.
Ibid   *Richard Wilkinson of Garsdall.* (as above)   1.5.9.   10s.
                                           0.14.4½ 10s.
                                           0.0.10½ 10s.

Two cows worth . . .   5.5.0.
Ibid   *Jno. Raw of Garsdall.* (as above)   1.18.3.   10s.
                                           0.16.10½ 10s.
                                                 10s.
                                           0.1.4.

One mare & one cow worth . . .   6.0.0.
Ibid. 1703   *Edward Raw of Garsdall* (as above)   1.3.3.   10s.
                                           0.15.1½ 10s.
                                           0.1.0.   10s.

One cow & one heffer worth . . .   4.10.0.
Ibid   *John Brown of Garsdall* (as above)   0.12.5.   10s.
                                           0.11.1.   10s.
                                           0.0.6.   10s.

Two bease worth . . .   4.10.0.
Ibid   *John Holme of Garsdale* (Tithes)   0.6.0.   20s.

One beast worth . . .   2.0.0.
Ibid   *George Holme of Garsdall.* (Tithes)   0.2.10.   20s.

One beast worth . . .   1.15.0.
Ibid   (George Capstacke of Dent had a beast
         worth £2.12.6. taken for tithes.)
31 o   11 mo.   The following Quakers of Grisdale, Garsdale
1705   & Dent were summoned to appear before
         two justices at Ingleton on the complaint of
         Jonathan Rose priest of Sedbergh and the
         tithe farmers for tithes and church dues, and
         had goods distrained with costs as above:
         Robert Dent, Garsdale.
         Ann Wilson, Garsdale
         Richard Wilkinson, Garsdale 1708.
         Thomas Harrison,
         Edward Raw,
         John Raw,
         John Capstack,
         Michaell Dawson, Grisedale.
         Robert Aycrigge, Grisedale.
         Elinor Dawson,
         Edmond Winn, Grisedale.
         James Harker, Grisedale.

Thomas Win, Grisedale.
Thomas Clemy, Grisedale.
John Win, Grisedale.
William Lambert, Grisedale.
Thomas Pratt,
Thomas Blayklinge,
John Shaw,
John Atkinson,

The Quakers of Grisdale and Garsdale were again sum moned to Ingleton and fined in 1706 & 1707. In the 1708 lists appearing at Ingleton John Hodgson of Garsdale appears. The costs charged in 1707 and 1708 are in the 5s. range.[30]

REFERENCES CHAPTER 10

(1) Besse, I, viii-lv.

(2) Second Period of Quakerism. Wm. C. Braithwaite, 39

(3) Ibid. 31.

(4) Hist. of Cumberland. R.S. Ferguson, 1890, 264.

(5) Second Period of Quakerism. op.cit. 40.

(6) Extracts 213-4. Sir Daniel Fleming to Sec. Williamson. May 1664. Later Records 27/8.

(7) Besse II, 17.

(8) H.M.C. E. of Lonsdale's MSS. Rep. XIII, app. part vii, 90. The undated list of 19 Appleby prisoners is probably that of 18. Mar, 1664/5 in a letter of John Thwaites, clerk of the peace, to Sir John Lowther in: C.R.O. Carlisle, D/Lons/L.13/I. In a bundle of Quaker Papers 1661-1664/5.

(9) C.R.O. Carlisle. E. of Lonsdale's MSS. D/Lons/L. Signed declaration of Sir Philip Musgrave, Sir John Lowther, John Dalston, & Edward Nevinson, 29 July 1664, committing 5 women to prison.

(10) Besse II, 17.

(11) C.R.O. Carlisle E. of Lonsdale's MSS. D/Lons/L. The places of origin of the prisoners are taken from H.M.C. E. of Lonsdale's MSS. Rep. XIII. app. part vii, 90-91. Ref. (8) above.

(12) Besse II, 17.

(13) C.R.O. Carlisle, E. of Lonsdale's MSS D/Lons/L. 28 Nov. 1664. Letter of Michael Langhorne of Askham from Appleby gaol to Sir John Lowther.

(14) Account of the Life, Travels and Christian Experiences of Samuel Bownas, 2nd. ed. 1761, p. 2. (C.U.L. 0.21.51.)

(15) Besse II, 19/20.

(16) Ibid. 20.

(17) C.R.O. Kendal. Accounts & Memoranda & Minute Book of Westmorland Quarterly Meeting 1658-1699. (93) Ref. WDFC/F/1. p. 37. Meeting on 7 of 2 mo. 1671 QS.

(18) Ejected of 1662. op.cit. 1101. Dodson was succeeded by Anthony Proctor, M.A./1673-1689.

F.P.T. 248, 272.

(19) Later Records. 223.

This work vol. II, Chapt. 8, under Ravenstonedale.

(20) Besse II, 23.

C.R.O. Kendal, WDFC/F/1/(51D). p. 183. Book of Sufferings Westmorland Quarterly Meeting, presentments from Ravenstonedale, Brough & Orton 1676-7.

(21) Later Records, 223.

(22) Besse II, 24.

(23) Ibid. 24/5.

(24) Ibid. 26/7.

(25) Ibid. 29/30.

(26) Ibid. 32.

(27) Ibid. 36/7.

(28) MS. copy of the Custome & Orders of the manor of Ravenstonedale written 2 Aug. 1586, and copied by James Bayliff of Ravenstonedale 1738, in the possession & by permission of Mr. C. Hollett of Sedbergh.

(29) Oxford Dict. of Christian Church. F.L. Cross, 1957, 1365.

(30) C.R.O. Kendal. Records of Westmorland Quarterly Meeting. Ref: WDFC/F/1 (51D). 4. 11 mo. 1703. and (p. 138) 31 of 11 mo. 1705. Q.S. Book of sufferings 1703-8. These lists of Garsdale & Grisdale Quakers are given to tie with the names which occur in the following registers.

CHAPTER 11

Testimony for Truth.

A modern reader of the two previous chapters has every reason to be astonished that, despite the wildness of some early Quaker invective against the clergy, and much that was wrong in the old systems of land tenures, and the worldliness of the church, the church should be so vindictive against its enemies. In truth, once the Quaker testimony against tithes was accepted, the old system of financing the established church would collapse. On the other hand an endowed parish ministry was one way of avoiding the preacher's begging bowl. Given good arguments on both sides, George Fox's claim that as Christ gave his Gospel freely, it should be given freely by its ministers, was incontrovertible. Compare these two documents:

(1) From the rector of Lowther to Sir John Lowther, May, 1664: 'This may certify your worship that John Wilkinson alias Crag of the Parkfoot hath not been at his parish of Lowther these four sundays last past, and so desire that the statute in that behalf provided may be executed upon him etc. William Smith rector ibid. Christopher Holm Churchwarden ibid. X his mark.'[1]

(2) George Whitehead and others writing in 1680: "We desire you to judge, whether these cruel and uncharitable proceedings of these clergymen towards us are consonant with the practice of the Ministers of Christ in the primitive times, or answer that Meekness and Christian Spirit manifested by them, in Instructing those that opposed, and not seeking to Destroy and Ruin them and their families, because they could not receive their Doctrine.'[2]

Richard Wilson of Knowscale, Garsdale, was an early convert to Quakerism. He may have come from Ravenstonedale, as he and his wife Katherine were members of the Dovengill Meeting from 1654/5. They appear to have travelled past Scale in Grisdale the home of Thomas and Elizabeth Win, and with them over the fells to Dovengill for their regular meetings. Initially, and for many years there was a small Meeting at Scale, but their chief source of strength was that at Dovengill. In

1660 Richard Wilson was among 209 Yorkshire Quakers who refused to take the Oath of Allegiance. In 1668 Thomas Winn and Richard Wilson had goods taken worth £3. for refusing to pay church rates.[3] In 1672 Richard was among 37 Yorkshire prisoners discharged under the General Pardon by the King's Letters Patent.[4] Thus even in this remote dale, the Quakers, no matter how humble, did not escape prosecution. The Quaker registers of Ravenstonedale and Grisedale which follow give the circumstances of the family. Richard & Katherine Wilson had the following children:

> Robert, born 1654/5, died 1702 or 1703.
> Peter (1), born 1656.
> Peter (2), born 1658.
> Thomas, born 1661.
> Richard, born 1664.
> Elizabeth, born 1667. (? bur. at Brigflats 1683).

The eldest son Robert was married 27th of 3rd month, 1691 Q.S. to Ann the daughter of Thomas Pratt of Sunbiggin, Orton. Thomas was a member of Ravenstonedale Meeting, who was prosecuted in 1696 for the non-payment of tithes.[5] Robert and Ann Wilson bore the following children:

> Richard, born 1692.
> Katherine, born 1693.
> Thomas, born 1693/4.
> Ann, born 1696.
> Hannah, born 1696. d. by 1705.
> George, born 1697. d. 1705.
> Robert, born 1699.
> Peter, born 1700, d. 1701.
> Isabel, born 1701, d. 1702/3.

This was an alarmingly large family to be raised on a small fellside farm. Disaster struck when Robert died in 1702/3 leaving a widow and five or six children. In the previous chapter[6] we read that in 1703 Richard Wilson was prosecuted by the vicar of Sedbergh for refusing to pay 6d. priest's dues. The justices charged 10s. for collecting it, and took pewter and bedding worth 11s. to discharge it. The financial position must have been grave. Richard Wilson made his Will in February 1705 and attempted to make the best out of limited resources. He was buried at Scale in Grisdale on the 2nd of the 7th month 1706 Q.S. His widow Katherine was buried there on the 24th of the 3rd month 1709 Q.S. By the time that Richard's Will was made another grandchild Hannah had died, leaving five.

In 1706 the young widow Ann was prosecuted at Ingleton by the tithe farmers; and for refusing to pay 16.11d. small tithes, with costs of 8s. a cow worth £1.11.0. was taken.[7] She was again fined in 1708 at Ingleton for refusing to pay small tithes of 7.3½2d.. and costs of 5s. and had a heffer worth £1.16.0. taken.[8]

In his Will of 27 Feb. 1705 Richard Wilson left his farm in Garsdale to his daughter-in-law Ann to use the profits towards the education of his grandchildren until the youngest reached the age of 21, with the exception that his widow Katherine should have his house for life, together with an annuity of £5 payable out of the farm. If Ann should fail to pay, Katherine may enter the lands and occupy them for the rest of her life. His two trustees were Christopher Mason of Cawgill, Dent, and Richard Wilkinson of Garsdale, both Quakers. They were empowered to use the profits of the farm to educate and maintain the grandchildren Richard, Thomas, Robert, Katherine and Ann until the youngest be 21. He left the farm to his two grandchildren Richard and Robert when the youngest of his grandchildren should reach the age of 21, on condition that Richard and Robert pay £40 between the remaining grandchildren. If either Richard or Robert should die before the age of 21, then his grandson Thomas shall take that half share, and the half share of the raising of the £40. To his son Richard he left 20s. to be paid if he came to claim it. Otherwise there was no mention of his children. So grave was his financial position that his moveable assets came to £9.11.11. and his funeral expenses 15.3d. The small sum represents his few cattle, sheep and hens, and means that they were almost destitute.[9]

In the light of the fate of the Wilson family, and of the finings given in the last chapter, there is no wonder that many dalesmen abandoned the financial and sacramental system of the old church, and embraced a free non-sacramental Christianity. This is referred to in the Epistle of the Yearly Meeting of 1764 subscribed by John Fothergill, M.D., Clerk to the Meeting:

'When ... about the Middle of the last Century,

these Nations were made as a Field of Blood, and Terror and Distress filled ever Corner of the Land; the Lord Almighty having secretly wrought, by the Spirit of His Son, in the Hearts of the People, to prepare them for further Manifestations of His Light and Truth, many were shaken from early Dependences, and engaged to look, for Succour and Support, to that Arm of Power which made and sustains all Things ...

This heavenly Virtue of the Word of eternal Life, thus wrought to the Sanctification of Individuals, and prepared many of them, as chosen Vessels to bear the Lord's name, and publish, from living Experience, the Power and All-sufficiency of that Truth, in which they had most surely believed. They were sent forth .. with Spirit and with Power, to call others who were asking the Way to Zion ...'[10]

Very soon after Fox's first convincements at Firbank in 1652 he wrote a letter to a small group of Friends established in the Brigflats district. It contained two principal points, Waiting upon God in the true Shepherd, and in minding purity:

'Everyone in your Measure wait upon God, who is the true Shepherd, and leads his Flock into green Pastures, and fresh Springs he opens daily: this ye will see and experience. And mind that which is pure in one another, which joins you together; for nothing will join, or make fit, but what is pure; nor unite, nor build, but what is pure. Therefore every particular, fear God; for whatsoever ye build (of yourselves) will not stand, but will tumble down again; Therefore wait every one in the Measure, which God hath given you; and none of you be Sayers (only) but Doers of the Word: And so, walk in the Truth, and be ye all Servants to it, and it will lead you out of the World.'[11]

We are here dealing with early idealism, not the later period when the Quaker merchants in the market towns incurred the wrath of Cobbett, that while waiting for the Spirit they were not above speculating in corn,[12] and had become fat in the land. Early Quakerism is remarkable for the heroic idealism in young men and women from the dales. In this spirit they exhibited a remarkable faith.

(a) In May 1701 Agnes the wife of Edmund Winn of Grisedale died sixteen weeks after the birth of a child. We can almost see her husband laboriously writing out these words in his farmhouse kitchen:

She 'was very weak at the time as to hir

outward body but exceedingly opn harted unto God whereby she received in that time great strength from God to shew forth his prais and often exhorted hir family to feare God with large promes there upon she gave hir family much swet advise and the day she dyed she had a desire to see hir children al that she might tak hir live of them and desiered of God to bles them al.'[13]

(b) in 1715 John Close, a young man of Grisedale felt moved in the humble Meeting house hard by the beck near Moor Rigg to leave the dale to visit meetings in Cumberland. The entry in the register puts its thus:

'John Close of Grisedale departed this life the 27th of the 11th month (1715) at Alenby in Cumberland and was buried in friends burying place att ye s'd Alenby the 29th of ye same. The said John Close was gone abroad in Truth's serves and being taken with the small pox in his journey was taken away by the same.'[14]

One can feel the sadness of that fellside farm, that they would see his face no more.

(c) 'In the year 1652, was *Richard Pinder* of Warth (Wath) in Ravenstonedale convinced, and about the year 1657 was called into the works of the ministry, and laboured much in many countreys, as Scotland, England, and two several times in Amirica, as particularly Barbadoes, Bermudas, New England, Jamaica, and severall other plantations, where he had considerable service.'[15]

He visited Scotland in 1657 at a very disturbed time. One sabbath at East Kilbride he addressed the assembled congregation before the arrival of the minister. He was arrested and imprisoned at Rutherglen. On the following sabbath he was put into the stocks for five hours outside the kirk. After this he was handed from constable to constable till he was finally bundled over the border into Cumberland. Those 'powerful threshers of the Word' the Scottish ministers, did not care to be addressed by these striplings from the northern dales.[16] From 1659 he was in the West Indies from which he published four tracts.[17] He appears to have returned to England in 1663 and married soon after; he and his wife Bridget produced four children between 1664 and 1671. From 1663 he and a number of Ravenstonedale Friends appear to have done much to support Francis Howgill and others in Appleby gaol. It is not clear whether Richard lived at Ravenstonedale or Kirkby Stephen. He was one of the signatories of the Epistle of the 1675 Yearly Meeting in London, which among other matters requested the keeping of records by Quarterly Meetings of all who had suffered for the cause.[18] His final writing seems to have been a Testimony to the life of William Dewsbury, published in 1689.[19] Richard died in Norwich on the 20th of the 10th month 1695. Q.S. and was buried there.

(d) *John Fothergill*, the son of Anthony of Trannahill, does not appear in the Quaker register of Ravenstonedale, though I have included his death. He may have been related to George Fothergill, who at the time was vicar of Orton.[20] He illustrates the point that many younger sons on the dales' farms had to leave home, and make their way in the world; this would account for his omission from the register of the Meeting.

'In that meeting called Ravenstonedale Meeting was that yonge man, called John ffuthergill, Trannahill, called early into the worke of the ministery, and richly furnished for the same, and laboured much in London and severall other parts of this nation, and continued faithful unto the end of his time in this world, died in London, the 25th day of ye sixth month 1665.'[21]

Besse gives four men who died in prison in 1665, including Fothergill. He was arrested in a Meeting at Guildford, and committed to prison in Southwark. After several months he died of fever in August 1665.[22]

(e) There are two additional Ravenstonedale names on overseas service. In 1689 *John Pinder* was in Maryland. On 7.11.1689 Anthony Pinder of Parrackmoor, yeoman, gave a receipt for £5. received from Richard Murthwaite of Rigg End, and George Murthwaite of Wath for the whole rent of Parrackmoor for 1688 and 1689 belonging to John Pinder. As there were two Johns in the Protestation Returns of 1641/2, a John son of Anthony born in 1657, and John son of Richard born in 1668 it is impossible to identify the John in Maryland in 1689. He may have been the John Pinder who received Fox in 1652;[23] that is more likely.

The other was *Anthony Robinson* of Dovengill. In 1701 William Edmundson of Little Musgrave returned from Ireland, and held Meetings at Kirkby Stephen, Little Musgrave, Crosby Garrett, Stainmore and Ravenstonedale. After visiting Appleby and Strickland Head 'Anthony Robinson came to us, he being newly arrived from Ireland'.[24] Anthony was the leader of the Dovengill Meeting. His manuscript register is in the Library of Friends' House, Euston Road, London.[25]

(f) After the first generation of Quakers had

died out, and after the Act of Toleration of 1689, though prosecution for tithes was as vigorous as ever, some Quaker communities seem to have been exhausted. Certainly the wide scattering of Quakers in the upper Eden valley seems largely to have dissolved. After the deaths of John Pinder, James Clerkson, and Anthony Robinson there are signs that Ravenstonedale Meeting was in difficulties. There is a total absence of recorded births for Ravenstonedale Meeting 1702-1717. This seems to be slackness.[26] The Ravenstonedale Meeting failed to contribute towards the Quarterly Meeting Stock at Kendal in 1696, 1697, 1698 and 1701. A Quarterly Meeting at Kendal on the 3rd of 8th mo.1701 heard:

'Friends of Sedbergh Meeting say they doe still continue on their care towards friends of Ravenstonedale Meeting as was formerly advised & hope that it doth prevail with them to stir them up to more diligence in their service to Truth etc = Also have brought from Ravenstonedale Meeting three collections which is all they are behind till this time.'

Ravenstonedale sent 2.6d. and Grisedale 6s. in 1702. There was a general collection in 1701 in Cumberland, Westmorland and Yorkshire to assist William Wilson of Newby Stones in the parish of Morland whose house and goods had been burned. Ravenstonedale sent 12s. towards this, Grisedale £1.10.0. Anthony Robinson and James Clerkson collected from Ravenstonedale, and Edmund Winn and Richard Wilkinson from Grisedale. In 1701 Sedbergh Meeting had from time to time held their Monthly Meetings at Ravenstonedale in order to induce a better attendance.[27] This discouraging picture changed when on the 8th of the 3rd month 1717 Q.S. Ralph Alderson of Northwaite married *Alice the daughter of William Burton of Scalegill Foot, Dent*. Alice had been a minister since 1707, and she induced new life into Ravenstonedale Meeting; she helped to span some of the difficult years in the middle of the century when poverty was so acute in the dales.

(g) The duty to give a testimony of faith, especially at the time of death, was common in Catholic and Protestant countries; the same applied to Quakers. In 1686 Barbara (aged 15) and Mary (aged 16) *the daughters of William and Isabel Skaife of Blacksyke, Warcop* caught smallpox and died. At the beginning of Barbara's illness she was visited by some neighbours; but she spoke to her Mother:

'Mother, suffer but a few to stay; when they have seen us, desire them to go into the house, for we have no need of such empty talk as is used among so many; but we would be quiet, that we may pray to the Lord to forgive us the faults we have committed; and if he spares us our lives at this time, I hope and believe we shall amend, and have a care of displeasing the Lord while we live.'

After she had been ill a month, and after warning her brother to live a godly life, she said to her mother:

'What thinkest thou of this forenoon?' Her Mother asked her what she meant; she replied, 'It will go far in my time in this world, for the Lord will ease me ere long, take away all my pain, and wipe away all tears from my eyes. Call in my father' said she, 'that he may see my departure'. Her father being come, he said, 'Barbara, how dost thou?' She replied, 'I am ready to leave this world; therefore, father and mother be content, and bear me company a little while.' And about the first hour in the afternoon she departed this life, as if she had fallen asleep.[28]

Barbara died in April and Mary in May 1686, and were probably buried at Birks.[29]

(h) It is a matter of degree as to who suffered most; the Quakers who lived on the fellsides who for the first 25 years were imprisoned for refusing to attend the parish church, or after 1689 had goods, cattle and crops taken in lieu of tithes; or those who left their quiet homes in the dales to go 'abroad on Truth's service.' One of the most eminent from the upper Eden valley was *William Edmundson* of the small hamlet of Little Musgrave. He and his brother Thomas were convinced by James Nayler after his release from Appleby gaol in January 1653. William's mother Grace died in 1631, and his father John in 1635.[30] The children were brought up by their mother's brother, who used them hardly. With the exception of William they all left as soon as they could, and eventually William was apprenticed to a carpenter in York. When the eldest brother came to man's estate he and the others had to sue the uncle for their portions. In 1650 William joined Cromwell's army in Scotland, and also took part in the battle of Worcester, and then was sent to the Isle of Man until its reduction. On his return to Chesterfield he first met the Quakers. In 1652 he recruited for the Scottish army in the north of England, and after taking his recruits to Scotland he obtained his discharge. He was persuaded by a brother serving in the army in Ireland to settle there as a merchant, and it was on his return in 1653 to buy goods that he met and was convinced by Nayler. On his return to Ireland he lost his goods at the customs because he refused to swear to the contents of his bills.

As it would take a book to recall his incredible sufferings and work for Irish Quakerism, in which he was imprisoned several times, had his house burned at least twice, a few points must suffice. So important was his testimony to the cause that his Life and Journal went through eight editions.[31] In 1654 he settled his business at Lurgan, but suffered from such depression that in 1655 he came to England to consult George Fox. He was comforted by his advice, and on his return sold his business and took a farm at Rosenallis near Mountmellick, in order to make his testimony against tithes. This was the base of his ministry for the rest of his life. In 1671 he went to America with Fox. In 1701 (as we have seen) he returned to his native land and visited his cousin Thomas Cleasby at Thringill near Nateby, and his old friend Lancelot Lancaster at Little Musgrave.[32] He was a tall man, a sincere, painful and diligent Quaker, solemn in deliberation, who suffered much from enemies and ill-health. After George Whitehead of Sunbiggin, he was the most considerable Quaker to emerge from the upper Eden valley; a great man. He died in 1712 after years of illness. Two sketches must suffice.

(1) in 1701 John Fothergill II of Carr End, then 26 went to Scotland, and then Ireland. Here he met

'our ancient and honourable friend William Edmundson. I went with some other friends to see him at his Lodgings, where he looked sternly and earnestly upon me, and said little; I sat down and little was spoken amongst us, but I observed he often case his EYE upon me. But when we parted from him, he seemed more free and cheerful to me.'[33]

(2) In 1690 King William III defeated the Irish - French forces at the battle of the Boyne. Edmundson described the fate of the Protestant families around Mountmellick in the following months. The defeated Irish - French army fled south, plundering and burning all the Protestant homes in their way. 'Now was wickedness let loose, and got an head.' Several Protestant families fled for their lives and found shelter with Edmundson and his family at Rosenallis. Every room in his house was filled with a family, and their cattle grazed in his fields. His house was plundered several times, and eventually Edmundson sent for the local chief and said that as the Protestants had lived peaceably with them, they wished to do so

still. But they should realise that when the English - Scots army came south their turn would come. The chief promised to keep his countrymen off, and in return Edmundson promised to assist the Irish when the English army arrived. The Irish promises, backed with many oaths, were vain; scarcely a night passed without English settlers being robbed.

On the arrival of the English army at Mountmellick the Irish were stripped of their cattle, and many prisoners were taken. Edmundson walked several miles to plead for the life of one of his neighbours, who was stripped naked ready for hanging, while an English solider put on his clothes. It took much persuasion, and not a little abuse from the soldiers before the condemned man was released and received his clothes, cattle and sons back again. When the English army settled in winter quarters at Mountmellick, the surrounding country was left to the mercy of the Irish raparees who plundered, murdered and burned far and wide. Edmundson's house was fired, his wife robbed of her outer clothes, and he and his two sons were taken away, and his cattle stolen. His wife never recovered from the cold that night. The next day the Irish threatened to shoot Edmundson and hang his two sons, but they were rescued by Lieutenant William Dunn, whose father Captain Dunn had been rescued by Edmondson when the English were about to hang him. The three were marched twenty miles to Athlone. After three days without food and little rest, the father and his two boys were in a pitiable state. An Irishman took pity on them and gave Edmundson a small piece of bread which he gave to the boys. On their arrival at Athlone they were mobbed by the rabble, and eventually taken to the Castle. Mercifully the governor knew something of Edmundson, and after some days a Quaker, John Clibborn who lived six miles away, pleaded with the governor, who allowed him to take Edmundson and his boys into his care.

While Edmundson was in Athlone his house was attacked again by the raparees who intended to burn Mountmellick. Edmundson's wife was stripped naked and driven through the winter night. Very shortly the English garrison attacked the raparees, slew many, and thus saved Mountmellick. There was much burning and killing on both sides. Eventually it was safe for Edmundson and his boys to travel to the next English garrison at Streams Town, where many English settlers had taken refuge.

When eventually Edmundson returned with some protection to Rosenallis, the Irish got it into their heads that he had betrayed them, and a band of men lay in wait to murder him, but he escaped. After some time the settlers felt free to leave the security of the English garrison, when some semblance of peace had been restored, to restart life on their small ruined farms. Thus Edmundson and his family returned to their home. But his wife died some months later from the chills she received those December nights.

After some months of repair and acute poverty Edmundson set out to visit the few small Quaker Meetings which had survived the war in the north. 'As we went to Dundalk, where the armies had been, one against the other, there were many bones and tufts of green grass, that had grown from the carcasses of men, as if it had been heaps of dung. Then I told Friends that were with me, that I declared it in public in the Word of Truth many years past ... that the Lord would dung the earth with the carcasses of men, and would spread them as dung upon the face of the earth. In that journey I had many sweet comfortable Meetings in the North; Friends hearts were glad, and were greatly refreshed in the Lord Jesus, and in one another. When clear of that Service I came to Mountmellick.'[34]

REFERENCES - CHAPTER 11

(1) C.R.O. Carlisle. Earl of Lonsdale's MSS. D/Lons/L. Letter of rector & churchwardens of Lowther to Sir John Lowther. May 1664.

(2) A Particular Account of the late and present Great Sufferings and Oppressions ... of Quakers upon Prosecutions in the Bishops' Courts presented for the serious Consideration of the King, Lords and Commons in Parliament by Wm. Mead, Geo. Whitehead & 19 others. London 15th of 9 mo. 1680. p. 3. (C.U.L.Syn.7.68.92).

(3) Besse II, 102, & II, 120.

(4) Besse II, 137.

(5) A Brief Account of the many Prosecutions of ... Quakers in the Exchequer, Ecclesiastical & other Courts for demands recoverable by the Acts made in the 7th & 8th Years of the Reign of King William the third etc. London 1736. p. 147. Thomas Pratt of Sunbiggin, parish of Orton. (C.U.L.8.39.11^1.)

(6) This work Vol. II, chapt. 10, ref. (30).

(7) C.R.O. Kendal. WDFC/F/1. Book of Sufferings (51D) of Westmorland Quarterly Meeting, 1706. 31. 11 mo. 1705/6.

(8) Ibid. 23. 8 mo. 1708.

(9) C. & W trans. M.C. XXIX, 1929. Quaker Wills & Contracts. W. G. Collingwood, no. 11. 27 Feb. 1705. Will of Richard Wilson of Knowscale, Garsdale. Now in C.R.O. Kendal.

(10) From a Collection of the Epistles of the Yearly Meeting Vol. I. 1675-1759. pub. 1760. Vol. II. Printed originals 1760-1843. Letter of Yearly Meeting 1764 signed by Fothergill. (C.U.L.7100.a.15.). John Fothergill (III) M.D. the son of John Fothergill (II) of Carr End, the eminent Quaker missionary.

(11) A Collection of the Epistles of George Fox. Vol. II, 1698. p. 12. 'To the Flock of God about Sedbergh.' (C.U.L.Syn.3.69.30.)

(12) Rural Rides, Wm. Cobbett. Penguin ed. 1983. 157.

(13) This work. vol. II. Burial register Grisdale & Garsdale. 1701

(14) Ibid. 1715.

(15) Hist. & Trads. of Ravenstonedale. W.Nichols II, 1914. p. 73.

Parish Registers of Ravenstonedale. Rev. R.W. Metcalfe. Richard s.o. John Pinder bapt. 14. Sept. 1634.

(16) The Story of Quakerism in Scotland. G.B. Burnet, 1952. 31.

(17) Cat. of Friends Books. Joseph Smith. II. 423/4.

(18) Epistles of the Yearly Meetings 1675-1759. London 1760. p. 2/3.

(19) Cat. of Friends Books, J. Smith op. cit. II, 423/4.

(20) This work, vol. I, chapt. 5. refs. (19) & (20).

Ravenstonedale par. reg. op. cit. Bapt. 15 Dec. 1633. John s.o. Anthony Fothergill.

For Anthony Fothergill of Trannahill: Notes & Queries 2nd. Ser. Vol. V. 1858. p. 321. The Fothergills of Ravenstonedale. Not too accurate.

(21) Hist. of Ravenstonedale op. cit. II. 73.

(22) Besse I, 693.

(23) For John Pinder in Maryland: C.R.O. Kendal. Receipt 7.11.1689 of Anthony Pinder of Parrackmoor

for £5. received from Richard Murthwaite of
Rigg End, & George Murthwaite of Wath
for the whole rent of Parrackmoor belonging
to John Pinder. Metcalfe-Gibson MSS. Infor-
F.P.T. 248.

mation of Arthur Duxbury, quaker of Hartley,
Kirkby Stephen.

(24) Journal of Wm. Edmundson. Friends Lib. 1833. vol. 4. 153.

(25) Library, Friends House, Euston Rd., London. MS: S.125.

(26) This work, Quaker register of Ravenstonedale; births.

(27) C.R.O. Kendal. Westmorland Quarterly (Men's) Meeting minute book, 1691-1743 passim.

(28) Piety Promoted, ed. J. Kendall, 1789, vol. I. 143. Barbara d.o. William & Isabel Skaife of Blackside, near Appleby.

(29) Ibid. 147/8. Mary d.o. William & Isabel Skaife. Both died 1686.

(30) Par. reg. Crosby Garrett, 1559-1812. ed. F. Haswell, 1945.

(31) Life of William Edmundson. Dublin, 1715. (C.U.L.Acton.d.8.201.) D.N.B. William Edmundson. 1627-1712.

Cat. of Friends Books. J. Smith I, 557-8. For Mary, Tryal & William Edmundson.

Some early Quaker Writings. 1650-1700. Hugh Barbour & Arthur O. Roberts, Michigan. 1973. 591.

(32) Journal. op. cit. 198, 201.

(33) An Account of the Life & Travels of John Fothergill, 2nd ed. London 1773, 34. (C.U.L.7100.c.323.)

(34) Journal of Wm. Edmundson, op. cit. 121-136.

CHAPTER 12

The Old Quaker Meeting

The present reader will ask: 'What was the old Quaker Meeting like?' Our answer comes from the third extract from Edmundson, on his return to the north in 1701:

(3) After visiting Swarthmore, Camsgill and Kendal: 'Then we went home with John Bleakling and next morning into Rissindale, accompanied with many Friends, where we had a large Meeting out of Doors; many came to it both Friends and Others from several places, being a First-Day of the Week, and the Lord mightily strengthened me, to declare the Word of Life, which reach'd many Hearts; then we went back to Sedber General Meeting, where many Friends came, both of Yorkshire, Lancashire, and Westmorland, and a powerful, heavenly Meeting it was, many Hearts were tender'd, and weighty things in the Lord's Power were Open'd, relating both to Doctrine and Gospel Order ...'

They then went to Kirkby Stephen and Little Musgrave.[1]

Frances Higginson vicar of Kirkby Stephen has an accurate description of a Meeting in 1653.

'For the manner of their Speakings, their Speaker for the most part uses the posture of standing, or sitting, with his hat on, his Countenance severe, his Face downward, his Eyes fixed mostly towards the Earth, his Hands and Fingers expanded, continually striking gently on his Breast; his Beginning is without a Text, abrupt and sudden to his hearers, his Voice for the most part low, his sentences incoherent, hanging together like Ropes of Sand ... sometimes full of sudden Pauses; his whole Speech is a mixt bundle of Words and Heaps of Nonsense, his Continuance in speaking is sometimes exceeding short, sometimes very tedious, according to the Paucity or Plenty of his Revelations. His admiring Auditors that are of his Way, stand the while like men astonished, listening to every Word, as though every Word was oraculous; and so they believe them to be the very words and dictates of Christ speaking in him.'[2]

It is this ethos which Fox communicated to his early hearers in Grisedale and Ravenstonedale in 1652, and which was to remain.

The best illustration of the discipline of silence comes from the life of John Griffith of Radnor.[3] He visited Ravenstonedale in 1753 after a visit to Preston Patrick:

'I had a Meeting next day at Ravenstonedale, which was a laborious trying time; my way was shut up as to ministry; friends seemed too much at ease in a profession. When this is the case, the life of religion is exceedingly depressed; so that those, who feel its state, must suffer therewith, until it please the Lord to raise his pure Seed, in judgement against evil in people's minds.'[4]

Not an encouraging picture. Griffith was to apply this discipline of silence a number of times, notably at a Meeting at Kirklinton in Cumberland, a then neglected and lonely parish. Before his visit in 1747:

'Friends having, without my knowledge, given notice to their neighbours, and to divers people of account in the world; it is like they expected great things from one come so far to visit them; and some perhaps hoped to get credit by that day's work; but we see sometimes, when man appoints, the Lord disappoints; which, in the issue, seems to have been the case here; as I sat, the meeting, which was very large throughout in silence, to the great mortification of many present, some of whom, one might have expected, from their appearance and pretensions, to have better understood the nature of spiritual worship, than to have been so anxious after words, or outward declarations; it proved, I think, as painful and exercising a meeting as ever I knew, to which the expectations of friends and others did not a little contribute. At the conclusion, I was fully satisfied that I had discharged the service required of me that day, in an example of silence, in which I had peace.'[5]

One can see perhaps the need of many christians in the remoter parts of the north in the mid-eighteenth century when poverty was acute for some word of cheer from a visitor who could see a wider horizon than theirs; and also the reason why the camp-meeting of later Methodism was to prove so acceptable. When Stephen Grellett visited the north in 1812 he came to Wensleydale:

'One (meeting) was held on a First-day afternoon, at the heads of Wensley and Bishopdale. The notice of it had been spread some days before, and people came from a distance of ten miles; several thousands attended. The Lord's power was felt in an eminent manner over us, and the everlasting Gospel was preached, to the tendering of many hearts. The meeting held upwards of three hours, but continued to the end in great stillness and solemnity. It appears that the spot which had been chosen for it, was a field belonging to the clergyman; he did not object to the choice made by the people, and it was the most suitable ground for the occasion. In these dales and among the hills I have felt much of the sufferings of the people; there is a great scarcity of grain amongst them; wheat is sold for 21s. to 22s., and oats, their chief food, at 11.6d. to 12s. per bushel. My horse had but poor fare, and I made as little do as I possibly could; but the Lord has strengthened me every way, blessed and reverend is his name! The business of many in these dales is to knit woolen stockings. They are so industrious that men, women and children, walking in the fields, or on the highways, keep knitting as fast as they can.'[6]

We have come to the end of a detailed and tedious tale. We have seen the distress of a remote dales' tenantry at the time of the Pilgrimage of Grace, and the dissolution of the monasteries; we have examined the nature of border-tenant-right, its slow development, and the struggle of lords with their tenants in the triangle of dales, Ravenstonedale, Mallerstang, Wensleydale, Grisdale and Garsdale; we have seen the division of farmholds in the later sixteenth century Mallerstang, creating a poor tenantry unable to resist hard times; we have seen the effect of James I's policy of extracting money from tenants in confirmation of their customary tenures; we have seen the effect of the Civil Wars and forced provisioning on the dales' farms, and the struggles for power during the Protectorate; and finally we have seen the story of Quakerism after 1660. Any hope that Quakers would be tolerated was dashed not only by their vituperative language against the clergy, but more especially by the rising of the Fifth Monarchy Men and the Kaber Rigg plot. Not least was the attitude of the landowners and returned royalists who had too many scores to pay off against the sectaries. The story of persecution from 1660 until long after the Toleration Act of 1689 is one of the most disgraceful in the history of the northern dales. And yet ... these men and women remained true to a faith they received through George Fox from 1652. They were given a Christian identity which had been lacking in the distant ministrations of the market town parish churches. Though Quakerism has vanished from the dales, the principle of a free church largely staffed by lay preachers outside the established church has continued in the Methodist chapels. Despite all the sufferings of the dalesmen from the sixteenth century, that they remained Christian is due to George Fox and the Religious Society of Friends.

Thomas Crosfield was rector of Spennithorne in Wensleydale from 1648/9. He was the son of Robert Crosfield of Strickland Roger, and the grandson of Martin Gilpin of the parish of Kendal. Thomas Crosfield wrote in his diary of 24th November 1653:

God out of evil can bring good, and why may he not out of the new sect of Quakers produce Glory to himself and good to his people, if they but with patience wait for his leisure.'[7]

Bishop Gilbert Burnet on dissenters:

'I will not deny that many of the dissenters were put to great hardships in many parts of England; I cannot deny it, and I am sure I will never justify it.

And I will boldly say this, that if the Church of England, after she is got out of this storm, will return to hearken to the peevishness of some sore men, she will be abandoned both of God and man, and will set heaven and earth against her.'[8]

A survey of early Quakerism in the dales is incomplete without reference to two friends, Edward Burrough and Francis Howgill, whose testimonies are among the most moving of the period, and complement each other's. Burrough's 'We went forth as commanded of the Lord' gives an excellent description of the message and suffering of early Quakers; Howgill's gives the spirit of their worship. It has proved impossible to exclude either.

We went forth as Commanded of the Lord. (Edward Burrough.)

Being prepared of the Lord, and having received Power from on high, we went forth as commanded of the Lord, leaving all Relations, and all things of the World behind us, that we might fulfill the work of the Lord into which he called us, and with Flesh and Blood ... we consulted not ... but of the Lord alone, who lifted up our heads above the World, and all fears and doubtings, and was with us in Power and Dominion, over all that which opposed us, which was great and mighty, and gave us power over it all, and to bind Kings in Chains ... and this is the Saints honour; and the Word of the Lord we founded, and did not spare, and caused the Deaf to hear, the Blind to see, and the heart that was hardened to be awakened; and the Dread of the Lord went before us, and behind us, and terror took hold upon our Enemies; And first of all our Mouthes were opened, and our spirit filled with indignation against the Priests and Teachers, and with them, and against them first we began to war, as being the Causers of the people to err, and the Blind-leaders, that carried the Blind into the Ditch, and against them, as the Fountain of all wickedness abounding in the Nations, and as being the issue of Prophaness ... who had made a prey upon us;

And in Steeple-houses we did visit them often, and in Markets and other Places, as the Lord moved, and made way for us, shewing unto all them ... that they were not Lawful Ministers of Christ, sent of Him, but were Deceivers and Antichrists;

We spared not publicly, and at all seasons to utter forth the Judgments of the Lord against them and their wayes, and against their Churches, Worships and Practices. This was our first work ... to thresh down the Deceivers, and lay them open, that all people might see their shame, and come to turn from them, and receive the knowledge of the Truth, that they might be saved.

This we did with no small Opposition nor danger; yea, oftentimes we were in danger of our lives, through beating, abusing, Punishing, Haling, casting over Walls, striking with Staves, and Cudgels, and Knocking down to the Ground, besides Reproaching, Scorning, Revilings, and Houtings at, and Scoffings, and Slanderings, and all abuse that could be thought or acted by evil hands and Tongues, and often carried before Magistrates, with grievous Threats, and sometimes put in the Stocks, and Whipped, and often Imprisoned, and many hard dealings ... of all this the North-countries may witness ... because of our faithfulness to the Lord, and for declaring against false Deceivers; for nothing save only the Hand of the Lord, and his Power could have preserved us ... and kept us in the Hollow of his Hand,

and under the Shadow of his Wings.

And though Rulers and People were combined against us, and executed their injustice and violence against us, yet the Lord made us prosper ... and the hearts of the People enclined towards us.

The Priests petitioned the Magistrates, and (they) gave forth Warrants for the apprehending of some, and made orders to break our Meetings, and that we should not meet in the Night-season; and such men might not pass abroad; and such stir and Opposition was made against us, it can hardly be expressed or declared; there were uproars in Steeple-houses, and uproars in Markets, and often haling before Magistrates, and (we were) abused, and threatened, and slandred, and all manner of evil done, and spoken against us, and great injustice, cruelty and Oppression acted against us.[9]

The Testimony of Francis Howgill, 1663

When it pleased the Lord to raise up the ancient horn of Salvation among us, who were reckoned in the North part of England, even as the outcasts of Israel, and as men destitute of great knowledge which some seemed to enjoy; yet there was more sincerity and true love among us, and desires after the living powerful presence of God, then was among many in that day, who seemed to make a great flourish, who ran into heaps and forms, but left the Cross behind them, and indeed were strangers to it; God out of his everlasting love did appear unto us according to the desire of our hearts who longed after him, when he had turned aside from the hireling Shepherds Tents, we found him whom our souls loved, and God out of his great love, and great mercy, sent one unto us immediately by his Power, a man of God, one of ten thousand to instruct us in the way of God more perfectly, who laid down the sure foundation, and declared the acceptable year of the Lord; who indeed made the mourners to rejoice, and the heavy hearted glad, which yet was terrible to all hypocrites and all formall profession; which testimony reached unto all our consciences, and entered into the utmost part of our hearts, which drove us to narrow search, and to a diligent inquisition concerning our state, which we did come to see through the Light of Christ Jesus which was testified of, and found it to be even what it was testified of; and the Lord of heaven and earth we found to be near at hand; and as we waited upon him in pure silence, our minds out of all things, his dreadful power and glorious Majesty, and heavenly presence appeared in our Assemblies, where there was no language, tongue nor speech from any creature; and the Kingdom of Heaven did gather us, and catch us all as in a Net, and his heavenly power at one time did draw many hundreds to Land, and we did come to know a place to stand in, and what to wait in, and the Lord did appear daily to us, to our astonishment, amazement, and great admiration, insomuch that we often said unto one another with great joy of heart "What, is the kingdom of God come to be with men? And will he take up his Tabernacle amongst the sons of men, as he did of old? And what, shall we that were reckoned as the outcasts of Israel, have this honor of glory communicated amongst us which were but men of small parts, and of little abilities, in respect of many other amongst men?"

Howbeit it seemed good unto the Lord to chuse the weak things, and the foolish things of this World, as to the aspect of men, that no flesh might glory, that no man because of his parts might glory, or because of his strength or wisdom might glory, but that the glory which is his, might only be given to him; unto whom be the glory of all his works, for ever and ever, Amen.

And from that day forward our hearts were knit into the Lord, and one unto another in true and fervent love, not by any external Covenant, or external Form; but we entered into the Covenant of Life with God, and that was as a strong obligation or bond upon all our Spirits, which united us one unto another, and we met together in the Unity of the Spirit, and of the bond of Peace, treading down under our feet all reasoning, questioning and contending about religion, or any part or parts, or practice or practices thereof, as to any external thing; and we waited at time or times as God did grant us opportunities; and the more we had and could obtain from our necessary occasions of this present life, the better we were, and the more we were confirmed and strengthened in our Hope and Faith, and holy Resolutions were kindled in our hearts as a Fire, which the Life kindled in us to serve the Lord while we had a being, and to make mention of his Name and Power whilst we did live, and to hold forth that Testimony which was committed to us in the signe of men and Nations, by doctrine, by practice, by a holy conversation; and mightily did the Word of God grow amongst us, and the desires of many were after the Name of the Lord. Oh happy day! Oh blessed day! the memorial of which can never pass out of my mind. And thus the Lord (in short) did form us to be a people for his praise in our generation.[10]

The House of God (John Ruskin)

'You have all got into the habit of calling the church "The House of God". I have seen over the doors of many churches, the legend actually carved, "This is the house of God and this is the gate of Heaven." Now, note where that legend comes from, and of what place it was first spoken. A boy leaves his father's house to go on a long journey on foot, to visit his uncle; he had to cross a wild hill-desert; just as if one of your own boys had to cross the moors to visit an uncle at Carlisle. The second or third day the boy finds himself somewhere between Hawes and Brough, in the midst of the moors at sunset. It is stony ground, and boggy; he cannot go one foot farther that night. Down he lies, to sleep, on Whernside, where best he may, gathering a few of the stones together to put under his head; - so wild the place is, he cannot get anything but stones. And there, lying under the broad night, he has a dream; he sees a ladder set up on earth, and the top of it reaches to heaven, and the angels of God are seen ascending and descending upon it. And when he wakes out of his sleep, he says, "How dreadful is this place; surely this is none other than the house of God, and this is the gate of heaven." This PLACE, observe; not this church; not this city; not this stone, even, which he puts up for a memorial - the piece of stone on which his head was lain. But this place; this windy slope of Whernside; this moorland hollow, torrent-bitten, snow-blighted! this ANY place where God lets down the ladder. And how are you to know where that will be? Or how are you to determine where it may be, but by being ready for it always? Do you know where the lightning is to fall next? You DO know that, partly; you can guide the lightning; but you cannot guide the going forth of the Spirit, which is as that lightning when it shines from the east to the west.'[11]

REFERENCES. CHAPTER 12.

(1) Journal op. cit. 198.

(2) A Brief Relation of the Irreligion of the Northern Quakers, op. cit. 12. This work Vol. 11. chapter 3. Ref. (7)

(3) Journal of John Griffith of Radnor, 1779. pp. 113, 115, 140, 158, 270, 347 & 359. (C.U.L. 7100.

c. 338).

(4) Ibid. 243.

(5) Ibid. 135/6, & 140.

(6) Memoir of the Life & Labours of Stephen Grellet by Benjamin Seebohm, 1860, vol. I. 203. (C.U.L.D.15.56).

(7) Diary of Thomas Crosfield, Fellow of Queens College, Oxford. F.S. Boas, 1935, xi-xii. & 103.

(8) Persecution Exposed in some Memoirs relating to the Sufferings of John Whiting and other Quakers. 2nd. ed. 1791. 520. (C.U.L. Ddd. 3.17).

(9) The Memorable Works ... of Edward Burrough, 1672, pp. 12, 13. Epistle to the Reader.

(10) A Testimony Concerning the Life, Death, Travels and Labours of Edward Burrough etc. by Francis Howgill, London 1663. p. 5. (C.U.L. Syn. 5.65.2. (13)

(11) The Crown of Wild Olive. John Ruskin. 1906 ed. Lecture II, at the Town Hall, Bradford. The placing of Whernside between Hawes and Brough is a bit of literary licence.

BIBLIOGRAPHY, Vol. III

Arnold, T. Select Works of John Wyclif. 1869.

Backhouse, James. Memoirs of Francis Howgill. 1828.

Barbour, Hugh, & Roberts, Arthur O. Some early Quaker writings 1650-1700. Michigan 1973.

Barclay, Robert. An Apology for the True Christian Divinity...as held by the People in Scorn called Quakers. 1701.

Baumann, Dr. Richard. Let your words be few. 1983.

Besse, Joseph. A Collection of the Sufferings of the People callecalled Quakers. 2 vols. 1753. There were several earlier edns., but this is the most complete.

Besse, Joseph. The Account of the Travels and Christian Experience in the work of the Ministry...of Samuel Bownas. 1756.

Bevan, Joseph Gurney. A Refutation of some of the Modern Misrepresentations of the Society of Friends. 1800.

Billing, Edward. A Mite of Affection manifested in Proposals, offered to all Sober and Free Born People etc. 1659.

Boas, F.S. The Diary of Thomas Crosfield, fellow of the Queen's College, Oxford. 1935.

Bolton, John (of Appleby). The tract giving the Dying Words of Francis Howgill (who died in Appleby gaol January 1668/9) pub. 1717. In Library of Friends House, Euston Road, London.

Bouch, C.M.L. & Jones, G.P. The Lake Counties 1961.

Bownas, Samuel. The Account of the Life, Travels and Christian Experience of, 1761.

Brailsford, H.N. The Levellers. Spokesman Books ed. 1976.

Braithwaite, Wm. C. The Beginnings of Quakerism. ed. of 1981.

Braithwaite, Wm. C. The Second Period of Quakerism. ed. of 1979.

Breay, Revd. John. Kirkby Stephen churchwardens' accounts 1658-1670. Cumberland & Westmorland Antiquarian Soc. N.S. LIV, 176.

Brierley, H. Parish Registers of Brough under Stainmore 1556-1706. 1923.

Bryant, Arthur. King Charles II. 1932.

Bugg, Francis, of Mildenhall. Testimony in: Catalogue of Friends Books, Joseph Smith. 1867.I.334.

Burnet, G.B. The Story of Quakerism in Scotland. 1952.

Burrough, Edward. A Declaration to the World of our Faith. 1659.

Burrough, Edward. The Everlasting Gospel of Repentance & Remission of Sins...A Message of Reconciliation to all People, particularly the People of Ireland. 1659.

Burrough, Edward. A Testimony concerning the Life, Death, Travels and Labours of Edward Burroughs (by Francis Howgill). 1663.

Burrough, Edward. The Memorable Works of a Son of Thunder, Edward Burrough, 1672.

Butler, David M. The Quaker Meeting Houses of the Lake Counties. (F.H.S.) 1978.

The Calendars of State Papers, Domestic and of the Committee for Compounding.

Canons and Constitutions of the Society of Friends 1668/9, pub. 1669.

Cobbett, William. Rural Rides. Penguin ed. 1983.

Coleridge, Hartley. Biographia Borealis 1833.

Coleridge, Hartley. Northern Worthies 1852.

Collingwood, W.G. A Book of old Quaker Wills. Cumberland & Westmorland Antiquarian Soc. N.S. XXIX, 1929.

Cross, F.L. The Oxford Dictionary of the Christian Church, 1957.

Cumberland & Westmorland Antiquarian and Archaeological Soc. O.S. & N.S.

Curwen, J.F. The Later Records of North Westmorland or the Barony of Appleby, 1932.

Dictionary of National Biography.
    Edward Burrough, 1634-1663.
    George Fox, 1624-1691.
    Edmund Grindal, 1519?-1583.
    Francis Howgill, 1618-1669.
    John Knewstub, 1544-1624.
    Nicholas Metcalfe, 1475?-1539.
    James Nayler, 1617?-1660.
    James Parnell, 1637?-1656.
    Anthony Pearson, 1628-1670?

Thomas Taylor, 1618-1682.

George Whitehead, 1636-1723.

Edmundson, William. A Letter of Examination to all you who have assumed the Place of Shepherds. 1672.

Edmundson, William. The Journal of the Life of, Friends Library, 1833.

Faraday, M.A. The Westmorland Protestation Returns of 1641. Cumberland & Westmorland Antiq. Soc. Tract series XVII, 1971.

Ferguson, R.S. Early Cumberland & Westmorland Friends. 1871.

Ferguson, R.S. The History of Cumberland. 1890.

Fogelklou, Emilia. James Nayler the Rebel Saint. 1618-1660. 1931.

Fothergill, John. (of Carr End), An Account of the Life and Travels in the Work of the Ministry of, 1754 & 1773.

Fothergill, John & Samuel (from Carr End), A Brief Account of the People called Quakers, Dublin. 1776.

Fox, George. The Journal of, ed. D.P. 1891.

Fox, George. The Journal of, ed. John L. Nickalls, 1975.

Fox, George. A Paper sent forth into the World why we deny the teachers of the World. 1652 et seq.

Fox, George. Newes coming up out of the North to the South, 1655.

Fox, George. A Declaration concerning Fasting and Prayer...and sheweth the Prayer that God accepts. 1656.

Fox, George. The Mystery of the Great Whore unfolded. 1659.

Fox, George. & Jo. Stubbs. The Divinity of Christ, and the Unity of those that bear Record in Heaven. 1669.

Fox, George. The Saints (or they that are born of the Spirit) their heavenly and Spiritual Washing...1683.

Fox, George. The Journal or Historical Account of the Work of the Ministry of that ancient Servant of Jesus Christ G.F. 1694.

Fox, George. A Collection of Many and Select and Christian Epistles of, 1698.

Fox, George. Gospel Truth, The Collected works of. 1706.

Fox, Dr. R.H. Dr. John Fothergill and his friends. 1919.

Friends Historical Soc. Journal of. XXXIII, 1936. 68. The Marriage Certificate of Alexander Fothergill & Ann Langton.

Friends Historical Soc. Journal of. vol. 51. 1965/7. p. 77. Anthony Pearson by Amy E. Wales.

Gilpin, John, of Kendal. The Quaker shaken, or a warning against Quaking. 1655.

Glover, T.R. Cambridge Retrospect 1943.

Griffith, John of Radnor. The Journal of, 1779.

Grellet, Stephen. A Memoir of the Life & Labours of, by Benjamin Seebohm. 1860.

Guy, Edward (of Appleby). A Funeral Verse on the death of Francis Howgill, 1671. from the catalogue of Friends Books, J. Smith. I. 898.

Higginson, Francis. (Vicar of Kirkby Stephen). Two tracts in one:
A Brief Relation of the Irreligion of the Northern Quakers, 1653.
A Brief Reply to some part of a very scurrilous Lying Pamphlet called Saul's Errand to Damascus (by G. Fox 1653). *Both in The Library of Trinity College, Cambridge.*

Historical Manuscripts Commission, Rep. XIII, app. Part vii, Earl of Lonsdale's MSS.

Holme, Wilfred (the Yorkshire poet). The Evill success of Rebellion from Time to Time...written in old Englishe verse by, (composed 1537) pub. 1572/3. Brit. Lib. cat. C.122.bb.20.

Howgill, Francis. The Great Case of Tythes (written in Appleby gaol), 1665.

Howgill, Francis. The Dawnings of the Gospel Day and its Light and Glory discovered, 1676.

Howgill, Francis. The Works of, 1676.

Kendall, J. Piety Promoted, 1789.

Kristenson, Gillis, Lund Studies in English, vol. 49. John Mirk's Instructions to parish priests.

Leake, Richard, (vicar of Killington). Foure Sermons, 1599. (Cambridge University Library).

Lilburne, John the Leveller. Come out of her my people, or an answer to the Questions of a Gentlewoman. 1639.

Lilburne, John the Leveller and others. The Declaration of John Lilburne etc. in the Tower: An Agreement of the Free People of England. 1649.

Matthews, A.G. Walker Revised, 1948.

Mayor, J.E.B. The History of the College of St. John the Evangelist, Cambridge, 1869.

Mead, Wm. & Whitehead, George and 19 Others. A Particular Account of the late and present Great Sufferings and Oppressions...of Quakers in the Bishops Courts, 1680.

Metcalfe, Revd. R.W. The parish registers of Ravenstonedale 1893.

Moderate Intelligencer, the. no. 207 of March 1 no. 210 of March 22 1649. In Cambs. Univ. Lib.

Nayler, James, his life, in: A Refutation of some of the Modern Misrepresentations of the Society of Friends. J.G. Bevan, 1800.

Nayler, James. The Power and Glory of the Lord shining out of the North into the South, 1653.

Nayler, James. A Discovery of the First Wisdom from Beneath, and the Second Wisdom from above...1653.

Nicholls, Revd. W. (Minister of Ravenstonedale). History and Traditions of Mallerstang Forest and Pendragon Castle, 1883.

Nicholls, Revd. W. History and Traditions of Ravenstonedale, c. 1914.

Nicholson, F. The Kaber Rigg Plot, 1663. Cumberland & Westmorland Antiquarian Soc. trans. N.S. XI, art. xvi.

Nicolson, J. & Burn, R. History of Cumberland & Westmorland 1777.

Nightingale, Benjamin. The Ejected of 1662 in Cumberland & Westmorland, 1911.

Notes & Queries, 2nd. Series, V. 1858.

Nuttall, Geoffrey F. Friends Historical Soc. Journal 1954. James Nayler, a fresh approach.

Overton, Richard, the Leveller. The Ordinance of Tythes dismounted, 1646.

Parnell, James, the Quaker. A Collection of the Writings of, 1675.

Pearson, Anthony, the Quaker. The Great Case of Tythes truly stated. 1659 & 1730.

Penney, Norman. The First Publishers of Truth, 1902.

Penney, Norman. Friends Historical Soc. Journal. vol. VII. 1910. Presentments at Episcopal visitations in Cumberland & Westmorland.

Penney, Norman, & Roberts, R.A. Extracts from the State Papers. 1913.

Piety Promoted, ed. J. Kendal 1789, vol. III.

Platt, A.E. A History of the Parish & Grammar School of Sedbergh, 1876.

Quakers, A Brief Account of the Many Prosecutions of, in the Exchequer, Ecclesiastical and other Courts in the 7th & 8th years of the reign of King William III, 1736.

Quakers, A Collection of the Epistles of the Yearly Meetings Vol. I. 1675-1759, pub. 1760. Vol. II a collection of the printed originals. 1760-1843, in the Cambridge University Library.

Quaker, Anti-. A broadsheet of 1700 containing extracts from the wilder Quaker books c. 1660 in the Cambridge University Library.

Robinson, Richard of Countersett. The testimony of, in Gospel Truth; the collected works of George Fox, 1706.

Rowse, Dr. A.L. The England of Elizabeth. Reprint Soc. 1953.

Ruskin, John. The Crown of Wild Olive, 1906 ed. Lecture II, at Town Hall, Bradford.

Sewell, J.S. The Friends Quarterly Examiner 1807. Vol. I. A Devotion on the Lord's Prayer.

Smith, A.R. Jabez-, Cumberland & Westmorland Antiquarian Soc. trans. N.S. LXXXIV. 1984. Anthony Pearson, an early Cumbrian Quaker.

Smith, Joseph. A Catalogue of Friends' Books 2vv. 1867.

Smith, William. The True Light shining in England. 1660.

Smith, William. Old Yorkshire, vol. 4. 1883.

Surtees Soc. Vol. XL. 1861. Depositions from York Castle 1663.

Taylor, Thomas. A Trumpet sounded from under the Altar; ten days persecution near an end. (Written in Appleby gaol to the people of Appleby and Bongate against Ambrose Rowlands, vicar of Appleby) 1658.

Taylor, Thomas. A Testimony of the True and Spiritual worship, and a Word of Consolation, 1670.

Thomason, George. Catalogue of pamphlets, books, manuscripts... 1640-1661. 1908.

Thornton, C. The Fothergills of Ravenstonedale, 1905.

Thwaite, H. Yorkshire Archaeological Soc. Record series CXXX, 1967: Abstracts of Abbotside Wills 1552-1688.

Tothill, W. Transactions of the High Court of Chancery both by practice and precedent. 1671.

Tuke, James Hack, in Old Yorkshire by Wm. Smith, 1883, vol. 4. 133. Dr. John Fothergill M.D.

Venn, J. Grace Book of the University of Cambridge, 1911.

Venn, J. & J.A. Alumni Cantabrigiae, from ancient times of 1751.

Victoria County History:
   N. Riding of York shire, 1968.
   Yorkshire III, 1968.
   Cumberland, 1968.

Vipond, Elfrida. George Fox and the Valiant Sixty. 1975.

Whaley, Revd. C. The Parish of Askrigg co. Yorks, including Low Abbotside and Bainbridge, 1890.

Whitehead, George (the Quaker of Sunbiggin, Orton). Jacob found in a strange land. 1656.

Whitehead, George. His Preface in: The many and select Epistles of George Fox, 1698.

Whitehead, George. The Christian Progress of that Ancient Servant and Minister of Jesus Christ, George Whitehead. 1725.

Whiting, John. A Catalogue of Friends Books, 1708.

Whiting, John. Persecution exposed in some Memories relating to the suffering of, 1791.

Willan, T.S. & Crossley, E.W. Yorkshire Archaeological Soc. Record Series, CIV, 1941. Three Seventeenth Century Yorkshire Surveys.

Williamson, Dr. G.C. Lady Anne Clifford, 1922.

Wilson, E. The Register of Sedbergh School, 1909.

Yorkshire Parish Register Soc. vol. 108, 1939. The parish registers of Wensley, 1538-1700.

As this volume contains a large number of names, this Index contains only key references to names and topics.

Rich, the. 34, 35, 36
Robinson, Anthony of Dovengill. 47, 51, 83
Robinson, Father Christopher of Wigton. 11
Robinson, Richard of Countersett. 13, 30, 70, 72
Rogerson, Sarah, marr. James Bayliff. 46
Ruskin, John. 90
Saint John's College, Cambridge. 10
Saul's Errand to Damascus, G. Fox. 1652. 17
Scaife, William of Warcop. (See Skaife). 51, 60
Sedbergh, Fox's visit, 1652. 16
  Monthly Meeting, 1693. 45
  Meeting, 1671. 74
  Fox's first letter to Friends at, 1652. 81
Sedbergh Chantry School. 10
Serious People, the. 35
Shaw, Richard, of Hanging Lunds, Mallerstang, Will of 1677. 64
Shorgill, Mallerstang. 10
Silent Heart, the. 24, 26
Silent worship. 26
Skaife, (Scaife) Barbara of Blacksyke, Warcop. 83
  Mary of same. 83
  William of same, husband of Isabel. 83
Southwell, Robert, solicitor of Court of Augmentations. 49
State Church, a. 38
Strickland Head Meeting. 70, 72, 73, 74
Sufferers, in the Commonwealth. 67
  in Westmorland 1652-1660. 68
  in Westmorland from 1660. 69
Sufferers:
  at Strickland Head. 72-3, 74
  at Ravenstonedale. 74-75
  at Grisdale & Garsdale. 76-78
Taylor, Christopher. 23, 51, 68
Taylor, Thomas. 23, 51, 68
Tithes.31
Thomson, Revd. Robert, vicar of Brough. 10
Thornton in Wensleydale, magistrates at. 75
Toleration Act, 1689. 75
Traders & Merchants. 36
Truth, the. 25
Turk, the. 37
Underbarrow Meeting. 74
Ward, Capt. Henry of Sunnybank, Grayrigg. 9, 51, 69
Wesley, Revd. John. 16
Wharton, Philip lord. 69, 74
Wharton, Sir Thomas lord.10
Whitehead, George of Sunbiggin. 29, 36, 80
Wilson, Ann (Pratt) wife of Robert. 80
Wilson, Edward, magistrate of Dalham. 75
Wilson, Katherine, wife of Richard. 80, 81
Wilson, Richard of Knowscale, Garsdale. 51, 80, 81
Wilson, Robert son of Richard & Katherine.,80-81
Winn, Agnes wife of Edmund of Grisdale. 81
Winn, Christopher, schoolmaster of Frostrow. 3-4
Winn, Thomas, of Grisdale. 51, 72
Wright, Thomas of Outhgill, Mallerstang. 68, 70
Wyckliff, John. 16
Yearly Meeting, 1676. 17
Zinzendorf, Nikolaus Ludwig, Graf von. 16